Intricate Patterns

Adult Coloring Book

Copyrighted Material © 2021 Mysa Digital Creations

All Rights Reserved

ISBN: 9798489236966

Intricate Patterns Series available on Amazon

Volume I
ISBN 9798489236966
(Less Intricate)

Volume II
ISBN 9798355488819
(Medium Intricate)

Volume III
Spiral Wiro Bound Format
ISBN 9788196119515
(Highly Intricate)

Volume IV
ISBN 9798858626244
(Highly Intricate)

Volume V
ISBN 9798871632079
This book is similar to
Volume 1 (Less Intricate)

Intricate Floral Tessellations Series available on Amazon

Volume I
ISBN 9798864734414

Volume II
ISBN 9798865419488

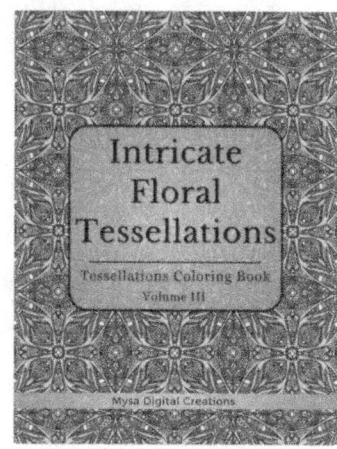

Volume III
ISBN 9798880453887

The First & New Release in the Mandala Animal Series!!

Originally hand drawn 35 Fascinating Intricate Animals with Detailed Style!!

Intricate Animals Coloring Book for Adults - Stunning Animals ready to enter your Artistic World of Imagination!!

Volume I - 8.5 * 11 inch coloring book

Intricacy - Medium

ISBN - 9798884098800

....

Sample Animals from the book:

   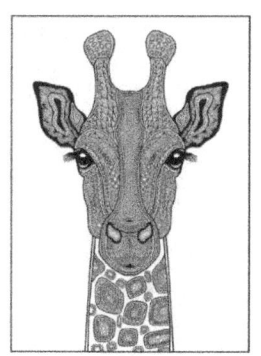

This book belongs to

_____

Color Swatch Sheet

Color Swatch Sheet

Note from the Author:

Thank you very much for purchasing this book!

- Each design in this book is authentic and we request you to completely relax by coloring them – it is now completely yours to color!
- A reflective state of being aware of the present moment is ***Mindfulness***.
- Coloring the patterns in the book helps to ***improve focus and attention*** towards practicing mindfulness – ***keeps the mind calm and relaxed***.
- I request you to appreciate yourself after finishing with each pattern to keep yourself inspired and definitely it feels good.
- Relax, Color and Keep Smiling! ☺

Quick Tips:

1. <u>**Please use a thick sheet behind the page before coloring, to avoid any ink blotting to the next page.**</u>
2. Start coloring from the center of the design, in order to avoid any smudging while coloring the outer portion of the design.
3. Verify color combinations using 'Color Swatch Sheet' provided in this book.

We hope you enjoyed and relaxed coloring the patterns in this book – they are designed with love and care by a human with no AI intervention.

Requesting to please leave a review on Amazon if you liked the patterns – it really means a lot!

Thank you!

The First & New Release in the Mandala Animal Series!!

Originally hand drawn 35 Fascinating Intricate Animals with Detailed Style!!

Intricate Animals Coloring Book for Adults - Stunning Animals ready to enter your Artistic World of Imagination!!

Volume I - 8.5 * 11 inch coloring book

Intricacy - Medium

ISBN - 9798884098800

....

Sample Animals from the book:

   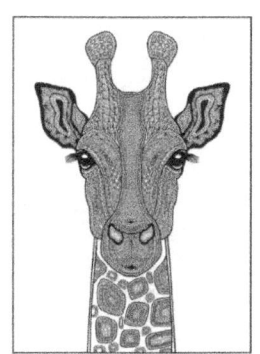

Intricate Patterns Series available on Amazon

Volume I
ISBN 9798489236966
(Less Intricate)

Volume II
ISBN 9798355488819
(Medium Intricate)

Volume III
Spiral Wiro Bound Format
ISBN 9788196119515
(Highly Intricate)

Volume IV
ISBN 9798858626244
(Highly Intricate)

Volume V
ISBN 9798871632079
This book is similar to
Volume 1 (Less Intricate)

Intricate Floral Tessellations Series available on Amazon

Volume I
ISBN 9798864734414

Volume II
ISBN 9798865419488

Volume III
ISBN 9798880453887

Enjoy coloring the other books in the Series!

Volume I
ISBN 9798489236966

Volume II
ISBN 9798355488819

Volume III
Spiral Wiro Bound Format
ISBN 9788196119515

Volume IV
ISBN 9798858626244

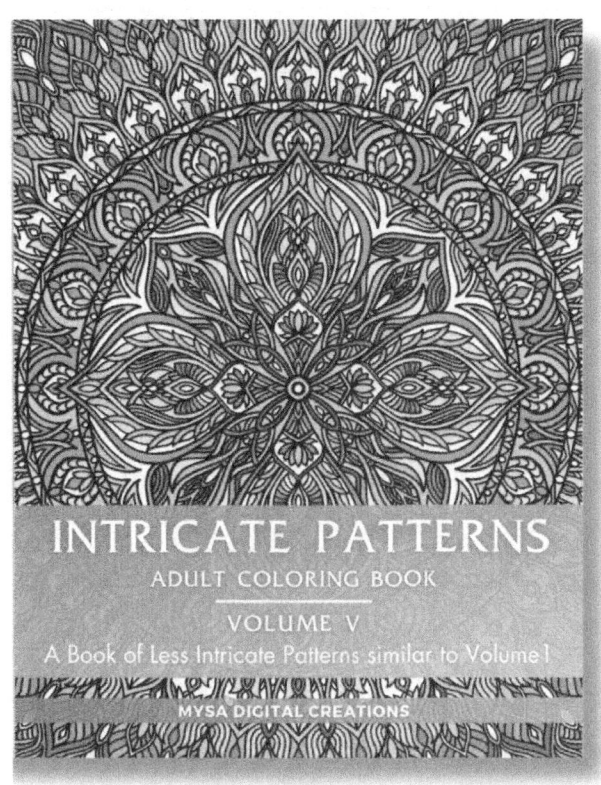

Volume V

ISBN 9798871632079

This book is similar to Volume 1
(Less Intricate Patterns)

Enjoy Coloring the trending style of Intricate Floral Tessellations Coloring Books from the new series!

Volume I
ISBN 9798864734414

Volume II
ISBN 9798865419488

Volume III
ISBN 9798880453887

Made in the USA
Las Vegas, NV
07 July 2024

92006158R00072

Pearson Australia
(a division of Pearson Australia Group Pty Ltd)
707 Collins Street, Melbourne, Victoria 3008
PO Box 23360, Melbourne, Victoria 8012
www.pearson.com.au

Copyright © Pearson Australia 2017
(a division of Pearson Australia Group Pty Ltd)
First published 2016 by Pearson Australia
2021   2020   2019
10 9 8 7 6 5 4

Reproduction and communication for educational purposes
The Australian *Copyright Act 1968* (the Act) allows a maximum of one chapter or 10% of the pages of this work, whichever is the greater, to be reproduced and/or communicated by any educational institution for its educational purposes provided that that educational institution (or the body that administers it) has given a remuneration notice to Copyright Agency Limited (CAL) under the Act. For details of the CAL licence for educational institutions contact Copyright Agency Limited (www.copyright.com.au).

Reproduction and communication for other purposes
Except as permitted under the Act (for example any fair dealing for the purposes of study, research, criticism or review), no part of this book may be reproduced, stored in a retrieval system, communicated or transmitted in any form or by any means without prior written permission. All enquiries should be made to the publisher at the address above.

This book is not to be treated as a blackline master; that is, any photocopying beyond fair dealing requires prior written permission.

Publisher: Alicia Brown
Development Editors: Zoe Hamilton, Antonietta Anello
Project Manager: Shelly Wang
Production Manager: Elizabeth Gosman
Editors: Vicky Chadfield, Marcia Bascombe, Aptara
Index: Brett Lockwood
Proof reader: Marcia Bascombe
Designer: Anne Donald
Copyright & Pictures Editor: Samantha Russell-Tulip
Desktop Operator: Ben Galpin, David Doyle, Aptara
Illustrator: DiacriTech
Printed in China

National Library of Australia Cataloguing-in-Publication entry (paperback)
Creator: Rickard, Greg, author.
Title: Pearson science SB7 / Greg Rickard [and thirteen others]
Edition: Second edition.
ISBN: 9781488656880 (paperback)
Series: Pearson science SB; 7.
Notes: Includes index.
Target Audience: For secondary school age.
Subjects: Science—Study and teaching (Secondary)
Science—Textbooks.
Dewey Number: 500

Pearson Australia Group Pty Ltd   ABN 40 004 245 943

Disclaimer/s
The selection of internet addresses (URLs) provided for this book/resource was valid at the time of publication and was chosen as being appropriate for use as a secondary education research tool. However, due to the dynamic nature of the internet, some addresses may have changed, may have ceased to exist since publication, or may inadvertently link to sites with content that could be considered offensive or inappropriate. While the authors and publisher regret any inconvenience this may cause readers, no responsibility for any such changes or unforeseeable errors can be accepted by either the authors or the publisher.

Some of the images used in *Pearson Science* might have associations with deceased Indigenous Australians. Please be aware that these images might cause sadness or distress in Aboriginal or Torres Strait Islander communities.

Practical activities:
All practical activities, including the illustrations, are provided as a guide only and the accuracy of such information cannot be guaranteed. Teachers must assess the appropriateness of an activity and take into account the experience of their students and facilities available. Additionally, all practical activities should be trialled before they are attempted with students and a risk assessment must be completed. All care should be taken and appropriate protective clothing and equipment should be worn when carrying out any practical activity. Although all practical activities have been written with safety in mind, Pearson Australia and the authors do not accept any responsibility for the information contained in or relating to the practical activities, and are not liable for any loss and/or injury arising from or sustained as a result of conducting any of the practical activities described in this book.

PEARSON Australian Curriculum
Writing and Development Team

Anna Bennett
Differentiation Consultant, Victoria

Ian Bentley
Former Head of Science, VCAA exam and trial exam writer, STEM investigation developer
Victoria

Christina Bliss
Science and senior Biology Teacher, VCE assessor Biology
Author and question writer,
Victoria

Donna Chapman
Science Laboratory Technician
Safety consultant, Victoria

Dr Warrick Clarke
Curriculum Writer, Science Communicator and Australian Post-Doctoral Research Fellow at UNSW.
Author, New South Wales

Jacinta Devlin
Science and senior Physics Teacher
Author, Victoria

Julia Ferguson
Education Officer,
Earth Science Western Australia
Author and reviewer,
Western Australia

Bob Hoogendoorn
Exam-style question writer
VCAA chemistry exam Assessor,
Victoria

Penny Lee
Science Laboratory Technician
Safety consultant, Victoria

Louise Lennard
Head of Science
Author and STEM investigation developer, Victoria

Greg Linstead
Former Head of Science, Deputy Chief Examiner, STAWA President
Author, Western Australia

Bryony Lowe
Director of Numeracy Improvement
Former Head of Science and Region Teaching & Learning Coach
Author and reviewer, Victoria

David Madden
Science Learning Area Manager at QCAA, Former Head of Science
Author and reviewer, Queensland

Fran Maher
Bioscience educator, Science teacher, Formerly a bioscience researcher
Author, Victoria

Rochelle Manners
Science and mathematics teacher
Co-ordinating author Teacher Companion, Queensland

Shirley Melissas
Teacher Librarian and Author
Development Editor, Victoria

Tamsin Moore
Science and senior Psychology teacher
Author, Western Australia

Natalie Nejad
Head of Science, Science and mathematics teacher
STEM investigation developer
Victoria

Malcolm Parsons
Education consultant, former teacher
Author, Victoria

Greg Rickard
Teacher, Former Head of Science
Coordinating Author, Victoria

Lana Salfinger
Teacher, Head of Science, IB Workshop leader in MYP Sciences
Author, Western Australia

Maggie Spenceley
Former Teacher, Curriculum Writer
Queensland Studies Authority
Author, Queensland

Jim Sturgiss
Teacher, Former Coordinating analyst (NSW Department of Education) reporting NAPLAN, Senior test designer for Essential Secondary Science Assessment (ESSA)
Author, Thinking Scientifically questions, New South Wales

Craig Tilley
STAV Trial Exam Coordinator,
VCAA Exam Assessor.
Author and exam-style question writer, Victoria

Jo Watkins
Chief Executive Officer,
Earth Science Western Australia
Author and reviewer, Western Australia

Dr Trish Weekes
Science Literacy Consultant,
New South Wales

Rebecca Wood
Science educator and tutor
Author, Victoria

Table of Contents

How to use this book vi
Acknowledgements xii

1 Working scientifically 1
1.1 Science and the laboratory 2
Working with Science 4
Science as a Human Endeavour 9
Review questions 10
Practical investigations 11
1.2 Practical investigations 14
Science as a Human Endeavour 18
Review questions 19
Practical investigations 21
1.3 Communicating 23
Working with Science 26
Review questions 27
Practical investigations 29
1.4 Planning your own investigation 31
Science as a Human Endeavour 34
Review questions 35
Practical investigations 36
Chapter review 37
Research questions 38
Thinking scientifically questions 39
Glossary 40

2 Properties of substances 41
2.1 Physical and chemical properties 42
Working with Science 45
Science as a Human Endeavour 46
Review questions 48
Practical investigations 49
2.2 Solids, liquids and gases 52
Science as a Human Endeavour 56
Review questions 58
Practical investigations 59
2.3 Changing state 61
Review questions 65
Practical investigations 66
2.4 Density 70
Science as a Human Endeavour 74
Review questions 76
Practical investigations 77
Chapter review 81
Research questions 82
Thinking scientifically questions 83
Glossary 84

3 Earth resources 85
3.1 Renewable and non-renewable resources 86
Science as a Human Endeavour 94
Review questions 96
Practical investigations 97
3.2 Energy resources 100
Working with Science 106
Science as a Human Endeavour 107
Review questions 109
Practical investigations 110
3.3 The water cycle 112
Review questions 118
Practical investigations 120
3.4 Water management 123
Science as a Human Endeavour 128
Review questions 130
Practical investigations 131
Chapter review 133
Research questions 135
Thinking scientifically questions 137
Glossary 138

4 Mixtures 139
4.1 Types of mixtures 140
Working with Science 143
Review questions 144
Practical investigations 146
4.2 Separating insoluble substances 149
Science as a Human Endeavour 154
Review questions 155
Practical investigations 156
4.3 Separating soluble substances 159
Review questions 163
Practical investigations 164
4.4 Purifying water 166
Science as a Human Endeavour 172
Review questions 174
Practical investigations 175
Chapter review 177
Research questions 178
Thinking scientifically questions 179
Glossary 182

5 Habitats and interactions ■ ■ ■ — 183

- **5.1 Living places** — **184**
  - Science as a Human Endeavour — 189
  - Review questions — 190
  - Practical investigations — 192
- **5.2 Food chains and food webs** — **194**
  - Review questions — 198
  - Practical investigations — 200
- **5.3 Impacts on ecosystems** — **201**
  - Science as a Human Endeavour — 206
  - Review questions — 208
  - Practical investigations — 209
- **5.4 Effects of industry** — **210**
  - Working with Science — 214
  - Science as a Human Endeavour — 215
  - Review questions — 216
  - Practical investigations — 217
- **Chapter review** — 220
- **Research questions** — 222
- **Thinking scientifically questions** — 223
- **Glossary** — 225

6 Classification ■ ■ ■ — 227

- **6.1 Using classification** — **228**
  - Review questions — 234
  - Practical investigations — 236
- **6.2 Animal kingdom** — **237**
  - Working with Science — 244
  - Science as a Human Endeavour — 245
  - Review questions — 247
  - Practical investigations — 249
- **6.3 Other kingdoms** — **250**
  - Review questions — 257
  - Practical investigations — 259
- **6.4 Classification systems** — **262**
  - Review questions — 269
  - Practical investigations — 271
- **Chapter review** — 273
- **Research questions** — 275
- **Thinking scientifically questions** — 276
- **Glossary** — 277

Key

■ ■ ■	Science Inquiry Skills
■ ■ ■	Biological sciences
■ ■ ■	Chemical sciences
■ ■ ■	Physical sciences
■ ■ ■	Earth and space sciences

7 Forces ■ ■ ■ — 279

- **7.1 What are forces?** — **280**
  - Science as a Human Endeavour — 284
  - Review questions — 286
  - Practical investigations — 288
- **7.2 Friction—a contact force** — **292**
  - Review questions — 296
  - Practical investigations — 298
- **7.3 Gravity—a non-contact force** — **301**
  - Science as a Human Endeavour — 305
  - Review questions — 306
  - Practical investigations — 308
- **7.4 Magnetic and electric fields** — **311**
  - Review questions — 317
  - Practical investigations — 319
- **7.5 Simple machines** — **323**
  - Working with Science — 328
  - Review questions — 329
  - Practical investigations — 331
- **Chapter review** — 336
- **Research questions** — 338
- **Thinking scientifically questions** — 339
- **Glossary** — 341

8 Earth in space ■ ■ ■ — 343

- **8.1 The night sky** — **344**
  - Review questions — 349
  - Practical investigations — 350
- **8.2 Discovering the solar system** — **352**
  - Science as a Human Endeavour — 357
  - Review questions — 359
  - Practical investigations — 360
- **8.3 Gravity and orbits** — **363**
  - Review questions — 369
  - Practical investigations — 370
- **8.4 Earth** — **373**
  - Working with Science — 376
  - Science as a Human Endeavour — 377
  - Review questions — 379
  - Practical investigations — 380
- **Chapter review** — 383
- **Research questions** — 385
- **Thinking scientifically questions** — 386
- **Glossary** — 387
- **Index** — **388**

How to use this book • STUDENT BOOK

Pearson Science 2nd edition has been updated to fully address all strands of the new **Australian Curriculum: Science** which has been adopted throughout the nation. Since some states have tailored the Australian Curriculum slightly for their own particular students, the coverage of the new **Victorian Curriculum: Science** is also captured in this new edition. We address inclusion by clearly indicating the additional content which enables flexibility to determine the approach, as well as the added bonus of an option to engage with **extension** and **revision** opportunities.

All aspects of the student books have been thoroughly reviewed by our **Literacy Consultant Dr Trish Weekes** and the result is **more accessible** content, **enhanced scaffolding** and **strengthened question and instructions sets**. The design is updated to improve the readability and navigation of the text.

In this edition, we retain a flexible approach to teaching and learning. A careful mix of **inquiry**, **STEM** and a range of **practical investigations**, along with **fully updated** content reflect the dynamic and ever-changing nature of scientific knowledge and developments. Combined with the improved and enhanced sets of questions, this series provides a rich assortment of choice, supporting a **differentiated approach**.

An integrated and research-based approach to science education, which ensures every student has engaging, supportive and challenging opportunities.

Be set

The **Chapter opening page** sets a context for the chapter, engaging students through questions that get them thinking about the content and concepts to come. The chapter learning outcomes are provided in student friendly language and give transparency and direction for the chapter. Each chapter is divided into self-contained modules. The **module opening page** includes an introduction that places the material to come in a meaningful context.

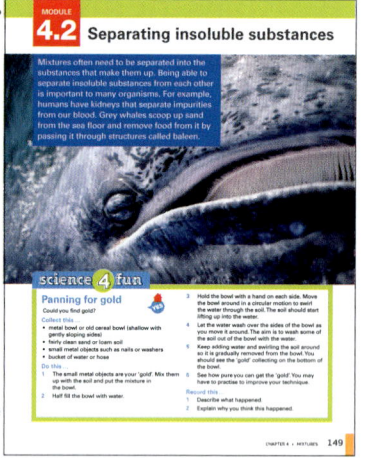

Be interested

Stunning and relevant **photos and illustrations** are purposefully selected to build understanding of the text. Students know when and how they should engage with artwork as each image is clearly referenced from within the text to develop understanding. Captions for every artwork, along with labels for more difficult images, build further meaning and understanding.

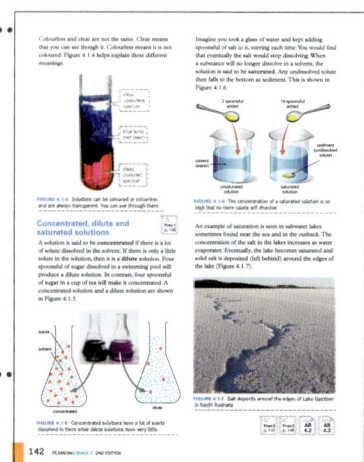

vi PEARSON SCIENCE 2ND EDITION

Be inventive

The **STEM4fun** activities are simple STEM-based applications. Students are given an open-ended problem and asked to create, design or improve something. These problems require students to draw on their acquired knowledge and skills, but are more about the process than the actual solution.

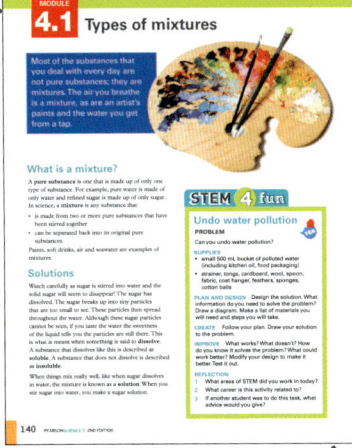

Be inquiring

Science4Fun are inquiry based activities. They pre-empt the theory and get students to engage with the concepts through a simple activity that sets students up to 'discover' the science before they learn about it. Broadly speaking, they encourage students to think about what happens in the world and how science explains this.

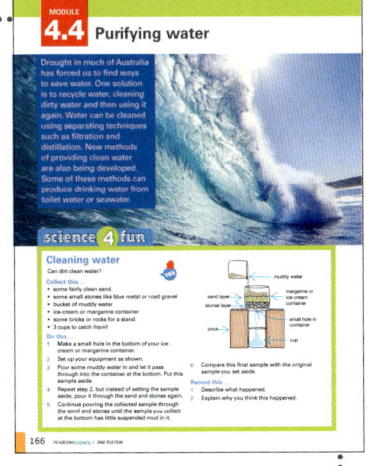

Be inspired

Working with science career profiles cast a spotlight on the diversity of career opportunities available through science with a focus on future science directions, STEM and women in science. Profiles include questions that to relate to the topic.

Be amazed

The **Science as a Human Endeavour** strand is addressed throughout the modules as well as in spreads. Many of the spreads have a special focus on Australian Scientists and highlight exciting developments, innovations and discoveries across all science fields. This feature also includes questions to help students build connections with the content they are learning and the relevance of these contributions.

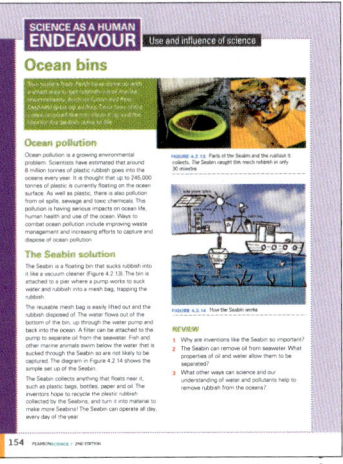

Be skilled

Skill Builders outline a method or technique and are instructive and self-contained. They step students through the skill to support science application.

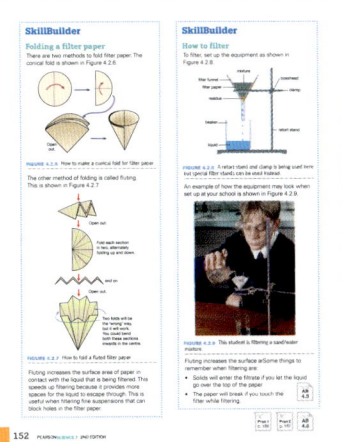

Be guided

Worked examples scaffold problems and techniques with a new thinking and working approach to guide students through solving problems and applying techniques to master and practice key skills.

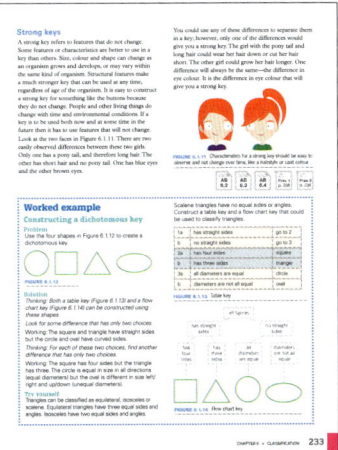

PEARSON SCIENCE 2ND EDITION

How to use this book *continued*

Be confident

Each module concludes with a comprehensive **module review** set that checks for understanding of key concepts and ideas developed through a carefully prepared range of Blooms categorised questions. Students enjoy the benefit of checkpoint opportunities to engage with module review questions at key points throughout the module.

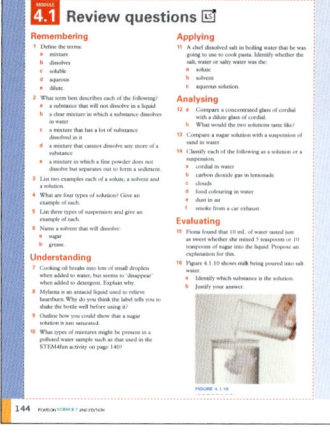
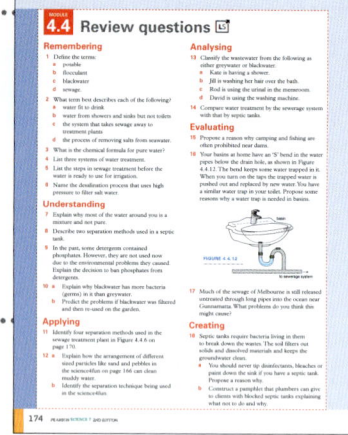

Be investigative

Practical investigations are placed at the end of each module. New Student Designed Investigations and STEM inquiry tasks provide students with opportunities to plan investigations, design and trial their plans to seek answers and solve problems. A timing suggestion assists with planning, whilst safety boxes highlight significant hazards. Full risk assessments, safety notes and technician's checklist and recipes are provided via ProductLink and eBooks.

Practical investigation icons appear throughout the modules to indicate suggested times for practical work. An icon will also appear to indicate where a SPARKlab alternative is available.

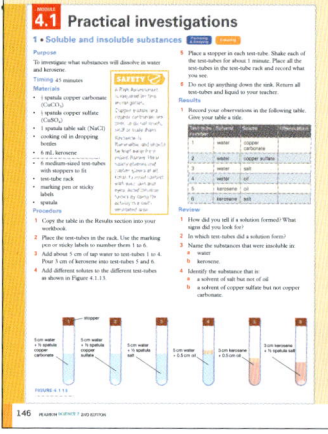
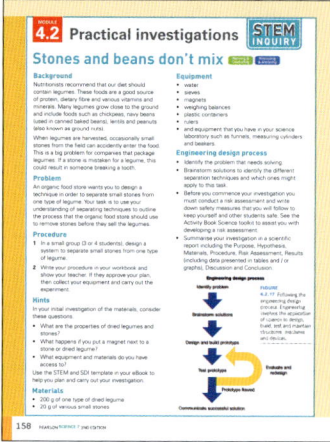

Prac 1
p. 175

Be extended

Each chapter concludes with an improved and richer assortment of questions organised within the Blooms structure, that bring together the learning of concepts from across a chapter. Apply knowledge and skills to answer questions, engage in fresh new opportunities for **inquiry** and extend into **research** to take your learning to a new level with the enhanced **Chapter Review**.

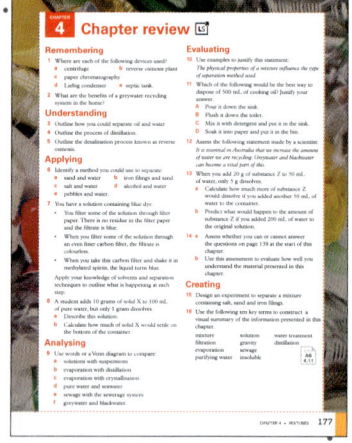

Be a thinker

Following the chapter review are **thinking questions** relevant to the chapter. These test students' science and interpretive skills.

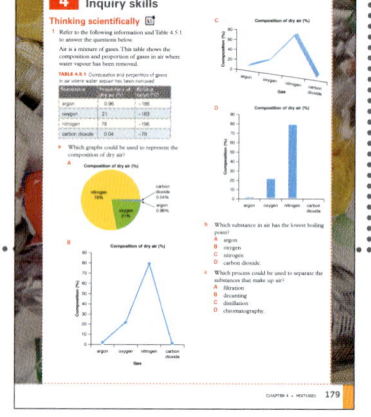

viii   PEARSON SCIENCE 2ND EDITION

Be supported

Every chapter concludes with an illustrated **glossary** that is an easy reference for additional support in comprehension of key terms. All key terms are bolded throughout the chapter.

Be reinforced

The **Activity Book** provides a set of worksheets for every student book chapter, giving lots of opportunities for practice, application and extension. Reference **Activity Book icons** indicate when the best time is to engage with a particular worksheet.

Be prepared

Focussed on supporting the greater **diversity of learners and pathways**, a 'step up' program has been developed to launch students into senior sciences, in addition to the 'core' science program. A series of **step up chapters**, written by experienced senior science teachers, have been developed with the view to providing all students with best chance of success.

The **Year 9 Student Book** features a step up chapter on **Psychology**. The **Year 10 Student Book** includes step up chapters for **Biology**, **Chemistry** and **Physics**. These chapters are referenced from the print text and are provided in full via the **eBook**. The eBook also contains **worksheets** specific to supporting the application and development of skills and knowledge from within the text.

All Year 10 Student book chapters include a new series of **Exam Style questions** to provide students practice and exposure in preparation for examinations.

Be progressed

Lightbook Starter contains **complementary sets of questions** for the module and chapter review sets from within the **student book**. This serves as alternate or additional assessment opportunities for students who enjoy the benefit of **instant feedback**, **hints** and **auto-correction** when engaging with this cutting-edge digital **formative** and **summative assessment** platform. Questions are all **tracked** against curriculum learning outcomes, making **progress** monitoring simple. A handy icon indicates the best time to engage with Lightbook Starter.

SERIES COMPONENTS

Pearson Science 2nd edition Teacher Companion

The Teacher Companion makes lesson preparation easy by combining full-colour student book pages with teaching strategies, ideas for class activities and fully worked solutions. All of the Activity Book pages are also included and are complete with model answers.

Be prepared
The **Chapter preview** provides an overview for planning purposes, including things to be aware of and organise ahead of commencing. The **pre-prep** also has an indicator of the time allocation to complete the chapter.

Be an expert
A further improved Teacher Companion places the support of **experts** alongside every Pearson Science 2e teachers, featuring wrap-around teaching and learning strategies and support from:
- Literacy Consultant: Dr Trish Weekes
- Differentiation Consultant: Anna Bennett
- School laboratory technicians: Penny Lee and Donna Chapman

Be confident
All practical activities have been trialled, reviewed, amended and replaced as necessary to ensure teachers and students can undertake practical activities that are tested, work and will yield effective results. Suggested replacement materials and equipment provided to make science more accessible.

Full risk assessments, safety notes and technician's checklist and recipes provided. Pracs and risk assessments have been updated to reflect new regulations around safety and materials in school science classrooms.

Be informed
Full **answers** including suggested findings and possible answers to practical activities, fully worked solutions and support for open-ended research, inquiry and STEM activities.

Pearson Science Lightbook Starter

Lightbook Starter offers a **digital formative and summative assessment tool** with **hints**, **instant feedback** and **auto-correction** of responses. Students and teachers also enjoy the visibility of learning through a **progress tracker** which shows student achievement against curriculum learning outcomes. Lightbook Starter provides questions with the most sophisticated auto-correction of answers.

Be ready
Commence each chapter with questions to establish a baseline for each student around prior knowledge. The **'before you begin'** section includes useful preparatory material with **interactive** resources to **activate prior knowledge** and **reteach key concepts**.

Be in control
Lightbook starter is written to enable teachers and students to use this digital assessment tool as an **alternative** (or additional practice) **to student book questions**. The Lightbook Starter structure mirrors the student book question set, thereby providing a complimentary alternative to the student book questions. This supports a fully integrated approach to digital assessment and feedback.

Be assisted
Module review questions (with **hints** and **solutions**), help students **check for understanding** of learning, revise and provide useful **formative assessment** to help teachers identify areas of weakness, great for lesson planning. These serve as a touchpoint throughout the chapter and students benefit from auto-corrected responses which provide **instant feedback** and support.

Be assessed
The **Chapter Review** in the student book has a complimentary **assessment** set in Lightbook Starter. Use this as an alternative to a class test at the end of a topic.

Be reflective
An integrated **reflection** set supports students in considering their progress and future areas for focus.

Be tracked
Enjoy seeing progress through the learning outcomes updated instantly in the **progress tracker**.

x PEARSON SCIENCE 2ND EDITION

Pearson Science eBook

Pearson eBook enables viewing and interaction with the student book online or offline on any device: PC or Mac, Android tablet or iPad and interactive whiteboard. This eBook retains the integrity of the printed page whilst offering easy to access resources, support and linked activities that will engage your students at school and at home.

The eBooks provide a fully integrated, digital learning platform. Enjoy the benefits of having the following digital assets and interactive resources at your fingertips:

* New interactive activities and lessons
* New Untamed Science videos
* Web destinations
* Student investigation templates and teacher support
* New step up Student Book and Activity Book chapters with answers at Years 9 & 10
* Full answers to all Student Book and Activity Book questions
* SPARKlabs
* Risk assessments
* Full teaching programs and curriculum mapping audits
* Chapter tests with answers

Pearson Science ProductLink

Additional student and teacher resources are available free when you purchase **Pearson Science 2nd Edition**. To access, visit www.pearsonplaces.com.au and log in. Click on 'Toolkit' then select 'ProductLink' and browse your title.

Professional Learning, Training and Development

Did you know that Pearson also offers teachers a diverse range of training and development product-linked learning programs? We are dedicated to supporting your implementation of Pearson Science, but it doesn't stop here.

Our courses align closely with Pearson Science Second Edition and offer an in-depth learning experience, combining both practical and theoretical elements, enabling you to implement the resource effectively in your classroom.

Find out more about our product-linked learning, workshops, courses and conferences at **Pearson Academy** www.pearsonacademy.com.au

Acknowledgements

All material identified by [AC Australian Curriculum] is material subject to copyright under the Copyright Act 1968 and is owned by the Australian Curriculum, Assessment and Reporting Authority 2016. ACARA neither endorses nor verifies the accuracy of the information provided and accepts no responsibility for incomplete or inaccurate information. In particular, ACARA does not endorse or verify that:

- The content descriptions are solely for a particular year and subject;
- All the content descriptions for that year and subject have been used; and
- The author's material aligns with the Australian Curriculum content descriptions for the relevant year and subject.

You can find the unaltered and most up to date version of this material at http://www.australiancurriculum.edu.au/
This material is reproduced with the permission of ACARA.

The Victorian Curriculum F–10 content elements are © VCAA, reproduced by permission. Victorian Curriculum F–10 elements accurate at time of publication. The VCAA does not endorse or make any warranties regarding this resource. The Victorian Curriculum F–10 and related content can be accessed directly at the VCAA website.

We thank the following for permission to reproduce copyright material.
The following abbreviations are used in this list: t = top, b = bottom, l = left, r = right, c = centre.

Cover image: Science Photo Library/Eric Heller
123RF: pp. 138tr, 172b, 225b, 259t, 310; alekseypatsyuk, p. 36 (tea); Philipe Ancheta, p. 16b; Rafael Ben-Ari, p. 82l; Philip Bird, p. 92t; Alen Ciric, p. 305l; Jostein Hauge, p. 84r, 62l; Imagedb China, p. 183; ingehogenbijl, p. 100; kateleigh, p. 335r; Sebastian Kaulitzki, p. 305r; kodda, p. 107l; kristo74, p. 188tr; Martin Kucera, p. 84bl; Steve Mann, p. 323t; Dmytro Nikitin, p. 87b; Atthidej Nimmanhaemin, p. 321; Ari Nousiainen, p. 151l; Sura Nualpradid, p. 279; Cornelia Pithart, p. 229l; Andriy Popov, p. 64r; wu ruiyun, p. 257; vladimir salman, p. 51; Brian Scantlebury, p. 44r; serezniy, p. 200; Maksim Shebeko, p. 161 (pot); Marek R. Swadzba, p. 247; Thawat Tanhai, p. 293r; Andrew Tichovolsky, p. 259b; Leah-Anne Thompson, p. 4bc; monthon wachirasettakul, p. 161br; Wavebreak Media Ltd, p. 238tl; Feng Yu, p. 36 (elastics).
AAP: RAMA SURYA, p. 215bl.
Age Fotostock: PhotoStock-Israel, p. 169.
Alamy Stock Photo: Roger Allen, p. 91t; Arco Images/Huetter, C., p. 251 (azolla); Arco Images GmbH, p. 266 (wallaroo); steve ball, p. 350; Holger Burmeister, p. 103l; John Cancalosi, p. 47r; culture-images GmbH, p. 294 (blue car); Elizabeth Czitronyi, p. 214r; dpa picture alliance, p. 328b; Daniel Dempster Photography, p. 99; John Daniels, p. 268 (galahs); Alan Dyer/VWPics, p. 387b; epa european pressphoto agency b.v., p. 172t; FLPA, pp. 182b, 188l; Fresh Start Images, p. 62tr; fStop Images GmbH, p. 284; Andrew Fox, p. 126l; Don Fuchs, p. 202r; Philip Game, p. 252tl; Oliver Gerhard, p. 104l; Paul Glendell, p. 328t; David Hancock, p. 151r; Nick Hanna, p. 214l; Brian Harris, p. 123; Steffen Hauser/botanikfoto, p. 267 (Wollemi); Tony Hertz, pp. 125, 138tl; Chris Howes, p. 211br; imageBROKER, p. 244tl; INTERFOTO, p. 70t; jaxpix, p. 136; John White Photos, p. 348b; Kim Karpeles, p. 323b; Marek Kasula, p. 268 (masked finch); Suzanne Long, p. 258l; Mary Evans Picture Library, p. 359; MaximImages, p. 302l; Nature Picture Library, p. 88t; Becky Nixon, p. 291; NSP-RF, p. 185tr; Paul Mayall Australia, p. 205r; PCN Photography, p. 283r; Gerry Pearce, p. 194t; Purestock, pp. 294 (hovercraft), 295t; Jochen Schlenker/robertharding, p. 185l; sciencephotos, pp. 6 (beam, spring), p. 316t; Martin Shields, p. 6 (electronic); Stanislaw Pytel, p. 71r; STOCK4B GmbH, p. 82r; Egmont Strigl, p. 150; Erik Tham, p. 376; The Natural History Museum, p. 245br; tingimage, p. 313; Barry Turner, p. 251 (livewort); Penny Tweedie, p. 267b; Masa Ushioda, p. 266 (box jellyfish); Genevieve Vallee, pp. 117r, 142br; David Wall, p. 125c, p. 129; WaterFrame, pp. 190, 241br; Andrew Watson, p. 91c; Dave Watts, pp. 185b, 245tr, 246, p. 278l; Westend61 GmbH, p. 4bl; Wildlight Photo, p. 253l; A. T. Willett, p. 316b; Ray Wilson, p. 268 (long-tailed finch and double-barred finch); Sam Wirzba, p. 213 (shorthorn).
Caroline Artzi: p. 372t.
Auscape International Photo Library: p. 87t; Attila Bicskos, p. 243tr; Nicholas Birks, p. 268 (bat); Jean-Paul Ferrero, pp. p. 207b, 229tr, 242 (barramundi); Wayne Lawler, p. 90r; Jaime Plaza Van Roon, p. 253cr; Dr David Wachenfeld, p. 239 (jellyfish).
The Bureau of Infrastructure, Transport and Regional Economics: Bureau of Infrastructure, Transport and Regional Economics (BITRE) 2015, 'The impact of side airbags and electronic stability control on Australian road fatalities', Information Sheet 68, BITRE, Canberra (CC BY 3.0), p. 340 (all).
CSIRO: Willem van Aken, p. 263l.
DK Images: Peter Gardner, p. 144.
Dreamstime: .shock, p. 228r; Ajn, p. 243cr; Anutkate, p. 240br; Chenke Chenke, p. 252 (gingko biloba); Musat Christian, p. 243br; Jan De Wild, p. 330 (hammer); Julius Elias, p. 254 (fruit); Charlie Hutton, p. 294 (red car); Gynane, p. 228l; Isselee, p. 265 (jaguar, leopard); Jakezc, p. 326; Kira Kaplinski, p. 252bl; Kellers, p. 250t; Anna Khomulo, p. 248b; Kikimorenok, p. 300; Ali Altug Kirisoglu, p. 227; Anthony Land, p. 242 (sting ray); Xidong Luo, p. 264; Marekp, p. 252 (cycad); Robyn Mackenzie, p. 327t; Ben Mcleish, p. 266 (Snake); Jacob Melrose, p. 273 (crab); Negativex_digital_photography, p. 268 (fire); Kevin Panizza, p. 238r; David Pruter, p. 239 (starfish); Airi Pung, p. 230 (basalt); Rambleon, p. 330 (scales); Smellme, p. 225tl; Vinicius Tupinamba, pp. 240tl, 248t.
Droughtmaster Australia: Kent Ward, p. 213 (droughtmaster).
Fairfax Photo Sales: Robert Peet, p. 95.
Fotolia: axway, p. 273 (oyster); Stéphane Bidouze, p. 273 (jellyfish); laurent dambies, p. 213 (wheat); Dejan Jovanovic, pp. 10c, 10r; Kuzmick, p. 41; pannoneantonio, p. 105; Production Perig, p. 52t; rekemp, p. 270t; wolfelarry, p. 273 (starfish).
Getty Images: Theo Allofs, p. 226; Theo Allofs/Minden Pictures, p. 201t; James L Amos, p. 31b; Andrew Bain, p. 330 (dam); Robin Bush, p. 189; Jason Edwards, p. 203l; Michael & Patricia Fogden, p. 128t; Jeff Foott, p. 149; Frank Greenaway, p. 34 (moth); David Hancock, p. 94; ML Harris, p. 267 (fern); Hemera Technologies, p. 225cr; Layne Kennedy, p. 168; Gary Lewis, pp. 210b, 225bl; Francois Xavier Marit, p. 295b; Lucia Meler, p. 143l; Jim Reed, p. 92b; Picture Researchers, p. 23; Tim Ridley, p. 70b; RubberBall Productions, p. 32; C Sohns, p. 184b; Dave Watts/Visuals Unlimited, Inc., p. 253tr; William West, p. 327b; Charles D. Winters, pp. 141l, 141tr, 145l, 311b; David Woodfall, p. 178.
Gollings Photography: John Gollings, p. 122.
ImageFolk: Liz Hafalia/San Francisco Chronicle, p. 55; Dennis MacDonald, p. 101; Viviane Moos, p. 207t; Jim Reed/Science Faction, p. 14; Roger Ressmeyer, p. 91b.
iStockphoto: rebecca ames, p. 255r; Arsty, p. 242 (eel); cavefish, p. 239 (urchin); Chris Fertnig, p. 294 (oil); Martina I. Meyer, p. 238bl; Tamara Murray, p. 237b; NoDerog, pp. 251 (spores), 277r; PEDRE, p. 242 (mouth); Noah Strycker, p. 273 (penguin).
Ron Kinsey: p. 253br.
Paul Kouris: p. 108.
Lochman Transparencies: p. 267 (Blue gum).
Monash University: Kara Rasmanis, p. 4t.

NASA: pp. 89, 343, 365b, 384; Boeing/Bob Ferguson, p. 52; Goddard Space Flight Center, p. 311t; Goddard Space Flight Center Image by Reto Stöckli, p. 112b; NASA image courtesy the MODIS Rapid Response Team, p. 203r; courtesy of nasaimages.org, p. 294 (ball); NASA image by Robert Simmon and Reto Stöckli, p. 86.

National Archive of Australia: (11145789), p. 205l.

National Geographic Creative: Frans Lanting, pp. 73r, 215tl; Carsten Peter, p.9.

National Maritime Museum: Justus Sustermans (1597-1681), National Maritime Museum, Greenwich, London, Caird Collection, p. 303r.

New Britain Palm Oil Limited: p. 215r.

Newspix: Darren England, p. 124l; Aaron Francis, p. 186r; Jeff Herbert, p. 34tl; Stuart Milligan p. 107r.

NHPA/Photoshot: p. 206br; p. 206bl.

Barnaby Norris: p. 357.

Pearson Education Asia Ltd: Cheuk-king Lo, p. 221.

Pearson Education Australia: p. 325 (all); Alice McBroom, pp. 16t, 47l, 31t, 5l; PEA CD, p. 265 (tiger, lion); p. 326

Royal Botanic Gardens Victoria: Adrian Vittorio, Courtesy of the Royal Botanic Gardens Victoria, p. 244r.

Seabin Project: p. 154r (all).

Science Photo Library: pp. 57l, 182t, p. 352; Andrew Lambert Photography, pp. 152, 160; BabakTafreshi, p. 347l; Dr Tony Brain, p. 254 (Giardia); CDC/Melissa Brower, p. 4br; Alex Cherney, p. 346t; Martyn F. Chillmaid, pp. 7 (blue flame), 142tl, 76; Carlos Clarivan, p. 113b; Clouds Hill Imaging Ltd, p. 44tl; Herve Conge, ISM, p. 188br; Tony Craddock, p. 104r; Martin Dohrn, pp. 63bl, 84tl; Patrick Dumas/Look at sciences, p. 5r; Dr Fred Espenak, p. 368tr; Eye of Science, pp. 88b, 161 (salt, sugar), 240bl, 294 (scales); Mark Garlick, pp. 348t; 368tl, 368bl, 375; Steve Gschmeissner, p. 255bl; Gary Hincks, p. 365t; Mikkel Juul Jensen, p. 364; Russell Kightley, p. 254 (euglena); Andrew Lambert, pp. 72, 141bl, 141br, 142bl; Lawrence Lawry, p. 44bl; Microfield Scientific LTD, p. 254 (yeast); Cordelia Molloy, p. 363b; NASA, pp. 303l, 302r, 344b, 356, 377; NASA/JPL/Space Science Institute, p. 363t; David Nunuk, p. 344t; Walter Pacholka, p. 347r; David Parker, pp. 373b, 349; Pekka Parviainen, p. 368br; Marie Perennou, p. 62br; Philippe Plailly, p. 65l; Power and Syred, p. 116c; Daniel Sambraus, p. 65l; John Sanford, p. 345l; 358 (all); Sinclair Stammers, pp. 17r, 40tr, 255tl; Power and Syred, pp. 161 (limescale), 293tl; Babak Tafreshi, p. 345r; David Taylor, p. 7 (yellow flame), 40br; TEK image, p. 153l; Sheila Terry, pp. 73l, 263tr; SPUTNIK, p. 301; Geoff Tompkinson, p. 159; Dirk Wiersma, p. 161 (copper sulfate), p.148; Detlev Van Ravenswaay, pp. 53, 346b, 366, 378.

Shutterstock: 1553054, p. 206t; 167119931, p. 3t; ADA_photo, p. 42; AJCespedes, p. 125b; Ricardo A. Alves, p. 27tl; Bragin Alexey, p. 83; Amble Design, p. 180; ARENA Creative, p. 281 (basketballer); Artiomp, p. 314 (drill); AustralianCamera, p. 119 (rainforest); Kevin Autret, p. 132; Evgeniy Ayupov, p. 195 (grasshopper); Nancy Bauer, p. 167 (dye); belizar, p. 223br; Dr. J. Beller, p. 274c; Mikhail Blajenov, p. 230 (freshwater); Oleg Blazhyievskyi, p. 197; B Brown, p. 167 (fertilisers); BMCL, p. 274r; bstoltz, p. 27br; Sebastien Burel, p. 119 (woodland); Robyn Butler, pp. 196l, 266 (Eastern Grey Kangaroo); Cameramannz, p. 235 (beans); Rich Carey, pp. 3 (ecology), 40bl, 187 (school of fish, coral); Marco Cavina, p. 230 (amethyst); Jacek Chabraszewski, p. 286; Chonnanit, p. 209; Clara, p. 274l; clearviewstock, p. 244bl; CLIPAREA l Custom media (bacteria), p. 195; Neale Cousland, pp. 34 (fire), 231; cynoclub, p. 20; Natalia D., p. 281 (dough); Esteban De Armas, p. 262; dirkr, pp. 230 (saltwater), 270b; Maslov Dmitry, p. 251 (sporangium); Pichugin Dmitry, pp. p. 3 (geology), 245bl; dotshock, p. 106r; dragunov, p. 102; Sebastian Duda, p. 237t, 278br; eltoro69, p. 230 (pipes); EpicStockMedia, pp. 166, 280; Greg Epperson, p. 3 (physics); Evikka, p. 314 (cooktop); EvrenKalinbacak, p. 93b; ffolas, p. 294 (rollerblade); FiledIMAGE, p. 194b; Fiore, p. 195 (sun); Mike Flippo, p. 36 (pinata); fotosav, p. 195 (grass); Sanit Fuangnakhon, p. 223l; gennady, p. 236; Germanskydiver, p. 307; ggw1962, p. 40tl; Matt Gibson, p. 145r; giSpate, p. 85; gnohz, p. 211tr; Volodymyr Goinyk, p. 116r; goodluz, p. 2; guentermanaus, p. 167 (rivers); Johnny Habell, p. 8b; R. Hall, p. 71l; Jacob Hamblin, p. 265 (spider); mark higgins, pp. 191, 196tr, 225tr; David Hilcher, p. 204br; Cyril Hou, p. 153r; Idea Studio, p. 293bl; Ilaszlo, p. 90l; iofoto, p. 210t; Ipatov, p. 34 (skier); Tischenko Irina, p. 235 (banana); Evgeniy Isaychev, p. 138bl; Eric Isselee, pp. 27tr, 204t, 229br, p. 265 (monkey, gorilla, wallaby), 273 (monkey); Andrea Izzotti, p. 187 (fish); jabiru, pp. 281 (roller coaster), 341; Marcel Jancovic, p. 297; Bernd Juergens, p. 330 (bottle opener); karenfoleyphotography, p. 61; kazoka, p. 243l; Cathy Keifer, p. 199; Kichigin, p. 63bc, 63br; Brian Kinney, p. 287; Serhiy Kobyakov, p. 235 (yellow apple); Georgios Kollidas, p. 355l; Vadim Kononenko, p. 57r; Levent Konuk, p. 314 (MRI); Zdenek Krchak, p. 34 (snow); Timur Kulgarin, p. 119 (still washing); Volodymyr Kyrylyuk, p. 322; Johan Larson, p. 213 (brahman); Rafael Ramirez Lee, p. 266 (Red Kangaroo); Gareth Leung, p. 195 (kookaburra); LianeM, p. 263br; Lena Lir, p. 74; Luis Louro, p. 292; LuckyKeeper, p. 277l; Lucky Business, p. 1; Robyn Mackenzie, p. 250 (flower); Tony Magdaraog, p. 196br; Cosmin Manci, p. 27bl; MarcelClemens, p. 387t; R. Gino Santa Maria, p. 140; mariait, p. 265 (horse); Aleksandr Markin, p. 167 (drinks); Alexander Mazurkevich, p. 258r; milias1987, p. 116b; Frances A. Miller, p. 230 (sedimentary); mlorenz, p. 245tl; Natykach Nataliia, p. 281 (spring); Sean Nel, pp. 119 (windy washing), 117l; Neveshkin Nikolay, p. 365c; Fedorov Oleksiy, p. 112r; Chris P., p. 373t; Pavel L Photo and Video, p. 314 (speakers); Edyta Pawlowska, p. 265 (boy); Bardocz Peter, p. 10l; Sergey Peterman, p. 304; photka, p. 139; Photographee.eu, p. 281 (sign); pics721, p. 187 (reef); Picsfive, p. 36 (tapes); I. Pilon, p. 335l; PKDirector, p. 119 (steamy rainforest); Rainer Plendl, p. 29; Leigh Prather, p. 54r; Belinda Pretorius, p. 103r; Production Perig, p. 45; Scott Prokop, p. 119 (cactus); Raimundas, p. 225br; Johanna Ralph, p. 212l; Alexander Raths, p. 167 (medicine); Sue Robinson, p. 254 (fungi); Huguette Roe, p. 93t; ruigsantos, p. 283l; RyFlip, p. 266 (children); Lisa S., p. 249l; schankz, pp. 265 (ant), 273 (ant); scyther5, p. 314 (credit card); Susan Schmitz, p. 232; Serg64, p. 324; Eremin Sergey, p. 330 (tweezers); Umberto Shtanzman, p. 187 (Earth); Asther Lau Choon Siew, p. 278tr; simez78, p. 228t; Alex Staroseltsev, p. 235 (apple); Wally Stemberger, pp. 124r, 138cr, StevenRussellSmithPhotos, p. 249r; Jeeranan Thongpan, p. 46; G Tipene, pp. 195 (rabbit), 241tr; Vitaly Titov, p. 265 (pigeon); Maksim Toome, p. 285; Gary Unwin, p. 195 (potoroo); Kristina Vackova, p. 240tr; James van den Broek, p. 266 (Spider); Francois van der Merwe, p. 127br; Anatolii Vasilev, p. 3 (astronomy); Marek Velechovsky, p. 223tr; Viktor1, p. 43l; Dolce Vita, p. 127tr; Chepko Danil Vitalevich, p. 3 (chemistry); Vaclav Volrab, p. 64l; wavebreakmedia, pp. 15l, 17l; Julian Weber, p. 235 (capsicum); Ashley Whitworth, p. 250 (forest); Steve Wood, p. 251 (moss); Bruce Works, p. 155; Sergiy Zavgorodny, p. 18; Zheltyshev, p. 202l; Czesznak Zsolt, p. 34 (fox).

Dimetra Skondras-Silva: p. 143r.

Maggie Spenceley: pp. 126r, 128b, 186b.

Spiire: p. 127l.

Kim Starr: Licensed under Creative Commons (CC BY 3.0), p. 267 (Grey iron bark).

Tunc Tezel: pp. 353; 387c.

Thinkstock: Amlani, p. 212r; Jolanta Dabrowska, p. 241tl; Mary Durden, p. 184t; Joanne Ingate, p. 54l; Jakub Jirsßk, p. 36 (ball); Jupiterimages, Brand X Pictures, p. 3 (psychology); Larisa Lofitskaya, pp. 15r, 40cr; Sean Nel, p. 239 (girl); QQQQcon, p. 106l; richmaj99, p. 3 (biology); fanelie rosier, p. 211bl; Vinicius Tupinamba, 171; vnlit, p. 43r; WTolenaars, p. 201b.

World Health Organisation (WHO): Reprinted with permission from the World Health Organization, http://www.who.int/mediacentre/events/2015/world-antibiotic-awareness-week/infographics/en/, accessed 17 July 2016, p. 26.

Wikimedia Commons: p. 352 (flags of Australia, Papua New Guinea, Samoa).

Every effort has been made to trace and acknowledge copyright. However, should any infringement have occurred, the publishers tender their apologies and invite copyright owners to contact them.

CHAPTER 1
Working scientifically

Have you ever wondered...
- why science is taught in schools?
- why scientists run experiments?
- why laboratories have rules?

After completing this chapter you should be able to:
- describe how science and technology impact society
- identify equipment appropriate to a task
- use diagrams to simplify situations
- describe how regulations on wearing seatbelts and safety helmets developed from scientific observations
- evaluate data to support or reject a hypothesis
- draw conclusions based on evidence
- construct and use tables, spreadsheets, graphs, keys and models
- describe patterns in data
- collaboratively plan how to investigate a problem
- identify controlled, dependent and independent variables
- compare data collected from different sources
- evaluate investigation methods and compare with others
- describe how different branches of science work together.

This is an extract from the Australian Curriculum
Victorian Curriculum F–10 © VCAA (2016); reproduced by permission

MODULE 1.1 Science and the laboratory

Scientists study the world around them to find out how it works. They investigate the living world of animals, plants, bugs and germs, and they study the planet and environments they live on and in. They investigate the physical world of substances like plastics and metals, and chemicals like water and acids. They explore forms of energy such as heat, light and sound. They even study things that are out of this world, like other planets, stars and galaxies.

STEM 4 fun

Can you create a phone?

PROBLEM
Create a phone that allows you to have a conversation when standing three metres apart.

SUPPLIES foam cups, plastic cups, paper cups, empty tins, wool, wire, cotton, cardboard, foil, twine

PLAN AND DESIGN Design the solution—what information do you need to solve the problem? Draw a diagram. Make a list of materials you will need and steps you will take.

CREATE Follow your plan. Construct your solution to the problem.

IMPROVE What works? What doesn't? How do you know it solves the problem? What could work better? Modify your design to make it better. Test it out.

REFLECTION
1 What area of STEM did you work in today?
2 In what career do these activities connect?
3 How did you use mathematics in this task?

Science is important

The world is very complex and is becoming more complex every day. New technology is constantly being developed and new issues are frequently hitting the headlines. For example, HD televisions, Blu-ray, smart phones and tablet computers were not common ten years ago. Laptop computers, mobile phones, email and the internet are only a little older. Likewise the issues of climate change were not heard of until relatively recently.

Developments in science have also caused argument and debate. Cloning, the use of stem cells to repair damage in the body, and genetically modified food have all been developed from scientific discovery. Society has split into those who support the use of these new discoveries and those who do not. Climate change, and what we as humans should do to control it, has also split society into those who believe that it is happening and those who do not. There is even debate among those who do believe it is happening: some believe that it is caused by human activity, while others believe it could be part of a natural cycle.

Whatever its cause, glaciers like the one in Figure 1.1.1 are melting at a higher-than-normal rate. Older issues, such as whether nuclear power should be used in Australia, are being debated again because of our increasing energy needs. As a future adult and voter you will need an understanding of science to help you decide what we should do about these issues and any new issues that arise. To make good decisions about our future, you will need an understanding of science.

FIGURE 1.1.1 Climate change: do we believe the evidence that temperatures are rising because of human activity or do we reject it based on other evidence?

The branches of science

The subject of science covers many different areas, ranging from acids to aardvarks, electricity to emus, rats to rocks, Venus to viruses, and much, much more. Science covers so many different areas that it must be split into different **branches** or **disciplines**, some of which are shown in Figure 1.1.2. Scientists tend to work in one particular branch of science. This allows them to explore it in detail and develop a deep understanding of it without being distracted by what is going on in the other branches.

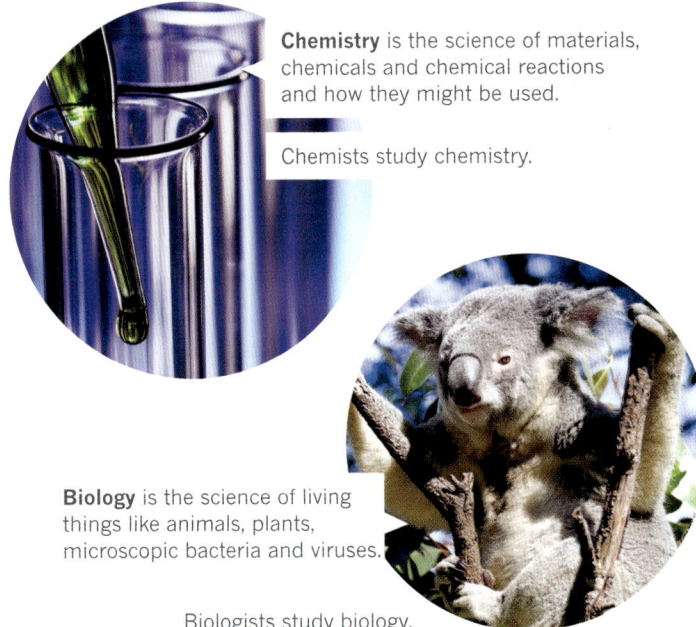

Chemistry is the science of materials, chemicals and chemical reactions and how they might be used.

Chemists study chemistry.

Biology is the science of living things like animals, plants, microscopic bacteria and viruses.

Biologists study biology.

Astronomy is the science of the planets, stars and the universe.

Astronomers study astronomy.

Ecology is the science of how living things affect each other and the environment in which they live.

Ecologists study ecology.

Physics is the science of matter and energy.

Physicists study physics.

Geology is the science of rocks, the Earth, earthquakes, volcanoes and fossils.

Geologists study geology.

Psychology is the science of how and why we behave the way we do.

Psychologists study psychology.

FIGURE 1.1.2 The main branches of science

CHAPTER 1 • WORKING SCIENTIFICALLY   3

Working with Science

BUSHFIRE AND CLIMATE SCIENTIST
Dr Sarah Harris

Understanding climate and bushfire patterns is an important part of predicting where and when bushfires might occur. By using this knowledge, firefighters can be more prepared and better equipped to manage bushfires. Bushfire and climate scientists use geology, biology, chemistry and mathematics to study, map and model fire and weather trends. Dr Sarah Harris is a bushfire and climate scientist at Monash University (Figure 1.1.3). In her work, she models climate and bushfires to forecast when bushfires might happen, to understand the impact of bushfires and to map planned burns. Dr Harris works with fire and emergency services, the Bureau of Meteorology and other government departments to work out the best ways to prepare for and manage bushfires to minimise their impact.

FIGURE 1.1.3 Dr Sarah Harris

Bushfires in Australia are frequent and severe. Scientists predict that climate change will increase extreme weather events such as drought and heatwaves. For this reason, bushfire and climate research will continue to be an important field of study. To become a bushfire or climate scientist, you will need a Bachelor of Science, majoring in environmental management or earth sciences. After your degree, you can continue studying to become a research scientist, or work for government departments. You might like this job if you enjoy working in teams, analysing data, observing patterns and using your knowledge to solve environmental problems.

Review
1. Why do you think bushfire and climate scientists are important?
2. Why do you think it is important that scientists work with the community and government departments?

Sub-branches of science

The branches of science are so broad that they are split into smaller sub-branches. For example, geology covers so much material that a geologist would find it impossible to study it all. Instead geologists tend to specialise by working in a sub-branch like petrology (the study of rocks), palaeontology (fossils), vulcanology (volcanoes) or seismology (earthquakes).

Likewise, physicists might specialise in acoustics (sound), optics (light) or mechanics (forces and energy) and chemists might specialise in organic, inorganic, analytical or physical chemistry.

There are so many types of living things that biologists specialise in the study of only one type of living thing, such as animals (zoologists study zoology), plants (botanists study botany) or germs (microbiologists study microbiology) (Figure 1.1.4). Even sub-branches are sometimes too big. For example, zoology covers so many different types of animals that it is split into smaller sub-branches such as insects (entomologists study entomology), spiders (arachnologists study arachnology) and fish (ichthyologists study ichthyology).

Prac 1 p. 11

FIGURE 1.1.4 Some of the sub-branches of biology (left to to right): zoology, botany, microbiology

SciFile

The many branches of science

There are lots of other very specific sub-branches of science. Some more examples include teuthology (the study of octopuses), mycology (the study of fungi), chiropterology (the study of bats), carpology (the study of fruits and seeds) and oology (the study of eggs).

The laboratory

A scientist works in a **laboratory**. Laboratories are where scientists run most of their experiments and make most of their observations, measurements and discoveries. Your idea of a laboratory is probably a large room equipped with Bunsen burners, sinks, glassware, balances and chemicals that is occupied by people in white coats and safety glasses. This is the type of laboratory that chemists tend to work in and the type of laboratory that you will eventually work in at school. It might look something like Figure 1.1.5.

FIGURE 1.1.5 To most of us, the laboratory is a place full of Bunsen burners, glassware and people in white coats.

Different scientists have very different ideas about what a laboratory is. For marine biologists, the laboratory could be a coral reef. The laboratory of a zoologist might be a rainforest, and a laptop computer and video camera could be their most important equipment. The laboratory of an astronomer will be wherever their telescope is mounted. Figure 1.1.6 shows a palaeontologist at work in her laboratory. Her equipment is most likely a spade and brushes to clear the soil away from around the fossil. Sturdy boots, overalls and a hat will be far more important to her than a white coat. Scientists like her will usually have another laboratory in which they can test the samples they collected outdoors. For example, an ecologist might collect samples of polluted water from a creek but then analyse them back in their other laboratory.

FIGURE 1.1.6 For palaeontologists, the laboratory could be the place in which a dinosaur fossil has been found.

Equipment

Tools and equipment are a necessary part of most jobs. A builder uses power drills and saws, nail guns and measuring tapes, while a chef uses ovens, pots and pans, sieves and measuring spoons. Scientists use equipment too, to help them carry out experiments and to help them describe what they observe more accurately. Each branch of science uses its own specific tools and equipment. An astronomer will not see much without a telescope, and a microbiologist needs a microscope to see bacteria that are invisible to the naked eye. Physicists need devices like ammeters and voltmeters to measure electrical current, and ecologists need pH meters to determine how acidic creek water is.

Technology also plays an important role. Devices like smartphones and tablets provide the ability to photograph and record video of investigations. Digital probes and sensors can be connected to devices to collect a range of data. Software enables scientists to work with the data they collect, create models, and share and engage with scientific research. However, there is a set of basic scientific equipment common to most laboratories, including the ones at school.

CHAPTER 1 • WORKING SCIENTIFICALLY 5

Balances

The beam balances, electronic balances and spring balances shown in Figure 1.1.7 can all be used to measure the **mass** of an object. Mass is a measure of how much matter there is in an object.

In the laboratory, mass is usually measured in grams (g) or kilograms (kg).

FIGURE 1.1.7 Different balances can be used to measure the mass of an object.

Glassware

Glassware such as beakers, conical flasks, test-tubes and watch-glasses allows you to mix and heat chemicals. Most glassware in the laboratory is made of Pyrex, a special type of glass that is less likely than normal glass to crack when it is heated to high temperatures or cooled quickly. Some common pieces of equipment are shown in Figure 1.1.8.

Beakers and conical flasks usually have markings up their sides, but the markings only indicate rough volumes. You would use a measuring cylinder to measure more accurate volumes. Volume is normally measured in the laboratory in millilitres (mL). Larger volumes are measured in litres (L).

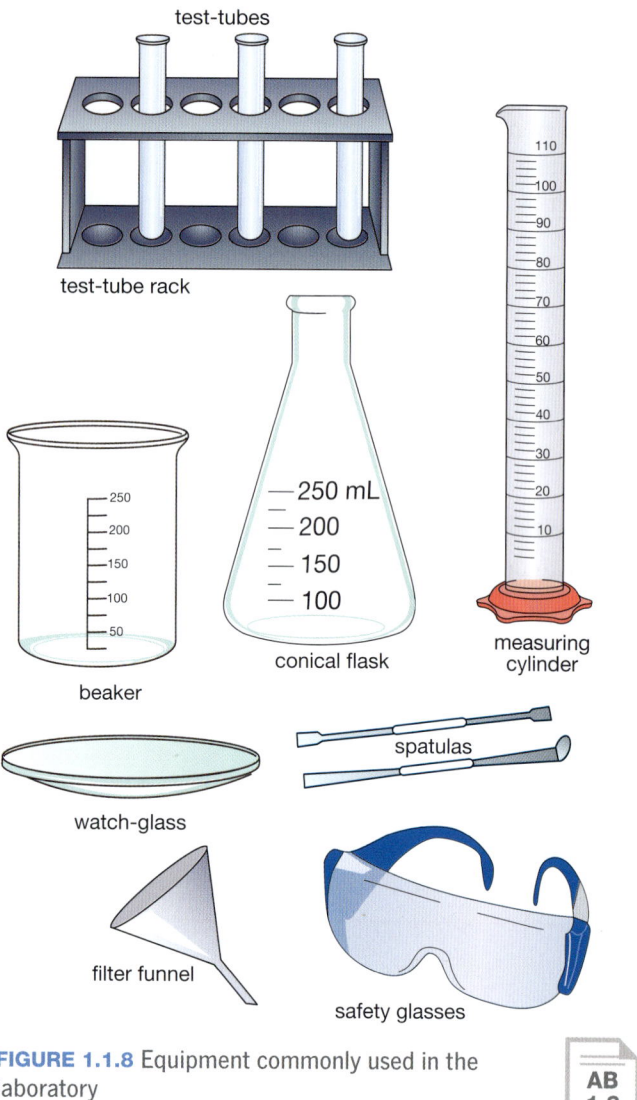

FIGURE 1.1.8 Equipment commonly used in the laboratory

Heating equipment

Hotplates and **Bunsen burners** are some of the most important and dangerous pieces of equipment that you will use in the school laboratory. Both get extremely hot and can cause serious burn injuries if you use them incorrectly.

The Bunsen burner

Figure 1.1.9 shows the parts of the Bunsen burner. The collar controls the amount of air that enters the burner as well as controlling the heat and colour of the flame. When you *shut* the airhole, very little air is able to mix with the gas. The gas does not burn well as it is the oxygen in air that is needed for fire to burn. It produces a pale yellow flame that is easily visible and relatively cool. This is shown in Figure 1.1.10. For these reasons, the yellow flame is called the **safety flame**. It is also a dirty flame, because it leaves a layer of black carbon soot on anything that is heated in it.

FIGURE 1.1.9 The Bunsen burner

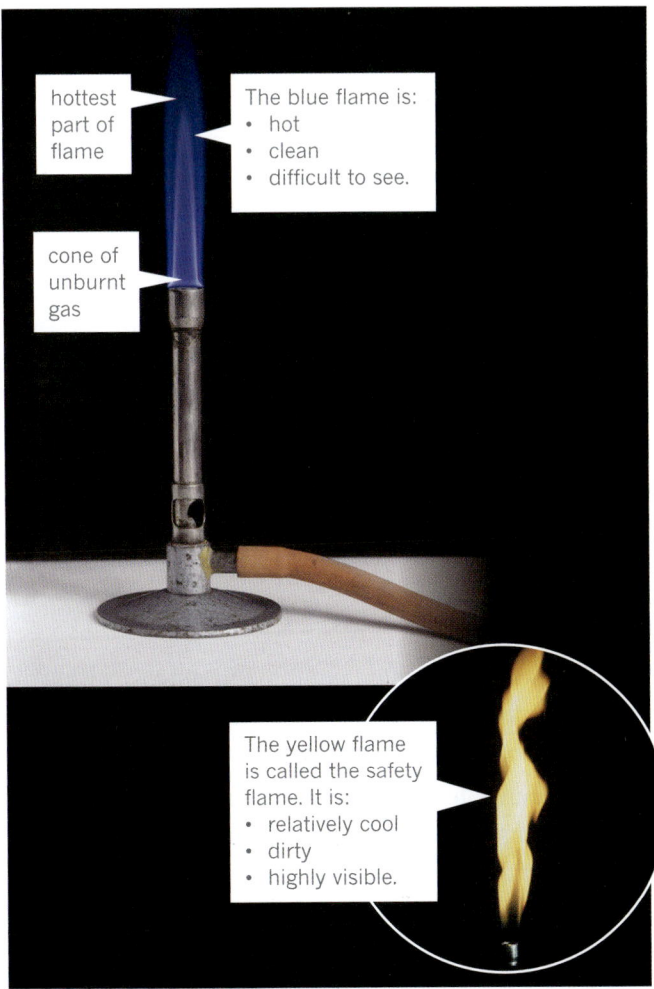

If you *open* the airhole, then a lot of air will enter, which means a lot more oxygen is able to enter. The gas will burn with no smoke, and will be extremely hot (about 1500°C). This flame is noisy. It has a blue colour and is sometimes difficult to see. At the very base of the flame, there is a small cone of unburnt gas. As Figure 1.1.10 shows, the hottest part of the flame is just above this cone.

FIGURE 1.1.10 The yellow flame is easy to see and relatively cool. The blue flame is much hotter and almost invisible. This makes it much more dangerous.

AB 1.2

Other equipment used for heating

A kitchen stove isn't very useful unless you have frying pans, saucepans, tongs and stirring spoons to help you cook the food safely. A hotplate and Bunsen burner also need additional equipment to help you heat objects safely. Some of this equipment is shown in Figure 1.1.11.

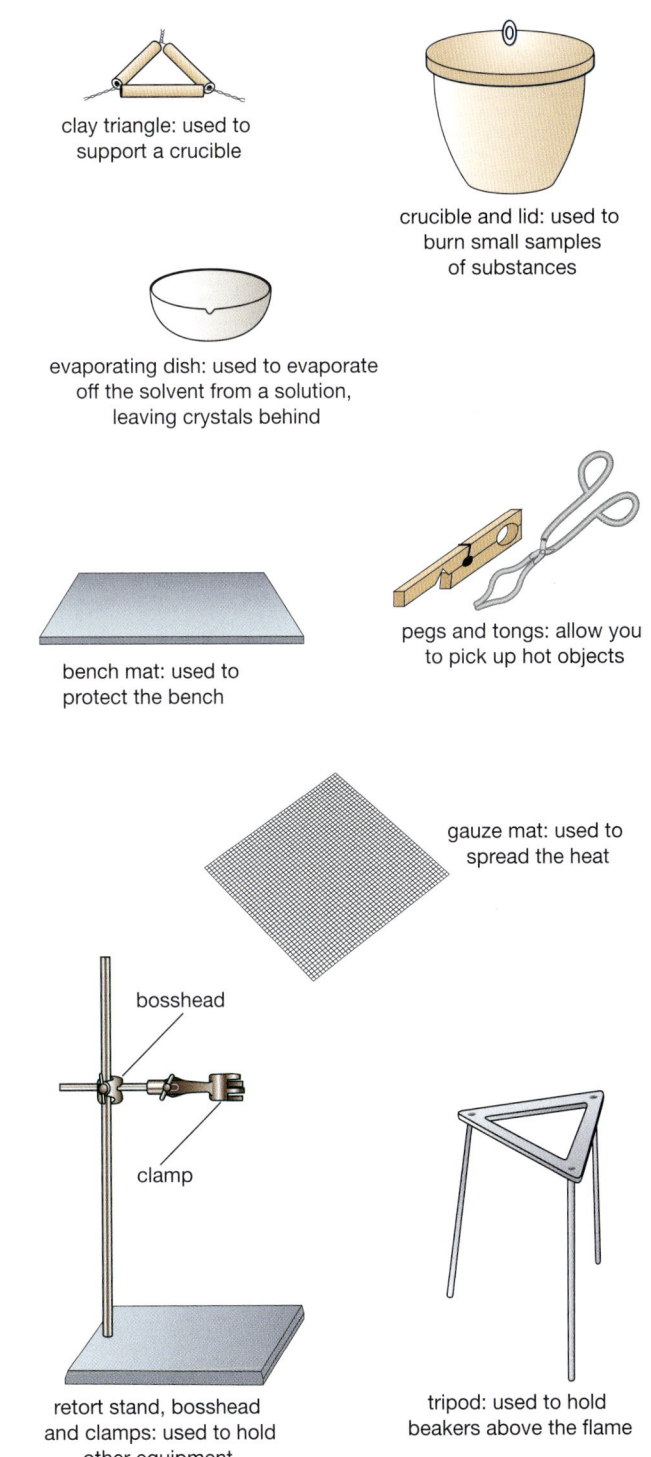

FIGURE 1.1.11 The hotplate and Bunsen burner need additional equipment to make them useful.

CHAPTER 1 • WORKING SCIENTIFICALLY **7**

Drawing equipment

Scientists do not draw equipment realistically but as simple two-dimensional (2D) line-drawings, 'splitting' the equipment down the middle to show its **cross-section**.

Figure 1.1.12 shows how scientists draw some of the most common equipment used in the laboratory.

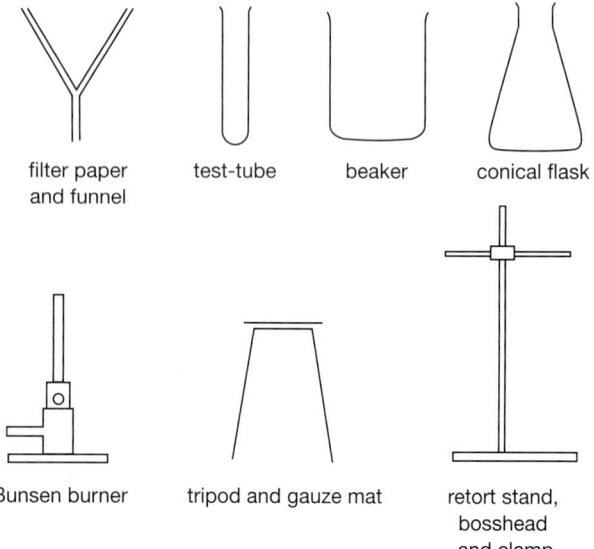

FIGURE 1.1.12 Scientists draw scientific equipment as simple, two-dimensional cross-sections.

Safety

Science can be fun. Experiments are part of that fun, but they can also be very dangerous. Hotplates and Bunsen burners can burn, and Bunsen flames can set clothes or hair on fire. Acids are corrosive and can burn badly, especially if splashed into your eyes (Figure 1.1.13). Many other chemicals are **toxic**, being poisonous if you sniff or taste them. Broken glassware can cut, and small fragments can easily enter your eyes.

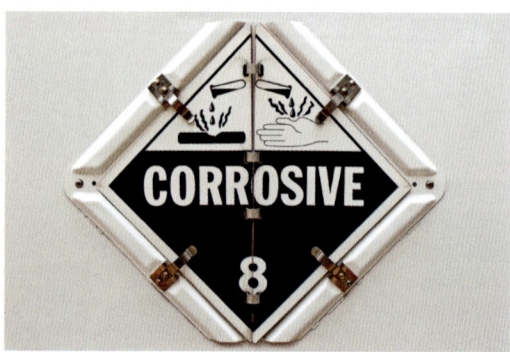

FIGURE 1.1.13 This warning sign lets you know a substance is corrosive.

Safety rules

The laboratory can be safe if we all follow some simple rules. Although each school, each laboratory and each teacher will have their own set of rules that you must follow, some rules are common to all laboratories:

- Always follow instructions from your teacher or laboratory technician.
- Move around the lab in a safe way. Do not run, push or shove.
- Always wear safety glasses when using chemicals.
- Do not eat, taste, drink or sniff anything in the lab.
- Treat all glassware with care.
- Make sure that test-tubes cannot roll off a bench when not in use.
- Always tell your teacher if you break something or if you are unsure about what to do.
- Hot glass that is placed under cold water will crack. Make sure glassware has cooled down before placing in cold water.

Your teacher and school will give you a list of any other rules that you need to follow in your laboratory.

Other rules apply when you are heating something:

- Always tie back long hair; otherwise it is a fire risk.
- When you need to leave a Bunsen burner on, turn it to a visible yellow safety flame.
- Only use matches to light Bunsen burners.
- Always use tongs to pick up objects that have been heated.
- When you are heating a test-tube, ensure that it is pointed away from everyone (including you).
- Hotplates and Bunsen burners, tripods and gauze mats remain hot for a long time. Allow them to cool before you pack them away.

Safety in the laboratory is really just common sense.

Your local experts

If you are confused about equipment, safety, or what you are supposed to do in a laboratory, then there are usually two experts you can turn to:

- Your science teacher is trained in science and has lots of experience in carrying out scientific investigations safely.
- Your laboratory technician (lab tech) will usually be found working behind the scenes in a science department. He or she may come into your laboratory to help your science teacher out, especially if an experiment is particularly dangerous. Your lab tech is trained in safety, the laboratory, its equipment and chemicals.

SCIENCE AS A HUMAN ENDEAVOUR
Use and influence of science

Scientists in Antarctica

Antarctica is one of the most remote and untouched places on Earth. It is incredibly cold, windy, dry and largely covered in ice. Due to its extreme conditions, very few land animals and plants can survive there. However, marine animals such as penguins, seals, whales and krill live in Antarctic waters, along with hundreds of different types of algae and bacteria.

SciFile
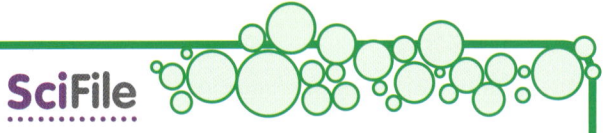

Antarctica is very, very cold!
Antarctica contains 90% of Earth's ice and 79% of its water. Its ice sheets are up to 4 km thick and cover 98% of its surface. The coldest temperature ever recorded was in Antarctica in 1983—the temperature dropped to −89.2°C.

FIGURE 1.1.14 These scientists are drilling into ice to collect ice core samples for research in Antarctica.

No humans live in Antarctica permanently, but 1000 scientists live there in winter and 4000 live there in summer. These scientists come from 28 countries and they work together on more than 100 projects in biology, astronomy, geology and environmental science. There are 76 research stations and 20–30 camps across the continent.

The unique conditions in Antarctica provide a natural laboratory that is unlike anywhere else in the world. Antarctic research from Antarctica has contributed to our scientific knowledge in several important areas.

Space science
Antarctica is an ideal place to observe space since there is no light pollution from cities and during winter it is almost always dark. Astronomers in Antarctica are detecting stars, galaxies, gravity waves and planets outside our solar system.

Climate change
Antarctica once had a much milder climate and important information about climate change is in the ice. Scientists drill and extract ice cores and rock to learn about past climate change to help predict the impacts of future climate change (Figure 1.1.14).

Oceanography
The ocean surrounding Antarctica helps to regulate Earth's weather. Studying this ocean helps scientists understand how changes in the ocean's temperature, currents and chemistry impact weather patterns.

Biological adaptation and conservation
The organisms that live in Antarctica provide scientists with information on how animals evolve, adapt and survive in extreme environments. With this information scientists are better able to manage and conserve its unique species and ecosystems.

REVIEW

1. Scientists often work with other scientists from different organisations or different countries. This is called collaboration. Why do you think collaboration is important in science?
2. Why is Antarctica an important place for scientific investigation?
3. Scientists from many different fields of science are working in Antarctica. What are some of the branches of science being used there?
4. Scientists often work with other scientists from different branches of science. Why do you think this is important?

MODULE 1.1 Review questions

Remembering

1. Define the terms:
   a. cross-section   b. toxic   c. safety flame.
2. What term best describes each of the following?
   a. the study of space
   b. the study of behaviour
   c. the study of chemicals.
3. List seven important branches of science.
4. Name an essential piece of equipment for:
   a. a microbiologist
   b. an astronomer.
5. What temperature can a blue Bunsen burner flame get to?
6. List four dangers that you will meet in the laboratory.
7. Draw 2D diagrams showing the following equipment:
   a. beaker   b. conical flask.

Understanding

8. Explain why everyone needs to have an understanding of science.
9. A biologist usually specialises in one sub-branch of biology. Explain why.
10. Why are all laboratories different?
11. a. The markings on beakers and conical flasks cannot be used to measure out volumes accurately. Explain why.
    b. What piece of equipment is used to measure volumes accurately?
12. A yellow flame will burn you if you are careless, but it is called the safety flame. Explain why.

Applying

13. Identify the branch and sub-branch of science being investigated in the STEM4fun on page 2.
14. Identify whether the following observations would be made by watching a yellow Bunsen burner flame or a blue Bunsen burner flame:
    a. dirty   d. extremely hot
    b. noisy   e. closed airhole.
    c. almost invisible

15. For each of the following investigations, identify the branch and sub-branch that is being studied.
    a. Abdul is counting how many eggs a cockroach has laid.
    b. Hon is studying the crystals embedded in a rock.
    c. Travis is investigating how light bends as it passes through glass.
    d. Lisa is photographing the bones of a dinosaur.
    e. Francesca is measuring the growth of a seedling.

Analysing

16. Refer to the contents pages (pages iv–v) and classify chapters 2–8 as biology, chemistry, physics, geology or astronomy (space).
17. What are the similarities and differences between a beaker and a conical flask?
18. Discuss what the following safety signs are saying.

a    b    c

Evaluating

19. Some branches of science cover two or more other branches. State what two branches of science are studied in biochemistry.
20. Propose reasons why:
    a. you should light a match before you turn on the gas to the Bunsen burner
    b. long hair should be tied back when you are using the Bunsen burner
    c. eating and drinking is banned in the laboratory
    d. you should turn a Bunsen burner to a yellow flame if you need to leave it.

Creating

21. You are using a Bunsen burner to heat water in a beaker. Construct a scientific diagram (2D line drawing) to show how your equipment looks.
22. Construct a sign that warns people that Bunsen burners are hot. Your sign must be in two colours only and use no words.

MODULE 1.1 Practical investigations

1 • Blowing up balloons `Questioning & Predicting` `Planning & Conducting`

In the laboratory, you will need to follow safety instructions and instructions on how to run experiments.

Purpose
To follow instructions to blow up a balloon in a strange way.

Timing   30 minutes

Materials
- up to 500 mL water
- 1.25 L PET plastic soft-drink bottle and cap
- balloon
- drawing pin

Procedure
1. Hold on to the open end of the balloon and drop the rounded end inside the soft-drink bottle. Secure the balloon by stretching its mouth over the mouth of the bottle as shown in Figure 1.1.15.
2. Put your mouth over the end of the soft-drink bottle and try to blow up the balloon. Record what happens.
3. Use the drawing pin to make a hole in the wall of the bottle near its base.
4. Try to blow up the balloon again. While keeping your mouth on the bottle, cover the pinhole with your finger. Record what you see.
5. Remove your finger. Record what you see.
6. Blow up the balloon again and cover the pinhole with a finger.
7. Pour water into the blown-up balloon. Remove your finger and record what you see.

Results
Record all your observations in your workbook.

Review
1. Propose a reason why:
   a. it was almost impossible to blow up the balloon without the pinhole
   b. the pinhole allowed the balloon to inflate
   c. a blocked pinhole kept the balloon inflated
   d. water rushed out of the balloon when your finger was removed from the pinhole.
2. Assess how well you followed the instructions for this experiment. For example, Question 1 outlines what should have happened. If you experienced all that, then you probably followed the instructions well. If you did not, or if you needed assistance along the way, then you probably did not follow the instructions well.

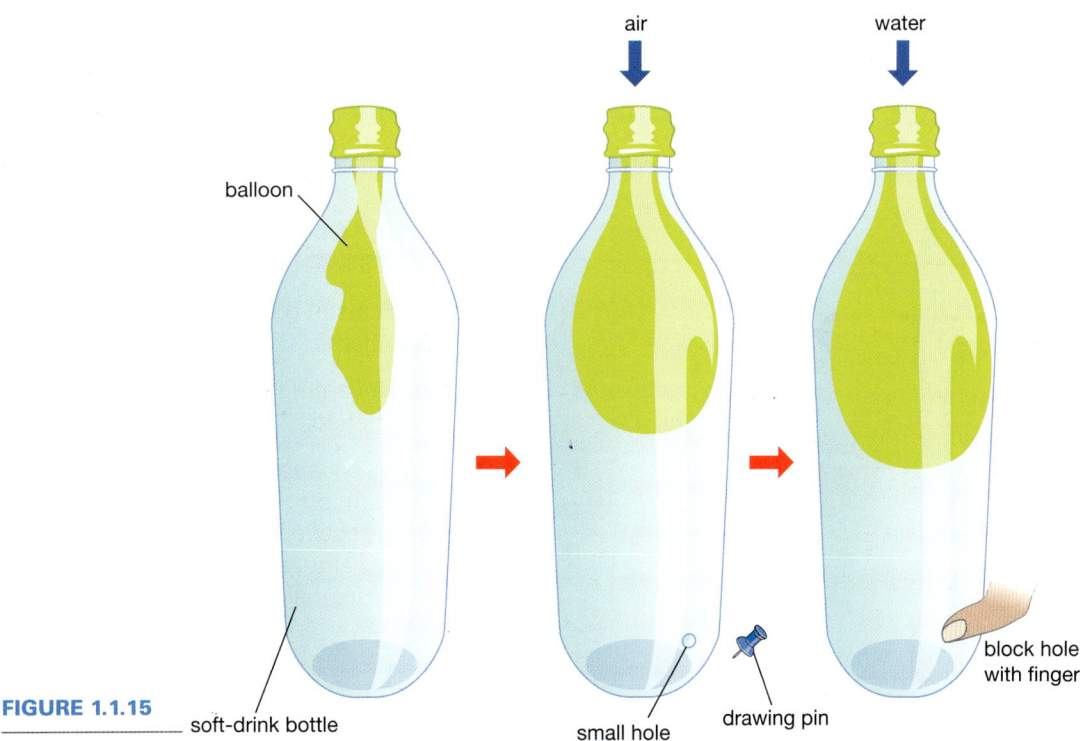

FIGURE 1.1.15

CHAPTER 1 • WORKING SCIENTIFICALLY

MODULE 1.1 Practical investigations

2 • The Bunsen burner

Purpose
To light a Bunsen burner and produce a yellow flame and a blue flame.

Timing
45 minutes

Materials
- Bunsen burner, bench mat and matches
- pin

Procedure
Copy the table in the Results section into your workbook. Give your table a title.

Part A: Lighting the Bunsen burner

1. Follow the instructions in the skill builder to light a Bunsen burner.
2. Switch between opening and shutting the airhole. Observe what colour flames are produced.
3. Turn off the Bunsen burner and allow it to cool.

Part B: Unburnt gas

4. Push a pin through the wood near the top of an unlit match. Balance the match on the top of the Bunsen burner so that the match head is in the centre of its barrel.
5. Light the Bunsen burner as usual and quickly turn it to a blue flame. Figure 1.1.16 shows the correct set-up.

SAFETY
Tie long hair back so it won't get in the flame.

Whenever you are not using the Bunsen burner, set its flame to yellow so that you can see it.

Equipment will be hot, so let it cool before packing it away.

Results
Record all your observations in your results table.

Airhole	Was the flame noisy or quiet?	Flame colour	Other observations
closed			
half-closed			
open			

Review
1. Why should the airhole be closed when you light a Bunsen burner?
2. Describe what happened to the match in the barrel of the Bunsen burner.
3. Explain your observations.

SkillBuilder

Lighting the Bunsen burner

1. Place the Bunsen burner on a heatproof bench mat and connect its hose to the gas jet.
2. Turn the collar of the Bunsen burner so that the airhole is completely closed.
3. Light a match.
4. Turn on the gas at the gas tap.
5. Hold the lit match about 1 cm over the top of the barrel.
6. If the match blows out then immediately turn the gas off and start again.
7. When lit, the Bunsen burner should produce a bright yellow flame.
8. To obtain a blue flame, turn the collar so that the airhole is opened.
9. This sometimes causes the flame to blow out. If it does, turn off the Bunsen burner and follow the steps above to light it again. Then, to obtain a blue flame, adjust the airhole so that it is not completely open.

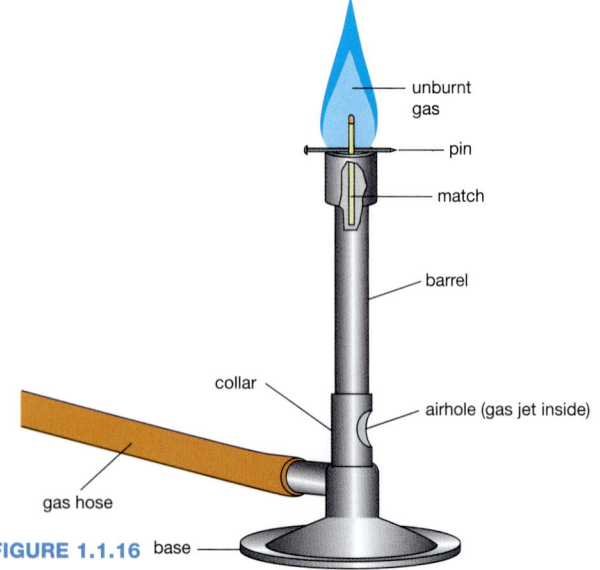

FIGURE 1.1.16

MODULE 1.1 Practical investigations

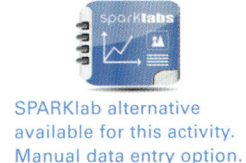

SPARKlab alternative available for this activity. Manual data entry option.

3 • Investigating the flame

Questioning & Predicting | Processing & Analysing

Purpose
To determine which flame is hot, which is cool, which is dirty and which is clean.

Timing 45 minutes

Materials
- Bunsen burner, bench mat and matches
- old, 'bald' gauze mat
- small piece of broken white porcelain
- tongs

Procedure
Copy the table in the Results section into your workbook. Give your table a title.

SAFETY
Tie long hair back so it won't get in the flame.
Whenever you are not using the Bunsen burner, set its flame to yellow so that you can see it.
Equipment will be hot, so let it cool before packing it away.

Part A: Hot or cool?
1 Set up and light the Bunsen burner.
2 Set it to a yellow flame.
3 With tongs, hold the gauze mat vertically in the flame so that it touches the top of the burner as shown in Figure 1.1.17.
4 Set the flame to blue and repeat step 3.
5 Carefully draw diagrams of any heat markings that you see.

Part B: Clean or dirty?
6 With tongs, hold the small piece of porcelain in a blue flame and record your observations.
7 Set the flame to yellow and repeat step 6.

Results
Record your observations in your results table.
Title:

Flame colour	Gauze mat	Porcelain
yellow		
blue		

Review
1 The wire of the gauze mat will glow red if it is really hot. Which flame (yellow or blue) made the wire glow red?
2 Describe the markings caused by the blue flame.
3 Where was the flame the hottest and where it was the 'coolest'?
4 Compare what happened to the porcelain in the yellow flame and the blue flame.
5 Which flame could be called 'dirty'?
6 Was this was the hot flame or the cool flame?

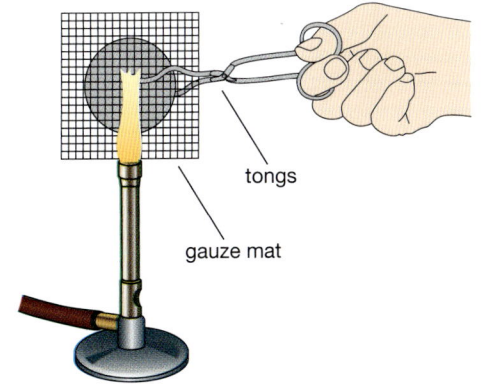
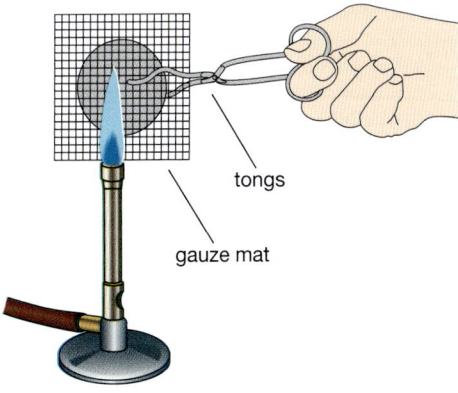

FIGURE 1.1.17

MODULE 1.2 Practical investigations

Scientists carry out experiments to investigate the world around them. They record their observations and measurements and analyse them so that patterns and trends become clear.

science 4 fun

Magic candles

Can you relight a candle from a distance?

Collect this...
- candle
- saucer or Petri dish
- matches

Do this...
1. Stand the candle upright on the saucer or Petri dish. Melt a little of its base to help it stick.
2. Light the candle and use all your senses except taste to make as many different observations as possible.
3. Gently blow the candle out and attempt to relight it by moving a lit match down the smoke trail as shown.

SAFETY
Candles, matches and hot wax can burn, so avoid touching the hot parts.

Record this...
1. Describe what happened.
2. Explain why you think this happened.

Experiments and fieldwork

A **practical investigation** tests a small part of the world around us. A practical investigation could be an **experiment** that is done entirely inside a laboratory. It might test the temperatures at which particular metals melt, how to make building materials fireproof, why some people are allergic to peanuts or how chocolate can be made even tastier. Practical investigations can also be fieldwork. In **fieldwork**, the laboratory is outside and observations and measurements are made on what is happening in nature. Fieldwork might gather information about the intelligence of dolphins, the types of insects living in a swamp, the diseases killing trees in a rainforest or the erosion happening on a mountain.

Scientists either design their own experiments and fieldwork or follow the instructions of other scientists who have performed them already. You will be doing this too. You will be given instructions for most practical activities, but some will require you and your team to plan and carry out your own investigations.

Observations and measurements

Although scientists use all of their five senses (sight, hearing, smell, taste and touch) to make observations, sight is probably the sense that gives them the most information. This is the sense being used in Figure 1.2.1. Scientists also use hearing, smell, taste and touch but often it can be far too dangerous to use some of these senses.

Scientists make either qualitative or quantitative observations.

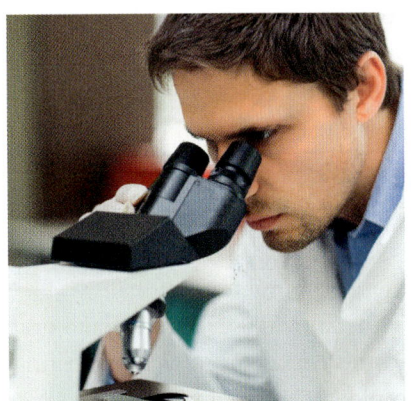

FIGURE 1.2.1 The main sense a scientist uses is sight.

Qualitative observations

Qualitative observations are descriptive and describe the qualities of things, such as their colour or shape or the sounds they make. They are recorded as diagrams or written down in words. Qualitative observations would be made about the noise a bird makes, the colour of its feathers, what it eats, and how it acts throughout the day. The appearance of shaving foam and the shape of a crab are qualitative observations too, as is the taste of the food in Figure 1.2.2.

FIGURE 1.2.2 The look, smell and taste of pizza are qualitative observations.

Quantitative observations

Quantitative observations involve numbers. If you say that a day is hot then you are making a qualitative observation. However, it doesn't really give an accurate idea of how hot the day is. There is no doubt about how hot the day is if you specify the temperature it reached: 43°C is hot in anyone's language! Measurements like this are quantitative observations. They are written as numbers and allow scientists to be more detailed and accurate in their observations. Distance, mass, time, temperature and volume are quantitative observations, since all can be written as numbers. For example, chips come in 200 gram bags, cans of soft drink hold 375 mL, water boils at 100°C, and it takes 60 minutes to fly from Melbourne to Sydney, a distance of 881 km.

Sometimes an optical illusion like the one shown in Figure 1.2.3 on page 16 will trick your senses into making qualitative observations that are incorrect. Measurement will usually indicate whether your senses were correct or not.

Prac 1 p. 21

> **SciFile**
> Michael Faraday, a nineteenth century scientist, made 53 different observations of a lit candle!

FIGURE 1.2.3 An optical illusion makes the floors (orange) of this building in Melbourne look as if they are at sloping at different angles. Measurement of the distance between the floors proves that they are all horizontal.

SciFile

Moonface!

The Moon often looks huge as it rises in the east but it is really just the same size as when it is somewhere else in the sky. Check this out by drawing around the Moon through a window using a drywipe pen. Come back and draw around it every half-hour to see what happens to the size of the Moon.

FIGURE 1.2.4 An optical illusion causes the Moon to look huge when it rises. As it rises, you can compare the Moon with the size of buildings and trees.

Units

Measurements are useless unless their units are included. Scientists use units from the metric system for their measurements.

- Distances, lengths and heights are measured in millimetres (mm), centimetres (cm), metres (m) or kilometres (km).
- Small masses are measured in grams (g). Heavier masses are measured in kilograms (kg) or tonnes (t).
- Volume is measured in millilitres (mL) or litres (L).

Some non-metric units are used as well. For example:

- time is measured in seconds (s), minutes (min) or hours (h)
- temperature is measured in degrees Celsius (°C).

The above units together form an internationally recognised system of units known as SI units. Each unit has its own symbol and there is a correct way of writing each symbol. For example, the symbol for millilitres is mL and not ML (which would mean a million litres). Likewise, the symbol for kilograms is kg, not Kg, KG or kgs.

Taking accurate measurements

Measurements are only worthwhile if they are accurate and they are recorded accurately and honestly. So that your measurements are as accurate as possible, make sure that:

- everyone in your team takes their own measurement. You can then calculate the average of everyone's values.
- you keep your eye level with the measurement (as in Figure 1.2.5)
- the measuring device starts at zero.

Mistakes are often made when measurements are recorded but you can avoid this if you take enough care. To reduce the chance of recording measurements wrongly:

- write down measurements (with their units) as soon as you take them. Do not try to remember measurements.
- avoid fractions like $\frac{1}{2}$ or $\frac{1}{4}$ in measurements. Use 9.5 kg rather than $9\frac{1}{2}$ kg.
- make sure that everyone in the group has a copy of the results before you leave the laboratory.

FIGURE 1.2.5 Keep your eyes level with your measurement.

SkillBuilder
Reading a meniscus

A **meniscus** is the curved shape formed by the surface of a liquid where it meets another surface. The meniscus is easy to see when the liquid is in a tube such as a measuring cylinder. Sometimes the meniscus curves upwards and sometimes it curves downwards. This could make measuring volumes a little difficult. Figure 1.2.6 shows how scientists measure the volume when a meniscus is present.

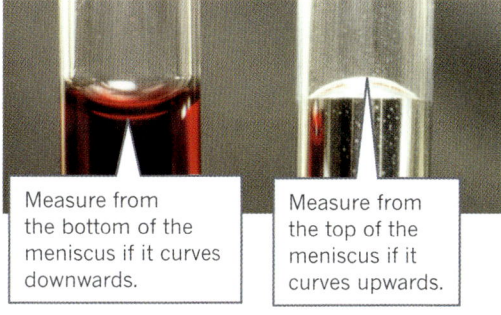

Measure from the bottom of the meniscus if it curves downwards.

Measure from the top of the meniscus if it curves upwards.

FIGURE 1.2.6 The surface of a liquid in a measuring cylinder forms a curve called a meniscus.

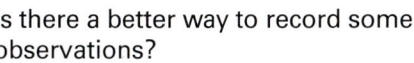

science 4 fun

Milk swirls

Is there a better way to record some observations?

Collect this …
- full cream milk
- food dyes (assorted colours)
- liquid dishwashing detergent
- shallow plate with flat bottom (such as a bread plate or dinner plate)

Do this …
1. Pour enough milk into the plate until it is 5 mm to 10 mm deep.
2. Place a single drop of food dye anywhere into the milk. Place single drops of other colours elsewhere.
3. Place 1 or 2 drops of detergent into the centre of the plate.

Record this …
1. Describe in words what happened.
2. Explain why it is sometimes difficult to produce a written record of what happened in an experiment.

CHAPTER 1 • WORKING SCIENTIFICALLY **17**

SCIENCE AS A HUMAN ENDEAVOUR
Use and influence of science

Science and the law

Scientists pay attention to the world around them and they make observations about it. These observations are the reasons for many of the laws and regulations that we all must follow every day.

For example, scientific evidence on the forces and motion involved in car and bike crashes has led to speed limits, and laws that make us wear seatbelts in cars and helmets when riding a bike or motorbike (Figure 1.2.7). In a similar way, scientific evidence on bushfires has led to laws determining days of total fire ban and the types of houses that are built in areas of high bushfire risk.

Scientific evidence has also been used to form laws and regulations that:

- make car manufacturers include airbags, crumple zones and crash-resistant fuel tanks
- control the type of houses built in areas at risk of floods or cyclones
- determine which drugs should be illegal, which should be available on prescription and which can be bought at the supermarket
- control the additives that can be put in food
- control how long food can be sold for ('use by' and 'best before' dates)
- determine unsafe levels of sound, chemicals and dust for workers
- control the type and amount of pollution that can be released into rivers, soil and the atmosphere
- preserve animals, plants and landscapes at risk of being lost forever.

Sometimes, scientific evidence leads to changes in global laws. For example, chemicals called chlorofluorocarbons were destroying the ozone layer. The ozone layer is a layer of gas around Earth that reduces UV radiation, so its destruction was putting us all at greater risk of skin cancer. Governments across the world have since banned the use of chlorofluorocarbons in everyday products like deodorants and hair sprays and in fridges. Similar laws will be required to limit the release of carbon dioxide to minimise global climate change.

FIGURE 1.2.7 Science has shown that helmets can protect you from serious head and brain injury.

In 2015, international leaders agreed to regulate the carbon dioxide emissions of their countries. This will probably lead to laws that restrict the use of fossil fuels like coal. These countries will look to replace fossil fuel usage with renewable energy sources.

REVIEW

1. Name the chemicals banned across the world that were destroying the ozone layer.
2. In 1970, Victoria became the first government in the world to make it compulsory to wear seatbelts when in a car.
   a. Suggest what evidence led to such a law.
   b. Other Australian states took longer to make wearing seatbelts compulsory. What evidence do you think eventually convinced them to adopt the law?
3. Different drugs are treated differently by the law. Suggest a reason why.
4. Propose a reason why laws now determine the type of houses that are allowed to be built in areas at risk of cyclones or bushfires.

MODULE 1.2 Review questions

Remembering

1. Define the terms:
   a. fieldwork
   b. quantitative observations.

2. What term best describes each of the following?
   a. practical investigation performed inside in a laboratory
   b. observations that do not include numbers.

3. State the five senses.

4. List three observations you may see from each of the following:
   a. a candle
   b. molten (melted) candle wax
   c. a candle flame
   d. the smoke from a candle that has been blown out.

5. What are the measurements shown in each of the measuring devices in Figure 1.2.8?

a.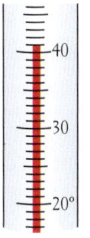
b.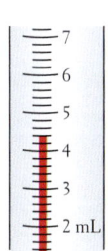
c.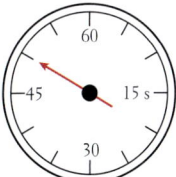
d.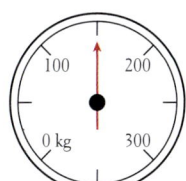
e.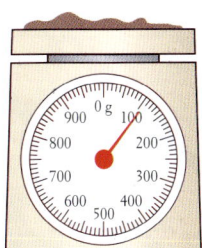
f.
g.

FIGURE 1.2.8

6. What is wrong with the way these measurements have been recorded?
   a. The mass of a mouse = $150\frac{1}{4}$ g.
   b. The car was travelling at 100.
   c. A full bottle of soft drink contained 1.25 mL.

7. Which of the abbreviations below are correct for these units?
   a. gram
      - A. gm
      - B. gms
      - C. G
      - D. g
   b. kilogram
      - A. kilo
      - B. kg
      - C. Kg
      - D. KG
   c. millimetre
      - A. mms
      - B. mm
      - C. Mm
      - D. mL
   d. litre
      - A. lt
      - B. mL
      - C. lit
      - D. L
   e. minutes
      - A. min
      - B. m
      - C. mins
      - D. ms

8. What volumes are indicated in test-tube A and test-tube B (Figure 1.2.9)

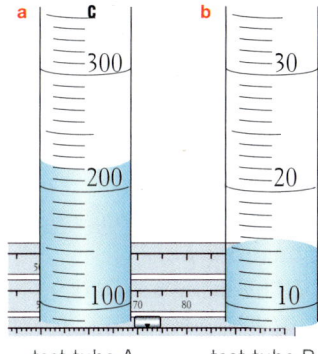

FIGURE 1.2.9

9. In the science4fun on page 17, detergent gathered together the fat in the milk, causing the liquid to swirl around. This pattern is nearly impossible to describe in words. What would be a better way of recording what happened?

Understanding

10. What advantages do quantitative observations have over qualitative observations?

11. Give an example to explain how optical illusions can lead you to make faulty observations.

CHAPTER 1 • WORKING SCIENTIFICALLY 19

MODULE 1.2 Review questions

Applying

12 Identify the best metric unit to use to measure the length of:
   a a bull-ant
   b the length of a cricket field
   c the distance between Brisbane and Sydney.

13 Identify the best SI unit to measure the:
   a mass of a mouse
   b time it takes to sneeze
   c mass of a person
   d volume of a swimming pool
   e temperature of a sick dog (Figure 1.2.10).

14 Sometimes it is too dangerous to use some of our senses. Identify which senses you would and would not use in the following investigations and complete Table 1.2.1.

FIGURE 1.2.10

TABLE 1.2.1 Using senses to investigate situations

Activity	Senses that would be safe to use	The sense that would give you the most information	Senses that would be unsafe to use
testing a new rat poison			
testing whether minced steak is OK to eat or is 'off'			
testing the lava flowing from a volcano			
testing how dangerous an acid is			
testing whether tomatoes are ripe			

Analysing

15 Classify the following observations as qualitative or quantitative.
   a The night was dark.
   b It took 15 minutes to walk to school.

Evaluating

16 When a candle is snuffed out, a trail of smoke rises from it. This smoke is unburnt gas. Propose how this trail of unburnt gas can be used to relight the candle.

17 Look at the images in Figure 1.2.11.
   a Assess whether the main lines in diagram S are the same length or not.
   b Assess whether the main lines in diagram T are parallel to each other.
   c Use a ruler to check whether you were correct or not.

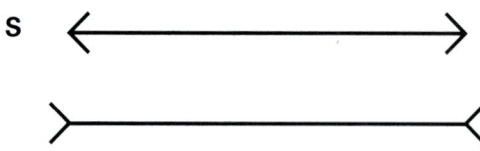

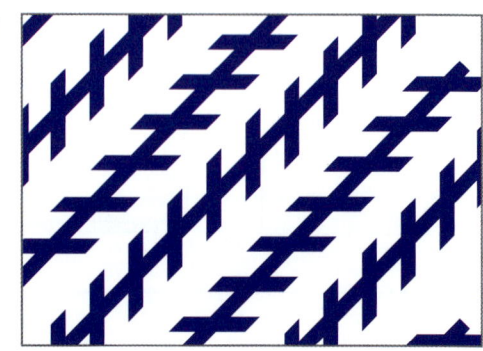

FIGURE 1.2.11

20 PEARSON SCIENCE 7 2ND EDITION

MODULE 1.2 Practical investigations

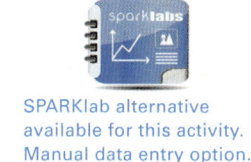

SPARKlab alternative available for this activity. Manual data entry option.

1 • Hot, hotter, hottest

Questioning & Predicting **Planning & Conducting**

Purpose
To compare qualitative with quantitative measurements.

Timing 30 minutes

Materials
- ice
- warm water
- 4 × 250 mL beakers or identical tubs
- thermometer or temperature sensor

SAFETY Do not use boiling water.

Procedure
1. Copy the table from the Results section into your workbook.
2. Fill four beakers and arrange them as shown in Figure 1.2.12.
3. Immerse (place) your left hand in the beaker containing cold water and your right hand in the beaker containing warm water. Leave your hands in the water for 30 seconds or so.
4. Remove your hands and put each hand into a beaker containing tap water.
5. Leave them there for 30 seconds or so. Does the water feel the same to both hands, or does one feel hotter?
6. In your table, rate what the temperature of the water in each beaker felt like—very hot, hot, cool or cold.
7. Use the thermometer to measure the actual water temperature of each beaker. Record the temperatures in your table.

Results
Record your observations in your results table. Give your table a title.

Beaker	What it felt like (very hot, hot, cool, cold)	Actual temperature (°C)
water–ice mixture		
tap water 1		
tap water 2		
warm water		

Review
1. What quantitative observations did you make in this activity?
2. Identify your qualitative observations.
3. Did your qualitative observations agree with your quantitative ones?
4. a Construct a conclusion for your investigation.
   b Assess whether your hypothesis was supported or not.

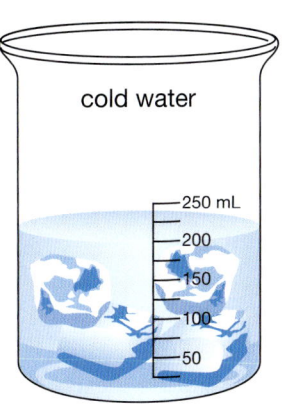 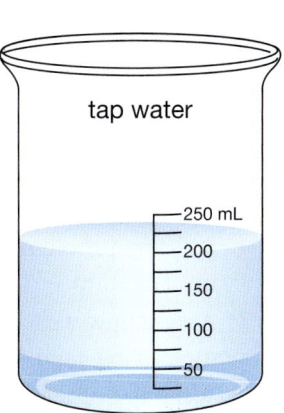 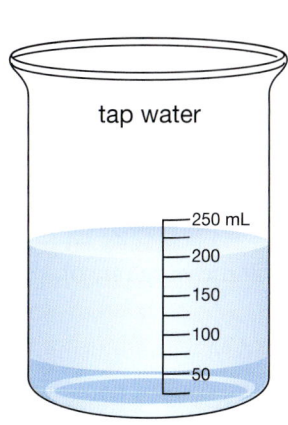 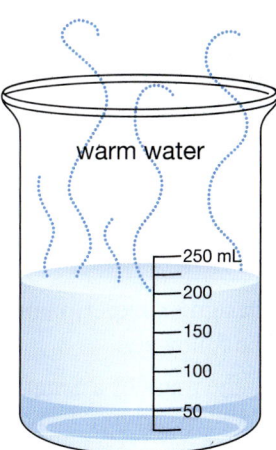

FIGURE 1.2.12

CHAPTER 1 • WORKING SCIENTIFICALLY 21

MODULE 1.2 Practical investigations

2 • Taking measurements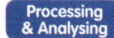

Purpose
To observe that not everyone takes the same measurement.

Timing 30 minutes

Materials
- access to a range of glassware that holds different volumes (such as a 250 mL beaker, 100 mL conical flask or a 100 mL measuring cylinder). Fill each with different quantities of water, a beam or electronic balance with a mass on it, a sheet of paper with a ruler to measure its length)
- A4 sheet of paper next to each piece of equipment

Procedure
Move around the laboratory and read the measurement for each piece of equipment.

Read each measurement at eye level.

Results
1. Construct a table similar to the one below in your workbook. Give your table a title.

Name of equipment	Measurement	Units

2. Record your measurement in the table and on the paper next to each piece of equipment.
3. After you finish, check all the measurements written on the pieces of paper and determine if they are all exactly the same.

Review
1. Everyone in a team will take slightly different measurements, even when measuring exactly the same thing. Propose reasons why.
2. Describe a way of using all the results on the paper to obtain an even better result.

• STUDENT DESIGN •

3 • When measuring is difficult

Purpose
To develop ways of taking measurements.

Timing 30 minutes

Materials
- small box of Smarties® or M&Ms®
- stack of A4 paper (recycled is OK)
- ruler
- watch or timer

SAFETY
A Risk Assessment is required for this investigation.

Procedure
1. Design an experiment that will measure one of the following:
   - the mass of a Smartie or M&M without using any weighing device
   - the thickness of a single sheet of A4 paper with a normal ruler
   - the time it takes for your heart to do one heartbeat.
2. Write your procedure in your workbook.
3. Before you start any practical work, assess your procedure. List any risks that your procedure might involve and what you might do to minimise those risks. Show your teacher your procedure and your assessment of its risks. If they approve, then collect all the required materials and start work.

Results
Record every measurement you take and every calculation you make.

Review
1. List any problems that you had in this investigation.
2. Assess how well your procedure worked for measuring each of the items.
3. What are other ways of measuring these quantities.
4. Whenever you design your own investigation, you need to show your teacher your planned procedure and your assessment of its risks. Propose a reason why.

MODULE 1.3 Communicating

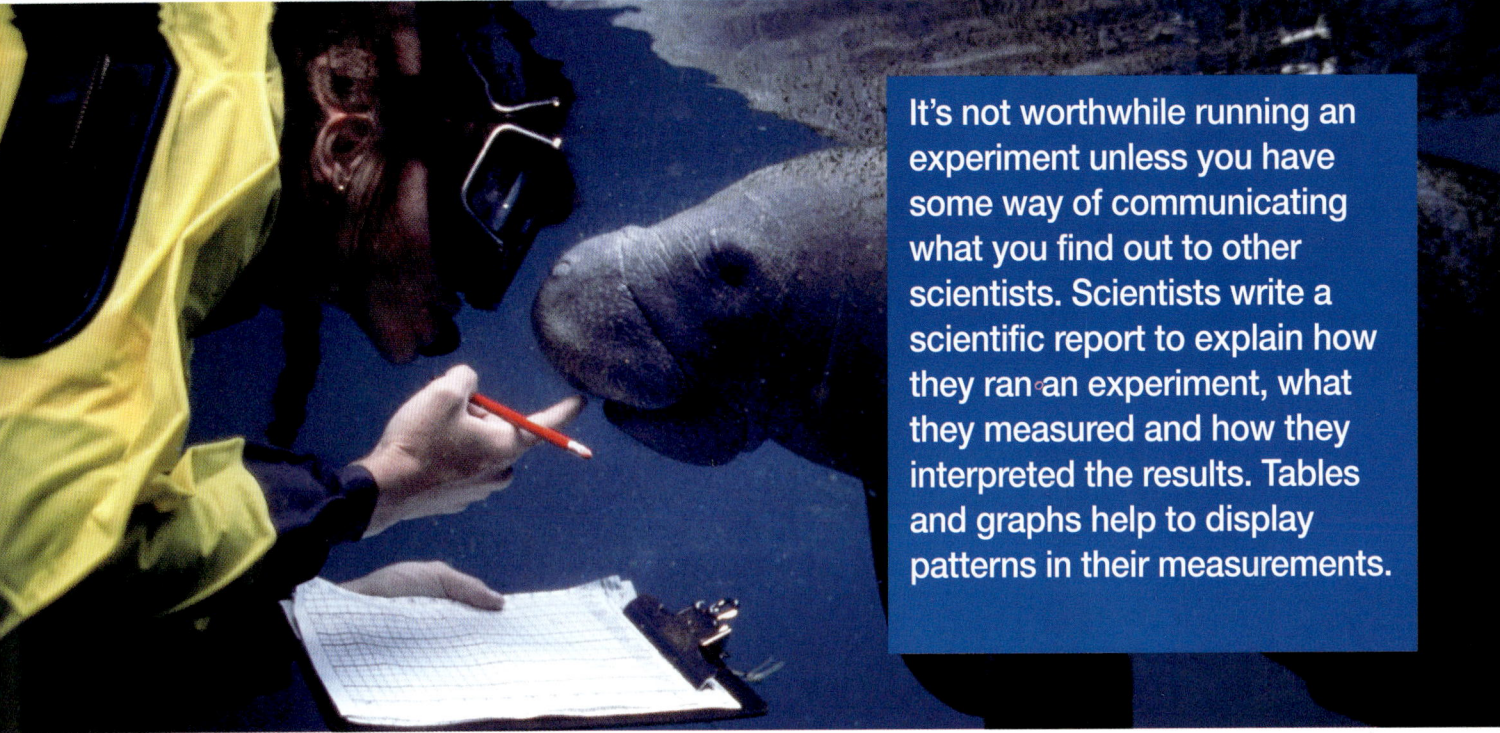

It's not worthwhile running an experiment unless you have some way of communicating what you find out to other scientists. Scientists write a scientific report to explain how they ran an experiment, what they measured and how they interpreted the results. Tables and graphs help to display patterns in their measurements.

science 4 fun

Broken whispers

Can a group communicate a piece of information accurately without writing it down?

Do this...
1. As a class or in a group, sit around in a circle.
2. One of you is to construct a short story that takes no more than two sentences to tell.
3. The story is to be passed on around your group by one person whispering it very quietly to another.
4. Compare the original story with the story that it ended up being.

Record this...
1. Describe what happened.
2. Explain why you think this happened.

Tables

Measurements and observations are easier to read and understand if they are displayed in tables. Tables also make trends (patterns) in the measurements more obvious. Each column in a table needs to have a clear heading that includes the units in which each measurement has been taken.

Computer programs such as Excel enable you to produce a digital table or spreadsheet on a computer or tablet. Spreadsheets can be programmed to automatically calculate values like totals and averages from your measurements. They can also use your measurements to construct different types of graphs.

Graphs

A graph shows trends in measurements even more clearly than tables do. The type of graph you construct depends on the types of observations you make.

Bar and column graphs

Some observations fall into **discrete** groupings. This means that all the observations can be sorted into definite categories and counted. No measurements are possible between each of the categories.

CHAPTER 1 • WORKING SCIENTIFICALLY 23

For example, animals fall into discrete groupings like kangaroos, ants, cockatoos and sharks. Other observations that have discrete values are makes of cars (such as Holden, Toyota, Ford, Mazda), sports (netball, football, golf, tennis), and building materials (timber, brick, concrete, glass).

Bar and **column graphs** are used when you have a set of observations that are discrete, such as the data in the table below. These discrete values are displayed on one of the axes of the graph while numbers are displayed on the other axis, as shown in Figure 1.3.1. Axes are the horizontal (left/right) and vertical (up/down) lines 'framing' the graph.

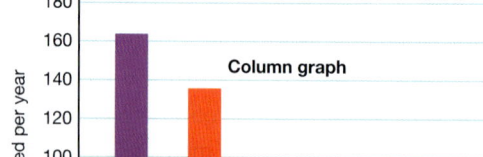

FIGURE 1.3.1 The table, column graph and bar graph all represent the same data. The data shows the five main causes of injury to the spine and the number of Australians injured each year.

Annual cause and incidence of spinal injuries in Australia

Cause of spinal injury	Average number injured per year
car crashes	164
falls	136
sports	24
surfing	20
diving	20

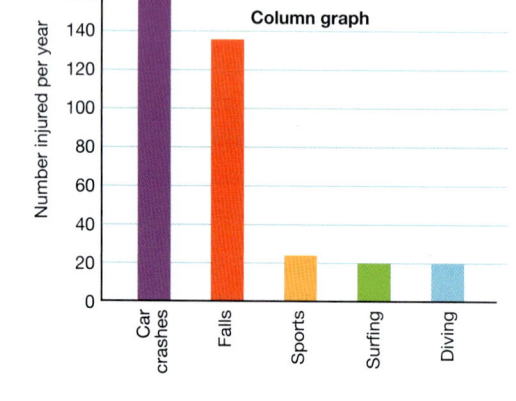

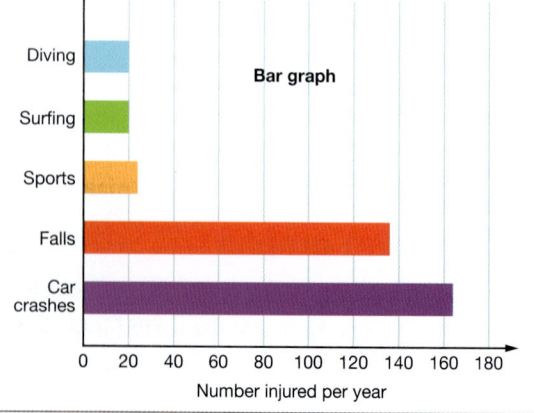

Pie graphs

Discrete groupings are also used to construct **pie graphs** or **sector graphs**. A pie graph shows the proportions of each grouping within a total. In a pie graph, the whole pie represents 100%, half the pie represents 50% and a quarter-pie represents 25%. As an example, Figure 1.3.2 shows the percentages of different animals living in a nature reserve.

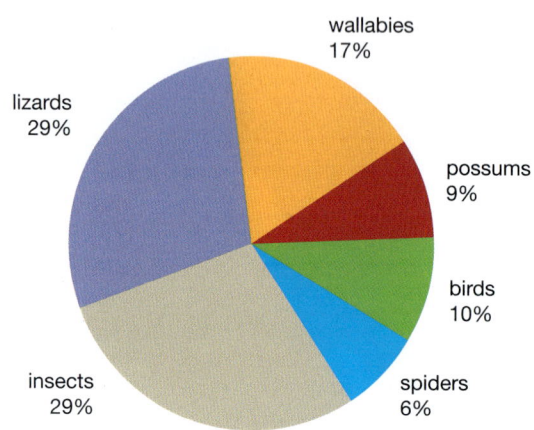

FIGURE 1.3.2 This pie graph shows the proportions of each animal in a nature reserve and not their real numbers.

Line graphs

Measurements involve numbers that are not discrete but **continuous**. This means that if you choose two numbers, then you can always find other numbers in between them. For example, in Figure 1.3.3 the numbers on the axis labelled 'Mass' go up by fives: 0, 5, 10, 15 and so on. There are other numbers between each of the labelled numbers: between 0 and 5 are 1, 2, 3 and 4. Between those numbers are even more numbers: between 1 and 2 are 1.1, 1.2 and so on. They are continuous.

Examples of continuous measurements include age, mass, length, time, volume, temperature and human height.

Line graphs require two sets of measurements that show continuous variation. One set of measurements is set out along the horizontal axis and the other is set out along the vertical axis.

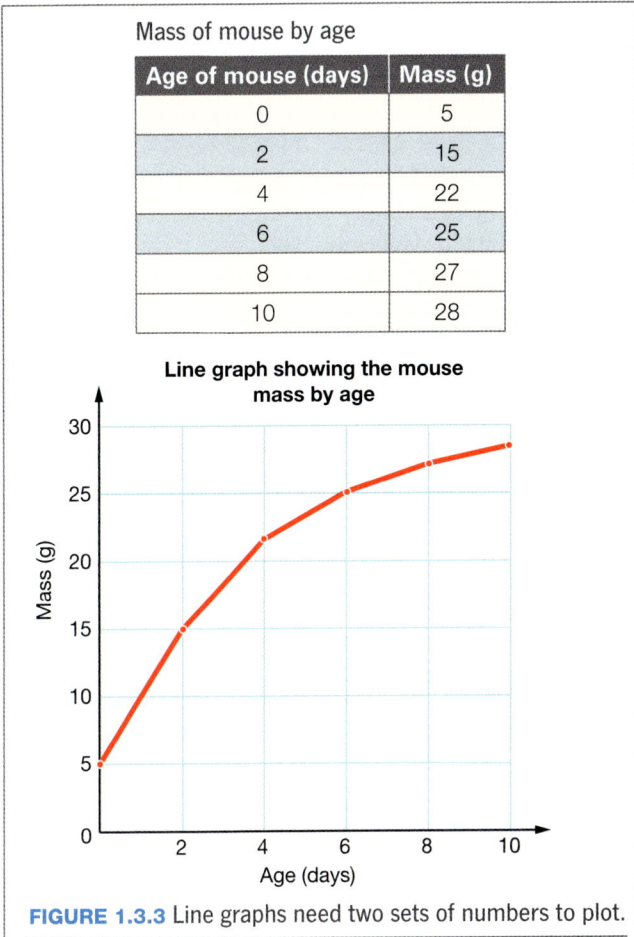

FIGURE 1.3.3 Line graphs need two sets of numbers to plot.

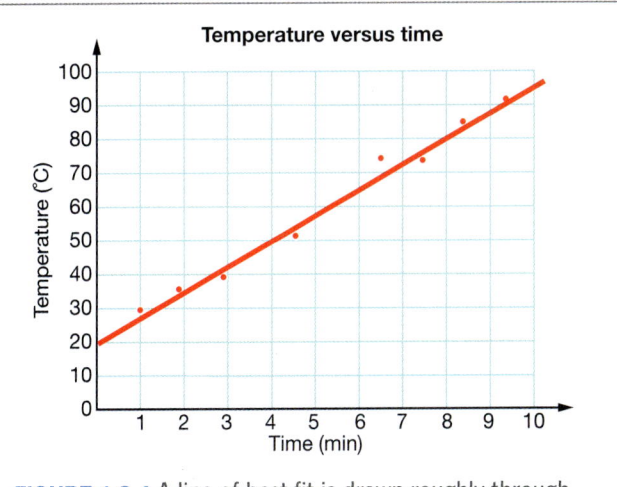

FIGURE 1.3.4 A line of best fit is drawn roughly through the middle of all the points. In this way, the line of best fit shows the trend or pattern in the graph.

Once you have plotted all the points on a line graph, there are two ways to connect the points:
- curve of best fit—connect the points from one to the next with a curved line (Figure 1.3.3)
- line of best fit—draw a straight line through the centre of all the points, making sure you have a balance between the number of points above and below the line (Figure 1.3.4).

These 'best fits' clearly show patterns that might exist in the measurements you took in the experiment.

Summary of graph types

Table 1.3.1 gives a summary of the different types of graphs and their features.

TABLE 1.3.1 Summary of graph types and their features

Graph type	Features
column/bar	• uses discrete quantities • each quantity is shown as a different column • allows comparison of quantities • column graphs are better for displaying data with negative values • bar graphs are better for displaying large amounts of data on the category (y) axis.
pie/sector	• uses discrete quantities • each quantity is shown as a different percentage or a fraction or slice of the pie. • the whole pie represents 100% • allows comparison of quantities.
line	• uses two sets of continuous measurements • uses a line or curve of best fit passing through the 'centre' of the points • trends in measurements are easy to see • can be used to estimate missing measurements.

CHAPTER 1 • WORKING SCIENTIFICALLY **25**

Scientific reports

Scientific reports are used by scientists to communicate to other scientists how they performed an investigation and what they found out by doing it. When reporting on an experiment, there is a common approach that scientists follow, outlined in Figure 1.3.5.

Title
- what was investigated

Purpose
- the **purpose** or **aim** describes what you wanted to show, prove or find out in an investigation
- can be a statement or a question
- one or two sentences
- often written as 'To investigate the effect of ... on ...'

Hypothesis
- the **hypothesis** is an educated guess about what you expect to happen in the investigation
- written as a short statement
- describes the different things you tested
- not always needed in a scientific report

Materials
- a list of all the important equipment, chemicals and materials that you used
- include quantities of substances and sizes of equipment (e.g. handful of rice, 250 mL beaker)

Procedure
- the **procedure** or **method** is a detailed list of what you did in the experiment, in the exact order you did it
- write in short, numbered steps
- include the quantities you used (e.g. 5 g, 2 spatulas, 10 mL)
- can include 2D scientific diagrams

Results
- **results** are a record of all the observations and measurements you took during the investigation
- observations can be written or can be diagrams, photos and videos
- preferably presented as written observations in a table
- include any graphs or calculations

Review
- **analysis** of your observations and measurements
- analyse any table, spreadsheet or graph you produced
- compare your findings with other groups or with information found from textbooks or the internet
- evaluate how you could make your investigation better
- construct a short **conclusion** that summarises what you found out in the experiment

FIGURE 1.3.5 How to write a scientific report

Working with Science

INFORMATION DESIGNER

For scientists to communicate effectively, they need to clearly and simply explain the ideas and messages behind what they have found. By turning scientific information into visual representations, scientists make it easier to understand.

The technology to study and visualise this information is continually improving. Because of this, opportunities for people with skills in graphic design and a good understanding of scientific data are expanding. Information designers use digital tools to present data in interesting and informative ways. Their skills can be used to create interest in science and deliver important scientific messages to the community (Figure 1.3.6).

FIGURE 1.3.6 This data on antibiotic resistance is presented in a visually engaging way.

To become an information designer, you need a qualification in graphic design or visual communication design (diploma or degree) and a good understanding of how data is collected, managed and analysed. If you think you might enjoy working with data and creating beautiful graphics that inform and engage people, then information design may be a career option for you.

Review
1. Why do you think it is important to communicate scientific findings to the community?
2. Scientific information can be communicated many different ways (e.g. on television, in the classroom, on science blogs, at the museum). What ways do you like to engage with science?

MODULE 1.3 Review questions

Remembering

1. Define the terms:
   a. continuous
   b. discrete.

2. What term best describes each of the following in a scientific report?
   a. what you intend to do
   b. educated guess
   c. the end.

3. Tables and spreadsheets can both display results from an experiment. What can a spreadsheet do that a table cannot?

Understanding

4. Explain why scientists would want to read what others have found out in experiments.

5. Why is a hypothesis different from a guess?

Applying

6. Adrian ran an experiment in which he tested how much sugar would dissolve in a hot cup of tea. Identify the best conclusion for his experiment.
   A. The experiment was fun.
   B. I learnt a lot from the experiment about sugar dissolving in hot tea.
   C. 3 teaspoons of sugar were able to be dissolved in a hot cup of tea.
   D. Tea tastes better when there is sugar dissolved in it.

7. Identify whether a column/bar, pie or line graph would best show the following results.
   a. the top speeds of different makes of cars
   b. the temperature of a room throughout a winter's day
   c. the percentages of your classmates who were born in Australia and overseas
   d. your height as you get older
   e. the types of animal with different numbers of legs (Figure 1.3.7).

FIGURE 1.3.7

8. Identify which of the graphs (A, B, C or D) best represents the results in Table 1.3.2.

TABLE 1.3.2 Pet ownership by percentage

Type of pet	Percentage (%)
dogs	50
cats	25
fish	13
birds	12

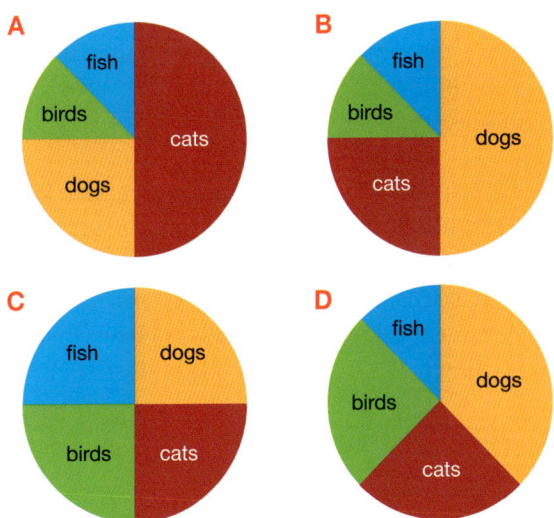

MODULE 1.3 Review questions

9 Use the key below to identify the term that best describes the trend shown in each of the line graphs in Figure 1.3.8.

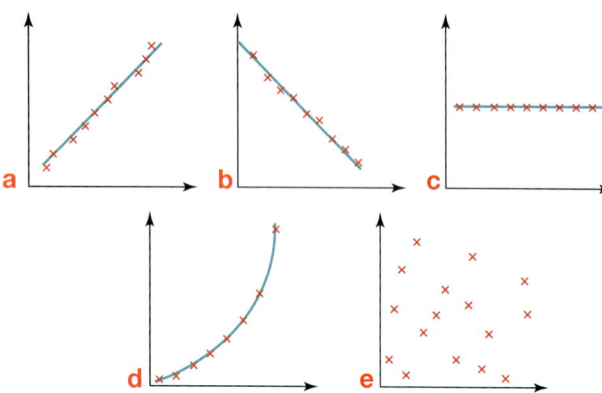

FIGURE 1.3.8

A	constant	B	increasing
C	decreasing	D	no trend shown

10 Use examples to show the difference between discrete measurements and continuous measurements.

11 a Describe what the term 'line of best fit' means.
   b Explain why a line of best fit is used instead of joining up points on a graph dot-to-dot.
   c Identify what is wrong with the graph in Figure 1.3.3 on page 25.

12 Imagine you whisper a message quietly in the ear of the person next to you who then whispers it to another person. The message is passed like this around the room and then eventually back to you.
   a Explain why the message you receive back is usually very different from the one you whispered.
   b Use this example to explain why results from an experiment should always be written down.

Analysing

13 Draw simple sketches to contrast a column graph with a:
   a bar graph
   b pie graph
   c line graph.

14 Construct a table for the poorly recorded results shown in Figure 1.3.9.

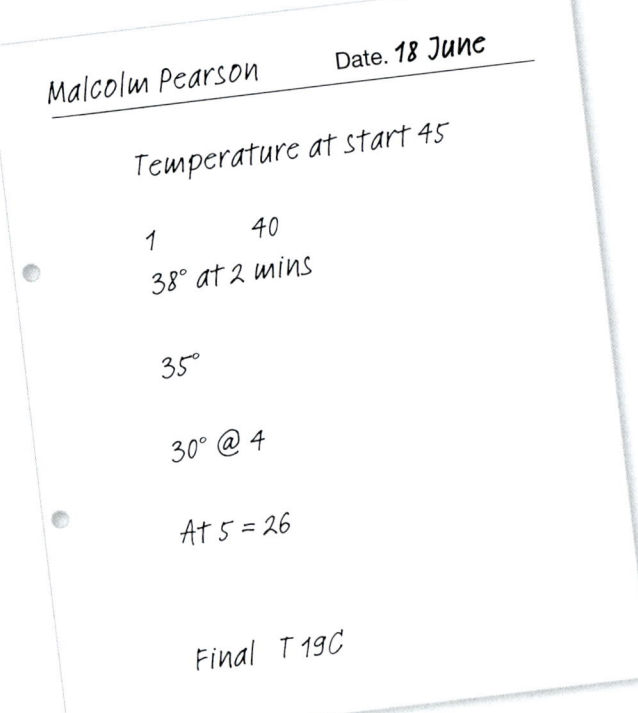

FIGURE 1.3.9

Creating

15 Construct a line graph from the data shown in Figure 1.3.9.

MODULE 1.3 Practical investigations

1 • Spaghetti predictions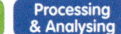

Purpose
To use a graph to predict unknown measurements.

Timing 75 minutes

Materials
- 4 lengths of dry spaghetti
- beam balance or electronic balance
- 30 cm ruler (with 1 mm markings)

Procedure
1. Break three lengths of spaghetti into three pieces each so that you end up with nine different lengths.
2. Measure the length and mass of each piece of spaghetti.

Results
1. Record the lengths and masses you measure in a table like that shown below. Give your table a title. Alternatively, use a spreadsheet to display your measurements.

Length of spaghetti (mm)	Mass of spaghetti (g)

2. Use this information to plot a line graph. Draw a straight line so that it passes roughly through the centre of your points. An example of a line of best fit is shown in Figure 1.3.10.

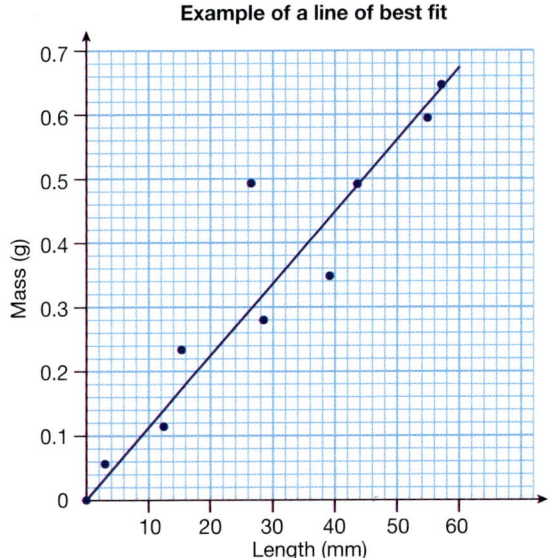

FIGURE 1.3.10

3. You have measured the length of nine bits of broken spaghetti and have plotted them as nine points on your graph. Mark a spot on your line of best fit between any two of your points.
4. For this spot, drop a line to the horizontal axis to find the length that spot represents. Then run a line across to the vertical axis to find the mass it is expected to be. This is a prediction and you now need to find out how accurate your prediction is. Add this predicted mass to your table.
5. To see how accurate your prediction is carefully snap the remaining piece of spaghetti so that one of its broken bits is the same length as you have just recorded in step 4.
6. Measure its mass.
7. Compare its actual, measured mass with its predicted mass.

Review
Construct a conclusion about the link between mass and length of spaghetti.

CHAPTER 1 • WORKING SCIENTIFICALLY **29**

MODULE 1.3 Practical investigations

• STUDENT DESIGN •

2 • Hot drinks cooling

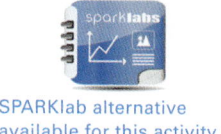

SPARKlab alternative available for this activity.

Questioning & Predicting
Communicating

Purpose
To compare the rates at which different cups of hot drink cool.

Hypothesis
Which do you think will cool faster—a cup of tea, coffee, or drinking chocolate? What about if it was in a cup or a mug, a large cup or a small cup? Before you go any further with this investigation, write a prediction in your workbook.

Timing 75 minutes

Materials
To be selected by students.

SAFETY
A Risk Assessment is required for this investigation.

Procedure
1. Design an experiment that will compare the cooling rates of:
   - cups, mugs and beakers
   - tea, coffee and drinking chocolate
   - tea or coffee with and without milk and sugar
   - different volumes of drink.
2. Write your procedure in your workbook.
3. Before you start any practical work, prepare a risk assessment. Show your teacher your procedure and your assessment. If they approve, then collect all the required materials and start work.

Hints
- Only test one thing at a time. For example, test the cooling in a cup, mug and beaker but keep everything else the same (such as drink volume and type of drink).
- When measuring temperature with a thermometer, read and record the measurement before you take the thermometer out of the drink.
- Use the STEM and SDI template in your eBook to help you plan and carry out your investigation.

Results
1. Record all your temperatures in a results table or spreadsheet similar to the following. If you choose a table, give your table a title.

Time (min)	Cup of tea	Beaker of coffee	Mug of drinking chocolate
0 (at the start)			
1			
2			
3			
4			

2. Plot the results of each drink as a line graph on a similar grid to that shown in Figure 1.3.11. Give your graph a title. Alternatively, use your spreadsheet to generate your graph.

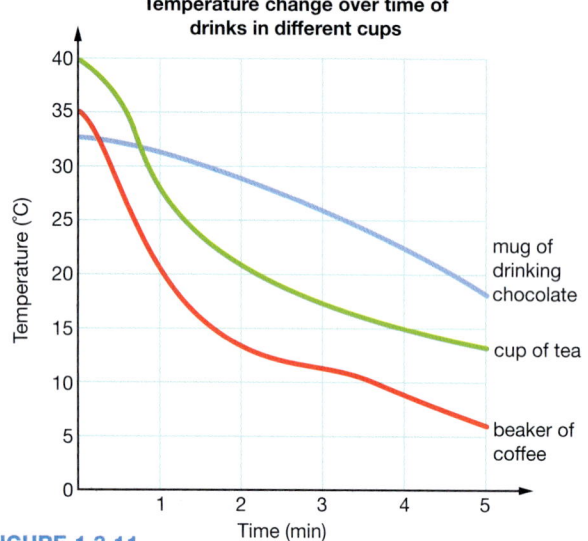

FIGURE 1.3.11

Review
1. Describe the trend or pattern that each graph showed. Was it increasing, decreasing, constant, unpredictable?
2. Which drink cooled the:
   a. fastest?
   b. slowest?
3. List as many factors as you can to explain why the drinks cooled at different rates.
4. Propose improvements that could be made to your experiment.
5. a. Construct a conclusion for your investigation.
   b. Assess whether your hypothesis was supported or not.

30 PEARSON SCIENCE 7 2ND EDITION

MODULE 1.4 Planning your own investigation

In most experiments, you will be given a detailed set of instructions. Sometimes you will need to plan your own investigation and decide what equipment and substances you use and how you intend to run the activity. Whatever you do in an experiment, you will need to run a fair test.

STEM 4 fun

Can you grow gummy bears?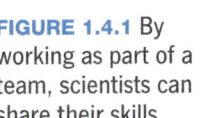

PROBLEM
Find the best way to increase the mass and length of a gummy bear.

SUPPLIES packet of gummy bears, cups, water, apple juice, vinegar, lemon juice, salt water, soda water, cordial, ruler, scales

PLAN AND DESIGN Design the solution. What information do you need to solve the problem? Draw a diagram. Make a list of materials you will need and steps you will take

CREATE Follow your plan. Produce your solution to the problem.

IMPROVE What works? What doesn't? How do you know it solves the problem? What could work better? Modify your design to make it better. Test it out.

REFLECTION
1. What area of STEM did you work in today?
2. How did you use mathematics in this task?
3. What did you do today that worked well? What didn't work well?

Teamwork

Science requires teamwork. In the laboratory, you will frequently work as part of a team, particularly when doing experiments, your own investigations or research. Working in a team allows you to pool everyone's talents. Scientists usually work in teams too. As Figure 1.4.1 shows, some teams have only two members. One way to organise a team is to find out what each person is already good at. For example, the best person to analyse and plot your measurements is probably someone who has used computer spreadsheets and graphing programs before.

FIGURE 1.4.1 By working as part of a team, scientists can share their skills.

CHAPTER 1 • WORKING SCIENTIFICALLY 31

Identifying variables

Many different factors influence what happens in an experiment. In science, these factors are known as **variables**. Think of the time it takes someone to run 100 metres. The time taken will depend on many variables, such as the age and fitness of the runner, the shoes being worn, the direction of the wind and whether the surface was grass, concrete or sand.

Any experiment that you carry out must be a **fair test**. To be fair, you should change only one variable at a time. Otherwise you won't be able to work out what variable caused any change. All the other variables must be controlled, being kept exactly the same.

In any experiment you should be able to identify the:

- **dependent variable**: this is what you are trying to measure. It depends on all the other variables. It might change as a result of a change in an independent variable. For the 100-metre run, the dependent variable is the time taken to run 100 metres.
- **independent variable**: this is what you are trying to test to see what effect it has on the dependent variable. For the 100-metre run, you might want to test what effect different running surfaces have on the time taken to run 100 metres. In this case, the running surface is the independent variable.
- **controlled variables**: these are all the other variables that you don't want to test right now. These are kept constant. In the 100-metre run, you are testing the surface, so every other variable needs to be kept the same. The age and fitness of the runner, the type of shoes they are wearing and the wind direction would all need to be kept constant.

FIGURE 1.4.2 The type of ball and the surface it is dropped onto are two variables that will affect the height to which the ball bounces.

Figure 1.4.2 shows a ball bouncing on a racquet. When a ball is dropped onto a surface such as a racquet, many variables influence the height the ball bounces back to. The height of a bounce (bounce height) is the dependent variable because it depends on other (independent) variables. Just a few of these are the:

- type of ball that is being bounced
- type of surface it is being bounced on
- height the ball drops from (drop height).

Let's say you decide to test how the drop height of a ball affects the bounce height. Your variables are therefore:

- dependent variable: bounce height. This is what you are measuring and will be the basis of your aim.
- independent variable: drop height. This is what you are changing.
- controlled variables: the type of ball and surface. These must be kept the same throughout the experiment.

Your purpose therefore would be: *To test how drop height affects bounce height.*

Developing a hypothesis

Think about what is likely to happen in the experiment. Write down what you think might logically happen. This is your **hypothesis**. For the ball-drop experiment, your hypothesis might be: *Increasing the drop height will increase the height the ball bounces to.* The prediction might be: *As the drop height increases, the ball bounce height will also increase.*

Developing your procedure

Your procedure must test the effect of only the independent variable you chose earlier. All other variables must be kept the same. In this ball-bounce experiment, you need to test one type of ball (such as a tennis ball) and one type of surface (for example, onto a concrete path). The only thing you can change is the height from which you drop the ball. Figure 1.4.3 shows how this might be done. If you want to change another variable, then you need to run a new and separate experiment.

32 PEARSON SCIENCE 7 2ND EDITION

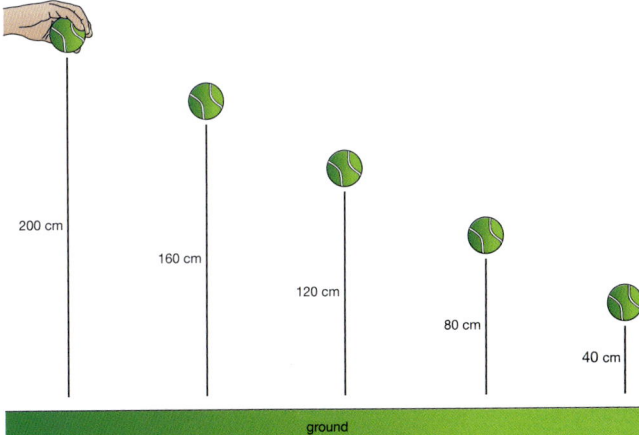

FIGURE 1.4.3 Try to test five or more different heights and make sure they are not too close to each other. Patterns are difficult to see if there are less than five measurements or if the measurements are too close together.

Choosing appropriate equipment

Once you have a rough procedure in mind, you can then work out what equipment you need.

For the bouncing tennis ball investigation, the starting height of the ball could be measured with a metre ruler or tape measure. The bounce height is more difficult to measure because the ball is moving all the time. You could mark off its height on a wall next to the bounce or you could video the motion on a smartphone, computer tablet or digital camera. You will need a hard flat surface to bounce the ball on.

Assessing risks

Before you start any actual practical work, you must assess how safe your planned procedure is. If there are any risks, then you need to find ways to minimise them or you need to change your procedure to something safer. For example, is there a chance you might get burnt? If so, then your team might need to wear heatproof gloves. In the bouncing ball investigation, dropping the ball from the roof would be spectacular but would also be very dangerous. To keep everyone safe, drop the ball from heights of less than 2 m instead.

Putting your results in a table

Here you are measuring drop height and bounce height. An appropriate results table would look like the one shown in Table 1.4.1. A spreadsheet would look very similar.

TABLE 1.4.1 Results table

Drop height (cm)	Bounce height (cm)
0	0
50	30
100	62
150	95
200	120
250	148

Plotting a graph

When plotting a graph, you first need to decide which type of graph you need to use. Line graphs are used when you have two sets of continuous measurements like height, mass or time.

The results from the ball-drop experiment have two sets of continuous numbers and so a line graph is the most appropriate graph to plot. It might look like the one in Figure 1.4.4.

Bar graphs are used when one set of results is discrete. For example, bar graphs would be a good way of showing the way bounce height changed when the type of ball or type of surface was changed.

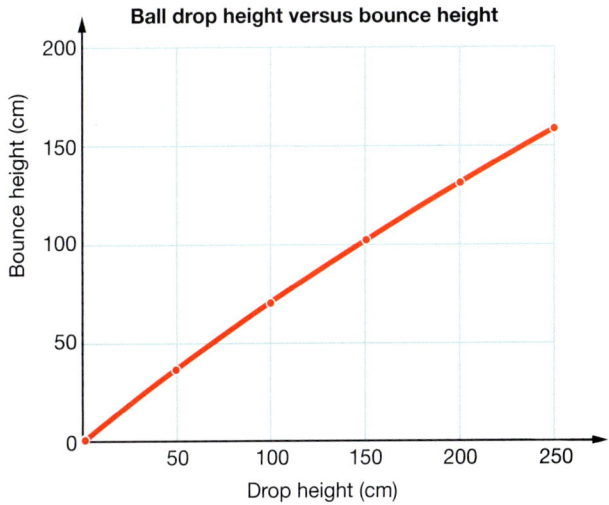

FIGURE 1.4.4 Two sets of measurements require a line graph.

Your conclusion

Your conclusion must answer the purpose or aim of your experiment. Depending on what you tested, an appropriate purpose and conclusion would be:

Purpose: To test what increasing drop height does to bounce height.

Conclusion: Increasing drop height causes bounce height to increase.

CHAPTER 1 • WORKING SCIENTIFICALLY   **33**

SCIENCE AS A HUMAN ENDEAVOUR
Nature and development of science

Teamwork across different branches of science

Big problems require big teams with a range of skills from different branches of science.

FIGURE 1.4.5 The mountain pygmy-possum is endangered. Teams of scientists are working to make sure it doesn't become extinct.

There are fewer than 500 mountain pygmy-possums (*Burramys parvus*) left in NSW. The species is classified as endangered (which means it might die out) and scientists are working to prevent it from becoming extinct. The possum lives in the mountains of the Kosciuszko National Park. In summer and autumn it eats Bogong moths, beetles, millipedes and spiders, and sometimes the seeds of plants. In winter, it hibernates, sleeping under a cover of snow that insulates it from the freezing cold. You can see a pygmy-possum in Figure 1.4.5.

To protect the possum, scientists need to find out why their numbers are falling. This research needs a variety of different skills that only come from being part of a team made up of scientists working in different branches of science (Figure 1.4.6).

REVIEW

1 Why do scientists from different branches of science need to work together to save the mountain pygmy-possum?

2 Sending a crew to Mars will require scientists with a wide variety of skills.
   a List some of the big problems these scientists will have to solve.
   b Identify the branches of science these scientists will need to specialise in to overcome these problems.

Ecologists need to find out whether the possums are being affected by the area being divided up into smaller parts by the local ski industry.

Botanists need to find out whether bushfires are damaging the plants whose seeds the possums eat.

Zoologists determined that foxes and feral cats were eating the possums.

Climate scientists need to find out whether less snow and a higher snowline will affect the possum's survival.

FIGURE 1.4.6 Branches of science working together

Chemists need to know whether the levels of arsenic in local Bogong moths and possum poo are similar to the levels found naturally.

34 PEARSON SCIENCE 7 2ND EDITION

MODULE 1.4 Review questions

Remembering

1. Define the terms:
   a. variables
   b. fair test.

2. What term best describes each of the following?
   a. a variable that is kept the same through an experiment
   b. the variable that is changed during the experiment
   c. the variable that changes naturally because another variable is changed.

3. In the STEM4fun activity on page 31, gummy bears were placed in different solutions. For this activity, what is a logical:
   a. aim
   b. hypothesis?

4. What advantages does working in a team bring?

5. List variables that are likely to affect the:
   a. amount of sugar that will dissolve in a cup of tea
   b. number of visitors to a swimming pool
   c. growth of a plant
   d. time taken to cook a potato
   e. number of times you go to the toilet in a day.

Understanding

6. Explain why only one variable should be changed in any single experiment.

7. Why must you assess risks when you are designing an investigation?

8. Explain why you should try to collect five or more results in an experiment.

Applying

9. Identify which of the following sets of drop heights would give the best idea of what happens when drop height is increased.
   A. 10 mm, 20 mm, 30 mm, 40 mm, 50 mm
   B. 5 cm, 10 cm, 15 cm, 20 cm, 25 cm
   C. 50 cm, 100 cm, 150 cm, 200 cm, 250 cm
   D. 10 m, 20 m, 30 m, 40 m, 50 m

10. Identify likely aims that would have led to these conclusions.
    a. Tennis balls bounced best on concrete. They did not bounce as well on short grass and bounced poorly on long grass.
    b. Superballs bounced best, followed in order by tennis balls and volleyballs. Squash balls were the worst bouncers.

11. Identify the variables that are likely to affect the amount of detergent froth produced when washing the dishes.

12. Use the rules for writing a good conclusion to write an appropriate conclusion that meets these aims:
    a. to test if fishing line is stronger than string
    b. to prove that water boils at 100°C
    c. to determine how much water a sponge can hold.

Evaluating

13. Bob ran an experiment on bouncing balls and recorded the following results.

Range of balls tested on different surfaces for bounce height

Ball	Surface	Drop height (cm)	Bounce height (cm)
tennis	sand	30	1
squash	concrete	300	30
golf	gravel	100	5
volleyball	grass	50	10

On the basis of his results, he claimed that squash balls bounced better than tennis balls.
   a. State the dependent variable that Bob tested.
   b. Identify how many variables Bob changed during the experiment.
   c. Assess whether the experiment was a fair test.
   d. Do you agree with Bob's conclusion? Justify your answer.

Creating

14. Georgie heard an old tale that if you want an avocado to ripen quickly, then it should be placed in a brown paper bag with a banana. She thought this sounded weird and wanted to see if it was true. Write an experiment for Georgie to test if the tale was true or not. Make sure that your test is fair.

MODULE 1.4 Practical investigations

• **STUDENT DESIGN** •

1 • Planning your own investigation

Purpose

To design and run an experiment that tests a single variable.

Timing 75 minutes

Materials

Choose your own, depending on your choice of topic.

SAFETY
A Risk Assessment is required for this investigation.

Procedure

1 List the variables that are likely to affect the:
   - bounce height of a ball
   - amount of sugar that can be dissolved in a cup of tea
   - adhesive strength of sticky-tape
   - stretch of an elastic band or another elastic material such as stockings
   - strength of paper.

Planning & Conducting   Processing & Analysing

2 Choose ONE of the topics listed in step 1 of the procedure and design an experiment that will test ONE of its variables. In your workbook, write a hypothesis that describes what you expect when you change that variable. For example, 'We expect that a tennis ball will bounce higher than a soccer ball when dropped from the same height.'

3 Write your procedure in your workbook.

4 Before you start any practical work, assess your procedure. List any risks that your procedure might involve and what you might do to minimise those risks. Show your teacher your procedure and your assessment of its risks. If they approve, then collect all the required materials and start work.

Results

Construct a table and a graph (column, bar or line graph) to display your results.

Review

1 a Construct a conclusion for your investigation.
  b Assess whether your hypothesis was supported or not.

2 Construct a scientific report describing what you did in your prac. In it, you should include a:
  a table of results
  b graph.

3 Identify other variables that would affect your experiment.

CHAPTER 1 Chapter review

Remembering

1. Define the terms:
   a. meniscus
   b. cross-section
   c. hypothesis
   d. variable.

2. Name the branch of science that studies:
   a. living things
   b. chemicals
   c. forces and energy
   d. behaviour
   e. the Earth
   f. space
   g. the environment.

3. List three sub-branches for each of:
   a. biology
   b. geology
   c. physics
   d. chemistry.

4. Name the two experts you can turn to in the laboratory.

5. State two metric units commonly used for:
   a. distance
   b. volume
   c. mass.

6. Which abbreviation is correct for these units?
   a. degrees Celsius
      A. deg C   B. deg
      C. °C   D. C
   b. seconds
      A. sec   B. secs
      C. S   D. s

7. What is one qualitative and one quantitative observation for each of the following?
   a. a can of soft drink
   b. yourself.

Understanding

8. Which of these observations are qualitative and which are quantitative?
   a. The cow went 'moo'.
   b. The car was travelling at 60 km/h.
   c. The Dockers won by 25 points.
   d. The Broncos won by a lot.

9. Describe the features of a safety flame.

10. Why are the senses of taste and smell rarely used in science?

Applying

11. Identify the equipment in these jumbled words.
    a. kaeber
    b. aluspat
    c. burccile.

12. Identify the best SI unit to measure the:
    a. time to run the 100 m sprint
    b. mass of a car
    c. volume of water in a sink.

13. Identify the type of graph (bar, column, pie or line) from the clues below.
    a. It shows percentages.
    b. It has two sets of measurements.
    c. It has discrete groups along its bottom, horizontal axis.
    d. It has discrete groups along its vertical axis.

Analysing

14. Compare the types of work done by a detective and a scientist.

Evaluating

15. Propose reasons why the Bunsen burner gas must be turned on after the match is lit.

16. a. Assess whether you can or cannot answer the questions on page 1 at the start of this chapter.
    b. Use this assessment to evaluate how well you understand the material presented in this chapter.

Creating

17. Use following ten key terms to construct a visual summary of the information presented in this chapter.

    | laboratory | equipment |
    | experiment | safety |
    | observations | measurements |
    | units | quantitative |
    | variables | qualitative |

AB 1.10

CHAPTER 1 • WORKING SCIENTIFICALLY   37

CHAPTER 1 Inquiry skills

Research

1 `Processing & Analysing` `Evaluating`

Three-part inquiry question

Select your entry point and complete the relevant parts of this inquiry. The Nobel Prize for Physiology or Medicine is awarded in most years. In 2005, it was awarded to a pair of Australian researchers: Dr Barry Marshall and Dr Robin Warren.

a What are the criteria used for the award of a Nobel Prize in Physiology or Medicine? What discovery or discoveries led to their being awarded the Nobel Prize? Explain why this research was so important.

b Describe the experiment performed by Dr Marshall. What hypothesis was Dr Marshall testing? What was the independent variable in the experiment? What was the dependent variable? What were some other variables that may have affected the outcome of the experiment? How did Dr Marshall control these? What evidence was collected by Drs Marshall and Warren that supported their hypothesis? Explain why it was so difficult for their conclusions to be accepted by the wider medical profession.

c After completing their initial investigations, Drs Marshall and Warren needed to try their proposed treatment on volunteer patients. What was the treatment proposed by Dr Marshall? Before any experiment can be performed using vertebrates (animals with backbones), including humans, they must be approved by an ethics committee. What are ethics committees? What is their function?

Consider that you are a member of the ethics committee evaluating the research of Drs Marshall and Warren and their proposed treatment. Discuss any issues that you can see with testing a new treatment on people. Make sure you consider the concept of 'informed consent' in your answer. Taking into account the issues that you have identified, would you give approval for the human trial to take place? Give reasons for your opinion.

2 `Processing & Analysing`

Fire blankets, eyewashes and fume hoods are common safety equipment in the laboratory. For each, find:
- an image
- what it is used for
- how it is used
- its location in your science laboratory.

Present your research as a plan of the laboratory with attached images and descriptions.

3 `Processing & Analysing`

Scientific investigations are regularly reported in the newspaper, on websites and in scientific magazines such as *Cosmos* and *Scientific American*. Find an article that discusses a scientific investigation and:
- give the names of the scientists involved
- summarise what they found out.

Present your information in whichever way you choose.

4 `Planning & Conducting`

Research the history of the metric (or SI) system of units.
Summarise the main events in its history as ten dot points.

5 `Planning & Conducting`

Scientists around the world eagerly awaited the landing of the Mars *Polar Lander* in 1999. One important mission of the lander was to search for water. However, after descending into the Martian atmosphere, the lander was never heard from again. Find:
- when it was launched from Earth
- what its mission on Mars was to be
- when it crashed
- what caused it to crash.

Present your research as four short paragraphs in a Word document, as four pages in a PowerPoint presentation or as four panels in a poster.

CHAPTER 1

Inquiry skills

Thinking scientifically

The Three Bears returned home and found someone had been eating their porridge. Being scientific bears, they were interested in how fast different-sized bowls cooled. They filled them with hot porridge and measured the temperature every minute. Their results are shown in the table.

TABLE 1.5.1 Temperature change over time in each bowl

Time (min)	Temperature of Papa Bear's porridge (°C)	Temperature of Mama Bear's porridge (°C)	Temperature of Baby Bear's porridge (°C)
0	60	58	61
1	55	48	50
2		39	48
3	45	31	30
4	40		20
5	35	18	10

1 Identify which bowl cooled the fastest.

Mama Bear then sketched line graphs to show what was happening. These are shown in Figure 1.5.1.

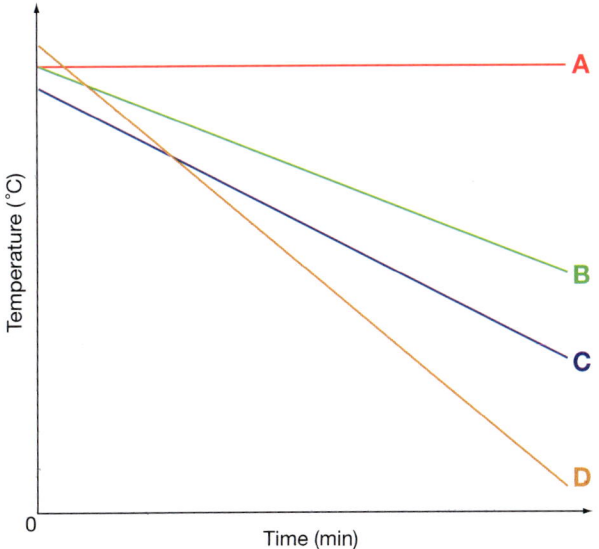

FIGURE 1.5.1

2 Which of the graphs in Figure 1.5.1 most likely represents each of the following?
  a Papa Bear's bowl
  b Mama Bear's bowl
  c Baby Bear's bowl.

3 Which of the following variables are unlikely to have much effect on the cooling of the porridge?
  A size of bowl
  B amount of porridge
  C amount of sugar in porridge
  D starting temperature of porridge.

4 Baby Bear misread his thermometer once. Which temperature reading is most likely to be wrong?
  A 50°C
  B 48°C
  C 30°C
  D 20°C

5 Papa Bear forgot to read his thermometer once. What was the most likely missing temperature?
  A 31°C
  B 53°C
  C 50°C
  D 18°C

6 Mama Bear also forgot to read her thermometer. What was the most likely missing temperature?
  A 30°C
  B 24°C
  C 20°C
  D 18°C

CHAPTER 1 • WORKING SCIENTIFICALLY   39

CHAPTER 1 Glossary

aim: what you are trying to do
analysis: looking for trends in the results
astronomy: the study of space
bar graph: used when one set of observations is discrete. Bars are horizontal
biology: the study of living things
branches: sub-groups of science. Also known as disciplines.
Bunsen burner: used in the laboratory to provide heat
chemistry: the study of chemicals and their reactions

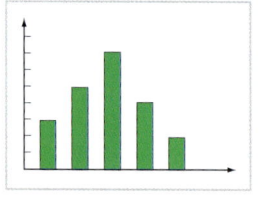
Bunsen burner

column graph: used when one set of observations is discrete. Columns are vertical.
conclusion: what you have found out
continuous: measurements that vary without breaking or falling into categories or groups
controlled variables: held constant throughout an experiment
cross-section: split down the middle
dependent variable: will change naturally as you change the other variables
disciplines: sub-groups of science. Also known as branches
discrete: measurements that fall into categories or groupings
ecology: the study of the environment
experiment: a practical investigation performed mainly inside a laboratory
fair test: changing only one variable at a time
fieldwork: a practical investigation performed mainly outside in nature
geology: the study of Earth

column graph

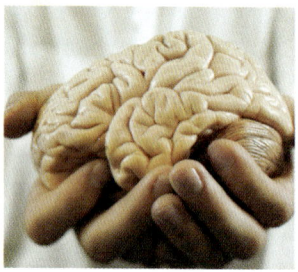
ecology

hotplate: heating device
hypothesis: educated guess
independent variable: what you change in an experiment
laboratory: where a scientist works
line graph: used when there are two sets of continuous measurements
mass: amount of matter
meniscus: curved surface of liquids in narrow tubes
method: tells how you did the experiment
physics: the study of forces and energy
pie graph: used to show proportions. Also known as a sector graph
practical investigation: experiment or fieldwork
procedure: tells how you did the experiment
psychology: the study of behaviour
purpose: what you are trying to do (aim)
qualitative observations: observations in words only
quantitative observations: measurements including numbers
results: the measurements and observations made in an experiment
safety flame: yellow flame
sector graph: used to show proportions. Also known as a pie graph
toxic: poisonous
variables: factors that influence an experiment

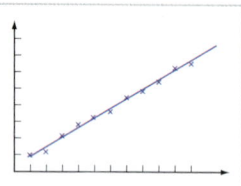
line graph

meniscus

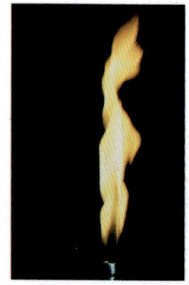
psychology

safety flame

AB 1.9

40 PEARSON SCIENCE 7 2ND EDITION

CHAPTER 2
Properties of substances

Have you ever wondered...
- why solids, liquids and gases appear so different?
- why clothes dry even when it's not hot?
- why you breathe out fog on a cold morning?
- why icebergs float?

After completing this chapter you should be able to:
- identify substances that can assist and harm our environment
- describe how new evidence has changed our understanding of the world
- classify changes as reversible or irreversible
- describe changes of state caused by heating and cooling
- explain melting, freezing and evaporating.

This is an extract from the Australian Curriculum
Victorian Curriculum F–10 © VCAA (2016); reproduced by permission

MODULE 2.1 Physical and chemical properties

There are millions of different substances in the world. Each can be identified by its properties. Properties describe a substance and how it acts. They include its appearance, what it does when heated or cooled, and how it reacts with other substances.

science 4 fun

What is foam?
Is shaving foam a solid, a liquid or a gas?

Collect this ...
- can of shaving foam
- plastic plate
- small mass (such as a 50c coin or a pebble)

Do this ...
1. Squirt a blob of shaving foam onto the plate. What does it look like? Does the foam flow or change shape without being pushed around?
2. Place the small mass on the top of the foam. Does it stay there or does it sink?
3. Squirt another blob of foam onto the plate. Put the plate into a cupboard so that it won't be touched. Leave it there overnight. What does the foam look like the next day?

Record this ...
1. Describe what happened.
2. Explain why you think it happened.

Physical properties

You can probably tell which objects and substances around you are solid, liquid or gas by the way they look and act. These are **physical properties**. Testing a substance for its physical properties does not change it into anything new. For example, crush a rock and it is exactly the same substance as before but in smaller pieces.

Some of the most useful physical properties of a substance are:

- whether it is a solid, liquid or gas at room temperature
- the temperatures at which the substance freezes or boils (known as its freezing point and boiling point)
- its appearance (such as its colour and texture, the shape of any crystals within it and whether it is shiny or dull)
- its density (how heavy it is compared to other substances of the same size)

- how hard or brittle the substance is (whether it is easily scratched or whether it crumbles)
- whether the substance dissolves in different liquids (known as solubility)
- its ability to let heat or electricity pass through it (known as its thermal and electrical conductivity).

Solids, liquids and gases

Substances exist in either a solid, liquid or gas form. These forms are known as the **states** of matter.

Solids, liquids and gases have very different physical properties. Think of the car in Figure 2.1.1. The bodies of cars only change shape when they are forced to do so, for example if they are in an accident or when they are broken up to be recycled. Also solids cannot be **compressed** (squashed to make them smaller). Try to compress a sugar cube and it might crumble, but the volume of sugar is exactly the same as it was before. The fact that solids do not change shape or size makes them useful for building cars and structures like bridges and skyscrapers.

Liquids:
- have fixed size and volume
- are able to flow
- take the shape of the container they are in
- are incompressible.

FIGURE 2.1.2 Liquids always flow to take up the shape of their container.

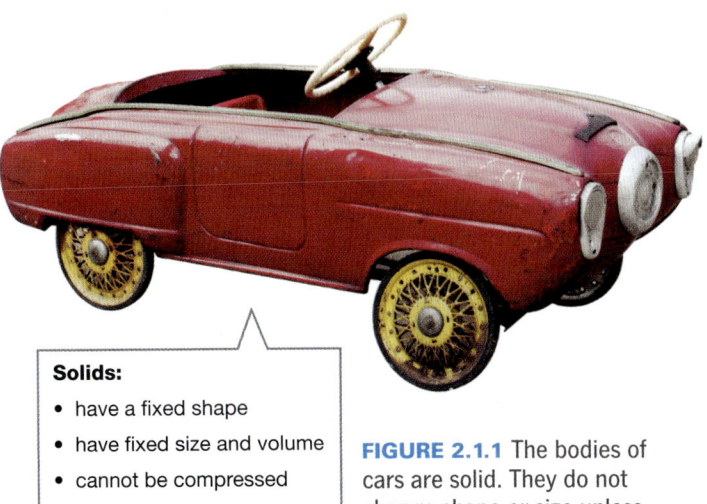

Solids:
- have a fixed shape
- have fixed size and volume
- cannot be compressed
- will usually sink when placed in liquids of the same material.

FIGURE 2.1.1 The bodies of cars are solid. They do not change shape or size unless they are in an accident or they are crushed to be recycled.

SciFile

No teardrops!

The shape of a raindrop depends on its size. None of them look like the teardrop shape shown in the weather report!

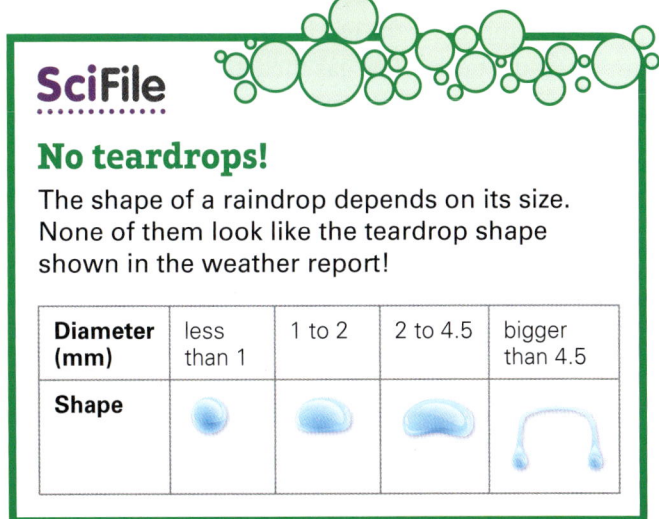

Diameter (mm)	less than 1	1 to 2	2 to 4.5	bigger than 4.5
Shape				

Liquids are similar to solids in that they don't change their size and are **incompressible** (unable to be compressed or squashed). They differ from solids in that they can flow and change shape. Think of orange juice: it splashes about and can be poured from one container into another, taking on a new shape as shown in Figure 2.1.2. The ability of liquids to squeeze along pipes and hoses without changing volume allows them to be used in hydraulic (powered by liquid) systems such as car brakes.

Gases are often invisible and many have no **odour** (smell). However, some gases do have an odour. Perfume, scent and fumes are words often used when people talk about gases that smell. Think of the perfume or scent of a rose like the one in Figure 2.1.3 on page 44, or the smell of chlorine fumes around some swimming pools. Water vapour is a gas that is invisible because it is colourless and spread too thinly for the gas to be seen. However, you can feel water vapour since it gives air its humidity. There is a lot of water vapour in the air on a humid day, making you feel sweaty and sticky.

CHAPTER 2 • PROPERTIES OF SUBSTANCES **43**

Gases:
- are often colourless, odourless and invisible
- will spread out to take the shape of the container
- have no fixed shape or volume
- can be compressed (pushed in to make them take up a smaller amount of space).

Chemical properties

Chemical properties describe how a substance reacts with other substances. When a substance reacts with another substance, an entirely new substance is formed. For example, when oxygen reacts with iron, a new substance, rust, is formed. Iron is grey, hard and often shiny, while the rust is red-orange, flaky and brittle. Likewise, paper burns and dynamite explodes, both reacting with oxygen and leaving behind ash and smoke.

Chemical properties include whether a substance:
- burns or explodes in oxygen (this is known as combustion)
- rusts or corrodes (known as corrosion) or is corrosion-resistant. For example, much of the shipwreck in Figure 2.1.5 has corroded away.
- is an acid like vinegar or a base like bicarbonate of soda or neutral like water (this is measured by its pH)
- reacts quickly or slowly with other chemicals (this is known as the rate of reaction). Explosions have a very fast rate of reaction.

FIGURE 2.1.3 This is a special type of photo called a Schlieren image. It shows the gaseous perfume rising from a rose.

Gases differ from solids and liquids in that they can be compressed. This property allows gases to be squeezed into small volumes such as barbecue gas cylinders. It also makes them useful in the gas struts or shock absorbers found in the suspension of bikes and cars. A bump compresses the gas in the struts, softening the impact of the bump. The gas then expands once more, pushing the strut back to its original shape.

Prac 1 p. 49   Prac 2 p. 50   Prac 3 p. 51

SciFile

The fourth state
There is a fourth state of matter but it is very rare on Earth. Plasma is a gas-like state that only exists at temperatures above 6000°C, making it common on stars but not here.

FIGURE 2.1.4 On Earth, plasma is found wherever high-voltage sparks are generated such as lightning bolts or in this plasma sphere.

FIGURE 2.1.5 The *SS Maheno* ran aground on Queensland's Fraser Island in 1935. Since then, much of the wreck has rusted away because its iron hull reacted with oxygen in the air and sea water.

Not solid, not liquid

PROBLEM

Can you create a substance that has properties of both a solid and a liquid?

SUPPLIES   flour, cornstarch, baby oil, liquid soap, water, spoon, bowl, measuring cups and measuring spoons

PLAN AND DESIGN   Design a method of weighing gas. What information do you need to solve the problem? Draw a diagram. Make a list of materials you will need and steps you will take.

CREATE   Follow your plan. Draw your solution to the problem.

IMPROVE   What works? What doesn't? How do you know it solves the problem? What could work better? Modify your design to make it better. Test it out.

REFLECTION

1. What area of STEM did you work in today?
2. How did you use mathematics in this task?
3. If another student was to do this task, what advice would you give?

Working with Science

ECOTOXICOLOGIST

Ecotoxicology is the study of the harmful effects of chemicals on plants and animals and the places where they live. Ecotoxicologists test areas where pollution is thought to have occurred. Action can then be taken to control any pollution found and to protect the area. Ecotoxicologists return regularly to monitor (check) if pollution levels are falling, suggesting that the action taken worked. Ecotoxicologists can also work out the best way to clean up major pollution from disasters, such as oil spills.

Ecotoxicology involves taking water, soil, plant and animal tissue samples and testing them for harmful chemicals (Figure 2.1.6). This information helps them to monitor and manage pollution. Ecotoxicologists test samples for substances such as heavy metals from industrial waste, chlorine from household cleaning products, pesticides and herbicides from agriculture, and phthalates from plastic bottles and containers. They also perform experiments to understand more about the effects of pollutants (substances harmful to the environment). This work can help them to develop tests for toxic chemicals and prepare guidelines for the safe use of chemicals that can become pollutants.

To become an ecotoxicologist, you need a Bachelor of Science majoring in chemistry and biology. Ecotoxicologists work in government departments, universities, environmental consulting groups, biotechnology institutes and non-government organisations. You might like this job if you enjoy working outside as well as in a laboratory and want to use your skills and knowledge to protect ecosystems.

Review

1. Why do you think it is important that ecotoxicologists monitor sites for pollution regularly?
2. What skills do you think are important for an ecotoxicologist to have?

FIGURE 2.1.6 Ecotoxicologists assess a water sample.

CHAPTER 2 • PROPERTIES OF SUBSTANCES   45

SCIENCE AS A HUMAN ENDEAVOUR
Use and influence of science

Biodegradability

Leave a sandwich in your schoolbag and a few days later you'll be left with a mess of rotting, smelly goo.

This happens because microscopic bacteria cause chemical reactions that break down and rot substances in sandwiches. Simpler substances like sugar, water and carbon dioxide are the result. However, the cling wrap or plastic container holding the sandwich is unlikely to have changed. The chemical properties of the bread, lettuce and tomato caused them to rot, while the chemical properties of the cling wrap or plastic container made them rot-resistant. For this reason, cling wrap and plastic are pollutants—they cause harm to the environment.

Biodegradable

Substances are classified as being **biodegradable** if bacteria or fungi break them down. Fruit, vegetables, flowers, wood, twigs and leaves are biodegradable since they can all be broken down quickly by bacteria and fungi. This is why they are put into composts—once they have broken down, they form simple substances that can then be used to fertilise other plants. The mould on the strawberries in Figure 2.1.7 shows that it is biodegradable. Animals are also biodegradable because bacteria quickly break them down into simpler substances once they die.

Anything made of natural, living substances (or from substances that once lived) is biodegradable. Some examples include:

- paper and cardboard (made from wood)
- cotton, hessian, linen fabrics (made from plants)
- woollen fabrics (made from the 'hair' of animals like sheep and goats)
- soaps (made from natural fats and oils).

Non-biodegradable

Non-biodegradable substances eventually break down but often take hundreds of years to do so. This is because non-biodegradable substances have structures that bacteria and fungi cannot pull apart.

FIGURE 2.1.7 Rot and mould show that these strawberries are biodegradable.

Examples of non-biodegradable substances include:

- polyethylene cling wrap (used to wrap food)
- most plastic shopping bags
- wrappers (used for lollies, chocolate bars and ice-creams)
- polystyrene (used for takeaway food)
- house paints
- glass (used for jam and sauce bottles)
- aluminium and steel cans (used for soft drinks and canned spaghetti)
- electronic waste (such as old computers, TVs, mobile phones and batteries).

Anything made from these substances remains in the environment as rubbish and pollution for many, many years. They might crush, break or rip into smaller pieces, but their chemicals are still there polluting the environment for a long time.

SCIENCE AS A HUMAN ENDEAVOUR

FIGURE 2.1.8 Many plastics can now be recycled. This reduces waste and stops their chemicals from polluting the environment.

What can we do?

Non-biodegradable substances cause pollution so it is a challenge to work out how to dispose of them. Most non-biodegradable substances can be burnt but they release toxic (harmful chemical) fumes and smoke unless the fire happens in special incinerators at extremely high temperatures. Glass, some plastics and electronic waste can be recycled (Figure 2.1.8). However, most non-biodegradable substances are simply thrown out. To minimise the impact of non-biodegradable substances on the environment, we all need to:

- use biodegradable packaging whenever possible, and buy food with no packaging or wrapped in paper or cardboard
- recycle or dispose of non-biodegradable packaging in bins, so that it will not end up on the street, rivers and oceans where it may catch and tangle fish, dolphins and birds like the one in Figure 2.1.9
- recycle glass, PET bottles and other plastics wherever possible
- re-use plastic shopping bags or use paper or re-useable cloth bags instead
- keep electronic waste until it can be deposited at council e-waste depots.

FIGURE 2.1.9 Most plastic bags are non-biodegradable and so they don't rot away. If they get washed into rivers and the ocean, wildlife can get caught up in them and can die.

Scientists have developed biodegradable plastics from plant-based substances but these plastics are more expensive than similar oil-based plastics. They can't be recycled and cannot be used for long-term packaging. For these reasons, their use is not yet widespread.

REVIEW

1. List four biodegradable and four non-biodegradable substances.
2. What evidence shows that fruit and cardboard are biodegradable?
3. A log in the forest grows mushroom-like fungi on it.
   a. Use this information to classify the log as biodegradable or non-biodegradable.
   b. Predict what will be left of the log after 10 years.
4. Classify faeces (poo) as biodegradable or non-biodegradable.

CHAPTER 2 • PROPERTIES OF SUBSTANCES 47

MODULE 2.1 Review questions

Remembering

1. Define the terms:
   a. compressed
   b. odour.
2. What term best describes each of the following?
   a. not able to be squashed
   b. how a substance reacts.
3. What are three words often used when talking about gases that have a smell?
4. State whether the following are solids, liquids or gases at normal room temperatures.
   a. a sugar cube
   b. ink
   c. air.
5. The following mixtures are made up of a variety of substances in different states. List the different states that exist in the different substances.
   a. soft drink
   b. chicken curry
   c. mud.
6. State two physical properties and one chemical property of a sheet of paper.
7. Gases are often invisible so sometimes they are detected using other senses. Which sense(s) are used to detect each of the following gases?
   a. the scent of food cooking
   b. the presence of air around you
   c. the purple vapours coming from crystals of iodine that are being heated
   d. the hissing sound of gas escaping from a BBQ gas bottle.

Understanding

8. Explain how the compressibility of gases makes them ideal for using in shock absorbers in the suspension of cars and bikes.
9. a. What causes humidity?
   b. Describe what a humid day feels like.

Applying

10. Shaving foam cannot be classified as a solid or a liquid because it has some of the physical properties of both. Identify the physical properties of shaving foam that could be used to classify it as:
    a. a solid
    b. a liquid.
11. It is easier to list the physical properties of a substance than its chemical properties. Use an example to explain why.

Analysing

12. Each of the following substances displays some properties of both liquids and solids. Think about the properties of each substance and use them to classify each substance as solid or liquid.
    a. sand
    b. toothpaste
    c. hair gel.
13. Shopping bags were once made out of thick paper but are now usually made of thin plastic.
    a. Compare the properties of thick paper and thin plastic.
    b. Use these properties to discuss why most shopping bags are now plastic, not paper.
14. The pistons in a car engine are forced up and down by petrol vapours exploding in the car's cylinders.
    a. What properties make petrol a good fuel for a car?
    b. Classify these properties as physical or chemical.
    c. Identify another substance that is needed for this explosion to occur.

Evaluating

15. Liquids flow to take up the shape of their container but on a surface they sometimes form small droplets instead. Propose a reason why the liquid doesn't spread across the surface.
16. Aluminium is an extremely light, corrosion-resistant metal. It is relatively expensive and so recycling it is cheaper than producing new aluminium. Steel is a much heavier and stronger metal than aluminium. Steel corrodes and so it rusts away over time. It is relatively cheap so it is rarely recycled.
    a. Given these properties, which would you consider to be the best metal to construct:
       i. the bodies of high-performance sports cars?
       ii. the bodies of cheaper, everyday cars?
       iii. the frames of skyscrapers?
       iv. the bodies of aircraft?
    b. Justify each of your choices.
17. Some toxic gases are coloured and so you can see them when in large quantities. What would you recommend your class do if you saw a coloured gas coming from a spilt container in your laboratory?

MODULE 2.1 Practical investigations

1 • Slime `Planning & Conducting` `Evaluating`

Purpose
To make slime and observe its properties.

Timing 45 minutes

Materials
Note: PVA tends to change consistency depending on the brand chosen and its age. The quantities of PVA and borax shown below may need to be altered slightly depending on the brand of PVA used.

- 10 mL 4–6% borax solution
- 25 mL PVA glue
- a few drops of food dye
- eye dropper/Pasteur pipette
- disposable medicine measuring cup
- 10 mL measuring cylinder
- 2 disposable plastic cups
- icy-pole stick
- disposable rubber gloves

SAFETY

A Risk Assessment is required for this investigation.

Borax may irritate if it is inhaled or it gets into the eyes or on the skin. Wear safety glasses and rubber gloves at all times.

Procedure
1. Use the measuring cylinder to measure out 10 mL of borax solution.
2. Use the disposable medicine measuring cup to measure out 25 mL of PVA glue.
3. Pour the PVA into a disposable plastic cup, using the icy-pole stick to scrape out the last bits.
4. Add a few drops of food dye to the PVA.
5. Pour the borax solution, all at once, into the cup containing the PVA and food dye. Stir thoroughly with the icy-pole stick.
6. Empty out the slime and rinse it gently under a slow-running tap.
7. Test your slime to find:
   - if it can be rolled into a ball
   - what happens when it is stretched
   - whether it flows to take the shape of a container
   - what happens when it is dropped.

Results
Record your results in a table like that shown below. Give your table a title.

Review
1. List the physical properties of your slime.
2. Use the physical properties of solids and liquids to classify your slime as solid or liquid.
3. Justify your classification.

Investigation	Observation	Is this property more like that of a solid or a liquid?
Can slime be rolled into a ball?		
What happens when slime is stretched?		
Does slime flow to take the shape of its container?		
What happens when a ball of slime is dropped?		

CHAPTER 2 • PROPERTIES OF SUBSTANCES

MODULE 2.1 Practical investigations

2 • The mass of a gas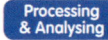

Purpose
To determine whether gas has mass.

Timing   30 minutes

Materials
- 2 balloons
- 3 lengths of string (each about 30 cm long)
- 1 m ruler
- needle (sharp enough to burst a balloon)

SAFETY A Risk Assessment is required for this investigation.

Procedure
1. Inflate both balloons until they are roughly the same size.
2. Tie their ends and tie a piece of string to the top of each balloon.
3. Tie one balloon to one end of the ruler and the other balloon to the other end as shown in Figure 2.1.10. Use the ruler markings to make sure that the strings are the same distance from the ends of the ruler.
4. Tie the third string to the middle of the ruler and hang the ruler from the edge of a table.
5. Balance the ruler so that it hangs parallel to the floor. Do this by sliding the middle string along the ruler until you find the balance point. The set-up is shown in Figure 2.1.10.
6. Puncture one of the balloons with the needle and observe what happens.

Review
1. Describe what happened.
2. What evidence supports the claim that gases have mass?

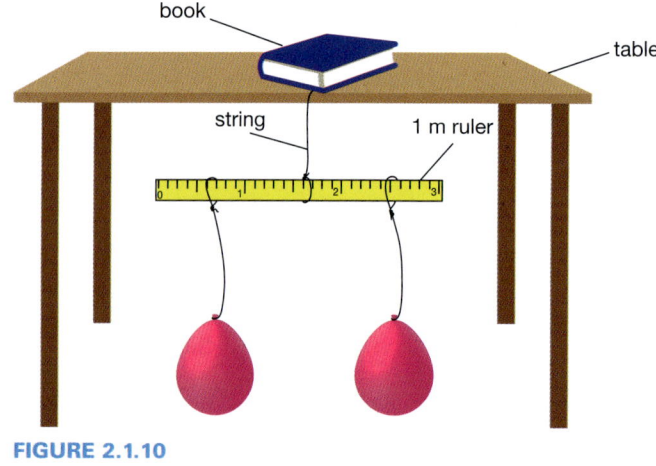

FIGURE 2.1.10

MODULE 2.1 Practical investigations

• STUDENT DESIGN •

3 • Oobleck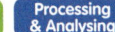

Oobleck is an easy-to-make slimy goo.

Purpose
To research and then design the best recipe to make oobleck.

Timing 45 minutes

Materials
To be selected by students.

SAFETY
A Risk Assessment is required for this investigation.

Procedure

1. Search the internet to find recipes or videos that show how to make oobleck. Print or save the recipe and save any video you find.
2. Summarise the main points of the recipe or video and write them in your workbook as your procedure.
3. Before you start making your oobleck, assess your procedure. List any risks that your procedure might involve and what you might do to minimise those risks. Show your teacher your procedure and your assessment of its risks. If they approve, then collect all the required materials and start work.
4. Once you have made your oobleck, test it by:
   • prodding it quickly with your finger
   • slowly lowering your finger into it
   • running the tests that were performed on slime in Prac 1.

Results
Record your results in a table like that used in Prac 1.

Review

1. List the properties of your oobleck that belong to:
   a liquids   b solids.
2. You can run easily across the wet sand at the edge of the sea. It firms up and becomes more solid under your feet. However, when you walk across wet sand it liquefies and you sink into it. Wet sand is classified as a non-Newtonian fluid.
   a Compare your oobleck with wet sand.
   b Both are specially classified as non-Newtonian fluids. List the properties of a non-Newtonian fluid.

SciFile

The Oobleck of Dr Seuss

In the book *Bartholomew and the Oobleck* by Dr Seuss, a king is so bored with ordinary weather that he instructs his wizard to create something new. A green goo called oobleck soon falls from the sky, gumming up the whole kingdom!

SciFile

Running on wet sand

The wet sand at the edge of the sea has the physical properties of a solid and a liquid. When you run across the wet sand, it firms up and becomes more solid under your feet. However, when you walk across it, it liquefies and you sink into it. For this reason, wet sand is given a special classification as a non-Newtonian fluid.

CHAPTER 2 • PROPERTIES OF SUBSTANCES **51**

MODULE 2.2 Solids, liquids and gases

Each of the states of matter has its own characteristic properties that can be explained using a simple model called the particle model.

science 4 fun

Get packing

Collect this ...
- 1 cup uncooked rice
- plastic or glass container (with lid)
- small ball that will fit in jar (such as a squash ball or ping-pong ball)

Do this ...
1. Pour uncooked rice into your container until it is half to three-quarters full.
2. Push the ball under the rice.
3. Put the lid on and shake the container jar sideways (not up and down).

Record this ...
1. Describe what happened.
2. Explain why you think this happens.

Models in science

Scientists often use models to test or explain something that is difficult to understand. Sometimes, the model will be a physical model like the aircraft shown in Figure 2.2.1. These models are commonly used by scientists and engineers to test how something acts under certain conditions.

For example, a model could be used to test how a building withstands an earthquake, how a car crumples in an accident or how a landscape will be changed by a flood.

FIGURE 2.2.1 Engineers use models and wind tunnels to test how new aircraft perform at high speeds. Problems can then be fixed before an expensive full-size aircraft is built.

Analogies

The heart is often compared with a water pump. This simple type of model is known as an 'analogy'. An analogy compares a common, everyday thing, like a pump, with a complex thing, like the heart. Analogies help us to understand how something complicated works. Likewise, a computer is sometimes used as an analogy for the brain.

Thought models

Models can also be 'thought' models. 'Thought' models help scientists imagine objects and events that are difficult to understand. This might be because the object or event is incredibly large. For example, the universe is so huge that it is difficult to imagine how it is arranged and how it began. For this reason, 'thought' models have been developed for our solar system and the Big Bang, the event which started the whole universe off around 13 billion years ago (Figure 2.2.2).

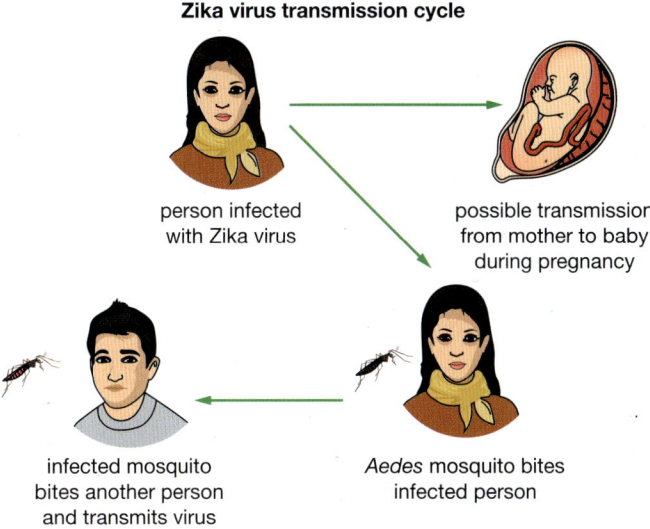

FIGURE 2.2.3 Thought model explaining spread of Zika virus

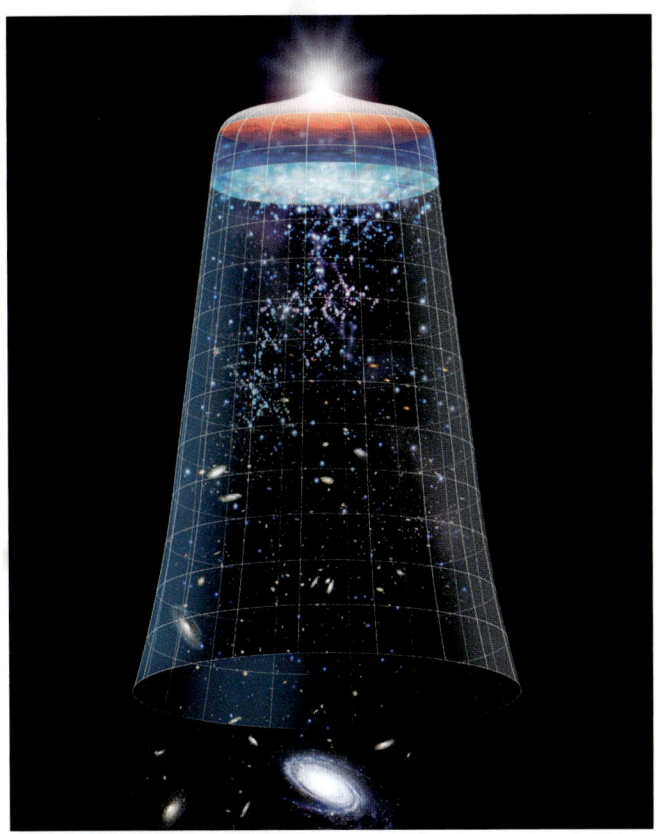

FIGURE 2.2.2 A computer artwork showing a 'thought' model that describes the development of the universe from the Big Bang to now.

Thought models are also helpful when you are trying to understand incredibly tiny things and what they do. For example, scientists and doctors use a model to explain how microscopic bacteria or viruses (germs) spread from one person to another during a disease outbreak (Figure 2.2.3).

Good scientific thought models are always supported by lots of scientific observations and evidence. Bad thought models are quickly dismissed because they don't have much real science behind them!

The particle model

The **particle model** is a 'thought' model that attempts to explain the properties of substances.

In the particle model, all substances are thought to be made of incredibly small, hard balls called particles. Each ball has energy and moves according to how much energy it has. If a particle has lots of energy, then it will move about a lot. If the particle has very little energy, then it will move about only a little bit. You add energy to a substance whenever you heat it, as heat is a type of energy. The more you heat a substance, the more energy the particles get and the faster they move. If you cool a substance, then the reverse happens: the particles move about less and move more slowly.

The particle model uses the following ideas:

- All substances are made up of tiny particles that are too small to see even with a normal microscope.
- Even if it is a very small amount, the particles always have energy and are moving.
- The particles move about more and move faster as temperature is increased.
- The closer the particles are to one another, the stronger the attraction between them.

CHAPTER 2 • PROPERTIES OF SUBSTANCES

Explaining solids

The particles in solids are closely packed in fixed positions. Forces between neighbouring particles form **bonds** that hold all the particles in the solid closely together. The particles in a solid have energy and **vibrate** (jiggle about) as shown in Figure 2.2.4. The particles don't break out of position but just vibrate on the spot. If you increase the temperature, this gives the particles more energy and so they vibrate more.

FIGURE 2.2.4 The particles in a solid are closely packed together and just vibrate on the spot.

Explaining liquids

In a liquid, the particles are still packed closely together but they are far more loosely bonded (joined) to their neighbours than the particles are in a solid. This is shown in Figure 2.2.5. The loose bonding allows the particles to move about and over each other, allowing the liquid to flow, drip and fill the bottom of whatever container it is in. As the liquid is heated, this movement gets faster.

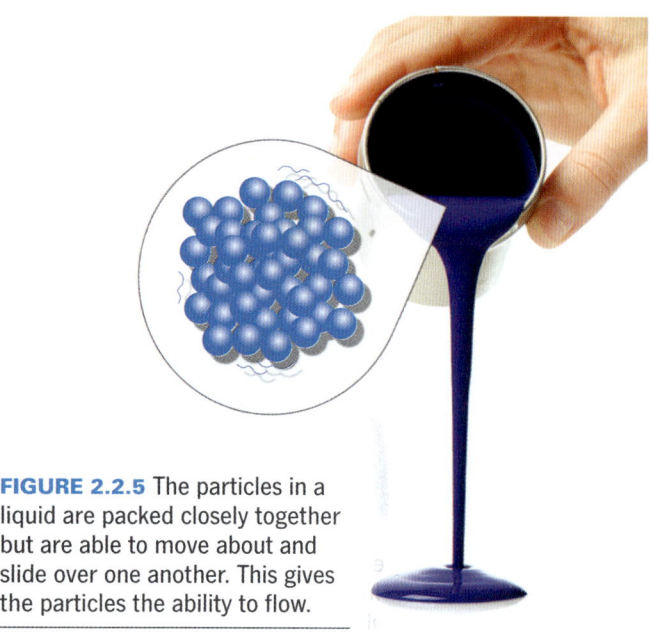

FIGURE 2.2.5 The particles in a liquid are packed closely together but are able to move about and slide over one another. This gives the particles the ability to flow.

Table 2.2.1 shows how the physical properties of solids are explained by the particle model.

TABLE 2.2.1 How the particle model explains the physical properties of solids

Property of solids	How it is explained in the particle model
fixed shape and does not flow	The particles are strongly bonded to their neighbours, fixing their positions.
incompressible	The particles cannot be pushed closer to each other because they are so closely packed that there is almost no space between them.
expand (get larger) when heated and contract (get smaller) when cooled	Heating causes the particles to vibrate faster, making them spread further apart and causing the solid to expand. Cooling slows down vibrations and the opposite happens.

Table 2.2.2 shows how the physical properties of liquids are explained by the particle model.

TABLE 2.2.2 How the particle model explains the physical properties of liquids

Prac 1 p. 59

Property of liquids	How it is explained in the particle model
flow to take the shape of the bottom of their container	Bonds are strong but loose enough to allow the particles in liquids to slip over one another.
incompressible	The particles cannot be pushed closer to each other because they are so closely packed that there is almost no space between them.
expand when heated and contract when cooled	Heating causes the particles to move over each other faster, making them spread further apart and causing the liquid to expand. Cooling slows down this movement, bringing the particles closer together and causing them to contract.

Explaining gases

The particles in a gas are spread far apart and have nothing holding them together. This lack of bond between particles allows them to move fast and in straight lines until they hit something. The particles could hit other gas particles or the walls of the container they are in. Any gas particle that hits a wall will bounce off, giving the wall a little push as it does so. The combined push of all the gas particles bouncing off the walls of their container is known as the **pressure** of the gas. The balloons in Figure 2.2.6 are kept inflated by the pressure of the gas particles trapped inside them.

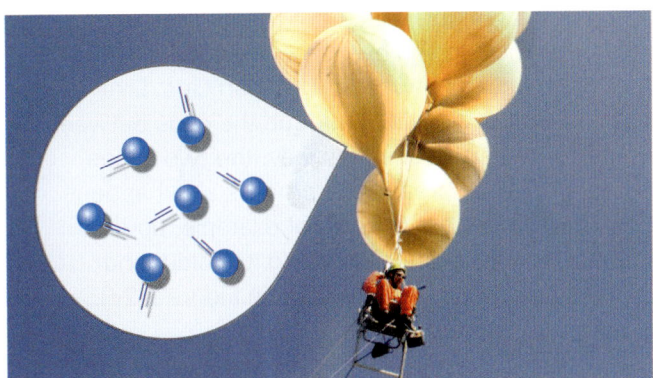

FIGURE 2.2.6 Gas particles push against the walls of the balloons. This pushing results in pressure which keeps the balloons inflated.

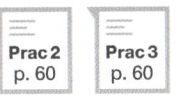

Table 2.2.3 shows how the physical properties of gases are explained by the particle model.

TABLE 2.2.3 How the particle model explains the physical properties of gases

Property of gases	How it is explained in the particle model
often invisible	The particles are spread so far apart that you cannot see the gas.
compressible	The particles are spread so far apart that there is plenty of vacant space between them. This space allows them to be pushed closer together.
spread to fill their container	There are no bonds between these particles as they are too far away from each other, and so they are able to move unrestricted by other particles. They travel until they hit the walls of their container.
expand when heated and contract when cooled	Heating causes the particles to move faster, making them spread further apart and causing the gas to expand. Cooling slows down this movement and the opposite happens.

science 4 fun

Pop the lid

Can heating a gas pop the lid off a soft-drink bottle?

Collect this ...
- hot tap water
- any size plastic soft-drink bottle with its lid
- any container a little bigger than the base of the soft-drink bottle

SAFETY Be careful handling hot water.

Do this ...
1. Remove the lid from the soft-drink bottle.
2. Run hot water from a tap into the container until it is about 5 cm deep.
3. Lightly wet the top of the lid and then place it UPSIDE DOWN on the bottle. It should stick slightly to it.
4. Carefully lower the soft-drink bottle into the container until the hot water reaches a few centimetres up the side of the bottle.

Record this ...
1. Describe what happened.
2. Explain why you think it happened.

SciFile

Colder than cold

As a substance is cooled, energy is removed from its particles, making them vibrate less and less. Eventually they have no energy at all and all vibrations stop. This happens at a temperature of absolute zero (−273°C). The particles can't move any slower and so absolute zero is the lowest temperature that is possible.

SCIENCE AS A HUMAN ENDEAVOUR
Nature and development of science

Indirect evidence and particles

Scientists have long wondered what makes up substances. The ancient Greeks thought that all substances were built up from incredibly tiny particles that they called *atomos* (meaning cannot be divided). We now call these particles *atoms*.

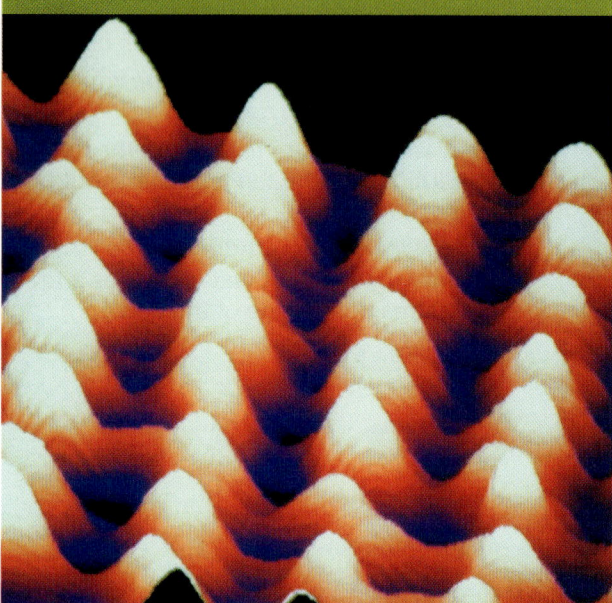

FIGURE 2.2.7 Each bump in this STM image represents an atom.

Atoms are too small to be seen with your eyes or even with a normal microscope. However an image of them can sometimes be achieved with a powerful type of microscope called a scanning tunnelling microscope (STM). You can see one of these images in Figure 2.2.7.

Even before the invention of the STM, scientists had an extremely good idea that substances were made from tiny atom-like particles.

This is because you don't always need to see something to know that it exists. Although atoms are 'invisible', observations throughout history have indicated that they existed. These types of observations are known as **indirect evidence**. You use indirect evidence every day—you know what you are having for dinner from smells coming from the kitchen, and you can often guess what's in a package by its weight and shape and the sounds it makes when shaken.

Diffusion

Perfume quickly spreads throughout the air of a room. Its smell gets weaker until eventually you can't smell it. This spreading process is called **diffusion**. In 1833, the Scottish chemist Thomas Graham (1805–1869) used the idea of particles to explain how diffusion might work. Perfume particles are constantly moving and over time they will move through the gaps between the air particles. Likewise, the air particles will move through the gaps between the perfume particles. In this way, the two gases diffuse (mix and spread). The process also happens when two liquids are mixed. For example, cordial diffuses through water, spreading its colour and flavour throughout. This is shown in Figure 2.2.8.

FIGURE 2.2.8 The twisted ribbon of orange liquid quickly diffuses through the water of the test-tube.

SCIENCE AS A HUMAN ENDEAVOUR

Brownian motion

Some of the most convincing indirect evidence for particles came from the work of the Scottish botanist Robert Brown (1773–1858). In 1827, Brown was using his microscope to study tiny pollen grains that were floating on some water. He expected the pollen grains to be still but they were moving about, as if pushed from all directions about by something in the water. His sketches of their motion are shown in Figure 2.2.9. Brown could not explain what was happening and it was 1905 before Albert Einstein (1879–1955) explained it—'invisible' particles in the water were constantly moving about, colliding with the pollen grains and pushing them around as they did so.

Brown was not the first to notice this type of motion. In 1785, Jan Ingenhousz (1730–1799) had observed similar movement in coal dust suspended in alcohol, and the ancient Roman Lucretius (99–55 BCE) wrote in around 60 BCE of dust particles jiggling about in a beam of sunlight (Figure 2.2.10). You may have already noticed something similar. This jiggling eventually became known as **Brownian motion**.

FIGURE 2.2.10 Lit by beams of sunlight, these dust particles seem to bounce about randomly—they are being pushed from all directions by tiny, invisible air particles colliding with them.

Review

1. Outline two pieces of indirect evidence that advanced our understanding of the particle model.
2. When cordial is added to water, the flavouring and sweetness spreads throughout the drink.
    a. What is the name for this process?
    b. Explain how this happens.
3. A drop of dye added to a swimming pool spreads and diffuses until eventually you can't see any of its colour. Use the particle model to propose a way this might happen.
4. a. Outline what Brownian motion is.
   b. Use the particle model to explain Brownian motion.
5. Dust particles in a beam of sunlight appear to jiggle about.
    a. Is this an example of diffusion or Brownian motion?
    b. Explain why the dust particles jiggle.

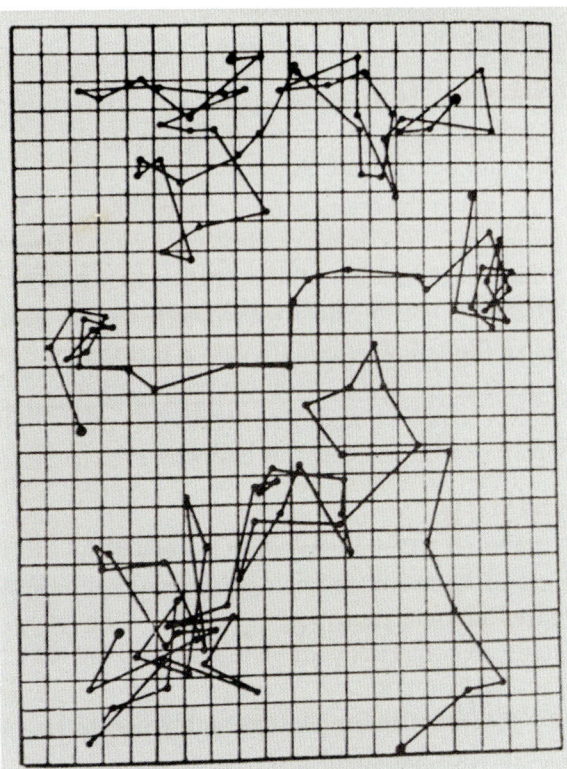

FIGURE 2.2.9 Robert Brown's original notes marking the positions of pollen grains every 30 seconds

CHAPTER 2 • PROPERTIES OF SUBSTANCES 57

MODULE 2.2 Review questions

Remembering

1. Define the terms:
   a. contract
   b. vibrate
   c. bonds.

2. What term best describes each of the following?
   a. get larger
   b. combined push of gas particles.

3. What is a commonly used analogy for:
   a. the heart?
   b. the brain?

4. Match the state of matter with the movement of its particles that describes it best.

solid	Particles move very quickly in straight lines.
liquid	Particles vibrate on the spot.
gas	Particles vibrate but can also move over one another.

5. Which state (solid, liquid or gas) has its particles:
   a. held together with the strongest bonds?
   b. a very long way apart?
   c. moving the fastest?
   d. moving the slowest?

Understanding

6. Why do manufacturers build scale models of cars before they start building the real thing?

7. Explain what happens to the particles in a substance when it is:
   a. heated
   b. cooled.

8. Explain why:
   a. solids have a fixed shape
   b. solids expand when heated
   c. liquids have the ability to flow
   d. liquids are incompressible
   e. gases are compressible
   f. gases expand to fill the space they are in.

9. You can usually smell fly spray and air fresheners when they are first sprayed into a room. After a while, you can't smell them. Explain why.

10. Predict what would happen in the science4fun activity on page 55 when the bottom of the soft-drink bottle is placed in:
    a. hot water
    b. ice water.

Applying

11. Absolute zero (−273°C) is the coldest temperature. Nothing can be colder. Use the particle model to:
    a. i. explain what happens to the motion of particles as they are cooled
       ii. predict what happens to the particles at −273°C.
    b. Use your answer to part a ii to suggest why nothing can be colder than absolute zero.

12. Use the idea of gas pressure to explain why:
    a. BBQ gas bottles need to have strong walls
    b. a balloon expands with every breath you blow into it
    c. a balloon goes flat if enough gas leaks out of it.

Analysing

13. Foam rubber has thousands of tiny air-filled holes in it. It is commonly used to make cushions in chairs and couches. Solid rubber has no holes in it. It is commonly used to make erasers.
    a. Compare the physical properties of foam rubber with solid rubber.
    b. Explain why foam rubber is ideal for furniture cushions.

Evaluating

14. Barbecue gas cylinders are usually weighed as they are being filled. Suggest a reason why.

15. The ball in the science4fun activity on page 52 rises when the container of rice is shaken. Use your understanding of how particles are packed to propose a reason why the ball rises.

16. LPG (liquefied petroleum gas) is formed by squeezing so much gas into a bottle that it converts into a liquid. Use the particle model to propose a reason why this happens.

Creating

17. Construct a Venn diagram showing which properties are shared between solids, liquids and gases and which properties belong to only one state. To construct your Venn diagram, follow these instructions.
    a. Draw a diagram like that in Figure 2.2.11 in your workbook.

MODULE 2.2 Review questions

b Identify which of the following properties is shared by all three states and write it in the overlap of all three circles.

has energy
changing shape
changing volume
incompressible
loosely packed
fixed shape
fixed volume
can be compressed
closely packed

c Identify the properties shared by solid and gas and list them in the overlap between them. Do the same for liquid and gas, and solid and liquid.

d Identify the properties displayed by only one state and list these in the appropriate spaces.

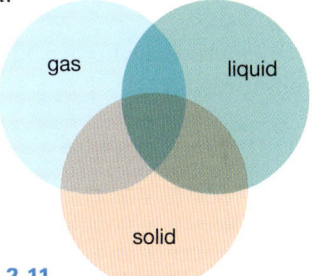

FIGURE 2.2.11

MODULE 2.2 Practical investigations

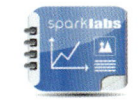

SPARKlab alternative available for this activity. Manual data entry option.

1 • Liquid thermometer

Purpose
To build a model thermometer.

Timing 45 minutes

Materials
- water
- 2 drops of food dye
- plasticine

- 250 mL conical flask
- clear drinking straw
- permanent marker pen

Procedure
1. Set up the apparatus as shown in Figure 2.2.12.
2. Carefully blow down the drinking straw. Water should rise up it. Stop blowing when the water rises about 1 cm above the plasticine plug.
3. Use the permanent marker to mark this water level as shown in Figure 2.2.13. This level represents the 'temperature' of the room today.

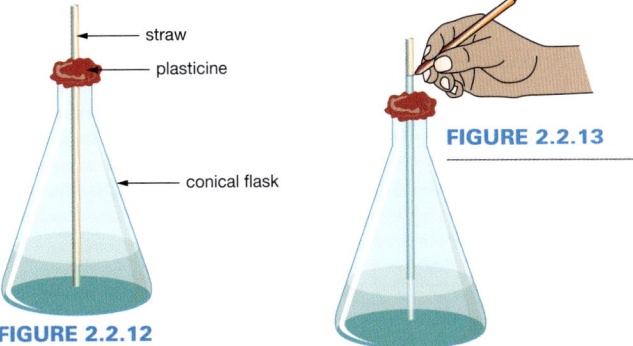

FIGURE 2.2.12

FIGURE 2.2.13

Results
Record what happens to the water level when you:

- hold the conical flask in your hands; don't squeeze but just let your hands warm it up (Figure 2.2.14)
- release your hold on the flask

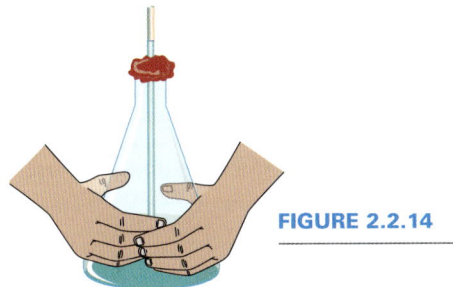

FIGURE 2.2.14

- watch the water reach the line again and then put the flask into a sink of cold water.

Review
1. Explain what happened in this experiment by copying the following sentences and choosing the correct term.
   a. Adding heat causes liquids to *expand/contract*. This caused the liquid to *rise/drop* in the drinking straw.
   b. Removing heat causes liquids to *expand/contract*. This caused the liquid to *rise/drop* in the drinking straw.
2. Thermometers usually do not use water but instead use alcohol (coloured red) or mercury. Propose a reason why.

CHAPTER 2 • PROPERTIES OF SUBSTANCES

MODULE 2.2 Practical investigations

2 • Compressing liquids and gases

 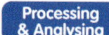

Purpose
To determine whether liquids and gases can be compressed.

Timing 45 minutes

Materials
- water
- plastic syringe (without needle)
- 250 mL beaker

SAFETY Do not use the syringe to squirt water at other people.

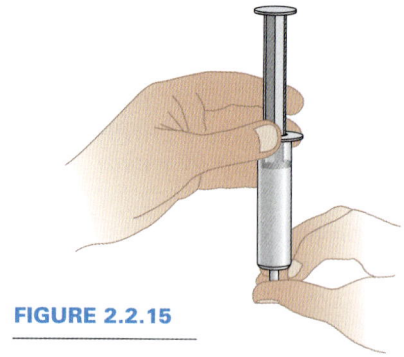

FIGURE 2.2.15

Procedure
1. Fill the beaker with water and use the syringe to suck up water until it is full.
2. Push the nozzle of the syringe against your finger as shown in Figure 2.2.15.
3. Push the plunger down and observe what happens. See if you can you compress the water.
4. Take the syringe apart, empty its water and re-assemble it.
5. The syringe is now full of air (with a little water that will help seal it). Once again, push the nozzle against your finger and attempt to push the plunger down. Observe what happens. See if you can you compress the air.

Review
1. Explain your observations in terms of the spacing of particles in liquids and gases.
2. Construct a conclusion for your investigation.

• STUDENT DESIGN •

3 • Pressure can protect

Purpose
To design and test a container that uses the pressure of a gas to protect an egg.

Timing 45 minutes

Materials
- 1 fresh egg (uncooked)
- 2 zip-lock bags
- 1 drinking straw
- sticky-tape

SAFETY A Risk Assessment is required for this investigation.

Procedure
1. Design:
   a. a container that uses air pressure and the materials listed above to protect a fresh egg when it is dropped onto a hard surface.
   b. an experiment that will test how far your container needs to drop for the egg to break.
2. Before you start constructing your container or start testing, assess your procedure. List any risks that your procedure might involve and what you might do to minimise those risks.

Show your teacher your procedure and your assessment of its risks. If they approve, then collect all the required materials and start work.

Hints
- Use the straw to inflate the bag.
- Sticky-tape can partly divide the bag to form cushions.
- Use the STEM and SDI template in your eBook to help you plan and carry out your investigation.

Results
Construct a table to show the results of your egg drops and the heights they were dropped from.

Review
1. What height was the egg dropped from when it eventually broke?
2. Explain how you used air pressure to protect your egg.

MODULE 2.3 Changing state

Liquid water freezes to form ice and frost on really cold mornings. As the day warms, ice and frost melt to form pools of liquid water. Ice-creams melt too, dripping down your arm if you're unlucky. Substances like water and ice-cream can be changed from one state into another by adding energy to them or by removing energy from them. This is done by heating them up or cooling them down.

Adding heat

Heating a solid, liquid or gas will usually just cause its temperature to increase. However, if you add enough heat, then the substance will change **state**. Given enough heat, solids will change into liquids and liquids will change into gases. You can see this in Figure 2.3.1.

science 4 fun

Freezing water

What does water do when it freezes?

Collect this …
- small plastic bottle (no cap needed)

Do this …
1. Fill a plastic bottle with water to the very top. Do NOT put the cap on.
2. Carefully stand it in a freezer and leave overnight.

Record this …
1. Describe what happened
2. Explain why you think this happened.

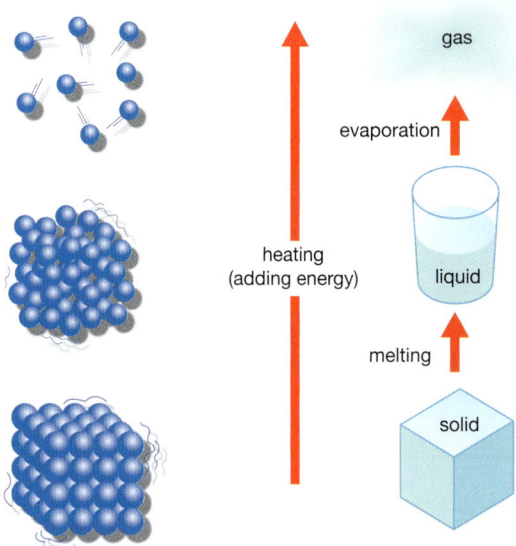

FIGURE 2.3.1 Heat makes particles move. If enough heat is added, then a solid will melt and a liquid will evaporate.

Melting

Melting is the process in which heat causes a solid to change into a liquid. Although the physical properties of the substance change, the substance itself is exactly the same as it was before. Ice (solid water) is exactly the same substance as the liquid water it melts into when heated.

CHAPTER 2 • PROPERTIES OF SUBSTANCES **61**

The solid wax that makes up a candle is exactly the same substance as the clear drips of wax that slide down its side.

Heat adds energy to the particles in a solid, making them vibrate faster. If you add enough heat, then the particles at the edges of the solid will be vibrating so violently that they will break free, allowing them to melt away from the others in the solid. You can see this happening at the edges of the melting butter in Figure 2.3.2.

FIGURE 2.3.2 Melting starts at the edges of the solid because these particles are the first to receive heat from outside.

Melting point

The temperature at which a solid melts is known as its **melting point**. A substance is solid below its melting point and is molten (a melted liquid) above it. For example, water, has a melting point of 0°C.

Different substances have different melting points, as Table 2.3.1 shows.

TABLE 2.3.1 The boiling, melting and freezing points of various substances

Substance	Boiling point (°C)	Melting point (°C)	Freezing point (°C)
ethanol (alcohol)	78	−114	−114
water	100	0	0
mercury	357	−39	−39
silver	2193	961	961

Evaporation

Evaporation is the process in which heat causes a liquid to change into a gas. Evaporation is sometimes also known as vaporisation. For example, heat causes liquid water to evaporate (or vaporise), turning it into the gas known as water vapour. Water evaporates at all temperatures because there is always some heat to make some particles move fast enough to break free from its liquid form. That's why clothes on the line eventually dry, even on cold days. On hot days, clothes dry faster because more water particles have enough energy to break free (Figure 2.3.3).

FIGURE 2.3.3 Evaporation happens at all temperatures but the rate of evaporation increases as temperature increases. This is why clothes dry faster on hot days than on cold days.

The bonds between the particles in a liquid are just strong enough to hold them all together to form a fixed volume of liquid. These bonds are too weak to stop the particles from moving about within the liquid, slipping and sliding over one another. Adding energy to a liquid causes its particles to move faster and loosens their bonds even more. If enough energy is added, then the particles at the liquid surface move so fast that they can break away completely from the rest of the particles in the liquid. They are now particles of gas, and escape into the atmosphere.

Prac 1 p. 66

SciFile

Sublimation

Most substances change from solid to gas in two stages: first they melt, and then they evaporate. A few substances change from solid into a gas directly, without going through a liquid stage. This process is called sublimation.

Two substances that sublime are dry ice (solid carbon dioxide) and iodine (Figure 2.3.4).

FIGURE 2.3.4 Iodine doesn't melt. Instead, the dark purple crystals sublime to produce a purple vapour (gas).

Boiling

Boiling is a special case of evaporation. Evaporation occurs at any temperature, but boiling only happens at a temperature known as the **boiling point**. Boiling is obvious because bubbles appear and break the surface of the liquid. These bubbles are formed by the evaporation of pockets of liquid deep inside the liquid. These pockets change into gas, which expands to form a bubble. The bubble then rises and escapes into the atmosphere when it reaches the surface of the liquid and breaks (pops).

Boiling point

The boiling point of a substance is the temperature at which it changes from a liquid into a gas. Water has a boiling point of 100°C. This represents the highest temperature that liquid water can reach. It is also the lowest temperature at which water vapour can exist.

Different substances have different boiling points, as Table 2.3.1 on page 62 shows.

Prac 2 p. 67

SkillBuilder

Identifying boiling

Boiling happens at a liquid's boiling point and is accompanied by the release of large bubbles from deep within the liquid. However, smaller bubbles appear well before boiling actually starts. These smaller bubbles appear because water contains dissolved gases—like the oxygen that fish use to breathe. These gases form bubbles soon after heating starts and can trick you into thinking that your liquid is boiling. The production of these small bubbles soon stops and it then takes some time for the big bubbles, which indicate that your liquid is boiling, to appear (Figure 2.3.5).

FIGURE 2.3.5 Continuous bubbling is a sign of boiling.

Removing heat

The temperature of a substance drops when heat is removed from it. A substance might change state if sufficient heat is removed from it, as seen in Figure 2.3.6.

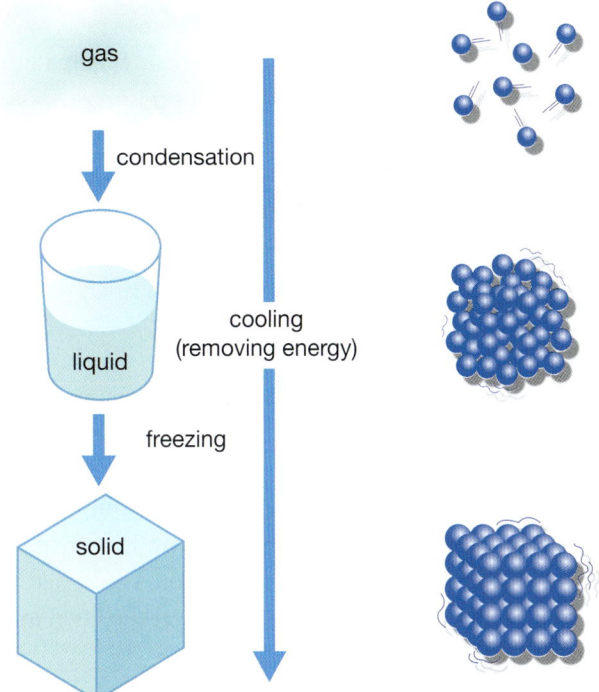

FIGURE 2.3.6 Cooling makes particles slow down. Substances will condense or freeze if enough heat is removed from them.

Freezing

Freezing occurs when heat is lost and a liquid changes into a solid. The process is sometimes known as solidification. Frost is dew (liquid water) that has frozen overnight. Snow is another form of ice. It is caused by water freezing or solidifying around specks of dust high in the atmosphere to form snowflakes. You can see two examples of snowflakes in Figure 2.3.7.

FIGURE 2.3.7 These snowflakes show some of the amazing shapes that can form.

CHAPTER 2 • PROPERTIES OF SUBSTANCES

As a liquid cools, energy is lost from its particles and the particles move more slowly than before. If you remove enough energy, then the particles will end up just vibrating on the spot. Bonds form between the particle, locking them into their position to form a solid of definite shape and size.

Freezing point

The **freezing point** is the temperature at which a liquid changes into a solid. Freezing is the opposite process to melting, and so freezing and melting occur at exactly the same temperature. For water, the freezing point is 0°C, the same as the melting point of ice.

Different substances have different freezing points, as Table 2.3.1 on page 62 shows.

Condensation

Condensation occurs when a gas loses heat and changes into a liquid. Your lungs are full of water vapour (gaseous water) that will condense into tiny droplets of liquid water when you breathe out onto something cold, like a window or mirror. Likewise, water vapour in the air will condense on a cold night to form droplets of liquid dew that will wet the lawn and spider webs, like the one in Figure 2.3.8.

FIGURE 2.3.8 The dew on this spider web is caused by water vapour condensing overnight.

As a gas is cooled, its particles slow down. When they have slowed enough, the individual particles begin to attract each other and form bonds that will tie their movement to the other particles in the substance. They now act as a group, forming droplets of liquid.

Steam is water vapour that has condensed to form a cloud of tiny but visible liquid water droplets in the air.

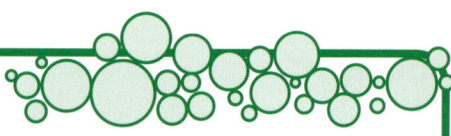

SciFile

Water breaks the rules

Whereas most substances contract when they freeze, water expands when it freezes to form ice. This is why containers of water and soft drink will often pop their top or split their sides if placed in the freezer.

Water vapour emerges as a gas from a kettle or from a hot iron (Figure 2.3.9) but quickly cools in the air to form a visible fog of tiny liquid water droplets.

FIGURE 2.3.9 Steam is created from the water used in the iron. The steam helps remove creases from clothes and linen.

SkillBuilder

Graphing changes of state

A substance changes state because heat causes bonds between its particles to break. The temperature will not change while this is happening, as the energy that was causing the particles to move is now being used to break the bonds between particles instead. This is shown by the flat sections on the graph of temperature versus time in Figure 2.3.10.

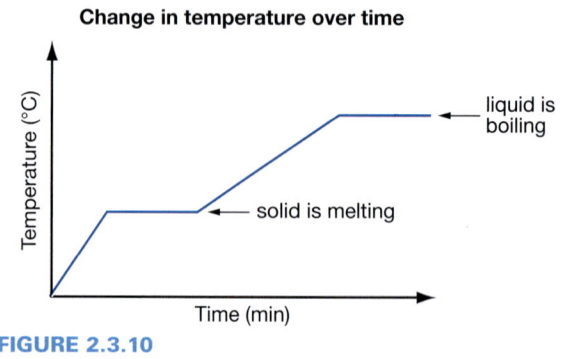

FIGURE 2.3.10

64 PEARSON SCIENCE 7 2ND EDITION

MODULE 2.3 Review questions

Remembering

1. Define the terms:
   a. melting
   b. condensation.
2. What term best describes each of the following?
   a. when something changes from a liquid into a gas
   b. when something changes from a liquid into a solid.
3. State the temperature at which liquid water:
   a. boils
   b. freezes.
4. State alternative words for the following terms.
   a. evaporation
   b. vapourise
   c. freezing
   d. solidify.
5. The melting point of candle wax is 46°C. What is its freezing point?
6. Recall the various changes of state by copying and completing Figure 2.3.11.

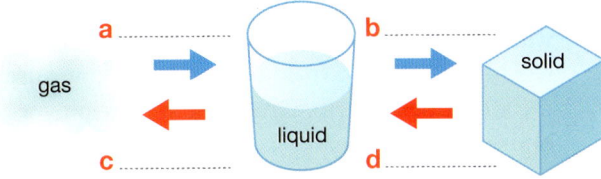

FIGURE 2.3.11

Understanding

7. Why are the melting point and freezing point of a substance at exactly the same temperature?
8. Describe the signs that show that water is boiling.
9. Why do solids melt at their edges first?
10. You hang out wet clothes on a clothes line. Explain why the water in the clothes evaporates despite the temperature never getting near the boiling point of water.
11. Explain how:
    a. snow forms
    b. dew forms
    c. frost forms.

Applying

12. Identify two substances that:
    a. melt at relatively low temperatures
    b. evaporate at relatively low temperatures.
13. Identify the change of state that happens when:
    a. ice-cream starts to drip
    b. jelly sets
    c. the bathroom mirror gets foggy.
14. Use the information from Table 2.3.1 on page 62 to predict what state ethanol, water, mercury and silver would be in at the following temperatures.
    a. −20°C
    b. 50°C
    c. 200°C
    d. 500°C
15. Sunglasses often fog up when you walk outside from an air conditioned building on a humid summer day. Use the idea of condensation to explain why.

Analysing

16. Contrast:
    a. steam and water vapour
    b. evaporating and boiling.

Evaluating

17. The addition of impurities such as salt to water lowers its freezing point and increases its boiling point. Use this information to propose reasons why:
    a. salt is spread on the roads in northern United States and Canada to help keep the roads clear of ice
    b. additives can stop a car radiator from boiling over
    c. ice-cream makers are cooled with a mixture of salt and ice.
18. A glass bottle full of water can shatter if left overnight with its cap on in the freezer. Propose a reason why.

MODULE 2.3 Practical investigations

1 • Rates of evaporation *Questioning & Predicting* *Evaluating*

Purpose
To determine whether water or alcohol evaporates faster.

Hypothesis
Which do you think will evaporate faster—water or the alcohol (that you find in substances like Deep Heat or Dencorub)? Before you go any further with this investigation, write a hypothesis in your workbook.

Timing 45 minutes

Materials
- 10 mL water (about $\frac{1}{2}$ tablespoon)
- 10 mL alcohol (about $\frac{1}{2}$ tablespoon)
- 1 cotton bud
- 2 × 250 mL beakers or similar to act as supports
- 2 × 100 mL beakers
- 1 sheet thick paper towel
- pencil
- sticky-tape
- plastic ruler
- plastic tweezers
- rubber gloves

SAFETY
A Risk Assessment is required for this investigation.

This kind of alcohol is extremely poisonous so do not sniff or taste it. It irritates eyes and open cuts so wear rubber gloves and safety glasses at all times. Alcohol is flammable so keep it away from all open flames.

Procedure

PART A

1. Use the cotton bud to paint a streak of water on a sheet of paper towel. Use the other end of the cotton bud to paint an identical streak of alcohol on the same sheet (Figure 2.3.12).
2. Lay the sheet of paper towel on your workbench. Note which streak disappears first.

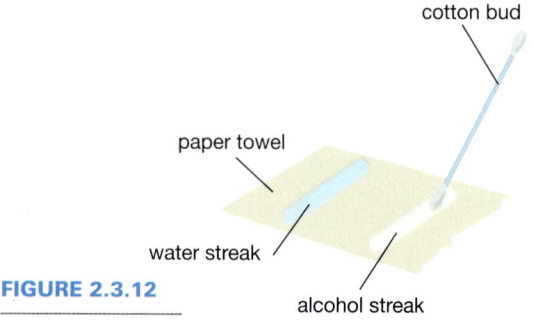

FIGURE 2.3.12

PART B

3. Set up the apparatus as shown in Figure 2.3.13, taping the pencil so that it cannot move.

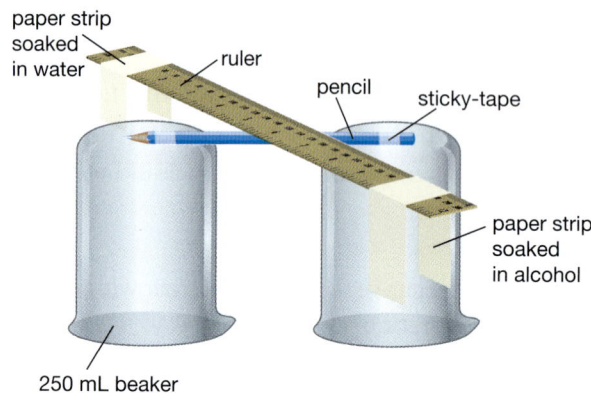

FIGURE 2.3.13

4. Cut two identical strips from a sheet of paper towel. Each strip needs to be about 3 cm wide and as long as the width of the sheet of paper towel. Label one strip 'Water' using a pencil.
5. Pour 10 mL of water into one of the 100 mL beakers and 10 mL of alcohol into the other.
6. Dip one strip marked 'Water' into the beaker of water so that it soaks it up. Use plastic tweezers to remove the strip from the water, making sure the strip does not rip. Drape the wet strip over one end of the ruler.
7. Roll the other strip of paper into a coil and place it in the beaker of alcohol. Once it has soaked up most of the alcohol, use the tweezers to quickly remove it and drape it over the other end of the ruler.
8. Quickly balance the ruler and its strips on the pencil, noting which is the water end and which is the alcohol end.
9. Watch what happens to the ruler as the substances start to evaporate.

Results
Part A: Record which streak 'disappeared' first.

Part B: Record which end of the ruler drops.

Review
1. Compare your results from Parts A and B.
2. The water and alcohol don't really 'disappear' in Part A. Describe what really happens to them.

66 PEARSON SCIENCE 7 2ND EDITION

MODULE 2.3 Practical investigations

3 The soaked paper strips in Part B become lighter as the experiment proceeds. Explain why.

4 The ruler becomes unbalanced if one of the substances evaporates faster than the other. Which end would drop if:
   a water evaporated faster than alcohol
   b alcohol evaporated faster than water.

5 a Use your answers to questions 1–4 to construct a conclusion for your investigation.
   b Assess whether your hypothesis was supported or not.

6 You used two different methods here to test the same thing.
   a Assess why this is considered good science.
   b Which do you consider was the best method (Part A or Part B) to determine answer the question 'Which evaporates faster?'
   c Justify your choice.

2 • Temperature graphs

Purpose
To determine what effect salt has on the melting and boiling points of water.

Hypothesis
What do you think will happen when salt is added to water–will it increase or decrease its melting and boiling points? Before you go any further with this investigation, write a hypothesis in your workbook.

Timing 45 minutes

Materials
- handful of crushed ice or ice cubes
- water
- about two large spatulas full of salt
- 250 mL beaker
- thermometer or temperature probe connected to datalogger
- stirring rod
- spatula
- stopwatch, watch or clock
- Bunsen burner, bench mat, tripod and gauze mat
- retort stand and clamp
- graph paper, ruler and grey lead pencil OR access to computer/tablet

A Risk Assessment is required for this investigation.

Tie long hair back so it won't get in the flame.

Whenever you are not using the Bunsen burner, sets its flame to yellow so that you can see it.

Water can spit when heated so wear safety glasses at all times.

Do not use the thermometer as a stirring rod.

Equipment will be hot so let it cool before packing it away.

Procedure

1 Copy the table from the Results section into your workbook. Alternatively, construct a spreadsheet with the same features or set the datalogger up to automatically record temperatures for you.

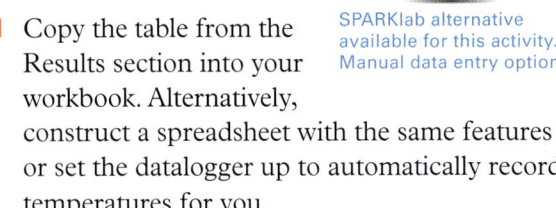

SPARKlab alternative available for this activity. Manual data entry option.

2 Your teacher will tell you which of the following two groups you and your lab partners will be part of:
   - the control group: this group will heat a mixture of tap water and ice
   - the salt group: this group will heat a mixture of salt, pure water and ice.

3 Both groups need to add crushed ice or ice cubes to their beaker so that the ice comes up to about the 100 mL mark.

4 Add water to the ice cubes so that it surrounds the ice and also comes up to about the 100 mL mark.

5 The salt group also needs to add salt (a couple of large spatula loads) to their ice–water mixture.

CHAPTER 2 • PROPERTIES OF SUBSTANCES   67

MODULE 2.3 Practical investigations

6 Set up the apparatus as shown in Figure 2.3.14.

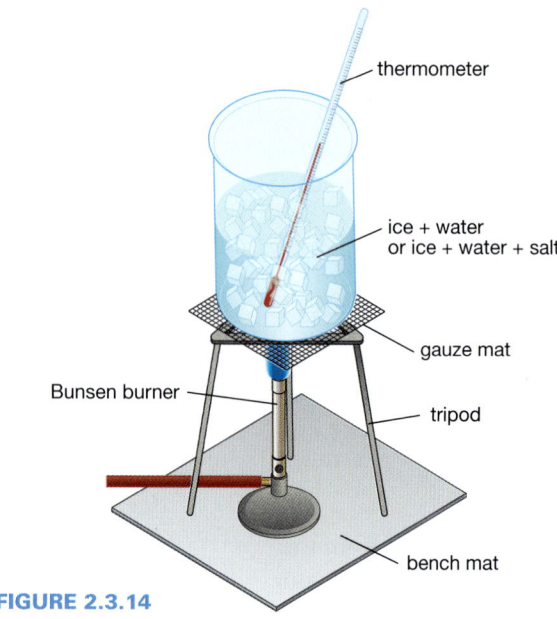

FIGURE 2.3.14

7 Measure and record the starting temperature of the ice–water or ice–water–salt mixture.

8 Light the Bunsen burner and turn the collar so that the airhole is open and the flame is blue. Start timing immediately.

9 Measure and record the temperature of the ice–water or ice–water–salt mixture every minute. Use the stirring rod to stir the mixture gently before measuring the temperature. Do NOT use the thermometer as a stirring rod.

10 Continue measuring and recording the temperature until the water has been boiling for 2 or 3 minutes. Once it is boiling, you may need to turn the collar on the Bunsen burner to partly close the airhole.

Results

1 Record all your measurements in a table or spreadsheet like the one below. If you are using a datalogger, then it will generate a table of results for you.

My group was the tap water group/salty group	
Time (min)	Temperature (°C)
0 (before heating starts)	
1	
2	
3	

2 Copy the graph template shown in Figure 2.3.15 onto graph paper. Ensure that the scale for your graph uses equal intervals. Plot your data on the graph and join the points with straight lines.

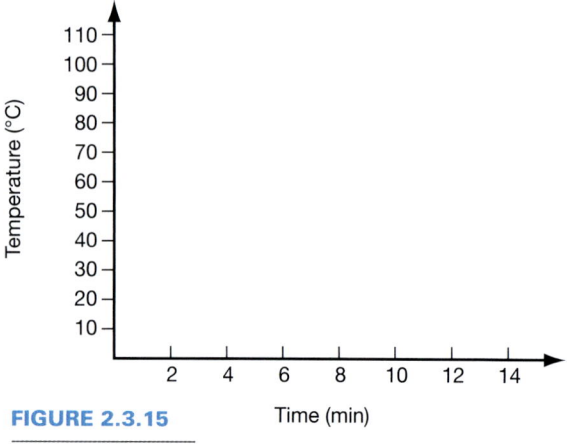

FIGURE 2.3.15

If you used a spreadsheet, use it to generate a scatter graph with a line. If you used a datalogger then print out the table of measurements and graph generated by it.

3 Your graph probably has two parts that are reasonably flat with little or no increase in temperature. Highlight those sections of your graph.

Review

1 Use your graph to find:
   a the melting point and boiling point
   b the water temperature 5 minutes after you started heating
   c the time it took your sample to reach 80°C
   d the likely temperature of your sample 10 minutes after it started to boil.

2 a Compare your graph with those of other groups.
   b Use the graphs to compare the melting and boiling points of salt water with those of tap water.

3 Figure 2.3.14 showed the equipment used in this prac in three dimensions (3D). Construct a scientific diagram that shows it in two dimensions (2D).

4 a Construct a conclusion for your investigation.
   b Assess whether your hypothesis was supported or not.

MODULE 2.3 Practical investigations

• STUDENT DESIGN •

3 • Role play *Planning & Conducting* *Evaluating*

This investigation is best performed in groups larger than 6 people.

Purpose
To model a solid, liquid and gas and their changes of state.

Timing 30 minutes

Materials
- masking tape
- a clear space of floor (a carpeted area is ideal)

SAFETY A Risk Assessment is required for this investigation.

Procedure
1. In your group, brainstorm ways of modelling with your bodies:
   - the bonds that hold particles together
   - the movement of particles in a solid, liquid and gas
   - what happens to these movements when the particles are heated.
2. Before you start anything else, assess your model and complete a risk assessment. Show your teacher for approval.
3. Use the masking tape to mark out a closed rectangle on the floor or on a grassed area.
4. Stand within the marked-out area with all the other students in the class.
5. Imagine you are all particles within a solid and that the masking tape represents solid walls. Move about to model what the particles would be doing when:
   - very cold
   - the solid is being heated
   - the solid is starting to melt
   - the liquid formed is being heated
   - the liquid is starting to evaporate
   - the gas formed is being heated.

Use the STEM and SDI template in your eBook to help you plan and carry out your investigation.

Review
1. Describe what happened when a particle broke its bonds with its neighbours.
2. Describe how the model showed:
   a. melting   b. evaporation.

• STUDENT DESIGN •

4 • Condensation *Questioning & Predicting* *Planning & Conducting*

Purpose
To observe condensation.

Hypothesis
Drops of liquid water (condensation) quickly appear on the outside of a glass beaker that contains ice and water. Where do these drops come from—from the beaker and its contents or from the air? Before you go any further with this investigation, write a hypothesis in your workbook.

Timing 45 minutes

Materials
- ice cubes
- water
- 2 zip-lock plastic bags (each large enough to hold a 250 mL beaker)
- 250 mL beakers
- drinking straw(s)

SAFETY A Risk Assessment is required for this investigation.

Procedure
1. Design an experiment that uses the above materials and which tests where the droplets of liquid water on the outside of a beaker come from.
2. Write your procedure in your workbook.
3. Before you start any practical work, assess your procedure and complete a risk assessment. Show your teacher for approval.

Hints
- Air has gaseous water vapour (humidity) in it. Suck the air out of a zip-lock bag and you will suck out the water vapour too.
- Use the STEM and SDI template in your eBook to help you plan and carry out your investigation.

Results
Construct labelled diagrams to show what happened.

Review
1. Compare the beakers that you tested.
2. Explain any differences you saw.
3. a. Construct a conclusion for your investigation.
   b. Assess whether your hypothesis was supported or not.

CHAPTER 2 • PROPERTIES OF SUBSTANCES   **69**

MODULE 2.4 Density

Some materials like lead, gold, granite and steel are very heavy for their size. Other materials like foam rubber, cork, balsa wood and feathers are so light that huge piles do not weigh much at all. Density determines how heavy a substance is and whether it floats or sinks in water.

science 4 fun

Salty lava lamp
Can you make your own lava lamp?

Collect this…
- cooking oil
- salt shaker
- food dye
- water
- tall glass

Do this…
1. Pour water into the glass until it is one-third full.
2. Add a few drops of food dye.
3. Pour in an equal quantity of cooking oil and observe which layer is on top.
4. Sprinkle salt into the glass and carefully observe what happens to the grains of salt.

Record this…
1. Describe what happened.
2. Explain why you think this happened.

Density: a physical property

Density is the physical property that determines whether a substance floats, sinks or bubbles up through water and other liquids.

Density also measures how much matter is packed into a space. It depends on how heavy a substance is, but is not the same as its weight or mass. For example, 1 kilogram of stones weighs exactly the same as 1 kilogram of polystyrene, which weighs as much as 1 kilogram of feathers. Density instead measures how much matter is packed into a specific space (Figure 2.4.1).

FIGURE 2.4.1 Stones are much more dense than feathers. This makes a small pile of stones weigh a lot more than a big pile of feathers.

Density and packing

The particles in a solid are usually packed more closely than they are in a liquid, making most solids a little denser than liquids of the same material—most solids sink when dropped into liquid made of the same substance.

When heated, the particles in solids and liquids move a little further apart, causing the substance to expand slightly. The substance takes up more space and so its density decreases. You can see this in Figure 2.4.2.

FIGURE 2.4.2 Density depends on the packing of the particles making up a substance. The more closely packed, the denser the substance will be.

When a gas is heated, its particles spread out even further, lowering its density even more. For this reason, hot air is less dense than cold air and will rise above it (Figure 2.4.3). This is why smoke rises—the air is hot and it carries soot and burnt material up with it. Likewise, bubbles of gas rise through the liquid, as seen in Figure 2.4.4.

FIGURE 2.4.3 The overall density of a hot-air balloon is less than the density of the air around it, allowing it to rise into the sky.

FIGURE 2.4.4 Gases are much less dense than liquids and will bubble upwards through liquid.

Mass, volume and density

Density depends on the amount of substance (its mass) and the space it takes up (its volume) and so its unit includes the units for mass and volume.

Density is normally measured in gram per centimetre cubed (g/cm^3). The densities of different gases, liquids and solids can be seen in Tables 2.4.1, 2.4.2 and 2.4.3.

TABLE 2.4.1 Densities of gases

Gas	Density (g/cm^3)
hydrogen (at 0°C)	0.00009
helium (at 0°C)	0.00018
air (at 40°C)	0.0011
air (at 0°C)	0.0013
oxygen (at 0°C)	0.0014

TABLE 2.4.2 Densities of liquids at 25°C

Liquid	Density (g/cm^3)
petrol	0.80
vegetable oil	0.91
water	1.00
honey	1.36
mercury	13.6

TABLE 2.4.3 Densities of solids

Solid	Density (g/cm^3)
polystyrene foam	0.03
wood (oak)	0.65
concrete	2.40
copper	8.90
gold	18.9

Density depends on mass

Mass measures how much matter is in a substance and is sometimes incorrectly referred to as weight. Scientists use grams (g) to measure small masses such as a twig, a mouse or a spatula load of chemicals, kilograms (kg) for heavier masses such as a dog or a human, and tonnes (t) for even bigger masses such as a car or an aircraft. Mass is measured using a beam balance, electronic balance or scales.

A substance will be denser if more mass is packed into the same volume. The four cubes shown in Figure 2.4.5 are all exactly the same volume but their masses are all different. This means that their densities are different too.

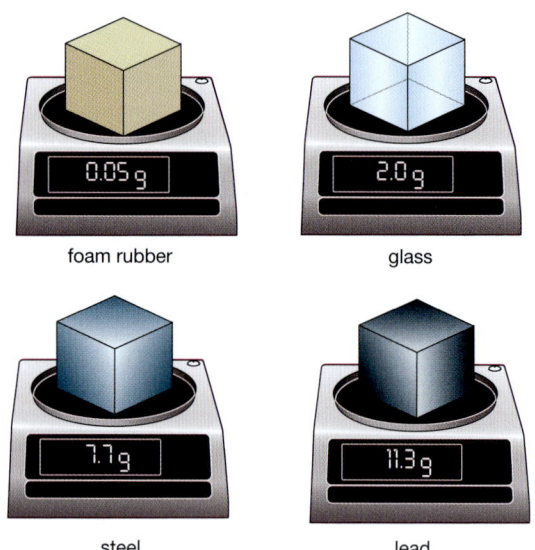

FIGURE 2.4.5 All of the cubes have exactly a volume of 1 cm^3. This makes the heaviest cube (lead) the densest and the lightest cube (foam rubber) the least dense.

SciFile

Danny Deckchair
Helium is a gas that is less dense than air. In 1982, US man Larry Walters tied 45 large helium-filled balloons to his aluminium garden chair and floated to a height of 4900 metres. After 45 minutes he punctured some of his balloons and crashed down among power lines. A similar flight was used in the plot of the 2003 Australian film *Danny Deckchair*.

Density depends on volume

Volume is the amount of space a substance takes up. Denser substances require less volume to pack in the same mass. Figure 2.4.6 shows that 10 g of brass has the smallest volume. This makes it denser than water and balsa wood.

FIGURE 2.4.6 These substances all have the same mass of 10 grams.

SkillBuilder
Calculating density

Density measures the mass packed into a certain volume. This can be represented by the mathematical formula:

$$\text{density} = \frac{\text{mass}}{\text{volume}}$$

Using symbols, this formula can be written as:

$$d = \frac{m}{V}$$

Mass is normally measured in grams (g) and volume in cubic centimetres (cm^3).

Worked example
Calculating density

Problem
Calculate the density of a pebble with a mass of 20 g and a volume of 10 mL.

Solution
Thinking: convert mL into cm^3
Working: V = 10 mL = 10 cm^3
Thinking: identify formula to use
Working: $d = \frac{m}{V}$
Thinking: substitute the values for mass and volume and calculate density
Working: $d = \frac{m}{V} = \frac{20}{10} = 2$ g/cm^3

Try yourself
Calculate the density of:
a a sausage with a mass of 30 g and a volume of 30 mL
b a piece of pine with a mass of 50 g and a volume of 100 cm^3.

Floating and sinking

Density determines how different substances will arrange themselves when mixed together. The densest substance will drop to the very bottom while the least dense will rise to the top.

For example, cooking oil floats on top of water because its density is less than that of water. A steel bolt sinks in water because its density is greater than that of water.

The density of water is $1.0\,g/cm^3$. Anything more dense than this will sink when placed in water. Anything less dense will float on top of the water. Figure 2.4.7 shows two types of rock of very different densities.

Prac 1
p. 77

Pumice is less dense than water and so it floats.

Obsidian is more dense than water and so it sinks.

FIGURE 2.4.7 Density determines whether things float or sink.

Water and ice

Water acts just like other liquids above 4°C and ice acts just like other solids below 0°C—it expands when heated and contracts when cooled. However, between 0°C and 4°C, water does the exact opposite : it expands when cooled and contracts when heated. Water at 4°C is denser than at any other temperature, and drops to the bottom of any pond, lake or swimming pool. Colder water floats on top of it, and any ice will float on the surface of that colder water. This is shown in Figure 2.4.8.

FIGURE 2.4.8 The water at the bottom of a pond, lake or swimming pool is always the densest. Even in freezing conditions, this layer is unlikely to drop below 4°C, giving fish some chance of survival.

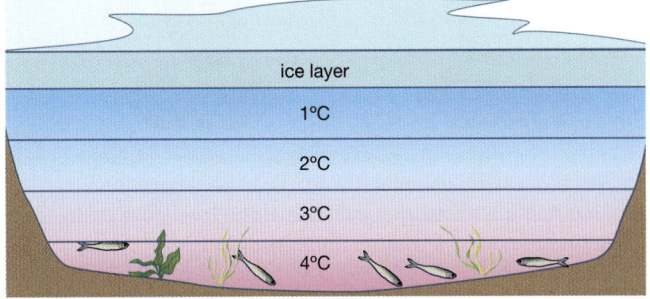

Icebergs

Thicker, heavier chunks of ice will be partly submerged (under water) with only their top exposed, forming an iceberg. Despite their huge size and mass, icebergs float because their density is less than that of pure water and seawater. Their densities are shown in Table 2.4.4.

TABLE 2.4.4 Densities of water

Substance	Density (g/cm³)
Ice	0.92
Pure water	1.00
Seawater	1.03

Icebergs are incredibly dangerous to ships because:
- they shift with ocean currents and winds, often into shipping lanes.
- 80–90% of the iceberg lies hidden below the water as shown in Figure 2.4.9. This hidden part doesn't melt as fast as the ice above the water, and so it usually extends wider than the ice visible above the water line. Any ship that comes near could hit this bulge, causing a hole and sinking the ship.

Although radar gives modern shipping some warning of a nearby iceberg, disaster can still happen. In 2007, the Canadian cruise ship MS *Explorer* hit submerged ice off Antarctica and sank. You can see the ship at the beginning of this module on page 70.

There was no radar in 1912 when RMS *Titanic* hit an iceberg and sank on its voyage from England to the USA. Although the crew knew that icebergs lay in the path of the ship and were watching out for them, it was a moonless night and the iceberg was only seen at the last moment.

FIGURE 2.4.9 Most of an iceberg lies below the surface of the water.

 AB 2.8   Prac 2 p. 78   Prac 3 p. 79   STEM p. 80

CHAPTER 2 • PROPERTIES OF SUBSTANCES **73**

SCIENCE AS A HUMAN ENDEAVOUR
Nature and development of science

Archimedes and the golden wreath

> Mass is easy to measure using balances and scales and the volume of simple shapes like cubes and cylinders can be calculated using simple mathematics. Determining the volume of oddly shaped objects is a little more difficult.

Archimedes (about 287–212 BCE) was the most important scientist and mathematician of ancient Greece, but he had a problem. According to a Roman story, King Hiero II of Syracuse had his goldsmith make a golden wreath (or crown) to be presented to the ancient Greek gods. It probably looked like the one in Figure 2.4.10. However, the king suspected that the wreath was made from cheaper silver rather than gold. Archimedes' task was to determine whether the wreath was made of pure gold.

Archimedes realised that density could help him. Pure gold is very dense and heavy for its size. Silver and gold/silver mixtures are less dense and so would take up more volume than if the crown was made of pure gold. Archimedes could easily measure the mass of the wreath with a simple balance but he also needed to measure the exact volume of the wreath. Archimedes wondered how he could measure its exact volume without destroying the precious wreath. He found his answer when he got into his bath and saw the water level rise. The water had risen because he **displaced** (took the place of) some of the water, pushing the water level up. He realised this would happen with any object and that the volume of water being displaced would be the same as the volume of the object. So excited with his discovery, Archimedes supposedly ran naked down the street screaming 'eureka, eureka' (I've found it, I've found it).

You too can measure the volume of an oddly-shaped object by submerging it in water. An easy way in the laboratory is to submerge it in a measuring cylinder. Figure 2.4.11 shows how.

FIGURE 2.4.10 Archimedes needed to determine whether a wreath was pure gold or made of cheaper materials.

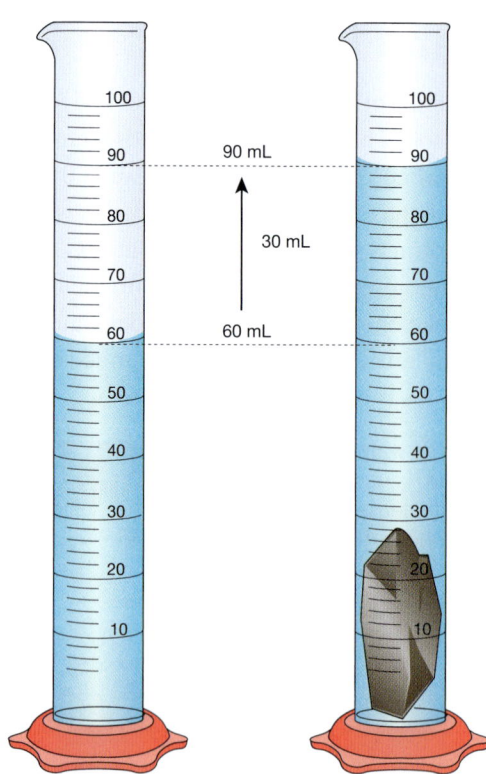

FIGURE 2.4.11 The volume of a solid can be determined by dropping it into a measuring cylinder. If the level goes up by 30 mL then the solid's volume must be 30 mL.

SCIENCE AS A HUMAN ENDEAVOUR

REVIEW

1. What does displace mean?
2. The pebble in Figure 2.4.11 had a mass of 60 g. Calculate its density.
3. The density of gold is 19.3 g/cm³ while the density of silver is 10.5 g/cm³.
   a. Use these densities to explain why a certain mass of gold will take up less volume than the same mass of silver.
   b. Calculate roughly how much bigger a mass of silver would be when compared with the same mass of gold.
4. Many scientists do not believe that Archimedes used his 'bathtub' method to determine if the wreath was pure gold or not. Many suggest that he used apparatus like that shown in Figure 2.4.12.

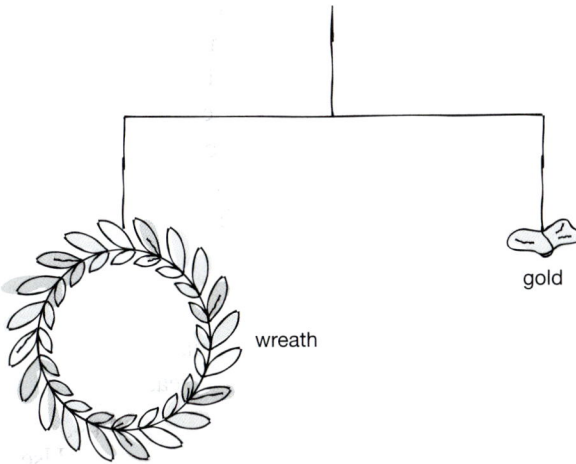

FIGURE 2.4.12

The diagrams in Figure 2.4.13 show three things that could happen once the balance was lowered into water.

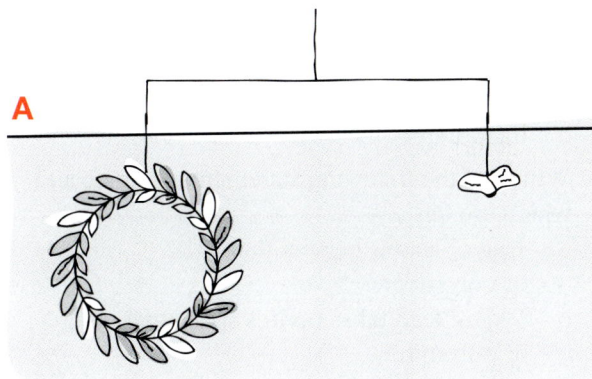

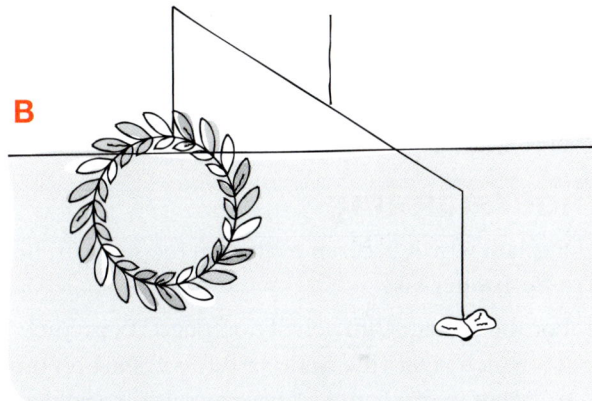

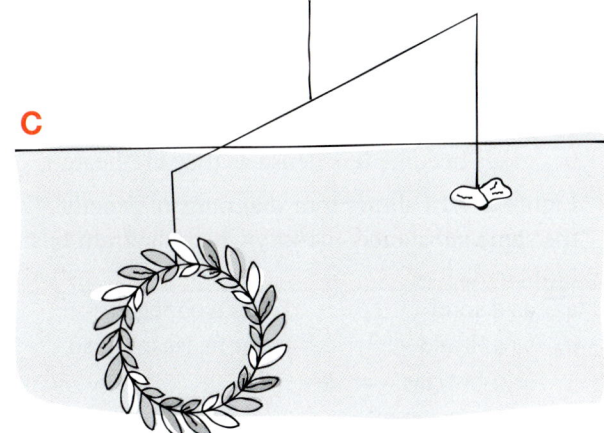

FIGURE 2.4.13

Predict what would happen (A, B or C) if the wreath was made of:

a. pure gold
b. a less dense substance like silver
c. a denser material like platinum.

MODULE 2.4 Review questions

Remembering

1. Define the term 'density'.
2. What term best describes each of the following?
   a. how much matter is in an object
   b. the quantity measured in mL.
3. Which of the following statements are true and which are false?
   a. 1 kg of lead is heavier than 1 kg of polystyrene.
   b. 1 kg of lead takes up less space than 1 kg of polystyrene.
   c. 1 kg of lead has the same density as 1 kg of polystyrene.
4. Arrange the following in order from least dense to most dense:
   ice   seawater   pure water at 1°C
   pure water at 4°C   water vapour

Understanding

5. Explain why it is easier to float in the sea than in a freshwater lake.
6. For the science4fun activity on page 70, predict:
   a. which layer (the water or oil) will start on top
   b. what might happen once the salt is sprinkled on top.

Applying

7. Use the particle model to explain why:
   a. gases are less dense than liquids and solids
   b. gases become less dense as they are heated.
8. Figure 2.4.14 shows four diagrams of exactly the same substance. Identify which diagram best represents it:
   a. as a solid
   b. as a liquid
   c. as a hot gas
   d. as a cool gas
   e. at its least dense.

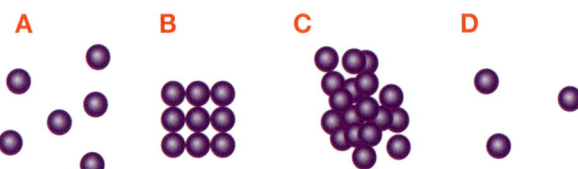

FIGURE 2.4.14

9. Use the densities in Tables 2.4.1, 2.4.2 and 2.4.3 on page 71 to explain why:
   a. lifesaving rings are usually made of polystyrene
   b. helium balloons rise
   c. spilt petrol forms a floating layer on top of water.

Analysing

10. Calculate the density of a solid that has a volume of 2 cm^3 and a mass of 3 g.
11. Figure 2.4.15 shows a density tower. The densities of the four liquids are:

    corn oil   0.93 g/cm^3
    methylated spirits   0.79 g/cm^3
    sugar syrup   1.83 g/cm^3
    water   1.00 g/cm^3

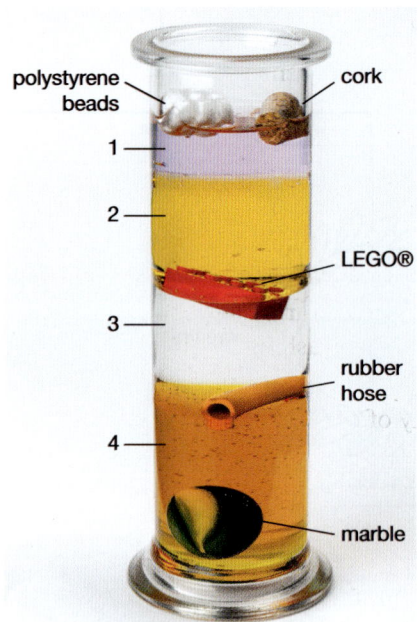

FIGURE 2.4.15

   a. Use the above densities to identify each of the numbered liquids.
   b. Five different solids float between the layers of liquid. Analyse where each solid is and match it with its most likely density:

      cork   0.25 g/cm^3
      polystyrene beads 1.30 g/cm^3
      LEGO brick   2.50 g/cm^3
      rubber hose   0.25 g/cm^3
      marble   0.96 g/cm^3

MODULE 2.4 Review questions

Evaluating

12 a   Are you more or less dense than water?
    b   Justify your answer.
13 Newspaper usually floats on water but then sinks after a while. Propose reasons why.

Creating

14 a   Construct a diagram showing a measuring cylinder containing all the liquids shown in Table 2.4.2 on page 71.
    b   Small lumps of wood, copper and gold were then dropped into the measuring cylinder. Modify your diagram to show where each would settle.

MODULE 2.4 Practical investigations

1 • Density tower

Purpose
To construct a tower of different liquids, layered according to their densities.

Timing 45 minutes

Materials
- 50 mL (maximum) each of corn syrup or honey, vegetable oil, ethanol or methylated spirits, coloured dishwashing liquid, water
- a variety of small solids (such as a cornflake, single penne pasta, cork, sultana, bolt)
- a few drops of food dye
- rubber stopper, grape, LEGO block
- large measuring cylinder
- small beaker
- digital camera or mobile phone (optional)

SAFETY
A Risk Assessment is required for this investigation.
Ethanol and methylated spirits are flammable so keep away from naked flames.
Wear safety glasses at all times.

Procedure
1 Carefully squeeze the honey into the measuring cylinder so that it forms a layer at least 1 cm thick on the bottom.
2 Carefully squeeze or pour a similar quantity of dishwashing liquid into the measuring cylinder. Do this by tilting the cylinder and slowly pouring the dishwashing liquid down its side.
3 Choose a food dye that is a different colour from the dishwashing liquid. Add a few drops of it to a small beaker of water. Tilt the cylinder again, and carefully pour the coloured water in to form a 1 cm layer.
4 Use the same method to pour a 1 cm layer of vegetable oil on top of the coloured water.
5 Add a few drops of food dye to a small beaker of ethanol or methylated spirits. Make another 1 cm layer by gently pouring the ethanol or methylated spirits down the side of the cylinder.
6 Stand the measuring cylinder upright and allow the contents to settle.
7 Gently lower the small solids, one by one, into the measuring cylinder.

Results
1 Construct a labelled sketch showing the layering of liquids in the tower, or take a photograph and add labels.
2 Record the level at which each small solid settles.

Review
1 Explain why:
    a   the liquids formed layers
    b   some objects floated and others sank.
2 Identify the least dense:
    a   liquid   b   object.
3 List in order from most to least dense all the:
    a   liquids you tested   b   solids you tested
    c   liquids and solids you tested.

CHAPTER 2 • PROPERTIES OF SUBSTANCES   77

MODULE 2.4 Practical investigations

2 • Icebergs and eggbergs

Questioning & Predicting · **Evaluating**

Purpose
To demonstrate how the different densities of fresh and salt water change how something floats.

Hypothesis
Which do you think is more dense—an ice cube or an egg? Before you go any further with this investigation, write a hypothesis in your workbook.

Timing   60 minutes

Materials
PART A: ICEBERGS
- 2 ice cubes
- salt
- water

- 250 mL beaker
- plastic 30 cm ruler
- spoon

PART B: EGGBERGS
- fresh uncooked egg
- salt
- water

- 2 tall glasses, tall beakers or large measuring cylinders, wide enough to take an egg
- spoon

Method
PART A: ICEBERGS

1. Three-quarters fill the glass or beaker with water.
2. Slide in a cube of ice.
3. Use the ruler to measure how much of the ice cube is above water and how much is below water.
4. Use a calculator to calculate the percentage of the ice cube that lies below the water.

$$\% = \frac{\text{how much ice cube is below water}}{\text{total height of ice cube}} \times 100$$

5. Use the spoon to remove the ice cube. Add salt to the water and stir. Keep stirring and adding salt until no more will dissolve.
6. Slide in another cube of ice and repeat your measurements.

PART B: EGGBERGS

7. Fill two tall glasses, tall beakers or large measuring cylinders with approximately the same amount of water.
8. Add spoonfuls of salt to one glass until no more will dissolve.
9. Use the spoon to lower the fresh egg gently into the glass of fresh (non-salty) water. Observe what happens.
10. Lower the egg into the glass of salt water. Observe what happens.
11. Remove the egg and pour out half of the salt water.
12. Very slowly add half of the fresh water, making sure that it does not mix with the salt water. The best way of doing this is by slowly pouring the fresh water down the inside of the glass.
13. Use the spoon to lower the egg gently into the water. Watch where the egg settles.

Results
Record your observations at each stage in Part A and Part B.

Review

1. What evidence suggests that salt water is more dense than fresh water?
2. List the following substances in order from most dense to least dense:

   egg   fresh water   ice cube   salt water

3. Use evidence from this experiment to explain why icebergs are dangerous to shipping.
4. The wreck of RMS *Titanic* was only discovered in 1985. Some scientists think that the wreck may not have hit the bottom immediately but settled somewhere in the water above it. Use observations made in this activity to explain how this might have happened.
5. a Construct a conclusion that compares the densities of ice cubes and eggs.
   b Assess whether your hypothesis was supported or not.
6. An egg that has gone 'off' will float in water whereas a fresh egg will sink. Propose why.

MODULE 2.4 Practical investigations

• **STUDENT DESIGN** •

3 • Calculating density

Purpose
To calculate the density of different objects.

Timing 60 minutes

Materials
- selection of small masses (such as pebbles, bolts, rubber stopper, LEGO blocks)
- large measuring cylinder
- access to electronic scales or beam balance

A Risk Assessment is required for this investigation.

Procedure

1. Design an experiment that:
   - identifies which of the selected objects sink and which float in water
   - gives the measurements you need to calculate the density of each object.
2. Write your procedure in your workbook.
3. Before you start any practical work, assess your procedure. List any risks that your procedure might involve and what you might do to minimise those risks. Show your teacher your procedure and your assessment of its risks. If they approve, then collect all the required materials and start work.

Hints
- You will need to measure the mass and volume of each object you have.
- Some objects might float so you will need a way of keeping them underwater without affecting your volume measurements.
- When using a measuring cylinder, make sure you read volumes from the bottom of the meniscus.
- Use the STEM and SDI template in your eBook to help you plan and carry out your investigation.

Results

1. Construct a table like the one below to record all your measurements and results from any calculations. Give your table a title. Alternatively, construct a spreadsheet for your results.

Object	Sink/float?	Mass (g)	Volume (mL or cm³)	Density (g/cm³)
ice-cube	float	2.3	2.5	2.3/2.5 = 0.92

2. Calculate the density of each object by dividing the mass by the volume:
$$d = \frac{m}{V}$$
A sample calculation has been done for you.
Alternatively, program your spreadsheet to calculate density for you.

Practical review

1. What is the density of water?
2. List the objects that:
   a. floated (if any)
   b. sank.
3. Compare the density of each object with the density of water.

CHAPTER 2 • PROPERTIES OF SUBSTANCES **79**

MODULE 2.4 Practical investigations

How can ships avoid sinking?

Background

Density is a measure of mass in a given volume. The density of seawater varies with water temperature and with the quantity of salt dissolved in the water (salinity). Plimsoll lines are drawn onto the hulls of ships to allow them to be loaded safely and to avoid the risk of sinking when a ship moves though water of varying temperature and salinity (Figure 2.4.16).

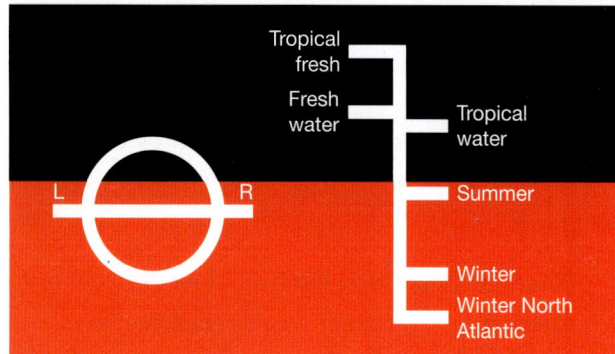

FIGURE 2.4.16 Plimsoll lines

The horizontal lines on the Plimsoll marking indicate where the water level should come up to on the loaded ship's hull. As a ship is loaded with more cargo, the weight of the cargo will push the ship further down into the water and the water line will come higher up the ship's hull. As the ship travels into different oceans, the salinity and temperature of the new ocean may not provide enough buoyancy for the loaded ship and the ship may sink.

Problem

One of Victoria's biggest export markets (approximately $2 billion per year) is the sale of dairy products to Japan and China. A shipping company wants to send dairy products to these export markets. They need to ensure that the ships do not sink when the density of water changes. The ships will leave Victorian ports in the winter, cross into tropical waters and arrive in Japan and China in summer months. How fully loaded should the ships be before they leave Victorian ports?

Procedure

1. Design and conduct a valid experiment to test how deep a loaded model ship sits in water of different temperature and salinity.
2. Write your procedure in your workbook and show your teacher. If they approve your plan, then collect your equipment and carry out the experiment.

Hints

In your investigation:
- make a model of your ship using a margarine container and load it with rice or sugar
- use the laboratory sink with the plug in as a test water tank

Materials

- pure (distilled) water
- table salt (sodium chloride)
- rice or sugar

Equipment

- empty margarine containers
- laboratory sink
- rulers
- thermometers
- permanent markers
- wooden spoon (or similar large stirrer)

Engineering design process

- Use the STEM and SDI template in your eBook to help you plan and carry out your investigation.
- Identify the purpose.
- Identify the independent, dependent and controlled variables and only change one independent variable at a time.
- Based on your purpose and the controls and variables, write a hypothesis for this experiment.
- Before you commence your investigation you must conduct a risk assessment. See the Activity Book Science toolkit to assist you with developing a risk assessment.
- Summarise your experiment in a scientific report including the Purpose, Hypothesis, Materials, Procedure, Risk Assessment, Results (including data presented in tables and/or graphs), Discussion and Conclusion.

CHAPTER 2 Chapter review

Remembering

1. State two physical properties each for:
   a solids   b liquids   c gases.

2. What happens to particles in the following states when they are heated?
   a solid   b liquid   c gas.

3. Name the opposite process to:
   a melting   b evaporation.

Understanding

4. Gases are less dense than liquids or solids of the same material. Explain why.

5. Describe the property that makes gases ideal for filling jumping castles.

6. Which of the following temperatures is most likely to be the melting point of butter?
   A −20°C   C 30°C
   B 0°C   D 100°C

7. Predict what might happen when you place an empty balloon around the rim of a conical flask with some water in it (Figure 2.5.1) and heat the flask.

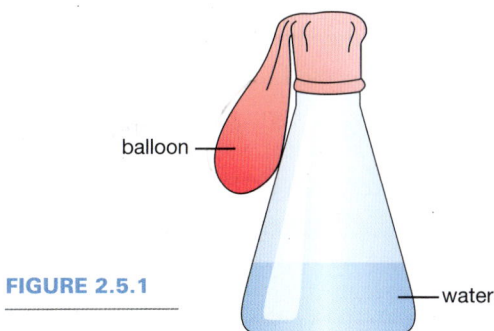

FIGURE 2.5.1

Applying

8. When you dive into a swimming pool, the water parts around you as you enter it. Use the particle model to explain:
   a what happens to the water particles as you dive in
   b why the swimming pool water gives you a 'punch' in the stomach when you do a 'belly flop' and not a clean dive.

9. Figure 2.5.2 shows a balloon full of gas. Which of the following diagrams best shows the gas and balloon after the gas is warmed up.

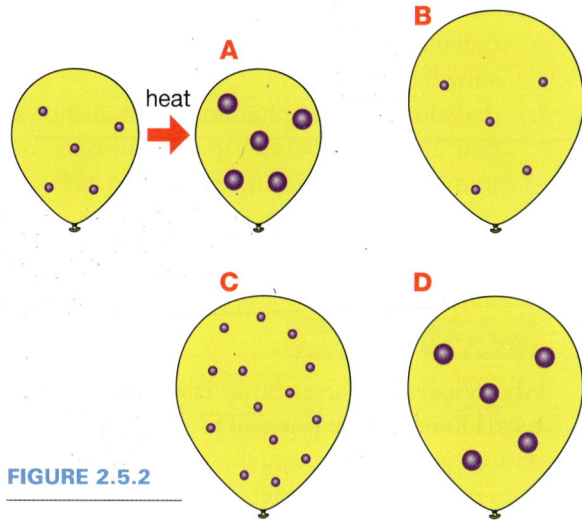

FIGURE 2.5.2

Analysing

10. Use the particle model to contrast:
    a melting and freezing
    b evaporation and condensation.

Evaluating

11. Suggest a reason why:
    a ships float despite the steel they are built from being denser than water
    b ships sink when badly damaged, allowing water to rush in.

12. a Assess whether you can or cannot answer the questions on page 41 at the start of this chapter.
    b Use this assessment to evaluate how well you understand the material presented in this chapter.

Creating

13. Use the following ten key terms to construct a visual summary of the information presented in this chapter.

matter	solid	liquid
gas	melt	freeze
evaporate	condense	
sublime	heat	

AB 2.10

CHAPTER 2 • PROPERTIES OF SUBSTANCES   81

CHAPTER 2 Inquiry skills

Research

1. **Planning & Conducting**

   Search the internet to:
   a. download 20 images of different shaped snowflakes
   b. download a video or animation that shows how exploding petrol vapour causes pistons to move up and down, powering a car
   c. download a video showing what supercooled water is and what happens when ice is added to it.

2. **Planning & Conducting** **Communicating**

   Aboriginal and Torres Strait Islander peoples have long used the physical properties of the natural materials around them to create items used in their everyday life. Research some of these materials. Some you might look at are:
   - waxes and resins used as glues saps, barks, oils, leaves and fruit used for bush medicine
   - bark, timber, leaves and fronds used for utensils, shelter and housing
   - plant fibres and animal sinews used for string and rope
   - stones, bones, shells, teeth, branches and roots used for tools, weapons and utensils
   - stalks and leaves used for weaving baskets (Figure 2.5.3).

   FIGURE 2.5.3

   Whatever materials you research, find:
   - an image or video of the material being used
   - how their physical properties makes them ideal for their particular uses
   - whether the use of the material was restricted to a particular region or is/was used Australia-wide.

   Present your research as a digital presentation.

3. **Planning & Conducting** **Communicating**

   Safe evacuation from a burning building depends on the different densities of hot, smoky air and cooler, smokeless air.
   a. Research evacuation procedures recommended by your state fire service.
   b. Describe how these procedures relate to the different densities of a fire.

   Present your findings as a pamphlet to be letter-boxed to all homes.

4. **Planning & Conducting** **Communicating**

   The older ice in a glacier or an iceberg often has an incredible blue colour (Figure 2.5.4). Find images of a glacier or iceberg that has this blue colouring.

   Explain:
   - what causes the blue colour
   - how it is connected to density
   - why there are different shades of blue in the ice.

   Present your research in digital form.

   FIGURE 2.5.4

CHAPTER 2 Inquiry skills

Thinking scientifically

1 Liquids do not always mix together. Sometimes one liquid floats on top of another. Alice filled a container with some liquids as shown in Figure 2.5.5. P, Q, R and S are different objects floating in the liquids.

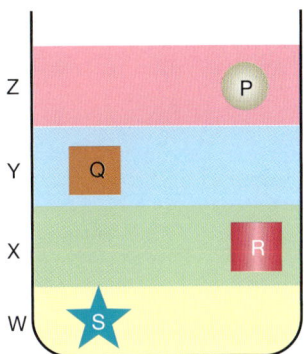

FIGURE 2.5.5

Which beaker shows what would happen if liquids X and Y were removed?

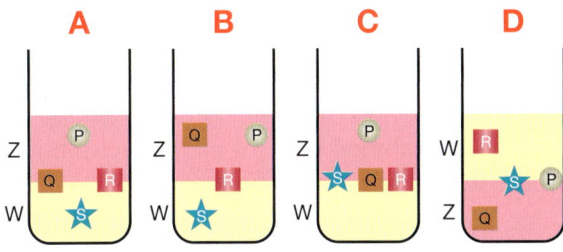

2 Angus placed a plastic cup in a plastic container filled with water. He marked the level of the water on the cup and the container (Figure 2.5.6).

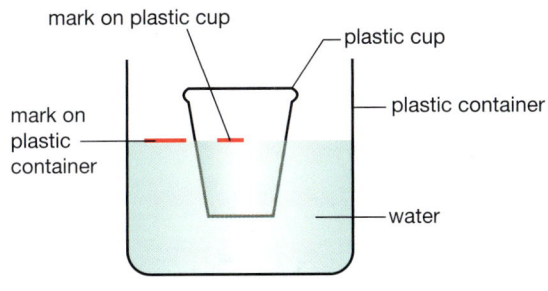

FIGURE 2.5.6

Angus then placed a heavy rock inside the plastic cup. Which beaker shows what he observed?

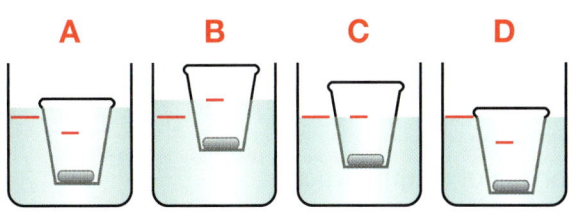

3 To find the density (d) of a substance, divide its mass (m) by its volume (V). That is, $d = \dfrac{m}{V}$.
The piece of granite in Figure 2.5.7 has a mass of 28 grams.

FIGURE 2.5.7

The volume of the granite was measured in a measuring cylinder by dropping it into 30 mL of water and measuring its displacement (Figure 2.5.8).

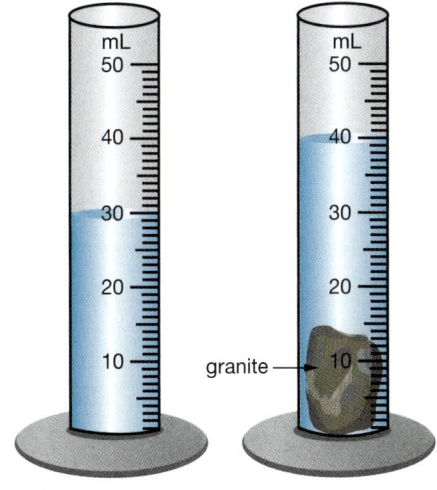

FIGURE 2.5.8

a The volume of the granite is
  A 10 mL   C 40 mL
  B 30 mL   D 50 mL.

b Calculate the density of the granite rock.
  A 0.36 g/cm³   C 28 g/cm³
  B 2.8 g/cm³   D 10 g/cm³.

CHAPTER 2 • PROPERTIES OF SUBSTANCES 83

CHAPTER 2 Glossary

biodegradable: bacteria or fungi breaks down the substance into simpler substances

boiling: the vigorous bubbling of a liquid when it is heated

boiling point: the temperature at which a liquid boils; 100°C for water

bonds: forces of attraction that hold particles together to form either a solid or liquid

Brownian motion: random motion of particles caused by being bumped and jostled by other particles

chemical properties: how substances react with other substances

compressed: squashed

condensation: occurs when the removal of heat changes a gas into a liquid

density: a measure of the mass per unit volume of a substance (unit: g/cm³)

diffusion: a process in which two liquids or gases mix

displace: when one object takes the place of another, for example a solid pushes water upwards

evaporation: heat changing a liquid into a gas. Also known as vaporisation.

freezing: occurs when the removal of heat changes a liquid into a solid

freezing point: the temperature at which a liquid freezes; 0°C for water

Boiling

chemical properties

incompressible: not able to be compressed or squashed

indirect evidence: facts and evidence from which something else can be inferred or reasoned

mass: measures how much matter is in a substance (unit: g)

melting: occurs when heat changes a solid into a liquid

melting point: the temperature at which a solid melts; 0°C for ice

non-biodegradable: does not rot or break down

odour: smell

particle model: the model used to help describe and explain the behaviour of particles in solids, liquids and gases

physical properties: describe the characteristics of a substance like its appearance, melting, freezing and boiling points and its hardness

pressure: combined push of gas particles bouncing off the walls of their container

states: solid, liquid, gas (also plasma at temperatures above 6000°C)

steam: condensation of water vapour, forming a visible fog of water droplets

vibrate: jiggle on the spot

volume: measures how much space is occupied by a substance (units: mL or cm³)

melting

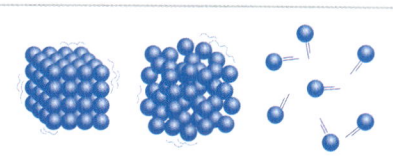
particle model

AB 2.9

CHAPTER 3
Earth resources

Have you ever wondered...
- what we need to survive on Earth?
- if we could run out of fuels such as petrol?
- where the electricity you use comes from?
- how clouds form?
- where the water goes in a storm?

After completing this chapter you should be able to:
- compare renewable and non-renewable resources
- describe resources in terms of the time taken to regenerate
- compare renewable and non-renewable sources of energy
- describe the water cycle in terms of changes of the state of water
- investigate factors that influence the water cycle in nature
- explore how human management of water impacts on the water cycle
- describe how water use and management rely on different areas of science and technology
- evaluate issues relating to the use and management of water within a community
- describe how water management affects farming, land management and gardening
- investigate how the knowledge of Indigenous Australians is being used to care for waterways.

This is an extract from the Australian Curriculum
Victorian Curriculum F–10 © VCAA (2016); reproduced by permission

AB 3.1

MODULE 3.1 Renewable and non-renewable resources

Humans need many things to stay alive, like food, air, water and shelter. Other living things have similar needs. These needs are met by the natural resources on Earth.

science 4 fun

In the soil
What is in soil?

Collect this...
- 3 × 2 L plastic soft-drink bottles
- 3 soil samples collected from very different areas
- serrated knife or hacksaw
- tablespoon

SAFETY
Wear rubber gloves and mask.
Always cut away from you when using a knife or hacksaw.

Do this...
1. Do this activity outside. Use the knife or hacksaw to cut 5 cm off the top of each plastic soft-drink bottle.
2. Add water to each bottle until it is about 5 cm from the top.
3. Pour a different soil sample into each bottle. Stop adding soil when the water level reaches 1 cm from the top of the bottle.
4. Leave the soil to settle for about 1 minute. If any animals such as insects or earthworms are found floating at the top, lift them out with the spoon, observe what they are and let them go.
5. Observe what happens to the soil in the container. Have another look after about 2 hours.

Record this...
1. Describe what you saw.
2. Explain the differences between each soil sample.

Natural resources

A **resource** is anything obtained from our Earth to satisfy a particular need of humans or other living things. Most natural resources are substances, such as rocks, air or water. However, sunlight is a vital resource too. Sunlight is not a substance but is a form of energy needed by almost all living things on Earth. Even though sunlight comes from space, it is considered to be an Earth resource.

The major natural resources of Earth are:
- living things (such as trees and chickens)
- air
- sunlight
- water
- rocks
- minerals (such as iron and gold) found in rocks
- fossil fuels (such as coal and oil) found in rocks
- soil.

All life depends on these resources. Protecting them gives all living things (including us) a better chance of survival.

Human-made resources

Not all resources are natural. Some are made by humans. Human-made resources start as natural resources. Some examples of these resources include:

- foods, such as pasta and bread, made from plant seeds (such as wheat, soy and rye)
- leather, made from animal skins (such as cowskins or pigskins)
- natural fibres, made from plants (such as cotton and linen) or animals (such as wool)
- wood (such as timber and bamboo) cut from trees and shrubs
- paper and cardboard, made from trees
- plastics (such as polystyrene) and synthetic fibres (such as polyester) made from oil
- fuels (such as petrol, diesel and kerosene) made from oil
- metals (such as copper and aluminium) made from minerals found in rocks
- glass, made from minerals found in sand
- ceramics (such as bricks and porcelain) made from clay
- cements, made from limestone, clay and other minerals found in rock
- medicines, made from plants, animals and minerals.

Renewable and non-renewable resources

Some resources, such as sunlight, are renewable and will never run out. Other resources, such as iron, are non-renewable and can never be replaced once used up.

A **renewable resource** is one that can be replaced by natural processes and that can be used again and again. Careful monitoring of these resources is required to ensure the resource isn't being used up faster than it is being renewed.

An example of a renewable resource is the timber in a forest. A forest can regrow after it has been cut down but it will take years to grow back to its original height. Although it takes time, the forest can be replaced with a new one. This is what is happening in Figure 3.1.1. In contrast, the forest may never regrow if all the trees are cut down at once. In this way, poor management of the resource can change it from renewable to non-renewable.

Air, water, sunlight and living things are considered to be renewable resources.

FIGURE 3.1.1 This blue gum forest is a renewable resource because it is regrowing as fast as other parts of the forest are being cut down.

Non-renewable resources are those that take a very long time to be replaced, usually much longer than a human lifetime. Coal, oil and natural gas take many millions of years to form. Therefore, they are non-renewable. We are using these **fossil fuels** far faster than they are being re-made and so they will eventually run out. Rocks, the minerals they contain, and soils are also non-renewable because they usually take thousands to millions of years to form (Figure 3.1.2).

FIGURE 3.1.2 Iron is a non-renewable resource. Here, iron ore from an open-cut mine is being loaded for export.

CHAPTER 3 • EARTH RESOURCES   87

Living things: a renewable resource

Living things are important resources for humans. We use different parts of the seeds, leaves, roots and stems of plants and the meat, fur and skins of animals to meet many of our everyday needs.

For example, farmers grow seed crops such as wheat, corn and rice and raise animals such as sheep, chickens and cows. Market gardeners grow fruit and vegetables such as peaches, oranges, lettuce, carrots, peas and tomatoes.

Wood and bamboo are important building materials. Eucalyptus trees (gum trees), she oaks, wattles and pines provide timber to build houses and furniture and to make other building products like the chipboard and MDF used to construct kitchen cupboards. Wood is also burnt for heating and cooking.

Plants provide cotton and linen for clothing and animals provide wool and leather. Important medicines are often made from plants too. For example, codeine is widely used for pain relief. It comes from the flower of the opium poppy flower, grown legally in registered farms in Tasmania and Victoria.

Living things are a renewable resource because they reproduce. A forest that has been cut down can regrow. Replacing some forests may take just a few decades, while other forests would take much longer to replace. Plantations are forests where trees are planted for timber. These can be replaced faster than a natural forest. Animals reproduce and so they are replaced by their offspring. Likewise, fish farms ensure that valuable fish like salmon and trout are harvested and replaced quickly.

Animals harvested from the wild are renewable as long as the populations are allowed to replace themselves. For example, if wild fish are caught faster than they breed then the fish will eventually disappear. An important food supply for humans (and other marine life) will then be lost. In many places in the world, wild fish stocks are falling because there are too many fish being caught too quickly (Figure 3.1.3). For example, yellow-fin tuna is being overfished, putting their survival at risk. To ensure fish like this remain a renewable resource, their numbers are constantly monitored (checked) and strict laws control how many fish can be caught.

FIGURE 3.1.3 Many types of fish are being caught faster than they can breed. What was once a renewable resource is now non-renewable.

SciFile

Feeding off others

Animals and plants use each other as resources too. This photo shows the head of a tapeworm, a parasite that lives inside the intestines of some animals, including humans. The tapeworm head has a ring of hooks at the top and below that a series of circular suckers that holds on to the intestine wall. The tapeworm has no mouth and absorbs digested food through its skin. There are many types of parasite, including other animals, fungi and plants.

Air: a renewable resource

The **atmosphere** is the very thin layer of air that surrounds Earth. Air is a mixture of gases and suspended particles such as dust, smoke and water vapour. The main gases in air can be seen in Figure 3.1.4.

About 21% of the air is oxygen gas. Oxygen is constantly used by animals and plants but is also constantly being replaced by plants. Green plants use a process called **photosynthesis** to combine carbon dioxide and water to make their own food. Photosynthesis is powered by the energy found in sunlight and the process releases oxygen back into the atmosphere. This allows the oxygen in the atmosphere to stay at about the same level.

Only about 0.04% of air is carbon dioxide. This is enough to supply plants with the carbon dioxide needed to carry out photosynthesis. Animals breathe out carbon dioxide so carbon dioxide is constantly being replaced in the air.

Scientists describe the movement of materials from one place to another and back again as a 'cycle'. Oxygen cycles from plants, through the atmosphere, to animals. Carbon dioxide completes the cycle, passing from animals, through the atmosphere, to plants. This cycle of oxygen and carbon dioxide is shown in Figure 3.1.5.

The most common gas in air is nitrogen (78%). Nitrogen is absorbed by plants and used to make proteins that help them to function and grow. Animals that eat plants use these proteins to help them to function and grow too. Nitrogen gas also has a cycle being absorbed by some organisms and released by others.

Prac 1
p. 97

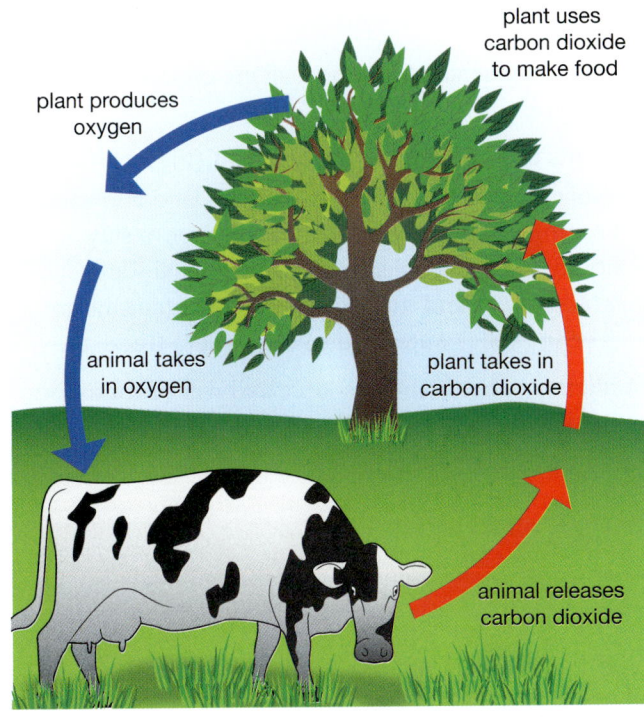

FIGURE 3.1.5 The cycle of oxygen and carbon dioxide between plants and animals renews these gases in the atmosphere.

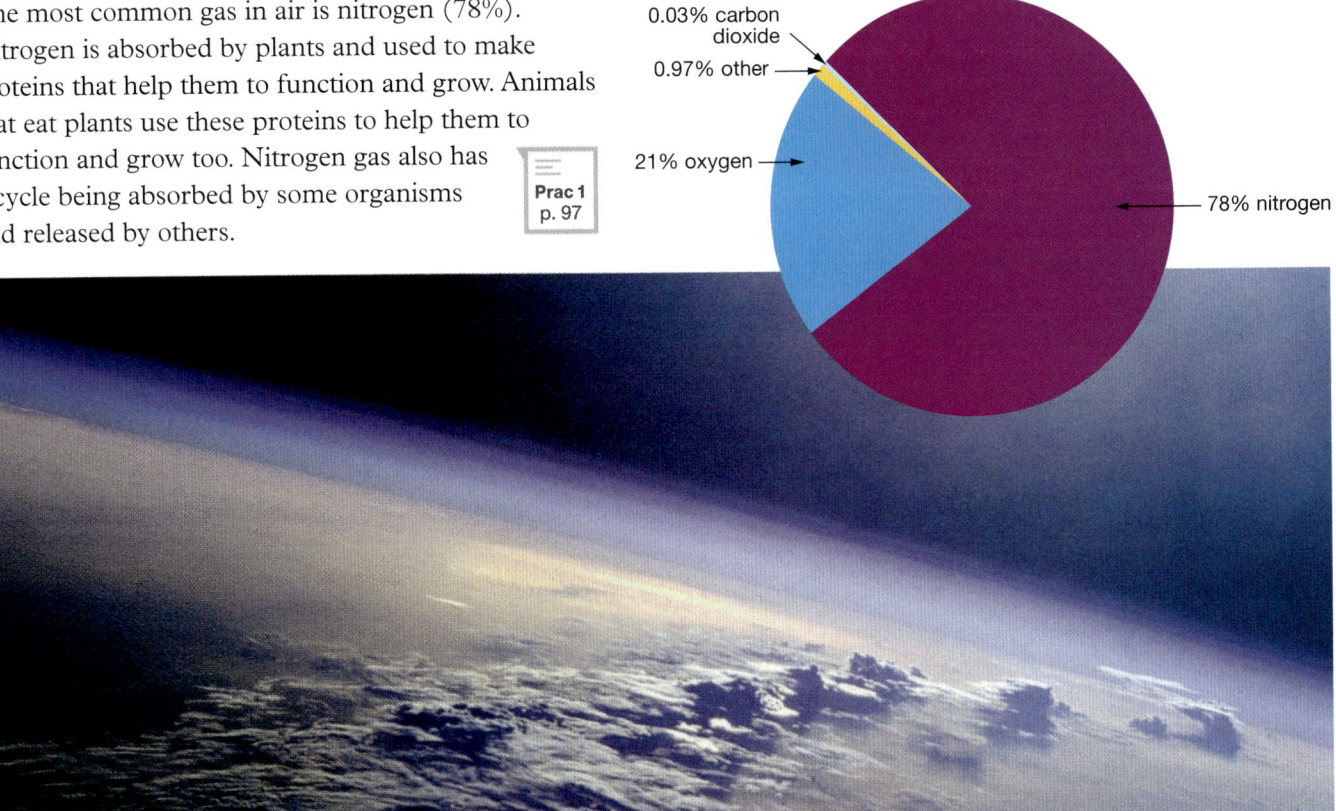

FIGURE 3.1.4 A thin layer of gases around Earth makes up our atmosphere. Most of the atmosphere is made of nitrogen gas.

CHAPTER 3 • EARTH RESOURCES   89

Sunlight: a renewable resource

Sunlight is essential for almost all life on Earth. This is because:

- plants use sunlight to produce food (Figure 3.1.6)
- sunlight warms Earth's atmosphere, land and water, keeping it warm enough for most water to stay liquid. If Earth cooled too much, then all water would freeze and turn to ice. Living organisms are 65–90% water water and so they would freeze too!

Sunlight is a renewable resource and will be for as long as the Sun keeps shining. The Sun is a star, and it will continue to shine for billions of years.

FIGURE 3.1.6 Green plants use photosynthesis to make their own food. Photosynthesis is powered by sunlight.

Water: a renewable resource

Water covers most of Earth's surface and all living things need it to survive (Figure 3.1.7). For this reason, water is Earth's most important resource.

Water is a renewable resource because it can move from place to place and replenish (replace) the water in an area. Only a tiny fraction of the water on Earth is made new each day. Some new water is made whenever:

- living things like trees burn
- fossil fuels like petrol and coal burn
- living things release energy in their bodies.

Scientists think that the total amount of water on Earth has not changed much since the planet formed billions of years ago.

FIGURE 3.1.7 Water is the most important resource on Earth because no living thing can survive without it.

SciFile
Life but not as we know it

On Earth, some living things do not need the energy from sunlight to survive. Deep in the oceans are underground volcanoes called geothermal vents where bacteria use energy from deep inside Earth instead of sunlight. These bacteria and any sea life that depend on them would survive even if the sun suddenly stopped shining.

SciFile
Living on other planets

Life cannot exist without water. For this reason, scientists searching for signs of life in space are only looking at planets and moons where water can be detected. Mars has recently been discovered to have water. Jupiter's moons Europa and Callisto also have water.

Rocks and minerals: non-renewable resources

Rocks provide two different resources:
- the rocks themselves
- minerals found in rocks.

There are many different types of rock. Some types are hard and can be used without altering them or removing any materials from them. Examples are basalt and bluestone. These rocks are used mainly for roads and buildings. Other types of rocks are soft, like limestone and sandstone. These rocks are easy to cut, so they are used in paving and walls. For example, Melbourne's Federation Square has walls made of sandstone and bluestone tiles. You can see it in Figure 3.1.8.

FIGURE 3.1.8 Rock is used to cover the buildings around Federation Square in Melbourne.

Rocks are made from substances called **minerals**. Minerals differ in their physical properties such as colour and hardness. You can see how minerals appear in a magnified view of a rock in Figure 3.1.9. Many minerals are important resources for us humans. A variety of minerals and their uses are shown in Table 3.1.1.

TABLE 3.1.1 Minerals and their uses

Mineral	Main use
bauxite	Contains aluminium which is used for making aircraft, drink cans, window frames, boats and cooking foil.
haematite	Contains iron which is used to make steel, which is used in car bodies, nails, ships and bridges.
malachite	Contains copper which is used in water pipes and electrical wiring.
halite	Contains sodium chloride (table salt) which is used in food preparation and medical applications.

FIGURE 3.1.9 This is a magnified view of a rock. Each different colour is a different mineral.

Rocks contain some of the minerals that are needed by living things. As the rocks gradually break down, they release minerals which end up in the water of oceans and lakes, and in the soil. From the water and soil, the minerals are taken up by plants and animals, providing them with necessary trace elements (substances needed but only in very small amounts).

Most of Earth's rocks formed millions of years ago, and took thousands to millions of years to form. Only small amounts of new rocks are being made today.

One place where new rocks form is around volcanoes. Volcanoes are weak spots in Earth's surface where hot liquid rock from inside the Earth flows or erupts out onto the surface. The hot liquid rock is known as magma when it is below the ground. If magma reaches the surface of the Earth, then it is known as lava. Over a few hours, lava cools to form new rock (Figure 3.1.10).

FIGURE 3.1.10 Igneous rock is formed when magma or lava cools and solidifies.

CHAPTER 3 • EARTH RESOURCES 91

Most magma never reaches the surface but instead cools underground to form rock. This may take thousands or millions of years.

Rocks formed when magma or lava cools are known as **igneous rocks**.

Other types of rocks form when fine rock particles like sand, silt and clay stick together and harden to become rock. These fine particles are called sediments and the type of rock formed is called **sedimentary rock**. Most sedimentary rocks form over many thousands or millions of years.

Only a tiny fraction of Earth's rocks is being replaced each year. The replacement takes so long that rocks cannot be considered to be renewable resources. Therefore the minerals in the rocks are considered to be non-renewable resources too.

Rocks also contain resources that are not minerals. Coal, oil and natural gas are energy sources that are found in or between layers of rock deep below the ground. The coal, oil and gas that we use today was formed from dead plants and animals that lived many millions of years ago. It takes millions of years for these resources to be made, and for this reason, fossil fuels are considered non-renewable resources.

Soil: a non-renewable resource

Rocks are **weathered** (broken down) by the action of rain, wind, chemicals and living things into smaller particles such as sand, silt and clay. The small particles are carried away by wind, water and ice in a process called **erosion** (Figure 3.1.11). The particles are then dropped somewhere when the wind, water or ice stops carrying them. This process is called **deposition** and the deposited (dropped) particles form layers of sediments.

Soils are made up of:
- sediments of fine rock particles like sand, silt and clay
- living things like worms and bacteria
- compost made from decaying leaf litter and animal waste and remains
- water
- dissolved minerals and gases.

In the mountains, rock can weather away to form new soil. However, the process is so slow that it can take thousands of years for the soil to build to a depth of a few centimetres.

FIGURE 3.1.11 The Colorado River in the USA has eroded the land around it so sediment has filled the river, giving it a brown colour. The weathering of surrounding rock and erosion has formed the Grand Canyon.

In river flood plains, soils will form because of sediments being carried there from other places. Although faster than weathering, it could still take decades to produce enough soil to promote plant growth. Depending on the vegetation or crop, a soil depth of 70 cm or more provides space and enough minerals for proper root development.

In general, the process of soil formation is so slow that soils cannot be considered to be renewable resources. For example, the soil blown away by the tornado in Figure 3.1.12 is unlikely to be replaced in the farmer's lifetime.

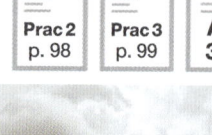

FIGURE 3.1.12 Tornadoes can strip soil from a farm and make it very difficult for any crops to grow.

Conserving resources

Non-renewable resources will run out unless we find ways to reduce the amount being used. Even renewable resources could become scarce if they are used faster than they form. This makes it important that we try to conserve our natural resources. As a community, we can:

- limit the amount of resources we use by stopping wastage. For example, turning off the lights when they are not needed helps save electricity and so less coal needs to be mined.
- recycle resources instead of throwing them away. For example, recycling cans and old computers means less aluminium, copper, lead and other metals need to be mined.
- increase the price of the resource to encourage people to use less of it and look for alternatives. For example, increasing the cost of water and electricity means that people waste less and use alternatives such as water tanks and solar panels.
- develop alternative resources or technologies. For example, electric cars and hybrid cars like the one in Figure 3.1.13 save oil. This allows oil to be used to make alternative resources like plastics.
- run public awareness campaigns to educate people on the need to conserve resources. For example, advertising campaigns encouraging 2-minute showers to save water so fewer dams and desalination plants need to be built.

SciFile

Recycle and save (the planet!)

Each aluminium can that you recycle saves about as much energy as it takes to run your TV for three hours!

FIGURE 3.1.13 Hybrid cars have both electric and petrol engines. Although currently more expensive to buy, hybrid cars save fuel and so are much cheaper to run.

SCIENCE AS A HUMAN ENDEAVOUR
Use and influence of science

Debating resources

Resources cause a lot of debate. Some people think that wind farms are ugly while others think that dams ruin the rivers they are built across. Coal mining provides a reliable source of energy, income and employment. However, coal mining also damages the environment. Communities often have differing views on what is more important—jobs or the environment.

FIGURE 3.1.14 An open-cut coal mine near Lake Macquarie, NSW.

Coal mining

Coal is a valuable resource to Australia. It is used to generate 73% of our electricity, provides a lot of people with reliable employment and provide the country with money from other countries who want to buy our coal. However, there are serious concerns about how it affects the environment. Environmental effects can include:

- dramatic changes to landscape (Figure 3.1.14)
- potential for fire in open-cut mines
- pollution of surface and ground water
- the release of carbon dioxide into the atmosphere when coal is burnt.

For these reasons, many people want Australia to gradually close its coal-fired power stations and stop exporting coal. To do this, we must all reduce consumption and switch to alternative energy sources. As Figure 3.1.15 shows, this has already started. Electricity consumption in Australia has recently dropped. Some reasons for this are:

- more solar panels being installed and more wind farms being used
- more energy saving five-star appliances such as refrigerators and washing machines
- more expensive electricity, encouraging us to use less.

Another approach is to develop technologies that remove carbon dioxide as it is being emitted from power stations.

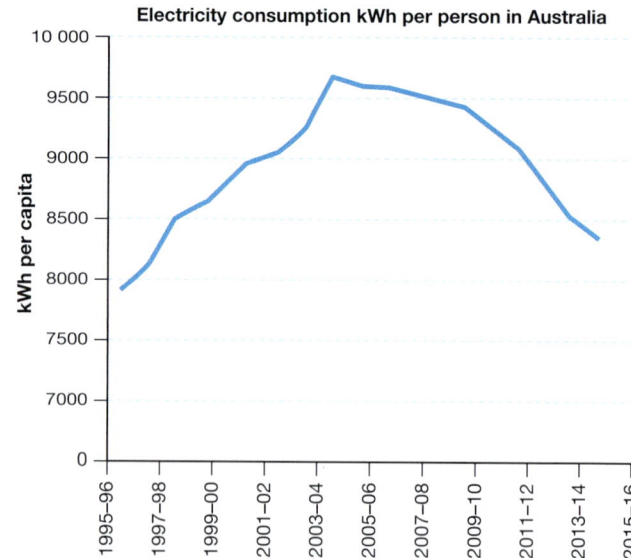

FIGURE 3.1.15 After many years of increasing electricity demand, there has been a recent drop in demand in Australia.

SCIENCE AS A HUMAN ENDEAVOUR

Carbon capture and storage

Carbon capture and storage isolates and captures carbon dioxide after coal is burnt. Once captured, the carbon dioxide is liquefied (changed into a liquid). It is then pumped underground into geological formations where it is to be stored. This is shown in Figure 3.1.16. Such 'clean coal technologies' aim to reduce greenhouse gas emissions generated when burning coal. Smallscale trials have been conducted, but the process has not yet been used on a large scale. Some scientists fear the process could trigger instability within the Earth, potentially leading to earthquakes.

Fracking

Sometimes new technology allows an entirely new type of mining. An example of this is **fracking**, in which water and other chemicals are pumped into rocks, causing them to fracture (break). The cracks allow resources to escape from the rock so that they can be extracted.

In Australia, fracking is used to release natural gas from coal. This gas is known as coal seam gas. However, there have been cases in the USA where fracking has contaminated water supplies. In rural Victoria, NSW and Queensland, groups have protested against the use of fracking (Figure 3.1.17).

FIGURE 3.1.17 A protest against using fracking to extract coal seam gas

People can have different views on which resources are more important. Those working in the mining industry claim that fracking is a safe process that will not damage water supplies if done carefully. Other groups, such as farmers or local residents, who are worried about water quality may be opposed to it.

REVIEW

1. Discuss the benefits and disadvantages of:
   a. coal mining
   b. fracking
   c. carbon capture and storage.
2. Why do farmers and miners have different views on using fracking to mine coal seam gas?
3. Evaluate the most appropriate approach for Australia to take regarding:
   a. carbon capture and storage
   b. fracking.
4. Justify the recommendations you made in question 3.

① Carbon dioxide can be pumped into abandoned coal mines. As carbon dioxide is pumped in, methane gas can be pumped out for use as an energy source.

② Carbon dioxide can be pumped into geological formations, such as deep saline aquifers, where it can be safely stored.

③ Carbon dioxide can be pumped into oil fields in which output is dropping. This process can increase oil recovery output from the oil field.

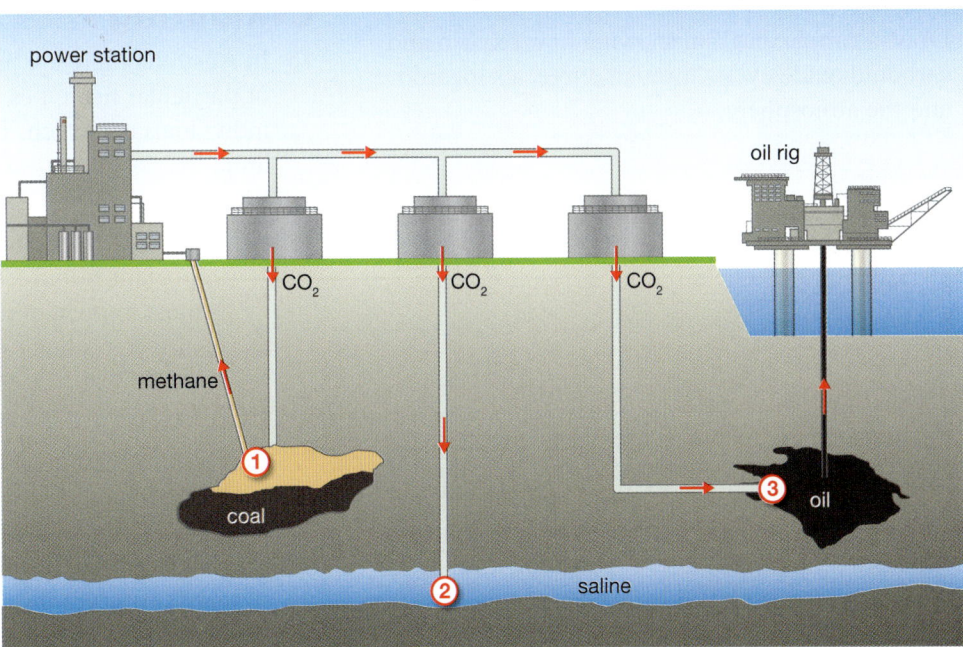

FIGURE 3.1.16 When coal is burnt, carbon dioxide is produced. Carbon dioxide can be used to extract methane gas, to help make oil fields more productive and it can be stored underground in a process called carbon capture.

CHAPTER 3 • EARTH RESOURCES   95

MODULE 3.1 Review questions

Remembering

1. Define the terms:
   a. resource
   b. sediment
   c. minerals.
2. Which term best describes each of the following?
   a. the thin layer of air around Earth
   b. the process by which plants make their own food
   c. the dropping of particles and sediment from air or water.
3. Name a product made from the following resources:
   a. sand
   b. wheat
   c. oil
   d. clay
   e. opium poppies
   f. bauxite.
4. What determines whether a resource is renewable or non-renewable?
5. List three examples of a:
   a. renewable resource
   b. non-renewable resource.
6. What is the percentage of oxygen, carbon dioxide and nitrogen in the atmosphere?
7. Draw a simple diagram showing how oxygen and carbon dioxide cycles through a tree, a kangaroo and the atmosphere.

Understanding

8. Group the following into renewable or non-renewable:
   a. pine trees
   b. water
   c. sand
   d. salmon.
9. Explain why the following are considered to be renewable resources:
   a. air
   b. farm animals.
10. Explain why the following resources are considered to be non-renewable:
    a. soils
    b. fossil fuels.
11. a. Outline how igneous rocks form.
    b. Some new igneous rock is being made every day yet rock is considered a non-renewable resource. Explain why.
12. The following resources are normally considered to be renewable. Explain how they could become non-renewable:
    a. trees in a forest
    b. crayfish or rock lobsters.

Applying

13. Use examples to explain how the following help to conserve resources:
    a. recycling
    b. public awareness campaigns
    c. increasing the price of resources.

Analysing

14. Compare:
    a. natural and made resources
    b. weathering and erosion
    c. igneous rocks and sedimentary rocks.

Evaluating

15. In Australia there are limits on the amount of particular fish types that fisheries and individuals can catch. This is often called the bag limit. Propose a reason why there is a bag limit for fishing.
16. a. Water and sunlight are both incredibly important resources. Which do you think is most important to life on Earth?
    b. Justify your choice.

Creating

17. Construct a plan involving five strategies you could use in your home to conserve natural resources. Include in your plan discussion of the resources that are being conserved and how your strategy conserves the resource.

MODULE 3.1 Practical investigations

• **STUDENT DESIGN** •

1 • Renewing air

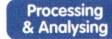

Purpose
To determine what a leaf needs to produce oxygen.

Timing
15 minutes + 45 minutes of occasional observation

Materials
- 4 × green leaves—each about the same size and from the same plant
- 100 mL distilled water
- 100 mL soda water
- 4 × 250 mL beakers
- stirring rod
- aluminium foil
- marker pen

Procedure
1. Pour about 100 mL of tap water into two of the beakers. Use the marker pen to label these beakers 'tap water'.
2. Pour about 100 mL of distilled water into another beaker. Label this beaker 'distilled water'.
3. Pour about 100 mL of soda water into the final beaker. Label this beaker 'soda water'.
4. Place one leaf in each beaker. Use the stirring rod to make sure the leaf is completely submerged (Figure 3.1.18).
5. Stir the 'soda water' beaker gently with the stirring rod to release any bubbles that might immediately appear.
6. Completely wrap one of the 'tap water' beakers in aluminium foil so no light can get in.
7. Place all four beakers in direct sunlight.
8. After roughly 45 minutes, unwrap the aluminium foil from the wrapped beaker.
9. Look to see if any bubbles form on the surface of the leaves in any of the beakers.

Results
Rank the beakers in order from the one with the most bubbles on the surface of its leaf to the one with the least bubbles.

Review
1. What substances do green leaves need to carry out photosynthesis?
2. List the substances that photosynthesis produces.
3. Bubbles in water are caused by a gas. What gas do you think caused the bubbles on the leaves?
4. Distilled water has no carbon dioxide dissolved in it. Tap water has some carbon dioxide while soda water has a lot. Compare the ranking of the beakers with the amount of carbon dioxide in each type of 'water'.
5. What evidence from this experiment suggests that photosynthesis requires each of the following for it to occur?
   a carbon dioxide
   b sunlight.

FIGURE 3.1.18

CHAPTER 3 • EARTH RESOURCES 97

MODULE 3.1 Practical investigations

• STUDENT DESIGN •

2 • Water-holding capacity of soil

This investigation is best performed in groups of 3 to 6.

Purpose
To compare the water-holding capacity of different soils.

Hypothesis
Which soil type do you think will be able to hold more water—sand, loam or clay? Before you go any further with this investigation, write a hypothesis in your workbook.

Timing 45 minutes

Materials
- 100 mL each of dry clay, loam and sand
- 3 plastic filter funnels
- retort stand and 3 clamps, or filter stands
- 3 × 100 mL beakers
- 50 mL measuring cylinder
- cotton wool
- rubber gloves

SAFETY
Do not inhale or touch the soil with bare hands—it can contain dangerous organisms (pathogens) and can also trigger asthma. Wear rubber gloves at all times and wash your hands afterwards.

Procedure
1. Set up the equipment as shown in Figure 3.1.19, with a cotton wool plug in the neck of each funnel. The plug should not be squashed down too tightly or it may block the funnel. The plug is only to stop soil particles escaping into the beaker.
2. Half fill each funnel with a different type of soil.
3. Pour 20 mL of water into each funnel and collect any water that comes through. If no water comes through a particular soil, add another 20 mL of water to that soil until some water runs through it.

Results
Record in a table how much water you added to each soil and how much water collected in the beaker.

Review
1. a Identify the soil which has the largest water-holding capacity and the soil that has the smallest capacity.
   b Justify your decision.
2. a Construct a conclusion for your investigation.
   b Assess whether your hypothesis was supported or not.
3. Outline some possible reasons why the soils had different water-holding capacities.
4. Soils described as 'well drained' allow much of the water that enters them to pass through them.
   a Based on this experiment, what characteristic of soils make them well drained?
   b Justify your answer.

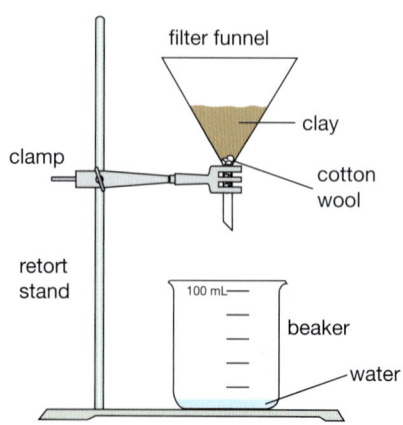
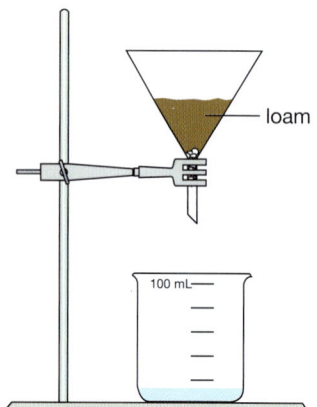
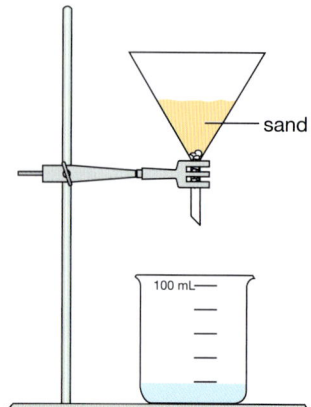

FIGURE 3.1.19

MODULE 3.1 Practical investigations

• STUDENT DESIGN •

3 • Erosion on a slope

Planning & Conducting *Evaluating*

Purpose
To test if the amount of soil erosion depends on the slope of the land over which the water runs.

Hypothesis
Which slope do you think will have the greatest erosion—a shallow or a steep slope? Before you go any further with this investigation, write a hypothesis in your workbook.

Timing 60 minutes

Materials
- 20 L dry sand
- 20 L dry loam
- plastic gutter
- bucket
- tap
- hand lens or microscope
- protractor
- wooden blocks or bricks
- rubber gloves

SAFETY
Do not inhale or touch the soil with bare hands—it can contain dangerous organisms (pathogens) and can also trigger asthma. Wear rubber gloves at all times and wash your hands afterwards.

Procedure
1. Design an investigation that will test how the angle of a slope affects the amount of soil erosion when water runs down it. Figure 3.1.20 shows water cascading down a hill. This fast flowing water will carry soil with it.
2. In your design you can use any equipment your teacher has provided or agreed to supply to you.
3. Decide in your group how you will proceed. Draw a diagram of the equipment you need and the procedure you will use to conduct your investigation.
4. Write your procedure in your workbook.
5. Before you start any practical work, assess your procedure. List any risks that your procedure might involve and what you might do to minimise those risks. See the Activity Book Science toolkit to assist you with developing a risk assessment.

Show your teacher your procedure and your assessment of its risks. If they approve, then collect all the required materials and start work.

Use the STEM and SDI template in your eBook to help you plan and carry out your investigation.

Results
Record your results and observations.

Review
1. Evaluate your procedure.
2. Outline how your procedure could have been improved.
3. a Construct a conclusion for your investigation.
   b Assess whether your hypothesis was supported or not.

FIGURE 3.1.20 Does the slope of the land affect the amount of soil erosion caused by water?

CHAPTER 3 • EARTH RESOURCES

MODULE 3.2 Energy resources

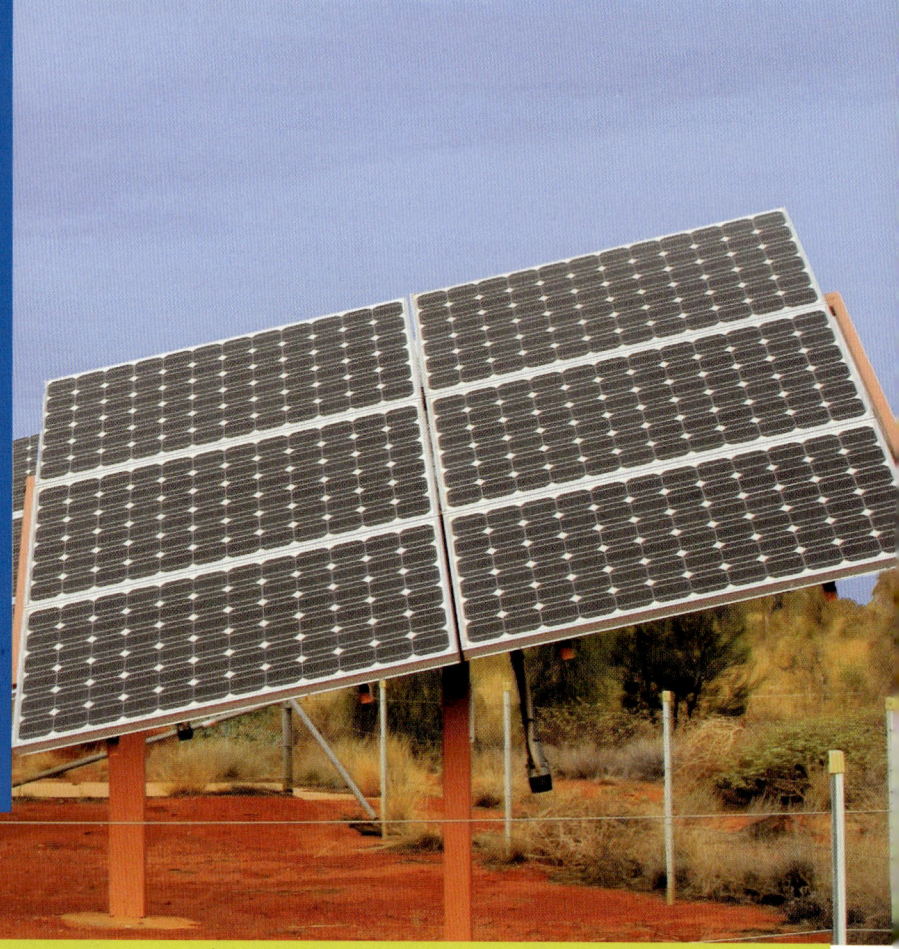

In Australia, most of our electricity comes from burning coal in power plants. Coal is a fossil fuel and all fossil fuels produce large amounts of the greenhouse gas carbon dioxide when burnt. This gives Australia one of the highest levels of greenhouse gas emissions per person in the world. Renewable resources such as wind, solar, tidal, hydroelectricity and biomass provide sustainable and clean alternatives.

STEM 4 fun

How to make a solar oven

PROBLEM

Can you make a solar oven that can stick two biscuits together by melting chocolate and marshmallows between them?

SUPPLIES   packet of digestive biscuits, thin pieces of chocolate, marshmallows, cardboard box, foil, glad wrap, foil tray, sticky tape, scissors, stick or skewer

PLAN AND DESIGN   Design the solution. What information do you need to solve the problem? Draw a diagram. Make a list of materials you will need and steps you will take.

CREATE   Follow your plan. Draw your solution to the problem.

IMPROVE   What works? What doesn't? How do you know it solves the problem? What could work better? Modify your design to make it better. Test it out.

REFLECTION

1. What field of science did you work in? Are there other fields where this activity applies?
2. In what career do these activities connect?
3. How did you use mathematics in this task?

Energy demand

Living things need energy to grow, reproduce and ultimately survive. Energy can be considered a resource too. Plants gain their energy from sunlight and animals gain their energy from the food they eat.

Humans need more than just the energy we get from our food. Early humans burnt fuels like wood and dried animal manure to keep warm, cook food and scare away wild animals. Our need for energy has risen dramatically since then. We now need energy to power televisions, computers, gaming consoles, washing machines, air conditioners, central heating systems, cars, aircraft and to recharge our smartphones. Lots of energy is required to manufacture (make) these appliances.

As you can see in Figure 3.2.1 Australia, the United States, Canada, the United Kingdom, Greece and Italy use much more energy per person than other less-developed parts of the world.

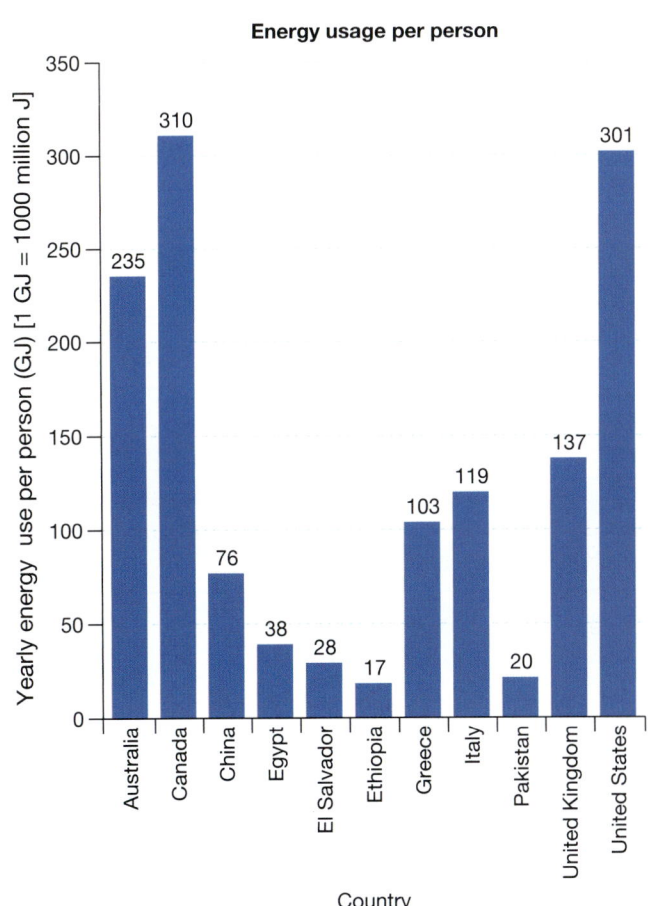

FIGURE 3.2.1 This column graph shows energy usage per person in 11 countries, including Australia.

Non-renewable energy sources

Like any resource, the sources where we get our energy from can be classified as non-renewable or renewable.

Fossil fuels and nuclear fuels are energy sources that either cannot be replaced or take many millions of years to do so. Once they are used, they are effectively gone forever.

Energy sources such as these are known as **non-renewable energy sources** (or simply non-renewables).

Fossil fuels

Oil, coal, gas and their products (such as petrol and diesel) are known as **fossil fuels**. Some 300 million years ago, the dead remains of prehistoric animals and plants were covered by layers of mud, sand and dirt. Pressure and heat below Earth's surface gradually transformed these remains into the different fossil fuels found today. The original source of energy for these fuels was the sunlight absorbed by the prehistoric plants. It was stored in their remains or in the remains of the animals that ate the plants.

Fossil fuels are excellent sources of energy for transport and for generating electricity.

In Australia, our main fossil fuel energy sources are:

- coal, burnt to produce steam that turns turbines in power plants to generate electricity
- petrol (a product of oil), burnt in car engines (Figure 3.2.2).

FIGURE 3.2.2 Most of our cars, trucks, motorbikes, aircraft and ships use fossil fuels for their energy.

CHAPTER 3 • EARTH RESOURCES **101**

- diesel (a heavy product of oil), burnt in the engines of trucks, tractors and some cars and trains
- aviation fuel (a light product of oil), burnt in jet and propeller engines in aircraft
- natural gas, burnt for cooking, central heating and hot water services
- LPG (liquefied petroleum gas), burnt for cooking and in some cars and buses.

Australia has lots of relatively cheap coal and also has reserves of oil and gas. We export coal and LNG (liquefied natural gas) to countries overseas. However, our need for petrol is greater than what we produce so we need to import large quantities of it.

Figure 3.2.3 shows that around 86% of Australia's electricity energy needs are obtained from fossil fuels. When burnt, all fossil fuels release large amounts of the greenhouse gas carbon dioxide. This increases the concentration of carbon dioxide in the atmosphere and is thought to contribute to climate change.

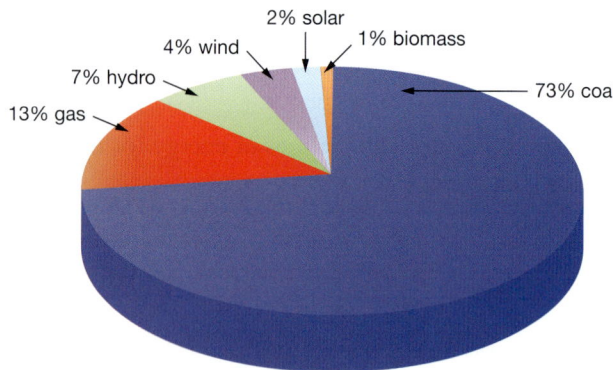

FIGURE 3.2.3 This pie chart clearly shows Australia's dependence on fossil fuels like coal.

Some new fossil fuels are currently being made in places like the sea bed but it will take millions of years to complete this process. For this reason, fossil fuels must be considered as non-renewable resources that will eventually run out.

SciFile

Nuclear Australia?

Australia has 31% of Earth's known uranium reserves and has three working uranium mines (Olympic Dam and Beverley in South Australia and Ranger in the Northern Territory). Australia has no nuclear power plants so almost all of this mined uranium is exported overseas. A very small amount is used in our only nuclear reactor at Lucas Heights in Sydney to produce radioisotopes. Radioisotopes are mainly used in medicine and engineering.

Nuclear fuels

About 6% of the world's energy comes from **nuclear fuels** such as uranium and plutonium. These are non-renewable sources of energy that are used as the main power source in many countries such as Japan, France and the USA. Small amounts of these fuels can produce large amounts of energy in a chain reaction in a process called nuclear fission. This chain reaction is carefully controlled in a nuclear power plant. The heat created is used to produce steam that turns turbines which then generate electricity. Nuclear power plants do not produce greenhouse gas emissions. However, the process of nuclear fission used produces wastes that remain radioactive for thousands of years. Long-term safe storage of these wastes remains a long-term problem.

Apart from their waste, nuclear power plants are usually safe. However, there have been at least 99 significant nuclear accidents since the first power plant started operating in 1952. The most devastating were at Three-mile Island (USA) in 1979, Chernobyl (Ukraine) in 1986 and Fukushima (Japan) in 2011. All released huge amounts of radioactivity that contaminated the districts around them. Over 70 000 people were evacuated from around Fukushima and more than 300 000 were evacuated from regions around Chernobyl. Both districts may remain unliveable for hundreds of years (Figure 3.2.4).

FIGURE 3.2.4 The city of Pripyat lies 3 km from Chernobyl. All 45 000 of its residents were evacuated two days after the accident. No-one is allowed to live in Pripyat now. These rusty dodgem cars were part its town fair.

Nuclear fuels like uranium were formed when the Earth formed and no more are being made. They are non-renewable resources.

Renewable energy sources

Renewable energy sources can be used over and over again. If we want to build an energy supply for the future and to limit greenhouse gas emissions then Australia needs to switch from fossil fuels to renewable sources. Power companies offer households the option to buy all or some of their electricity from a green power provider. You pay slightly more but you buy electricity that has been sourced from renewable energy.

Key sources of renewable energy are:

- moving water (hydroelectricity)
- biomass
- sunlight (solar energy)
- wind energy
- energy from the ocean (tidal)
- heat from within the Earth (geothermal energy).

A major problem with renewable energy sources is that their energy output is not continuous. Wind turbines, solar systems and wave generators rely upon the wind blowing, sun shining and waves breaking. Better methods need to be developed to store renewable energy when demand is low so that it can be used later when demand rises.

SciFile

Sugar rush

Most cars in Australia can run on E10 fuel. E10 is 90% normal petrol and 10% ethanol which is a biofuel usually made from sugar cane. By using E10, drivers use less petrol and the harmful chemicals like benzene and sulfur that are in it. Brazil produces vast crops of sugarcane and has long used ethanol made from sugarcane to power its cars. Its cars are essentially solar-powered!

Hydroelectricity

Gravity causes things to fall. For example, gravity causes water to spill from the dam in Figure 3.2.5, falling from a higher to lower level. The energy released in the fall can be used to turn turbines and generate electricity. This form of electricity is called **hydroelectricity**. The Snowy Mountains hydroelectric scheme in NSW is the largest hydroelectric power scheme in Australia. Hydroelectric schemes like this provide a renewable energy resource. However, they also change the way rivers flow and alter the environment.

FIGURE 3.2.5 The energy of falling water is used to turn turbines that generate electricity in a hydroelectric power station.

Biomass

Around 6% of the world's energy needs come from biomass. **Biomass** is material, such as dead plants, or animals and their wastes, from which energy can be obtained. These materials contain stored energy captured from the Sun. This energy can be released for use in many different ways:

- Heat energy is released when products such as wood, peat or dried manure (such as cow pats) are burnt.
- When organic wastes such as fruit peelings and grass clippings are put into landfill, they decompose, producing methane and carbon dioxide gases. This gas mixture, is called biogas. Biogas can be collected from landfill sites and the methane gas then used as a fuel. Biogas can also be produced from human sewage and animal wastes.

CHAPTER 3 • EARTH RESOURCES   **103**

- Biofuel is liquid fuel made from living things like plants or algae. For example, ethanol can be fermented from agricultural crops, such as sugarcane or corn, or from agricultural wastes, such as rice husks. Biodiesel fuel can be made from vegetable oils extracted from plant seeds, such as palm oil, sunflower, canola, soybean, sesame and linseed, or by harvesting algae.

AB 3.4 | Prac 1 p. 110

Solar energy

Light from the Sun is a valuable renewable resource. It can be used in many ways to provide energy:

- The direction a house faces (its orientation) can help to reduce the need for additional heating. For example, facing main windows towards the north allows warming sunlight into a house in winter. If this sunlight hits dark stone or concrete floors then its heat will be absorbed and stored, to be released later on at night.
- Sunlight can be used to heat water flowing through rooftop solar collectors to heat swimming pools and provide households with hot water and to heat swimming pools.
- **Solar cells** use materials called semiconductors to convert sunlight directly into electricity. Solar cells are useful for providing energy to remote areas and small-scale devices like garden lights. More commonly, they are arranged into panels (Figure 3.2.6). Solar panels are now commonly mounted onto the roofs of houses and factories to provide 'free' electricity. Any unused electricity is usually fed back into the city's electricity grid and the owner is paid for this extra electricity. Solar cells are expensive to produce but are now built with better efficiency (effectiveness) than ever before. This means that they produce more electricity and so quickly cover the cost of their production and installation. This makes them more affordable.
- Large-scale solar furnaces use vast arrays of mirrors to concentrate sunlight. Temperatures can reach 3500°C and this heat can then be used to generate electricity with no greenhouse gas emissions (Figure 3.2.7).

FIGURE 3.2.6 Solar panels are useful for providing electricity in remote areas.

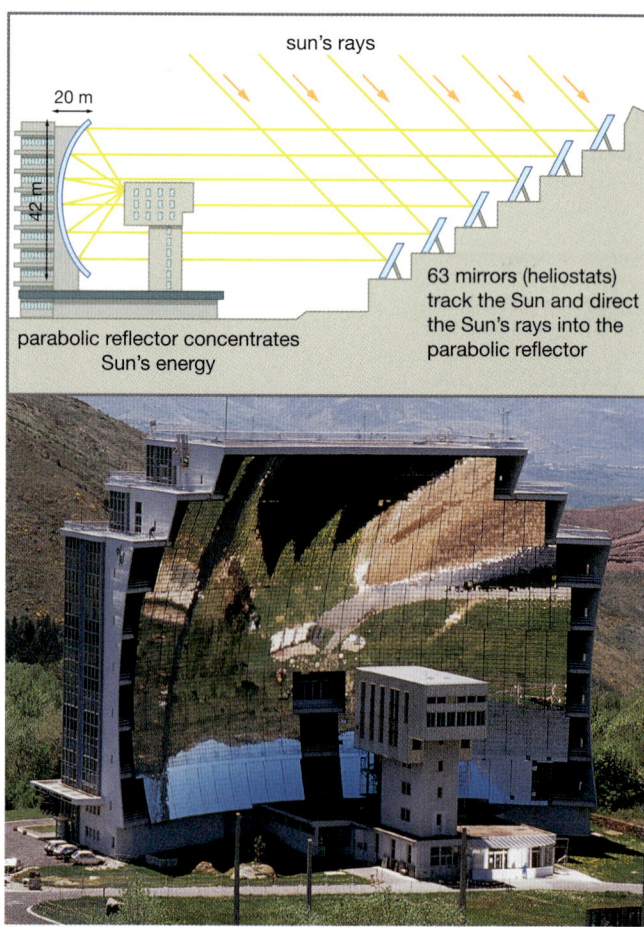

FIGURE 3.2.7 This solar furnace in France is used to generate electricity.

Wind energy

Wind energy is energy obtained by the movement of air by the wind. Wind energy has been used for centuries to power sailing ships and to turn windmills to grind grain. Windmills have long been used in Australia to pump water. Wind turbines are like large windmills but are used to generate electricity. South Australia generates approximately 27% of its electricity using 16 windfarms. You can see a wind farm in Figure 3.2.8. Nearby residents may object to wind farms because they produce some noise and birds may be injured by the blades as they spin.

Prac 2 p. 111

FIGURE 3.2.8 Wind farms release no greenhouse gases but they need to be located in areas with constant, strong wind.

Energy from the ocean

The ocean's waves and tides carry energy that can be converted into electricity. There are a number of different techniques that harness (collect) energy from the ocean. Although these techniques are generally expensive to set up, they offer a clean energy source once they are operating. Two methods of generating electricity from the tides use:
- oscillating wave columns, shown in Figure 3.2.9
- tidal barrages, shown in Figure 3.2.10.

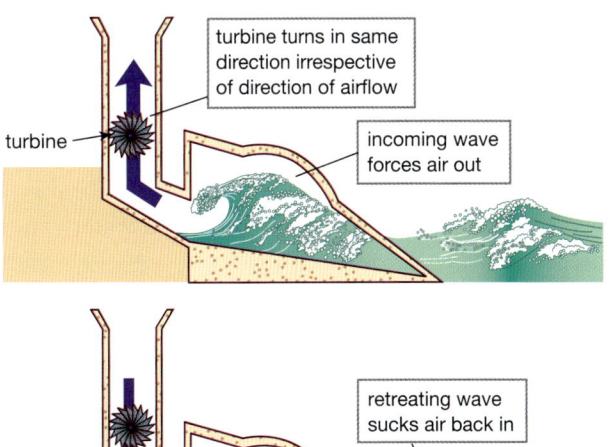

FIGURE 3.2.9 An oscillating wave column relies on the pressure of the waves to suck air in and out around a turbine to generate electricity.

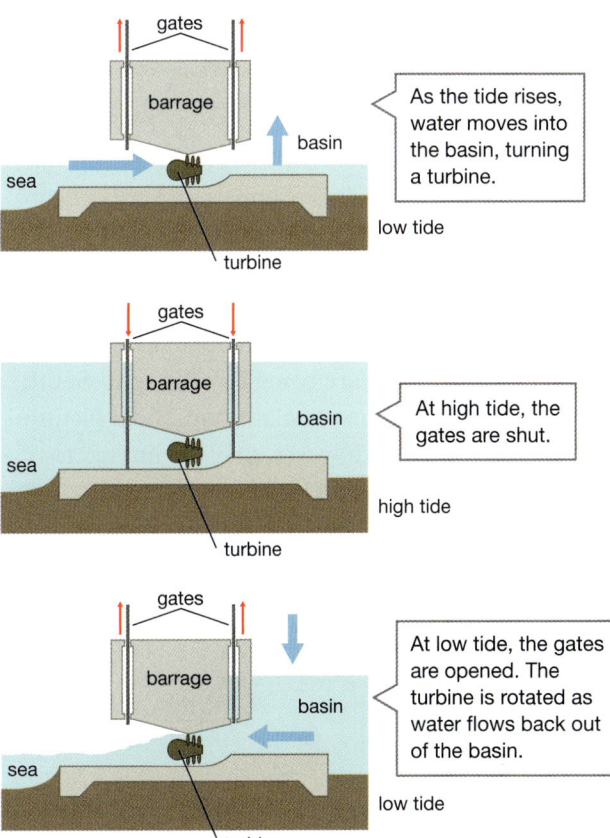

FIGURE 3.2.10 A tidal barrage uses a series of gates to control the tides flowing in and out of a large coastal river or basin of water.

CHAPTER 3 • EARTH RESOURCES **105**

Geothermal energy

Beneath Earth's crust lies molten magma (melted rock). In Iceland, Japan and New Zealand, this heat lies close to the surface and heated water may burst from the surface as a natural hot spring or geyser like the one shown in Figure 3.2.11. This source of heat is known as **geothermal energy**. This heated water can be used directly to generate electricity.

FIGURE 3.2.11 This steam is produced by geothermally heated water in Iceland.

Another way to use geothermal energy is to pump water underground through drilled channels and circulate it through the hot rock. The water is heated by the rock and is used to generate electricity when it returns to the surface. This process is shown in Figure 3.2.12. A geothermal power plant has been built at Birdsville, in Queensland, and plants are being developed in South Australia. Geothermal power plants tap into a plentiful natural energy source. However, they are limited to specific areas and can result in pollutant gases escaping from below Earth's surface.

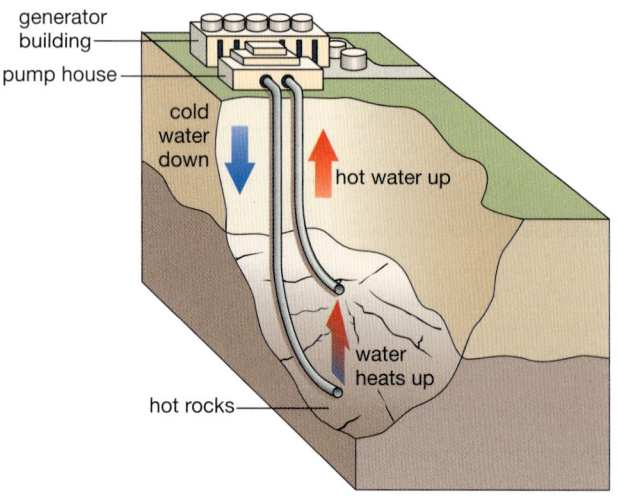

FIGURE 3.2.12 A geothermal power plant pumps cold water below the surface where it is naturally heated over hot rocks. It then returns to the surface.

Working with Science

RENEWABLE ENERGY ENGINEER

The growing need for clean, renewable sources of energy is creating many exciting job opportunities in the renewable energy area. Renewable energy engineers design and make renewable energy technology such as solar panels and wind turbines (Figure 3.2.13).

FIGURE 3.2.13 Solar panels in a solar energy field.

They use engineering principles to maximise the amount of energy that this technology can capture from renewable sources of energy (for example, wave action, solar and wind). This energy can then be used to provide electricity for our homes, transport and industry.

To become a renewable energy engineer, you will need to complete a Bachelor of Engineering, with subjects in renewable energy. Communication and problem solving skills are very important in this job. Renewable energy engineers work with a diverse range of people, such as engineers, architects, builders, members of the community and industry groups. The work of renewable energy engineers is helping us work toward a clean energy future and reducing climate change.

Review

1. What are three other jobs in the renewable energy sector?
2. How can people working in these jobs improve our quality of life and the health of our environment?

SCIENCE AS A HUMAN ENDEAVOUR

Use and influence of science

Citizen scientists

Our reliance on non-renewable sources of energy is putting enormous strain on Earth. Non-renewable resources, such as oil, coal and natural gas, can take thousands of years to form and cannot be replaced. Many of these non-renewable energy sources are also heavy polluters, contributing to air and water pollution and climate change. Right now, most of the world's energy comes from non-renewable sources. Australia is one of the biggest coal producers and exporters and most of our electricity comes from burning coal (Figure 3.2.14). This makes Australia one of the biggest carbon dioxide polluters in the world.

FIGURE 3.2.14 Most of Australia's electricity comes from burning coal.

To reduce pollution and avoid a global energy crisis, Australia needs to replace its use of non-renewable resources with clean, renewable sources of energy. Renewable resources are replenished quickly by natural processes and so are not likely to run out. Sunlight, wind, rain, waves and geothermal heat are all sources of renewable energy.

Many scientists are working toward developing efficient, affordable and sustainable sources of energy. However, professional scientists are not the only ones inventing solutions to global problems. Citizen scientists are people who don't work as scientists but volunteer their time to improving scientific research and knowledge. Citizen scientists are making important contributions to many areas of science. Cynthia Lam and Paul Kouris are two Australian citizen scientists who have invented devices that can generate electricity using clean, renewable sources of energy.

H2Pro

When she was a 17-year-old science student, Cynthia Lam (Figure 3.2.15) became concerned about the growing number of people who do not have access to clean water and electricity. This inspired her to create the H2Pro, a portable electricity generator and water purifier. The H2Pro uses a chemical reaction called photocatalysis. This reaction uses sunlight to activate a substance (such as titanium metal) that removes pollutants from water while generating electricity. Because no other power source is needed to run the H2Pro, it is a promising source of renewable energy and clean water for people living in remote locations.

FIGURE 3.2.15 Cynthia Lam with her invention the H2Pro.

SCIENCE AS A HUMAN ENDEAVOUR

Kouris Centri Turbine (KCT)

Paul Kouris (Figure 3.2.16) is a lawyer who first came up with the idea to build an electricity-generating water turbine 40 years ago! Over this time, he has tested many prototypes before finally developing the Kouris Centri Turbine (KCT). The KCT uses a vortex of water (water that is spinning around fast) to spin a turbine that then generates electricity. Paul's inspiration came when washing the dishes one day. When he pulled the plug from the sink, he saw the vortex of water in the drain and realised that it could be the power his turbine needed. The KCT can power one standard Australian home and about 20 African homes. The KCT shows great promise as an efficient source of renewable energy.

REVIEW

1. Why is it important that we replace non-renewable sources of energy with renewable sources of energy?
2. a Do you think that citizen scientists can play an important role in developing new renewable energy technology?
   b Justify your answer.
3. Why do you think it is important that citizens are involved in coming up with ways of reducing our use of non-renewable resources?
4. Imagine you could invent something to solve a local or global problem. What would it be?

FIGURE 3.2.16 Inventor of the Kouris Centri Turbine (KCT), Paul Kouris with his former business partner, Rohan Searle, and the KCT. The KCT uses a vortex of water and a turbine to generate electricity.

MODULE 3.2 Review questions

Remembering

1. Define the terms:
   a. biomass
   b. hydroelectricity.

2. What term best describes each of the following?
   a. fuels like coal, oil and gas
   b. using heat from deep underground.

3. What percentage of Australia's electricity is produced from each of the following?
   a. coal
   b. gas
   c. hydro schemes
   d. wind
   e. solar
   f. biomass.

4. List five examples of fossil fuels.

5. List five types of plant seeds that can be used to produce biodiesel fuel.

6. What are solar cells made of?

7. What percentage of South Australia's electricity is produced using wind?

8. Each situation a–h listed below describes different energy changes. Match the listed type of energy being used with the correct description in each case.

   hydroelectricity *tidal barrage*
   oscillating wave column *solar energy*
   biomass *geothermal energy*
   fossil fuel *wind energy*

   a. Wood is burnt in a camp oven to boil a kettle.
   b. Natural gas is used to heat a saucepan of pasta on a stove.
   c. Falling water turns turbines that generate electricity.
   d. Sunlight falling on a photovoltaic cell is directly converted into electricity.
   e. Turbines rotate as air flows through them and this is used to generate electricity.
   f. A turbine rotates in one direction and then the other as moving water sucks air past its blades.
   g. Water flows rapidly over a turbine, which is used to generate electricity.
   h. Water pumped below the surface of the Earth is heated and used to generate electricity.

Understanding

9. Outline how fossil fuels are formed.

10. Explain what happens if household solar panels produce more electricity than the house needs.

11. Outline five ways sunlight can be used as an energy source.

12. What are the advantages and disadvantages of the following?
    a. fossil fuels
    b. nuclear fuels.

Applying

13. a. Identify the source of energy that melted the chocolate and marshmallows in the STEM4fun activity on page 100.
    b. Use this evidence to explain why young children and animals should never be left in parked cars in summer.

Analysing

14. Compare the key advantages and disadvantages of two renewable energy sources.

15. Contrast:
    a. solar panels and solar furnaces
    b. hydroelectricity and energy from the ocean.

Evaluating

16. Suggest what is meant by the term 'green energy'.

17. Rank the countries in Figure 3.2.1 on page 101 from the one that uses the least energy per person to the one that uses the most.

18. Most modern cars turn off automatically when stopped at traffic lights. Suggest a reason why.

19. a. How far is Pripyat from Chernobyl?
    b. How many people were eventually evacuated from the surrounding districts?
    c. Pripyat was evacuated 2 days after the Chernobyl accident. Propose reasons why the incidence of cancer is higher than normal for those who were evacuated.

20. Some argue that Australia should take back nuclear waste produced overseas from our uranium. What do you think?

21. a. Which of the energy sources discussed in this module do you think are best suited to solve Australia's energy needs?
    b. Justify your choice(s).

MODULE 3.2 Practical investigations

SPARKlab alternative available for this activity. Manual data entry option.

1 • Energy from food (biomass)

The stored chemical energy in food can be used to produce biofuels. Food is also used to produce chemical energy inside your body.

Purpose
To burn a sample of food and calculate its energy content.

Timing 45 minutes

Materials
- food samples (such as Cheezels, crusty bread, Marie biscuit)
- Bunsen burner
- bench mat
- matches
- cork
- aluminium foil
- paper clip
- retort stand and clamp
- thermometer
- test-tube
- electronic balance
- small measuring cylinder

SAFETY
Do not use peanuts or any nut product because of possible food allergies.

Watch the burning food sample at all times.

Ensure that the room is well ventilated or complete this experiment inside a fume cupboard.

Procedure
1. Copy the results table below into your workbook. Alternatively, set up a spreadsheet with similar features.
2. Using the measuring cylinder, carefully measure 20 mL of water. Pour it into the test-tube.
3. Cover the cork with aluminium foil. Shape the paper clip like a hook and poke it into the cork.
4. Cut a small piece of your first food sample. Measure and record its mass in your table.
5. Set up the equipment as shown in Figure 3.2.17 so that the food sample will sit about 2 cm below the test-tube.
6. Measure and record the initial temperature of the water.
7. Use the Bunsen burner to set the food sample alight, and then carefully place the burning sample under the test-tube.
8. When the sample stops burning, measure the final temperature of the water and record this result.
9. Repeat the activity using two other food samples.

Results
1. Record all your measurements.
2. Calculate the change in water temperature by subtracting the initial temperature from the final temperature. Alternatively, programme your spreadsheet to calculate it for you.
3. For each sample, divide the change in water temperature by the mass of the sample.

Review
Compare the different samples and list them in order from the one that contains the most energy per gram to the one that has the least energy per gram.

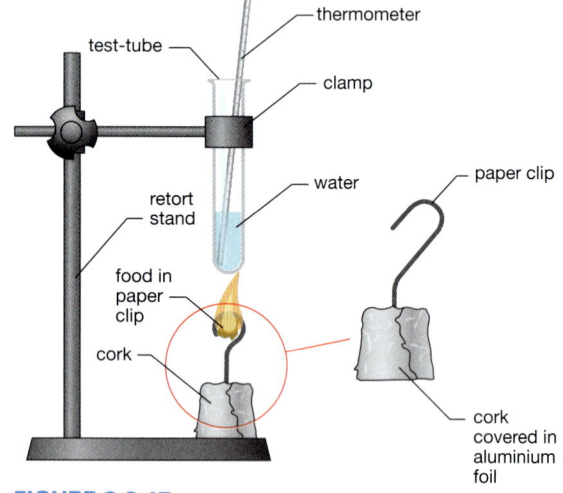

FIGURE 3.2.17

Results table

Food sample	Mass of sample (g)	Initial temperature of water (°C)	Final temperature of water (°C)	Change in water temperature (°C)	Change in water temperature ÷ mass of sample (°C g^{-1})
1					
2					

PEARSON SCIENCE 7 2ND EDITION

MODULE 3.2 Practical investigations

SPARKlab alternative available for this activity. Manual data entry option.

• STUDENT DESIGN •

2 • Harnessing the wind

Planning & Conducting
Evaluating

Purpose
To investigate the effect that wind direction has on wind power.

Hypothesis
Which direction of wind will make a turbine spin the fastest—will it be when the wind hits the turbine from straight in front or at an angle? Before you go any further in your investigation, write your hypothesis in your workbook.

Timing 60 minutes

Materials
- pedestal fan or a hairdryer
- pinwheel made from a sheet of light cardboard
- nail or drawing pin
- bamboo skewer
- protractor
- masking tape
- cardboard cylinder
- length of string
- paper clip

SAFETY
A Risk Assessment is required for this investigation. Do not operate the hairdryer near water or insert any materials inside the fan.

Procedure
1 Produce a cardboard pinwheel by following these instructions:
   i Enlarge the template of the pinwheel shown in Figure 3.2.18 and print it onto a sheet of paper or cardboard.
   ii Cut along the unbroken lines.
   iii Carefully bend each of the four corners towards the centre of the pinwheel.
   iv Secure the corners at the centre using a nail or drawing pin.
   v Press the nail into the bamboo skewer.
2 Design an experiment to test the speed at which the turbine will spin when wind hits the turbine from directly in front or when it hits from an angle. Figure 3.2.19 may give you some ideas.
3 Write your procedure in your workbook.
4 Before you start any practical work, assess your procedure. Assess any risks that your procedure might involve and what you might do to minimise those risks. See the Activity Book Science toolkit to assist you with developing a risk assessment. Show your teacher your procedure and your assessment of its risks. If they approve, then collect all the required materials and start work.

Use the STEM and SDI template in your eBook to help you plan and carry out your investigation.

Results
Present your results in a table.

Review
1 Construct a conclusion for your investigation.
2 Assess whether your hypothesis was supported or not.

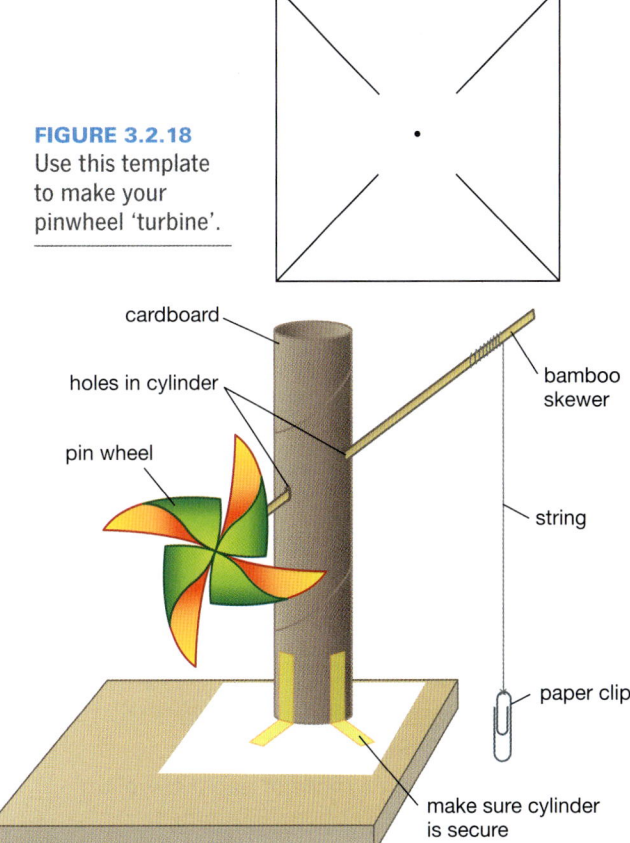

FIGURE 3.2.18 Use this template to make your pinwheel 'turbine'.

FIGURE 3.2.19 If the cylinder is unstable, tape it to a thick cardboard base so it is sturdy when standing upright.

CHAPTER 3 • EARTH RESOURCES

MODULE 3.3 The water cycle

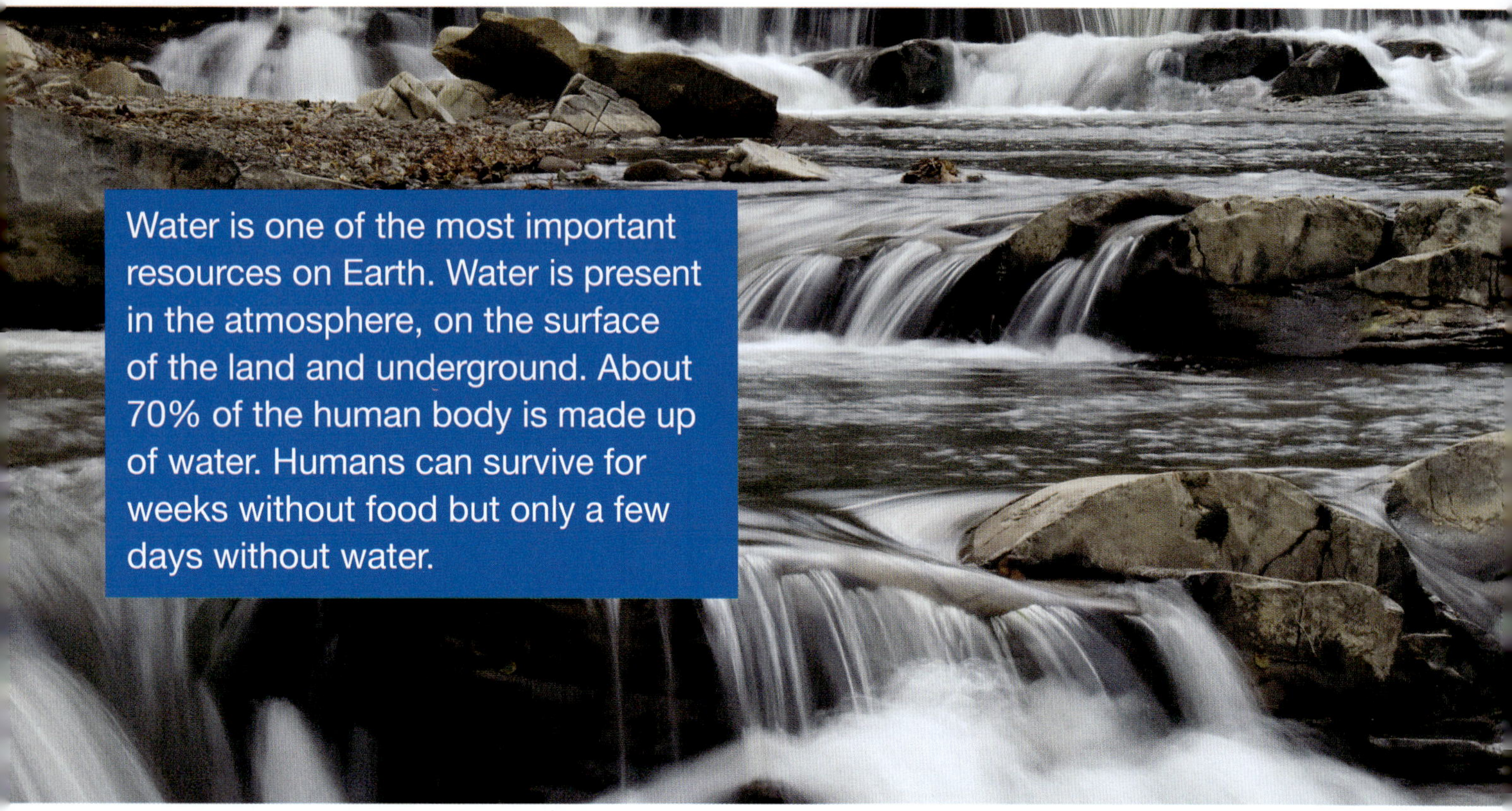

Water is one of the most important resources on Earth. Water is present in the atmosphere, on the surface of the land and underground. About 70% of the human body is made up of water. Humans can survive for weeks without food but only a few days without water.

science 4 fun

Dripping glass

Where does the water on the outside of the glass come from?

Collect this…
- cold water from the fridge
- glass
- sticky-tape or marker pen (optional)
- paper towel

Do this…
1. Half fill the glass with cold water.
2. Dry the outside of the glass with the paper towel.
3. Mark the level of the water with the sticky-tape or marker pen.
4. Place the glass on a piece of paper towel on a bench and leave for 5 to 10 minutes.

Record this…
1. Describe what happened.
2. Explain why you think this happened.

Water on Earth

Look at the map of the Earth in Figure 3.3.1. It shows that there is far more water than land. About 70% of Earth's surface is covered by water.

However, almost all (97.5%) of that water is in oceans, seas, bays and salt water lakes. This makes it unsuitable for drinking and most other uses.

FIGURE 3.3.1 Seventy per cent of Earth's surface is covered by water.

The other 2.5% is fresh water, but almost all of that is either trapped underground or frozen in glaciers and in the ice caps of the North and South poles, so it can't be used either! Only 0.01% of all water on Earth is renewable fresh water and is available for use. The tiny light blue spot in Figure 3.3.2 shows the very small proportion of water on Earth that is available for use by humans and other living things.

The water cycle

The water on Earth has been recycled over and over again since the planet was formed. This makes water a renewable resource.

The natural process of recycling water is known as the **water cycle** (Figure 3.3.3). As water moves through the cycle it changes state from liquid to gas and back to liquid again.

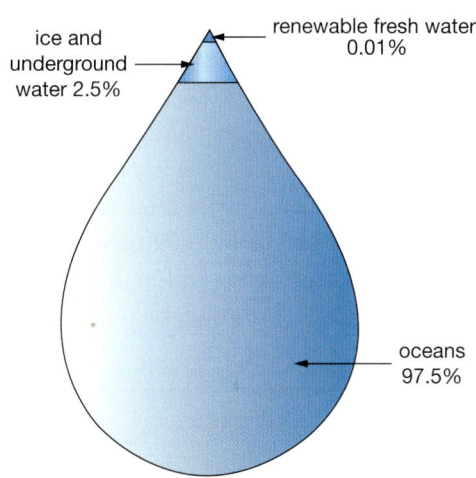

FIGURE 3.3.2 The amount of water available for our use is tiny compared to the total amount of water on Earth.

SciFile

Boiling water

Liquid water boils at 100°C.

At the top of Mt Everest there is less air pressure and so water boils at just 68°C.

Deep in the ocean, water pressure increases. Water near deep geothermal vents remains liquid at temperatures much higher than 100°C.

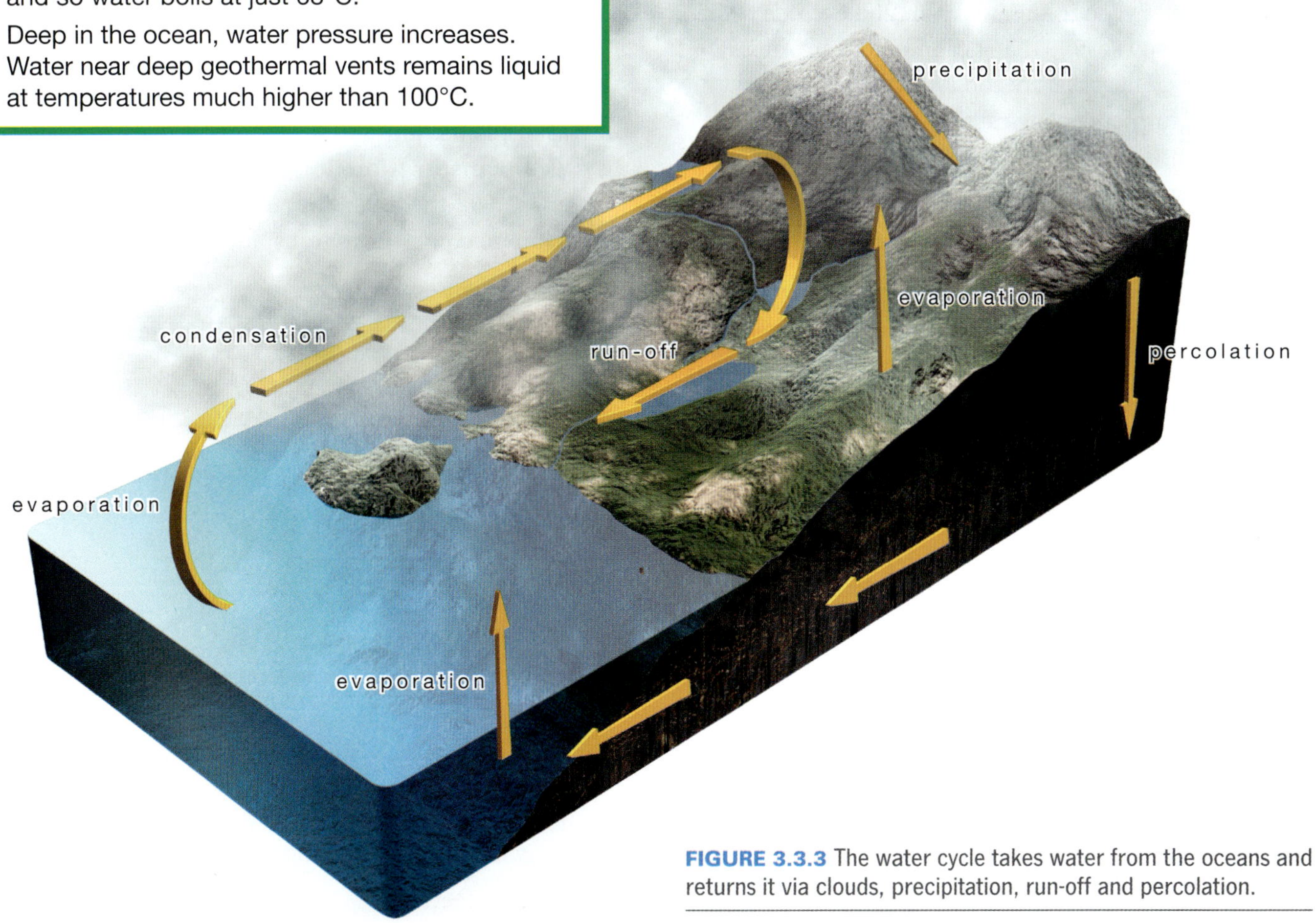

FIGURE 3.3.3 The water cycle takes water from the oceans and returns it via clouds, precipitation, run-off and percolation.

CHAPTER 3 • EARTH RESOURCES

Evaporation

Energy from the Sun causes water to evaporate from anything that is wet (Figure 3.3.4). The oceans are the largest bodies of water on Earth and roughly 86% of the evaporation in the water cycle happens there. Water in the seas, rivers and lakes evaporates too, as does the water in rainforests and even wet clothes hanging on the washing line. Liquid water on Earth has changed into water vapour in the atmosphere.

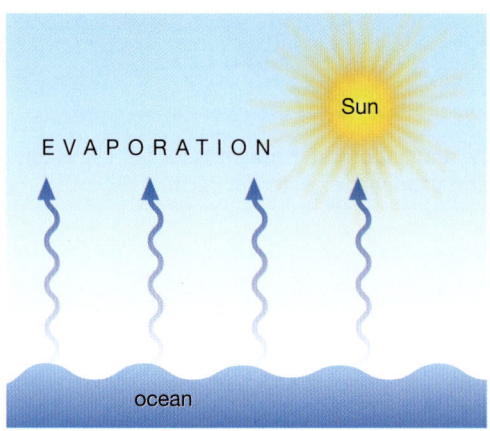

FIGURE 3.3.4 The process of water evaporating from a body of water

Condensation

As water vapour rises, it cools (Figure 3.3.5). Cool air holds less water vapour than warm air and eventually the air is so high and so cold that it cannot hold any more water vapour. The air has become **saturated** (full of water). Any further cooling causes water vapour in the air to condense, changing into tiny drops of liquid water. These tiny droplets form clouds.

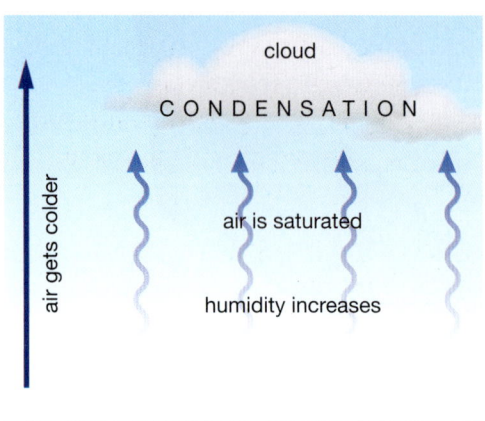

FIGURE 3.3.5 The process of water condensing in the atmosphere to form clouds

When the air cools further, the droplets of water combine to become larger and heavier droplets, which then fall back to Earth as **precipitation** (Figure 3.3.6). The precipitation may be in the form of liquid rain or it may be frozen, falling to Earth as snow or hail.

Run-off and percolation

Two things happen to the precipitation that falls on land.
- It may flow over the surface as **run-off**, moving back into rivers, lakes and streams, and eventually flow back to the oceans.
- It may soak down into the soil in a process called **percolation**.

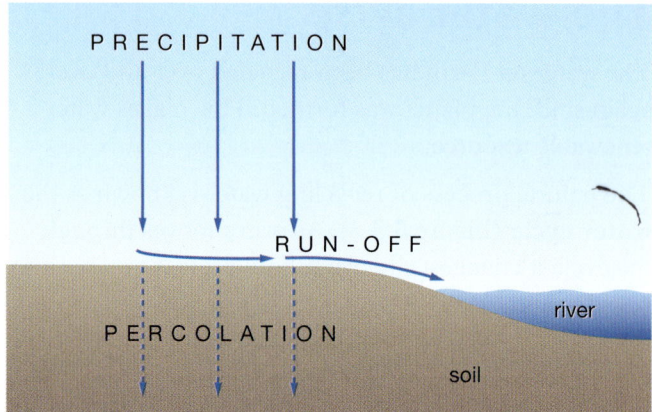

FIGURE 3.3.6 Precipitation either flows over Earth's surface as run-off or soaks into the ground through percolation.

Transpiration

Some of the water that percolates through the soil is taken up by the roots of plants. This water then moves up through the plant. The heat of the Sun causes some of this water to evaporate from the stems, flowers and leaves of plants. This evaporation of water from plants is called **transpiration**. It is shown in Figure 3.3.7. About 10% of the water vapour entering Earth's atmosphere comes from transpiration.

FIGURE 3.3.7 Transpiration is the evaporation of water from leaves and other parts of a plant. Transpiration returns water to the atmosphere.

Animals drink fresh water from rivers and lakes. This water is returned to the atmosphere as it evaporates from their bodies, or returned to the ground as urine.

Groundwater

Rainwater, rivers and dams are major sources of water for Australia. However, more than 20% of the water used in Australia each year comes from groundwater. **Groundwater** is water that exists underground. Most groundwater is not in underground lakes or rivers but is trapped in the tiny spaces between grains of sand or within pervious rocks. **Pervious rocks** are rocks that allow water to soak into them. They contain tiny spaces into which water can soak.

Sometimes the water within these pervious rocks can be extracted using a bore or well. The layer of rock is known then as an **aquifer**. Perth gets about 60% of its water from an aquifer.

The Great Artesian Basin

The Great Artesian Basin is one of the largest stores of groundwater in the world (Figure 3.3.8). About one-fifth of Australia sits on top of the Great Artesian Basin. Many millions of years ago there was an inland sea in Australia. Beneath the inland sea, rocks formed in alternating layers of pervious rock and impervious rock. **Impervious rock** does not allow water to soak into it. Movement of the land has exposed areas of the pervious rock, allowing water to soak into it and flow underground. The impervious rock above and below prevents the water from escaping. The result is a very large store of groundwater that forms the Great Artesian Basin. You can see its structure in Figure 3.3.9.

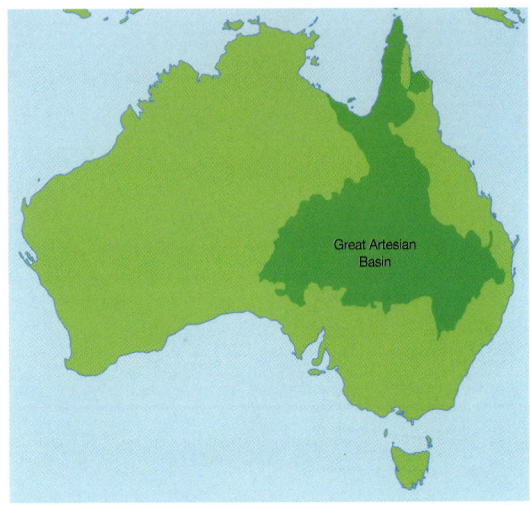

FIGURE 3.3.8 About one-fifth of Australia sits on top of the Great Artesian Basin.

It takes a very long time for the water to soak through the rock and into the aquifers. Some of the water in the Great Artesian Basin has been there for millions of years.

Factors affecting the water cycle

Some water particles might only take a few days to move through the water cycle, from ocean to atmosphere to land and back to ocean again. Other water particles might take thousands to millions of years because they percolated deep underground and are trapped in an aquifer like those found in the Great Artesian Basin. This water is still part of the cycle but cannot move onto a different stage in the cycle until it is carried up to the surface through a bore or well.

Many natural factors influence the rate at which water moves through the water cycle. They include the state the water exists in (solid, liquid or gas), air temperature and humidity, landscape, vegetation and the amount of available sunshine.

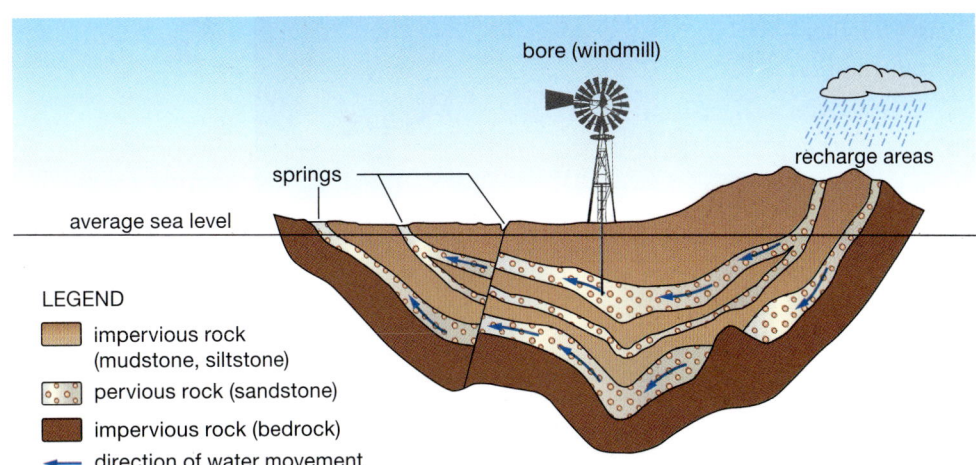

FIGURE 3.3.9 The Great Artesian Basin is made up of alternating layers of pervious and impervious rocks. The aquifers formed supply water to large areas of inland Australia.

FIGURE 3.3.10 The water in ice and snow is still part of the water cycle. However, it may be hundreds or thousands of years before the water is able to move on to the next stage of the cycle.

FIGURE 3.3.11 Plants have small openings called stomata. By opening and closing stomata, plants control the amount of water they lose through transpiration.

States of water

The ice and snow found at the North and South poles, in glaciers and on the top of high mountains is still part of the water cycle. However, this water is trapped in its frozen state and cannot move on to the next stage until it melts (Figure 3.3.10).

Plant roots only absorb liquid water from the soil. If the soil freezes in winter, then the plants stop taking up water. Many trees living in these conditions are deciduous, dropping their leaves in winter. Without leaves, trees lose very little water through transpiration. This way, the trees are able to survive until the weather warms and water in the soil melts.

Air temperature

The rate of evaporation from the ocean, sea and soil increases as air temperature increases. Higher temperatures also increase the rate of transpiration from plants.

Plants can slow transpiration down if they are losing water more quickly than they can take it in through their roots. Plants have special openings called **stomata** (singular: **stoma**) through which the water evaporates. You can see two stomata in Figure 3.3.11. Plants are able to close these openings if they are losing too much water. In this way plants are able to reduce the rate of transpiration and slow down the movement of water through the water cycle.

Humidity

Humidity is the amount of water vapour in the air. On a hot day with low humidity (little water vapour in the air), your sweat evaporates quickly off your skin, drying and cooling you. However, if the air is very humid (lots of water vapour in the air) then the sweat remains on your skin and you feel hot and sticky. This is what is happening in Figure 3.3.12.

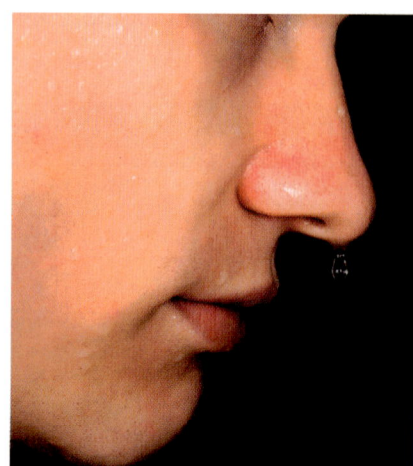

FIGURE 3.3.12 Your sweat doesn't evaporate when it is very humid because the air is already saturated with water vapour.

This happens because the rate of evaporation of water slows as humidity increases. Eventually, a point is reached where the air cannot hold any more water vapour. The air is then saturated. Evaporation and transpiration then stop.

Air movement

Air moving across a wet surface increases the rate of evaporation. Moving air carries away the saturated air, allowing evaporation and transpiration to continue. This is why turning on a fan makes you feel cooler and more comfortable on a hot, humid day: the breeze blows away the saturated air allowing your sweat to start evaporating again (Figure 3.3.13).

FIGURE 3.3.13 Air becomes saturated and evaporation is slow if there is no wind. Wind blows away moist air and so evaporation increases.

Landscape

Topography refers to the hills, valleys, rivers and other physical features of the landscape. The topography of an area affects run-off and percolation. Rain falling on smooth rock and steep slopes will quickly run over the surface and into streams and rivers. These streams and rivers will move the water quickly back into the ocean.

Where there are broken rock surfaces and areas of dense vegetation, run-off will be slower. Slower run-off allows more time for percolation to take place. Some soils like sand have many large spaces between the particles. Water can easily percolate into these soils and there is very little run-off (Figure 3.3.14). Other soils like clay have small particles that are closely packed together. It takes a long time for water to percolate through these soils and more of the water will flow over the surface as run-off.

FIGURE 3.3.14 Fraser Island in Queensland is the world's biggest island made of sand. Most rain percolates into the sand, but a few creeks carry run-off to the sea.

Hills and mountains experience more precipitation than low-lying areas. As air moves towards hills and mountains it rises to get over them. The rising air cools and the water vapour it holds condenses, resulting in clouds or precipitation. This means that clouds are often seen around mountains when there are otherwise few clouds around.

Vegetation

Vegetation describes the variety of plants that grow in a particular environment. Plants that grow well in one environment will not necessarily grow well in a different environment. For example, cacti and many Australian plants have spikes or small narrow leaves. These features reduce their rate of transpiration and help these plants conserve water so that they can survive in hot, dry climates. In contrast, plants growing in rainforests often have very large leaves. These plants receive plenty of water so a high rate of transpiration is not a problem.

Amount of sunshine

In nature the energy needed to evaporate water comes from the Sun. In parts of the world where there is a lot of sunshine, there is more evaporation than in areas with little sunshine and heavy cloud. This means that evaporation will be higher in deserts and on sunny plains than on permanently clouded mountaintops or in valleys that are always in the shadows.

CHAPTER 3 • EARTH RESOURCES   117

MODULE 3.3 Review questions

Remembering

1. Define the terms:
   a. aquifer
   b. topography
   c. vegetation.
2. What term best describes each of the following?
   a. rain, hail and snow
   b. air that cannot hold any more water vapour
   c. the holes in leaves that allow a plant to control its water loss.
3. a. How much of Earth's surface is covered in water?
   b. How much of this is saltwater and how much is fresh?
4. Draw a simple diagram that summarises the main stages of the water cycle.
5. List seven natural factors that influence the water cycle.
6. What part do animals play in the water cycle?
7. a. Which farmers can tap into water from the Great Artesian Basin?
   b. What would they use to do this?

Understanding

8. Explain why water is considered to be a resource that is in short supply when there is so much of it on Earth.
9. Explain why plants that grow in cold climates tend to lose their leaves during winter.
10. a. State three things that could happen to the rain that falls onto a field of grass.
    b. Predict the changes that would happen if:
       i. the soil of the field was very sandy
       ii. the soil was made of clay
       iii. the field was on a steep slope.
11. For the science4fun on page 112, predict what would happen to:
    a. the outside of the glass
    b. the level of water in the glass.

Applying

12. Identify the process that moves water from:
    a. rivers to the atmosphere
    b. atmosphere to clouds
    c. the atmosphere to freshwater lakes
    d. surface water to aquifers
    e. surface water to rivers.
13. Figure 3.3.15 shows a magnified view of soil in a particular area. It shows the relative size of the particles and the size of the spaces between them. Identify which layer would most likely represent:
    a. pervious rock
    b. impervious rock
    c. the layer that would store water as groundwater.

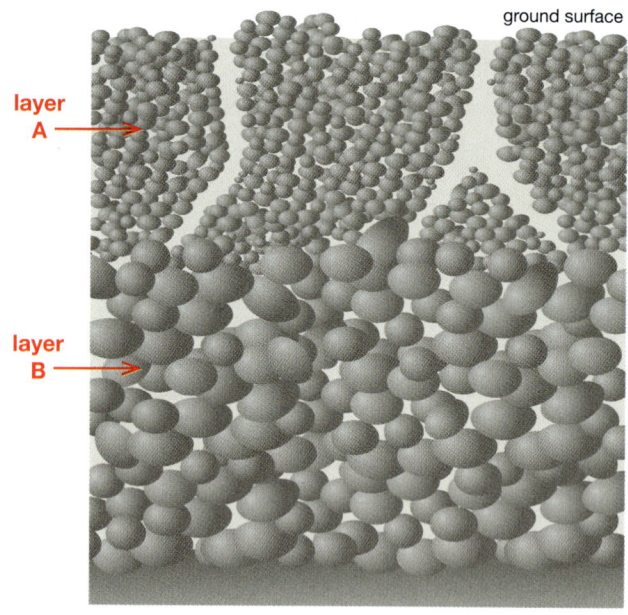

FIGURE 3.3.15

Analysing

14. Compare:
    a. evaporation and transpiration
    b. pervious and impervious rocks
    c. percolation and run-off.
15. Compare the formation of clouds in the atmosphere with the formation of water on the outside of a glass or can of cold soft drink.

MODULE 3.3 Review questions

16 Plants that grow in hot, dry environments are very different to those growing in hot and steamy rainforests (Figure 3.3.16). How are they different and how does this affect their transpiration?

FIGURE 3.3.16

Evaluating

17 a Figure 3.3.17 shows two different environments. Which would cause the greater rate of transpiration?
   b Justify your answer.

FIGURE 3.3.17

18 a Which set of clothes in Figure 3.3.18 would dry quicker?
   b Justify your answer.

FIGURE 3.3.18

19 To grow well, moss needs to be moist and avoid sunlight. Propose a reason why moss usually grows on the south side of trees in the southern hemisphere but on the north side of trees in the northern hemisphere.

Creating

20 Construct a diagram that demonstrates why cloud is more likely to form on the top of mountains than at their bases.

CHAPTER 3 • EARTH RESOURCES 119

MODULE 3.3 Practical investigations

1 • Model of the water cycle

Purpose
To model the water cycle.

Timing 30 minutes

Materials
- crushed ice (1 small handful)
- water at room temperature (about 50 mL)
- stopwatch
- 500 mL beaker
- clear plastic film
- small plastic bag
- tape (optional)

Procedure
1. Set up the equipment as shown in Figure 3.3.19.
2. Observe your model of the water cycle for about 20 minutes. Draw up a table and use this to record what happens in the first minute and after about 5 minutes and 10 minutes.

Results
1. Look at the underside of the plastic film (where the air in the beaker is in contact with the plastic). Describe the changes you observed:
   a. in the first minute of your investigation
   b. after about 5 minutes
   c. after about 10 minutes.
2. Use labelled diagrams to record any changes you observed.

Review
1. What part of the water cycle is represented by the water in the beaker?
2. a. Explain what was happening to the water in the beaker.
   b. What process in the water cycle does this represent?
3. a. Explain what was happening to the air in the beaker when it was in contact with the plastic film.
   b. What process in the water cycle does this represent?
4. How was precipitation represented in this model?
5. The equipment used in this investigation is shown in three dimensions (3D) (Figure 3.3.19). Construct a scientific diagram that shows it in two dimensions (2D).

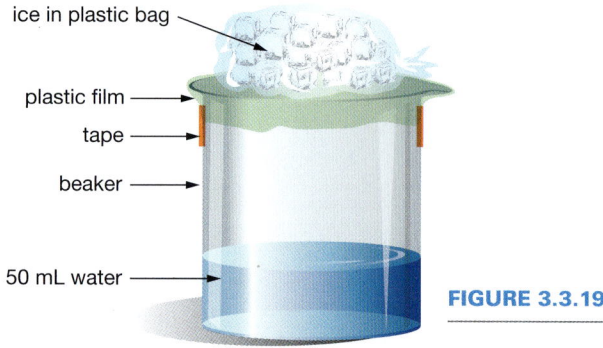

FIGURE 3.3.19

2 • Run off or soak in?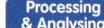

Purpose
To observe the percolation of water through different soils.

Hypothesis
Which soil do you think will allow the water to percolate into it the quickest—gravel, sand or clay? Before you go any further with this investigation, write a hypothesis in your workbook.

Timing 30 minutes

Materials
- approximately 140 mL each of very fine gravel, sand and clay soil
- 300 mL water
- 3 × 250 mL beakers
- 100 mL measuring cylinder
- marker pen and stopwatch

Procedure
1. Use the marker pen to label the three beakers: *gravel*, *sand* and *clay* (Figure 3.3.20).

FIGURE 3.3.20

MODULE 3.3 Practical investigations

2 Pour gravel into the 'gravel' beaker and sand into the 'sand' beaker until both are half full. Gently tap the side of both beakers to settle the contents. Add more gravel and sand if necessary.

3 Add some clay soil to the 'clay' beaker and push it down firmly. Add more clay and push it down again. Repeat this process until the beaker is half full.

4 Measure 100 mL of water and pour it into the top of the 'gravel' beaker. Pour it over the whole surface, not just in one place. Repeat for the 'sand' beaker and the 'clay' beaker.

5 Observe what happens in each beaker over the next 5 minutes.

Results
In your workbook, record:
- the way the water percolates through the gravel, sand and clay
- whether any water lay on top of any of the substances after 5 minutes.

Review
1 Why was it necessary to push the clay soil down firmly instead of just tapping the side of the beaker?
2 Which material did water percolate through:
 a the fastest?
 b the slowest?
3 Explain why water percolates through different substances at different rates.
4 a Identify the material from which run-off is most likely to occur.
 b Justify your choice.
5 a Construct a conclusion for your investigation.
 b Assess whether your hypothesis was supported or not.

• STUDENT DESIGN •

3 • Measuring evaporation

Purpose
To test the effect of sunshine on the rate of evaporation.

Hypothesis
Which do you think will evaporate faster—water in the sun or water in the shade? Before you go any further with this investigation, write a hypothesis in your workbook.

Timing 90 minutes
Materials
- water
- 2 shallow containers of the same size, material and depth, such as rectangular takeaway food containers
- ruler
- electronic balance (or kitchen scales that measure in 1 g intervals)
- marker pen

SAFETY
A Risk Assessment is required for this investigation.

Procedure
1 As a group, identify variables that might affect your investigation and design a way to control them.
2 Decide how your group is going to:
 - measure the amount of evaporation
 - measure or calculate how fast it is happening (its rate)
 - record your results.
3 Before you start any practical work, assess your procedure. List any risks that your procedure might involve and what you will do to minimise those risks. See the Activity Book Science toolkit to assist you with developing a risk assessment. Show your teacher your procedure and your assessment of its risks. If they approve, then collect the required materials and start work.

Use the STEM and SDI template in your eBook to help you plan and carry out your investigation.

CHAPTER 3 • EARTH RESOURCES 121

MODULE 3.3 Practical investigations

Review

1. a Calculate the amount of water lost from each container.
   b Compare the amount of water lost.
2. How did your results compare with the results from other groups?
3. Identify any factors that you were not able to control that might have affected your results.
4. a Construct a conclusion on the effect of sun and shade on the rate of evaporation.
   b Assess whether your hypothesis was supported or not.

MODULE 3.3 Practical investigations

Using less water at home

Background

El Niño refers to a major shift in weather patterns across the Pacific. It can last several months or up to a year. El Niño (meaning 'little boy' in Spanish) can lead to a drought in Australia. According to the Bureau of Meteorology the 2016 El Niño event was one of the three most significant El Niño events over the past 50 years. El Niño events result in reduced rainfall in Victoria which in turn reduces the amount of available water to fill dams. Fresh water from the Wonthaggi Desalination Plant (Figure 3.3.21) is used when rainfall cannot satisfy all of Victoria's water needs.

However, there is a good reason why Victoria should never use the plant unless absolutely necessary. The Victorian State Government has stated that powering the Wonthaggi Desalination Plant could use up to 90 MW of electricity per year. Although this provides the state with plenty of water, it also releases greenhouse gases from generating the electricity needed to run it. So saving water minimises the need for the plant and reduces greenhouse gases being emitted.

Problem

Design a water management system for a domestic house that limits the amount of water that the house draws from the central dam or desalination plant.

FIGURE 3.3.21 Wonthaggi Desalination Plant in Victoria

MODULE 3.4 Water management

In nature plants and animals get water from rain, rivers and natural stores such as lakes. In modern society, water is needed for cities, industry and agriculture. To meet these needs, water resources have to be managed differently. This management changes the movement of water through the water cycle.

science 4 fun

Ants and water
Can ants help locate a water source?

Collect this…
- shallow container for water

Do this…
1. Observe ants and note their behaviour.
2. Fill the container with water.
3. Place it on a path or on the grass in a partially shaded part of the garden close to the area you observed the ants.
4. Leave the container undisturbed for about an hour. Then observe the ants and note their behaviour.

Record this…
1. Describe any change in the behaviour of ants in the area.
2. Explain why this happened.

Storing water

Australia is the driest permanently inhabited continent. Rain may not fall as often as it is needed or when it is needed.

Water tanks

Tanks are a simple way of storing water collected from the roofs of buildings. For those living in the bush, tanks are often the only source of water for drinking and washing. In the cities, tanks are often used to water the garden or to flush the toilet, particularly during droughts when there are harsh water restrictions. Tanks do not affect the water cycle significantly since they only collect rain falling on the roof—the rest of the water still falls onto the Earth's surface, to percolate into the soil or run off into local rivers.

Dams and reservoirs

Another way of storing water is to build a dam wall across a gully, creek or river, holding back the running water to form a reservoir.

Most farms in Australia have small dams. The water collected is used for cattle and sheep to drink and may be used to water crops. Larger reservoirs are located near large town and cities to collect water for immediate use and to store it for the future. For example, the Wivenhoe Dam provides most of Brisbane's water. You can see it in Figure 3.4.1.

All dams interrupt the water cycle because water stored in them does not flow down the river and into the ocean. Water from the surface of the dam evaporates and is returned to the water cycle, but water deep in the dam may not be available for evaporation for a very long time.

FIGURE 3.4.1 Large dams are needed to collect enough water for the needs of cities. Brisbane gets most of its water from the nearby Wivenhoe Dam.

Dam floods!

In 2011 the Wivenhoe Dam was nearly filled to the brim with floodwater. Continuing torrential rains meant that the reservoir needed to hold more water than its size allowed. To enable the reservoir to receive this excess water the dam was opened. This released water into the Brisbane River, causing the river to rise up to 10 m and the flooding of nearly 2000 homes and much of central Brisbane.

Irrigation

Most of the farm crops grown in Australia have been introduced here from other parts of the world. This means that the wheat, cotton, rice, fruit and vegetables we grow do not have characteristics that allow them to grow with limited water. These crops need continuous supplies of water and farmers provide this water through irrigation. **Irrigation** is used in agriculture to provide water to crops using pumps, pipes and ditches.

There are three ways farmers commonly irrigate their land:
- spray irrigation
- flood irrigation
- drip irrigation.

Spray irrigation

In **spray irrigation**, a pump forces small droplets of water into the air. This is shown in Figure 3.4.2. The water falls on the soil and percolates down to the roots of plants. The water then moves up through the plant and is eventually lost back to the atmosphere through transpiration.

Spray irrigation is different to rain. When it rains, there are usually clouds in the sky and the air is very humid. This reduces the rate of evaporation from the soil and the plant leaves the water falls on. Spray irrigators can be used in bright sunshine. When this happens the tiny droplets of water quickly evaporate in the hot, dry air. In this way, a lot of the water that would normally percolate into the soil evaporates into the atmosphere instead and is wasted.

FIGURE 3.4.2 Spray irrigation

Flood irrigation

In **flood irrigation**, water is released into channels between the crop plants (Figure 3.4.3). The soil is soaked and water percolates down to the plant roots. However, the water will evaporate quickly if the soil and irrigation channels are not shaded.

FIGURE 3.4.3 Flood irrigation

Drip irrigation

Drip irrigation is a more modern method that either uses plastic tubing with regularly-spaced holes or mesh-like hoses which drip or ooze water directly into the soil (Figure 3.4.4). This way, evaporation is kept to a minimum. Less water is wasted and therefore less water is used, making it a useful irrigation method for hot areas. Drip irrigation is commonly used to water grape vines, strawberries, plants grown in containers and orchards of stone fruit trees (such as peaches and apricots). Home gardeners often use drip irrigation to water their own gardens.

FIGURE 3.4.4 Drip irrigation

Moving water around

Dams and pipes can be used to move water from an area where there is plenty of water to areas where there is not enough. For example, the Snowy Mountains Scheme uses 16 major dams and 225 km of pipes to shift water from the Snowy River to the dry inland of New South Wales (Figure 3.4.5). Building began in 1949 and was completed in 1974. Its location can be seen in Figure 3.4.6. The Snowy River is fed by melting snow and rain in the Snowy Mountains. This water once flowed quickly to the ocean but the scheme diverts (shifts) the water instead into the Murrumbidgee River. From there, the water is used to irrigate farms in the Murrumbidgee Irrigation Area. This has allowed the district to become one of the main wine and food producers in Australia.

FIGURE 3.4.5 Some of the 225 km of pipes in the Snowy Mountains Scheme

FIGURE 3.4.6 Map showing the locations of the Snowy Mountains Scheme and the Murrumbidgee Irrigation Area

CHAPTER 3 • EARTH RESOURCES **125**

The water used for irrigation is returned to the atmosphere through transpiration and evaporation from the soil. Irrigation water also percolates through the soil into the groundwater. Eventually, the excess flows via the Murrumbidgee and Murray Rivers into the ocean south of Adelaide.

After 1974, the Snowy River carried only 1% of its original water flows. Without regular, seasonal flooding, ecosystems along the riverbanks have changed and the river itself has become clogged with vegetation and sediments. In 2000, the NSW and Victorian state governments agreed to release more water down the Snowy. The aim was to increase it to 21% of its original flow, rising eventually to 28%. However, flows are still only 4% of what they were originally.

Stormwater

In nature, rain landing on soil percolates about 15 mm into the ground before there is any runoff. In cities, pervious soil is covered by impervious surfaces such as concrete and bitumen. Water that falls on roofs, roads and footpaths runs off immediately. This water is known as **stormwater**. It flows into stormwater drains like the one in Figure 3.4.7 then out to the ocean.

FIGURE 3.4.7 Water flowing off roofs, streets and other impervious city surfaces goes straight into stormwater drains. From there it goes directly to rivers and the ocean.

Using stormwater

In many parts of Australia, attempts are being made to use stormwater.

In some new suburbs, stormwater is being collected in tanks and pits. Harmful substances are removed and the water is used to irrigate parkland and sports fields and to water street trees.

Other examples where stormwater is used are described below:

- Water flowing into Blackman's Swamp Creek in Orange, NSW, is collected and piped to a nearby dam. This water is then added to the city's water supply.
- Baldwin Swamp in Bundaberg, Queensland, is a natural wetland that is a habitat for a wide variety of birds and animals. It is shown in Figure 3.4.8. Three drainage channels carry stormwater run-off from the city into the swamp. Rubbish is collected by council workers and pollutants are absorbed in the wetland. This leaves cleaner water to flow from the swamp into the Burnett River and Pacific Ocean.
- Albert Park Lake in Melbourne is an artificial lake that needs to be topped up to ensure that it can be used for sailing and rowing. For most of lake's history, it has been topped up with drinking water. This used up to 200 million litres of drinking water each year. After 2005, stormwater has been used instead. Pollution control ponds ensure that the stormwater is clean enough for people to use the lake.

FIGURE 3.4.8 Baldwin Swamp in Bundaberg, Queensland, is a natural wetland that uses stormwater. The swamp is home to over 150 species of birds and many other animals.

Rain gardens

Rain gardens are a small-scale way of dealing with stormwater. Figure 3.4.9 shows how rain gardens slow down the flow of stormwater and clean pollution from it before it enters creeks and rivers.

Stormwater is channelled into the rain garden bed. In the garden bed there is a layer of sand that filters the water. The filtered water is similar in quality to the water in undisturbed streams. It is not drinking quality but it is suitable for irrigation.

Rain gardens can be landscaped into suburban gardens as well as city parks, school yards and large nature strips that divide freeways. Figure 3.4.10 shows a working rain garden.

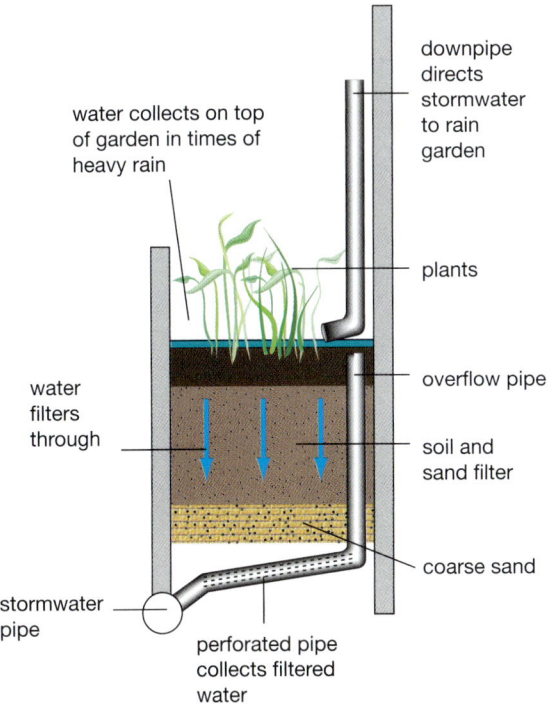

FIGURE 3.4.9 A rain garden cleans stormwater before it enters creeks and rivers.

FIGURE 3.4.10 Rain gardens are attractive and filter stormwater.

Changing vegetation

Changes in vegetation affect the water cycle of the area. Planting more trees means that more water will move out of the soil and more water will be transpired into the air. Low-growing shrubs and grasses reduce the amount of evaporation from the soil surface.

When trees are cut down and replaced with grass or bare soil, the movement of water over the land surface is changed. Trees, shrubs and long grass slow the rate at which water can flow over the ground. This means that there is more time for the water to soak into the soil.

Without vegetation, water moves quickly over bare ground and often carries large amounts of soil. This eroded soil is carried with the water as it flows into streams and rivers. Figure 3.4.11 shows the effect of this fast-moving water.

Prac 1 p. 131   Prac 2 p. 132

FIGURE 3.4.11 These channels in the soil have been created by erosion of soil by fast-flowing water.

AB 3.7

SciFile

Moving sand dunes

Sand dunes have no vegetation to hold them together, and so there is nothing to stop the wind from blowing the sand away. Old dunes can be destroyed and new dunes form in a continual cycle of erosion and deposition.

CHAPTER 3 • EARTH RESOURCES   **127**

SCIENCE AS A HUMAN ENDEAVOUR
Use and influence of science

Indigenous water use

Indigenous Australians are able to live in some of the driest parts of Australia. They can do this because they are able to use their observations to find sources of water. In the middle of a dry area, a ghost gum like the one in Figure 3.4.12 indicates where there is underground water. Ant trails also lead to underground water and dingo tracks lead to rock pools and waterholes.

FIGURE 3.4.12 The presence of a ghost gum indicates that water is nearby.

Traditional methods used by Indigenous Australians to obtain water include creating shallow wells and digging tunnels to reach water deeper underground. The mouth of the well or tunnel is covered to reduce evaporation and to prevent animals from drinking the water and polluting it.

In the past, the location of water sources determined the routes Indigenous Australians used to travel around the country. Vegetation, such as trees, often indicate the presence of water (Figure 3.4.12). Markings such as those in Figure 3.4.13 were made on the rocks to indicate where water could be found. In this way they were sure to have reliable sources of water.

FIGURE 3.4.13 These circular rock markings show that a number of waterholes are nearby.

SCIENCE AS A HUMAN ENDEAVOUR

FIGURE 3.4.14 Springs from the aquifers of the Great Artesian Basin were used by Indigenous Australians, native animals and later as watering points for cattle.

There are many **springs** where water from the Great Artesian Basin comes to the surface. One is shown in Figure 3.4.14. These springs were a major source of water for Indigenous Australians and for native plants and animals. Some European explorers and early settlers learned how to find water from the Indigenous people and so they too could get their water from springs.

In general, non-Indigenous Australians see water as a resource to be used. Indigenous Australians also view water as essential for survival but it is also an important part of their culture. There are many ceremonies, songs and customs which have been followed for thousands of years to make sure that rains come to keep the land, plants and animals healthy.

Early explorers were glad of the help Indigenous Australians could give them. However, Indigenous knowledge of land was usually not valued when decisions were being made about development of land and use of water. This is beginning to change as decision makers develop a respect for Indigenous knowledge. For example, in the Kimberley region of Western Australia the Karajarri people hold traditional knowledge of the wetlands.

Scientists studying the area for possible development found this knowledge to be very similar to their findings from fieldwork in the wetlands. However, the Karajarri described the information in a different way. Indigenous Australians are now involved in decision making relating to the use of water and any developments that may cause changes to water sources.

REVIEW

1. What are two observations Indigenous Australians used to help them find water sources?
2. Explain how Indigenous Australians protected underground water sources from pollution by animals.
3. What is different in the ways that Indigenous Australians and non-Indigenous Australians think about water?
4. Propose one reason for Indigenous knowledge now being part of decision-making about future developments that affect waterways.

MODULE 3.4 Review questions

Remembering

1. Define the terms:
   a. irrigation
   b. stormwater.
2. What term best describes each of the following types of irrigation?
   a. water sprayed out like rain
   b. water dripping out of a pipe.
3. State the:
   a. normal depth to which rain percolates into soil
   b. percentage of original water flow down the Snowy River now
   c. year in which the Snowy Mountain Scheme was completed.
4. What are the advantages of using tanks as water storage?
5. a. Explain why dams are built near large cities.
   b. Explain how a dam interrupts the water cycle.
6. At the end of winter the snow in the Snowy Mountains melts and the water flows into streams and rivers.
   a. What would have happened to that water before the Snowy Mountains Scheme was built?
   b. Describe what happens to the water from the Snowy Mountains now.
   c. What are the benefits of the Scheme?
   d. Describe problems the scheme has brought to the environment.
7. Describe two ways in which run-off from cities is being reduced.

Understanding

8. Water from rain gardens should not be used for drinking. Explain why.

Analysing

9. Compare the effect of drip irrigation, spray irrigation and flood irrigation by focusing on the effect they have on the water cycle.
10. Compare spray irrigation and a natural shower of rain.
11. Figure 3.4.15 represents an area where part of a forest has been cut down. Apply your understanding of the water cycle and use it to:
    a. explain how and why the humidity of the air at points A and B would be different
    b. explain how and why the rate of flow of water over the surface at points C and D would be different.

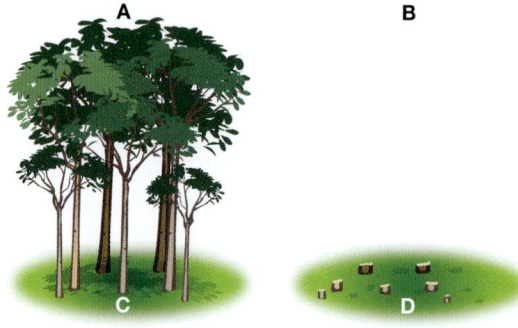

FIGURE 3.4.15

Evaluating

12. Imagine you are giving advice to an orchardist growing 1000 avocado trees in the Murrumbidgee Irrigation Area.
    a. Recommend what you think would be the best irrigation method to use.
    b. Justify your choice.
    c. Would your advice be different if the orchard is in the Ord River valley in Western Australia, where there is plenty of water and plenty of rain? Explain.
13. Seawater now reaches 7 kilometres further up the Snowy River than it did before the Snowy Mountain Scheme. Suggest a reason why.
14. Extra water is not released constantly down the Snowy River but is instead released in 'pulses', where a large quantity of water is released within a short time. Propose reasons why.

Creating

15. Imagine a city block in the middle of a large city such as Melbourne. Construct a diagram of the water cycle for that city block.

MODULE 3.4 Practical investigations

1 • Water from leaves

Planning & Conducting | Evaluating

Purpose
To extract water from leaves.

Hypothesis
Which leaves do you think will transpire and lose more water—leaves that are covered in hairspray or leaves that are not? Before you go any further with this investigation, write a hypothesis in your workbook.

Timing 24+ hours

Materials
- 2 × identical plastic bags approximately the size of an A4 piece of paper (make sure there are no holes in the bag)
- string
- access to trees with low branches
- marker pen
- 100 mL measuring cylinder
- hairspray

Procedure
1. Use the marker pen to write your team's name on the two plastic bags.
2. Select two twigs on your tree. Do NOT break the twig off but keep it on the tree.
3. Spray the top surfaces of the leaves on one twig with hairspray. Allow to dry.
4. Carefully slip a bag over each twig so that roughly the same numbers of leaves are enclosed in the bag (Figure 3.4.16).
5. Use the string to tie the bags on tightly.
6. Leave both bags in place for 24 hours.

Results
1. After 24 hours remove the bags from each twig. Be careful not to lose any of the water.
2. Carefully pour the water into the measuring cylinder.
3. Record the amount of water collected.

Review
1. Compare the water collected from each twig over 24 hours.
2. Compare your results with those of other groups.
3. For the unsprayed leaves, describe the changes in humidity that would occur during the 24 hours of the experiment.
4. What is the name of this process?
5. Why would this humidity condense overnight to form liquid water?
6. What is the name of the openings in the leaves of a plant and what are their purpose?
7. Predict what happened to these openings when the leaves were sprayed with hairspray.
8. Explain how this would affect the amount of water collected overnight.
9. a Construct a conclusion for your investigation.
   b Assess whether your hypothesis was supported or not.

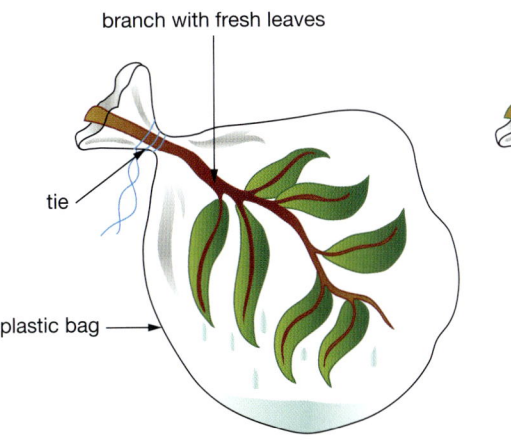 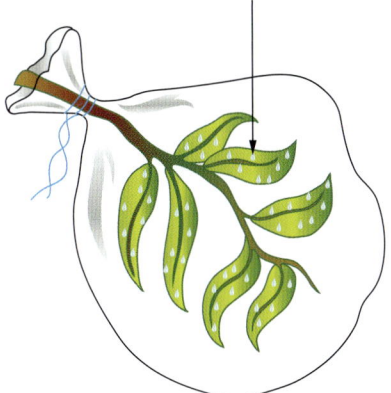

FIGURE 3.4.16

CHAPTER 3 • EARTH RESOURCES 131

MODULE 3.4 Practical investigations

• STUDENT DESIGN •

2 • More water from leaves

Purpose
To investigate factors affecting water loss from leaves.

Hypothesis
What factors do you think will affect the amount of water lost from leaves—amount of sunlight, type and number of leaves or some other factor? Before you go any further with your investigation, write a list of variables and how you think each one will affect the amount of water lost. Write a hypothesis for each variable in your workbook.

SAFETY
A Risk Assessment is required for this investigation.

Timing
45 minutes + observations over 24–48 hours

Materials
Materials as per Prac 1

Procedure
1. Before you start work, decide on which variable you are going to test. You might try:
   - leaves in the shade and in bright sunlight
   - old and young leaves
   - Australian native trees (such as eucalypts or melaleucas) and non-natives (such as camellias or roses)
   - green and variegated leaves
   - length of time for water collection.
2. Design an experiment that compares the amount of water lost from leaves when you change your chosen variable.
3. Revisit the hypothesis you wrote down earlier and make sure it covers the variable you are going to test. If not, then write a new hypothesis.
4. Write your procedure in your workbook.
5. Before you start any practical work, assess your procedure. List any risks that your procedure might involve and what you might do to minimise those risks. See the Activity Book Science toolkit to assist you with developing a risk assessment. Show your teacher your procedure and your assessment of its risks. If they approve, then collect all the required materials and start work.

Use the STEM and SDI template in your eBook to help you plan and carry out your investigation.

Hints
Make sure you only change one variable (such as sunlight). Keep all the other variables (such as type of plant and number of leaves) the same.

Results
Record your observations in your workbook.

Review
1. a. Create a conclusion for your investigation.
   b. Assess whether your hypothesis was supported or not.
2. a. Evaluate the procedure used in your experiment.
   b. What could you have done differently to improve the outcome?

FIGURE 3.4.17 Will leaves in sunlight or shade lose water faster?

CHAPTER 3 Chapter review

Remembering

1. What are two examples of each of the following?
   a. fossil fuels
   b. nuclear fuels
   c. renewable resources
   d. non-renewable resources
   e. devices that convert solar energy into electricity
   f. fuels made from biomass
   g. precipitation.
2. List ten energy-using devices in your home that probably did not exist 50 years ago.
3. What is the source of heat in water springing from a geyser?
4. What are three changes of state that water passes through in the water cycle?

Understanding

5. Explain the advantages of recycling metals instead of making them from natural resources.
6. Describe the effect that the ice sheets at the North and South poles have on the movement of water through the water cycle.
7. Figure 3.5.1 is a simplified diagram of the water cycle.
   a. Copy the diagram into your workbook.
   b. Modify the diagram by adding the names of the changes of state that are taking place.
   c. Predict places where water could stay for a long time before moving on.
   d. Predict places where the movement to the next part of the cycle could be fast.
8. Explain why the water we drink is recycled, even though it comes from dams or groundwater.

Applying

9. a. List the major sources of energy used in Australia to power appliances and for transportation.
   b. Predict what Australia's major energy sources might be in 50 years time.
10. Identify the energy being summarised below.
    a. moving air
    b. falling water
    c. waste food
    d. sunlight.
11. Identify the processes that are happening in the following examples.
    a. small particles of rock are carried away by the wind
    b. the formation of clouds
    c. the air is holding all the water vapour it can
    d. providing water to crops via ditches, pipes and pumps.
12. Identify the part of the water cycle that is represented in Figure 3.5.2.

FIGURE 3.5.2

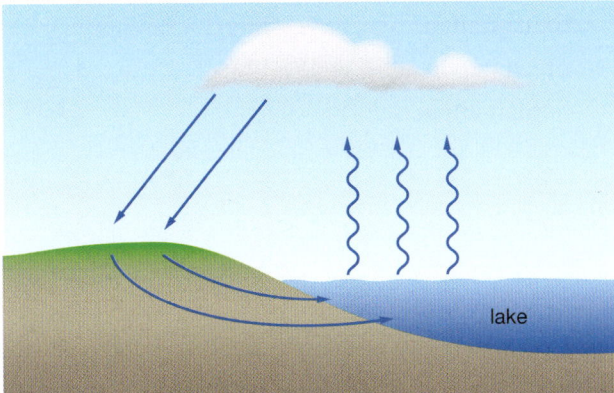

FIGURE 3.5.1

CHAPTER 3 • EARTH RESOURCES

CHAPTER 3 Chapter review

Analysing

13 Contrast:
   a renewable and non-renewable resources
   b pervious and impervious rocks
   c groundwater with water running off the ground.

14 Classify these energy sources as either renewable or non-renewable.
   • solar energy
   • oil
   • coal
   • wind energy
   • wave energy
   • tidal energy
   • LPG gas
   • geothermal energy
   • paper
   • uranium.

15 Compare the rate of evaporation on a windy day compared with the rate on a calm day.

16 Propose reasons why home gardeners are more likely to use drip irrigation and not spray or flood irrigation.

17 Compare living things and soils as resources, by discussing their:
   a classification as a renewable or non-renewable resource
   b importance as resources for humans
   c dependence on water to make them useful to humans.

Evaluating

18 Algae can grow in salty or waste waters and do not require the fresh water needed for many other biodiesel crops. Algae could potentially offer a good source of biofuel. Propose reasons why.

19 Suggest a reason why some clouds pass overhead without producing any rain.

20 Flexible solar cells are currently being developed for use instead of the rigid panels currently being used. Propose three ways in which flexible solar cells may be used in the future.

21 Renewable energy scientists are working to develop better ways to store energy. Explain why this technology is important.

22 In Australia there are laws that state how big each rock lobster (crayfish) must be before crayfishers can catch them. The laws also state that female crayfish carrying eggs cannot be caught. The eggs are tiny and are stuck underneath the tails.
   a Do you think these two laws makes sense?
   b Justify your answer.

23 a Assess whether you can or cannot answer the questions on page 85 at the start of this chapter.
   b Use this assessment to evaluate how well you understand the material presented in this chapter.

Creating

24 Use the following ten key terms to construct a visual summary of the information presented in this chapter.

   renewable resource
   non-renewable resource
   renewable energy source
   solar energy
   fossil fuels
   water cycle
   change of state
   transpiration
   precipitation
   human impacts

AB 3.10

134 PEARSON SCIENCE 7 2ND EDITION

CHAPTER 3: Inquiry skills

Research

1 *Processing & Analysing* *Communicating*

Research how the knowledge of Indigenous people in Australia has been used in protecting the environment during resource developments. In your research discuss a specific example for each of the following:
- major resource developments
- creating parks and reserves
- local government initiatives.

Present your findings in digital form.

2 *Planning & Conducting*

Many remote communities in Australia are located large distances away from the electricity grid. These communities generally rely on isolated diesel power stations. Such diesel power stations are affected by price variations in diesel fuel and also contribute greenhouse gases to the atmosphere.
- Research other sources of electricity that are being used or could be used in remote communities.
- Collect photos of some examples of other sources that provide energy.
- Link each photo of a source with its position on a map of Australia.
- Investigate factors that affect the cost of supplying electricity to remote communities.
- Summarise any improvements that are being made to the delivery of electric power in such regions.

Present your findings as a poster or as a digital presentation.

3 *Planning & Conducting*

More than 97% of all water on Earth is seawater. It would be very useful if we could drink it but we can't. Research to find out:
- how sea water compares with the water we drink
- what would happen to your body if you drank it.

Present your research as a series of tables, labelled diagrams, video and/or graphs.

4 *Planning & Conducting*

Hailstones are lumps of ice that may be the size of a grain of rice or as big as a tennis ball. Research the formation of hailstones to find:
- where they are formed
- what conditions cause hail to be created rather than rain
- why tropical summer thunderstorms often produce very large hailstones.

Present your research in digital form, including a series of labelled photos of diagrams.

5 *Processing & Analysing* *Communicating*

Design a project that would reduce the run-off from your school grounds and would make better use of stormwater.

Present your project as a series of labelled sketches or photos.

6 *Processing & Analysing* *Communicating*

Research any projects in your area that are designed to reduce the amount of stormwater flowing directly to rivers and oceans.
- Find a map showing the locations of rivers and creeks in your area.
- Identify locations where stormwater flows into these waterways.
- Find out different ways that stormwater is treated before release. Wetlands and rain gardens are only two methods. There are others.
- Record one advantage and one disadvantage of each method you identify.
- Locate on the map places where the different methods are used.

Present your findings as a poster or in digital form. In your presentation include a statement about the effectiveness of stormwater treatment in your area.

CHAPTER 3 Inquiry skills

7 *Processing & Analysing* *Communicating*

The construction of the Snowy Mountains Scheme reduced the flow of water in the Snowy River by 99%. Research the effects the loss of water had on the environment of the river.

Topics to consider include:
- The effect a reduced flow of water may have on the animals living in the water.
- Ways the plants on the riverbanks may be affected when the water level drops.
- The reaction of local landowners to changes that have occurred.
- Comments made by environmentalists about changes to water flow.
- If there are any plans to address any effects.

Present your findings as an illustrated report on the health of the Snowy River.

8 *Processing & Analysing* *Communicating*

The Aswan High Dam (Figure 3.5.3) was built on the river Nile in Egypt between 1960 and 1970. Research the Aswan High Dam or the Three Gorges Dam in China to:
- identify the reasons for the dam being built
- compare the flow of the river before and after the dam was built
- describe the effect that any changes have had on the environment downstream of the dam.

Present your findings as a poster or in digital form.

9 *Processing & Analysing* *Communicating*

Over recent years advertising campaigns have been used to educate the public regarding safe driving, the harmful effects of smoking and how to prepare for bushfires. Successful advertising campaigns focus on one message at a time.

The Clean Energy Council promotes the use of renewable energy sources in Australia.

Your task is to produce an advertisement for the Clean Energy Council. Your ad should emphasise the impact of fossil fuels on the environment and the importance of using more renewable energy. The advertisement must include pictures, diagrams or graphs to visually summarise reliable data.

Examples of the data that you might focus on in the advertisement could include:
- a comparison of Victoria's current usage of renewable energy with other Australian states
- the number of houses that have installed roof-top solar panels over the past 10 years.

Present your advertisement as a video or as a full page for a magazine.

FIGURE 3.5.3 Aswan High Dam, Egypt

CHAPTER 3
Inquiry skills

Thinking scientifically

1. A renewable natural resource is one that is replaced by natural processes that occur in a timescale less than an average human lifetime. A group of students was asked to classify some of Earth's resources into renewable resources and non-renewable resources. Their answer is shown in the following table.

Renewable resources	Non-renewable resources
1 rocks	7 wind
2 water	8 air
3 sunlight	9 coal
4 soil	10 petroleum
5 waves	11 natural gas
6 hydro-electric	12 nuclear

   Which resources (using the number) did the students classify incorrectly?
   A 1, 4, 7, 8
   B 2, 3, 9, 10
   C 5, 6, 11, 12
   D 9, 10, 11, 12.

2. A non-renewable energy source cannot be replaced. Identify which list below contains only non-renewable energy resources.
   A coal, oil, sunlight, wind
   B natural gas, sunlight, wind, tidal energy
   C oil, uranium, sunlight, tidal energy
   D natural gas, coal, oil, uranium.

3. The change of state from GAS → LIQUID represents:
   A the changes taking place in a cloud leading to rain
   B the change that takes place in saturated air as it cools
   C the change that takes place in leaves of trees with the Sun shining on them
   D the change of state necessary for water to be able to percolate through soil.

4. If the air temperature increased throughout the world, the rate at which water moves through the water cycle would:
   A stay the same
   B decrease
   C increase
   D increase in some areas and decrease in others.

5. As water goes through the water cycle again and again, the amount of water on Earth:
   A increases
   B decreases
   C stays the same
   D varies from time to time.

6. An experiment testing whether oxygen in air can be renewed was set up as in Figure 3.5.4. The flasks were placed in strong sunlight for a day. The gas collected in test-tube A made a glowing splint ignite. This proves that oxygen was present.

   Which of the following could you conclude from the results?
   A sunlight turns water into oxygen and carbon dioxide
   B plants take in oxygen from the air and release carbon dioxide
   C plants produce oxygen if they have sunlight and carbon dioxide
   D all the oxygen in the atmosphere comes from green plants.

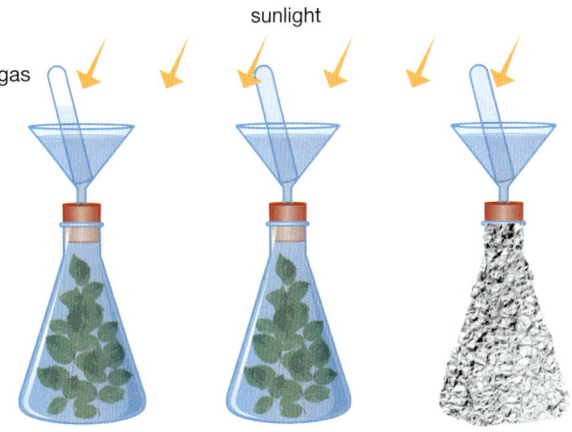

Flask A plant, water, carbon dioxide and light

Flask B plant, water and light, no carbon dioxide

Flask C plant, water and carbon dioxide, no light

FIGURE 3.5.4

Chapter 3 Glossary

aquifer: a layer of pervious rock from which water can be extracted using a bore or well

atmosphere: layer of gases above Earth's surface

biomass: all plant and animal matter found on Earth

carbon capture and storage: the process whereby carbon dioxide gas is isolated and captured for underground storage after coal is burnt

deposition: the dropping of sediments from moving water, air or ice

drip irrigation: tubes with holes in them that slowly drip water onto the ground

erosion: the removal of sediments from one place to another

flood irrigation: water is released in between crops in channels

flood irrigation

fossil fuels: fuels such as coal, oil and natural gas, formed from the remains of living things buried millions of years ago

fracking: a form of mining in which water and other chemicals are pumped into rocks, causing them to fracture (break)

geothermal energy: energy sources from heat below the Earth's crust

groundwater: water that exists underground

humidity: the amount of water vapour in the air

hydroelectricity: the process of using water falling from a height to turn turbines and generate electricity

igneous rock: rock formed by the cooling of molten rock, for example basalt

impervious rock: rock that does not allow water to soak into it

irrigation: used in agriculture to provide water to crops

minerals: substances found in rocks

non-renewable energy source: a source of energy that cannot be replaced after it is used, such as oil or coal

non-renewable energy source

nuclear fuel: a material that can be used to generate energy by splitting apart in a nuclear reaction

percolation: the process of water soaking into the soil

pervious rock: rock that allows water to soak into it

photosynthesis: the process by which plants use carbon dioxide, water and sunlight to make food

precipitation: any water falling from the sky

renewable energy source: a source of energy that can be replaced after it is used, such as solar or wind energy

renewable resource: a resource that is always being replaced naturally

resource: something that satisfies a particular purpose or need

renewable energy resource

run-off: rainwater not absorbed by the soil

saturated: not able to hold any more water vapour

sedimentary rock: rock formed by the compacting and sticking together of sediments, for example sandstone

solar cell: a device that absorbs solar energy and converts it directly into electrical energy

spray irrigation: where water droplets spray into the air

springs: places where underground water comes to the surface

stomata (stoma): holes in the leaves of plants that can be opened or closed to control water loss

spray irrigation

stormwater: rainwater that falls on hard surfaces that then runs off

topography: the hills, valleys, rivers and other physical features of the landscape

transpiration: the evaporation of water from plants

vegetation: the variety of plants that grow in a particular environment

water cycle: the recycling of water from ocean to atmosphere to land and back to the ocean

weathered: breaking down of rocks by the action of rain, wind, chemicals and living things into smaller particles

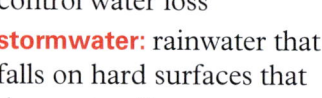
transpiration

wind energy: a form of renewable energy that converts energy from the wind into electrical energy

AB 3.9

CHAPTER 4
Mixtures

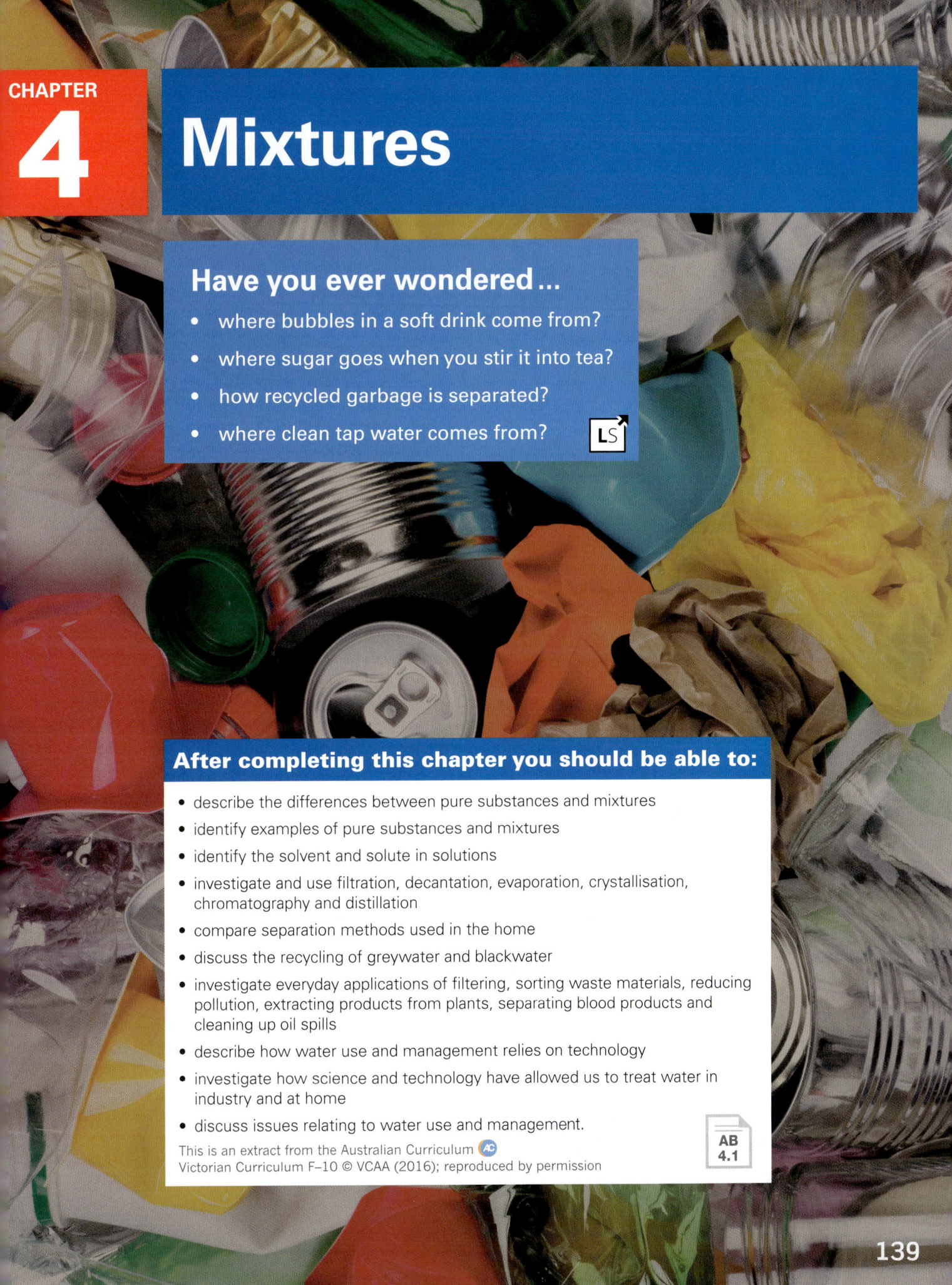

Have you ever wondered...
- where bubbles in a soft drink come from?
- where sugar goes when you stir it into tea?
- how recycled garbage is separated?
- where clean tap water comes from?

After completing this chapter you should be able to:
- describe the differences between pure substances and mixtures
- identify examples of pure substances and mixtures
- identify the solvent and solute in solutions
- investigate and use filtration, decantation, evaporation, crystallisation, chromatography and distillation
- compare separation methods used in the home
- discuss the recycling of greywater and blackwater
- investigate everyday applications of filtering, sorting waste materials, reducing pollution, extracting products from plants, separating blood products and cleaning up oil spills
- describe how water use and management relies on technology
- investigate how science and technology have allowed us to treat water in industry and at home
- discuss issues relating to water use and management.

This is an extract from the Australian Curriculum Victorian Curriculum F–10 © VCAA (2016); reproduced by permission

MODULE 4.1 Types of mixtures

Most of the substances that you deal with every day are not pure substances; they are mixtures. The air you breathe is a mixture, as are an artist's paints and the water you get from a tap.

What is a mixture?

A **pure substance** is one that is made up of only one type of substance. For example, pure water is made of only water and refined sugar is made up of only sugar. In science, a **mixture** is any substance that:

- is made from two or more pure substances that have been stirred together
- can be separated back into its original pure substances.

Paints, soft drinks, air and seawater are examples of mixtures.

Solutions

Watch carefully as sugar is stirred into water and the solid sugar will seem to disappear! The sugar has dissolved. The sugar breaks up into tiny particles that are too small to see. These particles then spread throughout the water. Although these sugar particles cannot be seen, if you taste the water the sweetness of the liquid tells you the particles are still there. This is what is meant when something is said to **dissolve**. A substance that dissolves like this is described as **soluble**. A substance that does not dissolve is described as **insoluble**.

When things mix really well, like when sugar dissolves in water, the mixture is known as a **solution**. When you stir sugar into water, you make a sugar solution.

STEM 4 fun

Undo water pollution

PROBLEM
Can you undo water pollution?

SUPPLIES
- small 500 mL bucket of polluted water (including kitchen oil, food packaging)
- strainer, tongs, cardboard, wool, spoon, fabric, coat hanger, feathers, sponges, cotton balls

PLAN AND DESIGN Design the solution. What information do you need to solve the problem? Draw a diagram. Make a list of materials you will need and steps you will take.

CREATE Follow your plan. Draw your solution to the problem.

IMPROVE What works? What doesn't? How do you know it solves the problem? What could work better? Modify your design to make it better. Test it out.

REFLECTION
1. What areas of STEM did you work in today?
2. What career is this activity related to?
3. If another student was to do this task, what advice would you give?

Solutes and solvents

When you make a solution, the substance that dissolves is known as the **solute**. In a sugar solution, the sugar is the solute. The substance that dissolves the other one is the **solvent**. So in this case the water is the solvent.

The soft drink in Figure 4.1.1 has sugars, preservatives and flavourings dissolved in water. There is also carbon dioxide gas dissolved in it to give the drink its bubbles. This shows that solutes don't always need to be solid. Table 4.1.1 shows other types of solutions made by combining solvents with solutes.

FIGURE 4.1.1 In soft drinks the solvent is water. The solutes are flavourings, sugars and preservatives. When you open the lid, you release pressure in the bottle, which causes dissolved carbon dioxide gas bubbles to rise to the surface.

TABLE 4.1.1 Common types of solutions

Type of solution	Examples
solid dissolved in a liquid	grease dissolved in petrol, sugar dissolved in water
liquid dissolved in another liquid	liquid detergent dissolved in water, oil dissolved in petrol
gas dissolved in a liquid	oxygen gas dissolved in water, oxygen gas dissolved in blood
gas dissolved in another gas	oxygen gas, carbon dioxide gas and water vapour dissolved in the other gases of the air

Most of the solutions you will meet in science and at home are aqueous solutions. An **aqueous solution** always has water as its solvent. Sugar dissolves in water, so a sugar solution is classified as an aqueous solution. Likewise, soft drink is an aqueous solution of sugars, preservatives, flavouring and carbon dioxide.

A particular solute will dissolve in some solvents and not in others. For example, grease will not dissolve in water but will dissolve in methylated spirits, petrol, turpentine and the fluids used by drycleaners. Particular solvents will dissolve some substances and not others. For example, water will dissolve detergent, but not oil. You can see this in Figure 4.1.2.

FIGURE 4.1.2 Oil will not dissolve in water but detergent will dissolve in water.

Solution or not?

Light passes easily through a solution, allowing you to see through it. This is one way of telling whether a mixture is a solution or not. Solutions are transparent (see-through). You can describe solutions such as this as 'clear', meaning you can see through them.

Solutions can be colourless, looking much like water. Other solutions are coloured. For example, blue copper sulfate solid dissolves in water to form a blue-coloured solution. You know that a solution has been formed because you can see straight through it. You can see its preparation in Figure 4.1.3.

FIGURE 4.1.3 Preparation of an aqueous solution of copper sulfate

CHAPTER 4 • MIXTURES   141

Colourless and clear are not the same. Clear means that you can see though it. Colourless means it is not coloured. Figure 4.1.4 helps explain these different meanings.

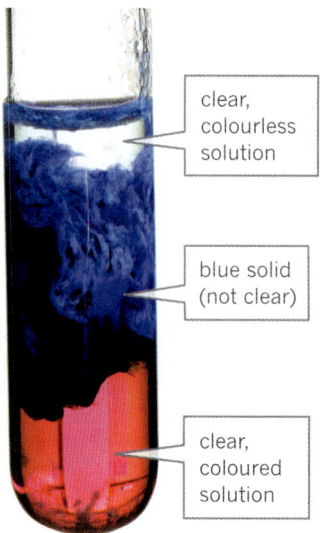

FIGURE 4.1.4 Solutions can be coloured or colourless and are always transparent. You can see through them.

Concentrated, dilute and saturated solutions

Prac 1 p. 146

A solution is said to be **concentrated** if there is a lot of solute dissolved in the solvent. If there is only a little solute in the solution, then it is a **dilute** solution. Four spoonsful of sugar dissolved in a swimming pool will produce a dilute solution. In contrast, four spoonsful of sugar in a cup of tea will make it concentrated. A concentrated solution and a dilute solution are shown in Figure 4.1.5.

FIGURE 4.1.5 Concentrated solutions have a lot of solute dissolved in them while dilute solutions have very little.

Imagine you took a glass of water and kept adding spoonsful of salt to it, stirring each time. You would find that eventually the salt would stop dissolving. When a substance will no longer dissolve in a solvent, the solution is said to be **saturated**. Any undissolved solute then falls to the bottom as sediment. This is shown in Figure 4.1.6.

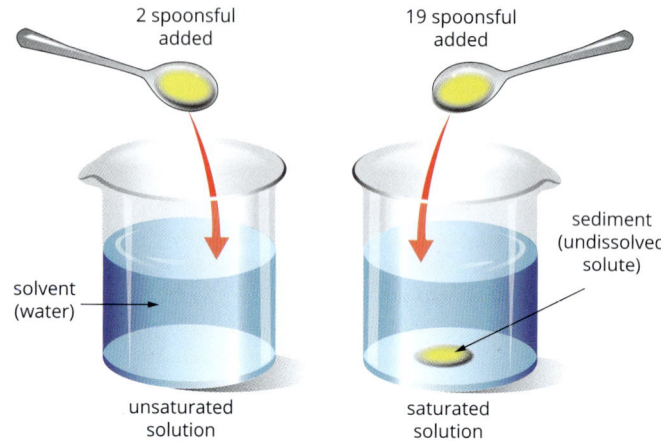

FIGURE 4.1.6 The concentration of a saturated solution is so high that no more solute will dissolve.

An example of saturation is seen in saltwater lakes sometimes found near the sea and in the outback. The concentration of the salt in the lakes increases as water evaporates. Eventually, the lake becomes saturated and solid salt is deposited (left behind) around the edges of the lake (Figure 4.1.7).

FIGURE 4.1.7 Salt deposits around the edges of Lake Gairdner in South Australia

Prac 2 p. 147 | Prac 3 p. 148 | AB 4.2 | AB 4.3

Suspensions

Sand does not dissolve when it is mixed into water. Instead it stays solid and spreads throughout the water. This type of mixture is called a **suspension**. In suspensions, substances like sand do not dissolve but **disperse** (spread) through a liquid or gas. Figure 4.1.8 shows dust floating in the air. This is another example of a suspension. Usually, the suspended particles are too large and heavy to stay in suspension and will fall and settle if left undisturbed. Sand mixed into a beaker of water will, after a while, settle on the bottom of the beaker. In the same way, dust in the air eventually drops to cover floors and other surfaces. Table 4.1.2 lists some different types of suspension.

TABLE 4.1.2 Types of suspensions

Type of suspension	Examples
solid suspended in a liquid	muddy water, sand in water
solids suspended in a gas	sand blown about in the air by the wind
liquids suspended in another liquid	oil paints, many medicines

FIGURE 4.1.8 Dust floating in the air forms a suspension of a solid (dust) in a gas (air). Eventually, the dust will settle onto the furniture and floor.

SciFile

Shake your bottle

Mylanta is an antacid liquid that eases heartburn. Like many medicines, it needs to be shaken up before you take it. If you don't, then one of the important ingredients might remain as a sediment on the bottom of the bottle and so you would receive an incorrect dose.

Working with Science

GREEN CHEMIST
Dr Deanna D'Alessandro

Green chemistry is a new and exciting area of science that aims to find environmentally responsible ways of making and using chemicals. Dr Deanna D'Alessandro (Figure 4.1.9) works at the University of Sydney developing materials that solve environmental problems. Dr D'Alessandro works in a laboratory with a team of scientists and students. One of her projects is developing materials called metal-organic frameworks that work like sponges, soaking up liquids and gases. These materials can be used to capture gases from the atmosphere, such as carbon dioxide or methane, or store hydrogen to fuel cars. Dr D'Alessandro is excited about making discoveries that can solve problems in the real world.

FIGURE 4.1.9 Dr Deanna D'Alessandro

To become a green chemist, you will need a Bachelor of Science, majoring in chemistry. After your degree, you can work in the industry or continue studying and become a researcher. A keen eye for detail, love of solving problems and curiosity about the world around you are great qualities to have as a green chemist.

Review

1. Why is green chemistry an important area of research in today's world?
2. What other types of scientists might a green chemist work with?

MODULE 4.1 Review questions

Remembering

1. Define the terms:
   a. mixture
   b. dissolves
   c. soluble
   d. aqueous
   e. dilute.

2. What term best describes each of the following?
   a. a substance that will not dissolve in a liquid
   b. a clear mixture in which a substance dissolves in water
   c. a mixture that has a lot of substance dissolved in it
   d. a mixture that cannot dissolve any more of a substance
   e. a mixture in which a fine powder does not dissolve but separates out to form a sediment.

3. List two examples each of a solute, a solvent and a solution.

4. What are four types of solution? Give an example of each.

5. List three types of suspension and give an example of each.

6. Name a solvent that will dissolve:
   a. sugar
   b. grease.

Understanding

7. Cooking oil breaks into lots of small droplets when added to water, but seems to 'disappear' when added to detergent. Explain why.

8. Mylanta is an antacid liquid used to relieve heartburn. Why do you think the label tells you to shake the bottle well before using it?

9. Outline how you could show that a sugar solution is just saturated.

10. What types of mixtures might be present in a polluted water sample such as that used in the STEM4fun activity on page 140?

Applying

11. A chef dissolved salt in boiling water that he was going to use to cook pasta. Identify whether the salt, water or salty water was the:
    a. solute
    b. solvent
    c. aqueous solution.

Analysing

12. a. Compare a concentrated glass of cordial with a dilute glass of cordial.
    b. What would the two solutions taste like?

13. Compare a sugar solution with a suspension of sand in water.

14. Classify each of the following as a solution or a suspension.
    a. cordial in water
    b. carbon dioxide gas in lemonade
    c. clouds
    d. food colouring in water
    e. dust in air
    f. smoke from a car exhaust.

Evaluating

15. Fiona found that 10 mL of water tasted just as sweet whether she mixed 5 teaspoons or 10 teaspoons of sugar into the liquid. Propose an explanation for this.

16. Figure 4.1.10 shows milk being poured into salt water.
    a. Identify which substance is the solution.
    b. Justify your answer.

FIGURE 4.1.10

MODULE 4.1 Review questions

17 Vitamin C is soluble in water. Vitamins A, D and K are soluble in oils. Chefs recommend that:
- vegetables are not soaked in water before or during cooking
- steaming or microwaving is better than boiling.

One reason for these recommendations is to stop heat destroying the vitamins. Propose another reason.

18 Solutions are transparent. This means that there are no particles in the solution big enough to reflect or scatter the light as it passes through. Figure 4.1.11 shows two test-tubes, A and B, that contain different mixtures. Green and red light is shone through both.
   a Identify the test-tube that contains a solution.
   b Justify your choice.

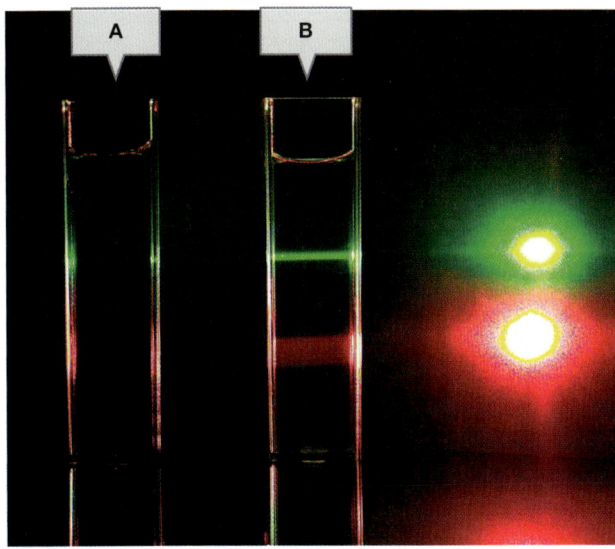

FIGURE 4.1.11

19 Figure 4.1.12 shows beams of sunlight passing through foggy air.
   a Identify whether the air is a solution or a suspension.
   b Justify your answer.

FIGURE 4.1.12

20 Two students, Dean and Erin both tested how well copper sulfate crystals dissolved in water. Dean used tap water, while Erin used distilled water. They each added copper sulfate a spoonful at a time, stirring each time to see if it dissolved. Dean used copper sulfate from a fresh jar, while Erin used recycled copper sulfate from other experiments. They each counted the number of spoons they added until the solutions became saturated.
   a Predict whether Dean and Erin are likely to get the same result.
   b Evaluate whether this is a fair test.
   c What do you think Dean and Erin could have done to improve their experiments?

MODULE 4.1 Practical investigations

1 • Soluble and insoluble substances

Purpose
To investigate what substances will dissolve in water and kerosene.

Timing 45 minutes

Materials
- ½ spatula copper carbonate ($CuCO_3$)
- ½ spatula copper sulfate ($CuSO_4$)
- 1 spatula table salt (NaCl)
- cooking oil in dropping bottles
- 6 mL kerosene
- 6 medium-sized test-tubes with stoppers to fit
- test-tube rack
- marking pen or sticky labels
- spatula

> **SAFETY**
> A Risk Assessment is required for this investigation.
> Copper sulfate and copper carbonate are toxic so do not touch, sniff or taste them.
> Kerosene is flammable and should be kept away from naked flames. Wear safety glasses and rubber gloves at all times to avoid contact with your skin and eyes. Avoid inhaling fumes by doing the activity in a well-ventilated area.

Procedure
1. Copy the table in the Results section into your workbook.
2. Place the test-tubes in the rack. Use the marking pen or sticky labels to number them 1 to 6.
3. Add about 5 cm of tap water to test-tubes 1 to 4. Pour 3 cm of kerosene into test-tubes 5 and 6.
4. Add different solutes to the different test-tubes as shown in Figure 4.1.13.
5. Place a stopper in each test-tube. Shake each of the test-tubes for about 1 minute. Place all the test-tubes in the test-tube rack and record what you see.
6. Do not tip anything down the sink. Return all test-tubes and liquid to your teacher.

Results
1. Record your observations in the following table. Give your table a title.

Test-tube number	Solvent	Solute	Observation
1	water	copper carbonate	
2	water	copper sulfate	
3	water	salt	
4	water	oil	
5	kerosene	oil	
6	kerosene	salt	

Review
1. How did you tell if a solution formed? What signs did you look for?
2. In which test-tubes did a solution form?
3. Name the substances that were insoluble in:
   a. water
   b. kerosene.
4. Identify the substance that is:
   a. a solvent of salt but not of oil
   b. a solvent of copper sulfate but not copper carbonate.

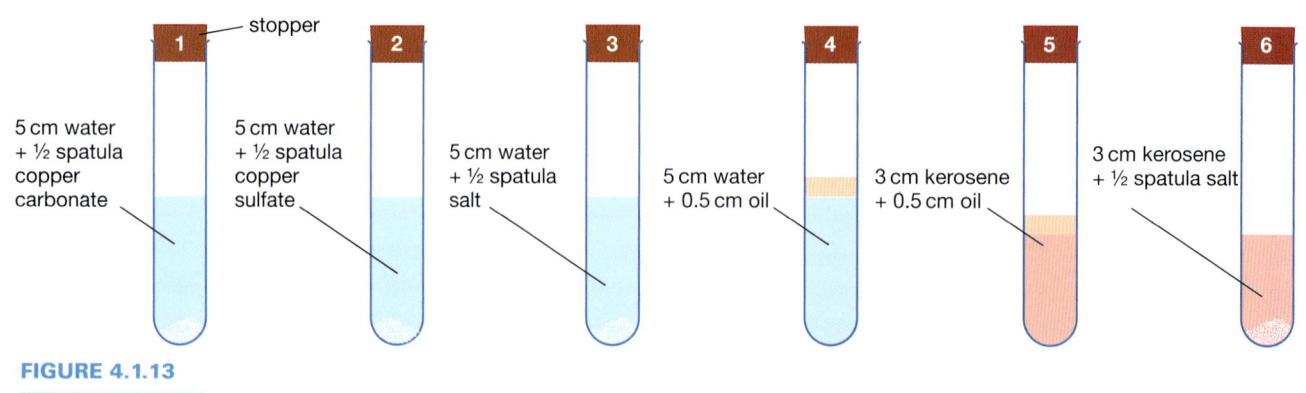

FIGURE 4.1.13

MODULE 4.1

Practical investigations

• STUDENT DESIGN •

2 • Dissolving and surface area   *Planning & Conducting*   *Evaluating*

Purpose
To test whether breaking up a solute into smaller particles can change how fast it dissolves.

Hypothesis
Which do you think will dissolve faster—a whole Sugarine® tablet or a crushed Sugarine tablet? Before you go any further with this investigation, write a hypothesis in your workbook.

Timing 45 minutes

Materials
- 2 Sugarine tablets
- 2 test-tubes and stoppers
- paper patty case
- 1 metal spoon
- method for timing the reaction such as a stopwatch, smart phone or tablet to film the experiment and then review to check the time. (optional)

SAFETY — A Risk Assessment is required for this investigation.

Procedure
1 Design an experiment that will test whether a crushed Sugarine tablet dissolves faster or slower than a whole Sugarine tablet. Figure 4.1.14 might give you some ideas on how to do this.

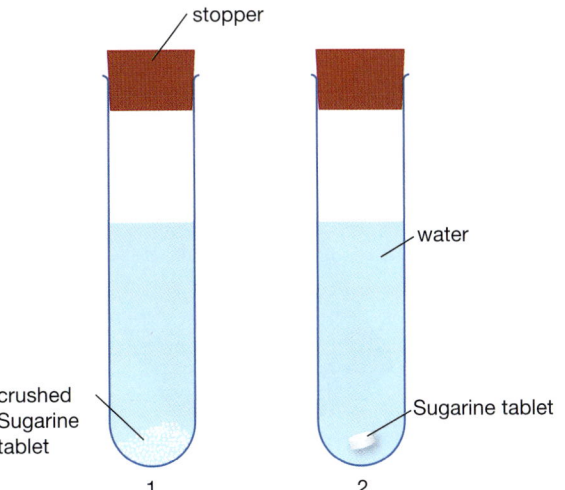

FIGURE 4.1.14

2 Write your procedure in your workbook.

3 Before you start any practical work, prepare a risk assessment. Show your teacher your procedure and your assessment. If they approve, then collect all the required materials and start work.

Hints
- Crush the tablets in the patty case to stop them spreading.
- You should use the same size test-tubes with the same amount of water in each.
- You only need to find out which tablet dissolves faster—you do not need to find the exact time each tablet takes to dissolve.
- Use the STEM and SDI template in your eBook to help you plan and carry out your investigation.

Results
Record which tablet (whole or crushed) dissolved first. If you measured the time taken for each to dissolve, then record the times as well.

Review
1 List the variables that you controlled (kept constant) during this experiment.
2 Which variable did you change?
3 a Construct a conclusion for your investigation.
  b Assess whether your hypothesis was supported or not.
4 In this investigation, it was not necessary to measure the length of time it takes for the two tablets to dissolve. Explain why.
5 You sometimes take an aspirin tablet or capsule when you have a bad headache. Capsules contain roughly the same amount of aspirin as a tablet. However, a capsule has its aspirin as small particles held in a shell that dissolves when you swallow it.
  a Which would you choose to relieve your headache faster—a capsule or a tablet?
  b Justify your choice.

CHAPTER 4 • MIXTURES **147**

MODULE 4.1 Practical investigations

• STUDENT DESIGN •

3 • Investigating dissolving *Planning & Conducting* *Questioning & Predicting*

Purpose
To investigate how things dissolve.

Hypothesis
Once you have decided which investigation to perform, write a hypothesis in your workbook.

Timing 45 minutes

Materials
Students to choose from:
- sugar
- copper sulfate ($CuSO_4$)
- salt
- 3 varieties of liquid dishwashing detergent
- source of grease (such as oil)

SAFETY A Risk Assessment is required for this investigation.

Procedure
1. Design an experiment that will answer **one** of the following questions.
   - Can sugar and copper sulfate both dissolve in the same container of water?
   - Is the amount of salt that can dissolve in water more or less than the amount of sugar that can dissolve in the same volume of water?
   - Can copper sulfate dissolve in a saturated solution of salt?
   - Are all dishwashing liquid detergents equally good at dissolving grease?
2. Write your procedure in your workbook. Include a diagram of your design for your experiment.
3. Before you start any practical work, assess your procedure. List any risks that your procedure might involve and what you might do to minimise those risks. Show your teacher your procedure and your assessment of its risks. If they approve, then collect all the required materials and start work.
4. Dispose of all residues from experiments as directed by your teacher.

Use the STEM and SDI template in your eBook to help you plan and carry out your investigation.

Results
Record your results and observations in your workbook.

Review
1. Construct a conclusion for your investigation.
2. Assess whether your hypothesis was supported or not.

FIGURE 4.1.15 Copper sulfate crystals

MODULE 4.2 Separating insoluble substances

Mixtures often need to be separated into the substances that make them up. Being able to separate insoluble substances from each other is important to many organisms. For example, humans have kidneys that separate impurities from our blood. Grey whales scoop up sand from the sea floor and remove food from it by passing it through structures called baleen.

science 4 fun

Panning for gold
Could you find gold?

Collect this…
- metal bowl or old cereal bowl (shallow with gently sloping sides)
- fairly clean sand or loam soil
- small metal objects such as nails or washers
- bucket of water or hose

Do this…
1. The small metal objects are your 'gold'. Mix them up with the soil and put the mixture in the bowl.
2. Half fill the bowl with water.
3. Hold the bowl with a hand on each side. Move the bowl around in a circular motion to swirl the water through the soil. The soil should start lifting up into the water.
4. Let the water wash over the sides of the bowl as you move it around. The aim is to wash some of the soil out of the bowl with the water.
5. Keep adding water and swirling the soil around so it is gradually removed from the bowl. You should see the 'gold' collecting on the bottom of the bowl.
6. See how pure you can get the 'gold'. You may have to practise to improve your technique.

Record this…
1. Describe what happened.
2. Explain why you think this happened.

CHAPTER 4 • MIXTURES 149

Magnetic separation

Your recycle bin at home contains a mixture of solids. It probably contains steel cans, glass jars, aluminium cans, paper, cardboard, plastic bottles and packaging. After collection, this mixture needs to be separated so that the different substances can be recycled and then re-used.

Magnets are a convenient way of separating any rubbish made of iron or steel. Iron is always attracted to magnets. As steel is made from more than 95% iron, it too is attracted to magnets. Magnets also attract the metals nickel and cobalt, but do not attract other metals such as aluminium, copper or gold or substances such as plastic, paper or glass.

Magnetic attraction allows iron and steel to be easily removed from piles of rubbish, leaving the non-magnetic materials behind. One way in which magnets are used to separate rubbish is shown in Figure 4.2.1. Magnetic separation is also used in the mining industry and in the scrap metal business.

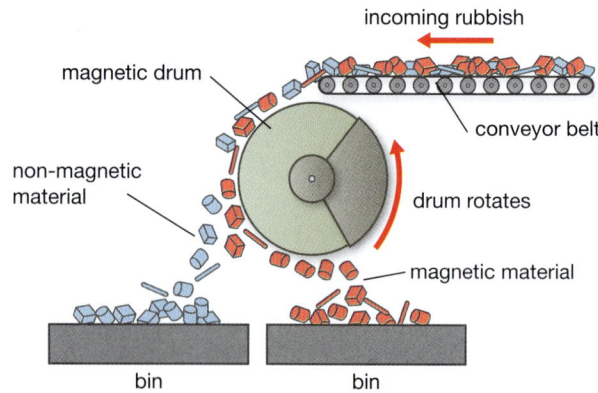

FIGURE 4.2.1 A rotating drum can be used to separate magnetic materials from rubbish.

Gravity separation

Not all mixtures contain a collection of solids like those in your recycle bin. Many mixtures are suspensions which contain insoluble solids dispersed through a liquid. **Gravity separation** uses gravity to separate heavier substances from a suspension. The heavier particles sink to the bottom of the container.

Gold panning uses gravity separation. As Figure 4.2.2 shows, the heavier and denser particles drop to the bottom of the pan, allowing the lighter, less dense mud and water to be poured off. Hopefully, gold will be down among those heavier particles!

FIGURE 4.2.2 Panning for gold uses gravity separation.

Decantation is a type of gravity separation that lets suspensions of solids or liquids separate naturally. The top layer can then be poured or scraped off. After vegetables are cooked in a saucepan of water, the water is poured off. This is decanting. If a bottle of wine is left standing up for a long time, sometimes sediment collects at the bottom of the bottle. If you pour the wine into a glass container (decanting), the sediment remains behind in the bottle.

Decantation can separate:

- oil and water—water sinks to the bottom with a layer of oil on top
- leaves and soil—soil falls to the bottom, with leaves on top
- rocks and water—rocks sink to the bottom with water covering them.

Decanting is used in many industries. Figure 4.2.3 shows how decanting can be used in science laboratories.

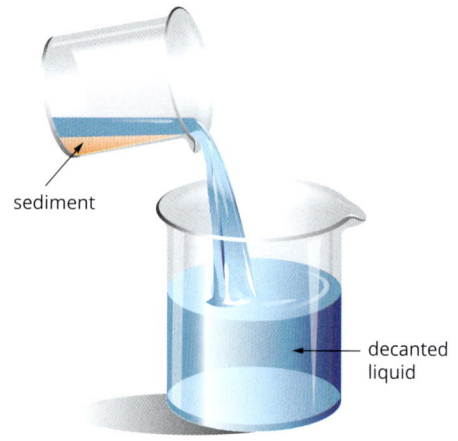

FIGURE 4.2.3 Decanting pours off the liquid to leave the solids behind.

150 PEARSON SCIENCE 7 2ND EDITION

Sieving

A sieve is a barrier with holes in it. Small solid particles can get through, but large ones cannot. The process is called sieving. Sieves are common in the kitchen. For example, lumps of flour are removed before baking by sifting the flour through a sieve called a flour sifter. A colander is a sieve that strains water from cooked vegetables and pasta and the wire basket in Figure 4.2.4 strains hot oil from the chips once cooked.

FIGURE 4.2.4 The wire basket chips are cooked in is a type of sieve.

Sieves are also used in industry and their holes can be graded to a specific size for the job they do. For example, a fishing net may be able to catch large fish but allows smaller fish and water to pass through. Sieves are used to separate apples into different sizes and are used in mining to ensure that only rocks of the correct size enter a rock crusher.

Filtration

Filtration, also known as filtering, is a widely used method of separating solids from liquids.

Filtration uses a **filter**. A filter is like a sieve in that it is a barrier with many, many small holes in it. These holes are smaller than the particles being separated and so these particles get caught in the filter. However, smaller particles pass straight through. Filters can take different forms, such as a mesh of fine fibres (like cotton wool) or even a rock that has fine pores (small holes). The larger particles that are trapped in the filter are known as the **residue**. The smaller particles (usually water) that pass through the filter are known as the **filtrate**.

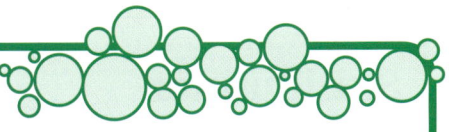

SciFile

Human filters

Your kidneys filter your blood removing wastes and producing urine. Your whole blood supply passes through your kidneys in about 1 hour. This means your blood has passed through your kidneys about 24 times in a day. From this you make about 1 litre of urine.

Filters are commonly used in everyday life. Filters are used to separate coffee grounds from filter coffee. Likewise, tea bags are a type of filter that allows water to move through them while keeping the tea leaves in the bag. Filters remove fluff from the water in washing machines and leaves from swimming pools. In cars, filters remove dirt and metal particles from the oil lubricating its engine and transmission.

Filters can also be used to separate solids from gases. The face mask shown in Figure 4.2.5 is a filter that separates dust from air. A similar filter is used in most vacuum cleaners. The filtered, clean air is then blown back into the room. Air conditioners, clothes dryers and air cleaners use filters to ensure the air is clean and free of dust and fluff.

Filters are also used in the laboratory. Several different methods are used, but the most common uses filter paper.

FIGURE 4.2.5 Builders, painters and plasterers work in dusty environments so they often wear face masks to stop dust entering their airways.

SkillBuilder

Folding a filter paper

There are two methods to fold filter paper. The conical fold is shown in Figure 4.2.6.

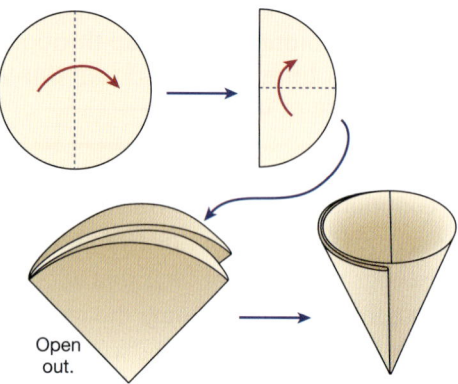

FIGURE 4.2.6 How to make a conical fold for filter paper

The other method of folding is called fluting. This is shown in Figure 4.2.7.

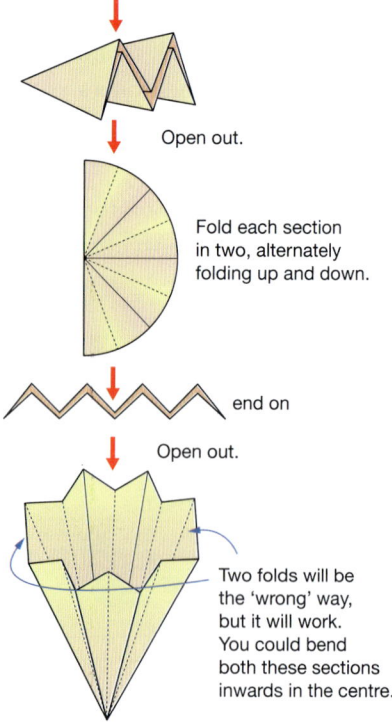

FIGURE 4.2.7 How to fold a fluted filter paper

Fluting increases the surface area of paper in contact with the liquid that is being filtered. This speeds up filtering because it provides more spaces for the liquid to escape through. This is useful when filtering fine suspensions that can block holes in the filter paper.

SkillBuilder

How to filter

To filter, set up the equipment as shown in Figure 4.2.8.

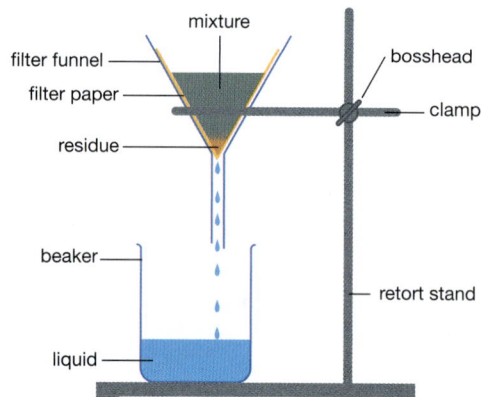

FIGURE 4.2.8 A retort stand and clamp is being used here but special filter stands can be used instead.

An example of how the equipment may look when set up at your school is shown in Figure 4.2.9.

FIGURE 4.2.9 This student is filtering a sand/water mixture.

Fluting increases the surface arSome things to remember when filtering are:

- Solids will enter the filtrate if you let the liquid go over the top of the paper
- The paper will break if you touch the filter while filtering.

Centrifuging

A simple **centrifuge** is shown in Figure 4.2.10. It has chambers arranged around the rim of a spinning tub. Any tiny particles suspended in the liquid are forced to the sides and then to the bottom of each chamber. The spinning process is called centrifuging.

FIGURE 4.2.10 A simple centrifuge is used to separate substances in the laboratory.

A common use of a centrifuge is in the spin cycle on a washing machine, in which the clothes are spun very fast in the bowl. Figure 4.2.11 shows how this works. Water is forced out of the clothes and through the holes in the bowl. It then drains away and is pumped out of the machine. In a similar way, salad spinners are used in the kitchen to dry washed lettuce.

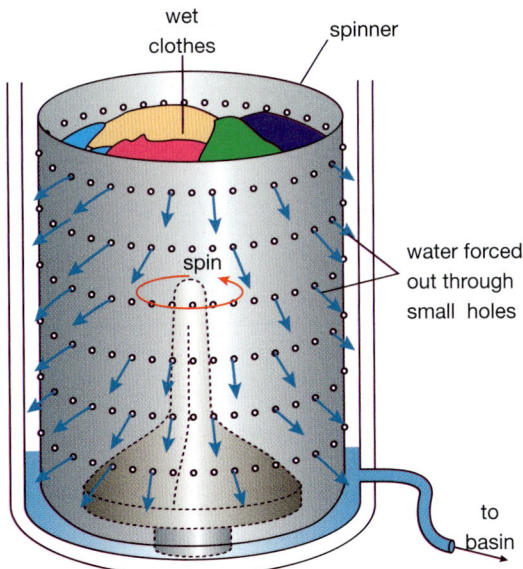

FIGURE 4.2.11 A washing machine spin cycle acts as a simple centrifuge.

There are many other designs for centrifuges. Some very complicated ones are used in mining. Centrifuging is also widely used in laboratories.

Centrifuging blood

Blood and its parts are very important in health care. After a serious accident or during surgery, people might need to receive a transfusion of whole blood. Sometimes only parts of blood are needed, such as red or white blood cells or liquid plasma (Figure 4.2.12). Whole blood can be separated into these parts by centrifuging. These parts can then be used directly or further separated to treat particular health conditions.

Plasma is used to treat burns patients. Some other conditions don't require plasma but instead need particular chemicals extracted from it. For example, chemicals called clotting factors are extracted from plasma to treat people who have haemophilia. Patients with this disease can bleed to death because their blood does not clot (thicken) to seal a cut.

Patients with anaemia have insufficient red blood cells in their blood. They can be given whole unseparated blood but this can stress their heart if they also have heart problems. Instead, they are given transfusions of red blood cells because these place less stress on the heart.

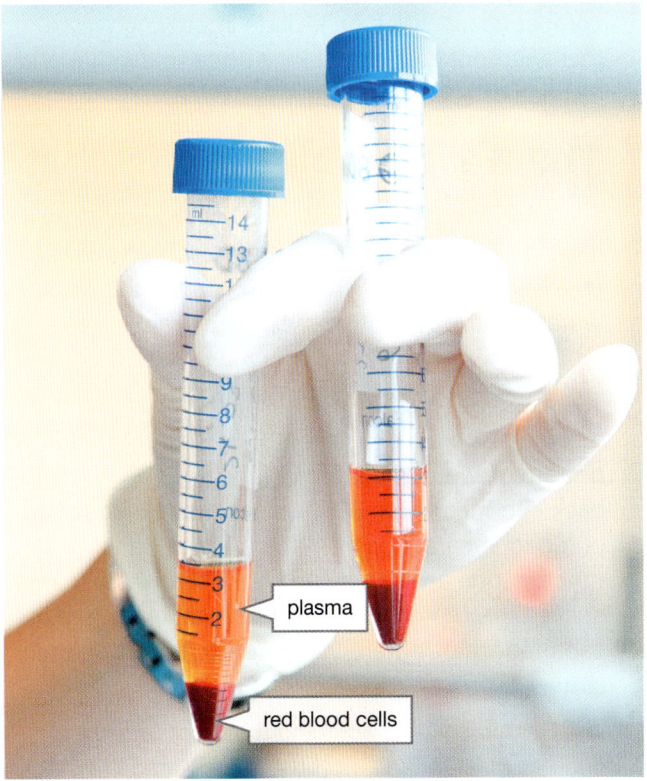

FIGURE 4.2.12 Blood that has been centrifuged separates out into layers.

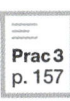

Prac 3 p. 157

CHAPTER 4 • MIXTURES **153**

SCIENCE AS A HUMAN ENDEAVOUR
Use and influence of science

Ocean bins

Two surfers from Perth have come up with a smart way to get rubbish out of marine environments. Andrew Turton and Pete Ceglinski grew up surfing. Their love of the ocean inspired them to clean it up and the idea for the Seabin came to life.

FIGURE 4.2.13 Parts of the Seabin and the rubbish it collects. The Seabin caught this much rubbish in only 30 minutes.

Ocean pollution

Ocean pollution is a growing environmental problem. Scientists have estimated that around 8 million tonnes of plastic rubbish goes into the oceans every year. It is thought that up to 245,000 tonnes of plastic is currently floating on the ocean surface. As well as plastic, there is also pollution from oil spills, sewage and toxic chemicals. This pollution is having serious impacts on ocean life, human health and use of the ocean. Ways to combat ocean pollution include improving waste management and increasing efforts to capture and dispose of ocean pollution.

The Seabin solution

The Seabin is a floating bin that sucks rubbish into it like a vacuum cleaner (Figure 4.2.13). The bin is attached to a pier where a pump works to suck water and rubbish into a mesh bag, trapping the rubbish.

The reusable mesh bag is easily lifted out and the rubbish disposed of. The water flows out of the bottom of the bin, up through the water pump and back into the ocean. A filter can be attached to the pump to separate oil from the seawater. Fish and other marine animals swim below the water that is sucked through the Seabin so are not likely to be captured. The diagram in Figure 4.2.14 shows the simple set up of the Seabin.

The Seabin collects anything that floats near it, such as plastic bags, bottles, paper and oil. The inventors hope to recycle the plastic rubbish collected by the Seabins, and turn it into material to make more Seabins! The Seabin can operate all day, every day of the year.

FIGURE 4.2.14 How the Seabin works

REVIEW

1. Why are inventions like the Seabin so important?
2. The Seabin can remove oil from seawater. What properties of oil and water allow them to be separated?
3. What other ways can science and our understanding of water and pollutants help to remove rubbish from the oceans?

MODULE 4.2 Review questions

Remembering

1. Define the terms:
   a. sieve
   b. gravity separation.
2. What term best describes each of the following?
   a. sieve with many small holes in it
   b. a machine with chambers spun at speed around an axle.
3. List examples of sieving and filtering around your home.
4. What is an example of centrifuging that is used at home?
5. What are two methods that can be used to separate a:
   a. solid from another solid?
   b. solid from a liquid?
   c. liquid from another liquid?
6. Draw a diagram that shows how to set up equipment for filtration.

Understanding

7. Outline how magnetic separation can be used to separate magnetic and non-magnetic metals from household rubbish.
8. Explain why particles of gold fall to the bottom of the pan when panning for gold.
9. a. Describe what a paper filter would look like if you could magnify it enough.
   b. Explain how filter paper works to filter out particles.
10. Filtration will not separate sugar from water. Explain why.
11. Construct a table in which you:
    a. list each of the five methods of separation in this module
    b. describe how each method works
    c. specify an example where it may be used.

Applying

12. Identify a method of separation that could be used for the following situations.
    a. You want fine clean sand without any sticks or stones from the soil in your garden.
    b. You drop nails into the sand in your backyard.
    c. You drop hundreds-and-thousands into the flour a baker is using for a cake.
    d. The gravel border along the driveway is covered by bark, and leaves and fine sticks are mixed with the gravel.
    e. Your tea bag breaks in your cup of tea.
13. Compare:
    a. gravity separation and centrifuging
    b. sieving and filtering
    c. the two methods of folding filter papers.

Analysing

14. Car air cleaners are structured as shown in Figure 4.2.15.
    a. Compare the air cleaner with a fluted filter paper.
    b. Describe why this design is effective as an air cleaner.

FIGURE 4.2.15

Evaluating

15. Propose a reason why vehicle air, fuel and oil filters need to be changed regularly.
16. Some washing machines do some test spins before starting the spin-dry cycle. After doing this, the machine may not spin the clothes but instead agitate them back and forth for a while, before trying another test spin. Propose a reason why the machine has been designed to do this.

Creating

17. Design an experiment to test whether cold water from a refrigerator filters faster than warm tap water.
    a. Which do you think will filter faster?
    b. Draw a diagram(s) to show how you intend to carry out your experiment.
    c. Describe the procedure you intend to use.
    d. Identify the independent variable, dependent variable and controlled variables.
    e. How will you make sure the test is fair?
18. In the laboratory, you are given a mixture of sugar, sand and gravel. Design a way of separating these three substances.

MODULE 4.2 Practical investigations

1 • Comparing filters

Purpose
To compare conical and fluted filter papers.

Hypothesis
Which filters faster—a conical filter paper or a fluted filter paper? Before you go any further with this investigation, write a hypothesis in your workbook.

Timing 45 minutes

Materials
- 1 spatula sand
- 1 spatula copper carbonate ($CuCO_3$)
- 1 spatula
- 2 funnels
- 4 filter papers
- 4 × 100 mL beakers
- 2 stirring rods
- 2 stopwatches or timers
- retort stand, bosshead and clamp or filter stand

> **SAFETY**
> A Risk Assessment is required for this investigation.
> Copper carbonate is toxic so do not touch, sniff or taste it.

Procedure
1. Place two funnels in the clamp or filter stand. Place a beaker under each funnel to collect the liquid.
2. Fold one filter paper into a conical shape and the other into the fluted shap eas shown in the SkillBuilder 'Folding a filter paper' on page 152 and in Figure 4.2.16. Place each filter in a funnel.
3. Collect one spatula of sand and place it in 40 mL of water in a beaker. Repeat for the other beaker.
4. Read the SkillBuilder 'How to Filter' on page 152. Make sure you understand how to filter before continuing.
5. Now pour the contents of one beaker into the conical filter paper. Start the timer as soon as the first water goes into the conical filter paper.
6. Pour the same amount of water from the other beaker into the fluted paper. Start the second timer as soon as the water goes into the fluted filter.
7. Add more of the sand and water mixture to each filter paper until all of the liquid has been filtered. Stop the timer when the filter stops filtering. Leave any remaining sand in the beaker. Note the time taken for each filter, and how clear the filtrate is.
8. Repeat steps 1–7 with new filter papers, but this time use copper carbonate instead of sand.
9. Dispose of all residues from experiments as directed by your teacher.

Results
1. Record the appearance of the filtrate, for both the sand and the copper carbonate.
2. Record the time it took for all of the liquid to pass through each filter.

Review
1. Compare the rate at which the two differently folded filter papers filtered each of the mixtures.
2. Construct a conclusion for your investigation.
3. Assess whether your hypothesis was supported or not.
4. Propose a reason why one folding method was better than the other.

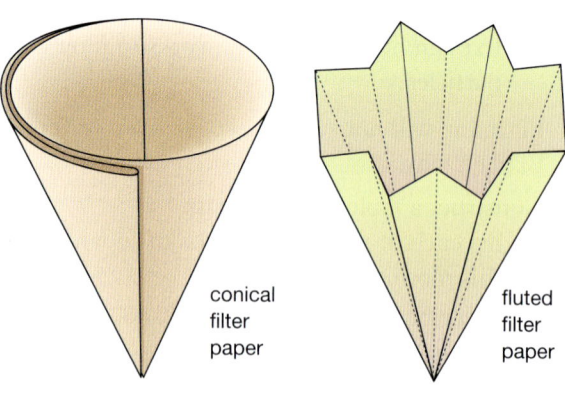

FIGURE 4.2.16

MODULE 4.2 Practical investigations

• STUDENT DESIGN •

2 • Separating solids

Purpose

To separate a mixture of sand, gravel, iron filings and salt.

Timing 45 minutes day 1, 10 minutes day 2

Materials

- 1 spatula each of sand, gravel, iron filings and salt
- water
- 100 mL beaker
- 4 spatulas
- magnet (wrapped in plastic)
- equipment including filter paper, funnels, beakers
- fly wire 20 cm square
- electronic scales

SAFETY
A Risk Assessment is required for this investigation.

Procedure

1. Use different spatulas to measure out one spatula each of sand, gravel, iron filings and salt.
2. Weigh each sample separately using the electronic scales and record the mass of each.
3. Combine all four substances together in a beaker.
4. Design a method to separate these four solids from each other so that you recover all four substances.
5. Write your procedure in your workbook.
6. Make sure you weigh each component once you have separated it at the end. Compare this with the initial mass and total, to see how accurate and careful your separation techniques have been.
7. Before you start any practical work, list any risks that your procedure might involve and how you can minimise those risks. Show your teacher. If they approve, then start work.

Hints

- Make sure the magnet stays covered in its plastic.
- Salt crystals form if salt solution is left to evaporate for a few days.
- Results from Module 3.3 Prac 3 may help you (if you did it).
- Use the STEM and SDI template in your eBook to help you plan and carry out your investigation.

Review

Construct a report using the headings listed in Figure 1.3.5 on page 26.

• STUDENT DESIGN •

3 • Oil spills

Sorbents are materials that can soak up substances. Sorbents are commonly used to soak up oil that has spilled into the sea, rivers or lakes.

Purpose

To compare three different sorbents that could be used to clean up oil spills.

Hypothesis

Which sorbent do you think will soak up more oil—paper towel, cotton balls or a sponge? Write a hypothesis in your workbook.

Timing 45 minutes

Materials

- 50 mL cooking oil
- detergent (for cleaning up)
- equal masses of cotton balls, paper towel and kitchen sponge
- 3 plastic cups
- tweezers
- 2 wide-mouth jars
- access to timer

SAFETY
A Risk Assessment is required for this investigation.

Procedure

1. Carefully read the list of materials provided.
2. Design a method that will allow you to compare how well cotton balls, paper towel and a kitchen sponge absorb cooking oil that has been mixed with water.
3. Write your procedure in your workbook.
4. Before you start any practical work, list any risks that your procedure might involve and how you can minimise those risks. Show your teacher. If they approve, then start work.

Use the STEM and SDI template in your eBook to help you plan and carry out your investigation.

Review

1. Construct a conclusion for your investigation.
2. Assess whether your hypothesis was supported or not.
3. Construct a report using the headings listed in Figure 1.3.5 on page 26.

CHAPTER 4 • MIXTURES 157

MODULE 4.2 Practical investigations

Stones and beans don't mix

Background
Nutritionists recommend that our diet should contain legumes. These foods are a good source of protein, dietary fibre and various vitamins and minerals. Many legumes grow close to the ground and include foods such as chickpeas, navy beans (used in canned baked beans), lentils and peanuts (also known as ground nuts).

When legumes are harvested, occasionally small stones from the field can accidently enter the food. This is a big problem for companies that package legumes. If a stone is mistaken for a legume, this could result in someone breaking a tooth.

Problem
An organic food store wants you to design a technique in order to separate small stones from one type of legume. Your task is to use your understanding of separating techniques to outline the process that the organic food store should use to remove stones before they sell the legumes.

Procedure
1. In a small group (3 or 4 students), design a system to separate small stones from one type of legume.
2. Write your procedure in your workbook and show your teacher. If they approve your plan, then collect your equipment and carry out the experiment.

Hints
In your initial investigation of the materials, consider these questions.
- What are the properties of dried legumes and stones?
- What happens if you put a magnet next to a stone or dried legume?
- What equipment and materials do you have access to?

Use the STEM and SDI template in your eBook to help you plan and carry out your investigation.

Materials
- 200 g of one type of dried legume
- 20 g of various small stones

Equipment
- water
- sieves
- magnets
- weighing balances
- plastic containers
- rulers
- and equipment that you have in your science laboratory such as funnels, measuring cylinders and beakers.

Engineering design process
- Identify the problem that needs solving.
- Brainstorm solutions to identify the different separation techniques and which ones might apply to this task.
- Before you commence your investigation you must conduct a risk assessment and write down safety measures that you will follow to keep yourself and other students safe. See the Activity Book Science toolkit to assist you with developing a risk assessment.
- Summarise your investigation in a scientific report including the Purpose, Hypothesis, Materials, Procedure, Risk Assessment, Results (including data presented in tables and / or graphs), Discussion and Conclusion.

Engineering design process

Identify problem → Brainstorm solutions → Design and build prototype → Test prototype → Prototype flawed → Communicate successful solution (with Evaluate and redesign loop)

FIGURE 4.2.17 Following the engineering design process. Engineering involves the application of science to design, build, test and maintain structures, machines and devices.

MODULE 4.3 Separating soluble substances

The soluble substances in a solution are far too small to settle or be trapped in filter papers. Different methods are therefore needed to separate them from the solvent they are dissolved in. In the photo a separation method called chromatography is being used to separate pigments in black dyes.

STEM 4 fun

Colourful black-and-white butterfly

PROBLEM

Can you use black marker and white paper to create a colourful butterfly?

SUPPLIES a range of different black markers and pens, dropper, straws, plastic or paper cups, water, methylated spirits, different white paper including filter paper, tissue paper, copy paper

PLAN AND DESIGN Design the solution. What information do you need to solve the problem? Draw a diagram. Make a list of materials you will need and steps you will take.

CREATE Follow your plan. Draw your solution to the problem.

IMPROVE What works? What doesn't? How do you know it solves the problem? What could work better? Modify your design to make it better. Test it out.

REFLECTION

1. What field of science did you work in? Are there other fields where this activity applies?
2. What did you do today that worked well? What didn't work well?

CHAPTER 4 • MIXTURES 159

Chromatography

Chromatography is a process that can separate a mixture by making it move through another substance. This substance could be a gel, column of liquid or strip of paper, like that shown in Figure 4.3.1. When a piece of paper with ink on it is placed in water, the water will move up the paper. Water is the solvent. As the water moves up the paper, it dissolves the dyes from the ink and carries the colours with it as it moves higher up the paper. The process is called chromatography.

Chromatography works because different substances in the dyes have different levels of attraction to the paper. Substances that are strongly attracted to the paper are harder for the solvent (water) to move along, so these substances do not move very far. Weakly attracted substances move the furthest along the paper. In this way, the different substances in the dye are separated.

Chromatography is very important in industry. It is used to find out what is in oil and gas, and to identify chemical pollutants in water samples taken from rivers or the sea.

Chromatography is also used by pharmaceutical manufacturers to analyse plants and animals for possible useful medical drugs and to test the quality of their products.

FIGURE 4.3.1 Paper chromatography separates mixtures such as inks and dyes.

STEM p. 165

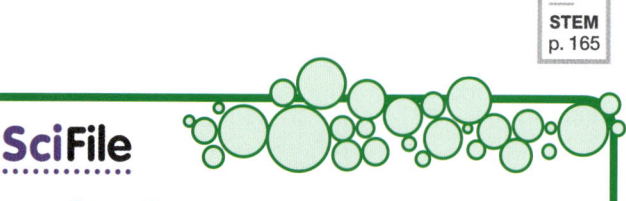

SciFile

Lawbreakers beware!
Chromatography can catch you out! It can help catch drug cheats in sports by identifying banned drugs in urine. Chromatography can also be used to identify the ink used to write a letter, and that ink can be matched to your pen.

science 4 fun

Candy crystals
Can you grow big candy crystals?

Collect this...
- sugar (sucrose)
- water
- food colouring (optional)
- flavouring (optional)
- clean glass jar
- clean cotton or string
- pencil or icy-pole stick
- metal saucepan
- stove

Do this...
1. Pour 3 cups of sugar and 1 cup of water into the saucepan.
2. Heat, stirring constantly, until all the sugar has dissolved. Try not to boil the solution. A few drops of food colouring and ½ teaspoon of flavouring can be added, but this may slow your crystal formation.
3. Cool the sugar syrup in the refrigerator until it is at about room temperature.
4. Soak the string in the syrup and then hang it to dry in the air.
5. Set up your equipment as shown in the diagram.

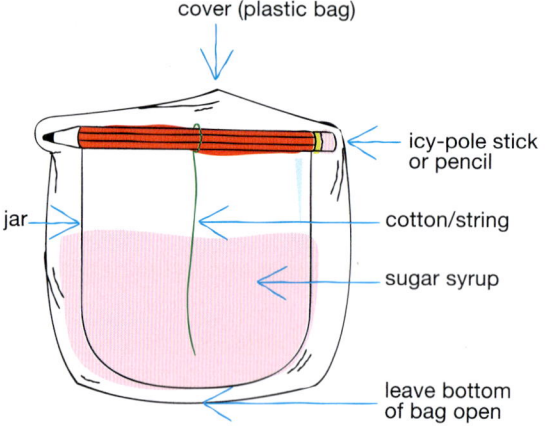

6. You can eat the candy after the week. Do not eat the string.

Record this...
1. Describe what happened.
2. Explain why you think this happened.

Evaporation

When pools of water lie on a road, or wet clothes are placed on the washing line, the sun will heat up the water. As the water heats, it changes state and becomes a gas, a process known as **evaporation**. As more of the water evaporates, the pool of water or wet clothes will become dry. Water evaporates at any temperature above 0°C. Water does not have to be boiling to evaporate. However, evaporation speeds up at higher temperatures. This explains why clothes dry more quickly on a hot day than a cold one.

If the water has any solute dissolved in it, then evaporation will leave that solute behind. For example, sea water is an aqueous solution of salt dissolved in water. After swimming in the sea, the water on your skin evaporates, leaving a thin layer of salt behind.

Evaporation is used in kitchens at home and in restaurants. For example, when cooks make a sauce or gravy, they heat the mixture so that water evaporates (Figure 4.3.2). As the mixture loses water, the sauce gets thicker and its flavour gets stronger.

FIGURE 4.3.2 Evaporation removes the water from sauces making them thicker and richer.

Evaporation is commonly used in the laboratory to separate a solvent from its solute. The solution can be left in the air to evaporate using the heat of the room, but a Bunsen burner or hotplate speeds the process up. The solute is left behind in the evaporating dish, while the solvent (usually water) is lost to the air. This means that you can only collect the solute.

Crystallisation

The solute left behind by evaporation often forms crystals. You can see some different crystals in Figure 4.3.3. Crystals have distinctive shapes because the solute particles lock into one another like pieces of a jigsaw.

As the solvent evaporates, the solution becomes more and more concentrated. Eventually the solution becomes so concentrated that it is saturated. The solute particles start to lock in with one another, and the crystals grow as more of the solvent evaporates. This process is called **crystallisation**. Smaller crystals form when the solvent evaporates quickly. In contrast, larger crystals form when the solvent evaporates slowly.

FIGURE 4.3.3 Crystals come in a variety of different shapes. They form because the solvent evaporates, leaving solute crystals behind.

Evaporation and crystallisation are used in industry to remove soluble substances from solutions and to purify substances. For example, salt producers make salt by using the heat from the Sun to evaporate water from pools of salt water. This leaves crystals of salt behind to be collected (Figure 4.3.4).

FIGURE 4.3.4 Salt crystals recovered from sea water have been scraped into piles.

Crystallisation is also used in industry to purify substances such as pharmaceuticals (medical drugs). A solution may have unwanted substances dissolved in it as well as substances that are wanted. The unwanted substances are called **impurities**.

CHAPTER 4 • MIXTURES **161**

The particles of impurities generally do not have the same shape as the solute particles. So if you crystallise the solute, the impurities will not have the right shape to lock into the growing crystals (Figure 4.3.5). Instead, the impurities stay in solution and the crystals formed stay pure.

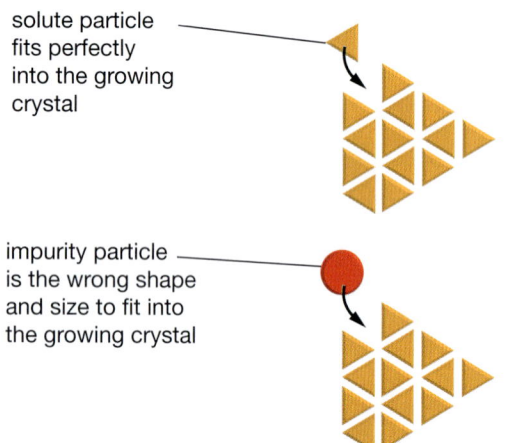

FIGURE 4.3.5 Impurities have the wrong shape to lock into crystals. Crystallisation is often used to purify substances such as medical drugs.

Distillation

Evaporation is the process in which a liquid turns into a gas. Condensation is the opposite: a gas cools to form a liquid. **Distillation** uses both evaporation and condensation to separate substances.

Evaporation loses the liquid solvent to the atmosphere, but sometimes you need to keep the liquid as well. In distillation, the gas is condensed back into a liquid so that it can be collected. If the solvent is water, distillation first evaporates off the water. Distillation then cools the water vapour so that it condenses back into liquid water. The apparatus that converts the gas back to the liquid is called the condenser. Figure 4.3.6 shows a special apparatus called a Liebig condenser that is often used in the laboratory.

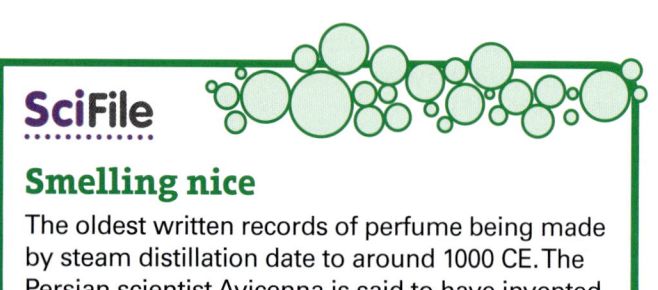

SciFile

Smelling nice

The oldest written records of perfume being made by steam distillation date to around 1000 CE. The Persian scientist Avicenna is said to have invented the process to make rose water. There is now a perfume named Avicenna in his honour.

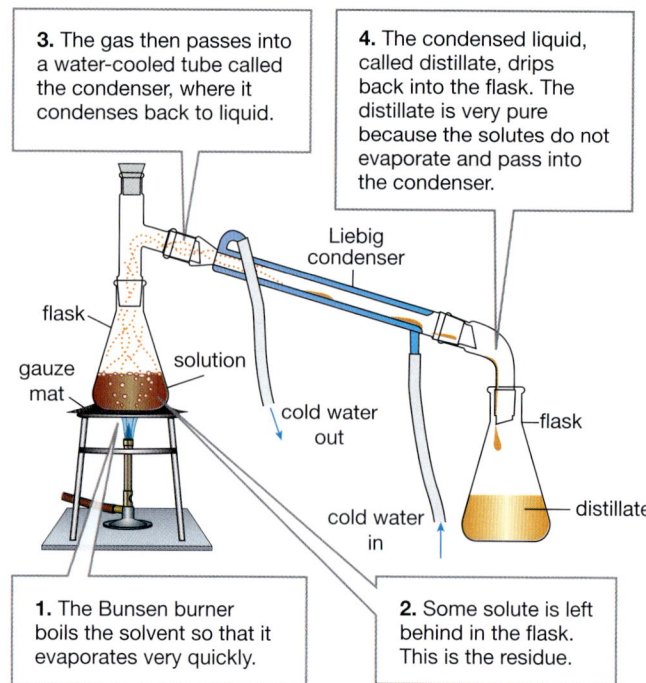

FIGURE 4.3.6 Distillation is often carried out in the laboratory using a Liebig condenser.

Distillation is able to separate several liquids from each other if they have different boiling points. For example, alcohol has a boiling point of 78°C while water boils at 100°C. These two liquids can therefore be separated by distillation. When the mixture reaches 78°C, the alcohol evaporates leaving the water behind. The alcohol vapours then condense back into liquid alcohol inside the condenser. After all the alcohol has evaporated, the mixture's temperature will increase and the water will evaporate when it reaches 100°C. When this water vapour reaches the condenser it too condenses back into its liquid form. Whatever solute was dissolved in the original solution is left behind.

As well as separating solutions in laboratories, distillation is used in:

- producing alcoholic drinks such as vodka and bourbon
- separating crude oil into petrol, diesel, lubricating oils and other components
- removing impurities from drinking water
- separating oxygen, nitrogen and argon from air for industrial use
- perfume manufacture.

MODULE 4.3 Review questions

Remembering

1. Define the terms:
   a. evaporation
   b. impurities.
2. What term best describes each of the following?
   a. the separation of ink by water moving up paper
   b. solute left behind after the solvent has evaporated.
3. Match the following separating methods with its correct description. Choose from A, B or C.
   a. chromatography
   b. evaporation
   c. distillation

   A. a process using evaporation and condensation to separate and recover both solute and solvent
   B. a process that can separate a mixture by making it move through another substance like a paper strip
   C. a process in which heat changes a liquid into a gas, allowing recovery of the solute but not the solvent
4. Name the separation process used to:
   a. separate different coloured substances from food colouring or ink
   b. collect salt crystals from seawater
   c. make alcoholic drinks like gin and whisky.

Understanding

5. Explain the process by which chromatography can separate substances.
6. Explain the process by which distillation can separate a solute and a solvent and allow you to recover both substances.
7. You are making copper sulfate crystals in the laboratory by evaporating water from a solution of copper sulfate. Describe how you could:
   a. make the crystals rapidly
   b. form larger crystals by evaporating the water slowly.

Applying

8. Identify a separation method that could be used for each of the following purposes:
   a. to purify water from a washing machine enough to drink it
   b. to recover the sugar from a bag that you accidentally dropped into a saucepan of water while you were cooking.
9. Draw a diagram that shows how crystallisation stops impurities from becoming part of a growing crystal.

Analysing

10. If you are lost in the bush and have no drinking water, you can make a 'bush still' to try to collect some.
    a. Compare the 'bush still' shown in Figure 4.3.7 with distillation apparatus.
    b. How can this be considered an example of distillation?

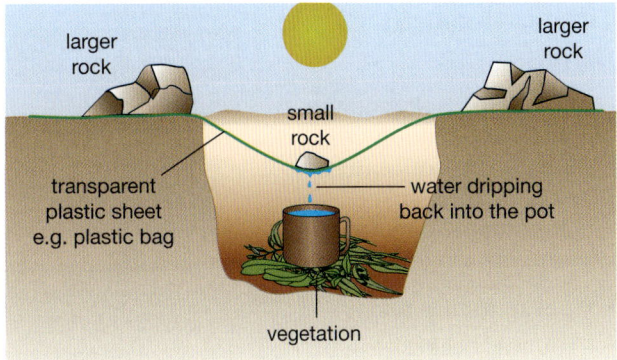

FIGURE 4.3.7

11. Compare evaporation of water and boiling of water.

Evaluating

12. a. Identify the process used in the STEM4fun on page 159 to separate the colours in marker pen inks.
    b. What do you think would happen if you swapped the tissue paper with paper that attracted the colouring more strongly.
    c. Justify your answer.
13. A whisky maker wants to concentrate the alcohol in his mixture. Alcohol boils at 78°C and water boils at 100°C. If you were the whisky maker, would you choose evaporation or distillation? Justify your choice.
14. When you dry your bathers after swimming in the sea, they are crisp with salt. However, if you rinse them in fresh water first, they dry clean and salt-free. Propose a reason why the two methods of drying produce such different results.
15. When evaporating a solution to produce pure crystals of a solute, there are also impurities left behind. Design an experimental method to separate the impurities and the crystals.

MODULE 4.3 Practical investigations

1 • Slow and fast evaporation *Questioning & Predicting* *Communicating*

Purpose
To grow salt (sodium chloride) crystals and compare their sizes when formed by fast and by slow evaporation.

Hypothesis
Which do you think will produce larger crystals—slow evaporation or fast evaporation? Before you go any further with this investigation, write a hypothesis in your workbook.

Timing 45 minutes

Materials
- 2 × 50 mL salt (sodium chloride) solution OR 2 × 50 mL concentrated alum (potassium aluminium sulfate) solution
- 2 evaporating basins
- 100 mL beaker
- Bunsen burner, bench mat, tripod and gauze mat or hotplate

SAFETY
A Risk Assessment is required for this investigation.

Tie long hair back. Turn the Bunsen burner flame to yellow when it is not being used. Allow equipment to cool before packing it away.

Procedure

SLOW EVAPORATION
1. Pour 50 mL of your solution into one of the evaporating basins until it is about one-quarter full. Set it aside somewhere in the room where it will not be disturbed. Observe what happens over the next day or so.

FAST EVAPORATION
2. Collect about 50 mL of solution in your beaker, and set up the equipment as shown in Figure 4.3.8. Do not turn on the Bunsen burner or hotplate yet.
3. Pour the solution into your evaporating basin until it is about half full.
4. Heat the solution with a hot flame with the Bunsen burner airhole about half open, watching carefully that material does not 'spit' out of the basin. If it does spit, close the collar on the Bunsen burner a little, or use the gas hose to move the Bunsen burner carefully in and out of the tripod. If you are using a hotplate then start with high heat and then turn it down as the solution starts to evaporate.
5. When only a small pool of the liquid is left, turn the Bunsen burner or hotplate off. The rest of the liquid will evaporate with the heat left in the basin.
6. Allow the basin to cool for several minutes.

Review
1. Describe the crystals formed by fast and slow evaporation.
2. a Construct a conclusion for your investigation.
   b Assess whether your hypothesis was supported or not.
3. Figure 4.3.8 shows the equipment used in this prac in three dimensions (3D). Construct a scientific diagram that shows it in two dimensions (2D).
4. Use the results of this prac to help you explain why salt crystals often form around the edges of salt lakes.

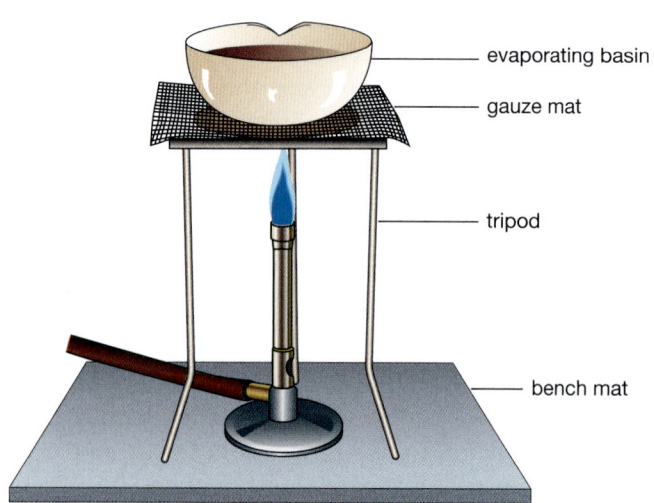
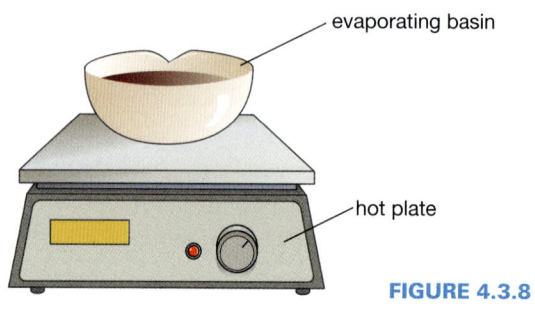

FIGURE 4.3.8

MODULE 4.3 Practical investigations

Do leaves contain the same colours?

Background
Simon enjoys walking home from school in April when there are many autumn leaves on the ground. He had always wondered why leaves change colour in autumn so he collected a few leaves of different colours and took them to his science class the following day. Simon's science teacher thought this was a very good question and asked if anyone in the class might know the answer? A couple of students thought that it might be due to the leaves dying since they no longer had access to water via the tree branches. Simon's teacher explained that leaves are normally green in colour due to a pigment called chlorophyll which is important in the process of photosynthesis. When leaves start to change colour in autumn, the chlorophyll breaks down and other colours that were also present in the leaf can later be observed.

Problem
Simon's class wanted to find out the range of different colours that could be found in leaves. Simon's teacher asked the class to use their knowledge of separating mixtures using the technique of chromatography to see if they could answer this question.

Procedure
1. Design and conduct a valid experiment that will separate the different colours contained in different leaves at any time of the year.
2. Write your procedure in your workbook and show your teacher. If they approve your plan, then collect your equipment and carry out the experiment.

Hints
- Many of the pigments in leaves are water soluble.
- Suitable solvents could include ethanol (methylated spirits) or acetone (nail polish remover).
- Use the STEM and SDI template in your eBook to help you plan and carry out your investigation.

Materials
- Leaves of different colours from the same or different trees

Equipment
- chromatography or filter paper
- beakers
- mortar and pestle
- methylated spirits
- acetone

Engineering design process
- Identify the purpose
- Identify the independent, dependent and controlled variables and only change one variable at a time.
- Based on your purpose and the controls and variables, write a hypothesis for this experiment.
- Before you commence your investigation you must conduct a risk assessment and write down safety measures that you will follow to keep yourself and other students safe. See the Activity Book Science toolkit to assist you with developing a risk assessment.
- Summarise your experiment in a scientific report including the Purpose, Hypothesis, Materials, Procedure, Risk Assessment, Results (including data presented in tables and / or graphs), Discussion and Conclusion.

Engineering design process

Identify problem → Brainstorm solutions → Design and build prototype → Test prototype → Prototype flawed → Communicate successful solution (with Evaluate and redesign loop)

FIGURE 4.3.9 Following the engineering design process. Engineering involves the application of science to design, build, test and maintain structures, machines and devices.

CHAPTER 4 • MIXTURES 165

MODULE 4.4 Purifying water

Drought in much of Australia has forced us to find ways to save water. One solution is to recycle water, cleaning dirty water and then using it again. Water can be cleaned using separating techniques such as filtration and distillation. New methods of providing clean water are also being developed. Some of these methods can produce drinking water from toilet water or seawater.

science 4 fun

Cleaning water

Can dirt clean water?

Collect this...
- some fairly clean sand
- some small stones like blue metal or road gravel
- bucket of muddy water
- ice-cream or margarine container
- some bricks or rocks for a stand
- 3 cups to catch liquid

Do this...
1. Make a small hole in the bottom of your ice-cream or margarine container.
2. Set up your equipment as shown.
3. Pour some muddy water in and let it pass through into the container at the bottom. Put this sample aside.
4. Repeat step 2, but instead of setting the sample aside, pour it through the sand and stones again.
5. Continue pouring the collected sample through the sand and stones until the sample you collect at the bottom has little suspended mud in it.

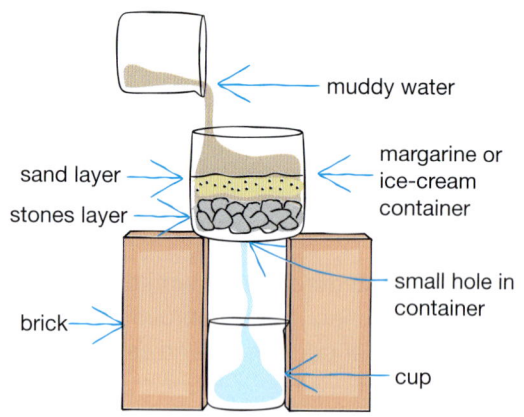

6. Compare this final sample with the original sample you set aside.

Record this...
1. Describe what happened.
2. Explain why you think this happened.

166 PEARSON SCIENCE 7 2ND EDITION

The need for water

Water is the most important substance needed for life. It is essential, because without it all living things die.

As humans, we need water for more than just drinking (Figure 4.4.1). We need water to grow our food. We also use water as a solvent that dissolves:
- soap and detergent in our showers, sinks and carwashes
- sugars and flavourings in soft drinks and fruit juices
- chemicals used in industry, in the preparation of foods, medicines, fertilisers, paints, adhesives and paper
- minerals underground in a process called leach mining.

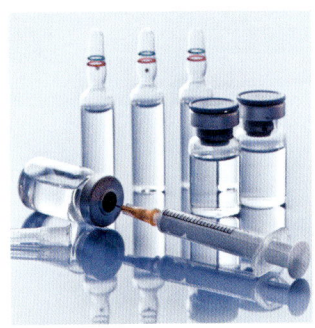

FIGURE 4.4.1 Water is used as a solvent in industry to make many products such as medicines, dyes, drinks and fertilisers.

Water also dissolves minerals in rocks and many of these are needed by plants for their growth. These minerals are also needed by animals that eat the plants.

SciFile

Too much water
It is possible to drink too much water. A man in the UK died after drinking about 7 litres of water in a short period. Excessive amounts of water like this can cause a condition where sodium is flushed out of the body and brain cells are damaged.

Is water pure or a mixture?

The term *water* means different things to different people. To scientists, water is a pure chemical with the chemical formula H_2O. However, to everyone else, water is what comes out of a tap and is found in rivers, lakes, swimming pools, rain and the sea.

In these cases, water is not pure but is an aqueous solution with H_2O as its solvent, or a suspension H_2O. Sometimes it's both. For example, seawater is both an aqueous solution and a suspension, containing water, dissolved salt, floating particles like sand, and living things like seaweed, bacteria and fish. Seawater also has dissolved oxygen in it, which is used by all the organisms that live there, and dissolved carbon dioxide, which is used by seaweed.

Water in rivers and lakes contains dissolved oxygen, as well as bacteria and possibly particles of dirt, forming a muddy suspension (Figure 4.4.2). Swimming pools contain dissolved chlorine or other treatment chemicals.

FIGURE 4.4.2 The mixing of these two rivers shows that one is relatively clear while the other has a lot of mud floating in it as a suspension.

Tap water is a mixture of many substances. Some of these enter the water naturally through contact with soil and rock. Others are added deliberately by water authorities to protect public health. What is in your water depends on the source of the water, and how it was treated.

CHAPTER 4 • MIXTURES **167**

Water treatment

Water that is obtained from dams, rivers and aquifers is never pure. It also contains other substances. Most of these substances come from the rocks and soil that the water passes over.

These unwanted substances can cause health and other problems if not removed before the water is used. For example, rubbish washed from gutters into rivers, dams and lakes encourages microscopic disease-causing bacteria to grow in the water. Likewise, pollutants might be toxic. The high salt content of groundwater rusts away hot water systems and washing machines, often causing them to burst. Clay and other sediments can also block pipes and clog motors.

Drinking water

Water fit to drink is called **potable water**, while water unfit to drink is known as non-potable. Water from dams and groundwater goes to a treatment plant before it is supplied as potable water to homes and businesses.

There are five stages of water treatment as shown in Figure 4.4.3. These stages are:

1 Flocculation—The fine solid particles like clay are separated out of the water. Chemicals called flocculants are added to make the tiny clay particles clump together.

2 Sedimentation—after an hour the water passes into a sedimentation tank where these clumps settle to the bottom.

3 Filtration—The water is pumped through filters to remove any remaining particles.

4 Sterilisation—Chlorine is added to kill micro-organisms like bacteria.

5 Fluoridation—Fluoride is added to reduce the chance of tooth decay.

Water filters like the one shown in Figure 4.4.4 can be used to remove impurities and added chemicals from potable water. Generally this is not needed in Australia.

Prac 1 p. 175

FIGURE 4.4.4 Some people use filters to clean their water of impurities.

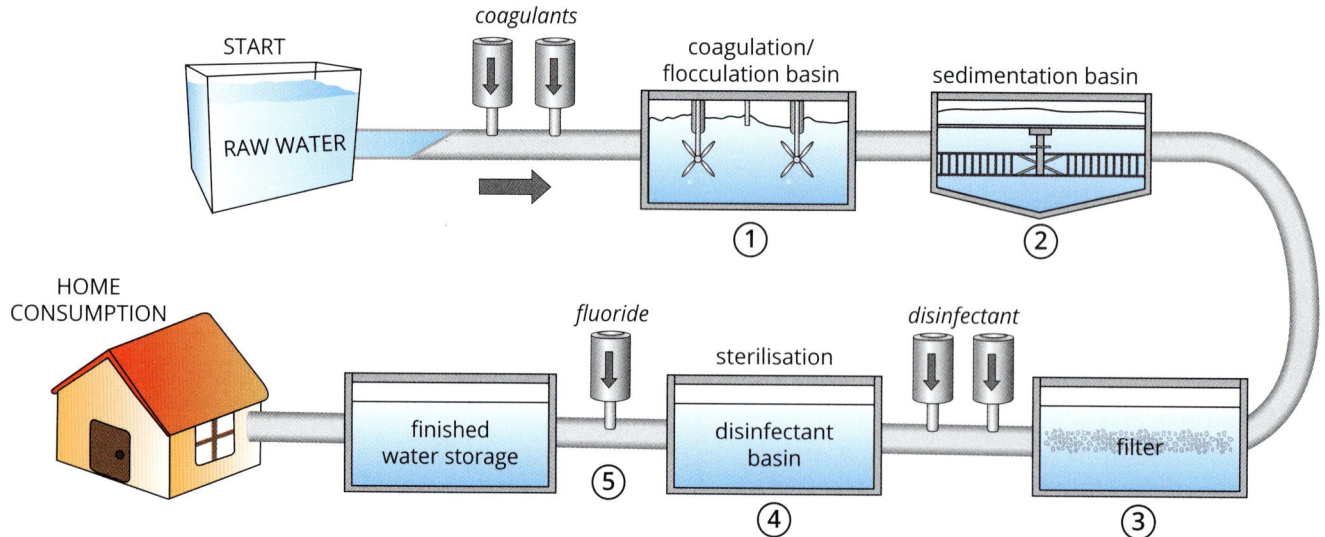

FIGURE 4.4.3 Drinking water treatment plant

Desalination

Dams, lakes and groundwater may not be able to supply all of Australia's needs in the future. This is because the water in them comes from rainfall, and rainfall is declining in many parts of the country. Another source of drinking water is salt water, such as seawater or water from salt lakes or salty rivers. Before we can drink this, the salt must be removed. **Desalination** is the process of removing salts such as sodium chloride from the water.

Desalination can be achieved by distillation, but distillation in this form doesn't work well on a large scale. The desalination process is also quite expensive. Another process of removing salt from seawater is via reverse osmosis. This too is expensive as it requires a lot of energy. Reverse osmosis places salt water under high pressure, which forces it through a very fine filter or membrane. The membrane has microscopically small holes that only the water particles pass through. The salt is left behind. In this way the salt is separated from the water. A reverse osmosis plant is shown in Figure 4.4.5.

FIGURE 4.4.5 Reverse osmosis desalination plants have been built near Perth, Sydney, Melbourne and the Gold Coast to treat seawater and make it into drinking water.

Wastewater treatment

Wastewater is any water that has been used and disposed of because it is no longer clean. This includes all water disposed from homes, shops, offices and factories and the runoff from roads, gardens and irrigation. **Sewage** is wastewater from kitchens, bathrooms, toilets and laundries.

Sewage can be classified as:

- **blackwater**—this is wastewater that comes from toilets and kitchens. This wastewater contains urine, faeces (poo), toilet paper and anything else that gets thrown down the toilet. Blackwater also includes food wastes washed down the sink and wastewater from dishwashers.
- **greywater**—this is wastewater that comes from showers, baths and laundries. It contains a large range of substances such as detergents, soaps, shampoo, grease and hair.

Due to its contents, blackwater contains many more bacteria (germs) than greywater. The bacteria use some impurities, mainly food scraps and faeces, as food.

The sewerage system

Most homes and businesses in cities are connected to the **sewerage system**. This is a system of underground pipes that carry blackwater and greywater away to a waste treatment plant. This plant then makes the water safe enough to pump into the ocean or to be used to irrigate crops and vegetable gardens. A typical sewage treatment plant is shown in Figure 4.4.6 on page 170.

Prac 2
p. 176

CHAPTER 4 • MIXTURES   **169**

Septic tanks

Septic tanks are used to process sewage from houses and businesses located beyond the sewerage system, usually in the country or outer suburbs. Septic tanks are made up of a series of concrete or plastic tanks buried underground close to the building they serve. They process both blackwater and greywater and the treated water soaks through the bottom of the final tank to join groundwater in the aquifers. You can see how a typical septic tank works in Figure 4.4.7.

SciFile

The world's smelliest job?

Septic tanks have to be emptied out from time to time when the solids build up too much. The worker may have to take the lid off the tank to clear blockages. You need a strong stomach and an ability to cope with bad smells in that job.

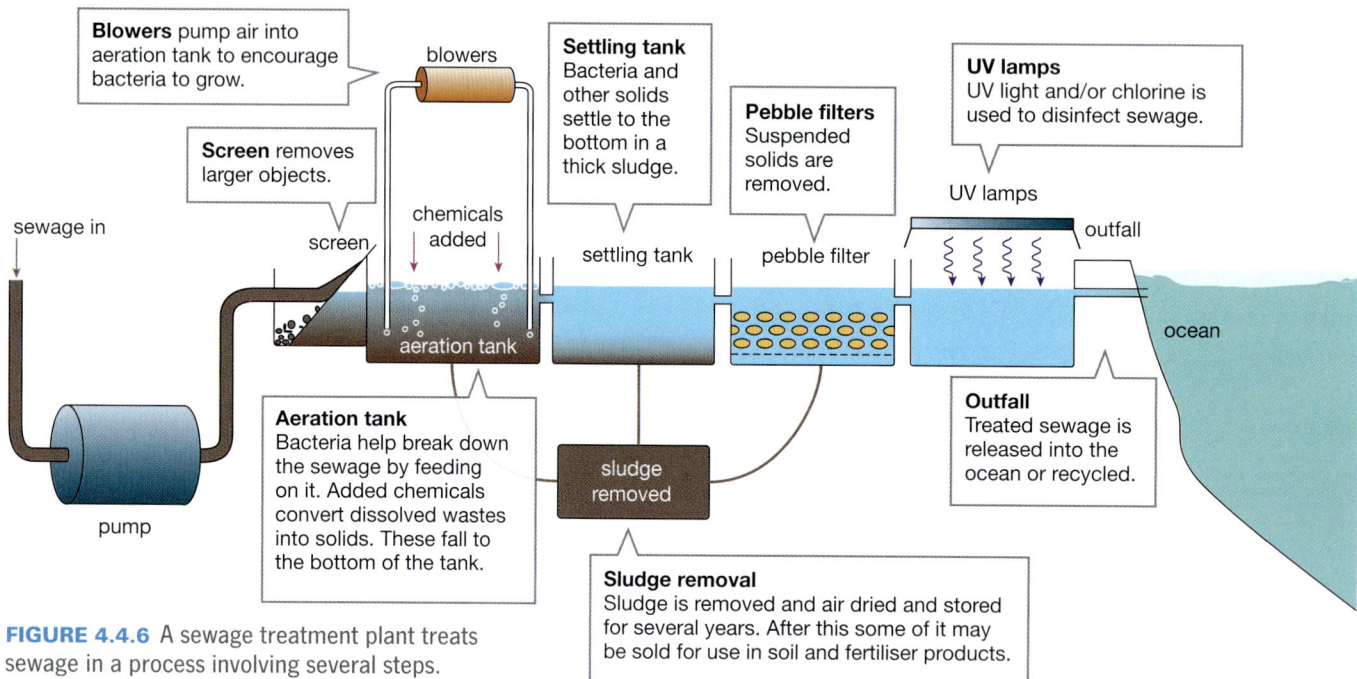

FIGURE 4.4.6 A sewage treatment plant treats sewage in a process involving several steps.

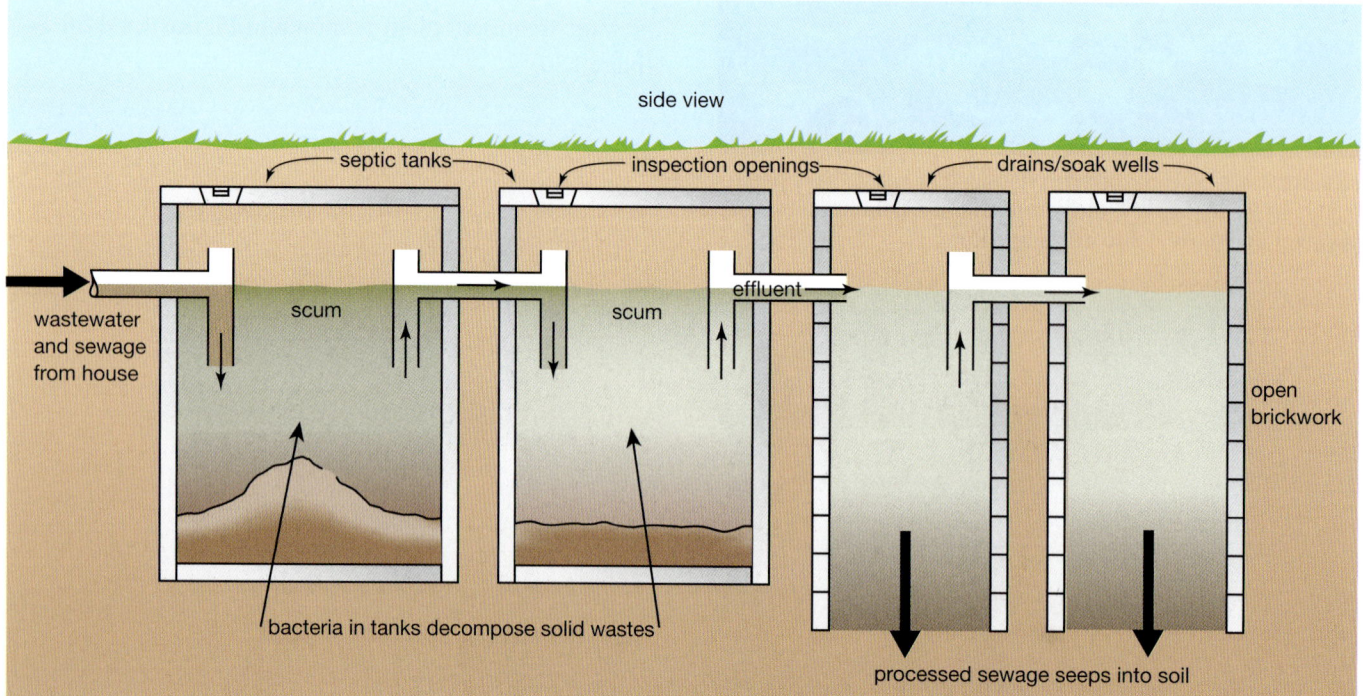

FIGURE 4.4.7 Septic tanks consist of tanks and soak wells. Processed sewage then seeps into the soil.

Greywater recycling systems

Greywater recycling systems are small systems used in homes to recycle and reuse the greywater from laundries, showers and baths. The water is cleaned and is then used in laundries, to water the garden and to flush toilets. However, the water is not clean enough to be used for drinking or washing.

A plan of a greywater recycling system is shown in Figure 4.4.8. The system uses an underground tank in which special bacteria decompose wastes in the greywater. Then the water is passed through a very fine filter to remove the bacteria and other particles and impurities. Finally the cleaned water is stored in another chamber to be re-used.

Toilets and gardens use a lot of water so using greywater in these areas, saves the drinking water that would otherwise have been used.

Protecting the environment

Our water and our environment will be cleaner if we all stop putting the wrong things down the toilet or sink. Some simple actions we can all take are listed below.

1. In the bathroom: Put medicines, nappies, women's sanitary products, razor blades and cotton buds in the bin instead of down the toilet or sink.

2. In the kitchen: Wipe the oil off pots and pans with paper towel instead of pouring excess oil down the sink. Then put the towel in the bin, along with any food scraps.

3. In the laundry: Use less detergent in the laundry. Most people use more detergent/washing powder than the manufacturer recommends. Choose detergents that are phosphate- and nitrate-free since these chemicals cause algal blooms in lakes and rivers. These blooms then produce toxic chemicals that kill fish.

4. On the street: Put rubbish in bins. Otherwise it will be washed into the rivers and into the sea via the nearest stormwater drain next time it rains.

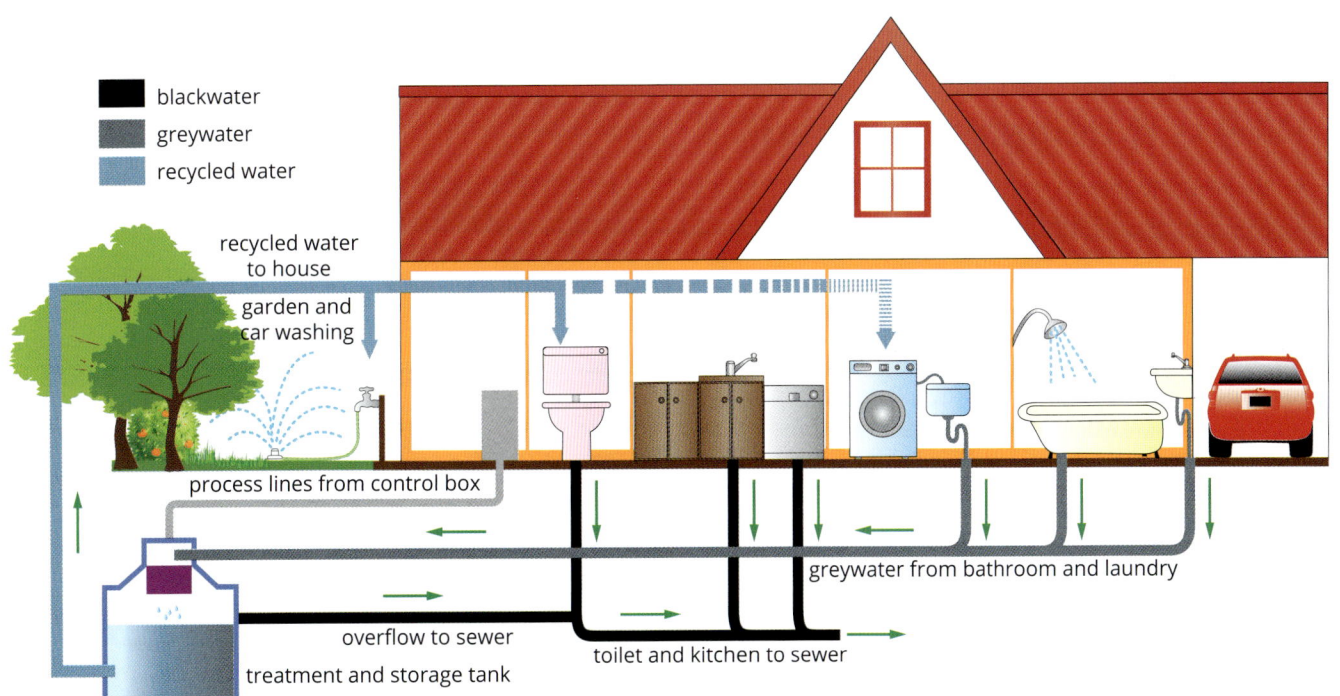

FIGURE 4.4.8 A domestic greywater recycling system

SCIENCE AS A HUMAN ENDEAVOUR
Use and influence of science

Drinking recycled sewage

At present in Australia, recycled sewage water is only used for irrigation of crops and public parks. However, the Australian Government has stated that it is almost certain that we will soon use recycled sewage for drinking water (Figure 4.4.9).

FIGURE 4.4.9 Singapore's recycled wastewater, bottled and ready to drink

Why is it being considered?

Australia is the driest inhabited continent (Figure 4.4.10). With regular droughts and an increasing population we simply do not have enough water available to meet the demand. This is why water authorities are trying to find alternative water supplies and looking for ways to reduce water usage. Currently, water use in Australia is increasing rather than decreasing.

Should we use it?

The proposals to recycle sewage for drinking water have caused a lot of debate. For example, Toowoomba residents in south-east Queensland rejected the proposal to recycle their wastewater. One reason against using it is the 'yuk factor'. This means people don't like the thought of drinking recycled water. However, tests have shown that people cannot taste the difference between tap water, bottled water and recycled water.

FIGURE 4.4.10 Parts of Australia are very dry. Recycling sewage is a possible solution to our shortage of water.

SCIENCE AS A HUMAN ENDEAVOUR

Water authorities in Australia believe that there is no scientific or health reason against recycling wastewater for drinking. This is based on the conclusions of much scientific research. Recycled wastewater is successfully used to top up drinking water supplies in the United States, Namibia and Singapore (Figure 4.4.9).

How would it be done?

Recycling wastewater

Some uses of recycled wastewater are shown in Figure 4.4.11. The main proposal at present is that Australia should adopt indirect potable (drinkable water) re-use. This means first sending wastewater to a water treatment plant, where it is highly treated to make it safe. The highly treated water is then pumped back into an existing drinking water source such as a reservoir, river or aquifer. The reservoir or aquifer uses natural processes to treat the water, such as filtration by soil particles and decomposition by bacteria. When the water is needed, it is pumped out of the reservoir to another water treatment plant.

Recycling sewage

Reverse osmosis is one of the processes that can be used for recycling sewage. In Toowoomba, for example, the wastewater would have been treated using filtration, reverse osmosis, ultraviolet disinfection and oxidation processes to destroy microorganisms. Reverse osmosis is already used around the world to provide water for industry and drinking water on ships.

REVIEW

1 Explain why some authorities are looking at sewage as a potential source of drinking water.
2 Name the process most likely to be used in Australia to recycle sewage.
3 Create a flow chart that shows the process of turning wastewater into potable water
4 List the advantages and disadvantages of using recycled sewage as a major water supply.
5 Should Australia plan to use recycled sewage in the future? Use evidence from your summary in question 4 to support your answer.

AB 4.8

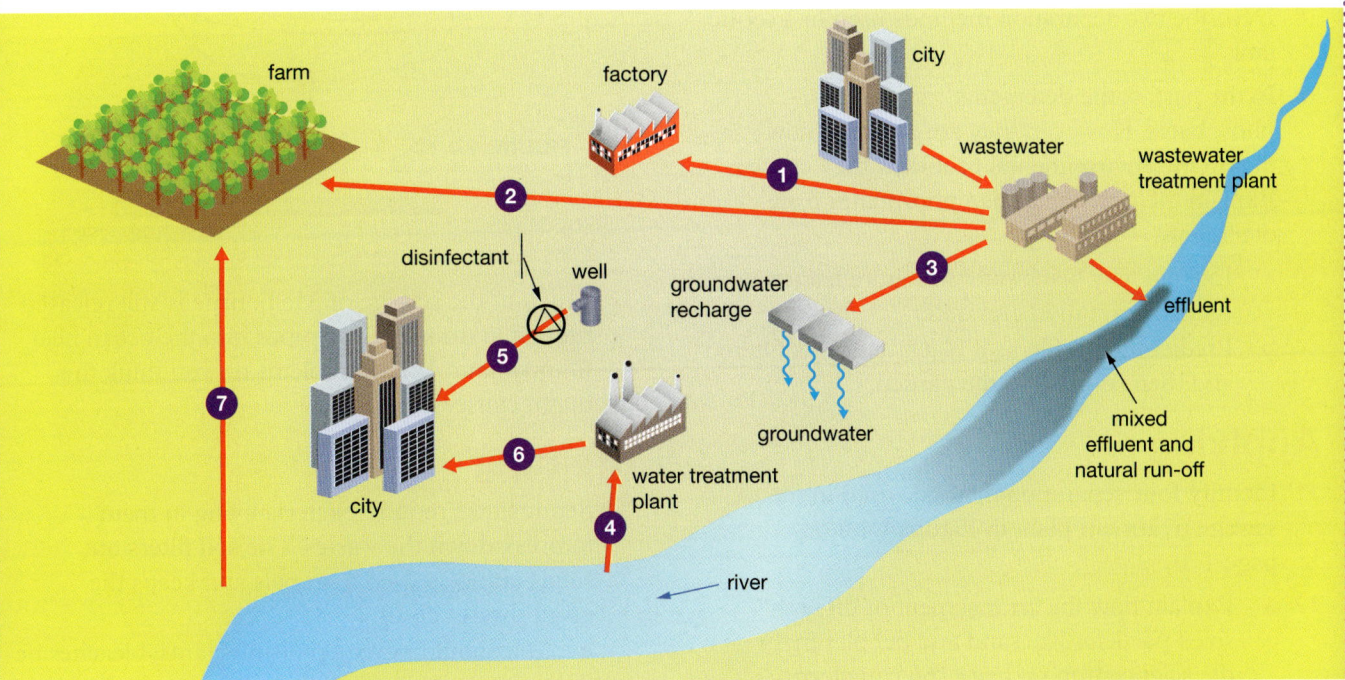

1 Direct industrial re-use
2 Direct agricultural re-use
3 Groundwater recharge
4 Indirect potable re-use from river
5 Indirect potable re-use from well
6 Potable water supply system
7 Indirect agricultural reusable re-use from river

FIGURE 4.4.11 Some possible uses of recycled wastewater

MODULE 4.4 Review questions

Remembering

1. Define the terms:
   a. potable
   b. flocculant
   c. blackwater
   d. sewage.

2. What term best describes each of the following?
   a. water fit to drink
   b. water from showers and sinks but not toilets
   c. the system that takes sewage away to treatment plants
   d. the process of removing salts from seawater.

3. What is the chemical formula for pure water?

4. List three systems of water treatment.

5. List the steps in sewage treatment before the water is ready to use for irrigation.

6. Name the desalination process that uses high pressure to filter salt water.

Understanding

7. Explain why most of the water around you is a mixture and not pure.

8. Describe two separation methods used in a septic tank.

9. In the past, some detergents contained phosphates. However, they are not used now due to the environmental problems they caused. Explain the decision to ban phosphates from detergents.

10. a. Explain why blackwater has more bacteria (germs) in it than greywater.
    b. Predict the problems if blackwater was filtered and then re-used on the garden.

Applying

11. Identify four separation methods used in the sewage treatment plant in Figure 4.4.6 on page 170.

12. a. Explain how the arrangement of different sized particles like sand and pebbles in the science4fun on page 166 can clean muddy water.
    b. Identify the separation technique being used in the science4fun.

Analysing

13. Classify the wastewater from the following as either greywater or blackwater.
    a. Kate is having a shower.
    b. Jill is washing her hair over the bath.
    c. Rod is using the urinal in the mensroom.
    d. David is using the washing machine.

14. Compare water treatment by the sewerage system with that by septic tanks.

Evaluating

15. Propose a reason why camping and fishing are often prohibited near dams.

16. Your basins at home have an 'S' bend in the water pipes below the drain hole, as shown in Figure 4.4.12. The bend keeps some water trapped in it. When you turn on the taps the trapped water is pushed out and replaced by new water. You have a similar water trap in your toilet. Propose some reasons why a water trap is needed in basins.

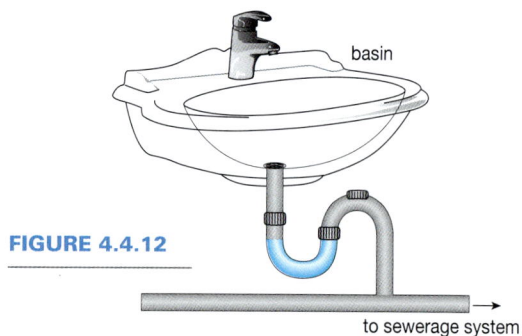

FIGURE 4.4.12

17. Much of the sewage of Melbourne is still released untreated through long pipes into the ocean near Gunnamatta. What problems do you think this might cause?

Creating

18. Septic tanks require bacteria living in them to break down the wastes. The soil filters out solids and dissolved materials and keeps the groundwater clean.
    a. You should never tip disinfectants, bleaches or paint down the sink if you have a septic tank. Propose a reason why.
    b. Construct a pamphlet that plumbers can give to clients with blocked septic tanks explaining what not to do and why.

MODULE 4.4 Practical investigations

1 • Flocculation

Purpose
To compare different chemicals as possible flocculating agents.

Timing 30 minutes

Materials
- muddy water
- test flocculants (1 M solutions in dropper bottles)
  - potassium aluminium sulfate (alum)
  - aluminium sulfate
  - sodium carbonate
  - sodium hydrogen carbonate
  - sodium chloride
  - iron(II) sulfate
  - calcium chloride
- 2 × 100 mL beakers
- filter funnel
- filter paper
- filter stand
- test-tube rack
- 7 small test-tubes

SAFETY
A Risk Assessment is required for this investigation.

All the chemicals should be considered to be toxic, so do not touch, sniff or taste them.

Procedure
1. Filter the muddy water to remove large particles.
2. Use the filtrate (the leftover water from Step 1) to half fill the seven test-tubes. Label each tube with a code so you know which flocculant you will add to it.
3. Add five drops of your first test flocculant to the first test-tube, add five drops of the second to the second test-tube, and so on , as shown in Figure 4.4.13. Record your observation on each test-tube in a table.
4. Filter one of the clearest test-tubes and observe the filtrate and residue.
5. Dispose of all residues from experiments as directed by your teacher.

Review
1. Identify the test materials that appeared to be flocculants.
2. Is there any way of telling which substance was the best flocculant? Explain.
3. Explain how this experiment is relevant to our lives.

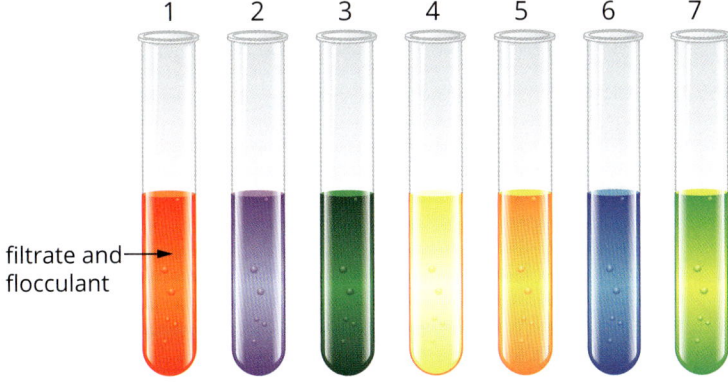

FIGURE 4.4.13

CHAPTER 4 • MIXTURES 175

MODULE 4.4 Practical investigations

• STUDENT DESIGN •

2 • Sewage treatment

Purpose
To design and construct a model of a sewage treatment plant (Figure 4.4.14).

Timing 90–120 minutes

Materials
- 500 mL of a mixture of water, vegetable oil, mud, sand, gravel and paper
- potassium aluminium sulfate
- equipment chosen by students

SAFETY
A Risk Assessment is required for this investigation.

Procedure
1. In your group, decide what are the essential features of a sewage treatment plant.
2. Design a model of a sewage treatment plant. The method of separation should model the processes used in a real sewage treatment plant (Figure 4.4.14). You are only modelling the sewage treatment processes. Some processes are too difficult, time consuming or dangerous to actually do in a laboratory. Do not actually aerate the mixture, use real ultraviolet light or add chlorine. You can pretend you are doing these processes by using materials to simulate the processes.
3. Draw your design in your workbook and write how you intend to separate the mixture.
4. Before you start any practical work, assess your model and how it will work. List any risks that it might involve and what you might do to minimise those risks. Show your teacher your design and your assessment of its risks. If they approve, then collect all the required materials and start work.

Hints
- Fly wire is a good sieve.
- You can simulate aerating the mixture by blowing into a plastic tube.
- A lamp can simulate a UV steriliser.
- You could 'pretend' that a salt solution is chlorine.
- Use the STEM and SDI template in your eBook to help you plan and carry out your investigation.

Review
1. Compare your model with a real sewage treatment plant.
2. Evaluate the performance of your design.
3. Discuss the relevance of this practical activity to everyday life.

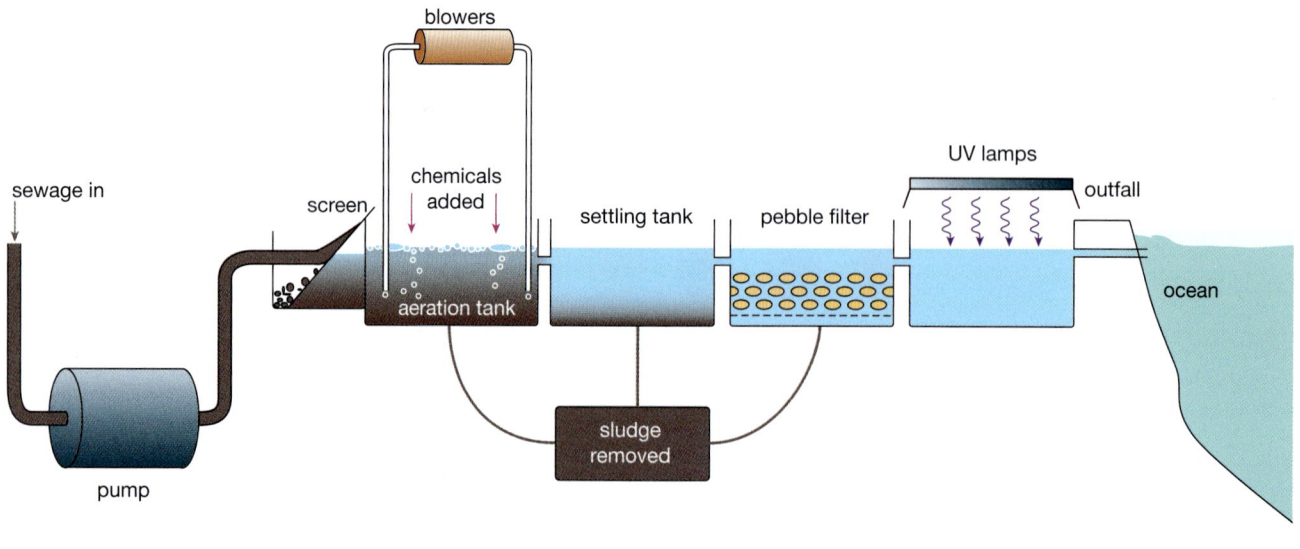

FIGURE 4.4.14 The typical stages for sewage treatment

CHAPTER 4 Chapter review

Remembering

1. Where are each of the following devices used?
   a. centrifuge
   b. reverse osmosis plant
   c. paper chromatography
   d. Liebig condenser
   e. septic tank.
2. What are the benefits of a greywater recycling system in the home?

Understanding

3. Outline how you could separate oil and water.
4. Outline the process of distillation.
5. Outline the desalination process known as reverse osmosis.

Applying

6. Identify a method you could use to separate:
   a. sand and water
   b. iron filings and sand
   c. salt and water
   d. alcohol and water
   e. pebbles and water.
7. You have a solution containing blue dye.
   - You filter some of the solution through filter paper. There is no residue in the filter paper and the filtrate is blue.
   - When you filter some of the solution through an even finer carbon filter, the filtrate is colourless.
   - When you take this carbon filter and shake it in methylated spirits, the liquid turns blue.

   Apply your knowledge of solvents and separation techniques to outline what is happening at each step.
8. A student adds 10 grams of solid X to 100 mL of pure water, but only 1 gram dissolves.
   a. Describe this solution.
   b. Calculate how much of solid X would settle on the bottom of the container.

Analysing

9. Use words or a Venn diagram to compare:
   a. solutions with suspensions
   b. evaporation with distillation
   c. evaporation with crystallisation.
   d. pure water and seawater
   e. sewage with the sewerage system
   f. greywater and blackwater.

Evaluating

10. Use examples to justify this statement:
    The physical properties of a mixture influence the type of separation method used.
11. Which of the following would be the best way to dispose of 500 mL of cooking oil? Justify your answer.
    A. Pour it down the sink.
    B. Flush it down the toilet.
    C. Mix it with detergent and put it in the sink.
    D. Soak it into paper and put it in the bin.
12. Assess the following statement made by a scientist:
    It is essential in Australia that we increase the amount of water we are recycling. Greywater and blackwater can become a vital part of this.
13. When you add 20 g of substance Z to 50 mL of water, only 5 g dissolves.
    a. Calculate how much more of substance Z would dissolve if you added another 50 mL of water to the container.
    b. Predict what would happen to the amount of substance Z if you added 200 mL of water to the original solution.
14. a. Assess whether you can or cannot answer the questions on page 139 at the start of this chapter.
    b. Use this assessment to evaluate how well you understand the material presented in this chapter.

Creating

15. Design an experiment to separate a mixture containing salt, sand and iron filings.
16. Use the following ten key terms to construct a visual summary of the information presented in this chapter.

    mixture   solution   water treatment
    filtration   gravity   distillation
    evaporation   sewage
    purifying water insoluble

    AB 4.11

CHAPTER 4 Inquiry skills

Research

1 `Evaluating` `Communicating`

Research three methods of cleaning up pollution from oil spills in the ocean. Choose methods that use separation techniques you have studied such as filtering, gravity separation or centrifuging. In your answer:
a   Outline each method.
b   Identify the separation technique each method uses and explain how each method works.
Present your findings in digital form.

FIGURE 4.5.1 Cleaning up ocean oil spills can be achieved by several methods. This string of polystyrene floats (called a boom) has trapped oil floating on the ocean's surface.

2 `Communicating`

Research two separation methods used in either the food industry or the wine industry.
a   Name the methods used.
b   Explain the purpose of each separation method.
Present your research as diagrams, photos or videos illustrating the equipment used in the separation method.

3 `Evaluating` `Communicating`

Water shortages are becoming a reality in many places in Australia. There are many possible solutions to this. Consider the following list of possible strategies a government may use and discuss by providing points for and against each strategy.
• increase the price of water
• impose severe water restrictions
• increase fines for using water without permission
• build more water treatment plants
• improve water recycling methods in the home and industry
• public awareness campaigns.

4 `Evaluating` `Communicating`

One way of trying to save water is by using alternative toilet designs. One alternative design is the composting or dry toilet, which can be used instead of the flushing toilet usually found in homes. Research the different types of toilets used around Australia.
a   Include a diagram of each type of toilet.
b   Explain how each toilet works.
c   Propose reasons why composting toilets are not more widely used in homes.
Present your research as a pamphlet to homeowners or a display for a home show.

5 `Processing & Analysing` `Communicating`

Research the water purification process called reverse osmosis.
a   Describe the basic process of reverse osmosis using a diagram.
b   Compare the process of reverse osmosis with filtration.
c   Include a diagram showing:
    • a typical reverse osmosis unit that can be used in a home to purify tap water
    • how a desalination plant uses reverse osmosis.
d   Include a map showing a desalination plant that uses reverse osmosis nearest to your home.
Present your research in digital form.

CHAPTER 4
Inquiry skills

Thinking scientifically

1 Refer to the following information and Table 4.5.1 to answer the questions below.

Air is a mixture of gases. This table shows the composition and proportion of gases in air where water vapour has been removed.

TABLE 4.5.1 Composition and proportion of gases in air where water vapour has been removed

Substance	Proportion of dry air (%)	Boiling point (°C)
argon	0.96	−186
oxygen	21	−183
nitrogen	78	−196
carbon dioxide	0.04	−79

a Which graphs could be used to represent the composition of dry air?

A
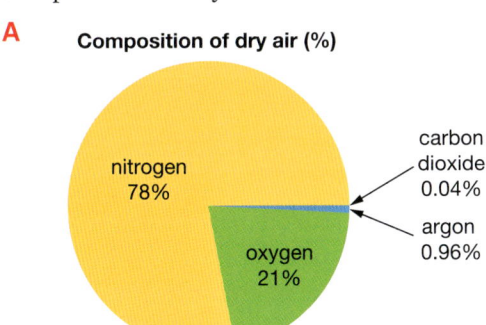

B
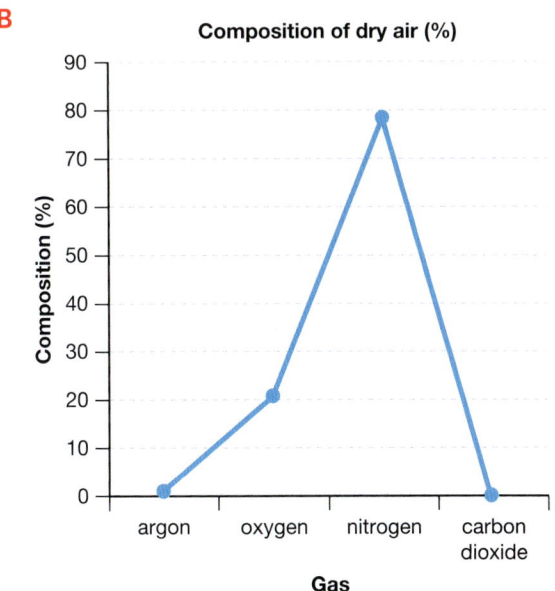

C
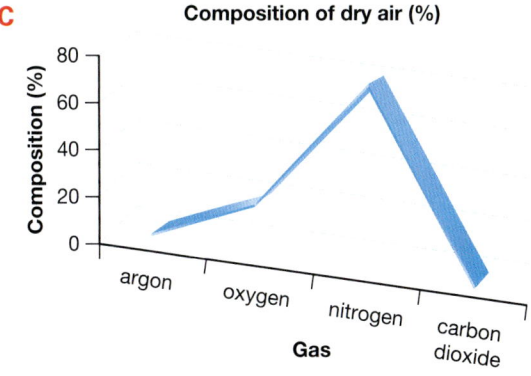

D
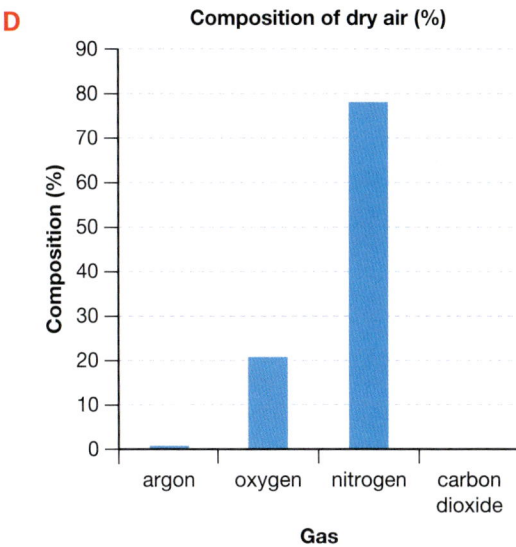

b Which substance in air has the lowest boiling point?
A argon
B oxygen
C nitrogen
D carbon dioxide.

c Which process could be used to separate the substances that make up air?
A filtration
B decanting
C distillation
D chromatography.

CHAPTER 4 • MIXTURES 179

CHAPTER 4

Inquiry skills

2   Refer to the following data to answer the questions below.

Soda is a mixture.

The bubbles in soda water come from carbon dioxide gas (CO$_2$) dissolved in water (Figure 4.5.2).

FIGURE 4.5.2

The amount of carbon dioxide in water depends on the temperature of the water (Figure 4.5.3).

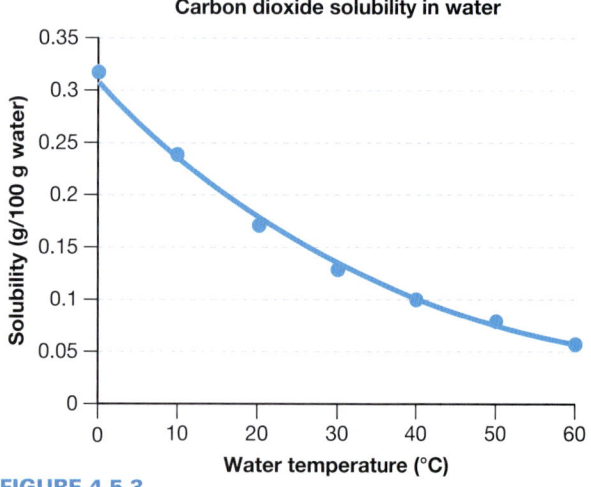

FIGURE 4.5.3

a   What is the trend in the above graph?
   A   erratic
   B   increasing
   C   decreasing
   D   unchanging.

b   What is the solubility of CO$_2$ at 25°C?
   A   0.05 g/ 100 g
   B   0.15 g/ 100 g
   C   0.16 g/ 100 g
   D   0.70 g/ 100 g.

c   What would the solubility of CO$_2$ at 70°C be?
   A   0.03 g/ 100 g
   B   0.05 g/ 100 g
   C   0.06 g/ 100 g
   D   0.10 g/ 100 g.

d   What is the independent variable in the graph?
   A   water
   B   solubility
   C   temperature
   D   carbon dioxide.

e   What is CO$_2$ in this mixture?
   A   solute   B   aquifer
   C   solvent   D   solution.

f   Carbon dioxide can trap heat in the atmosphere. Carbon dioxide is naturally dissolved in the ocean waters.
   What will be the effect of climate change warming the ocean waters?
   A   The oceans will begin to fizz.
   B   More carbon dioxide will be dissolved in the oceans.
   C   The rate of change to hotter climates will be increased.
   D   The rate of change to hotter climates will be decreased.

3   Jan tested how well certain substances dissolved in cold and hot water. Her results are shown in Table 4.5.2.

TABLE 4.5.2 How well substances dissolve in hot and cold water

Substance	Colour of substance	Did it dissolve in cold water?	Did it dissolve in hot water?
E	white	no	no
F	yellow	no	no
G	white	no	yes
H	white	yes	yes
I	brown	yes	yes

Identify which pair of substances could be separated from each other by dissolving one of them in hot water and then filtering out the one that did not dissolve.
   A   H and I   B   E and G
   C   G and I   D   E and F

CHAPTER 4 Inquiry skills

4 Michael and Andrew used the procedure shown in Figure 4.5.4 to separate copper sulfate from water from an aqueous copper sulfate solution.

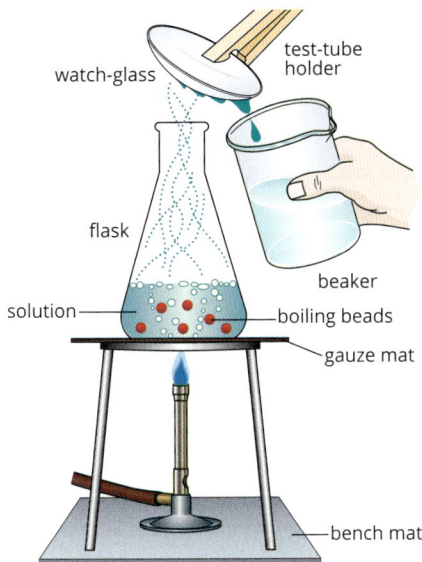

FIGURE 4.5.4

a Identify the main separation method that resulted in the liquid in the beaker.
b If they continue to heat the conical flask, predict what it will contain at the end.
c Identify three possible safety issues with the experiment.
d How successful do you think this method of separation is? Predict some problems with the process.
e Identify equipment that would do a better job of separating the copper sulfate solution.

5 Scientist Jane noticed that where muddy water from a river met the ocean, it became clear fairly quickly. Scientist Jim suggested that the sediment settled because the river slowed down when it met the sea and the particles were too heavy to stay suspended in the water. When experiments with the muddy river water were conducted it was found that the mud particles stayed suspended in the test-tube when the water was left to settle. Jane disagreed with Jim, and proposed a different hypothesis.
a What hypothesis do you think Jane proposed? State a likely hypothesis.
b Use results from an experiment you have already performed to support your answer.

CHAPTER 4 Glossary

aqueous solution: solution that has water as its solvent

blackwater: wastewater from toilets and kitchens

centrifuge: device that spins very fast to separate solids from liquids, or liquids from other liquids

chromatography: a method of separating a mixture by making it move over or through another substance that stays still

concentrated: there is a lot of solute in the solvent

crystallisation: formation of crystals as a dissolved substance solidifies

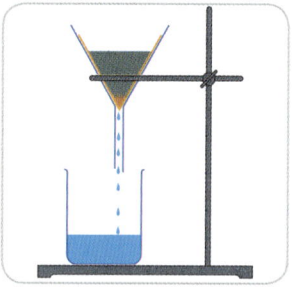

crystallisation

decantation: separation by pouring liquid off the top of a mixture of solid in liquid, or liquid in liquid

desalination: removing dissolved salts such as sodium chloride from water

dilute: when there is little solute in the solution

disperse: when particles spread without dissolving

dissolve: break up into tiny particles that are smaller than the eye can see

distillation: a process that uses evaporation and condensation to separate solids from liquids or liquids from liquids, enabling the recovery of both

evaporation: a process that uses heat to make a liquid solvent change state to a gas, and leave behind the solute it had dissolved

filter: screen or membrane used in filtration

filtrate: liquid that passes through the filter paper

filtration: separation of solids or liquids from a liquid or gas by using a barrier with holes smaller than the particles being separated

gravity separation: a method of separating two components from a suspension by using the force of gravity to separate heavier particles to the bottom

filtration

greywater: wastewater from shower/bath and laundry

impurities: unwanted substances

insoluble: substance that does not dissolve in a particular solvent

mixture: a substance made from two or more pure substances that have been stirred together and that can be separated to recover the original substances

potable water: drinkable water

pure substance: a substance made of only one type of material

residue: solid left in the filter paper after filtration

saturated: as much substance as possible is dissolved in a solvent

septic tank: concrete or plastic tanks placed underground that process sewage from homes and businesses outside the sewerage system

sewage: wastewater from toilets, bathrooms, kitchens and laundries that may contain human waste and other organic chemicals or harmful chemicals

sewerage system: system of pipes underground that collects wastewater from homes and businesses and takes it to treatment plants

soluble: able to be dissolved

solute: a substance that dissolves to make a solution when it is mixed into another substance

solution: when a substance dissolves in another, forming a clear mixture

solvent: a substance that dissolves another substance

suspension: mixture in which a substance will not dissolve in another and quickly separates out if left to stand

wastewater: water that has been used and disposed of because it is no longer clean

suspension

CHAPTER 5
Habitats and interactions

Have you ever wondered...
- why different things live in particular environments?
- how to show the relationships between living things?
- how our actions affect the things living around us?

After completing this chapter you should be able to:
- explain how Australian plants and animals are adapted to survive and reproduce in their environment
- construct and interpret food chains and food webs
- classify organisms according to their position in the food chain
- describe the role of micro-organisms within food chains and webs
- investigate how the introduction or loss of one species affects the food chains and food webs it belongs to
- describe the effect of human activity on local habitats, such as deforestation, agriculture and the introduction of new species
- outline how living things can change the environment and affect other living things
- investigate ways to control the spread of the cane toad and rabbits
- investigate the use of fire by traditional Aboriginal people
- describe how traditional and Western scientific knowledge can be used to care for Country/Place
- describe the effects of palm oil production in Sumatra
- outline the contributions of Australian scientists to local environmental projects and the study of human impact
- outline how human activity can have positive and negative effects on the sustainability of ecosystems.

This is an extract from the Australian Curriculum
Victorian Curriculum F–10 © VCAA (2016); reproduced by permission

183

MODULE 5.1 Living places

Some living things live in hot dry environments such as the deserts of inland Australia. Others, like this turtle, live in a marine environment.

science 4 fun

What lives in your local area?

Do this ...

Go for a walk to try to find five living and five non-living things around your backyard, local park or in your neighbourhood.

Record this ...

1. Describe the area in which you saw living things.
2. Explain why you think things would be living in this particular area.

Habitats

Living things come in many shapes and sizes. All living things, such as plants, animals and bacteria, are known as **organisms**. An organism is anything capable of carrying out the processes required for life such as growth, reproduction and movement. Scientists have identified more than eight million kinds of organisms living on our planet.

The place where an organism lives is called its **habitat**. The habitat of an organism must provide everything that it needs to survive. Your habitat would include your home, school and local area.

Organisms can sometimes find suitable habitats in a wide range of areas. For example, the red kangaroo shown in Figure 5.1.1 can be found in arid and semi-arid regions from the extreme north of the east coast, to the south-west of mainland Australia. They live in open grassland with scattered trees that provide shade and shelter.

FIGURE 5.1.1 The Australian desert is the habitat of the red kangaroo.

184 PEARSON SCIENCE 7 2ND EDITION

Habitat requirements

Every living thing has particular needs, and will live only where these needs are met by the resources available in the habitat. Some of the resources a habitat must provide for an organism to survive and reproduce include:

- food
- water
- shelter and living space
- a suitable temperature
- mating partners for reproduction
- gases such as oxygen.

The Australian freshwater crocodile (Figure 5.1.2) lives in freshwater creeks and rivers of northern Australia. There it can find the birds, frogs and fish that it eats. The females need sandy riverbanks in which to dig nests and lay their eggs. The resources in the river and the surrounding area meet the Australian freshwater crocodile's needs, so this is its habitat.

FIGURE 5.1.2 The habitat of the Australian freshwater crocodile

The needs of living things can be divided into two types:

- **biotic factors**. These are living factors that include partners for mating, organisms to eat, and organisms they may compete with for food and shelter.
- **abiotic factors**. These are non-living factors that include water, light, wind, soil and temperature.

The number of organisms of the same type, living in the same habitat, will vary over time depending on the availability of food, water, living space and mating partners.

Adaptations

To survive in their habitat, organisms have adaptations. **Adaptations** are characteristics that assist organisms to survive and reproduce. Adaptations help organisms to get food and water, protect themselves, build homes and reproduce.

Figure 5.1.3 shows some of the crocodile's adaptations that allow it to survive and reproduce in its environment.

FIGURE 5.1.3 Adaptations of the Australian freshwater crocodile

The spotted-tailed quoll (Figure 5.1.4) is a marsupial that lives in the forests of eastern Australia, from Queensland to Tasmania. The quoll's dark colouring is an adaptation that makes it well camouflaged. This allows it to sleep in hollow trees and rock crevices without being seen by other animals that would hunt it for food. A quoll uses its sharp claws and teeth to catch live rats, birds and reptiles. It will also eat dead remains of other animals.

FIGURE 5.1.4 The spotted-tailed quoll is the largest meat-eating marsupial on Australia's mainland.

CHAPTER 5 • HABITATS AND INTERACTIONS **185**

Quolls can see in dim light which allows them to be **nocturnal**. This means that they are active and hunt at night. These features are all adaptations that make the quoll well suited to its environment.

Native trees growing in some parts of Australia need to survive frequent fires. Some trees have buds buried deep within the trunk where they are protected from the heat of the fire. Normally these buds do not sprout. However, if a fire destroys most of the leaves on the tree, these buds grow and quickly cover the tree with new leaves, as shown in Figure 5.1.5.

FIGURE 5.1.5 After fire destroyed the leaves of this tree, buds hidden deep in the trunk grew and produced new leaves.

This adaptation of eucalyptus trees has enabled them to survive harsh Australian bushfires.

All plants need light if they are to survive. Plants use the energy from sunlight to help them make their food. Plants growing in dense rainforests often have adaptations such as hooks on stems and leaves, or long, thin threads called tendrils to help them climb over other plants to reach the sunlight. Smilax shown in Figure 5.1.6 is a common plant in Australian forests. It sends out tendrils that coil around neighbouring branches.

This adaptation enables plants to reach the light, which may otherwise be restricted to the limited light on the forest floor.

FIGURE 5.1.6 Tendrils are adaptations that enable Smilax to climb over other plants to reach the light.

Adaptations enable animals to:
- protect themselves from predators (camouflage)
- survive hot and cold temperatures, and wet and dry seasons
- move from place to place
- catch and eat food
- take in oxygen
- reproduce.

Adaptations enable plants to:
- protect themselves from grazing animals
- take in oxygen and carbon dioxide
- take in water
- capture light
- reproduce.

STEM 4 fun

Surviving in the desert

PROBLEM
Pretend you have made a new discovery of an animal or plant that can survive in the desert. What does it look like?

SUPPLIES
- pictures of desert animals and plants
- research on the environment of a desert
- research the structures and behaviours required for survival in a desert

PLAN AND DESIGN Design the solution. What information do you need to solve the problem? Draw a diagram. Make a list of materials you will need and steps you will take.

CREATE Follow your plan. Draw your solution to the problem. Create a clearly labelled diagram of your final animal or plant.

IMPROVE What works? What doesn't? How do you know it solves the problem? What could work better? Modify your design to make it better. Test it out by explaining your animal or plant to others.

REFLECTION
1. What area of STEM did you work in today?
2. In what career do these activities connect?
3. If another student was to do this task, what advice would you give?

Environmental conditions

An organism needs to be well adapted to environmental conditions to survive. The term **environment** is used to describe all the things that affect a plant or an animal in its habitat. Many factors may shape and change an environment, including:

- the temperature
- whether it is wet or dry
- whether it is windy
- the quality of the air
- the water quality
- the type of soil
- the plants, animals, bacteria and fungi that live there.

The study of the interactions between living things and their environment is called **ecology**. **Ecologists** are scientists who study these interactions.

Living together

The **biosphere** is the place where all life as we know it exists. The biosphere consists of the surface of the Earth and its atmosphere. The biosphere is made up of many ecosystems, such as forests, wetlands or coral reefs. An **ecosystem** is a system formed by organisms interacting with each other and their non-living surroundings in a balanced way. In an ecosystem, there are many habitats. The relationship between the biosphere, ecosystems and habitats is demonstrated in Figure 5.1.7.

The organisms in an **ecosystem** are **interdependent**. Interdependent means that the organisms depend on each other for survival.

Another term used for two different kinds of organisms that live together is **symbiosis**. The relationship between these two different organisms can be positive, negative or have no impact on the individuals.

FIGURE 5.1.7 The relationship between biosphere, ecosystems, habitat and the organisms that live there.

CHAPTER 5 • HABITATS AND INTERACTIONS   187

There are three main types of interdependence or symbiosis.

1. **Commensalism:** In this kind of relationship between two organisms, one organism benefits and the other is not affected. For example, the cattle egret as seen in Figure 5.1.8 will follow cattle and water buffalo as they graze (look) for food. As these animals graze, insects are flushed out of the grass as they move. The egrets catch and eat the insects when they fly from the grass. In this relationship the egret benefits greatly, but there is no effect on the herbivore.

FIGURE 5.1.9 An example of mutualism is the lichen you can see growing on this tree branch. In this relationship, a fungus and an algae form what is known as lichen. They both benefit from the relationship with each other and neither of them is harmed.

FIGURE 5.1.8 An example of commensalism is the cattle egret following cattle to eat the insects disturbed by the cattle. This is a relationship of commensalism because the egret benefits and the cattle are not affected.

2. **Mutualism:** This is an interaction where both the organisms benefit from the relationship and neither is harmed. In many cases, neither organism can exist without the other. Figure 5.1.9 shows lichen growing on a rock. Lichen consists of a fungus and algae growing together. The algae makes its own food using energy from sunlight and the fungus uses this food. The fungus provides the algae with a protected place to live.

3. **Parasitism:** In another type of relationship, one organism (the **parasite**) lives on or in another organism (the **host**). The parasite obtains food and shelter from its host, but often harms or may even kill the host in return. Heartworm is a parasite that lives in the hearts of dogs. The worms breed rapidly and can clog up the dog's heart, as shown in Figure 5.1.10. The worm uses the dog for shelter and food, but if left untreated the dog often dies. Heartworm is easily prevented by applying treatment on the skin, giving a regular tablet or seeing the local vet for an annual injection.

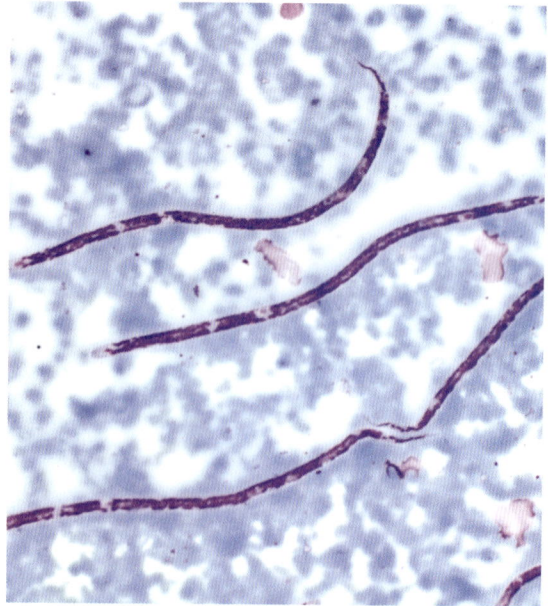

FIGURE 5.1.10 An example of parasitism is heartworm. This is the heart of a dog that has been infected with heartworm. This is an example of parasitism because the dog is the host and the heartworm is the parasite.

SCIENCE AS A HUMAN ENDEAVOUR
Use and influence of science

Regrowing a forest

Ravensworth State Forest is one of the largest areas of remnant woodland in the Hunter Valley of New South Wales. **Remnant vegetation** is the patches of native vegetation that have survived when surrounding areas have been changed by activities such as grazing or forestry.

FIGURE 5.1.11 The green and golden bell frog is a threatened species that was once found in the Ravensworth State Forest.

A number of threatened species live in this forest such as the squirrel glider and the spotted-tailed quoll, as well as several species of bats. The green and golden bell frog (*Litoria aurea*), shown in Figure 5.1.11, is a threatened species that lived in the forest in the past. Ponds in the state forest have been improved with the aim of reintroducing this frog and other amphibians to the area.

Ravensworth State Forest was used for grazing and as a source of timber for more than 100 years. Logging ceased in 1986 and grazing was stopped in 1995. However, a coal mine was established in the area in 1993 and it is still in production. To compensate for disturbing the forest the mining company purchased 430 hectares of neighbouring land, which has now been included as part of Ravensworth State Forest.

The company that owns the mine is working with government bodies and experts from the University of Newcastle to regenerate areas of forest. The aim is to restore habitat for threatened species and other species living in the area. Scientists are carrying out research to find the best ways to:
- conserve the existing plant and animal life in the area
- restore the grazing land and logged forest to native woodland forest.

In the future, the regenerated forest will be linked to other areas of native vegetation. The aim is to provide habitat corridors along which native animals can move as they search for food and breeding areas.

Topsoil that was originally taken from the mine site has been spread in areas to allow native regrowth of native plant species from seeds in the soil. A wide variety of plants is now found in the area. These plants vary from tall trees to small shrubs and grasses, and provide habitat for many different animals. Surveys have shown that more than 220 species of animals now live in Ravensworth State Forest.

REVIEW

1. a Explain what the term 'remnant vegetation' means.
   b Explain why the woodland in Ravensworth State Forest is called remnant woodland.
2. Describe how the native animals in Ravensworth State Forest benefit from the forest regeneration.
3. Explain the importance of using soil from Ravenswood State Forest to regenerate areas that were once grazed.

CHAPTER 5 • HABITATS AND INTERACTIONS

MODULE 5.1 Review questions

Remembering

1. Define the terms:
   a. habitat
   b. abiotic factors
   c. adaptations
   d. ecology.

2. Which term best describes each of the following?
   a. living things
   b. living factors
   c. active and hunts by night
   d. organisms that depend on one another.

3. List the resources that are provided by the habitat of an organism.

4. What adaptations help the following Australian animals catch their prey?
   a. crocodile
   b. spotted-tail quoll.

5. List adaptations that allow:
   a. eucalypts to survive bushfire
   b. Smilax to reach sunlight.

6. Predict possible causes of a change in the number and type of organisms living in an area.

Understanding

7. Explain why some organisms are found over a very wide area, whereas others live in very restricted areas.

Applying

8. Use an example to outline what scientists mean when they say that organisms are interdependent.

9. Use examples to help define the following terms.
   a. biosphere
   b. ecosystem.

10. Identify two examples of symbiosis not listed in the text.

Analysing

11. Compare commensalism and mutualism.

12. a. List the benefits and/or harm that each of the organisms bring to the following relationships.
    b. Classify each relationship as commensalism, mutualism or parasitism.
       i. a leech sucking on the blood of humans and other mammals
       ii. bees carrying pollen from one flower to another as they collect nectar
       iii. rainforest vines using hooks and tendrils to climb up large trees to reach the light
       iv. cleaner fish taking the parasites off the gills of large carnivorous fish as seen in Figure 5.1.12.

FIGURE 5.1.12 A cleaner fish (blue) cleaning the gills of a carnivorous fish (orange)

Evaluating

13. Use your understanding of adaptations to assess why a particular type of organism cannot just move to another area if its habitat is destroyed.

14. Many Australian animals are nocturnal.
    a. Name an animal that is nocturnal.
    b. Nocturnal animals need particular adaptations. Identify one such adaptation.
    c. What do you think are some of the advantages that come from an animal being nocturnal?

MODULE 5.1 Review questions

15 What adaptations do you think an animal or plant would need to live in:
   a an environment that is very hot?
   b an environment that is very cold?
   c an environment that has a large number of predators?

16 In a tropical rainforest, very little light reaches the ground because of the dense canopy formed by the trees. Imagine that one very large tree falls.
   a What probable changes in abiotic factors would occur in the area of the forest where the tree fell?
   b Propose ways in which the changes would affect the plants and animals living in the immediate area.

17 Imagine that there is a sudden change in the number and type of organisms living in an area. What do you think could be possible causes?

Creating

18 Think about a koala living in the Australian bush (Figure 5.1.13). Construct a concept map of the biotic and abiotic factors that would be in the koala's environment. Include any adaptations that the koala would need to survive in its environment.

19 Work in a small group to design a model of a specific ecosystem. On your model, include labels that:
   a state the type of ecosystem
   b identify the abiotic factors that would affect the organisms in this ecosystem
   c name the organisms that live in this ecosystem
   d describe how the organisms in this environment interact
   e identify two symbiotic relationships in this ecosystem.

FIGURE 5.1.13 A koala

MODULE 5.1 Practical investigations

1 • What lives in your schoolyard?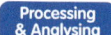

Purpose
To investigate the small organisms that are living in various habitats of the school grounds.

Timing 30 minutes

Materials
- small paintbrush
- protective gloves
- magnifying glass
- sweep net
- 4 m of string
- 4 weights (stones will do)
- field guide
- large resealable plastic bags
- map of school grounds

> **SAFETY**
> Some stinging insects may be captured, so gloves should be worn by the person who has to hold the net and shake the animals into the plastic bag. If there are any animals still caught in the net, avoid contact. Use a paintbrush to remove them.

Procedure
1. Choose the location for your experiment. If possible, each group should choose a location with a different type of ground cover. Draw a sketch of your location, noting the types of plants and the ground conditions. Take photographs if you can.
2. At your location, measure a square area that has sides of one metre. Mark the area using the string and weights. This is the area that will be swept.
3. To sweep an area for organisms make a 'figure 8' in such a way that the open side of the net is always facing away from you.
4. At your site brush your net back and forth over the surface to 'sweep' the area and capture any organisms.
5. Hold the bag halfway up to make sure that the organisms do not escape.
6. While another student holds the resealable bag, place the net over it, loosen your hold and turn it inside out into the bag. Carefully shake and remove the net from the bag, being sure to seal it so that the organisms do not escape.
7. Observe the organisms through the resealable bag and try to identify them using your field guide. Count the numbers of each type of organism.
8. Release any organisms that you have found.

Results
1. Record the time and date of your experiment and describe the area in which you made your observations.
2. Construct a table showing the appearance and number of each type of organism at your site.
3. Record your results along with those of other members of your class on your map of the school grounds.
4. As a class, prepare a poster of what lives in the school grounds.

Review
1. Compare the numbers and different types of organisms caught at the various sites.
2. Which site was the most successful in terms of the:
   a number of organisms caught?
   b variety of organisms caught?
3. Discuss the differences between the sites that could cause these variations.
4. What other factors that could have led to this result?
5. Classify the organisms into groups according to the environmental conditions each preferred. Examples include: dry or moist; long grass or short grass; sun or shade.
6. a Discuss whether or not you would expect the same organisms in your sweep if you conducted this experiment at:
      i   different times of day
      ii other times during the year.
   b Propose reasons for any variation.
   c Describe a way of testing your predictions.

5.1 Practical investigations

2 • Looking at earthworms

Purpose
To investigate how worms behave in their habitat.

Timing 30 minutes

Materials
- trowel
- gloves
- containers
- stereomicroscope or magnifying glass
- sheet of white paper or a white tile
- spray bottle containing water

SAFETY
Make sure that you are wearing gloves and that you don't directly inhale any dust. It is important that the worms are treated with care and are not harmed during your investigation. Take care to look after them and then return them to where you collected them, once you have finished.

Procedure
1. Dig for worms in the garden (Figure 5.1.14). Choose a place where the soil is moist.
2. Place the worms in a container with some loose soil. Keep the worms moist at all times and make sure they don't escape.
3. In the classroom, gently place one of the worms on the white paper.
4. Look at the earthworm through a stereomicroscope. Make notes about its appearance. Sketch what you see.
5. Observe the way the worm moves.
6. Use the stereomicroscope or magnifying glass to look carefully at the underside of the worm close to its head.
7. Run your finger very gently from the back to the front of the worm's underside.
8. When you have finished, return the earthworm to a natural habitat under some leaves in a moist, shady location.

Review
1. Describe the shape of the worm and how this helps it move through the soil.
2.
   a. Describe how the shape of the worm changed as it moved.
   b. How did this change in shape helps the worm move forward?
   c. What do you think was happening inside the worm to cause these changes in shape?
3.
   a. Describe what you felt and/or saw on the underside of the worm.
   b. How do you think this feature helped the worm move?
   c. Deduce why it is difficult to pull a worm from its burrow.
4. Worms are well adapted to living underground. Identify the adaptations you observed.

FIGURE 5.1.14 An earthworm in the soil

CHAPTER 5 • HABITATS AND INTERACTIONS 193

MODULE 5.2 Food chains and food webs

Healthy ecosystems usually contain many different habitats and a variety of organisms. The organisms living there interact in different ways. Food is one of the most important needs of all living things. Therefore one of the relationships between organisms is a feeding relationship. Some organisms do the eating. Other organisms are eaten.

science 4 fun

Predators in the garden

Can I see predators at work in the garden?

Collect this…

A magnifying glass could be useful but is not essential.

Do this…

1. Sit quietly in the garden or in an area of parkland where there are flowers, bushes and trees.
2. Observe the insects, birds and other animals such as lizards that are moving around.
3. Use your magnifying glass to observe insects moving around on the plants.

Record this…

1. Describe any situations where an animal was feeding.
2. Explain which organism was the predator and which was being eaten.

Predators and prey

An organism needs to live in a habitat where it can find enough food. Plants make their own food from gasses in the air, nutrients in the soil and energy from the sun. Animals must consume other animals or plants to get the nutrients they need to survive. Animals that eat other animals are called **predators**. For example, a wedge-tailed eagle will hunt and eat rabbits. The wedge-tailed eagle is a predator of the rabbit. The animal that is eaten is the **prey**. The rabbit in Figure 5.2.1 is the prey of the wedge-tailed eagle.

FIGURE 5.2.1 The wedge-tailed eagle is the predator. The rabbit is its prey.

194 PEARSON SCIENCE 7 2ND EDITION

If two animals eat the same sort of food and they live in the same habitat, they must compete for their food; they are **competitors**. Rabbits (Figure 5.2.2) were introduced into Australia during the 1830s and they compete with many Australian animals for food, living space, water and shelter.

FIGURE 5.2.2 The Australian long-nosed potoroo and introduced rabbits compete for food, shelter, living space and water.

Food chains

Plants and animals use energy in growing and in day-to-day activity. This energy must come from somewhere. Plants get their energy from sunlight, and animals get their energy from the food they eat. For example, grass uses the energy from sunlight to make the food it needs to be able to grow. A grasshopper may eat the grass to get the energy it needs and a kookaburra might eat several grasshoppers to get the energy it needs. When the kookaburra dies, bacteria will help to decompose its body. In this way, the bacteria get the energy they need and return the nutrients stored in the body of the kookaburra to the soil for plants to use in growth.

As shown in Figure 5.2.3, the arrows in a **food chain** show the direction of energy flow.

The sun gives the grass energy to grow. The grass gives the grasshopper energy when it eats the grass. The grasshopper gives the kookaburra energy and, when the kookaburra dies, it gives the bacteria energy.

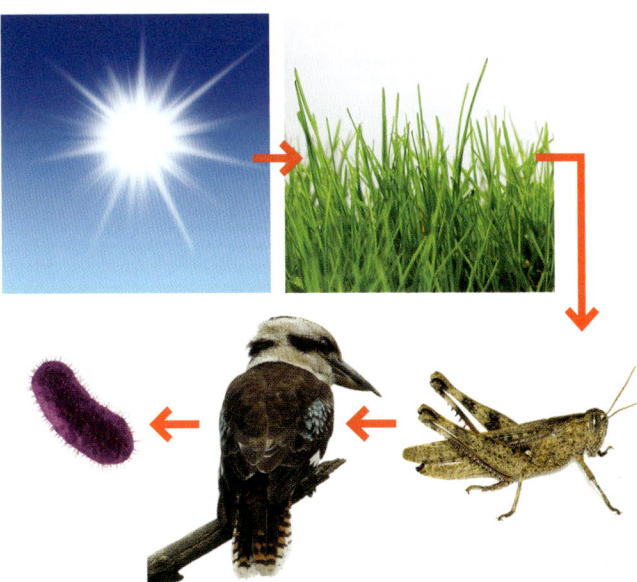

FIGURE 5.2.3 Food chains start with the Sun, and usually end with bacteria or fungi.

A food chain is usually drawn as a simple flow chart like this:

Sun → grass → grasshopper → kookaburra → bacteria

The food chain flow chart above demonstrates the direction of energy flow. Energy flow is shown by the arrows, they always point in the direction where the energy goes. The Sun is not an organism but is often included because it is the original energy source.

Producers, decomposers and consumers

Food chains start with the Sun. The Sun gives out light energy. Plants trap the Sun's energy in their leaves using a chemical called **chlorophyll**. Inside the leaves of a plant a process called **photosynthesis** occurs (Figure 5.2.4). The process of using energy to convert water and carbon dioxide into glucose and oxygen is called photosynthesis.

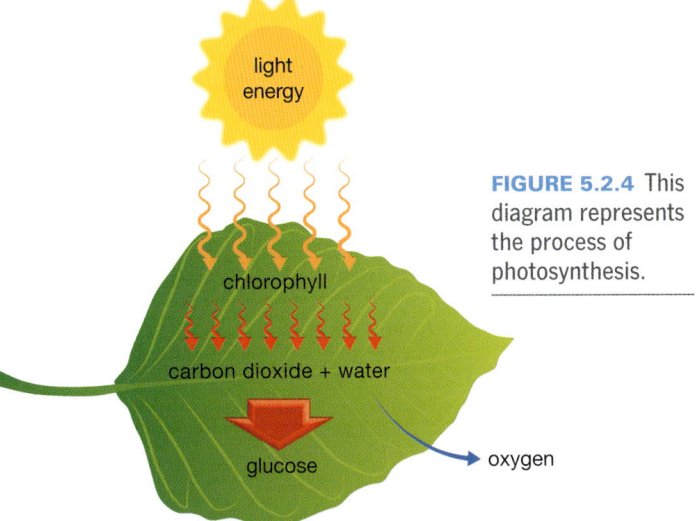

FIGURE 5.2.4 This diagram represents the process of photosynthesis.

CHAPTER 5 • HABITATS AND INTERACTIONS **195**

Plants can produce their own food and so they are called producer organisms or **producers**.

Animals cannot make their own food and must consume (eat) plants or other animals to get the energy and nutrients they need. Animals are therefore called **consumers**. Consumers such as grasshoppers, kangaroos or koalas that eat only plants are known as **herbivores**.

FIGURE 5.2.5 Wombats are herbivores. They eat native grass, plant roots and bulbs, and bark.

Consumers, such as dingoes, kookaburras and quoll, which eat only other animals are called **carnivores**.

Omnivores are consumers that eat plants and animals. Humans have a varied diet and are considered omnivores. The Australian bandicoot has a varied diet that includes insects, fungi and vegetation so they are also omnivores.

Decomposers break down the remains of dead plants and animals in addition to breaking down any waste products left by living animals. Decomposers break down the remains of dead plants and animals in addition to breaking down any waste products left by living animals. Decomposers, such as fungi are very important for any ecosystem as they make up the last part of food chains. If they were not in the ecosystem the plants would not get the essential nutrients they require and dead matter and waste would build up. Decomposers release the nutrients from dead matter into the atmosphere, water and soil increasing the levels of available nutrients in the soil.

When an animal dies, a **scavenger** such as a Tasmanian devil (Figure 5.2.6), fox or rat will find dead animals or plants and eat them. While they eat them they are breaking them into smaller bits.

FIGURE 5.2.6 Tasmanian devils are scavengers. They feed on dead animals such as the kangaroo in this image.

Scavengers start the process of 'recycling' dead animals and waste but they are not decomposers—scavengers do not return essential nutrients back to the soil.

Once the scavengers have done their part the decomposers take over and complete the breakdown. The soil contains millions of bacteria and fungi ready to spring into action when there is something to decompose. Bacteria are microscopic, meaning that they cannot be seen without a microscope. In contrast, many fungi can be easily seen. An example is the fungus in Figure 5.2.7 living on a dead tree. Decomposers reduce dead animals, plants and waste into elements such as carbon and nitrogen. These elements become part of the soil and can then be used by the living plants and animals that consume them.

Consumers are further classified into primary secondary or tertiary consumers. **Primary consumers** are herbivores. Herbivores eat plants, algae and other producers. In the desert ecosystem, the hopping mouse that eats grass and seeds is a primary consumer.

FIGURE 5.2.7 The fungi on the tree stump are decomposer organisms. Fungi break down the materials that the tree is made from, returning these materials to the soil.

196 PEARSON SCIENCE 7 2ND EDITION

Secondary consumers eat herbivores. A snake that lives in the desert and eats a hopping mouse would be a secondary consumer (Figure 5.2.8).

FIGURE 5.2.8 This snake is a secondary consumer because it eats a mouse.

Tertiary consumers eat secondary consumers. A barn owl living in the desert would prey on and eat the snake. In this case the owl is a tertiary consumer. There may be many levels of consumers in a food chain before it finally reaches the top predator. A top predator in a food chain is also called an **apex predator**. An apex predator has no natural predators except humans. In this desert ecosystem the apex predator would be the wedge-tailed eagle.

In this food chain:

Sun → grass → desert hopping mouse → snake → barn owl → wedge-tailed eagle

Producer → primary consumer → secondary consumer → tertiary consumer → apex predator

In another food chain, the owl may eat the hopping mouse. The barn owl could then be eaten by the wedge-tailed eagle. The new food chain would look like this:

Sun → grass → desert hopping mouse → barn owl → wedge-tailed eagle

Producer → primary consumer → secondary consumer → apex predator

Food webs

AB 5.6

A **food web** is made up of all of the food chains in an ecosystem. As seen above a living thing will be part of many food chains. A food chain is a possible path that energy may take as it moves through the ecosystem. A food web is produced when all of the food chains in an ecosystem are joined together. A small food web is shown in Figure 5.2.9.

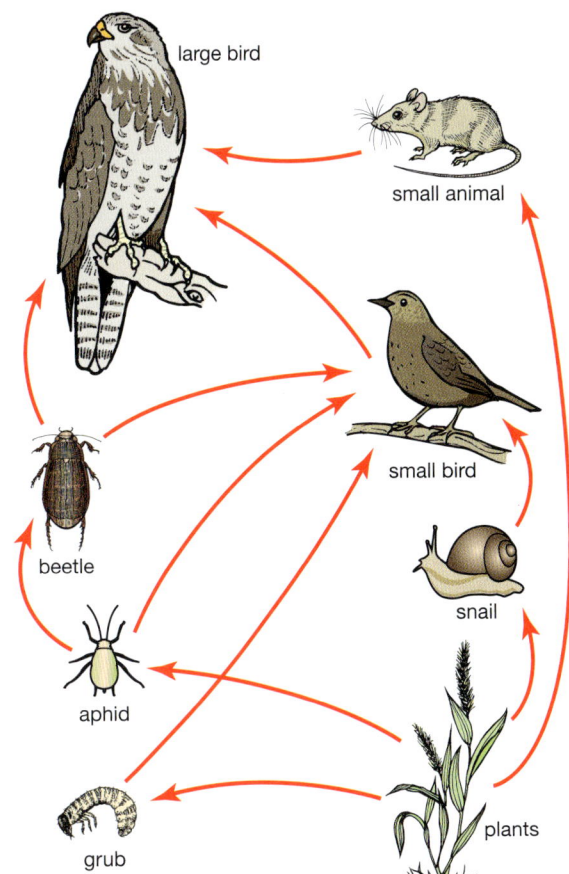

FIGURE 5.2.9 A food web clearly identifies the flow of energy in the whole ecosystem. In this ecosystem the organisms are part of a small food web. Within this food web, there are at least four different food chains.

Changes often occur in food webs as the populations of different organisms increase, decrease or disappear altogether. In the pond ecosystem shown in Figure 5.2.10 some animals or plants might be in the pond for only a short time each year; for example, tadpoles might be an abundant food source for fish one week, but if they become frogs the next week they will no longer be available to the fish but instead could be a food source for the kookaburra.

AB 5.7   AB 5.8

FIGURE 5.2.10 A pond ecosystem is home to a variety of organisms.

Prac 1 p. 200

CHAPTER 5 • HABITATS AND INTERACTIONS   **197**

MODULE 5.2 Review questions

Remembering

1. Define the terms:
   a. prey
   b. carnivore
   c. consumer
   d. decomposer.

2. Which term best describes each of the following?
   a. an animal that eats other animals
   b. an animal that only eats plants
   c. organisms that make their own food
   d. the process plants use to make their food.

3. State what the arrows in a food chain indicate.

Understanding

4. Why is the Sun always included as the original energy source in food chains?

5. Explain why a producer is the first living thing in a food chain.

6. Group the following organisms as producers, consumers or decomposers.

   grass

   fungi

   grasshopper

   mouse

   bacteria

   eagle

   acacia tree

7. Discuss whether humans are:
   a. producers or consumers
   b. carnivores, herbivores or omnivores
   c. an apex consumer or a lower-order consumer.

Applying

8. In the food web shown in Figure 5.2.9 on page 197, identify the:
   a. producer
   b. primary consumers
   c. secondary consumers
   d. apex predator.

9. Identify three food chains that are contained within the food web shown in Figure 5.2.9.

10. Match each of the following organisms to the appropriate term.

Term	Organism
producer	snail
herbivore	small bird
omnivore	eucalyptus tree
carnivore	bacteria
decomposer	hawk

11. Use the organisms in question 10 to draw a food chain.

Analysing

12. Compare the role of scavengers and decomposers in an ecosystem.

13. Use examples to discuss the importance of decomposers in the environment.

14. Classify the organisms in the pond ecosystem shown Figure 5.2.10 on page 197 as producers, herbivores, omnivores or carnivores.

15. Greg said that humans are scavengers because we buy meat and vegetables that are no longer living. Lana disagreed. Discuss.

MODULE 5.2 Review questions

Evaluating

16 a Figure 5.2.11 shows a Venus flytrap. This plant catches insects and uses them as a source of nutrients. Do you think that a carnivorous plant like a Venus flytrap is a producer or a consumer?
   b Justify your response.

FIGURE 5.2.11 Venus flytrap

17 What do you think could happen in the food web shown in Figure 5.2.12 if the number of:
   a small birds decreased?
   b large birds increased?
   c plants decreased?

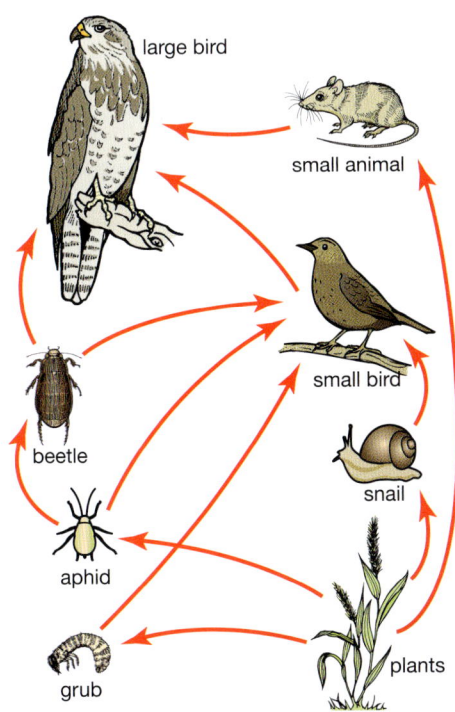

FIGURE 5.2.12

Creating

18 Use the following information to construct a food web.
   - algae (a producer)
   - snail (eats algae)
   - small fish (eats algae and snails)
   - water beetle (eats small fish)
   - frog (eats beetles)
   - snake (eats beetles and frogs)
   - decomposers (break down dead animals).

19 Using a set of six cards, write your own name on one card. On the other cards write the names of five plants and animals that you could eat.
   a Use these cards to construct a food chain in which you are:
      i   a primary consumer
      ii a secondary consumer
      iii an apex predator.
   b Discuss how easy was it to make the food chains, and whether you had to make other cards.

20 Ecosystems rely on producers, consumers and decomposers. Design a role-play for each of the following situations.
   a All the consumers in an ecosystem are removed.
   b All the producers in an ecosystem are removed.
   c All the decomposers in an ecosystem are removed.

CHAPTER 5 • HABITATS AND INTERACTIONS   199

MODULE 5.2 Practical investigations

1 • Woolly web

Note: This is a whole-class activity.

Purpose
To create a food web using students connected by pieces of wool.

Timing 30 minutes

Materials
- information about feeding relationships in a particular habitat such as the pond ecosystem on page 197.
- small balls of wool or string (start with five for each student)
- card to make labels
- marker pen
- paperclips (one per student)

Procedure
1. Each student selects an organism from the list of organisms found in the habitat.
2. Using the card and marker pen, create a name label so that you can be identified. Attach it using a paperclip.
3. Using the information about feeding relationships, identify the organisms that you will use as a source of food.
4. Start with the producer organisms. Connect the producers to the herbivores that eat them, extending the wool from the producer's right hand to the herbivore's left hand. The producer organisms and the herbivore hold opposite ends of a piece of wool. The wool represents an arrow in the food web.
5. The carnivores then connect to the herbivores they eat, by holding opposite ends of a piece of wool (wool from the right hand of the herbivore should extend to the left hand of the carnivore).
6. Any carnivores that eat other carnivores are then connected until all the feeding relationships are created by pieces of wool.
   The wool always goes from the right hand of the organism being eaten to the left hand of the predator.
7. Identify one organism that will be eaten—the prey. The student representing that organism gently pulls on one piece of wool so that the energy moves along the food chain from the prey to the predator. The predator then pulls on all of his/her strings so that the energy moves to the next level. Continue in this way until the energy reaches the consumers at the ends of all the food chains.
8. Repeat the exercise, starting with organisms at different levels in the food web.

Results
Observe the effect on other parts of the food web, of the changes you have made.

Review
1. What effect will a change have to the levels in a food web:
   a. above it?
   b. below it?
2. If an organism disappeared from a habitat, what could happen to the food web at its:
   a. higher levels?
   b. lower levels?
3. Explain why it is an advantage for organisms to have a variety of food sources.
4. Identify any of the higher consumers that would be left with no food source if one of the primary consumers in your food web was to disappear from the area.
5. What will happen to your food web if a producer organism is removed from the area?

MODULE 5.3 Impacts on ecosystems

Environmental conditions in ecosystems change. Fire, flood, cyclone and drought may cause widespread changes that have both short-term and long-term consequences. Introduced animals change relationships within ecosystems.

Sustainable ecosystems

Ecosystems that are diverse and are able to provide the needs of the organisms living there over a long period of time are **sustainable ecosystems**. They are sustainable because they are maintained without being used up or destroyed.

In sustainable ecosystems, there are a wide variety of **species** or different types of organisms found there (Figure 5.3.1). There are many different habitats for these species. Most species have a variety of food sources, so if one food source is in short supply they can use another.

Natural ecosystems are sustainable ecosystems. Human activities can change ecosystems. This can result in sustainable or unsustainable environments. Humans can influence ecosystems so that species leave the ecosystem because their needs are no longer met. If the species cannot find a suitable place to live then it is in danger of becoming extinct.

Prac 1 p. 209

science 4 fun

No food!

How would things change if all the supermarkets closed down?

Collect this ...

No equipment is needed.

Do this ...

Imagine how life in your area would change if all the supermarkets were closed down.

Record this ...

1. Describe what you think would happen in the short term of two weeks and in six months.
2. Explain how this relates to the destruction of a natural environment and the effect on the organisms that lived there.

FIGURE 5.3.1 The valleys of the Blue Mountains are sustainable ecosystems that provide the resources for a variety of species.

CHAPTER 5 • HABITATS AND INTERACTIONS **201**

When a species becomes extinct, every individual of that species has died. Extinction can be caused by climate change, disease, destruction of habitat, natural disasters or the development of a new species that is better adapted to the environment.

Traditional use of fire

Fire causes rapid changes in ecosystems. Fire has been an important part of Australian ecosystems since before humans lived on the continent. In large areas of Australia the plants are adapted to fire.

For example, more than 400 Australian species of plants will germinate after being exposed to smoke. Examples are species of Acacia, grass trees and Banksia. **Germination** is when a plant grows from a seed. Without smoke or fire many Australian plant species will not grow from seeds. Another important adaptation is the ability to recover quickly after fire has destroyed their leaves. An example of example of an Australian plant that does this is the eucalyptus (gum tree).

Indigenous Australians used fire as a tool for hunting. Kangaroos and wallabies escaping from the fire could be captured more easily by hunters. Traditional burning patterns used frequent low intensity fires, such as the fire in Figure 5.3.2. Forests were replaced by open woodlands and grasslands. There was an increase in grazing for animals, such as the kangaroos the Aboriginal people used for food. Plants used as food also flourished.

FIGURE 5.3.2 Traditional Aboriginal burning practices used low-intensity fires that burned the grass and low shrubs without destroying the leaves at the tops of the tallest trees.

Different areas were burned at different times, leaving a mosaic pattern which provided a variety of habitats for different plants and animals. In turn, this provided a variety of foods for the Aboriginal people.

When Europeans arrived in Australia, traditional Aboriginal burning practices gradually stopped. Many of the ecosystems they had created changed.

SciFile

Smoke in a bottle!

In 2004 a team of Australian scientists including Dr Kingsley Dixon and Dr Gavin Flematti were working at Kings Park Botanic Gardens in Western Australia. There they discovered the chemical in smoke that promotes germination. This was an important discovery as the chemical could potentially be added to soil or water to aid in germination.

Fuel reduction burning

Many people in Australia are afraid of fire and want to prevent fire. However, when there is a long time between fires, the amount of fuel available causes an intense fire like the one in Figure 5.3.3. When an intense fire goes through an area many of the native animals are incinerated and plants are killed.

Regular burning is one way of reducing the amount of fuel available for a fire. This practice is called **fuel reduction burning** (FRB). If a fire burns in an area that has been burnt recently, it will spread up to six times more slowly and be up to 20 times less intense.

FIGURE 5.3.3 Intense wild fires are very destructive and may cause the death of large numbers of plants and animals.

FRB turns an intense fire into a low-intensity fire. Firefighters can control low-intensity fires more easily. Animals such as kangaroos can escape from a slow-spreading low-intensity fire and move into unburnt areas. Lizards and other reptiles can escape by hiding under logs or in a hole. Birds may lose their nests but usually the breeding season is past before the time of the year when there is a higher fire risk.

After a low-intensity fire, animals such as kangaroos and wallabies move back into the area within a few days. Plants quickly produce new shoots, as seen in Figure 5.3.4. These shoots provide food for the animals.

FIGURE 5.3.4 A forest floor erupts in a carpet of green bracken fern after a fire. Kinglake National Park, Victoria, Australia

Conservationists are concerned that frequent burning reduces the number of different types of living things able to survive in an area. However, scientists in Western Australia have studied the effects of FRB in a variety of ecosystems and have found that the variety of living things is not affected. That is, the ecosystems in the burnt areas still have all the same types of plants and animals as before, but the actual numbers of individuals may be less.

Carefully planned burns can be used to create a variety of habitats. Unburnt areas provide a refuge for animals escaping the fire. Recently burnt areas provide habitats for animals that prefer open areas. The dense vegetation of areas left unburnt for a few years provide small birds and other animals with protection from predators. Planned burns also create fire breaks that stop wildfires from burning particular habitats.

Botanists recognise that fire is a necessary part of the environment. Botanists study thousands of plants to find out what happens to the plants during a fire and how regrowth occurs after a fire has gone through. Using this information botanists hope to be able to work out how frequently burning should take place and how intense the fires should be to manage environments so that they are sustainable.

Fire monitoring technology

Different parts of Australia have different times of the year when fires are most likely to occur. These times are known as the **fire season**. In southern Australia the 2001–2002 fire season was a bad one and following it, Australian scientists and government agencies developed a new fire-monitoring system. This system uses satellites that have Moderate Resolution Imaging Spectroradiometer (MODIS) sensors. Using observations from these satellites, fires in remote areas can be identified and fires in less remote areas can be monitored. Emergency agencies can then decide how best to use their resources to the fight the fires effectively. Less than an hour after the observations are made using MODIS, the Water and Land Division of CSIRO has a picture of the location and intensity of fires, like the one in Figure 5.3.5.

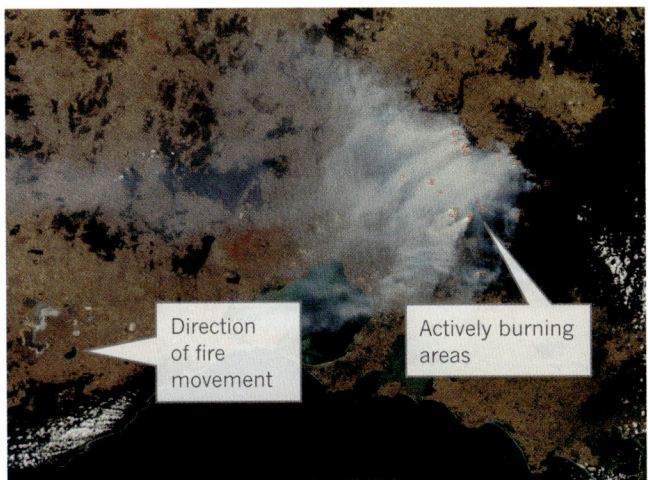

FIGURE 5.3.5 Bushfires continued in the mountains east of Melbourne, Australia, on February 13, 2009. This image from the Moderate Resolution Imaging Spectroradiometer (MODIS) on NASA's Aqua satellite shows the fires and thick smoke spreading to the west.

Introduced species

Many species of plants and animals have been introduced into Australia. These include:

- most of the animals and plants we use as food such as cattle and wheat
- pet animals such as cats and dogs
- animals used for transport and recreation such as the horse and the camel
- many ornamental plants used in parks and gardens such as the jacaranda and roses.

The wool, cotton and leather used to make clothes and furnishings come from introduced species. The majority of the introduced species have benefited humans. The same is not true for other introduced species such as the rabbit, cane toad and the fox as shown in Figure 5.3.6.

FIGURE 5.3.6 The fox was introduced into Australia from Europe in the 1860s to provide sport for hunters.

Animal control

Animal control is often needed to restore native environments and assist farmers. Introduced animals, such as rabbits, foxes and cats, cause widespread damage to ecosystems, eating native animals and destroying efforts to grow crops through digging and eating seedlings. Animals such as rabbits also compete with cattle and sheep for the food that farmers' crops provide. Native animals such as dingoes can cause problems for farmers by killing lambs for food. Rabbits eat the crops that farmers grow for their cattle and sheep. This leads to farmers building fences to protect their animals from both native and introduced predators.

Dingo fence

Dingoes were a problem for farmers in the late 1800s. Between 1880 and 1885 a fence was constructed to protect the sheep and cattle of southern Queensland from attack by dingoes and other wild dogs. The path followed by the fence is shown in Figure 5.3.7. The aim of the fence was to keep the dingoes out of the farming areas of southeastern Australia. The fence has brought benefits and disadvantages. The advantage is that fewer sheep are killed and eaten by dingoes. Also the numbers of emus and kangaroos are greater where there are no dingoes. The disadvantage is that the greater numbers of kangaroos and emus inside the fence compete with the sheep for the grass. This means that farmers cannot graze as many sheep per hectare.

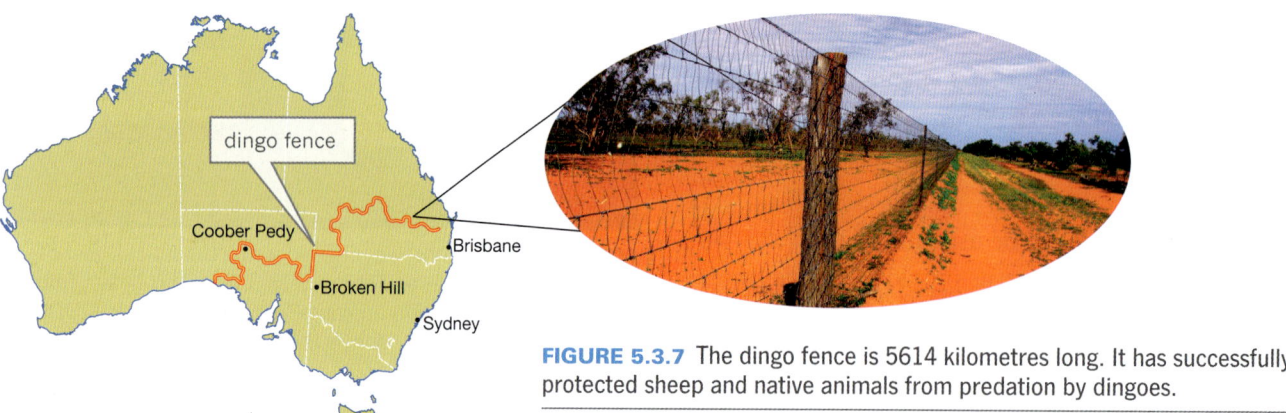

FIGURE 5.3.7 The dingo fence is 5614 kilometres long. It has successfully protected sheep and native animals from predation by dingoes.

Rabbit proof fence

Rabbits were introduced to Australia with the arrival of European settlers in Botany Bay on the First Fleet in 1788. The number of rabbits was very small to begin with but a further introduction in 1859 caused their numbers to increase rapidly. By the late 1800s rabbits were a plague and had spread across into Western Australia. A **plague** means that there were a very large number of rabbits and they were causing damage to the environment.

Rabbits were damaging crops and eating all the grass, leaving nothing for the cattle to feed on. By digging their burrows rabbits were causing millions of dollars worth of damage to grazing land. Sights like those seen in Figure 5.3.8 were common. To protect their livelihood, farmers trapped and shot the rabbits in large numbers.

FIGURE 5.3.8 In many parts of Australia rabbits were present in plague numbers as shown by the photograph above taken near Adelaide in 1961.

The rabbit-proof fence was built to protect crops and grazing land in Western Australia. There are three parts that make up the rabbit-proof fence. They stretch a total of 3253 kilometres. It is the longest unbroken fence in the world as shown in Figure 5.3.9.

SciFile

Record extinction

Australia holds the record for the highest extinction rate of mammals over the last 200 years with more than 29 species becoming extinct. Predators that were introduced to Australia by settlers, such as foxes and feral cats, have had a major role in many of these extinctions.

FIGURE 5.3.9 Construction of the rabbit-proof fence started in 1901. However, rabbits were found to its west even before the fence was completed in 1934. This required a second and then third section of fence to be built.

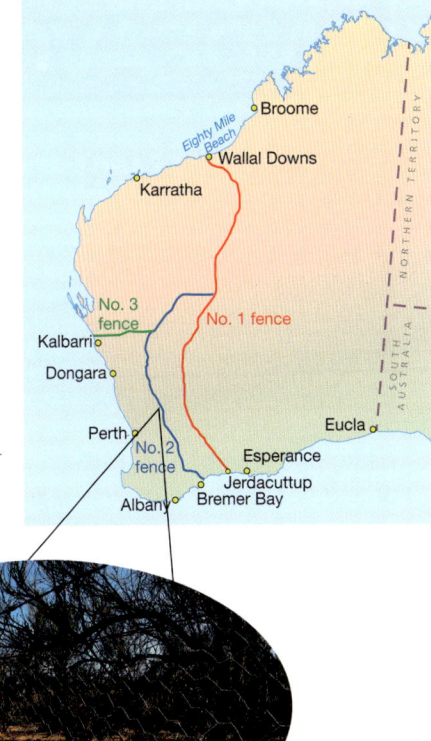

The rabbit-proof fence brought other benefits too. It has protected the livelihood of farmers by excluding dingoes, emus, foxes and goats. It also creates a 20-metre wide fire break along its total length.

In the 1950s the myxoma virus was introduced into the rabbit population. It caused a disease called myxamatosis which killed most of the rabbits in some areas. Rabbit populations have since increased again because of two factors:

- The virus did not spread well through the central areas of Australia.
- The effectiveness of the virus in killing rabbits reduced over time. This most likely happened because some rabbits had a natural immunity or resistance to the virus. These resistant rabbits would survive the disease and go on to breed, leading to a population of myxoma-resistant rabbits.

AB 5.9

CHAPTER 5 • HABITATS AND INTERACTIONS

SCIENCE AS A HUMAN ENDEAVOUR
Use and influence of science

Biological control

One method of controlling unwanted pests is to introduce a predator or an animal that will compete with the pest for food or shelter (a competitor).

Using one type of organism to control the numbers of another type of organism is called **biological control**. This includes introducing a disease-causing organism (bacteria or virus) that will kill the pest species but not other species.

The following are three examples of biological controls that have been tried in Australia.

Prickly pear

The prickly pear cactus (Figure 5.3.10) was first bought to Australia in 1788 as a food source for a valuable insect, known as the cochineal scale insect. This insect produces red pigment and has been used to make red dye for clothing since the 15th century. Because the red dye was such a valuable resource, the British settlers brought cochineal-infested cactus from Brazil and attempted to farm the insects in Australia. The cochineal insects died but the prickly pear cactus thrived, spreading across eastern Australia. The cactus moth (*Cactoblastis cactorum*) was introduced into Australia in 1925 in an attempt to control the spread of the prickly pear cactus. The cactus moth lays its eggs on the prickly pear cactus and, after hatching, the larvae (caterpillars) bore into the leaves and eat almost all of the cactus (Figure 5.3.11).

FIGURE 5.3.10 The prickly pear cactus

The prickly pear cactus is the only food source for the cactus moth larvae in Australia, so once the cactus had been eradicated, the moths soon died out. Here, biological control was successful because most cacti had been eaten within a few years. There are still patches of prickly pear cactus in Australia today, but it is controlled to prevent it spreading.

FIGURE 5.3.11 The cactus moth (*Cactoblastis cactorum*). The caterpillars (larvae) of this moth eat the prickly pear cactus.

SCIENCE AS A HUMAN ENDEAVOUR

Rabbit plagues

Sometimes biological controls do not work as planned. An example of this is the biological control that was introduced to control rabbits in Australia (Figure 5.3.12). Rabbits eat crops and pasture for farm animals, as well as burrowing (digging) through the soil. In 1995 a virus, the calicivirus, was being researched as a possible method of control. The virus was accidentally released into the wild ahead of schedule. In the first few weeks, millions of rabbits died. Grazing land regenerated quickly. The results looked promising until it was realised that the foxes that relied on the rabbits for food were now eating small native mammals instead.

It was also discovered by Dr Tanja Strive from Australia's CSIRO that some rabbits have natural immunity natural immunity to calicivirus. The rabbits developed resistance to calicivirus, as they did to the myxoma virus that was introduced to control rabbit populations in Australia in 1950.

FIGURE 5.3.12 Plagues of rabbits can quickly destroy the land. Scientists tried to control the spread of rabbits in Australia with poisons and viruses.

Cane toads

The most famous Australian biological control story is that of the cane toad (Figure 5.3.13). Cane toads can weigh up to 1.3 kg, live for up to 15 years and produce 40 000 eggs per year.

Cane toads are native to South America and were first introduced in Queensland, Australia in 1935 to control cane beetles. Cane beetle larvae hatch underground and eat the roots of the sugar cane, killing the plant or stunting its growth.

FIGURE 5.3.13 Cane toads are spreading across northern Australia into Western Australia and down the east coast into northern New South Wales. This cane toad is eating a frog.

As a control agent, cane toads were a failure. They did not eat the cane beetle; instead the cane toads found many other things they preferred to eat. A cane toad eats anything it can swallow, including insects, mice, small snakes, lizards and even young cane toads. Poison from glands on its back kills many potential predators such as snakes and even crocodiles.

The cane toad's broad diet and lack of predators have allowed it to reproduce and spread rapidly. Cane toads are now found across most of northern Australia and their range is expanding every year. They are now as far west as Kakadu National Park in the Northern Territory and northern Western Australia and as far south as northern NSW.

Currently there is no way to get rid of cane toads, although scientists continue to research ways to control their spread and remove them from the environment. The only methods that currently work are:

- physically removing cane toads
- fencing small areas so that the toads cannot get through.

REVIEW

1. Why was the cane toad introduced into Australia?
2. List two reasons why the prickly pear was introduced into Australia.
3. Discuss whether calicivirus has been successful or unsuccessful as a biological control agent for rabbits in Australia.
4. Explain why the introduction of the cactus moth is considered a success while the introduction of the cane toad is considered a disaster.
5. Why do you think environmentalists are extremely concerned about the presence of cane toads in Kakadu National Park in the Northern Territory?
6. Propose reasons why society should support research into biological controls.

MODULE 5.3 Review questions

Remembering

1. Define the terms:
   a. fire season
   b. FRB
   c. MODIS.

2. Which term best describes each of the following?
   a. plants growing from seeds
   b. different types of organisms
   c. ecosystems that can provide the needs of organisms for a long time.

Understanding

3. What is the difference between a low-intensity fire and an intense fire?
4. Describe changes in ecosystems caused by the traditional burning practices used by Indigenous Australians.
5. a. How did Indigenous Australians create a mosaic pattern in the vegetation?
   b. Explain the benefits of having such a mosaic pattern.
6. Predict the benefits of fire reduction burning:
   a. for the wildlife in an area
   b. for the firefighters responsible for the area.
7. Outline the benefits to wildlife of planned burning programs.
8. Discuss the benefits and disadvantages of having the dingo fence.

Applying

9. Use examples to describe three different ways that humans can affect ecosystems.

Analysing

10. Compare a sustainable and an unsustainable ecosystem.
11. Compare the way Indigenous Australians used fire with the attitude of Europeans settlers to fire.
12. Many of the native Australian species of animals have soft pads on their feet, whereas introduced animals such as cows, sheep and horses all have hard hooves. Analyse the impact this would have on the Australian soil and germination of native species of plants.

Evaluating

13. Over 400 species of Australian plants have improved germination rates when exposed to smoke. What do you think are the advantages of using smoke and smoke products to germinate Australian native plants?
14. In some forests only the largest trees are taken out by loggers. What changes do you think removing only the largest trees would have on the other organisms living in the forest?
15. Discuss ways in which observations from MODIS can help protect Australian homes, industry and farming land.
16. In an area of the Flinders Ranges in South Australia, foxes were preying on the yellow-footed rock wallaby. In 1993, foxes were excluded from an area and for the next nine years the number of wallabies in the area was counted. The results are shown in Figure 5.3.14.
    a. Use the information in the graph to evaluate the effect on the wallaby population of removing the foxes.
    b. Propose reasons why the numbers decreased in 2002.

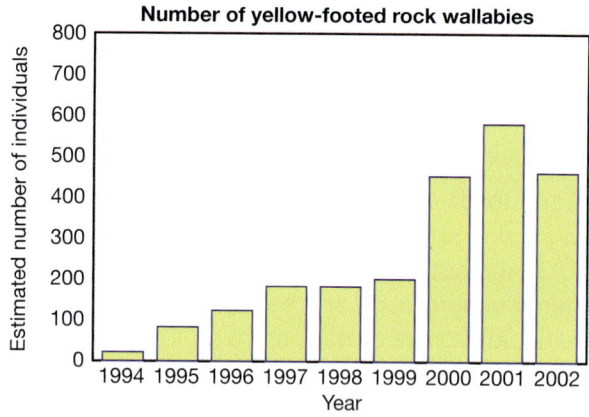

FIGURE 5.3.14

Creating

17. Design an experiment that would demonstrate the effect of excluding a particular animal from an area (for example excluding cows, sheep or goats from an area of grazing land). You will need to decide:
    - which animal to study
    - how to keep these animals out
    - how to capture information before and after the experiment about the condition of the area
    - how long experiment should go for
    - how you will record your data.

MODULE 5.3 Practical investigations

1 • Creating a terrarium

A terrarium is a glass jar or any other glass container, which contains plants and other structures so that it looks like a miniature garden or forest.

Purpose
To create a miniature environment.

Timing 60 minutes

Materials

FIGURE 5.3.15 Carefully layer the terrarium and add plants of different colours, shapes and sizes as this will add to the effect of the finished product.

SAFETY Always wear a mask when using potting mix.

- rocks, size will depend on the size of the container
- activated charcoal to filter the water and help to prevent the growth of fungi
- potting mix
- small plants of different sizes and colours
- decorative rocks or pebbles
- clear glass or plastic container—any container will do, a glass bowl overturned on a plate, goldfish bowl, or empty jar or softdrink bottle
- spray bottle containing water

Procedure

1. You are to design and build a terrarium that reproduces the main features of a particular environment. Whatever environment you choose, follow the following instructions to build your terrarium.
2. Start with a layer of rocks, about 2–3 cm, at the bottom of your container (Figure 5.3.15). These will help the soil drainage, so the roots of your plants won't get water-logged.
3. Add a 1 cm layer of charcoal then add potting mix until the container is up to half-full.
4. Plant your plants. When you remove them from their little pots, carefully pull the roots apart and remove some of the old soil so they will fit nicely in the terrarium.
5. Arrange them so that there is some space to breathe and grow.
6. Pat down the soil so they don't get uprooted easily.
7. Add decorative pebbles, rocks or whatever you like to make your terrarium look like a little garden world.
8. Water the plants using the spray bottle. Remember to consider the type of plants in the terrarium; some plants will need more water than others.

Hints
You will first need to decide what type of environment you want to create. Some plants have very different needs to others. For example you could create a desert or coastal environment that contains succulents like cactus or pigface and need very little water. Alternatively you could create a lush tropical environment including ferns and moss, which like a moist, humid environment.

Review

1. What is the name for the miniature environment you have created?
2. Explain why it is important to wear a mask when using potting mix.
3. Describe how you can create a moist humid environment in your container.
4. Compare your miniature environment with those of other groups.
    a. What criteria can you use to measure the 'success' of each?
    b. How does your miniature environment rate against those criteria?

CHAPTER 5 • HABITATS AND INTERACTIONS **209**

MODULE 5.4 Effects of industry

As the human population grows, cities get larger and industry expands. These changes mean that the area available for natural environments is reduced. Many species have been badly affected. However, many industries are now trying to make their operations more sustainable.

Species diversity

Human actions have caused many native species to become extinct. A species is said to be **extinct** when nobody has seen it in the wild for over 50 years and the last known individual has died. In the past 200 years more than 125 species of Australian native plants and animals have become extinct. Hunting, changes to the environment, and habitat loss have caused many more species to become threatened.

Threatened organisms can be classified into one of three groups, depending on how great the threat to their survival appears to be.

Endangered species are close to extinction and very small numbers remain. Examples are the Gouldian finch, the blue whale, the loggerhead turtle and the Leadbeater's possum (Figure 5.4.1).

FIGURE 5.4.1 The Leadbeater's possum is an endangered species.

Vulnerable species are experiencing a rapid population decline and are in danger of becoming extinct if the drop in numbers continues. Examples of vulnerable animals are the green turtle, the painted honeyeater, the Mallee fowl, the chuditch and the numbat.

Rare species have low numbers and are often spread out over a large area. Although the populations may be small, they are not decreasing. Rare organisms include the eastern wallaroo, the leafy sea dragon and the alpine tree frog.

science 4 fun

I need mining and forestry

What products of the mining and forestry industries do you use every day?

Collect this ...
- paper and pencil

Do this ...

Look around your home or school and list the products that are made of:
- wood, paper and cardboard (from the forestry industry)
- metal (from the mining industry).

Record this ...
1. Describe the range of products you identified.
2. Explain how your life would be different without these products.

210 PEARSON SCIENCE 7 2ND EDITION

Effect of an industry

Sumatra is one of the islands of Indonesia. Its position is shown in Figure 5.4.2. It has a huge range of plant and animal species, some of which are found only on this island.

FIGURE 5.4.2 Sumatra is one of many islands that make up the country of Indonesia.

The Sumatran elephant, rhinoceros, orangutan and tiger as shown in Figure 5.4.3, are four species that are critically endangered because their habitat is disappearing. These species live in the rainforests of Sumatra. However, Sumatra has lost almost 50% of its rainforests in the past 35 years.

FIGURE 5.4.3 Sumatra is the only place where this tiger is found. It is the smallest of the tigers and there are fewer than 400 individuals left in the wild.

The rainforests of Sumatra are logged and burned, and then oil palm plantations are established. One such plantation is shown in Figure 5.4.4. These plantations are not suitable habitats for Sumatran tigers, orangutans, rhinos and elephants. Indonesia is the world's largest producer of palm oil and the industry brings money into the country and provides employment for many people.

FIGURE 5.4.4 Palm oil plantations such as this one are replacing rainforest on the island of Sumatra.

Logging

Trees growing in Australia's forests are a valuable source of timber. Timber is used in construction, furniture making and as wood pulp for the production of paper. Figure 5.4.5 shows how the forests, and the habitats the forests contained, are destroyed when the trees are removed. Animals' homes and food sources are lost. More light is able to reach the ground and the types of plants able to grow there change.

In Australia the aim is to manage the forests in a sustainable way. Sustainably managed forests should:

- provide timber both now and into the future
- protect forest environments to maintain biodiversity
- provide benefits for the local community.

FIGURE 5.4.5 Large trees provide food and shelter for a variety of organisms. These organisms all lose their homes when old trees are cut down.

CHAPTER 5 • HABITATS AND INTERACTIONS   211

Mining

Mining is an important industry in Australia. Gold, copper, nickel, aluminium and iron ore are some of the minerals mined. Coal is also mined in many states of Australia including Victoria, Queensland and New South Wales. Coal is a very important industry for Australia as it is used to generate over 65% of our electricity. In 2013–2014, Australia produced 431 million tonnes of coal, 375 million tonnes of which was exported to countries such as Japan, Korea and China. This makes coal an important source of income for Australia.

However, mining has the potential to cause major damage to environments. Many mines are open-cut mines like the one in Figure 5.4.6. In open-cut mining, the surface plants and animals are removed then soil and rock is scraped away to access the resource underneath. All the habitats that were present are destroyed. Sometimes poisonous chemicals from the mines can pollute waterways, causing damage to these habitats and the organisms that live in them. Loose soil also washes into rivers and creeks and destroys the habitat of water plants that cannot grow in muddy water.

FIGURE 5.4.6 The super pit gold mine at Kalgoorlie in Western Australia is Australia's largest open-cut mine.

The mining industry in Australia is controlled by state and federal regulations. The aim of these regulations is to minimise any harmful effects on the environment. Before mining projects are approved, possible effects on water, biodiversity, air quality, noise and greenhouse gas emissions are assessed. The possible effects on the environment are balanced against benefits to the community and the economy. For this reason, mining companies and state authorities will usually work together to reduce and repair some of these harmful environmental effects.

Agriculture

In Australia, a large proportion of the total land area has been cleared of native **vegetation**. The vegetation in an area is the plants that are usually found in that particular area or habitat. The land is now used to graze animals or to grow crops such as the wheat seen in Figure 5.4.7. These agricultural areas provide very different habitats from the native vegetation. Fertilisers and pesticides used on the crops may wash into rivers from the farmland, causing changes in river and wetland ecosystems.

FIGURE 5.4.7 Vast fields of wheat cannot provide the same habitats as those provided by native vegetation.

Scientists have developed new varieties of crops and breeds of animals better able to cope with Australian conditions. Scientists have also developed ways of growing consistently good quality fruit and vegetables that can be produced as cheaply and quickly as possible.

Salt-tolerant wheat

In parts of Australia soils have a high salt content. The salt occurs naturally, but some land management practices have brought the salt closer to the surface. Not all plants can grow in salty soils. For example, if the salt reaches the leaves of wheat, the plant cannot carry out photosynthesis. As the area of salty land increases, the amount of food produced decreases.

Durum wheat (Figure 5.4.8) is used to make pasta and couscous. Durum wheat is particularly sensitive to salt and about 69 per cent of Australia's wheat-growing area is affected by high levels of salt in the soil.

FIGURE 5.4.8 Durum wheat is used to make pasta. Its yield is very low when it is grown in salty soils.

In 2012, Australian scientists from the University of Adelaide produced a variety of durum wheat that is able to grow in soil with high levels of salt. The scientists created the new variety by using two varieties of wheat. The parent plants used were:

- a modern variety of durum wheat that produces a large amount of grain—it has a high yield.
- an ancient wheat variety that can remove the salt from the water as the water moves from the roots to the leaves. However, the old variety has a low yield (i.e. it does not produce much grain).

The new variety of wheat scientists have created has characteristics of both parent plants—the high-yield characteristic of modern wheat, and an ability to tolerate salt. It has taken about 15 years of research to create this new variety. Now that scientists have been successful in making salt-tolerant durum wheat, they hope to use this knowledge to create a variety of bread wheat that is able to grow in salty soils.

Droughtmaster cattle

Cattle are not native to Australia and were originally imported from Europe. The conditions in Australia are very different from Europe and farmers often struggled to keep their cattle in good condition for the beef market. In the early 1900s, pioneer cattle breeders in North Queensland saw a need for cattle that:

- could tolerate hot weather
- could make best use of the limited nutrition provided by the native pasture grasses
- could walk long distances to access water and feed
- were resistant to ticks
- produced good quality meat
- give birth to their calves easily.

Brahman cattle (Figure 5.4.9) originally came from India. They have more sweat glands than European cattle, which makes them better able to tolerate hot weather. Their oily skin helps repel insect pests and they are more resistant to parasites and disease.

Shorthorn cattle are a breed from the United Kingdom that produce good meat. Some of the original Australian Shorthorns came from England with the First Fleet in 1788. By 1820 the colonies were self-sufficient in meat by grazing Shorthorns.

In the early 1930s, the cattle breeder R.L. (Monty) Atkinson mated Brahman cattle with beef Shorthorn cattle. This process of mating one breed of cattle with another is known as **cross breeding**. At each generation the offspring that showed the best characteristics were selected and then mated. After many years of cross breeding, animals with all the desired characteristics were produced. This new breed was called Droughtmaster. It is now found in all Australian mainland states. It is able to cope with harsh conditions and is now the second-most common breed in Australia.

FIGURE 5.4.9 Droughtmaster cattle have characteristics of both Brahman and Shorthorn cattle.

Working with Science

URBAN FARMING

Urban farming is a food growing system that is located in cities or towns. Vacant blocks, nature strips, rooftops and building walls are used for growing a diverse range of food plants, with the aim of making urban spaces as productive as possible (Figure 5.4.10). Urban farming is becoming more popular as more people want to grow their own food in a sustainable way. Growing food in cities and towns reduces the environmental and economic costs of transport and connects the community to their food source. This has lots of positive effects for the health of individuals, the community and the environment.

Urban farmers design food growing systems to be as energy efficient as possible. Part of their job is to understand the characteristics of food plants and animals and how they will interact to improve the system. Lots of careful planning and design goes into developing an urban food garden. To work as an urban farmer or garden designer, training in areas such as Horticulture (Certificate or Diploma) and Landscape Design (Certificate or Diploma) will give you the skills you need.

FIGURE 5.4.10 Rooftop gardens can turn bare spaces into productive, food growing havens.

Review

1. What are some of the benefits of growing food in cities and towns?
2. Why is it important to look for sustainable options for growing our food?

Urbanisation

Towns and cities are built on land that was once a natural ecosystem. The native vegetation has been replaced with houses, shops, offices, industries, roads, and new parks and gardens. When more cities are built and more people go to live in them, this process is called urbanisation. The animals that once lived among the native vegetation no longer have their habitat and have had to move away. However, there are some animals that live in urban areas and appear to thrive there. Possums such as the brushtail possum in Figure 5.4.11 are a common sight in cities. They often live in the space between the ceiling and roof of houses and use vegetable gardens and fruit trees as a source of food.

FIGURE 5.4.11 Possums thrive in cities. They are often seen travelling from place to place along electricity and telephone wires.

SciFile

Cow cancer

Eye cancer is the most common form of cancer in cattle. It is a skin cancer affecting the eye and eyelids. Eye cancer is more common in cattle with light colouring around their eyes. The red colouring of the Droughtmaster is not just in their coat, it is also in their eyes giving them protection against eye cancer.

SCIENCE AS A HUMAN ENDEAVOUR
Use and influence of science

Sustainable palm oil

Palm oil is the most widely used vegetable oil in the world. It is a common ingredient in thousands of household products such as shampoo, soap, make-up, biscuits, breakfast cereal, bread and chocolate.

FIGURE 5.4.12 An aerial view of lowland rainforest in Borneo, Malaysia that has been cleared for palm oil plantations.

Most of the world's palm oil comes from Indonesia and Malaysia where plantations of the palm oil tree are grown. To make room for the plantations, rainforests are rapidly being cleared (Figure 5.4.12). As the global demand for palm oil increases, so too does the clearance of rainforests. The deforestation is devastating populations of rhinos, orangutans (Figure 5.4.13), tigers and elephants and forcing indigenous people off their land. The clearing of rainforest also increases carbon dioxide emissions and contributes to climate change.

The palm oil industry is important for the livelihoods of many small scale farmers and the economy of Indonesia and Malaysia. Rather than boycotting the industry because of unethical practices, environmentally and socially responsible farming of palm oil needs to be encouraged.

FIGURE 5.4.13 Orangutans rely on the rainforests of Indonesia and Malaysia for their habitat. Palm oil plantations have replaced most of their habitat over the last 20 years, leading to large reductions in orangutan populations.

Environmental groups have been working towards making palm oil farming practices sustainable.

Together, the Roundtable on Sustainable Palm Oil (RSPO) and the Palm Oil Innovation Group (POIG) are working with palm oil producers to develop more environmentally responsible practices. They have committed to:

- protect areas of high conservation value from deforestation
- protect wildlife and their habitat
- ensure that companies report their greenhouse gas emissions and work with companies to reduce their greenhouse gas emissions, and water, pesticide and fertiliser use
- partner with indigenous communities to ensure that their land rights are respected and that human rights are upheld.

Palm oil workers' rights are also protected to make sure that they are paid fair wages and have safe working conditions. The RSPO and POIG are working with small farmer groups to ensure they have the support, training and resources they need to adopt sustainable practices (Figure 5.4.14). By fulfilling these commitments, the RSPO and POIG believe that the palm oil industry will be transformed and palm oil produced sustainably.

FIGURE 5.4.14 Many small palm oil plantations are run by family groups.

REVIEW

1. Why is it important that our use of natural resources is sustainable?
2. How are environmental organisations helping to protect the habitat of rainforest species in Indonesia and Malaysia?
3. How can you make a positive difference to the palm oil industry?

MODULE 5.4 Review questions

Remembering

1. Define the terms:
   a. extinct
   b. rare species
   c. cross-breeding.

2. Which term best describes each of the following?
   a. plants usually found in an area
   b. close to extinction
   c. rapidly declining population.

3. List three ways in which humans can affect ecosystems.

4. Name two Australian species in each of the following categories.
   a. endangered
   b. vulnerable.

5. What characteristic has helped the new variety of durum wheat survive in Australian soils?

6. Look around you. List ten objects or materials in the classroom that have been obtained from mining or forestry.

Understanding

7. a. Define the term 'open-cut mining'.
   b. How does this type of mining causes damage to the environment?

Applying

8. Loss of biodiversity is an increasing problem. Discuss how zoos have an important role to play in conserving biodiversity.

9. Identify the useful characteristics of Droughtmaster cattle that came from:
   a. Brahman cattle
   b. Shorthorn cattle.

Analysing

10. Compare the three groups of threatened species.

Evaluating

11. Are all introduced species pests? Justify your answer.

12. Propose reasons for Australian cattle needing to be able to walk long distances when European cattle do not.

Creating

13. A wildlife corridor is a strip of native vegetation that links patches of bushland. In many cases the patches of bushland are no longer big enough to provide for all the needs of organisms living in this habitat. Linking the patches of bushland allows animals to reach their food sources, shelter and breeding grounds.

    In Figure 5.4.15 there are several isolated patches of bushland. Your task is to modify this area to include wildlife corridors. Some conditions on the use of the land are also listed in the figure. Design this area to include wildlife corridors so that the animals can move between the various areas. You may need to consider how to form links across roads.

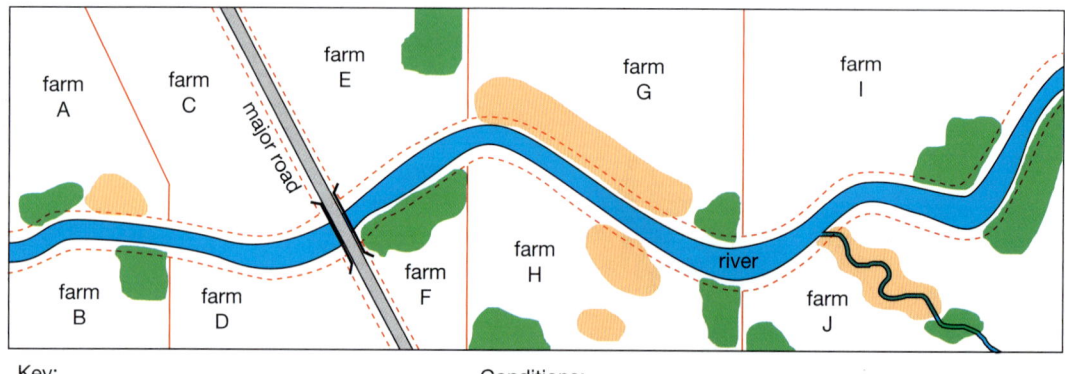

Key:
- farm boundaries
- present bushland
- swampy areas – unproductive farmland

Conditions:
- Farmers don't own land along the river. It is public land 15 m either side of the river's edge
- Farmers have the right to use water for stock
- Farms A, C and G unlikely to cooperate in the wildlife corridor project

FIGURE 5.4.15

MODULE 5.4 Practical investigations

1 • Taking cuttings

Purpose
To grow new plants from cuttings.

Timing 30 minutes

Materials
- healthy parent plant (geranium, pelargonium or coleus) large enough to provide 5 cuttings
- rooting hormone
- soilless potting mix such as vermiculite (enough to fill the pots)
- sharp knife, box cutter or Stanley knife
- 5 small plant pots or yoghurt containers with holes pierced in the base
- 5 plastic bags large enough to fit over the pots
- pencil
- marker pen
- camera or smartphone (optional)

SAFETY
Take care with sharp instruments.
Do not inhale the rooting hormone or dust from the potting mix as it may contain bacteria or other contaminants.

FIGURE 5.4.16

Procedure
1. Label the pots 1 to 5.
2. Fill each of the five pots with potting mix.
3. Use the pencil to make a hole at least 3 cm deep in the middle of the potting mix. This is where the cutting will be placed.
4. Cut off 5 pieces of stem about 8–10 cm long. The stems should have leaves but no flowers.
5. Carefully cut off all but the top four leaves.
6. At this stage you could take a photograph of your cuttings.
7. Dip the cut end of your cuttings into the rooting hormone. If the stem is dry you may have to moisten it to make sure the hormone sticks to it.
8. Carefully place one cutting into each of the pots and press the potting mix firmly round the cutting.
9. Give the pot enough water to dampen the potting mix thoroughly.
10. Place a plastic bag over each pot. This will act like a mini greenhouse (Figure 5.4.16).
11. Put the pots in a warm light position.
12. After one week observe and record any changes in the cuttings. Carefully remove the cutting in pot 1 and note any evidence of root growth. Take a photograph of the cutting.
13. Repeat step 12 each week for four more weeks observing the root growth in each of the numbered pots in turn.

Results
Record the changes you observed in the cuttings such as new leaves, an increase in height or evidence of roots.

Review
1. Propose a reason why it was important that some leaves were present on your cuttings.
2. Describe the changes in the cutting over 5 weeks.
3. What differences would you expect if rooting hormone was not used?
4. What relationship do you think exists between changes in root growth and changes in the upper part of the plant?
5. Compare your results with those from other groups.
6. Assess your experimental method and suggest improvements.

CHAPTER 5 • HABITATS AND INTERACTIONS   217

MODULE 5.4 Practical investigations

• STUDENT DESIGN •

2 • Investigating environmental impacts

Questioning & Predicting | *Planning & Conducting*

Purpose
To observe the impact of chemicals such as fertilisers, pesticides or salinity on plant growth.

Hypothesis
How do chemicals from industry, agriculture and the clearing of natural vegetation impact soil and plant health? Before you go any further with this investigation, write a hypothesis in your workbook.

Timing
60 minutes + daily observations and plant maintenance

Materials
Access to plant seeds or seedlings such as tomatoes, beans, wheatgrass

SAFETY
A Risk Assessment is required for this investigation.

Procedure
1. Plan an experiment to test the impact of one of the following on plant growth. Remember to set up a control set of plants to observe changes against:
   - the salinity of the soil (consider adding salt, bicarbonate of soda or lime to the potting mix)
   - the application of excess fertiliser
   - the exposure to pollutants (consider spraying the plants with pollutants like washing detergents or pyrethrum sprays).
2. Write your procedure in your workbook.
3. Before you start any practical work, assess your procedure. List any risks that your procedure might involve and what you might do to minimise those risks. Show your teacher your procedure and your assessment of its risks. If your teacher approves, then collect all the required materials and start work.

Hints
- To assist in your observations over time, it may be helpful to also take photographs to support your observations of the plants.
- Use the STEM and SDI template in your eBook to help you plan and carry out your investigation.

Results
Construct a table showing what you measured and the results you obtained.

Review
1. Describe the change in plants you observed during the period of your investigation.
2. Compare your findings with those from other groups.
3. Construct a conclusion for your investigation.
4. Assess whether your hypothesis was supported or not.

MODULE 5.4 Practical investigations

SPARKlab alternative available for this activity

• STUDENT DESIGN •

3 • Taking control of plants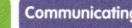

Purpose
To investigate the effect of changes in light on the growth of plants.

Timing
45 minutes

Materials
- a range of plants, such as grass, alfalfa, cress
- different coloured cellophane (blue, green, red, clear)
- cardboard box
- black paper
- digital camera
- measuring tools (rulers, balances, measuring cylinders)
- light source

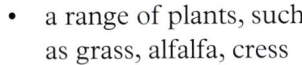
A Risk Assessment is required for this investigation.

Procedure

1. Decide what aspect of light you will study, for example, the direction where the light is coming from, or the quality of the light that is reaching the plant. This will be the controlled variable.
2. Use some of the above materials, or materials you select, to design a way of controlling the amount or quality of light that is reaching the plants.
3. Think about ways in which all the other variables can be kept the same.
4. Decide how you are going to measure or record the response of the plant. The digital camera could be useful for this purpose.
5. Check that the experiment you have designed is a fair test.
6. Write your procedure in your workbook.
7. Before you start any practical work, assess your procedure. List any risks that your procedure might involve and what you might do to minimise those risks. Show your teacher your procedure and your assessment of its risks. If your teacher approves, then collect all the requirements and start work.

Hint
- Quality refers to how bright the light is. The plants could be in full sunlight, in heavy shade or somewhere in-between.
- Use the STEM and SDI template in your eBook to help you plan and carry out your investigation.

Results
Present your results in a way that identifies patterns.

Review

1. Compare the response of different plant species to the variable you studied.
2. Identify situations where plants in a natural environment could be exposed to changes in the direction or quality of light.
3. Use your results to discuss how changes in the environment can affect plants.
4. Could your procedure be used by ecologists to investigate plant behaviour?
5. Discuss the things that worked well and those that did not in this experiment.
6. Assess how the experiment could be improved.

CHAPTER 5 • HABITATS AND INTERACTIONS

CHAPTER 5 Chapter review

Remembering

1. State why a producer organism is normally part of every food chain.
2. What is the original source of energy for food chains?
3. List these in order from largest to smallest:
   habitat, biosphere, ecosystem.
4. List these groups of organisms in order of most to least threatened:
   rare, vulnerable, endangered.
5. What are three outcomes of sustainably managed forests?

Understanding

6. Explain why the habitat of an organism is sometimes referred to as its address.
7. Figure 5.5.1 shows a food web where an eagle is the consumer at the top of the food chains.
   a. Predict what would happen to the number of eagles in the area if foxes were introduced.
   b. Modify the food web to include the foxes.

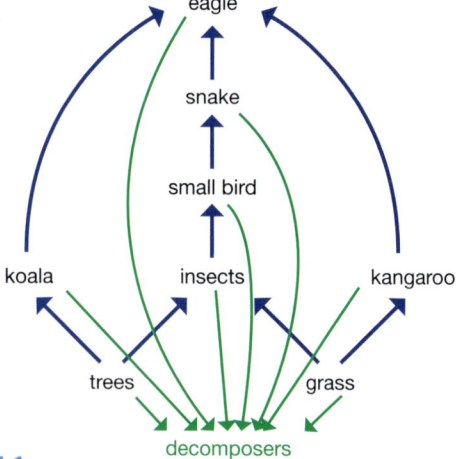

FIGURE 5.5.1

8. Explain why it is necessary to produce new breeds of animals and varieties of plants for Australian conditions.

Analysing

9. Compare the roles of prey and predator in a habitat.
10. Classify the organisms in the following list as either producers or consumers:

    cat, magpie, rose, eucalypt, sparrow, worm, ant, grass, daisy.

11. Classify the following as biotic or abiotic environmental factors in a wetland ecosystem:

    water birds, water temperature, crocodile, rate of water flow, amount of salt in the water, water plants, frogs, fish.

12. Use the information in Figure 5.5.2 to answer the following questions.
    a. Identify the organisms that compete with each other for food.
    b. Which organism would be affected most by the use of insecticides (chemicals that kill insects)?
    c. Predict the consequences for the remaining organisms in the food web if bandicoots became extinct in the area.

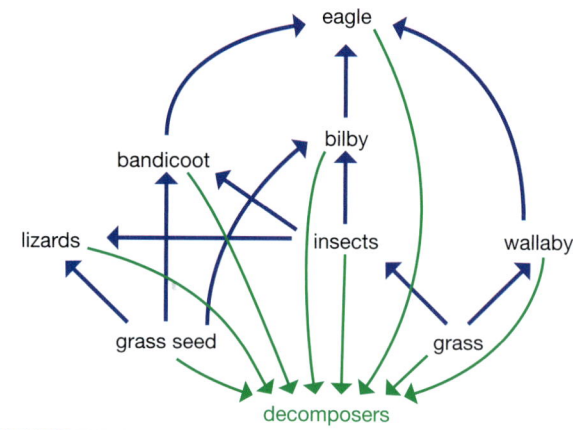

FIGURE 5.5.2

Evaluating

13. Propose reasons why humans are able to live in so many environments.
14. a. Use information from the chapter to list ways that human activity affects ecosystems.
    b. Classify the effects as positive or negative.
    c. In what ways do you think the negative effects would make the ecosystem unsustainable?
    d. In what ways do you think the positive effects would make the ecosystem stronger, increasing its sustainablitly?

CHAPTER 5 Chapter review

15 Lantana is a large flowering shrub that is native to Central and South America (Figure 5.5.3). It was introduced into Australia in 1841 as an ornamental garden plant that could be cut into a hedge. In the wild it grows rapidly along creek banks. It forms very dense bushes that prevent light from reaching the ground. Lantana grows in areas that are difficult to access and it is not easy to remove. It has a prickly stem and the leaves are poisonous to livestock if eaten. Its seeds are contained in a cluster of fleshy black berries that birds love to eat.

FIGURE 5.5.3 Lantana

Use the information about Lantana to answer these questions.
- **a** In what ways do you think lantana could affect:
  - **i** the growth of native Australian plants?
  - **ii** the number and species of native animals living in an area?
- **b** List actions that could be taken to prevent the spread of Lantana in Australia.

16 **a** Assess whether you can or cannot answer the questions on page 183 at the start of this chapter.
   b Use this assessment to evaluate how well you understand the material presented in this chapter.

Creating

17 **a** Use the following lists of organisms to construct food chains.
   - **i** grass, snake, frog, grasshopper
   - **ii** eucalypt, kookaburra, caterpillar
   - **iii** shark, large fish, small fish, snail, water plants
   b Label each organism as a primary, secondary or tertiary consumer or a producer.

18 Design an experiment that will demonstrate how a particular animal affects its environment. For example, how do cows, rabbits or goats affect grazing land and what would happen if they were excluded? You will need to decide:
- which animal or animals are to be studied
- how these animals will be prevented from getting into the study area
- what information needs to be collected about the area at the beginning of the experiment so that it can be compared at a later date
- how long the experiment should run for
- how the data will be recorded.

19 Create a flier to make people aware of a species that lives in your state that is becoming threatened. It could be an animal or a plant. Whichever species you choose, include the following in your research.
- Find images or video of the species.
- Find its proper biological Latin name (called its binomial name, which includes genus and species).
- Describe its normal habitat.
- Outline the changes to its habitat that are causing the decrease in its numbers.
- Find if and how human activity has caused these changes.
- Propose action that could be taken to conserve this species.

20 Use the following ten key terms to construct a visual summary of the information presented in this chapter.

environment biotic factors
abiotic factors habitat
food chain producer
consumer photosynthesis
endangered species adaptation

AB 5.12

CHAPTER 5 Inquiry skills

Research

1 *Processing & Analysing | Communicating*

Research a particular parasite that affects humans. For that particular parasite:
- find images or video of its size
- outline how humans can become infected with it
- describe the symptoms the parasite causes and the long-term effects on health if not treated
- outline the treatment (if any) to rid the body of the parasite or control it.

Present your research as a PowerPoint presentation or as a digital poster.

2 *Processing & Analysing | Communicating*

Research a habitat in your local area. It could be a local creek, a forest, a beach or a park. For your chosen habitat:
- collect images of plants and animals that live there
- use these animals and plants to construct a food web for the habitat.

Present your food web as a poster.

3 *Processing & Analysing | Communicating*

Research the food eaten by a koala, a great white shark, an emu and a Tasmanian devil. For each one:
- produce a food chain or food web showing what they eat and what eats them
- identify which level they belong to as a consumer (a primary, secondary, tertiary consumer and/or an apex consumer).
- use your food chains/webs to deduce which of these animals would be most affected if one of their food sources disappeared. Justify your choice.

Present your findings as a poster.

4 *Processing & Analysing | Communicating*

Cyclones and drought also affect ecosystems. Research either a cyclone or a drought to find:
- how extreme a weather pattern needs to be before it is classified as a cyclone or a drought
- images or video of a cyclone and drought
- how they change ecosystems and the environment
- ways in which humans can minimise their effects.

Present your research as a digital document that includes images and video.

5 *Evaluating | Communicating*

Research efforts to eliminate cane toads and rabbit plagues in Australia. Find:
- detailed reasons why cane toads and rabbits were introduced
- the year(s) and locations they were released
- evidence of how they changed their environments and how they affected the organisms living there
- images of the damage they cause or have caused
- different techniques used to get rid of or control them
- the advantages and disadvantages for the environment of each technique. If more than one control technique has been used, then rank them from the one you think is best to the one you think is worst. Include the reasons for your ranking.

Present your findings and ranking in digital form.

6 *Processing & Analysing | Communicating*

Research a local environmental management project.
- Outline the major features of the project.
- Describe the reasons the project was set up and the expected benefits to the community.
- Identify the types of scientists involved in the project and the role that each scientist has.

Present your research as an illustrated Word document.

7 *Processing & Analysing | Evaluating*

Our diets provide nutrients, water and energy that we need to grow and stay healthy. Different foods provide varying amounts of energy. But where does this energy originate?

Your task is to choose five different foods with varying energy levels and with your knowledge of food chains produce a flow chart going backwards to show where the energy in each food originates. Include at least one type of meat, fish, fruit and processed food in your comparison.

CHAPTER 5 Inquiry skills

- Design and produce food chain flow charts for five different foods showing where the energy in food originates.

Present your findings to show similarities and differences in the origins of energy in our food supply.

Hints
- Be sure to reference all sourced material as soon as you access it rather than trying to remember at the end of the task.
- Remember the difference between a food chain and a food web.

8 *Processing & Analysing* *Communicating*

Identify one Australian scientist who is studying the human impact on environments. Find:
- the human impacts this scientist is researching
- the changes in human behaviour that the scientists suggests have to be made.

Present your findings as an illustrated Word document.

9 *Processing & Analysing* *Evaluating*

Cassowaries (*Casuarius casuarius johnsonii*) are found in the rainforests of northern Australia (Figure 5.5.4). They are very important to the ecosystems. In fact, cassowaries are a keystone species.

FIGURE 5.5.4 A cassowary showing its prominent headcomb and very large feet

a What is a keystone species? Discuss what makes the cassowaries so important to the rainforest.

b Cassowaries have relationships with many other rainforest organisms. Mutualism, commensalism and parasitism are all possible relationships that organisms could have with another species. Identify one example of each of these that the cassowary has with another species. Explain how the relationship fits the description. Draw a food web including the three organisms that you have named along with the cassowary and at least ten other forest dwellers.

c Cassowaries are well suited to their rainforest environment. Look at the following pictures of the cassowaries. Identify at least three adaptations that you can observe. Explain how these adaptations could help it to live in the forest or to reproduce successfully.

d Cassowaries are considered to be an endangered species. Consider all that you have discovered about them. Discuss the possible effects on the rainforest if they were to become extinct. Could the cassowary survive if rainforest loss continues? Explain why or why not.

Present your research as a set of answers to the above tasks.

Thinking scientifically

1 Environmental factors may be biotic (living) or abiotic (non-living). Identify the list that has these sorted correctly.

  A *biotic*: soil, predators, living space, bacteria, parasites

  abiotic: water, prey, light, wind, rock

  B *biotic*: prey, living space, parasites, predators, wind

  abiotic: soil, water, bacteria, light, rock

  C *biotic*: soil, predators, rock, bacteria, light

  abiotic: water, parasites prey, wind, living space

  D *biotic*: predators, prey, bacteria, parasites

  abiotic: water, living space, light, wind, rock, soil

CHAPTER 5 Inquiry skills

2 First-order consumers feed directly on producers. A producer can manufacture its own food from energy in sunlight. From the food web in Figure 5.5.5, identify the group of organisms that are all first-order consumers.
 A tadpole, water beetle, snail
 B water beetle, frog, small fish
 C kingfisher, snail and algae
 D snail, tadpole, algae

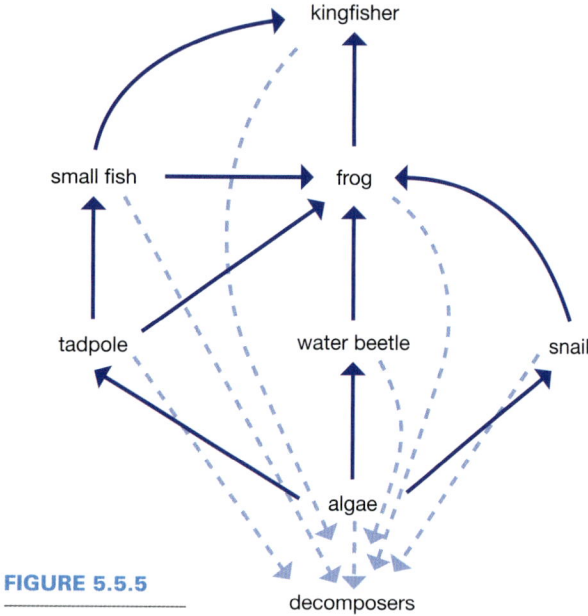

FIGURE 5.5.5

3 From the food web in Figure 5.5.5, identify the organism that is both a second-order and a third-order consumer.
 A small fish   C frog
 B kingfisher   D snail

4 Identify the plant in Figure 5.5.6 that would be adapted to get the most water from its environment.

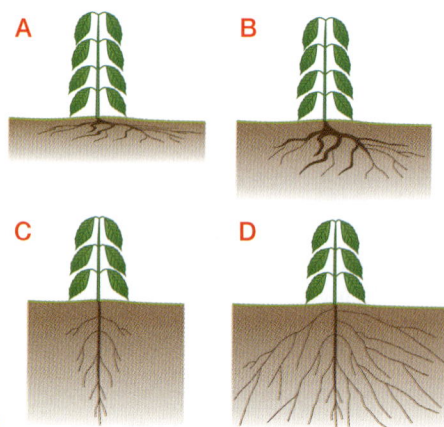

FIGURE 5.5.6

5 The fish shown in Figure 5.5.7 is adapted to its habitat; it has characteristics that assist it to survive in its environment.

 Which characteristics will help it swim through the water?
 A the dark colour of its tail and fins
 B the long spines in its back fin
 C its streamlined shape
 D its gaping mouth and small teeth.

FIGURE 5.5.7

6 Figure 5.5.8 shows the changes in the numbers of different animals found in an area for a period of 40 years. You are asked to interpret the information in this graph.
 a Describe the general trend in the population of the native animals (red-necked wallaby and eastern grey kangaroo).
 b Describe the general trend in the population of the rabbit—an introduced species.
 c Compare the changes in the rabbit population with the changes in the population of the eastern grey kangaroo.
 d What may have caused the drop in grey kangaroo numbers in 1885?
 e Identify the animals that are competing with the eastern grey kangaroo for food.

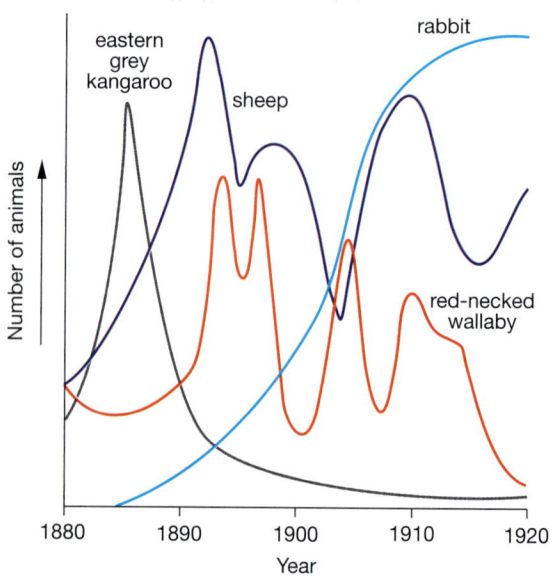

FIGURE 5.5.8

224 PEARSON SCIENCE 7 2ND EDITION

CHAPTER 5 Glossary

abiotic factors: non-living factors in the environment

adaptations: characteristics that help an organism to survive in its environment

apex predator: predator that has no natural predators except humans

biological control: a method of controlling unwanted pests by using a natural predator or disease

biosphere: the place where all life exists; consists of Earth and its atmosphere

biotic factors: living factors in the environment

carnivore: a consumer that eats only other animals

chlorophyll: the chemical in plants that traps energy from the Sun and gives plants their green colour

carnivore

commensalism: an interaction between two organisms where one of them benefits but the other one is not affected

competitors: organisms that have the same food source and live in the same habitat

consumers: organisms that must eat other organisms to get the energy and nutrients they need. Animals are consumer organisms.

cross breeding: the process of mating one breed of plant or animal with another breed of that plant or animal (e.g. cattle)

decomposers: organisms that get the energy they need by breaking down dead matter and waste products

ecologists: scientists who study the interactions between living things and their environment

ecology: the study of the relationship between organisms and their surroundings

ecosystem: a balanced system formed by organisms interacting with each other and their non-living surroundings

endangered species: species that are close to extinction and very small numbers remain

endangered species

environment: all the conditions that affect a plant or animal in its habitat

extinct: a species that has not been seen in the wild for more than 50 years, and of which the last known individual has died

fire season: times of the year when fires are most likely to occur

food chain: the flow of energy from organism to organism in a series of feeding relationships

food web: a number of food chains combined

fuel reduction burning: regular burning to reduce the amount of fuel available for a fire

germination: the process by which a plant grows from a seed

habitat: the place where an organism lives

herbivore: an animal that eats only plants

host: an organism in or on which a parasite lives

herbivore

interdependent: depending on each other for survival

mutualism: an interaction between organisms where both organisms benefit from the relationship and neither is harmed

mutualism

nocturnal: active or hunting at night

omnivore: an animal that eats both plants and animals

organisms: all living things

omnivore

CHAPTER 5 • HABITATS AND INTERACTIONS 225

Chapter 5 Glossary

parasite: an organism that lives on or in a host, taking food or shelter from the host. The host gets nothing in return and may be harmed.

parasitism: an interaction where one type of organism (the parasite) lives on or in another type of organism (the host); the host is usually harmed or even killed

photosynthesis: the process used by plants to make their own food

plague: unusually large numbers of an organism and they are causing damage to the environment

population: a group of organisms of the same species, which live in the same area

predator: an animal that eats other animals

prey: an animal that is eaten by a predator

primary consumer: a consumer that only eats plants, algae and other producers

producer: an organism able to manufacture its own food; plants are producer organisms

rare species: species that has low numbers, often spread out over a large area; the population is not decreasing

remnant vegetation: native vegetation that remains unchanged when surrounding areas have been changed by activities such as grazing or forestry

scavenger: an animal that finds dead animals or plants and eats them

secondary consumer: a consumer that eats a primary consumer

species: different types of living things

sustainable ecosystem: an ecosystem that is diverse and able to provide for the needs of the organisms living there over a long period

symbiosis: another name for interdependence

tertiary consumer: a consumer that eats a secondary consumer

vegetation: the plants that are usually found in that particular area or habitat

vulnerable species: species that is experiencing a rapid population decline and is in danger of becoming extinct if numbers continue to fall

vulnerable species

CHAPTER 6
Classification

Have you ever wondered ...
- how many types of living things there are on Earth?
- why we put things in groups?
- why some people group things differently from others?
- how scientists communicate?

After completing this chapter you should be able to:

- outline the reasons for classifying organisms such as identification and communication
- group a variety of organisms on the basis of similarities and differences describe how biological classification systems have changed over time
- describe how biological classification systems have changed over time
- classify organisms using hierarchical systems such as kingdom, phylum, class, order, family, genus and species
- use scientific conventions for naming species
- use provided keys to identify organisms surveyed in a local habitat.

This is an extract from the Australian Curriculum
Victorian Curriculum F–10 © VCAA (2016); reproduced by permission

AB 6.1

227

MODULE 6.1 Using classification

If you tell someone you play a team sport, then you are communicating information about yourself. If you add the sport is netball and you play wing attack, then you are giving more detailed information. This helps the person understand more about what you are like.

You may have a friend who also plays sport but they play football, not netball. So you have some things in common and other things that are different.

Your pencil case

How could the things in your pencil case be classified?

Collect this...
- the contents of your pencil case

Do this...
1. Tip the contents of your pencil case out on the table.
2. Sort the contents into groups and give names to each group.
3. List the items included in each group under the group name.
4. Re-sort the contents into different groups, and again list the items included in each group.

Record this...
1. Describe how you decided what to include in the groups.
2. Explain which of the groupings was most useful.

You use it every day

Classification is the process of putting things into groups. It is a skill needed in many areas of life, not only in science.

Next time you walk round a supermarket, think about the way products are grouped. Biscuits are all in the same aisle, with the savoury biscuits separated from sweet and chocolate biscuits. Canned items are usually together, but the canned fruit is separated from the baked beans and soups, and fresh fruit is organised as in Figure 6.1.1.

FIGURE 6.1.1 Fruit and vegetables in the supermarket are sorted into groups. This makes it easier to find the type of vegetable you need or the variety of apple you want to buy.

228 PEARSON SCIENCE 7 2ND EDITION

Music you download is classified in a variety of ways. This allows you to find the music by searching via artist, album, composer or genre (such as rock, pop and dance).

Grouping things in this way makes it easier to find a particular item or similar items to the one you are looking for. Imagine what shopping day would be like if the hundreds of supermarket items were placed on the shelves at random. Similarly it would be nearly impossible to find a song by your favourite band if there was no organisation to the way the songs were grouped.

Your group

At school you may be classified by age or year level, whether you are a girl or boy or even by which sport you do. The group you are placed in depends on the reason you and others are being grouped. You are part of all these groups at different times and have things in common with the other members of each group.

Groups change

Just as you are placed in different groups, plants and animals are often grouped in different ways too. For example, the grass making up a garden's lawn is looked after and encouraged to grow. However, if the grass escapes from the lawn area and into a national park, the grass is now considered to be a pest and is dug out or even poisoned. The plant that belongs in one place is a weed in another place. **Weed** is not a name given to a special group of plants, but is a classification for any plant growing where it does not belong (Figure 6.1.2).

FIGURE 6.1.2 A weed is just a plant growing where it does not belong.

Introduced species

Many plants have been introduced into Australia from overseas. Some introductions were intentional and have brought benefits. Many food crops, such as wheat, potatoes, tomatoes and apples, were introduced by early European settlers and are still cultivated and controlled.

Other introduced plants have created problems. Lantana (*Lantana camara*) has a pretty flower and was introduced to Australia in the 1840s (Figure 6.1.3). It now grows out of control in parts of Australia and has already invaded over 4 million hectares of farmland, woodlands and forests. This is an area equal to about two-thirds the size of Tasmania! Scientists believe that, if not controlled, lantana could invade an area of 35 million hectares across New South Wales, Queensland, Western Australia and Northern Territory. Because the plant spreads rapidly and is toxic to livestock who eat it, lantana is classified as a Weed of National Significance.

FIGURE 6.1.3 Lantana (*Lantana camara*) is a weed species introduced from South America.

Animals have also been introduced to Australia for food (for example cattle and sheep), transport (horses and camels), hunting (rabbits and foxes, as shown in Figure 6.1.4) and to control other pests (the cane toad was introduced to control a beetle ruining sugar cane crops).

FIGURE 6.1.4 The red fox (*Vulpes vulpes*) is a pest that kills native wildlife.

CHAPTER 6 • CLASSIFICATION **229**

Some of these animals have become a major problem for Australian wildlife. Foxes eat wildlife, rabbits eat vegetation normally eaten by wildlife, while poisonous cane toads will kill any snakes, crocodiles and birds that eat them. These introduced animals are known as **pest species**.

Why classify?

Scientists classify things to make it easier to identify things and communicate with other people. Giving an object, substance or organism a name ensures everyone knows what they are talking about.

In order to classify something, you have to find out its characteristics and make a judgement about how similar it is to other things.

Classification is an important skill used in all branches of science. Scientists observe ways in which objects are similar and group them together. Chemists classify substances such as those in Figure 6.1.5 and group them using names such as metal or non-metal, and crystalline or non-crystalline. Geologists classify rocks as sedimentary, igneous or metamorphic (Figure 6.1.6), and astronomers classify heavenly bodies into groups such as stars, planets, comets and meteors.

Sedimentary rocks are laid down in layers.

FIGURE 6.1.6 Geologists classify rocks using characteristics such as how hard they are, their colour, and how they were formed.

Basalt is formed in the Earth's surface following a volcanic eruption.

copper

amethyst

FIGURE 6.1.5 Chemists group substances according to their characteristics. Copper is classified as a metal, along with iron and tin. Amethysts form purple crystals and can be grouped with other crystalline substances such as sugar and salt.

The importance of identification

Australian crocodiles

Saltwater crocodiles (*Crocodylus porosus*) and freshwater crocodiles (*Crocodylus johnsoni*) are two closely related species found in Northern Australia. An example of each type of crocodile is shown in Figure 6.1.7. Saltwater crocodiles inhabit coastal and tidal areas.

saltwater crocodile | freshwater crocodile

FIGURE 6.1.7 Saltwater crocodile and freshwater crocodile are two closely related species found in Northern Australia.

Freshwater crocodiles are found inland in wetlands and rivers. Despite their name, saltwater crocodiles can be found in freshwater habitats, particularly after floods.

Table 6.1.1 compares the characteristics of saltwater and freshwater crocodiles.

TABLE 6.1.1 Saltwater and freshwater crocodiles

	Saltwater crocodiles	Freshwater crocodiles
size	3–6 metres	1–3 metres
mass	up to 1 tonne (1000 kg)	up to 100 kg
behaviour	Aggressive predators that hunt wallabies, pigs, cattle and even horses. They will attack and kill humans.	Eat insects, fish, birds and small mammals. Less aggressive than their saltwater relatives. Attacks on humans are rare and only tend to occur when disturbed or provoked. No fatalities have been recorded.

FIGURE 6.1.8 Signs like this one are used to warn people of the presence of saltwater crocodiles.

SciFile

Powerful bite

Saltwater crocodiles are the largest living reptile in the world. They have the strongest bite in the animal kingdom. Their bite strength is 4 times as strong as that of a lion!

Crocodiles and people

Northern Australia is popular with tourists for camping, bushwalking and swimming. Park Rangers need to be able to identify both types of crocodiles and communicate this information to the public and tour operators. One method of communication is via signs (Figure 6.1.8). Swimming in a waterhole inhabited by freshwater crocodiles is reasonably safe, but it is not a good idea to be anywhere near water that is occupied by a saltwater crocodile.

Apart from size there are other differences that can be used to identify crocodiles. Saltwater crocodiles have broad powerful snouts and their teeth vary in size. Freshwater crocodiles have long thin snouts and their teeth are smaller and much the same size. Rangers and scientists use these features to identify and communicate about crocodiles.

Introducing keys

Biologists classify living things. Scientists who specialise in grouping and naming living things are known as **taxonomists**, and the science of grouping and naming things is called **taxonomy**. Once the characteristics of organisms have been described this information can be used to develop a key. A key is a tool that can then be used to identify unknown organisms.

The simplest type of key is a dichotomous key. The word *dichotomous* means *cut in two*. A **dichotomous key** is a series of choices that leads to the identification of an object. At each stage of using a dichotomous key you are given two choices. Each choice leads to another two choices and so on, until there are no more choices and the object is identified.

Two ways of writing keys are as flow charts or tables. Buttons have been used to construct the two keys shown in Figure 6.1.9 on page 232.

Keys work best if the features used to make the choices are easy to observe, with everyone knowing exactly what they mean. Take height as an example. A person's height is easy to observe, but words such as tall or short can be interpreted in different ways. You would probably describe someone taller than you as 'tall'. As Figure 6.1.10 on page 232 shows, that same person might be described as short by an even taller person. Therefore tallness is not a good and reliable feature for a key. Descriptions of height such as 'greater than 1.5 metres in height' are more reliable.

CHAPTER 6 • CLASSIFICATION **231**

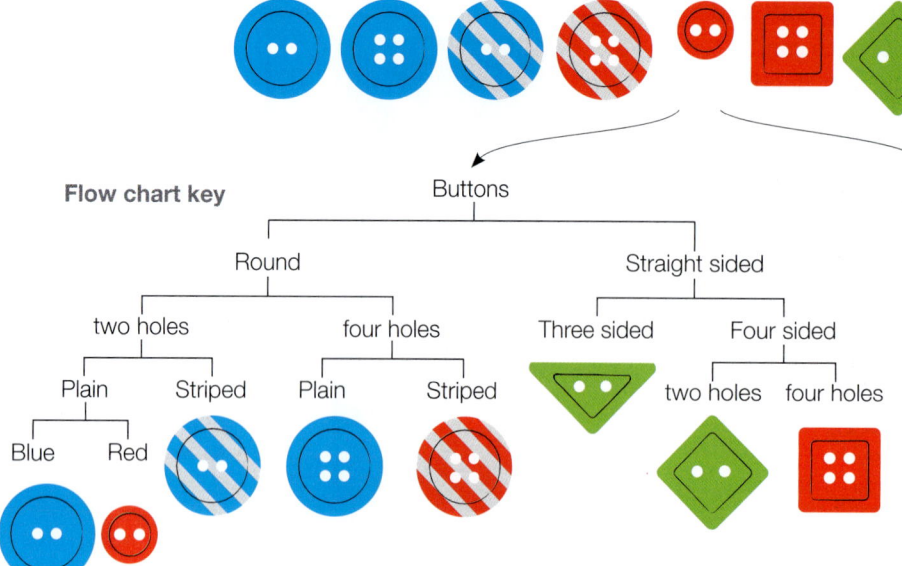

FIGURE 6.1.9 These buttons can be classified using different keys.

FIGURE 6.1.10 Qualitative descriptions, such as tall or short, are subjective, with different interpretations. Quantitative measurements are more reliable because they are definite.

SciFile

Harmless or deadly?

It is important to be able to tell the difference between Australian snakes so that the correct antivenom can be given for a snake bite. Of the world's top ten deadliest snakes, six are native to Australia. These include the brown snake, death adder and copperhead.

Strong keys

A strong key refers to features that do not change. Some features or characteristics are better to use in a key than others. Size, colour and shape can change as an organism grows and develops, or may vary within the same kind of organism. Structural features make a much stronger key that can be used at any time, regardless of age of the organism. It is easy to construct a strong key for something like the buttons because they do not change. People and other living things do change with time and environmental conditions. If a key is to be used both now and at some time in the future then it has to use features that will not change. Look at the two faces in Figure 6.1.11. There are two easily observed differences between these two girls. Only one has a pony tail, and therefore long hair. The other has short hair and no pony tail. One has blue eyes and the other brown eyes.

You could use any of these differences to separate them in a key; however, only one of the differences would give you a strong key. The girl with the pony tail and long hair could wear her hair down or cut her hair short. The other girl could grow her hair longer. One difference will always be the same—the difference in eye colour. It is the difference in eye colour that will give you a strong key.

FIGURE 6.1.11 Characteristics for a strong key should be easy to observe and not change over time, like a hairstyle or coat colour.

Worked example
Constructing a dichotomous key

Problem
Use the four shapes in Figure 6.1.12 to create a dichotomous key.

FIGURE 6.1.12

Solution
Thinking: Both a table key (Figure 6.1.13) and a flow chart key (Figure 6.1.14) can be constructed using these shapes.
Look for some difference that has only two choices.
Working: The square and triangle have straight sides but the circle and oval have curved sides.
Thinking: For each of these two choices, find another difference that has only two choices.
Working: The square has four sides but the triangle has three. The circle is equal in size in all directions (equal diameters) but the oval is different in size left/right and up/down (unequal diameters).

Try yourself
Triangles can be classified as equilateral, isosceles or scalene. Equilateral triangles have three equal sides and angles. Isosceles have two equal sides and angles.

Scalene triangles have no equal sides or angles. Construct a table key and a flow chart key that could be used to classify triangles.

1a	has straight sides	go to 2
b	no straight sides	go to 3
2a	has four sides	square
b	has three sides	triangle
3a	all diameters are equal	circle
b	diameters are not all equal	oval

FIGURE 6.1.13 Table key

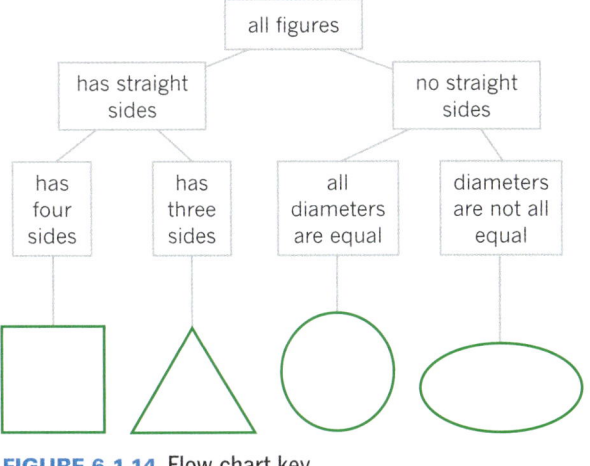

FIGURE 6.1.14 Flow chart key

CHAPTER 6 • CLASSIFICATION **233**

MODULE 6.1 Review questions

Remembering

1. Define the terms:
   a. classification
   b. weed
   c. taxonomy.

2. What term best describes each of the following?
   a. introduced animals that become a problem for wildlife
   b. a key where there are two choices at each stage
   c. a key based on features that never change.

3. What type of scientist names and classifies living things?

4. You are classified in different ways depending on the purpose.
   a. Name two groups you are in at different times.
   b. Choose one of these groups and list two different ways people are classified within this group.

Understanding

5. Explain why we need to group things together.
6. How does classification make shopping at the supermarket easier?
7. Explain what is meant by a strong key.
8. Predict what could happen if a key used features that were not obvious or reliable.
9. a. Some plants are called weeds while others are not. How can you decide whether something is a weed or not?
   b. Would 'weed' or 'not a weed' be a good alternative to use in a key? Explain your answer.
10. Crocodiles in Australia are classified into two groups: saltwater crocodiles and freshwater crocodiles.
    a. List two observable differences between the two types of crocodiles.
    b. Explain why it is important to be able to identify and name what type of crocodile is present in a habitat.

Applying

11. a. Use the key shown in Figure 6.1.15 to describe:
       i. a motorbike
       ii. rollerblades.
    b. Modify the key so that it includes a tricycle.

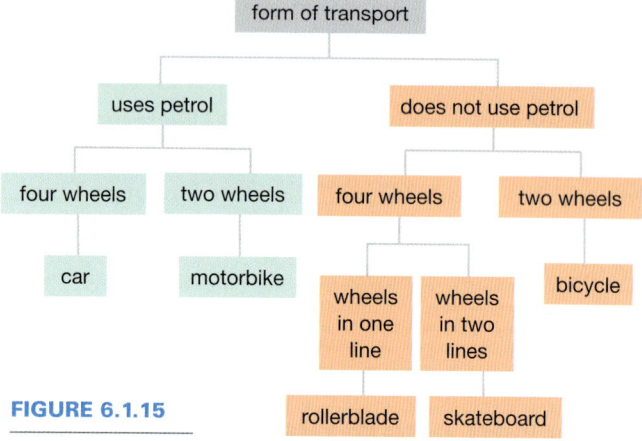

FIGURE 6.1.15

12. The shapes in Figure 6.1.16 can be grouped in more than one way. Identify the structural features that would best separate these shapes into classification groups.
    a. Identify the headings you would use to separate these shapes into groups.
    b. List the shapes under each group heading.

FIGURE 6.1.16

Analysing

13. Classify the following objects into three groups.

    pencil   boot   book   chalk
    comic   shoe   crayon   sandal

MODULE 6.1 Review questions

14 **a** Classify the five objects shown in Figure 6.1.17 into two groups in at least three different ways.
    b For each grouping, what feature did you use?
    c Discuss the usefulness of each feature you chose.

FIGURE 6.1.17

15 Analyse the cars in a car park and list characteristics that could be used to classify them.

Evaluating

16 The most popular way for most people to find a new house to buy is by looking online. Most property websites have a general search function and the ability to search by suburb. There are also other headings that can be used.
    a How does being able to search by suburb assist people to find a house to buy?
    b Propose other ways that a house buyer may wish to search for a new house. Evaluate each of these ways.

17 **a** In the key shown in Figure 6.1.18, identify which features make it a strong key and which are not useful.
    b Justify your decisions.

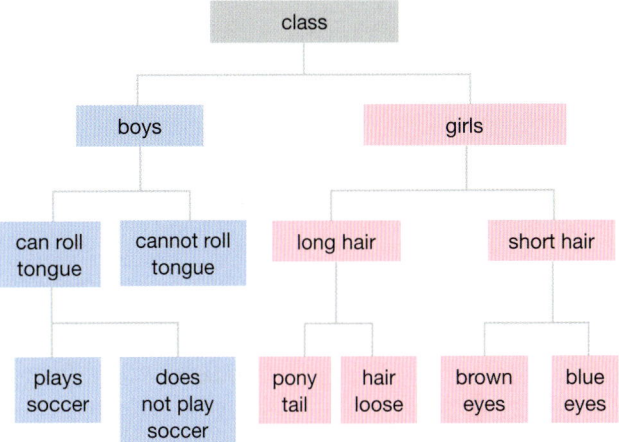

FIGURE 6.1.18

18 **a** Which of the following characteristics would be useful when constructing a key to identify varieties of dog?
- loud bark/quiet bark
- pink tongue/black and pink tongue
- short hair/long hair
- large ears/small ears
- wags tail/does not wag tail
- black/brown
- straight hair/curly hair
- hair hangs over eyes/hair not over eyes.

    b Justify your choices.

Creating

19 Construct a key using these terms:

cricket	playing field
soccer	tennis racquet
chess	netball
tennis	hockey stick
squash court	

20 **a** Construct keys that could be used to identify the objects from Figures 6.1.16 and 6.1.17.
    b Share your key with other members of the class. Compare the choices that were used.

CHAPTER 6 • CLASSIFICATION   **235**

MODULE 6.1 Practical investigations

1 • Sorting pasta

Purpose
To construct a dichotomous key using pasta.

Timing 45 minutes

Materials
- 6 different types of dry pasta
- paper and pencil

Procedure
1. Describe each type of pasta, making a note of the similarities and differences.
2. Use the differences to construct a dichotomous key.

Results
Present your key as both a table and a flow chart.

Review
1. Describe any difficulties you had in sorting the types of pasta.
2. Explain why you selected the characteristics you used to create the key.
3. Ask another student to try using your key. Discuss with them any improvements you could make to the key.
4. Is your key a strong key? Justify your answer.

• STUDENT DESIGN •

2 • Class key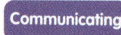

Purpose
To construct a dichotomous key to identify each member of the class.

Timing 45 minutes

Materials
- class members

Procedure
1. Brainstorm and list differences that could be used to distinguish between class members.
2. Decide if these differences would make a strong key.
3. When you have decided on the first choice, the members of the class should form the two groups.
4. For one of these groups, decide on the next choices that will allow each student to be identified.
5. Repeat for the other group.
6. Record the choice used at each step.
7. Construct the key showing this classification.
8. Some less obvious characteristics that could be used to classify the class are:
   - ability to roll tongue
   - ear lobes attached or free
   - length of second toe compared to big toe
   - dimples in cheek
   - dimple in chin
   - widow's peak.
9. Now use these characteristics to organise the class first into two groups, then four, then eight and so on.

Use the STEM and SDI template in your eBook to help you plan and carry out your investigation.

Review
1. Explain why a class member who is absent on the day the key was created could not be identified using the class key.
2. What would happen if you tried using the key to identify that class member?

MODULE 6.2 Animal kingdom

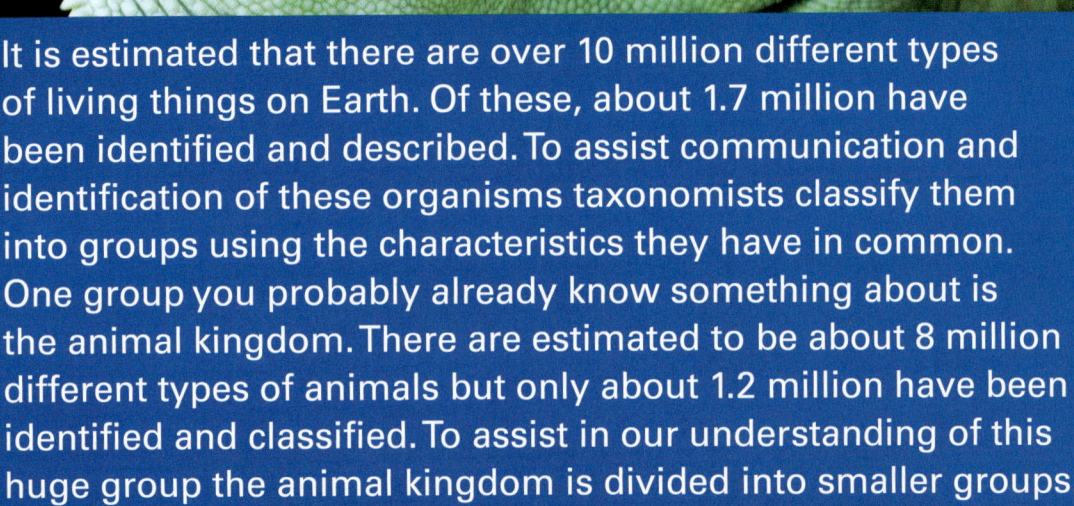

It is estimated that there are over 10 million different types of living things on Earth. Of these, about 1.7 million have been identified and described. To assist communication and identification of these organisms taxonomists classify them into groups using the characteristics they have in common. One group you probably already know something about is the animal kingdom. There are estimated to be about 8 million different types of animals but only about 1.2 million have been identified and classified. To assist in our understanding of this huge group the animal kingdom is divided into smaller groups.

science 4 fun

Evidence of animals

Can you tell if animals are present even if you cannot see them?

Possums made all these scratch marks as they climbed the tree.

Collect this…
- a magnifying glass (optional)
- notepad and pen or digital camera.

Do this…
1. Make careful observations as you walk to and from school, wander round the school grounds, go to a park, beach or for a walk in the bush.
2. Record evidence that animals have been there. The evidence could include holes in leaves where they have been eaten, footprints, soil and gravel thrown up by ants making a nest, scratches on bark where claws have been used to climb trees, and shells or crab sand balls on the beach.

Record this…
1. Describe the place or places where you saw most evidence of animal activity.
2. Explain why the animals were likely to have been there.

Kingdom

Scientists sort organisms into groups to help them make sense of the millions of different types of living things.

The first level of classification sorts living things into a small number of groups. Each group has a very large number of organisms in it, and each organism shares important characteristics with others in their group. Although similar in many ways, the organisms in each group still have many, many differences. **Kingdom** is the name given to the group at this first level of classification.

Currently taxonomists sort all living things into five kingdoms. One kingdom is the **animal** kingdom. You could probably produce a long list of animals that would include kangaroos, rosellas and snakes. However, bees, worms and jellyfish are animals too. Four members of the animal kingdom are shown in Figure 6.2.1.

FIGURE 6.2.1 The boy and his dog are both members of the animal kingdom and so are the frog and the bee sitting on its head.

The organisms of the animal kingdom are then divided into smaller groups according to the characteristics of the animal.

Animal phyla

Animals are often described as **vertebrates** (animals with backbones) or **invertebrates** (animals without backbones). Although this difference is very important, these terms are not always used in the scientific classification of animals.

Scientists have made a large number of observations of living things. The presence or absence of a backbone is only one of the observations. Using the similarities and differences taxonomists have grouped all the known members of the animal kingdom into nine smaller groups which are together called **phyla**. Each of the smaller groups is known as a **phylum**. The nine phyla are shown in Figure 6.2.2.

Animals
- Poriferans
- Cnidarians
- Echinoderms
- Annelids
- Nematodes
- Platyhelminths
- Molluscs
- Arthropods
- Chordates

FIGURE 6.2.2 Eight of the animal phyla in this key do not have backbones; they are invertebrates. The phylum Chordates includes all the animals with backbones—the vertebrates.

Poriferans

Poriferans are commonly called sponges. A typical sponge is shown in Figure 6.2.3.

Poriferans live in the water and most are found in marine environments. They are full of pores (holes) through which water passes, carrying their food. They filter the food out of the water, and for this reason they are known as filter feeders. The wastes along with water are pushed out through an opening at the top of the sponge.

FIGURE 6.2.3 This yellow tube sponge grows to about 80 cm tall. It pushes so much water through its body as it feeds that divers can feel a current of water near the top of it.

SkillBuilder

Symmetry in organisms
Organisms are often described as having radial symmetry or bilateral symmetry.

Radial symmetry
A cut in any direction through the middle will result in identical halves.

Bilateral symmetry
There is only one position where a cut produces identical halves.

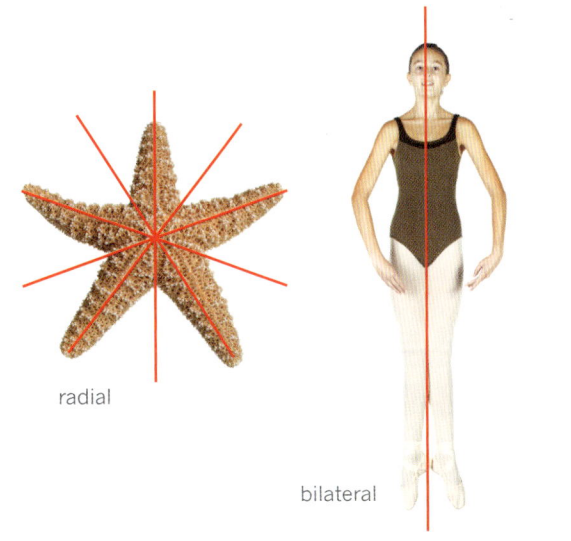

Cnidarians

Jellyfish (sea jellies), sea anemones and coral polyps belong to the **cnidarians** (pronounced as 'nidarians'). They have radial symmetry and only one body opening. Food goes into the body through this opening and waste comes out of the same opening. Cnidarians have stinging cells, which they use to catch food. Cnidarians are not interested in using humans for food, but the poison from their stinging cells will cause you intense pain if you get tangled in their tentacles.

Some cnidarians like the box jellyfish will not just hurt but will kill you within minutes. The poison causes animals that get tangled to have a heart attack. The box jellyfish is responsible for 100 human deaths each year. You can see it in Figure 6.2.4.

FIGURE 6.2.4 The venom produced by the stinging cells of the box jellyfish (*Chironex fleckeri*) is one of the most poisonous in the animal kingdom.

Echinoderms

Starfish (more correctly known as sea stars), brittlestars, sea urchins and sea cucumbers belong to the **echinoderms**. They all live in the ocean, usually in shallow water near the coast. Starfish, brittlestars and sea urchins have a spiny skin, which you can see in Figure 6.2.5, but the skin of sea cucumbers is leathery. All echinoderms have a chalky layer under their skin, which forms a protective armour. One thing common to all echinoderms is that they have radial symmetry.

FIGURE 6.2.5 There are over 6000 species of echinoderm. Here are two species: an orange starfish, and the black spines of a sea urchin.

Annelids

The most familiar **annelid** is the earthworm, shown in Figure 6.2.6. Other annelids are leaches and ragworms (often used as bait for fishing). Look closely at an annelid and you will see rings along the length of its body. These rings are segments or divisions within the body, and give the group their common name of 'segmented worms'. These animals have bilateral symmetry. Annelids are found in water and in damp places on land.

FIGURE 6.2.6 Annelids have two body openings—one at the front where food enters and one at the back from which wastes leave.

Nematodes

Nematodes are roundworms. They have bilateral symmetry like annelids, with long tapered bodies that are pointed at each end, but they do not have segments. They are commonly found in damp soil, in water, and as parasites in the bodies of other organisms. **Parasites** are organisms that live on or in another organism, called a host. They get their food from the host, but the host gets nothing in return and may be harmed. Heart worm, a common disease of dogs, is caused by a nematode. Even humans can be hosts to parasitic nematodes, like the one shown in Figure 6.2.7. You would know if you were infected with them because they cause stomach pain, vomiting and diarrhoea.

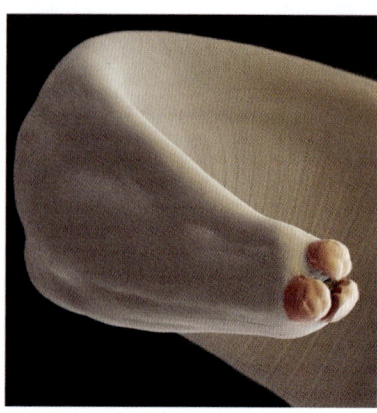

FIGURE 6.2.7 *Ascaris lumbricoides* is a parasitic nematode that inhabits the human intestine. They can grow up to 35 cm in length.

Platyhelminths

Platyhelminths are flatworms. They have bilateral symmetry with the body flattened top to bottom (Figure 6.2.8). They live in water or very moist places.

FIGURE 6.2.8 There are over 12 000 species of Platyhelminths. They range in size from around a millimetre to 15 metres in length. The species shown here is the gold-dotted flatworm, which lives in the ocean and can grow to 7 cm in length.

Molluscs

Molluscs are members of the second largest phylum in the animal kingdom. Snails, slugs, oysters and mussels belong to this group. All of them live in water or in very moist places. They come in a wide variety of shapes and sizes, but all have bilateral symmetry, have well developed internal organs, and have a muscular foot which they can use to move along. Some molluscs have a shell for protection like the snail in Figure 6.2.9.

FIGURE 6.2.9 The protective shell of the snail is clearly visible.

Arthropods

Arthropods form the largest animal phylum, with over one million species described. This phylum includes:

- insects
- scorpions and spiders (Figure 6.2.10)
- crustaceans like prawns, crabs and lobsters.

FIGURE 6.2.10 Flies and spiders, crabs, prawns and millipedes are all arthropods.

Arthropods are found everywhere—on land, in the air and in water. They are able to survive on dry land because they have a waterproof **exoskeleton**—a skeleton on the outside of the body. The skeleton does not bend, so the limbs of arthropods (legs and antennae) are jointed to allow the animals to move. Inside, the body is divided into segments. These are sometimes visible as lines across the exoskeleton.

AB 6.6

Chordates

Chordates have a nerve cord running down their backs, which gives this group its name. Most chordates have skeletons inside their body (an **endoskeleton**), and most of the chordates have a series of small bones protecting the nerve cord.

The small bones are called **vertebrae**, and together they are called the **vertebral column** or backbone. The group of chordates that has a backbone is commonly called the vertebrates. The cockatoo shown in Figure 6.2.11 is an example of a chordate.

Most of the larger animals you see around you are vertebrates. Dogs, cows, birds, fish and humans are all vertebrates.

FIGURE 6.2.11 Birds are examples of chordates. They have a spine and spinal cord.

All chordates have bilateral symmetry. They are divided into **classes** based on a range of characteristics that includes the way they breathe, their skin covering, body temperature, and how they reproduce. The eight classes of chordates are shown in Figure 6.2.12.

Chordates
- Chordates without backbones
- Agnatha
- Chondrichthyes
- Osteichthyes
- Amphibians
- Reptiles
- Aves
- Mammals

FIGURE 6.2.12 Classes of chordates

SciFile

Spineless?

All chordates have a nerve cord but not all have a backbone to protect it. Some, like sea squirts, have a rod of cells known as a notochord lying below the nerve cord. Adult sea squirts look just like a bag of jelly. They filter food from the water and then squirt out the water when they are finished with it.

CHAPTER 6 • CLASSIFICATION **241**

There are three classes of chordates that are commonly called fish: agnatha, chondrichthyes and osteichthyes. They all live in water and breathe using gills. They are **ectothermic**, which means that their body temperature varies with the temperature of the water they live in.

Agnatha

The **agnatha** are jawless fish. There are many fossils of jawless fish, but the only living representatives are hagfish and lampreys like the one in Figure 6.2.13. They have an internal skeleton made of **cartilage**. This is more flexible than bone—it is cartilage in the wobbly bit at the end of your nose. Agnatha have a fin along their backs. Their mouth is a round sucker, lined with horny teeth, which they use to attach themselves to other fish. All agnatha are parasites.

FIGURE 6.2.14 Rays are members of the class Chondrichthyes. Their side fins are extended to resemble wings.

FIGURE 6.2.13 Lampreys are shaped like an eel. Their mouth is like a suction cup that attaches to its host. Horny teeth scrape the skin away so that the lamprey can suck blood.

Chondrichthyes

Sharks and rays belong to the class of chordates called **chondrichthyes**. Their skeleton is also made of cartilage, which gives them their common name of cartilaginous fish. Unlike the jawless fish, they have proper jaws and teeth. Sharks and rays have fins on the side of their bodies as well as along their backs as shown in Figure 6.2.14, and this helps them to be agile swimmers.

Osteichthyes

The **osteichthyes** are bony fish. They have fins on the back and sides of their body and have proper jaws and teeth. What makes them different from the other fish is their skeleton made of bone. Tuna, goldfish, eels, sea horses and lungfish all belong to this group. Figure 6.2.15 shows a barramundi, an example of a bony fish.

FIGURE 6.2.15 The barramundi (*Lates calcarifer*) is found in river estuaries and in the ocean around the north of Australia, from Fraser Island, Qld in the east around to Shark Bay, WA in the west.

Amphibians

Frogs, like the one shown in Figure 6.2.16, toads, newts and salamanders are all amphibians. **Amphibians** are chordates that live both in and out of water. Their eggs are laid in water, and the larvae or tadpoles must live in water because they breathe through gills. The body then changes shape allowing the adult to live on land, breathing air using lungs. Their lungs are not very effective, and amphibians also take in oxygen through their skin. To be able to do this their skin must remain moist.

All amphibians are ectothermic, so are not found in very cold areas.

FIGURE 6.2.16 Amphibians must keep their skin moist, and usually live near water or in very moist places.

Reptiles

Reptiles such as crocodiles, lizards and snakes like the one in Figure 6.2.17 are ectothermic, and have a dry, scaly skin. They breathe using only their lungs. Most lay eggs with a leathery shell on land. While most spend their whole life cycle on land, there are exceptions. Sea snakes spend all their lives in water, and some cannot move on land at all. Sea snakes do not lay eggs—instead they give birth to live young. Some land snakes and lizards also do this. Tiger snakes and blue-tongue lizards are two Australian examples.

FIGURE 6.2.17 The common death adder (*Acanthophis antarcticus*) is found in eastern NSW and Queensland and southern SA and WA. It is one of the most venomous snakes in Australia and its bite can cause death within six hours.

Aves

Aves is the biological name for birds. Birds are different from other groups because they have feathers covering their body and lay hard-shelled eggs. All birds have wings, including those that cannot fly. Penguins use their wings to swim in the same way as other birds move their wings to fly (Figure 6.2.18). Birds are **endothermic**, meaning that they generate their own heat and are able to control their body temperature. This allows them to remain warm in cold environments.

FIGURE 6.2.18 All birds have wings and most can fly, even big birds like flamingos (*Phoenicopterus roseus*). Although this Humboldt penguin (*Spheniscus humboldtii*), cannot fly in the air, they move their wings as if they are flying underwater.

CHAPTER 6 • CLASSIFICATION 243

Mammals

The class **Mammals** includes all the animals that have a body covering of hair, and feed their babies on milk produced by the mother. Like birds, mammals are endothermic. Mammals are divided into three subclasses based on the way they reproduce.

- **Placentals** are mammals that nourish the baby inside the mother's body by a placenta and the baby is born at a developed stage. Placental mammals include seals, dingoes, horses, humans, humpback whales and flying foxes (Figure 6.2.19).
- **Monotremes** lay eggs. This subclass consists of the platypus and two species of echidna. One species of echidna is shown in Figure 6.2.20.
- **Marsupials** give birth to a tiny undeveloped young that climbs into the pouch where it is fed on milk. The young marsupial grows and completes its development in the pouch. Most of the world's species of marsupials are Australian.

FIGURE 6.2.19 The grey-headed flying fox (*Pteropus poliocephalus*) is a placental mammal found in Australia.

FIGURE 6.2.20 A short-beaked echidna (*Tachyglossus aculeatus*) is a mammal that lays eggs—a monotreme.

Prac 1 p. 249

Working with Science

PLANT CLASSIFICATION

Angharad Johnson: Collections database officer and photographer

The Royal Botanic Gardens Victoria manages a huge collection of over 1.5 million dried plant, algae and fungi specimens in the National Herbarium of Victoria (NHV). The collection is an important resource for scientists, historians and land managers. Many people work to ensure that the collection is maintained and arranged in a systematic order.

FIGURE 6.2.21 Angharad Johnson works as a collections database officer at the Royal Botanic Gardens Victoria.

In the herbarium, specimens are stored according to their biological classification. The NHV is currently entering specimen information into an online database, Australia's Virtual Herbarium and imaging specimens, as part of the Global Plants Initiative (GPI). The GPI is an international project that involves digitising herbarium collections from all over the world and bringing them together in an online database.

Angharad Johnson (Figure 6.2.21) is a Digitising and Database Officer at the Royal Botanic Gardens Victoria who is working on the GPI. Angharad's work involves scanning and photographing specimens from the NHV's collection, checking the specimens' information and updating the database. Her job requires attention to detail, good record-keeping skills and knowledge of plant classification. A qualification in botany or horticulture (diploma or degree) can help you gain these skills. Angharad's work plays an important role in making the valuable information stored in the herbarium accessible to anyone from anywhere in the world.

AB 6.7

Review

1. Why do you think it's important to make resources, such as the National Herbarium of Victoria (NHV), more accessible?
2. Why is a classification system important in places like herbariums and museums?

SCIENCE AS A HUMAN ENDEAVOUR

Nature and development of science

Is this a real animal?

FIGURE 6.2.23 When explorers first described a platypus it caused problems for taxonomists.

By the end of the eighteenth century, naturalists in Europe had described, named and classified many living things. They were confident that they understood the animal kingdom and that their classification system would be able to include any new species that were discovered.

Explorers to Africa and America tested these ideas when they brought back organisms never seen before, such as giraffes, opossums, hippopotamuses and armadillos (Figure 6.2.22). A bigger stir was yet to come!

In 1798 the Governor of New South Wales, John Hunter, watched an Aboriginal hunter spear a small animal in the Hawkesbury River, near Sydney. Hunter sent the skin to England, where taxonomists described this strange animal as having characteristics of a fish, bird and quadruped (four-footed animal). It was about the size of a cat, had a bill like a duck, four short legs and webbed feet (Figure 6.2.23). They had not seen anything like it before and it did not fit into their classification system.

Other specimens of skins, like the one shown in Figure 6.2.24, and skeletons arrived and were examined by Dr George Shaw, an experienced naturalist. He wondered if the animal was a hoax or trick. At that time, Chinese sailors had a reputation for their skill in stitching together parts of different animals to create a non-existent animal that they then sold to European sailors. Despite very close examination, George Shaw could not find any evidence of this being a hoax. There were no cut marks or stitched parts.

FIGURE 6.2.22 Animals such as the armadillo (*Dasypus novemcinctus*) and the hippopotamus (*Hippopotamus amphibius*) challenged European scientists' systems of classification.

FIGURE 6.2.24 Using dried skins like this one, European scientists tried to imagine what a platypus looked like and how it lived. It is not surprising that they were confused at first.

CHAPTER 6 • CLASSIFICATION 245

SCIENCE AS A HUMAN ENDEAVOUR

Complete, preserved specimens arrived in 1800, accompanied by descriptions from people who had observed the animal. Shaw was then able to confirm that the animal was no hoax. It was a new type of animal. The question then became whether it was a mammal. The animal:

- had fur like a mammal
- was warm-blooded (endothermic) like a mammal and a bird
- had a beak like a bird
- lived in water like an amphibian.

At this stage the naturalists did not know that the platypus laid eggs (like a bird or reptile) and produced milk for its young (characteristic of a mammal). It was many years before scientists were able to gather all the information they needed to describe this new animal in detail and decide how to classify it. A new group of mammals was created—the monotremes. This group includes the echidna and the platypus (Figure 6.2.25).

FIGURE 6.2.25 The large webbed feet of the platypus make it an efficient swimmer. The duck-like bill is used to find prey in muddy creek beds.

REVIEW

1. Why did scientists first think that the skin of the platypus was a hoax?
2. The classification systems of the eighteenth century were not able to include animals such as the giraffe, the kangaroo or the platypus. Propose a reason why.
3. Scientists found the platypus very difficult to classify. Give as many reasons as you can to explain this.

SciFile

Using electricity

When the platypus dives to find food it closes its eyes and nostrils. It cannot see, nor can it smell its prey. The platypus searches for food using its electro-sensitive beak. The beak is so sensitive it can detect tiny electrical signals from the muscles of small arthropods and worms as they move around.

MODULE 6.2 Review questions

Remembering

1. Define the terms:
   a. vertebrates
   b. exoskeleton
   c. phyla
   d. ectothermic.

2. What term best describes each of the following?
   a. the first level of classification
   b. sponges
   c. the skeleton inside the body
   d. jawless fish.

3. a. List the nine phyla of animals.
   b. Give an example or a common name for each.

4. Name the phylum:
   a. that describes the largest number of animal types
   b. to which humans belong.

5. List evidence that would show that animals are living in your garden.

Understanding

6. a. Describe how an exoskeleton and an endoskeleton are different.
   b. Name a group of animals that has an exoskeleton.
   c. Name a group of animals with an endoskeleton.

7. Explain why frogs need to live in damp places but lizards can survive in dry areas.

Applying

8. Use material from this module to fill in the main characteristics of each animal phyla. Add extra rows to the table as needed.

Phylum	Where it lives	Symmetry	Number of body openings	Type of skeleton	Other features

9. a. Copy the shapes in Figure 6.2.26 into your workbook, then for each add all lines of symmetry in a different colour.
   b. For each diagram, identify whether it represents radial or bilateral symmetry.

FIGURE 6.2.26

10. A group of students found the animal shown in Figure 6.2.27 in a forest in France. Some students suggested it was a lizard and others thought it was a salamander.
    a. What characteristics would the students look for to work out whether it was a lizard or a salamander?
    b. Identify the unknown animal as a lizard (a reptile) or a salamander (an amphibian).

FIGURE 6.2.27

MODULE 6.2 Review questions

Analysing

11 Compare annelids with nematodes.
12 Contrast:
    a an endothermic animal with an ectothermic animal
    b platyhelminths and nematodes.
13 Classify the following as endothermic or ectothermic:
    shark, kookaburra, koala, frog, python, human, lizard, poodle
14 Classify the following as having an endoskeleton or an exoskeleton:
    trout, prawn, eagle, mosquito, scorpion, kangaroo, human, crab
15 Compare the characteristics used to classify:
    a a shark and a barramundi
    b a frog and a lizard
    c a kangaroo and a platypus.
16 Use the following description to classify the organism.

    This organism was collected from the ocean. It has a soft body with long tentacles. After I touched the tentacles my hand was stinging.

Evaluating

17 Examine the animals shown in Figure 6.2.28.
    a Classify each into a phylum.
    b Justify your decisions.

    i

    ii

    FIGURE 6.2.28

18 Propose reasons why animals without a skeleton often live in water.
19 The animal kingdom is classified into nine phyla. A different way of dividing the animal kingdom is to divide it into two large groups—the invertebrates and vertebrates.
    a Describe the main differences between vertebrates and invertebrates.
    b List the phyla that are invertebrates.
    c Name the phyla that includes the vertebrates.
    d Assess the following statement:
       All vertebrates are chordates but not all chordates are vertebrates.

Creating

20 a Construct a Venn diagram like the one in Figure 6.2.29. Write the characteristics of each phylum in the appropriate circle, with shared characteristics written in the overlap.
    b Use this to compare the three chordate classes commonly called fish.

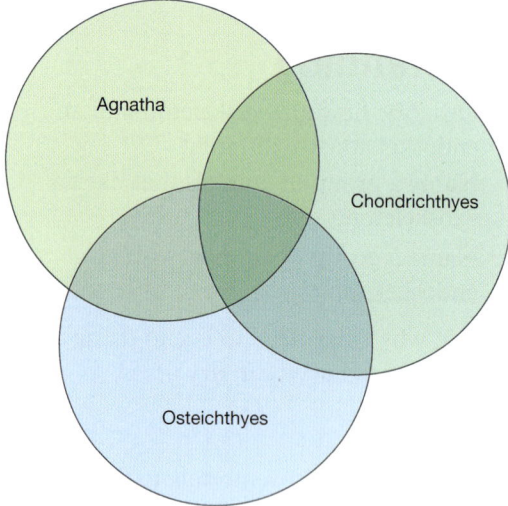

FIGURE 6.2.29

248 PEARSON SCIENCE 7 2ND EDITION

MODULE 6.2 Practical investigations

1 • Classifying animals  Processing & Analysing

Purpose
To use structural features to classify animals into their different phyla.

Timing
45 minutes

Materials
- multiple photos or printouts of animals from the 9 different phyla (at least 2 animals per phylum)
- assorted skeletons, shells, preserved specimens, fossils

SAFETY
The liquids used to preserve some older animal specimens are hazardous so do not use any specimens preserved this way.

Procedure
1. Copy the table from the Results section into your workbook. Make sure you include enough rows for all the animals on display.
2. Around the laboratory are labelled photos, skeletons, preserved specimens and fossils of a variety of different animals. Move around the laboratory and for each animal record:
   - its name/s (common and/or biological)
   - the type of specimen you looked at (photo, skeleton, preserved specimen or a fossil)
   - its distinctive characteristics and structural features.

There are photos of two animals to get you started in Figure 6.2.30.

Results
1. Use your observations to complete the results table. An example has been provided for you as a guide.
2. Use the characteristics and structural features to identify the phyla for each animal you looked at. Use this book to assist you when necessary.

Animal	Specimen type	Characteristics or structural features	Phyla
e.g. starfish	e.g. preserved	e.g. radial symmetry	e.g. echinoderm

Review
1. a Which phyla were the easiest to identify?
   b Explain what made them easy to identify.
2. Are there any phyla that might easily be confused with one another? Explain why they could be confused.
3. a List any difficulties you had in classifying the animals.
   b Explain a situation where one of these difficulties led to an incorrect identification.

FIGURE 6.2.30 slug butterfly

CHAPTER 6 • CLASSIFICATION **249**

MODULE 6.3 Other kingdoms

Living things are divided into five kingdoms. You know the animal kingdom and you are probably familiar with another—plants. The next three get a bit harder to name. It is likely that you have seen organisms from the fungi kingdom in the form of mushrooms and toadstools. You are less likely to be familiar with organisms from the other two kingdoms, Monerans and Protists, because they can only be seen using a microscope.

Plant kingdom

The **plant** kingdom, like the animal kingdom contains a large number of very different organisms. Some are shown in Figure 6.3.1.

The organisms in the plant kingdom are classified by the way they reproduce and whether they have organised transport systems, that transport substances such as water and nutrients.

Importantly all plants can make their own food. They do this using the energy from the sun in a process called photosynthesis.

Instead of the kingdom being subdivided into phyla as in the animal kingdom, the plant kingdom has **divisions**. The divisions are then divided again into classes.

FIGURE 6.3.1 The tall trees and the ferns growing under them are all members of the plant kingdom. So too is the waratah. This one has bright red flowers.

science 4 fun

Plants you eat

What parts of plants do you eat?

Collect this ...
- samples or images of various fruits and vegetables such as cauliflower, capsicum, cucumber, pea, celery, carrot, broccoli, apple, spinach leaves

Do this ...
1. For each fruit or vegetable, decide which part of the plant it represents. For example, is it the root, stem, leaf, leaf stalk, flower, fruit or seed?
2. Make a list of fruits and vegetables with the name of the plant part beside it.

Record this ...
1. Describe the part of plants that is most commonly eaten.
2. Explain why this might be the case.

Plant divisions

Figure 6.3.2 shows the major divisions and some classes of the plant kingdom.

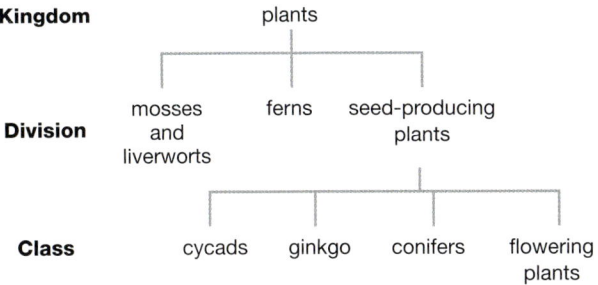

FIGURE 6.3.2 Key to the plant kingdom

Mosses and liverworts

Mosses and **liverworts** (Figure 6.3.3) are usually very small because they do not have any tissues to transport water or nutrients through the plant. They absorb water from the atmosphere through their leaves. Therefore, they mostly live in damp places where they are not in danger of drying out. Mosses and liverworts reproduce using single cells called **spores** that grow into a new plants.

moss   liverwort

FIGURE 6.3.3 Mosses and liverworts are low-growing plants often forming a mat on a rock, tree or soil surface.

Spores are produced in special structures known as **sporangia**. Moss sporangia can be seen in Figure 6.3.4. They grow from the top of the leafy moss plant. The spores develop in the capsule at the end of the stalk. When the spores are ripe the capsule opens and the spores are blown out by the wind. When the spore lands in a suitable area, the spore will grow into a new moss plant.

FIGURE 6.3.4 The capsule and the stalk together form the moss sporangium. The spores develop inside the capsule.

Ferns

Ferns have a **vascular system** consisting of hollow tubes or vessels which transport water and nutrients throughout the plant. They also reproduce using spores produced in structures known as sporangia, like those in Figure 6.3.5.

Ferns have been around for a very long time. The first ferns appeared on Earth about 360 million years ago – long before flowering plants. Ferns vary in size. Azolla is a water fern that is only a few centimetres across (Figure 6.3.6). In contrast, tree ferns such as the lacy tree fern in Figure 6.3.7 on page 252 can grow to a height of 15 metres.

FIGURE 6.3.5 The spores are produced in the sporangia (dark spots) on the back of the fern leaf.

FIGURE 6.3.6 Azolla may be small but it grows very rapidly. It quickly covers the surface of a pond giving it a pinkish tinge.

CHAPTER 6 • CLASSIFICATION **251**

FIGURE 6.3.7 The lacy tree fern (*Cyathea cooperi*) is one of the tallest Australian tree ferns.

Seed-producing plants

Seed-producing plants reproduce using seeds. Seeds are more complex than spores. One cell within the seed becomes the new plant. There are many other cells in the seed. These other cells provide food for the developing plant until the leaves are formed. The division of seed-producing plants has four classes:

- cycads
- ginkgo
- conifers
- flowering plants.

Cycads and ginkgos

Cycads and **ginkgos** have separate male and female trees. Male trees produce pollen in cones, and female trees produce seeds. There is only one living member in the ginkgo class—Ginkgo biloba. Examples of a cycad and a ginkgo are shown in Figures 6.3.8 and 6.3.9.

FIGURE 6.3.8 Cycads have separate male and female plants.

SciFile

Largest flower

The largest flower in the world is found in South-East Asia. It can be up to one metre in diameter and weigh 11 kg. Its name is *Rafflesia arnoldii*. Its smell is like rotting meat.

FIGURE 6.3.9 Ginkgo biloba is sometimes called the maidenhair fern tree.

Conifers

Most **conifers** produce the male (pollen-bearing) and female (seed-bearing) cones on the same tree. Cypress, fir and pine belong to this class. Australian conifers include the hoop pine (*Araucaria cunninghamii*), Huon pine (*Lagarostrobos franklinii*) and Wollemi pine (*Wollemia nobilis*).

The Wollemi pine is an ancient tree. It has been found in fossil records dating back 90 million years. Living trees were discovered in 1994 in the Blue Mountains 200 kilometres west of Sydney. You can see a Wollemi pine in Figure 6.3.10.

Male cones are 5–11 cm long and reddish-brown in colour when mature and ready for the pollen to be released. They are produced lower in the tree than the female cones.

Female cones are green, 6–12 cm long and 5–10 cm in diameter. They take about 18–20 months to mature. Then they break down to release the seeds.

FIGURE 6.3.11 Cones of the Wollemi pine

FIGURE 6.3.10 The Wollemi pine grows to a height of 40 metres. It produces multiple trunks from the base. This characteristic has helped it survive fires and other natural disasters.

The male cones and female cones of the Wollemi pine seen in Figure 6.3.11 are produced on the same tree. Each of the points on the female cone is the end of a scale. One seed develops on each scale. The seeds are protected in the cone until ready to be released. Then the mature cone breaks down releasing the seeds. The seeds are small with thin papery wings. The wings help the seeds to blow in the wind.

Flowering plants

Flowering plants produce seeds fully protected inside the female part of the flower, which is known as the ovary. Many of the flowers produced by flowering plants are used to attract pollinators such as bees, flies, moths, birds or bats. Grasses, with less showy flowers, are pollinated by wind.

About 65 per cent of all flowering plants are pollinated by insects. Flowers have many characteristics that help them to attract insects, such as having bright colours, a perfume and nectar.

Nectar is a sugary liquid inside a flower that some insects use as food. When an insect visits a flower to collect the nectar, pollen sticks to its body. The insect then carries the pollen to the next flower and it pollinates the flower, helping it to reproduce. The shape of the flower limits the variety of insects that can pollinate it. For example, nectar at the base of a long tube-shaped flower can only be reached by insects with long mouthparts such as butterflies, moths and bees.

SciFile

Shaking the pollen out

Hibbertia is a common flower in coastal sand dunes. Its pollen is released by vibrations caused by the buzzing of certain bees. The blue banded bee and many Australian carpenter bees hold on to the plant and buzz, causing the plant to vibrate so the pollen is released.

Prac 1
p. 259

Prac 2
p. 261

Fungi kingdom

Mushrooms and toadstools and the bracket fungi and mould shown in Figure 6.3.12 are **fungi** that are big enough to be easily seen. That is, they are **macroscopic**. Other fungi, such as the yeast in Figure 6.3.13, are so small that they can only be seen through a microscope—they are microscopic.

Unlike plants, fungi cannot make their own food, and therefore they must feed on other organisms. Fungi are the main cause of decay (or rotting) in fruit and vegetables. Fungi are **decomposers** responsible for breaking down wastes like faeces and dead organisms and returning the nutrients they contain to the environment.

FIGURE 6.3.12 Bracket fungi often grow on the trunks of dead trees. The blue-green mould growing on this orange is a fungus called *Penicillium*.

FIGURE 6.3.13 Yeast is a fungus used in the manufacture of beer and to make bread rise. This image shows yeast magnified thousands of times.

Fungi are the source of some medicines. For example the antibiotic penicillin is prepared from *Penicillium*, a blue-green mould. Penicillin is used to fight bacterial diseases.

Protist kingdom

Most organisms in the **protist** kingdom are very small or microscopic and live in water. One type is shown in Figure 6.3.14. The protists are more diverse than any other kingdom, and they are grouped together because they do not fit any other kingdom.

FIGURE 6.3.14 The euglena has a whip-like tail called a flagellum that moves it through the water and acts like a boat's propeller.

Protists vary in the way they move, the way they feed, and how they live. Some contain the green pigment chlorophyll and can make their own food. Others catch and eat food from the water around them. Protists, in turn, become an important source of food for many aquatic organisms. Most protists are not harmful to humans, but some cause disease. These diseases tend to be more common in tropical climates. For example, amoebic dysentery, which causes severe pain and diarrhoea, is caused by drinking water contaminated with protists (Figure 6.3.15).

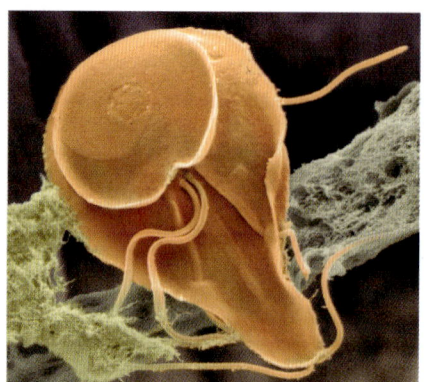

FIGURE 6.3.15 Giardia is a protist that causes cramps, explosive diarrhoea and nausea.

SciFile

Protists colonies

Some protists, such as this volvox, live in colonies. Each individual has flagella and chloroplasts and can make its own food. Individuals are held together by a jelly-like substance, and they all swim around together using their flagella in a coordinated way.

Monera kingdom

The **Monera** kingdom includes all the organisms known as bacteria. You can see some bacteria in Figure 6.3.16. This kingdom is so diverse that some taxonomists believe it should be divided into two kingdoms or even into three major groups.

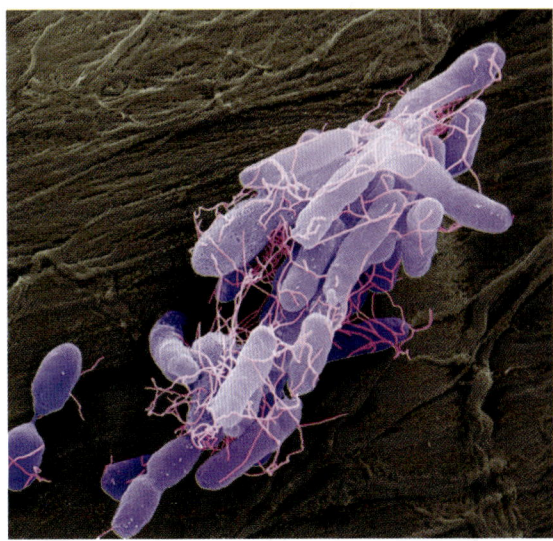

FIGURE 6.3.16 Bacteria belong to the monera kingdom. The bacteria here have been magnified and the image coloured so that they can be seen clearly.

Many people associate bacteria with disease and infections, but most bacteria are harmless and some are actually good for you. *Lactobacilli* are bacteria that occur naturally in dairy products. Bacteria also live in your intestines where they help your digestion. Along with fungi, bacteria are decomposers responsible for breaking down wastes and returning the nutrients they contain to the environment.

Most bacteria rely on other organisms for their food. Examples are the decomposers and the bacteria that live inside your body. However, bacteria such as cyanobacteria or sulfur bacteria make their own food.

Bacteria live in many different places, ranging in temperature from hot springs (Figure 6.3.17), where the temperature reaches 300°C, to the ice fields of Antarctica.

FIGURE 6.3.17 An aerial photo of a geyser and boiling pond. The water in this bubbling geyser is very hot. Bacteria able to live in temperatures between 50°C and 60°C form a brown scum at the edge of the water.

A closer look at kingdoms

Snails, jellyfish and birds obviously belong to the animal kingdom, while wattles, ferns and pine trees are obviously plants. However, outward appearances aren't always an accurate way of classifying living things. To accurately identify the kingdom an organism belongs to, you need to look more closely. You need to look through a microscope at what it is made up of—its cells.

Cells

All living things are made up of building blocks called **cells**. Cells are so small that they can only be seen using a microscope. All living things in the plant and animal kingdoms are made up of millions of cells. They are **multicellular**—*multi* means many. Some fungi are also multicellular but other fungi have only one cell making the entire living thing. These fungi are **unicellular**—*uni* means one. All living things in the monera and protist kingdoms are unicellular.

The cells of all organisms have parts in common:
- cell membrane—the 'skin' that holds the cell together.
- nucleus—the control centre of the cell.
- cytoplasm—a watery, jelly-like mixture that contains many smaller parts.

However, not all cells are the same. When cells are looked at using a microscope, differences can be seen. These differences can be used to place the organisms in different kingdoms. How the organism feeds is another characteristic used to separate the kingdoms. The main characteristics of the five kingdoms are shown in Table 6.3.1.

TABLE 6.3.1 Characteristics of the five kingdoms

Kingdom	Characteristics		Examples
animal	Animals are made up of millions of cells. Their cells have a membrane forming the boundary of the cell, a nucleus and cytoplasm inside the cell. Animals obtain their energy by feeding on other living things.	(diagram of animal cell showing nucleus and cell membrane)	pelican, human, frog, spider, jellyfish
plant	Plants are made up of millions of cells. Their cells have a cell wall outside the cell membrane. The cell wall helps support the plant and give it its shape. Many plant cells also contain tiny structures called chloroplasts in the cytoplasm. A substance called chlorophyll within the chloroplasts give plants their green colour. Using chlorophyll, plants are able to manufacture their own food from carbon dioxide and water—a process called photosynthesis.	(diagram of plant cell showing cell membrane, nucleus, cell wall, chloroplast containing chlorophyll)	grass, daisy, gum tree, moss
fungi	Fungi can be made up of many cells or a single cell. The cells of fungi have a cell wall and do not contain chloroplasts. The cell wall is made up of a different substance to that of plants. Fungi feed mostly on dead material from other living things.	(diagram of fungi cell showing nucleus, cell wall, cell membrane)	moulds, toadstools, mushrooms, yeast
protist	Protists are single-celled organisms. Protist cells may be plant-like or animal-like.	(diagram of protist cell showing nucleus, choloroplast)	protozoa, algae
monera	Monerans are single-celled organisms. Their cells have a cell wall but do not have a clearly defined nucleus. All monerans are very simple and microscopic.	(diagram of moneran cell showing cell wall, cell membrane)	bacteria, cyanobacteria

MODULE 6.3 Review questions

Remembering

1. Define the terms:
   a. conifer
   b. division
   c. fern
   d. macroscopic.

2. What term best describes each of the following?
   a. the building blocks that make up all living things
   b. structures that make spores
   c. only able to be seen using a microscopic
   d. organisms responsible for breaking down wastes and dead organisms.

3. Name the kingdom in which you will find all the organisms without a distinct nucleus in their cells.

4. Name the classes of seed-bearing plants.

5. a. What is the main difference between organisms that are unicellular and those that are multicellular?
   b. Name one kingdom in which all the organisms are:
      i. multicellular
      ii. unicellular.

Understanding

6. Plants and fungi are classified in different kingdoms but they also have a number of things in common.
   a. Describe the characteristics that plants and fungi have in common.
   b. Explain why plants and fungi are in different kingdoms.

7. Fungi can be beneficial to humans but they can also cause problems. Describe one benefit and one problem caused by fungi.

8. Describe the plant kingdom, highlighting the features that make it different from the other kingdoms.

Applying

9. Humans regularly eat plants as part of their diet. Usually they don't eat the whole plant but just a part of it. Name two plants we eat that come from the following things:
   a. leaves
   b. stalks
   c. seeds
   d. roots
   e. fruit.

   ginger plant

Analysing

10. Compare the characteristics used to classify:
    a. a moss and a fern
    b. a pine tree and a flowering gum tree
    c. a fern and a pine tree.

11. Compare the protist and monera kingdoms.

12. Explorers in a previously unknown area have found some very unusual organisms. These are two descriptions from one of their notebooks. Classify these organisms into their correct kingdoms.
    a. The organism was shaped like a semicircle with a radius of about 8 cm. It was found on the side of a tree. Looking through the microscope, I could see many cells that all looked very much alike. There was a distinct cell wall. The cells were colourless.
    b. The organism was seen when I looked at some water under a microscope. It was still very small when I had the microscope on its highest power. I could see that the organism was unicellular but I could not see a distinct nucleus.

MODULE 6.3 Review questions

13 Classify these plants from their descriptions.
   a It is less than one centimetre tall and when the leaves were examined under a microscope no vascular tissue could be seen.
   b Dark spots were visible on the back of the leaf and there was vascular tissue running along the middle of the leaf.
   c It is a tree over 20 m tall that has needle-like leaves and produces seeds in cones on its branches.

Evaluating

14 One organism was described as *macroscopic*. Another organism was described as *microscopic*. Propose what is the main difference between them.

15 The Wollemi pine was discovered in 1994 (Figure 6.3.18). Scientists classified it as a conifer.
   a What characteristics would the scientists have used to classify it in this class?
   b What other class of plants might they have considered before deciding it was a conifer?
   c Justify your answer.

FIGURE 6.3.18

16 Plants that produce nectar are giving something to the insects that pollinate them. Propose why this relationship between plants and insects has come about.

17 The flowering plant *Rafflesia arnoldii* (Figure 6.3.19) produces a huge flower that smells like rotting meat. For this reason it is commonly known as the corpse flower. Like many flowering plants it relies on insects for pollination.
   a What type of insects do you think pollinate the corpse flower?
   b Justify your answer.

FIGURE 6.3.19 *Rafflesia arnoldii* (corpse flower)

Creating

18 a Construct a flow chart key that could be used to identify which of the five kingdoms an unknown organism belongs to.
   b Compare your key with at least one other student.
   c Evaluate your key.

MODULE 6.3 Practical investigations

1 • Dissecting a flower

Planning & Conducting **Communicating**

Eighty per cent of all plants on Earth are flowering plants. Most of our food comes from flowering plants directly or by providing food for animals we eat. Humans also rely on flowering plants for medicines, timber and many other products. All flowering plants produce flowers at some time in their lives. Flowers are the reproductive organs of flowering plants.

Purpose
To dissect a flower and identify the major parts involved in reproduction.

SAFETY Scalpels and razor blades are very sharp. Handle with care.

Timing
60 minutes

Materials
- a flower; a large flower such as a lily or an iris works best (Figure 6.3.20)
- hand lens or magnifying glass
- razor blade or scalpel, probe, forceps
- dissecting board
- paper
- glue

FIGURE 6.3.20 (a) Lily flower (b) iris flower

Procedure
1. Place the flower on a dissecting board.
2. Use Figure 6.3.21 to identify the stem, sepals and petals of your flower (some structures may not be present, depending on the type of flower used).

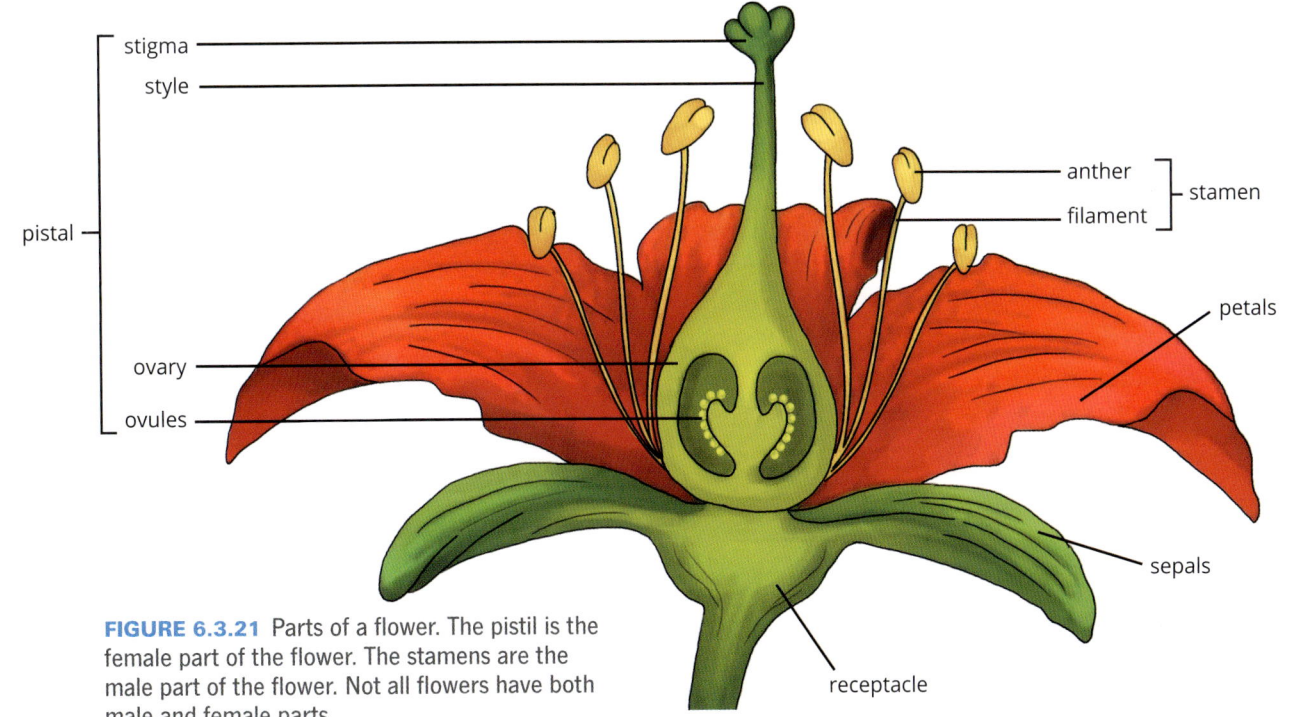

FIGURE 6.3.21 Parts of a flower. The pistil is the female part of the flower. The stamens are the male part of the flower. Not all flowers have both male and female parts.

CHAPTER 6 • CLASSIFICATION **259**

MODULE 6.3 Practical investigations

3 Carefully remove the sepals and petals. Do this by pulling them down towards the stem.

4 Look carefully at the sepals and petals. Use your hand lens if you have one. In your workbook, write a description of each. Include their colour, texture and size. Put the sepals and petals to one side.

5 Identify as many of the other parts of the flower as possible.

6 Remove the stamens and gently tap the anther on to a sheet of clean white paper. Examine the pollen with a hand lens. As before, describe the pollen. Put the stamens with the petals and sepals.

7 Carefully remove all structures except the pistil.

8 Examine the stigma. Touch the surface gently. Describe the stigma.

9 Cut the ovary in half length-wise. Examine the inside of the ovary. You may be able to identify the ovules. Draw what you see.

10 When you have completed your dissection reconstruct your flower by gluing the parts onto a new sheet of paper.

Review

1 Use Figure 6.3.21 on page 259 to label all the structures you have identified.

2 Use your labelled reconstructed flower and the information in this module to propose a function for each part of the flower. Write this next to each name on your reconstructed flower.

3 Compare your labelled reconstructed flower with that of at least one other student. List the similarities and differences.

4 Suggest reasons for these differences. Justify your suggestions.

MODULE 6.3 Practical investigations

2 • Classifying plants in a local habitat
Planning & Conducting | Processing & Analysing

Purpose
To use a provided key to identify and classify some of the plants in a local habitat such as your own garden, the school grounds or a local park.

Timing
60 minutes

Materials
- pencils and paper
- hand lens or magnifying glass
- camera (optional)
- access to reference material such as this student book, internet

SAFETY
Some plants have prickles and thorns and others can cause skin irritations. Do not handle soil. Wash your hands after you have completed the activity.

Procedure
1. Choose a location in your local area. Suitable areas include your own garden, the school grounds, a local park or state or national park.
2. Choose a plant you wish to classify.
3. Photograph or make a sketch of the plant you are classifying. Include key features such as shape of leaves and other structures, flowers if present, fruits, cones and so on. Include an estimate of overall size.
4. Use the key shown in Figure 6.3.22 to classify the plant. If you have access to reference material use this to assist you classify the plant.
5. Next to your photo or sketch write the steps it took to get to that identification.
   For example:
   true stems and leaves → cones → conifers
6. Repeat steps 2–5 for five more but different plants. Remember plants can be very big or very small. Choose a variety of them.

Review
1. Did you have any difficulties using the key and identifying your chosen plants? Explain.
2. What additional information would have helped overcome these difficulties? Explain how this would assist
3. What types of plants appear to be most common in your local habitat? Is this surprising? Propose reasons for this finding.

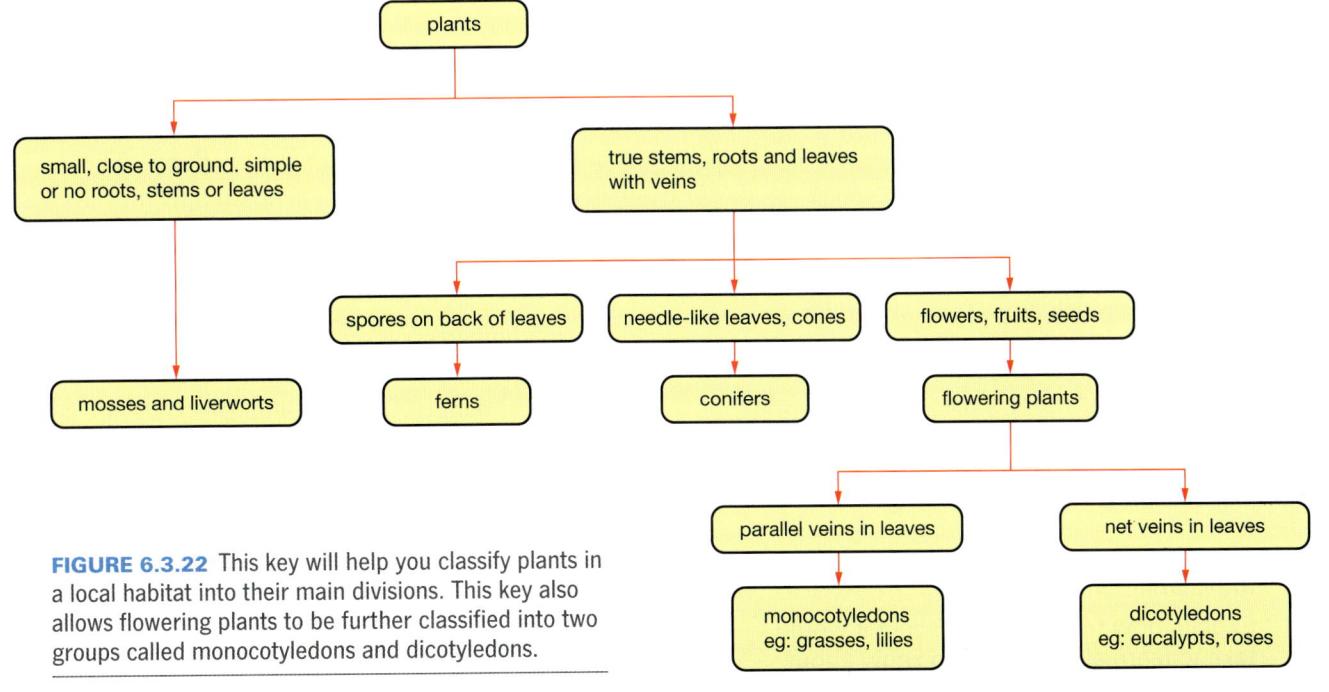

FIGURE 6.3.22 This key will help you classify plants in a local habitat into their main divisions. This key also allows flowering plants to be further classified into two groups called monocotyledons and dicotyledons.

CHAPTER 6 • CLASSIFICATION **261**

MODULE 6.4 Classification systems

People have always identified, grouped and given names to the organisms that are important to them. Different people of different cultures create different classification systems that are related to how and where they live. Over time these classification systems change.

science 4 fun

Observing

Collect this …
- a pet animal, or a place where you can observe an animal closely
- paper and pencil
- digital camera (optional)

Do this …
1. Imagine that your life could depend on knowing as much as you can about this animal. Observe the animal very closely. No observation is too small. Remember that observing uses more senses than just sight.
2. Record as many observations as you can of the animal.

Record this …
1. Describe any new things you learnt about the animal.
2. Explain how much time and care it would take to learn all there was to know about the habits of an animal in the wild.

History of classification

Humans have always tried to make sense of the world around them. One way is to classify things. The categories chosen would depend on how they lived and what was happening around them.

Ancient humans

For early humans one very good reason for classification would have been survival. Animals would have been classified as dangerous and not dangerous. For example, the sabre-toothed tiger twould have been classified as a dangerous animal.

Plants were probably classified as edible and poisonous. Plants that were found to act as medicines would need to be carefully identified before being used (Figure 6.4.1). It would have been important to communicate this information to the rest of the group or tribe so it is likely that names and descriptions were given to these different groups.

As humans developed farming there is evidence that animals were classified into five groups—wild animals, domestic animals, flying animals, creeping animals and water animals.

FIGURE 6.4.1 Indigenous Australians used ground tea-tree leaves as an antiseptic to treat wounds. Tea-tree oil is a very effective antiseptic that is still used today. This is a commercial tea tree plantation that has been harvested.

SciFile

Sabre-toothed lion?

Sabre-toothed tigers became extinct about 13 000 years ago. There were three species of sabre-toothed tigers, all in the genus Smilidon. Evidence suggests that sabre-toothed tigers were more closely related to modern day lions than tigers.

More recent times

Aristotle was a Greek philosopher who lived from 384 to 322 BCE. He studied and wrote about many subjects including physics, astronomy and living things. Aristotle divided organisms into plants and animals. He then divided animals into animals with blood and animals without blood. He further classified animals on the basis of how they moved and reproduced. Aristotle's system of classification was used until the 1600s.

Figure 6.4.2 shows a portrait of the Swedish scientist Carl Linnaeus (1707–1778). Linnaeus organised the classification of living things into a hierarchy with Kingdom at the top and species as the lowest level. His classification system had two kingdoms Vegetabilia and Animalia.

FIGURE 6.4.2 Carl Linnaeus classified all living things into two kingdoms. He also developed the binomial system for naming organisms.

Since Linnaeus, the number of kingdoms has been increased from two to three to four and in recent times to the five kingdom system that most taxonomists now use. Other systems that include more than five kingdoms have been suggested, but the most common remains the five kingdom system.

Common names

In Europe, the plant shown in Figure 6.4.3 is called purple bugloss. It was introduced into Australia where it has become a major weed. As it spread, it became known by different common names including salvation Jane, Paterson's curse and blueweed.

FIGURE 6.4.3 Purple bugloss has come to be known by many different names in Australia.

Using common names for living things creates confusion as people from different areas will not know which name goes with which living thing.

CHAPTER 6 • CLASSIFICATION **263**

Standardising names

In the eighteenth century scientists used descriptions as a way of naming living things and as new organisms were discovered, the descriptions would become longer.

For example, *Canis* is part of the scientific name for a dog (a canine). If a new species of dog was found in the woods, then it could be the 'canine' that 'lives in woods'. If another canine was found living in the woods it would have to be described differently. It could be the 'canine' that 'lives in woods; dark coat in winter; found only in the north'—and so the names expanded.

Another example is the carnation in Figure 6.4.4. It needed nine words to describe it: *Dianthus floribus solitaris, squamis calycinus subovatus brevissimis corollus crenatis*. It literally means 'the dianthus that has single flowers with very short scales and toothed petals'.

FIGURE 6.4.4
Linnaeus renamed the carnation so that it had only two names: *Dianthus caryophyllus*.

Linnaeus thought that there must be a better system. He organised the classification of organisms into a hierarchy (order), with kingdom at the top and species as the lowest level. **Genus** is the name given to the level above **species**. The name of an organisms has two parts—the genus it belongs to and a descriptive name for its species. With this, binomial naming (also known as binomial nomenclature) was born.

Latin was used as the language for naming because it was a language then understood by all well-educated people throughout Europe.

Binomial nomenclature is now used internationally regardless of the language spoken in the country the organism or scientist comes from. The system has been used for plants since 1753, for animals since 1758, and for bacteria since 1980. Using one system overcomes the confusion of using common names.

Scientific naming

When scientists discover a new organism they observe it carefully, describe it, look for ways in which it is similar to species they know, and then decide which group it belongs to. Once this has been decided they give it a name. The name will be used by all scientists throughout the world to describe the organism.

The name given to a newly described organism is not random. Taxonomists use the binomial naming system that gives every species a unique two-part name.

- The first part of the species name tells you the genus to which the organism belongs, and always starts with a capital letter.
- The second part tells you the species within that genus. This part of the name always starts with a lower case letter. When the names are typed, italics are used. When names are written, they are underlined.

For example, the animals shown in Figure 6.4.5 are *Panthera leo*, *Panthera onca*, *Panthera pardus* and *Panthera tigris*. They all belong to the same genus because they all have the same first part to their name, Panthera. If they are in the same genus then they must be fairly similar to each other. However, they are not all the same species. You can tell that because the second part of their name (their species name) is different. You are more likely to recognise the animals by their common names—lion, jaguar, leopard and tiger.

Linneaus and Banks

Linnaeus corresponded with the botanist Joseph Banks, who sailed to Australia with Captain Cook on the *Endeavour* in 1768. Also on board was Daniel Solander, one of Linnaeus's students. Between them Banks and Solander collected more than 1000 species of plants new to science. The banksia is an Australian native plant named after Banks.

AB 6.5

FIGURE 6.4.5 All these species belong to the same genus, *Panthera*.

Levels of classification

Kingdom is the first level of classification and contain the largest number of organisms. The kingdoms are divided into smaller groups in which the organisms are more similar, as Figure 6.4.6 shows. The second level of classification is into phyla (singular: phylum). In the plant kingdom the phyla are called divisions.

- Phyla and divisions are then divided into **classes**.
- Classes are divided into **orders**.
- Orders are divided into **families**.
- Families are divided into **genera** (singular: genus).
- Genera are divided into species.

Moving down through the levels in the classification system, the groups become smaller in that they have fewer types of living things in them. Figure 6.4.7 shows how organisms become more similar as you move through the levels of classification.

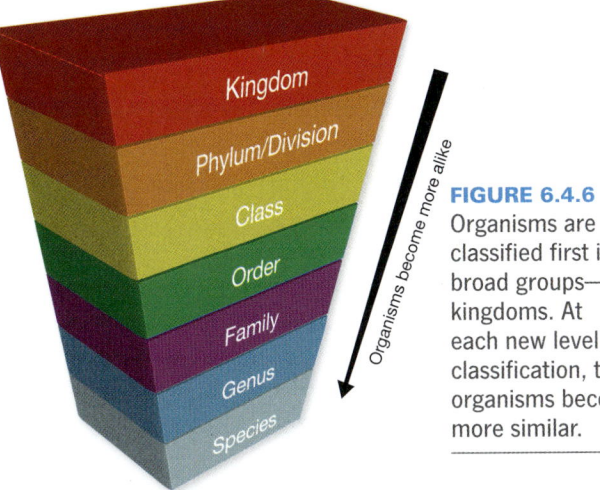

FIGURE 6.4.6 Organisms are classified first into broad groups—kingdoms. At each new level of classification, the organisms become more similar.

FIGURE 6.4.7 Organisms are classified first into broad groups—kingdoms. At each new level of classification, the organisms become more similar.

CHAPTER 6 • CLASSIFICATION 265

Worked example
Constructing a mnemonic
A mnemonic is a way of helping you remember things. One way of trying to remember a list is to make a sentence using familiar words with each word starting with the first letter of each word in the list.

Problem
Construct a mnemonic to remember the order of the groups in biological classification.

Solution
Thinking: List the words in the order you need to remember.

Working: **K**ingdom **P**hylum **C**lass **O**rder **F**amily **G**enus **S**pecies

Thinking: Take the first letter of each word and give that word a familiar word, that's easy for you to remember. Select words that can be linked together to make a sentence.

Working: **K**eep **P**lacing **C**ake **O**rders **F**or **G**ood **S**tudents

Try yourself
Construct another mnemonic that would help you remember the order of the groups in biological classification.

Organisms of the same species are most similar, but they are not identical. Look around at the people in your classroom or in the street. All the individuals in Figure 6.4.8 belong to the same species (*Homo sapiens*), but you can easily see that they are not all identical.

FIGURE 6.4.8 All humans belong to the one species but they are not all identical.

Classifying Australian organisms
When European scientists came to Australia they described and named the plants and animals they found here. Taxonomists have given all Australian species a scientific name.

The red kangaroo, the eastern grey kangaroo and the common wallaroo have characteristics in common and this is reflected in their classification illustrated in Table 6.4.1. All belong to the same kingdom, phylum, class, order and family.

The classification also shows that according to scientists the eastern grey kangaroo and the common wallaroo are most alike. They also belong to the same genus.

TABLE 6.4.1 Classifications of three macropods

Common name	Red kangaroo	Eastern grey kangaroo	Common wallaroo
Kingdom	Animal	Animal	Animal
Phylum	Chordate	Chordate	Chordate
Class	Mammal	Mammal	Mammal
Order	Diprotodon	Diprotodon	Diprotodon
Family	Macropod	Macropod	Macropod
Genus	*Magaleia*	*Macropus*	*Macropus*
Description of species	*rufa*	*giganteus*	*robustus*
Scientific name	*Magaleia rufa*	*Macropus giganteus*	*Macropus robustus*

How similar or different other animals are can be seen in their classification. The red bellied snake belongs to the same phylum as the kangaroos and wallaroo. However the box jelly fish and funnel web spider have only the kingdom in common. These classifications are shown in Table 6.4.2.

TABLE 6.4.2 Classifications of three animals

Common name	Red-bellied snake	Box jellyfish	Funnel-web spider
Kingdom	Animal	Animal	Animal
Phylum	Chordate	Cnidaria	Arthropod
Class	Reptile	Cubozoa	Arachnid
Order	Squamata	Cubomedusae	Aranaea
Family	Elapidae	Carybdeidae	Hexathelidae
Genus	*Pseudechis*	*Carybdea*	*Atrax*
Description of species	*porphyriacus*	*rastonii*	*robustus*
Scientific name	*Pseudechis porphyriacus*	*Carybdea rastonii*	*Atrax robustus*

The Sydney blue gum, grey iron bark, Wollemi pine and lacy tree fern all belong to the plant kingdom. The classification in Table 6.4.3 shows that the blue gum and iron bark are closely related. The other plants are different at the level of division.

TABLE 6.4.3 Classifications of four plants

Common name	Sydney blue gum	Grey iron bark	Wollemi pine	Lacy tree fern
Kingdom	Plant	Plant	Plant	Plant
Division	Magnoliophyta	Magnoliophyta	Pinophyta	Pteridophyta
Class	Magnoliopsida	Magnoliopsida	Pinopsida	Pteridopsida
Order	Myrtales	Myrtales	Pinales	Cyatheales
Family	Myrtaceae	Myrtaceae	Araucariaceae	Cyatheaceae
Genus	*Eucalyptus*	*Eucalyptus*	*Wollemi*	*Cyathea*
Description of species	*saligna*	*paniculata*	*nobilis*	*cooperi*
Scientific name	*Eucalyptus saligna*	*Eucalyptus paniculata*	*Wollemi nobilis*	*Cyathea cooperi*

Indigenous classification

Indigenous people all over the world have complex and effective classifications of plants and animals, but they do not look like the five-kingdom system used by scientists. Indigenous classifications help the people of a tribe or local area to communicate about the plants and animals that are important to them.

The Indigenous people of Australia have sophisticated classification systems that suit the way they live in their environments (Figure 6.4.9). The classifications take into account relationships the Indigenous people recognise between the living and non-living parts of the environment, and group together things that are used in similar ways.

The classification system used by the Yolngu of Arnhem Land (Northern Territory) begins by creating two groups—things that have life, and things that do not. Things that have life are further divided into three groups:

- things that move themselves, such as the Sun and planets, or the water and fire (Figure 6.4.10 on page 268)
- things that breathe and reproduce. This group includes all plants and animals except humans
- humans.

FIGURE 6.4.9 Indigenous Australians make sense of their world by classifying things into groups that are important to them.

FIGURE 6.4.10 The Yolngu people of Arnhem Land classify fire as 'something that could move itself'.

Things that breathe and reproduce

Things that breathe and reproduce are then subdivided into nine different sets. For example:

- *guya* is the name for a group that includes all fish
- *dharpa* is all plants with woody stems
- *warrakan* includes all land or freshwater mammals, birds and reptiles, with the exception of snakes. Figure 6.4.11 shows some *warrakan*.
- *bäpi* is the group to which snakes, legless lizards and worms belong.

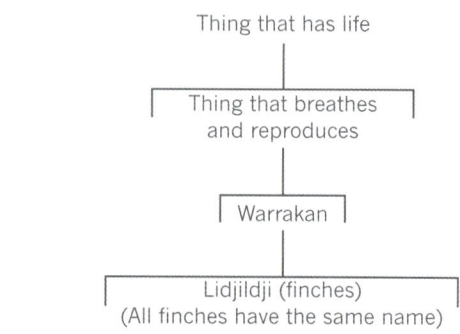

FIGURE 6.4.11 The Yolngu group animals according to how they move. Birds and bats are in the same group—the *warrakan butthunamirr*—because they can both fly. Biological classification uses differences between birds and bats to place them in separate groups at the level of class. Galahs are named *Eolophus roseicapillus* and the lesser long-eared bat is named *Nyctophilus geoffroyi*.

Some of the nine groups are further subdivided. For example:

- *guya* are subdivided according to where they live: near the surface of the water, near the bottom, in rivers, in fresh water, or among reefs and rocks
- *warrakan* are grouped according to whether they fly, walk, crawl or slide.

Comparing classifications

The hierarchy of classification used by the Yolngu is similar to, but much simpler than, the biological classification. The scientific classification of three finches found in Arnhem Land can be used as an example (Figure 6.4.12).

The classification used by the Yolngu is shown in Figure 6.4.13. It is a lot simpler.

There are no specific names for the different finches: they are all *lidjildji*. They only give specific names to things that are of special use or significance.

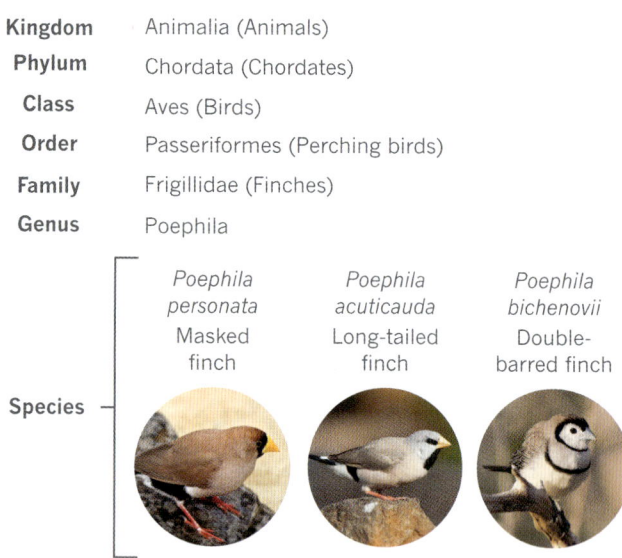

FIGURE 6.4.12 Scientific classification of finches

FIGURE 6.4.13 The Yolngu have a simple classification of the finches of northern Australia.

 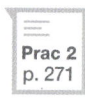

MODULE 6.4 Review questions

Remembering

1. Define the terms:
   a. class
   b. order
   c. species.

2. What term best describes each of the following?
   a. the level in the classification system below order and above genus
   b. the level in the classification system below family and above species.

3. Family, kingdom, genus, class, phylum and species are different levels of classification.
   a. List them in order from the level that has the greatest number of different types of organisms to the level that has only one type of organism.
   b. List them in order from the level that has the most similarities to the level with the fewest similarities.

4. Who developed the binomial system of classification?

5. What animals would the Yolngu people place in the following groups?
   a. *guya*
   b. *warrakan*.

6. What is the Yolngu name for each of the following?
   a. plants with woody stems
   b. snakes and legless lizards.

Understanding

7. Describe some of the difficulties that could arise if only common names were used for plants and animals.

8. Explain what the term *binomial nomenclature* means.

9. Explain why the Yolngu people do not have named for all the different types of finches.

Applying

10. Below are the names of four plants:
    - *Acacia gunnii*
    - *Tristania conferta*
    - *Eucalyptus gunnii*
    - *Acacia conferta*.

    Although you probably do not know what the plants look like, identify the ones that are most closely related.

11. a. Who developed a classification system that was based on plant/animal and blood/no blood?
    b. Use this classification system group the following organisms.
       i. jellyfish
       ii. bird
       iii. mushroom.

Analysing

12. Discuss the following statement and explain why you agree or disagree.
    Two organisms that are in the same family will be more alike than two organisms that are in the same phylum.

13. As people explore new habitats, they find new organisms that have to be described and named. Discuss the advantages of having the binomial system of classification compared to the system used before Linnaeus.

Evaluating

14. The eastern pygmy-possum (*Cerartetus nanus*), the common brush-tailed possum (*Trichosurus vulpec*), the mountain pygmy-possum (*Barramysula parvus*) and the short-eared possum (*Trichosurus caninus*) are all possums found in eastern Australia.
    a. Identify the possums that are most similar.
    b. Explain why you made that choice.
    c. Propose a reason for them all being commonly known as possums when biologists classify them differently.

MODULE 6.4 Review questions

15 Refer to the following plant names:
   - *Eucalyptus robusta*
   - *Grevillea banksii*
   - *Metrosideros robusta*
   - *Grevillea ericifolia*
   - *Eucalyptus banksii*.

   a i Identify which of the listed organisms would be most closely related to *Grevillea robusta*.
      ii Justify your response.
   b i Select other species in the list that are related to each other.
      ii Explain your selection.
   c i State how many species are represented in this list.
      ii Justify your response.
   d i State how many different genera (plural of genus) are represented in the list.
      ii Justify your response.

16 The magpie with the biological name *Pica pica* (Figure 6.4.14) is a common bird in Europe. *Cracticus tibicen* (Figure 6.4.15) is a familiar Australian bird and is also commonly known as the magpie. Biologists do not consider these two birds to be similar. Propose reasons for the European magpie and the Australian magpie both having the same common name.

17 Four organisms, A, B, C and D, all belong to the same kingdom.

   A and D belong to the same class.
   A and C belong to the same genus.
   B and C belong to the same order.
   a Deduce which two organisms are most alike.
   b Use this information to answer the question: 'Do organisms A and B belong to the same order?'
   c Justify your decision.

FIGURE 6.4.14 The European magpie (*Pica pica*)

FIGURE 6.4.15 The Australian magpie (*Cracticus tibicen*)

18 There are many different Indigenous classification systems for living things. Propose reasons for there being many different Indigenous classification systems for living things in Australia.

Creating

19 Create a mnemonic to help you remember the animal phyla.

20 Construct a concept map showing the characteristics of the five kingdoms.

MODULE 6.4 Practical investigations

1 • Pictorial key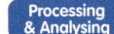

Purpose
To create a picture wall that represents the five kingdoms.

Time 45 minutes

Materials
- digital camera
- sticky-tape or Blu Tack
- cardboard
- marker pen

Procedure
1. Brainstorm where it would be possible to find representatives of the five kingdoms.
2. Decide which kingdoms you will be able to photograph for yourselves.
3. Decide which kingdoms you will need to obtain images from other sources such as the internet.
3. Make a name card for each of the kingdoms and attach it to the wall or poster.
4. Take photographs of 3 or 4 different representatives of each kingdom and attach them to the wall under the name card.
5. Try to sort the photos within the plant and animal kingdoms into smaller groups. You could also add information about the classification of the organism to the back or underneath the photograph.

Review
1. Compare the number of photographs you have for each kingdom.
   a. Which kingdom was most difficult to photograph directly? Explain why.
   b. Was there a kingdom that you could not photograph for yourselves? If so, explain why you could not.
   c. Which kingdom was the easiest one to photograph? Explain why.
2. a. Which photograph did you find most interesting?
   b. Explain why it interests you.
3. Do you think your photographs truly represent the variety of organisms in that kingdom? Explain your answer.

2 • Classifying weather

Purpose
To compare calendars from two groups of Indigenous Australians.

Time 45 minutes

Materials
- pen
- paper

Procedure

PART A

1. Analyse the information presented in calendars from two Indigenous groups: the Wardaman people of Northern Territory and the Brambuk people of Victoria (Figure 6.4.16 on page 272).
2. Compare the calendars with the temperature and rainfall statistics from the Australian Bureau of Meteorology (Figure 6.4.17 on page 272) for Katherine in the Northern Territory near where the Wardaman people live, and Ararat in Victoria near where the Brambuk people live.

PART B

3. Create a personal calendar by drawing a circle at least 10 cm in diameter. Divide it into 12 equal segments. Label the segments with a month of the year.
4. Into the calendar place the events that are important to you and that occur at the same time each year. Consider events such as sports seasons, birthdays, family holidays, school terms, and seasons of the year.

CHAPTER 6 • CLASSIFICATION   271

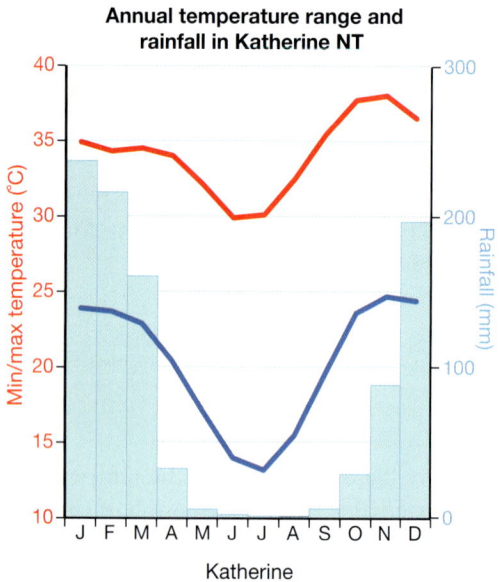

FIGURE 6.4.16 Indigenous calendars

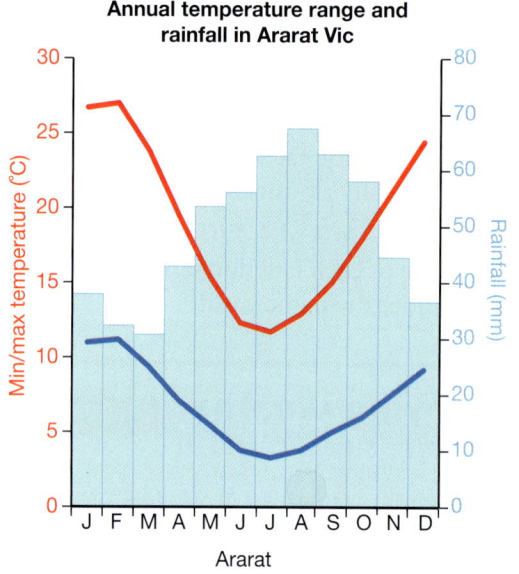

FIGURE 6.4.17 Temperature and rainfall statistics

Review

Take care to observe the scales on these graphs when interpreting them and answering questions.

PART A

1 What information is classified in the calendars and graphs?

2 Compare the information included in the two Indigenous calendars. Suggest reasons for the differences.

3 Compare the calendar of the Wardaman people with the statistics for Katherine, and the calendar of the Brambuk people with the statistics for Ararat. Assess the accuracy of the information gathered by the Indigenous people.

4 Discuss the uses made of the calendars in Indigenous society and the uses made of the information from the Bureau of Meteorology in society today.

PART B

5 Compare the information included in your calendar and the Indigenous calendars.

6 Propose reasons for any differences.

CHAPTER 6 Chapter review

Remembering

1. Define the term 'classification.'
2. a How many kingdoms are there in the current system of classification?
   b Name the kingdoms.
3. Name the type of scientist who places things in groups.
4. People classify things and use classification systems everyday. List examples of classification you experience most days.
5. Which phylums are described as having the following?
   a stinging cells
   b an exoskeleton
   c a single muscular foot
   d a nerve cord.

Understanding

6. Why aren't the products in supermarkets arranged in alphabetical order?
7. Explain how classification is used in:
   a clothing shops
   b online music stores.
8. Explain why characteristics such as hair length or style, or the presence of facial hair, would not make a strong key.
9. Describe the characteristics that cause plants and animals to be placed in separate kingdoms.
10. The Protist kingdom could be called the 'kingdom of misfits'. Explain.

Applying

11. The two animals in Figure 6.5.1 look very different. Refer to Table 6.3.1 on page 256 to explain why they are both classified as animals.

FIGURE 6.5.1

12. Identify characteristics that could be used in a key to identify the creatures in Figure 6.5.2.

FIGURE 6.5.2

13. Identify the kingdom and phylum to which the organisms shown below belong.

Analysing

14. Contrast the following kingdoms:
    a plant and animal
    b monera and protist
    c plant and fungi.

CHAPTER 6 • CLASSIFICATION **273**

CHAPTER 6 Chapter review

15 Use the following information to classify each of these organisms into a kingdom and, if possible, phylum/division.
   a Found when pond water was examined under a microscope. It is green and appears to be a number of cells grouped together within a thin 'skin'. Flagella are visible attached to each cell. A nucleus is visible within each cell.
   b Large organism standing about two metres tall. A soft brown hair covers its body. It had a pouch-like structure on the front of the body. At times a small head appeared out of the pouch.
   c Small green leaves are arranged in a spiral around something that looks like a stem but it has no vascular tissue. This organism is about one centimetre tall. It was found in the shade behind a rock.

16 Analyse the key in Figure 6.5.3 to identify its strengths and weaknesses.

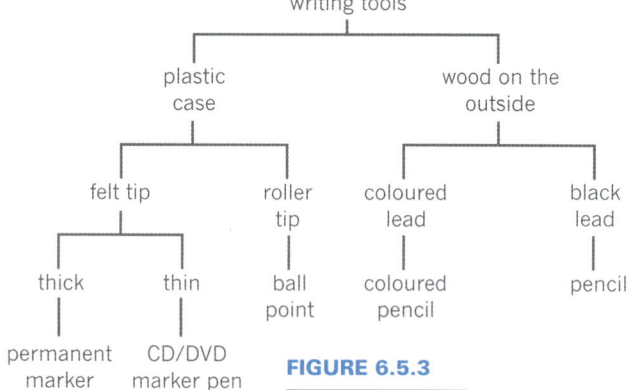

FIGURE 6.5.3

Evaluating

17 a List the three classes of animals that are often grouped together as fish.
   b Propose reasons why most people group these classes together as fish.

18 The West, South and East Alligator rivers are rivers in the Northern Territory. They were named after early explorers mistook saltwater crocodiles living in these rivers for alligators. Many people today still confuse American alligators and Australian saltwater crocodiles.
   Use the information in Tables 6.5.1 and 6.5.2 to answer the following questions.
   a Which two organisms are most closely related? Justify your answer.
   b Why do you think people often confuse American alligators and saltwater crocodiles?
   c What are two characteristics that all three organisms would share?

TABLE 6.5.1 Comparison of alligators and crocodiles

Description	American alligator	Saltwater crocodile	Freshwater crocodile
length	2–5 metres	3–6 metres	1–3 metres
maximum weight	500 kg	1000 kg	100 kg
behaviour	moderately aggressive will attack and kill humans	very aggressive attack and kill humans	shy avoid humans

TABLE 6.5.2 Classification of alligators and crocodiles

	American alligator	Saltwater crocodile	Freshwater crocodile
Kingdom	Animal	Animal	Animal
Phylum	Chordate	Chordate	Chordate
Class	Reptile	Reptile	Reptile
Order	Crocodilia	Crocodilia	Crocodilia
Family	*Alligatoridae*	*Crocodylidae*	*Crocodylidae*
Genus	*Alligator*	*Crocodylus*	*Crocodylus*
Species	*mississippiensis*	*porosus*	*johnsoni*

19 a Assess whether you can or cannot answer the questions on page 227 at the start of this chapter.
   b Use this assessment to evaluate how well you understand the material presented in this chapter.

Creating

20 a Create names for each of the creatures in Figure 6.5.2.
   b Construct a strong table key to classify them.

21 Use the following ten key terms to construct a visual summary of the information in this chapter.

kingdom   species
classification   taxonomy
dichotomous key plants
animals   protists
monera   fungi

AB 6.10

274 PEARSON SCIENCE 7 2ND EDITION

CHAPTER 6 Inquiry skills

Research

1 *Planning & Conducting* · *Evaluating*

Visit a supermarket to research the way:
- meat is classified
- frozen foods are classified.

Present your findings as a diagram or table. Evaluate the classification of either the meat or frozen foods.
Why do you think it is organised this way? Suggest improvements to the organisation.

2 *Planning & Conducting* · *Communicating*

It is estimated that over 80% of all known animal species are arthropods. Many scientists consider this phylum to be the most successful on Earth. Without doubt they are one of the most important groups of organisms to humans. Research the arthropods. Include the following in your research.

- What classes to taxonomists divide the arthropods into?
- List the characteristics used by scientists to separate the classes.
- Find images or video of animals in each class.
- Identify two classes of arthropods that include animals that can be harmful to humans. Explain how they are harmful to humans.
- Identify two classes of arthropods that include animals that help humans. Explain how they are helpful to humans.
- Why do many scientists consider the arthropods to be the most successful phylum on Earth?
- Construct a dichotomous key for the phylum.
- Have other members of the class use your dichotomous key. Evaluate the usefulness of your key based on feedback.

Present your findings as a poster or digital presentation.

3 *Processing & Analysing* · *Communicating*

Research a plant of your choice. Include:
- which division it belongs to
- the structural features that place it in that division
- where it lives
- ways in which it is important for humans.

Present your research as a poster, information, leaflet or PowerPoint presentation

4 *Evaluating* · *Communicating*

A classification system by Indigenous Australians divides plants into 'plants used for medicine' and 'plants used for food'.
Research Indigenous Australian bush medicine. Include information on the following:

- which plants are used as medicines
- which part of the plant is used and how the medicine is prepared
- how the medicine is taken or applied
- the name of the medicine, if it has one
- whether any of these medicines been used in, or contributed to the development of commercially available medicines.

Present your findings as a poster.

5 *Evaluating* · *Communicating*

Pumas are native to North and South America. Depending on the region, they are also called mountain lions, cougars or panthers. Scientists mostly refer to them as pumas.
Research pumas to find the following information:

- What is the scientific name for pumas?
- Suggest why pumas have so many common names. How might this create confusion or problems?
- Classify pumas at all levels from kingdom to species.
- Is the puma more closely related to the lion or domestic cat? Give reasons for your answer.

The puma is often referred to as the largest of the small cats whereas lions and tigers are referred to as big cats.

- There are five members of the big cat grouping. Name these.
- Name two other members of the small cat grouping.
- Is small and big cats a useful classification?

Present your findings as a list of answers to the above questions. Use tables and dot points wherever possible.

CHAPTER 6 • CLASSIFICATION 275

CHAPTER 6 Inquiry skills

Thinking scientifically

1 The aliens below belong to three different family groups. Which two aliens belong to the same family?
   - A 1 and 5
   - B 2 and 3
   - C 4 and 6
   - D 5 and 8

2 Which alien belongs to the same family as alien 9?
   - A 8
   - B 6
   - C 7
   - D 3

Jo's groups	Kai's groups
Spider Scorpion	Spider Scorpion Tick
Housefly Tick Mosquito	Housefly Mosquito

3 Which characteristic did Jo use to create the groups? Justify your answer.

4 Which characteristic did Kai use to create the groups? Justify your answer.

5 Students created this key for their group.

1	a	male	go to 2
	b	female	go to 5
2	a	straight hair	go to 3
	b	curly hair	go to 4
3	a	can roll tongue	Mark
	b	cannot roll tongue	Yasu
4	a	brown eyes	Hans
	b	grey eyes	Jack
5	a	straight hair	Jane
	b	curly hair	Mai

How many people in the group have straight hair?
   - A 1
   - B 2
   - C 3
   - D 4

Use the information below to answers questions 3 to 5.

Two students were given this information about some animals and asked to put them into groups.

Animal	Number of legs	Number of pairs of wings	Number of body parts	Other characteristic
spider	8	0	2	poisonous
housefly	6	1	3	feeds on nectar
tick	8	0	2	feeds on blood
scorpion	8	0	3	poisonous
mosquito	6	2	3	feeds on blood

CHAPTER 6 Glossary

agnatha: jawless fish with an internal skeleton made of cartilage. Examples are hagfish and lampreys.

amphibians: chordates that live both in and out of water

animal: one of the five kingdoms of living things; multicellular organisms with cells that have a membrane as the outer layer and a distinct nucleus

annelids: phylum of the animal kingdom consisting of the segmented worms. Examples are earthworms and leeches.

amphibians

arthropods: animals with an exoskeleton and jointed limbs. Examples are crabs and insects.

aves: animals with feathers covering their body; lay hard-shelled eggs and are endothermic

cartilage: flexible material from which the skeletons of agnatha and chondrichthyes are made

cells: the building blocks of all living things

chondrichthyes: fish with proper jaws and teeth, a skeleton made of cartilage and fins on the sides of their bodies as well as along their backs. Examples are sharks and rays.

chordates: animals with a nerve cord running down their backs, and an endoskeleton

class: the level under phylum in the classification of living things

classification: the process of putting things into groups

cnidarians: animals with radial symmetry, one body opening and stinging cells. Examples are jellyfish, sea anemones and coral polyps.

conifers: plants that bear their seeds on cones and have male and female cones on the same tree. Example cypress, fir and hoop pine.

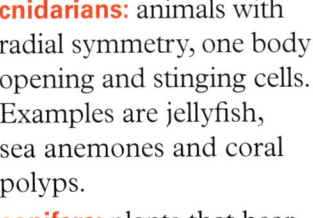
cnidarians

cycads: plants that bear their seeds in cones and have male and female cones on separate plants

decomposers: bacteria and fungi responsible for the natural breakdown of wastes

dichotomous key: a key with two choices at each stage

division: the level below kingdom in the classification of plants

echinoderms: radially symmetrical animals. Examples are starfish, sea urchins and sea cucumbers.

ectothermic: animals with a body temperature that varies with the temperature of their surroundings

echinoderms

endoskeleton: a skeleton inside the body

endothermic: animals with a body temperature controlled internally

exoskeleton: a skeleton on the outside the body

family: the level in the classification system below order and above genus

ferns: plants that reproduce using spores and have a vascular system for transporting food and water throughout the plant

flowering plants: plants that produce seeds fully protected inside an ovary

ferns

fungi (singular: **fungus**): one of the five kingdoms of living things; multicellular or unicellular organisms with a cell wall as the outer covering and a distinct nucleus

fungi

genus (plural: **genera**): the level in the classification system below family and above species

ginkgo: trees with separate male and female plants. Pollen is produced in cones. The female tree produces fleshy-coated seeds

invertebrates: animals without backbones

kingdom: the first level of classification

CHAPTER 6 • CLASSIFICATION **277**

CHAPTER 6 Glossary

liverworts: plants with no vascular tissue which reproduce using spores

macroscopic: able to be seen without the help of a microscope

mammals: a class that includes all the animals that have a body covering of hair and feed their babies on milk produced by the mother

marsupials: a subclass of mammals that give birth to immature young that are suckled in a pouch. Examples are koala, kangaroo and wombat.

microscopic: cannot be seen without the help of a microscope

molluscs: phylum of animals that are bilaterally symmetrical, have well-developed internal organs, and have a muscular foot which they use to move along

Monera: one of the five kingdoms of living things; single-celled organisms without a distinct nucleus

monotremes: a subclass of mammals that lays eggs. Examples are echidna and platypus

monotremes

mosses: plants with no vascular tissue that reproduce using spores

multicellular: made of many cells

nematodes: phylum of the animal kingdom consisting of the roundworms

order: the level in the classification system below Class and above Family

osteichthyes: the bony fish. Examples are tuna, barramundi, eels, sea horses and lungfish

parasite: organism that lives on or in another organism called a host; it gets its food from the host, but the host gets nothing in return and may be harmed

pest species: an animal species that causes problems and is not wanted in an area

phylum (plural: **phyla**): the second level of classification of living things, below Kingdom and above Class

placentals: a subclass of mammals that nourish the baby inside the mother's body by a placenta, and in which the baby is born at a more mature stage. Examples are dingo, horse and human.

plant: one of the five kingdoms of living things; multicellular organisms with a cellulose cell wall as the outer layer and a distinct nucleus

platyhelminths: phylum of the animal kingdom consisting of the flatworms

platyhelminths

poriferans: phylum of the animal kingdom consisting of the sponges

protist: one of the five kingdoms of living things; single-celled organisms with a distinct nucleus

reptiles: animals with scales covering their body; ectotherms, most of which lay eggs with leathery shells

seed-producing plants: plants that reproduce using seeds

species: the last level of classification of living things

sporangia: special structures in which spores are produced

reptiles

spores: single cells that grow into a new moss plant, fern or fungus

taxonomist: a scientist who specialises in grouping and naming things

taxonomy: the science of grouping and naming things

unicellular: made of only one cell

vascular system: systems of hollow tubes or vessels which transport water and nutrients around an organism

vertebrae: the individual bones of the vertebral column

vertebral column: the series of small bones protecting the nerve cord found in most chordates

vertebrates: animals with backbones

weed: a group name for any plant growing where it does not belong

AB 6.9

CHAPTER 7
Forces

Have you ever wondered...
- why cars are designed with crumple zones?
- why competitive swimmers wear a cap or shave their head for a race?
- how you can lift a car using a jack?

After completing this chapter you should be able to:
- investigate common situations in which forces are balanced, such as objects that are not moving
- identify changes that take place when different forces are acting
- investigate common situations where forces are unbalanced, such as falling
- describe how technological developments have reduced impact forces in car safety features and footwear design
- analyse situations where friction opposes motion and produces heat
- discuss how a sports scientist can improve an athlete's performance
- use the term 'field' in describing forces acting at a distance
- identify that gravity pulls objects towards the centre of the Earth
- distinguish between the terms 'mass' and 'weight'
- describe what happens when magnets are brought close together
- describe how charged objects behave when brought close to each other
- investigate simple machines such as levers, pulleys, gears or inclined planes.

This is an extract from the Australian Curriculum
Victorian Curriculum F–10 © VCAA (2016); reproduced by permission

MODULE 7.1 What are forces?

Forces act on you all the time. When you surf, you can feel many forces pushing and pulling you in different directions. Gravity always pulls you down, towards planet Earth. This force can be balanced by the support of the surfboard acting upwards. Forces of the waves push you towards shore, and friction from the air and water pull you back out to sea. Surfing requires your body to balance all those forces acting on you. If they're not balanced, then down you go!

science 4 fun

Unbalanced diet

Can you balance a soft-drink can on its side?

Collect this …
- empty soft-drink can
- water

Do this …

This activity is best done outside or on a bench that can easily be wiped down.
1. One-third fill an empty soft-drink can with water.
2. Try to balance the can by placing the ridge at its base on a bench at an angle of about 45°.
3. See if you can let the can go without it tipping over!

Record this …
1. Describe what happened to the can.
2. Explain why you think this happened.

Push or pull

A **force** is an interaction between two objects. This force, or interaction can be a push or a pull. Forces always happen in pairs. The girl in Figure 7.1.1 pushes on the handle of the pram. As she does this, the handle of the pram pushes back on the girl's hand. Similarly, when the girl pulls the cord attached to the toy boat, this cord pulls back on the girl's hand.

Force is measured using a unit called the **newton** (symbol N). This unit is named after the English scientist Sir Isaac Newton (1642–1727). It takes a force of about 1 N to lift an apple.

FIGURE 7.1.1
A force is a push or a pull that acts between two objects.

280 PEARSON SCIENCE 7 2ND EDITION

What forces do

All around you, things move, or are in motion. When something changes the way it is moving, a force has acted. Some examples are shown in Figure 7.1.2.

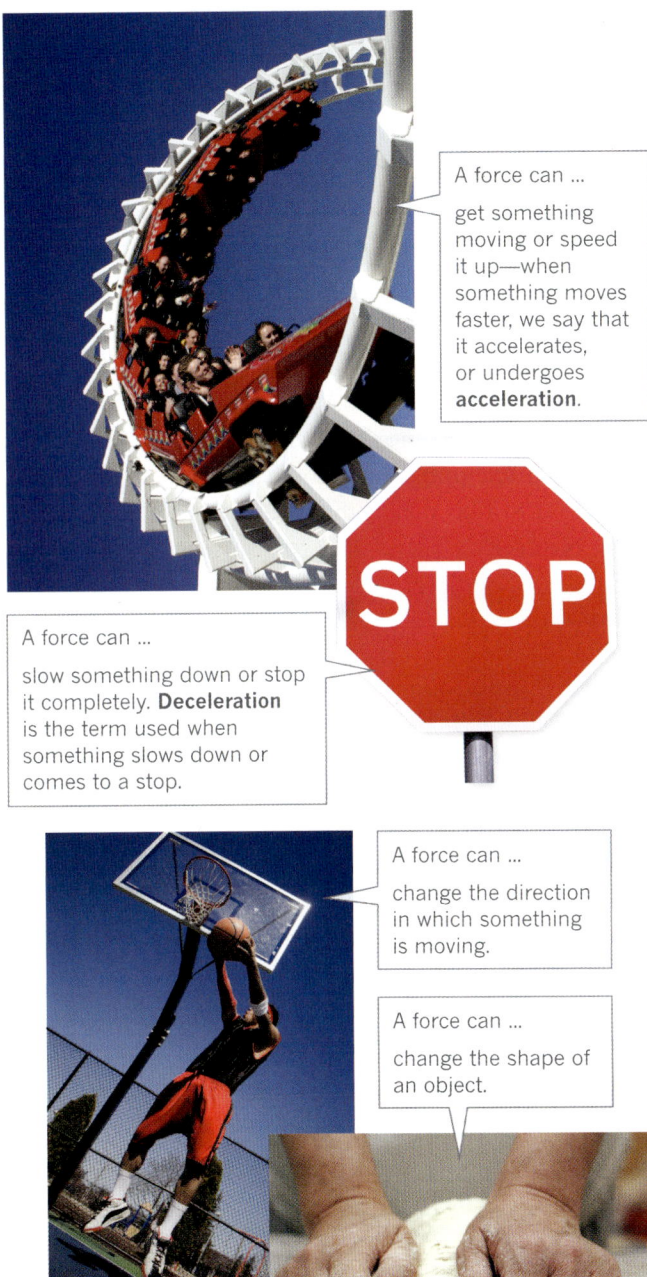

A force can ...
get something moving or speed it up—when something moves faster, we say that it accelerates, or undergoes **acceleration**.

A force can ...
slow something down or stop it completely. **Deceleration** is the term used when something slows down or comes to a stop.

A force can ...
change the direction in which something is moving.

A force can ...
change the shape of an object.

FIGURE 7.1.2 Forces are needed to cause a change in the motion of an object.

AB 7.6

Measuring forces

A spring can be used to measure a force. A spring is a spiral of wire that returns to its original size and shape after being stretched or squashed when the force is removed (Figure 7.1.3).

FIGURE 7.1.3 A force can stretch or squash a spring. When the force stops, the spring returns to its original size and shape.

The larger the pulling force, the more the spring is stretched and the higher the reading on the scale. The spring balance shown in Figure 7.1.4 operates in this way. Some bathroom and kitchen scales use a spring that is squashed or compressed to measure force. Digital scales rely upon objects squashing a special type of crystal called a piezoelectric crystal. This is a crystal that produces an electric current when squashed. The larger the current, the more the object weighs.

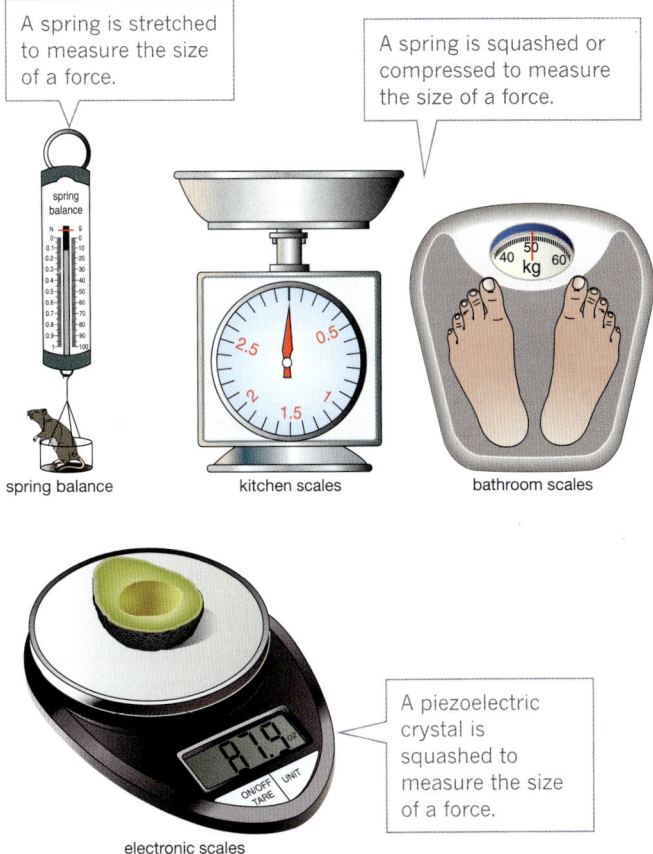

A spring is stretched to measure the size of a force.

A spring is squashed or compressed to measure the size of a force.

spring balance   kitchen scales   bathroom scales

A piezoelectric crystal is squashed to measure the size of a force.

electronic scales

FIGURE 7.1.4 When you squash or stretch a spring or compress a special type of crystal, you can measure the size of a force.

CHAPTER 7 • FORCES   **281**

Drawing forces

Many forces can act on an object at the same time. You can show these forces in a diagram such as Figure 7.1.5 by representing each as an arrow. The size of the arrow represents the size of the force, so the bigger the arrow, the bigger the force. Force A is the largest of these three forces and force C is the smallest.

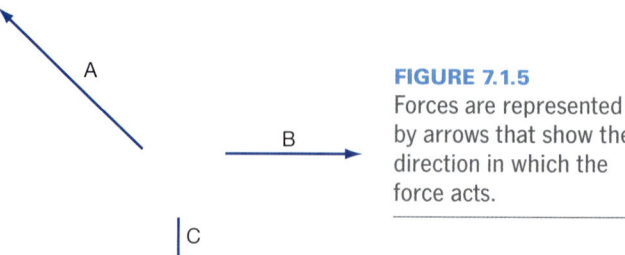

FIGURE 7.1.5 Forces are represented by arrows that show the direction in which the force acts.

Balanced forces

The forces acting on an object can be balanced or unbalanced. When sitting on a chair, the force of gravity pulls you downwards, towards Earth. The chair supports you by pushing upwards. This balances the downwards force of gravity. This balancing act is shown in Figure 7.1.6.

FIGURE 7.1.6 The downwards force of gravity is balanced by the upwards support force from the chair. The forces acting on this person are balanced.

Balanced forces don't always mean that the object is stopped—it might be travelling at the same speed without changing directions (Figure 7.1.7). Consider Nishika, about to ride her bike. To take off, Nishika must accelerate, pedalling quickly and hard to produce a force large enough to push her forwards. Another force is acting against her: friction. Forces of friction could slow her down, such as the roughness of the road and the air she pushes through. To speed up, Nishika keeps accelerating. Her pedalling needs to provide a driving force that is bigger than the force of friction acting in the opposite direction. As Nishika continues her journey, she may travel at a constant speed without slowing down or speeding up. When this happens, the driving force from her pedalling is cancelled out by the friction forces pushing her backwards. At this stage, her motion is constant and all of the forces acting on her are balanced.

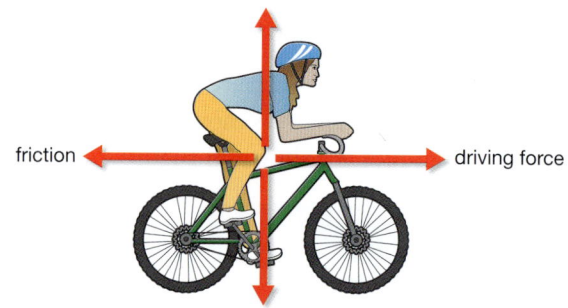

FIGURE 7.1.7 All the forces acting on Nishika are balanced: the driving force caused by her pedalling, the friction acting against her, the upwards support from the bike seat and the downward force of gravity.

Unbalanced forces

Whenever the forces acting on Nishika are unbalanced, her motion will change. Motion always changes in the direction of the unbalanced force, as can be seen in Figure 7.1.8. This means that the forces are unbalanced when Nishika:

- starts moving (by pedalling fast and hard)
- speeds up (by pedalling faster and harder)
- slows down (by using the brakes)
- comes to a stop (by using the brakes)
- changes direction (by turning the handlebars).

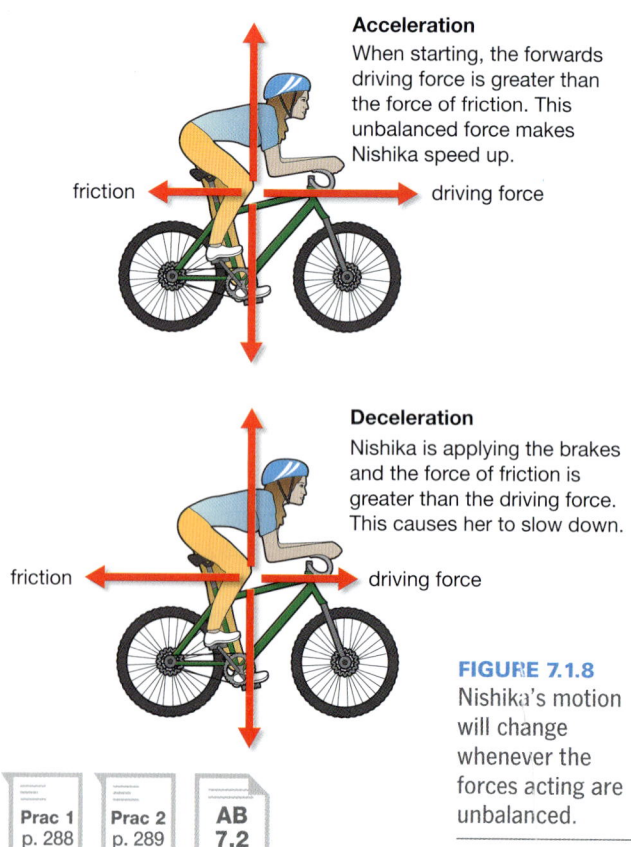

Acceleration
When starting, the forwards driving force is greater than the force of friction. This unbalanced force makes Nishika speed up.

Deceleration
Nishika is applying the brakes and the force of friction is greater than the driving force. This causes her to slow down.

FIGURE 7.1.8 Nishika's motion will change whenever the forces acting are unbalanced.

Prac 1 p. 288   Prac 2 p. 289   AB 7.2

282 PEARSON SCIENCE 7 2ND EDITION

Inertia

When you put your schoolbag down in your bedroom, it will stay there until something happens to it. Someone could lift it, push it or pull it to make it move; but if left alone, your schoolbag will stay as you left it. This ability of the schoolbag to remain unchanged is called its **inertia**. Everything and everyone possesses inertia. Inertia can be described as the tendency to resist any change in motion.

SciFile

Runaway success

In 1924, in Germany, Adolf (Adi) Dassler produced an athletic shoe made from goatskin, leather and chrome. Naming the shoe after himself, he called it Adidas. Jesse Owens wore Adidas shoes when he won four gold medals at the 1936 Olympic Games. This helped to make the brand famous.

Adi's older brother, Rudolph, broke away from the family company after a dispute. He established the Puma company in 1948.

Reducing impact force

Forces act on you all of the time. If these forces are balanced, then you will be still, or moving at a constant speed. If the forces are unbalanced, then your motion will change. Some of the forces that act on you in a collision can be large enough to break bones or damage internal organs.

Reducing impacts in sport

If you are riding a skateboard along the footpath and catch a wheel on a stone then your skateboard can stop moving. However, *you* will continue moving forwards until something makes you stop. Unfortunately this is likely to be the hard surface of the footpath ahead.

A properly fitted helmet, mouthguard and elbow, wrist and knee pads reduce the size of impact forces on you when something goes wrong while skateboarding, rollerblading or rollerskating. These accessories absorb some of the impact force in a collision and reduce the risk of serious injury (Figure 7.1.9).

FIGURE 7.1.9 Professional skateboard riders wear helmets and pads to lessen the impact force in a collision.

Footwear is also designed to reduce the force involved in the collision between a person's foot and the ground when walking, running or playing sport. The type of shoe worn needs to be suited to the type of activity. Running shoes are designed to cushion the toe and heel because it is these parts of the foot that are most affected by the impacts involved while running. Cushioned heels also spread the force over a larger area of the sole of the foot. Figure 7.1.10 shows the cushioning support of a running shoe.

AB 7.5

FIGURE 7.1.10 The cushioned sole of a shoe absorbs impact from running forces. A raised arch prevents the foot from rolling inwards.

CHAPTER 7 • FORCES **283**

SCIENCE AS A HUMAN ENDEAVOUR
Use and influence of science

Car safety features

Statistics show that human error is to blame in over 90% of severe car accidents.

Imagine being dropped off at school in a car with no driver. Car manufacturers around the world are developing driverless, or autonomous cars. Such cars use radar to sense their surroundings and GPS to navigate a route for driving. With no tired or distracted drivers behind the wheel, experts predict that our roads will be much safer when driverless cars are common. A knowledge of forces at work helps to make the cars you do travel in today safer.

When a car stops suddenly, its passengers continue to move forwards until they hit something that stops them. This is inertia at work. If the windscreen, dashboard or steering column stops them then they will usually hit the object head-first. This concentrates impact forces on their brain and they can be seriously injured or killed.

The number of road fatalities in Australia halved between 2005 and 2014 (Figure 7.1.11). Experts believe that this is due to a number of factors, which include safer cars, safer roads and improved law enforcement such as random breath testing and speed cameras.

Crash testing is used to assist the development of safer cars and to inform consumers of the safety rating of new cars on the market.

FIGURE 7.1.12 Crash testing in a laboratory enables scientific measurement of the forces in a collision.

Figure 7.1.12 shows what happens to crash test dummies the instant after a car hits a wall at 56 km/h. The ANCAP (Australasian New Car Assessment Program) uses a system of star ratings of 1 to 5 stars to indicate how safe a car will be in an accident.

The simplest way of preventing serious injury is to wear a seatbelt. A seatbelt holds you in place during a collision and minimises the impact forces on you by spreading them across your chest. Being slightly elastic, seatbelts also reduce the size of the impact force on your chest. Airbags (front, side and curtain) and front and rear crumple zones, as shown in Figure 7.1.13 reduce impact forces even further.

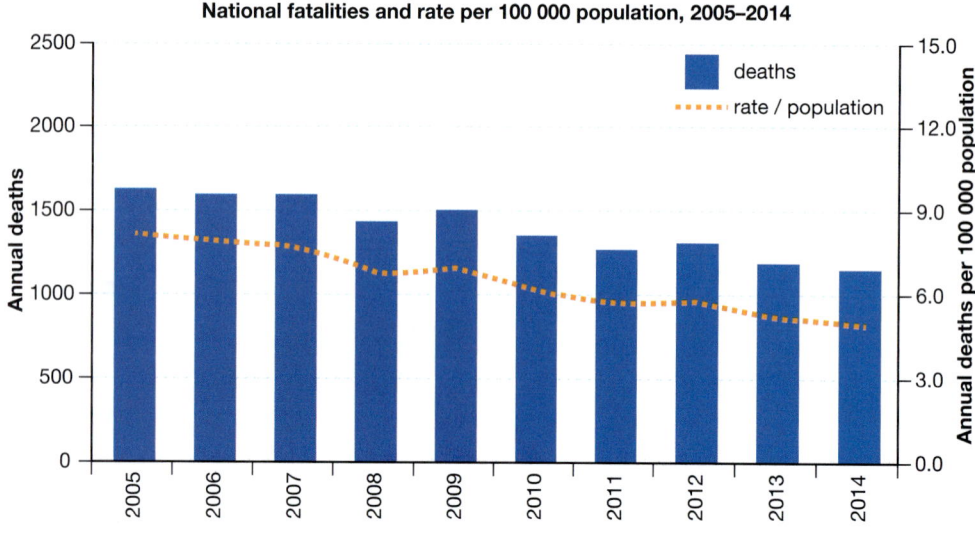

FIGURE 7.1.11 The number of people killed on Australia's roads has decreased over the last 10 years.

SCIENCE AS A HUMAN ENDEAVOUR

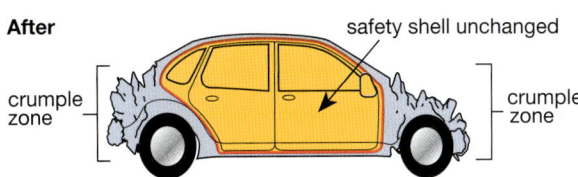

FIGURE 7.1.13 The safety shell of a car is usually made from steel to protect its passengers. The engine compartment and the boot are made to collapse on impact.

In the case of cars with electronic stability control (ESC), an on-board computer detects when the driver is about to lose control of the car due to turning the steering wheel too sharply. The computer attempts to restore control by reducing power from the engine and applying the brakes.

It's better to avoid a car accident in the first place and so modern cars include crash avoidance features or active safety features. These features are designed to reduce the chance of an accident occurring.

They include:
- good quality tyres inflated to the correct pressure
- high-intensity headlights
- automatic or swivelling headlights
- well-maintained windscreen wipers and washers
- automatic windscreen wipers
- a well-maintained braking system
- ABS (anti-lock brakes)
- brake assist
- cameras and sensors for reversing
- traction control
- Electronic Stability Control (ESC)
- night vision
- intelligent speed assist (ISA).

Passive safety features are crash protection features that are designed to lessen the impact of a force if and when an accident does occur. They include:
- correctly adjusted 3-point seatbelts and seatbelt reminder lights
- front and side airbags
- crumple zones
- side impact protection systems
- laminated windscreens
- no sharp features protruding from the dashboard of the car.

Some common passive and active safety features are shown in Figure 7.1.14.

REVIEW

1. List three recent advances in car safety design.
2. a If you could only have three crash avoidance features, which would you choose?
   b Justify your choice.
3. Explain how an airbag can save lives in a car accident.
4. Joel is driving along a road in the rain. He accelerates too quickly around a turn and feels the car starting to skid. Which active safety features could assist Joel?
5. Although experts predict that the roads will be safer with driverless cars, there are people who believe the opposite. Discuss the advantages and the disadvantages of using autonomous cars.

Prac 3 p. 290   Prac 4 p. 291

FIGURE 7.1.14 Active safety features lessen the chance of a collision occurring. Passive safety features reduce the impact of forces in the case of a collision.

CHAPTER 7 • FORCES   285

MODULE 7.1 Review questions

Remembering

1. Define the terms:
   a. force
   b. acceleration
   c. inertia.

2. What term best describes each of the following?
   a. the unit of force
   b. slowing down
   c. when different forces add up to zero.

3. List five ways a force can change motion.

4. Which of the following statements are true and which are false?
   a. If the forces acting on an object are balanced, then it is not moving.
   b. You supply a force when you squeeze a tube of toothpaste.
   c. Helmets, elbow pads and sunglasses all reduce the impact of forces in a collision.
   d. In a front-on collision, passengers continue to move forwards once the car has stopped.

5. List the following forces in order of size from smallest to largest.
   a. a car accelerating down a road
   b. typing a text message on a phone
   c. turning a key in a lock
   d. cutting a slice of bread from a loaf
   e. pushing a couch across the floor
   f. a rocket launching into space.

Understanding

6. Fill in the gaps in the statements below by selecting the correct word.
   push   motion   newton   force   spring
   a. All around us, things move or are in ____.
   b. Whenever there is a change in motion, a ____ has acted.
   c. A force can be a ____, a pull or a twist.
   d. A force can be measured using a ____ balance.
   e. The unit used to measure force is called the ____.

7. Describe an example of a force that:
   a. speeds up an object's motion
   b. changes an object's direction.

8. Explain how a spring balance is used to measure force.

9. The spring balance and kitchen scales shown in Figure 7.1.4 on page 281 both use a spring to measure the size of a force. Outline how the spring is used in each case.

10. Refer to the figure below of Nishika riding a bike.

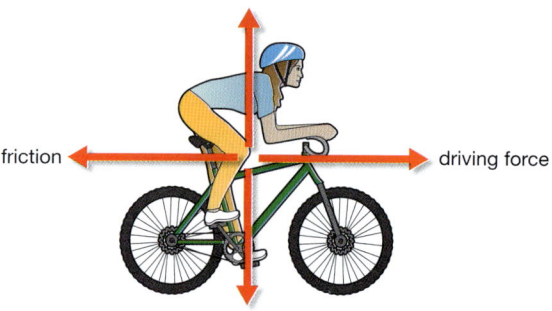

   a. Which forces act on Nishika when she travels at a constant speed?
   b. Why are the opposing forces in the above diagram shown equal in size?

MODULE 7.1 Review questions

Applying

11 Identify the direction of movement of objects acted upon by the forces given in Table 7.1.1.

TABLE 7.1.1 Movement of objects acted on by a force

Force to left (N)	Force to right (N)	Force upwards (N)	Force downwards (N)	Direction of movement
10	10	10	0	
20	30	0	0	
25	5	15	15	
30	30	10	50	
40	40	100	100	

12 Mylinh pushes a full shopping trolley with a force of 220 N and her four-year-old son also pushes with a force of 90 N.
  a Calculate the total pushing force acting on the trolley.
  b Mylinh continues pushing the trolley without realising her son has run in front of the trolley. State what pushing force she needs to apply to stop the trolley from moving.

Analysing

13 Forces can be represented by arrows.
  a Compare the forces shown in Figure 7.1.15 by stating which:
    i   force is the largest
    ii two forces are the same size
    iii two forces act in the same direction.
  b If forces B and E acted on an object, predict which direction the object would move.

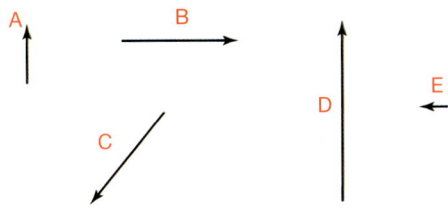

FIGURE 7.1.15

14 Classify each of these actions as a push, pull or twist force.
  a sweeping the floor
  b dragging a heavy sports bag along the floor
  c throwing a cricket ball
  d hitting a golf ball
  e tightening wheel nuts on a car
  f closing your front door from the inside of the house
  g closing your front door from outside your house.

Evaluating

15 Imagine you are travelling in a cart on a rollercoaster like the one in Figure 7.1.16. When reaching the end of the ride your carriage is brought to a rapid stop.

FIGURE 7.1.16

  a Will your head move forwards or backwards as you stop?
  b Use the term 'inertia' to explain why your head moves in this way.
  c People with specific health conditions, such as back or neck injury are advised not to go on certain rides at theme parks. Propose reasons why these recommendations are made.

Creating

16 A force is an interaction between two objects. If one of these objects is you, then if you push a door, the push is an interaction between your hand and the door handle. When you push against the door handle, it pushes back on your hand. Construct a short story in which you describe at least ten force interactions that you are involved in on a particular morning before school.

MODULE 7.1 Practical investigations

SPARKlab alternative available for this activity

1 • Looking at forces   *Planning & Conducting*   *Evaluating*

Forces act all around you, all of the time. Whenever the shape or motion of an object changes, you know that an unbalanced force has acted.

Purpose
To observe a range of forces in action.

Timing 30 minutes

Materials
- lump of Plasticine®
- textbook
- tennis ball
- plastic cup
- pencil case
- ruler
- bucket
- retort stand and clamp
- spring with hanging mass
- hairdryer
- table tennis ball
- balloon
- woollen fabric
- magnet
- paperclip
- plastic straw

Procedure
1. Copy the table below into your workbook.
2. Complete each of the tasks in the table, recording your observations as you go.

Results
Record all your observations in the appropriate columns of your table.

Review
1. How did you know that a force was acting in each task?
2. List any objects that changed shape as a result of the force.
3. State whether any of these changes in shape were permanent.
4. Did the tennis ball change its shape at any stage of its journey?
5. Discuss whether a table tennis ball could remain stationary even when two people blow air on it from two straws.

Observing forces

Task	Changes observed in the motion or shape	What produced the force?
Prop up one end of a textbook with your pencil case or another object to make a ramp. Roll a tennis ball down it.		
Rub woollen fabric against an inflated balloon, and bring the balloon towards someone's hair.		
Point an end of a bar magnet towards a paperclip.		
Drop a tennis ball and try to catch it when it bounces.		
Blow a table tennis ball across a bench using a plastic straw.		
Use a straw to blow bubbles in water in a cup. (Do not drink it.)		
Push your pencil case across the bench using a ruler.		
Squash a lump of Plasticine.		
Push an inflated balloon into a bucket of water and then let the balloon go.		
Suspend a hanging mass from a spring that is fixed to a retort stand. Carefully extend the mass down 2 cm and then release.		
Balance a table tennis ball in stream of warm air directed upwards from a hairdryer.		

288 PEARSON SCIENCE 7 2ND EDITION

MODULE 7.1 Practical investigations

2 • Measuring forces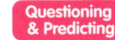

Purpose
To estimate and then measure the size of some common forces.

Timing
30 minutes

Materials
- spring balance
- 10 slotted 50 g masses and base/hook
- selection of items found in the laboratory

Procedure
1. Copy the table shown below into your workbook. If some of these items are not available, suggest an alternative but similar simple task.

Size of forces

Task	Estimate size of force required (N)	Measured force (N)
pulling a pencil case along a bench		
lifting a test tube rack		
lifting a laptop lid		
unzipping a laptop bag or pencil case		
lifting a 100 g mass		
lifting a 200 g mass		
lifting a 300 g mass		
dragging a 300 g mass along a bench top		

2. Estimate the size of each force and then measure for the situations above. Some possible set-ups are shown in Figure 7.1.17.
Record all of your measurements in the table as you go.

Review
1. State whether you needed to use a larger force to lift the 300 g mass or the 100 g mass.
2. Propose why this is the case.
3. Why do you think you needed to use a larger force to lift the 300 g mass than to drag it along a bench top?
4. Look at the sizes of the forces needed to lift the 100 g, 200 g and 300 g masses. Can you propose a link between the size of the mass and the force needed to lift it?
5. Use your answer to question 4 to predict the size of the force needed to lift a 500 g mass. Test your prediction using masses and a spring balance.
6. Use your answers to questions 4 and 5 to predict the size of force needed to lift a 40 kg (or 40 000 g) girl into the air.

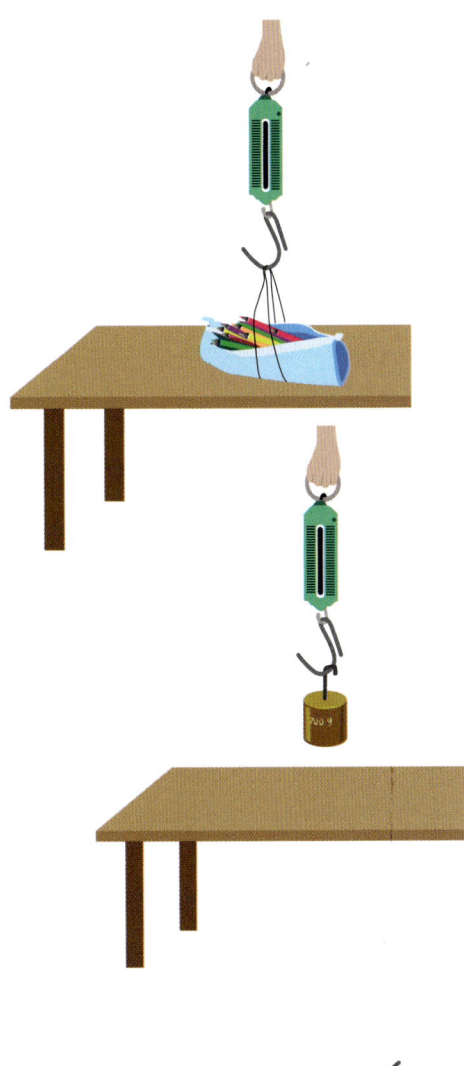

FIGURE 7.1.17

MODULE 7.1 Practical investigations

3 • Crash test dummies

Purpose
To model crash test dummies and describe their motion in different types of collisions.

Hypothesis
What do you think will happen to a dummy that is on a trolley that collides with a wall? What do you think will happen to dummies on trolleys that are in a head-to-tail collision? Before you go any further with this investigation, write a hypothesis for each question in your workbook.

Timing 30 minutes

Materials
- about 50 g of Plasticine
- talcum powder
- trolley
- toothpicks
- block of wood
- ruler or measuring tape
- ramp
- books or bricks to make ramp and a barrier
- video camera or mobile phone

Procedure

PART A: COLLISION WITH A BARRIER

1. Construct a model crash test dummy of a person from Plasticine and toothpicks.
2. Set up a ramp to a height of about 50 cm. Place a brick 30 cm in front of the ramp as shown in Figure 7.1.18.
3. Place crash dummy A on a trolley. Lightly powder the dummy with talcum powder to prevent it sticking to the trolley.
4. Release the trolley from the top of the ramp, and watch the motion of dummy A carefully (or record its motion) as it hits the brick.
5. Repeat the test three times and record your observations.

PART B: COLLISION BETWEEN TWO VEHICLES

6. Join with another group. Remove the brick and place one trolley and dummy B in its place.
7. Release dummy A from the top of the ramp and record what happens to dummies A and B when the trolleys collide.
8. Repeat this test three times.

Review

1. Part A: Collision with a barrier
   a. How does the motion of dummy A change on impact?
   b. Explain these changes in terms of inertia.
   c. Which safety features would protect dummy A in this impact?

2. Part B: Collision between two vehicles
   a. How does the motion of dummy A change on impact?
   b. Explain these changes in terms of inertia.
   c. Which safety features would protect dummy A in this impact?

3. a. Construct a conclusion for your investigation.
   b. Assess whether your hypothesis was supported or not.

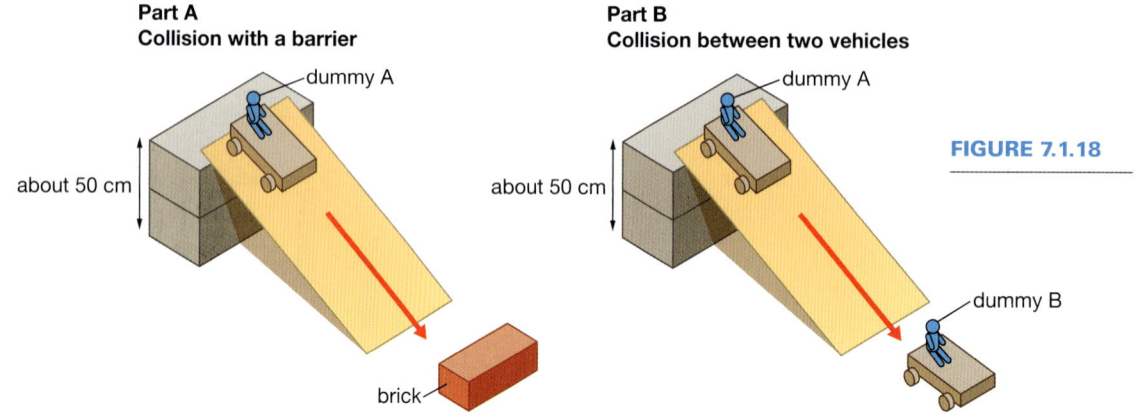

FIGURE 7.1.18

MODULE 7.1 Practical investigations

• STUDENT DESIGN •

4 • A force-measuring device

Purpose
To construct a device that can measure the size of a force.

Timing: 45 minutes

Materials
Students could select materials such as elastic bands, springs, or other elastic material in their design. Figure 7.1.19 could give some ideas.

SAFETY
A Risk Assessment is required for this investigation.

Procedure
1. Design a device that will stretch or compress when acted on by a force.
2. Write your procedure in your workbook.
3. Before you start any practical work, assess your procedure. Assess any risks that your procedure might involve and what you might do to minimise those risks. Show your teacher your procedure and your assessment of its risks. If they approve, then collect all the required materials and start work.

Use the STEM and SDI template in your eBook to help you plan and carry out your investigation.

Hints
Once you have assembled your device, you will need to calibrate it. This means that you need to make a scale that links the extension or compression of your device with a reading of force measured in newtons (N). To calibrate your device, you need to know that the reading of a hanging 100 g mass corresponds to a force of 1 newton.

Results
In your workbook, draw a diagram of your force-measuring device.

Review
1. Explain what is meant by the term 'calibration'.
2. Assess the effectiveness of your design for measuring forces.
3. Propose any improvements you could make to your design.

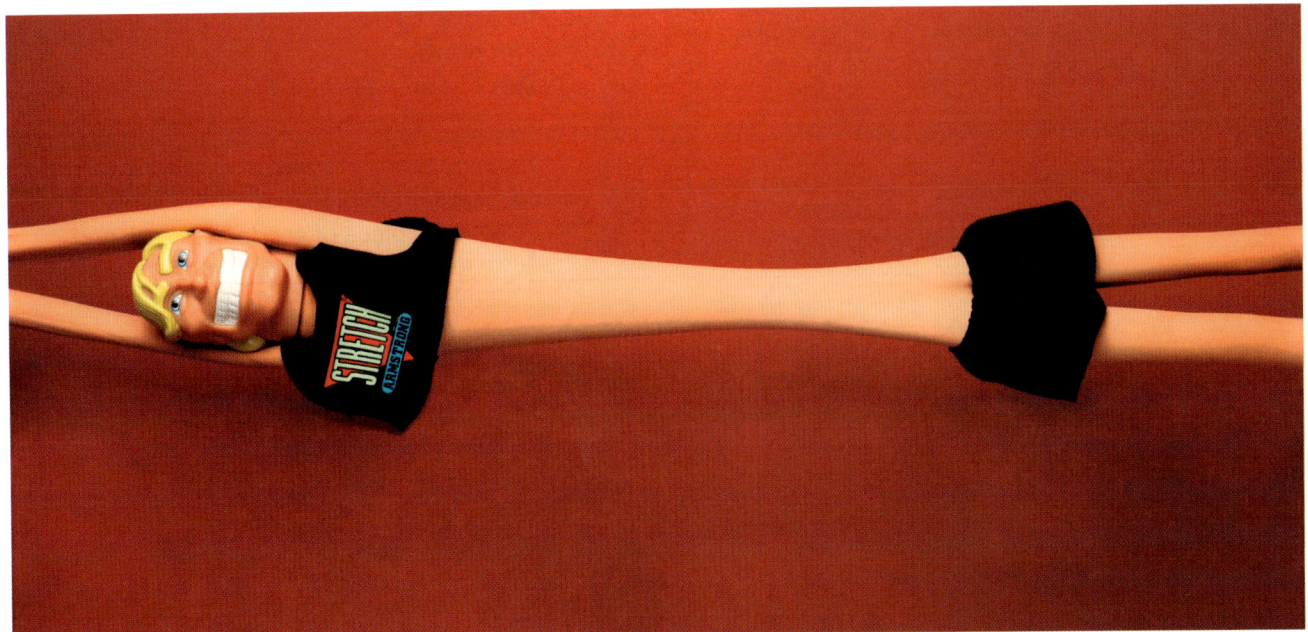

FIGURE 7.1.19 This toy is made of rubber so it can be stretched.

MODULE 7.2 Friction—a contact force

Things that are moving continue to move unless a force makes them stop. The force that makes most moving objects stop is friction. Friction exists whenever two surfaces are in contact. Friction is the force that provides the grip needed by cars and your shoes to get moving, change direction and slow down. Friction can be a problem. It causes machines with moving parts to heat up, which wastes energy.

What is friction?

Roll a soccer ball along a patch of grass and it will slow down and eventually stop. The force that slows the ball down is **friction**. Friction occurs whenever one object tries to move over another. Both surfaces are in contact so friction is called a **contact force**. Friction always acts in a direction opposite to motion. You can see this in Figure 7.2.1.

FIGURE 7.2.1 Friction always acts in the opposite direction to motion.

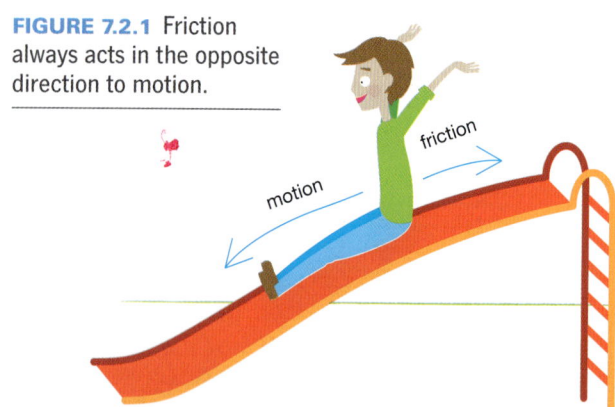

science 4 fun

Warming up

Collect this ...
- block of wood
- piece of sandpaper

Do this ...
1. Rub your hands together as quickly as you can for a minute. How do they feel?
2. Now rub a piece of sandpaper back and forth over a piece of wood for a couple of minutes. Feel the surface of the wood.

Record this ...
1. Describe what happened in each case.
2. Explain why you think these observations happened.

Two sheets of sandpaper will appear to 'stick' when you try to slide them over each other. This is because the grit on one sheet grabs and catches bumps on the other. This causes friction, and collisions between these bumps create heat.

All surfaces have bumps on them, even 'smooth' materials such as glass or steel. Figure 7.2.2 shows the microscopic bumps on the 'smooth' surfaces of a contact lens. An ice sheet is a very smooth surface (Figure 7.2.3). Try to walk on ice and you will slip because the friction is so low. You may have already worked this out and suffered a few bruises as a result!

FIGURE 7.2.2 These ridges are microscopic bumps on the surface of a plastic contact lens, viewed with an electron microscope.

FIGURE 7.2.4 More friction exists between the heavier box and the floor than between the lighter box and the floor. This makes the heavier box harder to move.

FIGURE 7.2.3 The puck used in ice hockey travels long and fast because of the low friction between it and the ice.

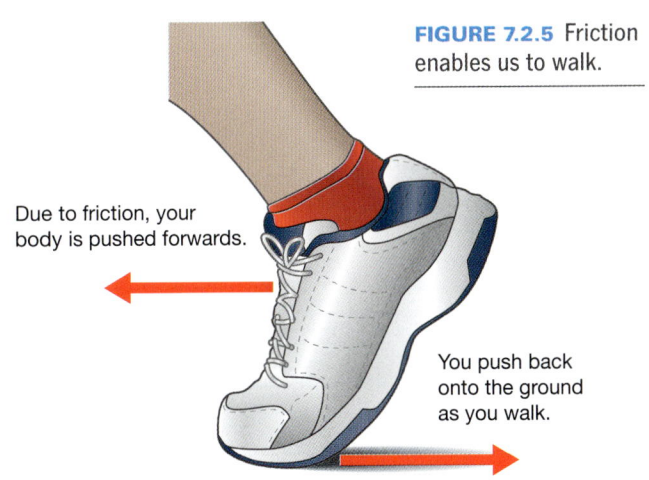

FIGURE 7.2.5 Friction enables us to walk.

Due to friction, your body is pushed forwards.

You push back onto the ground as you walk.

Factors affecting friction

Prac 1 p. 298

Friction depends on:
- how rough the surfaces in contact are
- how hard the surfaces are pushed together.

The greater the weight of a sliding object, the larger the force of friction, as shown in Figure 7.2.4.

Useful friction

When you walk, you push your foot backwards against the ground. The force of friction acts in the opposite direction to push you forwards. For this to happen, there must be enough **traction** (grip) between your feet and the ground, otherwise you will slip. This is shown in Figure 7.2.5. Without friction you could not walk, run, ride a bike or travel in a car, and you could not pick things up (Figure 7.2.6).

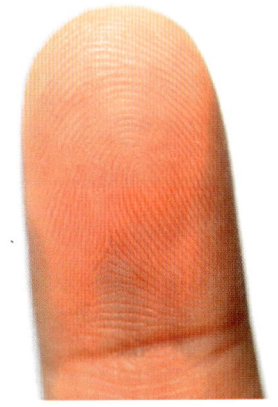

FIGURE 7.2.6 The ridges and grooves seen in your fingerprints increase the friction between your fingers and the objects you grasp.

CHAPTER 7 • FORCES 293

Unwanted friction

You rely on friction in your daily life, but it also has some unwanted effects. Moving parts in a machine or engine are gradually worn away and made thinner by friction. Friction also produces heat. Much of the energy put into a car, an aircraft, a mixer or an electric knife, is converted into heat caused by friction. This makes the machine less efficient and wastes energy, because it is not being converted into the useful forms of energy required. The friction of moving parts in a car engine would quickly cause it to overheat if the car did not have a radiator. A car radiator releases excess heat to the air that passes through it as the car drives along.

Friction between an object and the air around it slows its motion. This type friction is called **air resistance**, or drag. Scientists can study the way that air flows over an object using a wind tunnel. In a wind tunnel, air and smoke is blown at high speed over the object being tested, as if the object itself is travelling fast through air. Smooth smoke lines indicate low friction whereas bunching and breaking up of the smoke lines indicate higher friction. You can see this in the smoke pattern left behind the tennis ball and car in Figure 7.2.7.

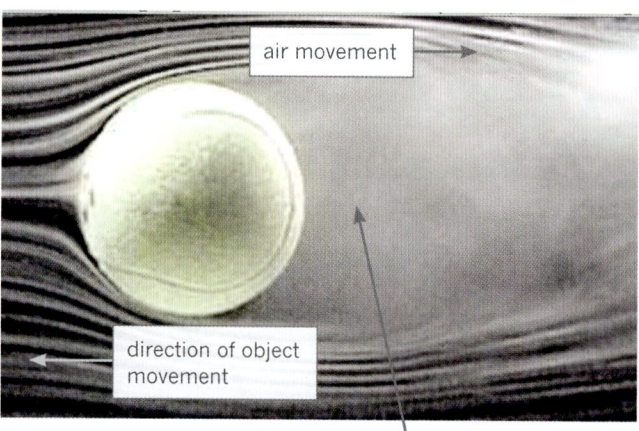

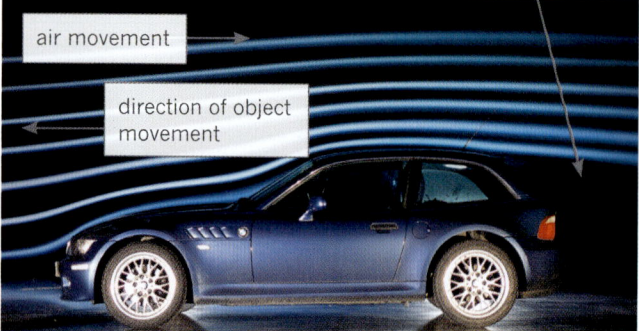

FIGURE 7.2.7 A wind tunnel is forcing air from left to right, as if the tennis ball and car are moving right to left. Highly disturbed or bunched-up air indicates high friction.

Reducing friction

Reducing friction makes machines more efficient, cheaper to run and longer lasting. Friction can be reduced by a number of different methods. Some are shown in Figure 7.2.8.

Rolling surfaces produce less friction than sliding surfaces. Skateboards and rollerblades have ball bearings in the hub of their wheels, allowing them roll more freely over the axle.

An effective way to reduce friction is to stop moving parts being in contact with each other. A hovercraft travels on a blanket of air with very little friction.

Oil and grease are lubricants that reduce friction between moving parts by making their surfaces smoother. That is why a car engine needs oil.

Vehicles, such as cars and aircraft, are all designed to have a streamlined shape. These shapes allow air to flow over and around them more freely, and reduce drag.

FIGURE 7.2.8 There are a number of ways friction can be reduced.

SciFile

Low-drag shark

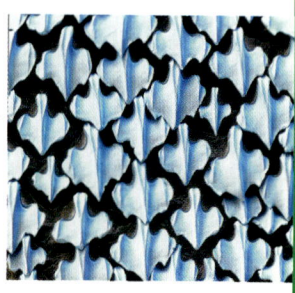

These are shark scales. Each is made from dentine, is coated in dental enamel and measures about a half a millimetre. The base of each scale is made from bone and attaches the scale to the shark's skin. The shark's scales reduce churning of the water as the shark moves, and allow it to glide more smoothly as it seeks its prey.

science 4 fun

Making a low friction vehicle

Collect this ...
- CD or DVD (or small diameter plastic plate with a hole punched in the middle)
- the top of a sports bottle with a push/pull opening
- a balloon
- strong glue (such as Superglue)

Do this ...
1. Glue the bottom of the closed sports bottle top to the centre of the CD/DVD so that the holes in each line up. Make sure it is completely sealed.
2. Blow up the balloon. Do not tie the end but twist the neck of the balloon to hold the air in.
3. While still making sure the air stays in the balloon, stretch the neck of the balloon over the top of the sports bottle top.
4. Gently pull open the sports bottle top and carefully allow the balloon to untwist itself.
5. Push the CD/DVD slightly to start it moving.
6. The balloon will deflate quickly but you can remove it and repeat these steps.

Does your hovercraft move more slowly over different surfaces?

Record this ...
1. Describe to another student, by using a drawing, how to re-create your hovercraft design.
2. Explain how the hovercraft moves on different surfaces.

SciFile

Swimsuit friction

Each year FINA, the international body that governs swimming, releases a list of approved swimwear. Before 2010, some swimmers gained an advantage by wearing suits containing polyurethane. Polyurethane doesn't let water soak through. Pockets of air can be trapped inside the suit, making the swimmer more buoyant. As a result, the swimmer swims closer to the surface and friction is reduced, giving the competitor an edge. These swimsuits are now banned as they gave swimmers an unfair advantage.

 Prac 2 p. 299
 Prac 3 p. 300
 AB 7.3
 AB 7.4
 AB 7.7

CHAPTER 7 • FORCES

MODULE 7.2 Review questions

Remembering

1. Define the terms:
   a. friction
   b. contact force.
2. What term best describes each of the following?
   a. the force of friction between a moving object and the air
   b. oil or grease.
3. What are three everyday activities you couldn't do without friction?
4. Which of the following are true and which are false? Friction:
   a. acts in the same direction as an object's motion
   b. is smaller for heavier objects sliding across a floor
   c. makes a machine more efficient.

Understanding

5. Predict what life would be like if you had no fingerprints.
6. Cars have cooling systems which pump water through the engine. This water absorbs heat and releases some of it into the air via a radiator.
   a. Why do cars produce so much unwanted heat?
   b. Predict what would happen to a car with water leaking from its radiator.
7. Why are ball bearings in the hubs of skateboard wheels?
8. Your grandmother has asked you to shift her refrigerator to the other side of the kitchen. Describe three ways you could reduce friction to make the task easier.
9. Wood and sandpaper heat up when rubbed against each other.
   a. Where did this heat come from?
   b. Predict whether using a coarse or fine sandpaper would produce more heat.

Applying

10. a. Identify the surfaces that are in contact:
       i. when you kick a football
       ii. when you swim at the beach
       iii. as you walk down the street
       iv. as you push a broken-down car.
    b. Explain how friction assists in each of the above situations.

Analysing

11. Imagine an ice-skater performing a routine on ice.
    a. Compare the friction on the ice and on a footpath.
    b. Discuss how this difference allows the ice-skater to move differently on the ice.
    c. The base of an ice skate is a narrow blade. Explain how this shape helps to lessen friction.
12. Rank the situations below from those that would experience the most friction to those that would experience the least.
    - a couch being dragged across carpet
    - a waxed pair of skis travelling on snow
    - an ice-hockey puck hit across the ice
    - a child's tricycle being pulled along the footpath.

Evaluating

13. a. Compare the surfaces that mountain bikes and road bikes typically ride over.
    b. Propose a reason why:
       i. mountain bikes have much rougher tyres than road bikes
       ii. mountain bikes are much heavier than road bikes.

MODULE 7.2 Review questions

14 A minibus is travelling along a flat road.

   a What are two sources of friction acting on the vehicle?
   b In which direction do these forces act?
   c What does the driver need to do to maintain the speed of the minibus?
   d The surfboard is now removed from the roof-rack.
      i Explain whether the friction acting on the minibus would increase or decrease.
      ii Justify your answer.
   e Predict what would happen if the tyres on the minibus were not properly inflated. Use friction to justify your answer.

15 The blades of an electric mixer are hot after beating some cream. Why do you think this happened?

16 Weightlifters rub chalk onto their hands before attempting a lift. The chalk absorbs any sweat on the weightlifter's palms.
   a Propose why weightlifters use this chalk.
   b Predict what could happen if they use too much chalk.

Creating

17 Imagine that you wake up one morning and the force of friction no longer exists. Create a role-play or story or a flow chart in which you describe what happens when you attempt five everyday tasks, such as getting dressed, brushing your teeth, cooking and eating your breakfast, getting to school, and sitting in class.

18 A hovercraft is a vehicle that moves on a cushion of air to reduce friction. The maglev train moves over a layer of air due to magnetic forces that push the train up off its guiding track.
   a Create a drawing of your own method of transportation that is almost frictionless.
   b Describe how your vehicle will work and why it has low friction.

MODULE 7.2 Practical investigations

SPARKlab alternative available for this activity

1 • Friction and mass

Purpose
To investigate how increasing mass affects the size of friction.

Hypothesis
Do you think there will be more or less friction associated with pulling a larger mass than a smaller mass? Before you go any further with this investigation, write a hypothesis in your workbook.

Timing 30 minutes

Materials
- wooden block with hook
- spring balance or force sensor
- 200 g masses

Procedure
1. Copy the table below into your workbook. Alternatively, construct a spreadsheet with similar columns.
2. Place the wooden block on a benchtop.
3. Attach the spring balance to the block of wood as shown in Figure 7.2.9.
4. Measure the size of the force needed to keep the block moving at a constant speed. This is equal to the force of friction. Record this in your results table.
5. Repeat step 4 twice and record the results.
6. Add a 200 g mass on top of the block of wood. Measure the friction between the block and the benchtop three times and add these results to the table.
7. Repeat the friction measurements for 400, 600, 800 and 1000 g (1 kg) masses on the block, recording three results for each test.

Results
1. Calculate the average of your results in the table by adding the three forces and dividing by 3. Alternatively, program your spreadsheet to calculate the average for you.
2. Construct a line graph showing your results. Place mass added to the block on the horizontal axis (0, 200, 400, 600, 800 and 1000 g) and the friction force on the vertical axis (in newtons).

Review
1. What happened to the size of the force of friction as the mass on the wooden block increased?
2. Describe a situation in which you have noticed this link between friction and mass.
3. Propose any improvements that could be made to the design of this experiment.
4. a Construct a conclusion for your investigation.
   b Assess whether your hypothesis was supported or not.

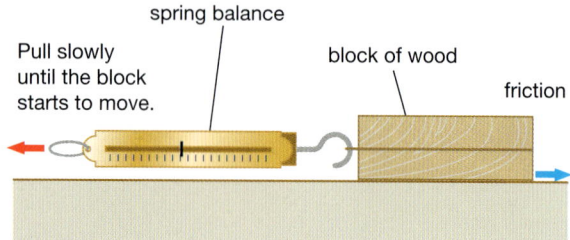

FIGURE 7.2.9

Average forces on block

Object moving	Average friction force (N) measured on blocks of differing mass			Average friction (N)
	Trial 1	Trial 2	Trial 3	
wooden block				
wooden block + 200 g				
wooden block + 400 g				
wooden block + 600 g				
wooden block + 800 g				
wooden block + 1000 g				

MODULE 7.2 Practical investigations

2 • Reducing friction *Questioning & Predicting* *Evaluating*

Purpose
To reduce the force of friction between a block of wood and a wooden ramp.

Hypothesis
Which materials do you think will have the greatest and the least friction when a wooden block is slid across them? Rank the materials you are testing in order from the one you think will produce the least friction to the one that produces the greatest friction when a block slides along it. Before you go any further with this investigation, write your ranking in your workbook.

Timing 45 minutes

Materials
- wooden block, each surface covered with a different material (such as lino, carpet, sandpaper, waxed paper)
- wooden ramp
- protractor
- 3 pieces of dowel

Procedure
1. Copy the table in the Results section into your workbook.
2. Place the wooden block on a marked position near the end of a plank of wood. In your table, record the type of surface that is in contact with the ramp (sandpaper, felt etc.). Call this test 1.
3. Slowly lift the end of the plank that the block is on, holding the other end of the plank so that it does not slip on the benchtop (Figure 7.2.10).
4. Record this angle in your table.
5. Repeat the test until you have tried all four different materials glued onto your block. Give each test a new number and record your measurements in the table.
6. Place the three pieces of wooden dowel parallel to one another to act as rollers. Place the block on wooden dowels and repeat the experiment. Once again, record the angles for each of the different surfaces.

Results
1. Record your results in the table.

Angle of slide

Test number	Surface	Angle at which block starts to slide
1		
2		

2. Construct a bar or column graph that compares the angle at which the block started to slide for each surface.

Review
1. Construct a diagram on which you label the direction of friction acting on the block.
2. The larger the angle at which the block started to move, the larger the friction between the block and the ramp. Assess whether you were correct in predicting which block experienced the most friction.
3. Rank the tests from the one that showed the most friction to the test that showed the least.
4. Rank the surfaces in order of traction or grip, from the surface that showed the most to the surface that showed the least.
5. Identify two examples where lubricants, rollers or waxing are used to reduce the force of friction.
6. a Construct a conclusion for your investigation.
   b Assess whether the ranking you made in your hypothesis was correct or not.

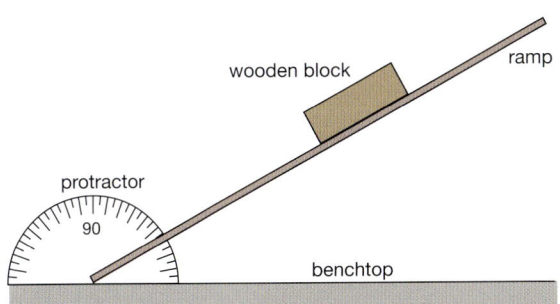

FIGURE 7.2.10

MODULE 7.2 Practical investigations

• STUDENT DESIGN •

3 • Investigating friction in the home

Questioning & Predicting | *Communicating*

Purpose
To investigate the friction produced when operating a household device.

Timing 60 minutes

Materials
- household furniture and devices to be investigated
- string, weights, spring balance, stopwatch or digital timer and other materials as required

SAFETY — A Risk Assessment is required for this investigation.

Procedure
1. Decide which sliding or other mechanism you will examine. For example:
   - a door handle as it turns
   - a suitcase moving on rollers
   - the runners in a drawer as it slides (Figure 7.2.11).
2. In your workbook, write a procedure explaining how you intend to examine the mechanism.
3. Before you start any practical work, assess your procedure. Assess any risks that your procedure might involve and what you might do to minimise those risks. Show your teacher your procedure and your assessment of its risks. If they approve, then start work.

Use the STEM and SDI template in your eBook to help you plan and carry out your investigation.

Results
In your workbook, draw a diagram that shows where friction is experienced.

Review
1. Describe how the mechanism examined works.
2. How can the friction in the device be reduced?

FIGURE 7.2.11

MODULE 7.3 Gravity—a non-contact force

After being lifted 39 km above the surface of the Earth in a helium-filled balloon, Felix Baumgartner jumped out. In his fall, he reached speeds of 1350 km/h before opening a parachute and safely landing. In everyday life, you don't feel the effects of gravity quite as dramatically as Felix, but you do feel its effects constantly.

science 4 fun

Centre of mass

The centre of mass or centre of gravity is a point where you can imagine all of an object's mass is concentrated. This point can be inside or outside the object. Where is your centre of mass when you sit and when you bend down?

Collect this...
- chair
- wall
- coin

Do this...

Part A
1. Place the back of the chair against a wall.
2. Your partner is to sit on the chair, with their feet flat on the floor in front of the chair.
3. Put your thumb on their forehead.
4. Ask your partner to stand up.

Part B
1. Stand with your back to a wall.
2. Your partner is to put a coin on the floor, near your feet.
3. Try to pick up the coin.

Record this...
1. Describe what happened.
2. Explain why you think this happened.

CHAPTER 7 • FORCES 301

What is gravity?

All objects attract each other. There is a force of attraction between you and your schoolbag, as there is between you and everything around you. **Gravity** is this force of attraction. The more mass a pair of objects have, the stronger the pulling force of gravity between them. As a result, you are pulled strongly towards the Earth and the Earth is pulled strongly towards you. The Earth has much more mass than you, so the pull you exert on it is barely noticeable. However you can feel its pull! It's what causes you to fall off a skateboard and the the ride in Figure 7.3.1 to suddenly drop on its track. In comparison, you and your schoolbag have a much smaller mass, so the force between you and your bag is very, very small.

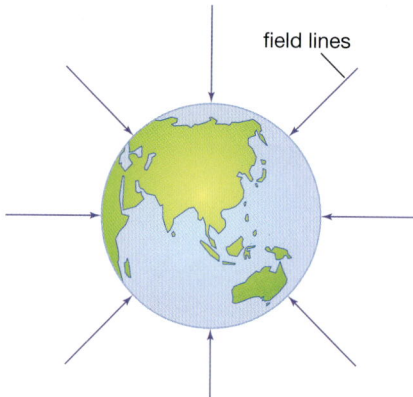

FIGURE 7.3.2 These field lines show the direction of a gravitational field around Earth. Any mass inside this field will pulled by gravity in this direction.

The planets of our solar system lie within the Sun's gravitational field. As a result, they are pulled towards the Sun by a gravitational force. This force is not strong enough to pull Earth or any of the other planets onto the Sun, but it is strong enough to keep them from escaping into deep space. Planets orbit the Sun in paths as shown in Figure 7.3.3. Similarly, our Moon and various artificial satellites are pulled into an orbit of the Earth because they lie within Earth's gravitational field.

FIGURE 7.3.3 Gravitational attraction keeps moons in orbit around massive planets, and planets in orbit around more massive stars like the Sun.

FIGURE 7.3.1 On the Giant Drop on the Gold Coast in Queensland, passengers fall 120 m in just 5 seconds!

Gravitational fields

If you throw a ball into the air, you know it will fall back to Earth. If an object lies within a region called the Earth's **gravitational field**, then a gravitational force will act upon it. This region is called a **force field**. Gravity acts through a force field, without direct contact. It can be described as a **non-contact force**. Figure 7.3.2 shows the direction of Earth's gravitational field.

Comparing mass and weight

Some people mistakenly think that mass and weight are the same. However, to scientists they are very different quantities.

Mass

Mass is the amount of matter in an object. Your mass remains the same if you travel to other planets, because the matter you are made from remains the same. Mass is measured in kilograms (kg). Smaller masses, such as the ingredients of a cake, are measured in grams (g). The mass of a large object, such as a car or truck, is measured in tonnes (t).

Mass is spread throughout an object but can be thought of as being concentrated in a point called its **centre of mass**. Since gravity works on mass, this point is also known as the centre of gravity. From the centre of mass, you can work out how stable an object will be. For example, the car shown in Figure 7.3.4 is stable because its centre of mass lies above its base. The car will remain firmly planted on the ground. In contrast, the truck is unstable and will topple over—its centre of mass lies outside its base.

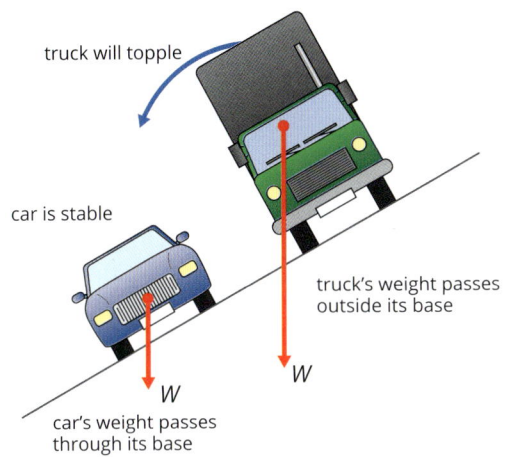

FIGURE 7.3.4 The car's centre of mass lies above its base so it is stable. The truck will topple because the centre of mass lies outside its base.

Weight

Weight is the name given to the pulling force of gravity on an object. Like all forces, weight is measured in newtons (N). Your weight depends not only on your mass, but also on the strength of the gravitational field of the planet or moon you are on. For this reason your weight on the Moon is only one-sixth of that on Earth (Figure 7.3.5).

FIGURE 7.3.5 The last person to stand on the Moon was Eugene Cernan in 1972. He had exactly the same mass as on Earth. The Moon's gravity is only one-sixth that of Earth's so his weight on the Moon was only one-sixth of what it was back on his home planet.

Falling

Drop an autumn leaf and a stone from the same height and the stone will always hit the ground first. For many centuries, this caused people to believe that heavier things fell faster than lighter ones. The Italian scientist Galileo Galilei (1564–1642) performed experiments with falling objects. He realised that the reason some things fell faster was not because they weighed more, but because they had a smaller surface area than other things. Air is pushed out of the way as an object falls.

An object with a small surface area experiences less air resistance as it cuts through the air compared to an object with a larger surface area. This can be seen in Figure 7.3.6. The weight force of the feather is smaller than the weight force of the hammer, because the feather has a smaller mass than the hammer.

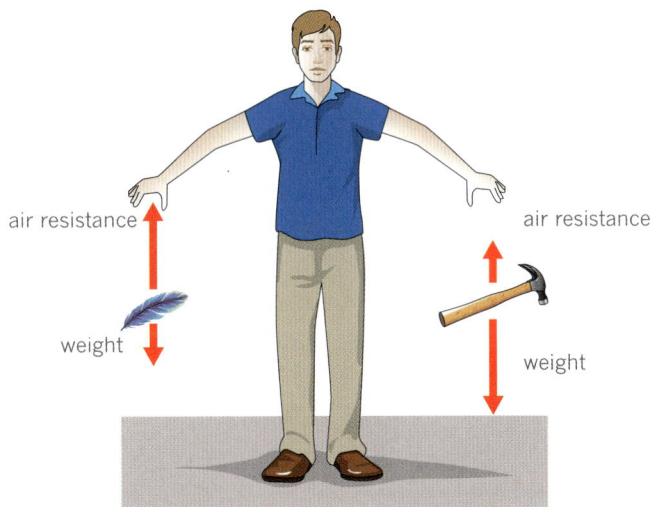

FIGURE 7.3.6 A feather falls more slowly than a hammer because it experiences a larger force of air resistance.

SciFile

Real or legend?

At the time of Galileo Galilei, people believed that heavier objects fell faster than lighter objects. Galileo believed that all objects were affected equally by gravity, but fell at different rates due to differences in the air resistance affecting each. Legend has it that Galileo dropped two balls made from the same material but of different masses from the Leaning Tower of Pisa to prove his point.

CHAPTER 7 • FORCES   303

Due to its shape, the feather experiences a larger air resistance force as it falls than the air resistance experienced by the hammer. The net force on the feather as shown in the diagram is upwards. This means it is slows down as it falls. The net force on the hammer is downwards, so the hammer speeds up as it falls. The difference in the way the feather and hammer fall is due to air resistance. If dropped on the Moon, where there is no air, the hammer and feather hit the ground at the same time.

A leaf has a greater surface area than a stone of the same mass. Hence it experiences a greater force of friction (air resistance) when falling in air. This slows its motion and causes it to flutter as it falls (Figure 7.3.7).

FIGURE 7.3.7 A leaf flutters as it falls, because it has a relatively large surface area and experiences more air resistance than other more compact objects.

SciFile

Looking to escape?
Could you permanently jump off the Earth if you jumped really, really high and really, really fast? Not unless there is something superhuman about your leg muscles! To escape from Earth's gravity, you'd need to jump faster than 40 000 km/h!

Terminal velocity

As an object's speed increases, its air resistance also increases. This means that the air resistance on a falling object increases as it falls. Eventually, the air resistance acting on the object equals its weight force. When this happens, the forces acting on the object are balanced and the object then falls at a constant speed. This speed is called **terminal velocity**. This situation is shown in Figure 7.3.8.

The terminal velocity of a skydiver without a parachute is far too great to survive a landing on Earth. Opening a parachute provides a much larger surface area, which greatly increases the force of air resistance and slows the skydiver down.

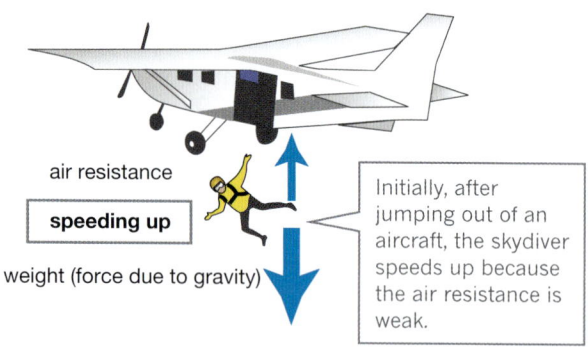

Initially, after jumping out of an aircraft, the skydiver speeds up because the air resistance is weak.

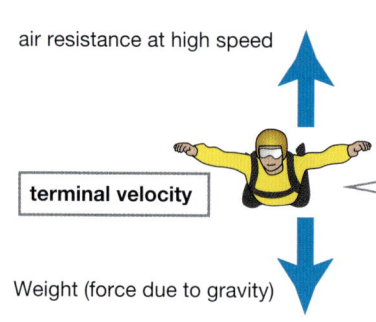

The skydiver is pulled down by gravity so he speeds up. As he falls more quickly, air resistance increases. Air resistance then becomes stronger until the force of air resistance balances the force of gravity.

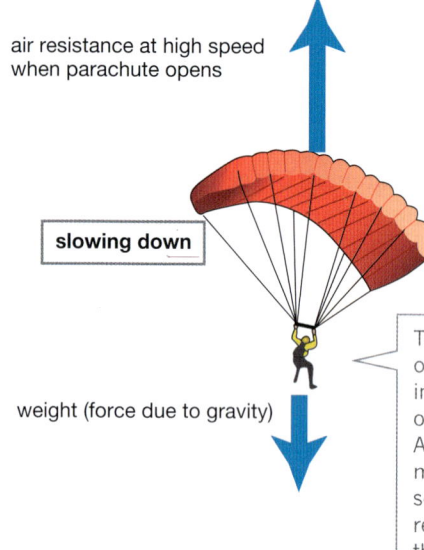

The surface area of the skydiver is increased when he opens his parachute. As a result, there is more air resistance, so the force of air resistance is greater than gravity and the skydiver slows down.

FIGURE 7.3.8 The motion of a skydiver depends upon the relative sizes of the forces of air resistance and weight.

SCIENCE AS A HUMAN ENDEAVOUR
Use and influence of science

Sports science

In sport, a slight advantage of one athlete over another could mean the difference between winning or losing. For this reason, sports scientists apply scientific ideas and techniques to improve the performance of athletes.

FIGURE 7.3.9 A sports scientist will examine the technique of an athlete and will try to minimise the risk of injury.

To help an athlete better their performance, a sports scientist will use knowledge from physics, engineering, psychology, science skills and biomechanics (the study of human motion) (Figure 7.3.9).

For example, the understanding of forces and how they work will allow them to:

- help an athlete reduce friction in the air or water—for example, by shaving their legs, wearing streamlined helmets when cycling and swimming with an efficient stroke that minimises splashing or turbulence
- develop a method to throw a cricket ball or baseball with a desired curve or spin
- keep their centre of gravity low so they will remain balanced when performing gymnastics, pole vaulting or high jumping.

Engineering will assist in the design of equipment to assist an athlete. Examples are lightweight and efficient bikes, more flexible pole vaults and golf clubs that will deliver maximum impact to a ball.

Good scientific method and inquiry skills will allow sports scientists to make observations, collect and interpret data and use it to improve the athlete's performance (Figure 7.3.10). Heart rate data, blood tests, high-speed video or computerised sensors may be used to gather data. A sports scientist can then analyse such information to instruct an athlete on how to improve a sporting technique or to make changes to their exercise plan.

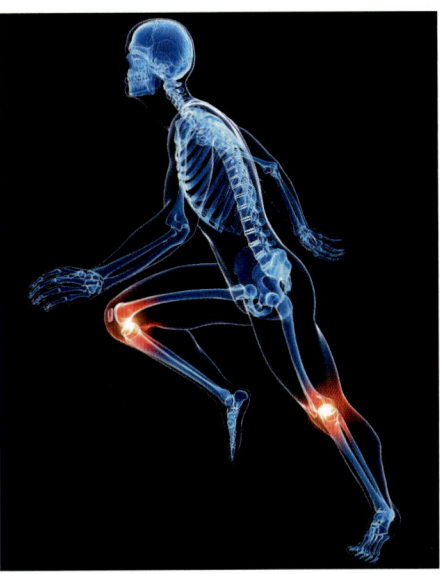

FIGURE 7.3.10 Sports scientists work with athletes to monitor the physical fitness and strength of the athlete.

An understanding of nutrition is required to design a diet that is tailored to the athletics they are helping.

Sports scientists will use psychology to help an athlete prepare mentally for their sporting competition, to make effective decisions and to cope with the demands of being in the spotlight.

Finally, biomechanics will allow scientists to work out what causes injuries and to try to prevent them from happening. If injuries do happen then they will work with an athlete to develop an exercise and training plan to strengthen the athlete and give them the best possible recovery time.

REVIEW

1. What are three workplaces that may employ a sports scientist?
2. Outline three ways in which the work of a sports scientist is similar to the work of a scientist in a laboratory.
3. Do you think a sports scientist will always be able to improve the performance of all athletes. Discuss.
4. Some sports scientists have pushed the boundaries too far by introducing athletes to banned performance enhancing drugs. What is your opinion on the use of performance enhancing drugs in sport? Discuss.

MODULE 7.3 Review questions

Remembering

1. Define these terms:
   a. gravity
   b. weight.
2. What term best describes each of the following?
   a. the amount of matter in an object
   b. falling at a constant speed.
3. Which of the following words correctly complete the following sentences?
   a. Gravity is a *contact/non-contact* force.
   b. Gravity *pulls/pushes* objects towards the Earth.
   c. All objects naturally *attract/repel* each other.
   d. Objects of the same mass fall at different speeds due to their *weight/surface* area.
4. What unit used to measure the following?
   a. mass
   b. weight.

Understanding

5. Explain what a force field is, giving two examples.
6. The lines in Figure 7.3.11 represent Earth's gravitational field.
   a. Describe what happens to an object that is located in the region of this field.
   b. Describe what happens to the strength of this gravitational field as an object moves further away from Earth.
   c. Explain why gravity is called a non-contact force.

7. Two forces act on a skydiver falling towards Earth.
   a. Name these two forces.
   b. Draw a diagram showing the forces on the skydiver while she is accelerating as she falls.
   c. Eventually the two forces are balanced. Explain how this affects the skydiver.

Applying

8. a. A person's mass changes throughout life. Describe three ways this can happen.
   b. A person's mass can stay the same but their weight can change. What would happen to their weight if they travelled to the Moon?
   c. Identify a place on Earth where their weight would be very slightly less than normal.

Analysing

9. Gravity pulls people downwards regardless of where they are on Earth. How is this possible? Use a diagram to assist you to explain how.
10. a. Compare gravity on the surface of the Moon with gravity on the surface of Earth.
    b. Describe how this would make you feel when walking on the Moon.
11. Compare mass and weight by listing their similarities and differences.
12. A tennis ball, a cricket ball and a shot put are dropped at the same time. The path of the tennis ball as it falls is shown in Figure 7.3.12.

    Copy the diagram and draw where the cricket ball and shot put would roughly be when the tennis ball is at the spots shown.

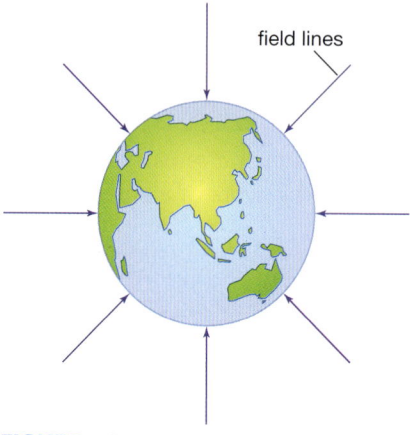

FIGURE 7.3.11

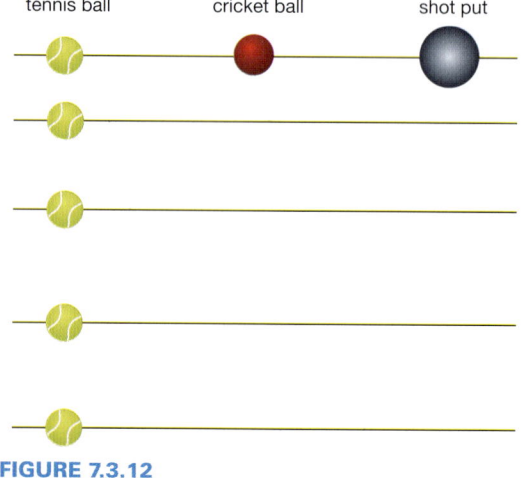

FIGURE 7.3.12

MODULE 7.3 Review questions

Evaluating

13 Min-Jee drops a leaf and a small rock from the top of a playground slide.
   a Predict which will hit the ground first.
   b Assess whether gravity acts differently on objects because of their different mass.
   c Predict what Min-Jee would observe if her experiment was repeated on the Moon.

14 When you get up from a chair you push your body forwards.
   a Where do you think your centre of mass is when you are sitting on a chair?
   b When you stand up, you bend forwards. Propose a reason why.

Creating

15 According to the ancient Greek philosopher Aristotle, heavy objects contain more gravity than light objects, so they fall faster. Construct a response to Aristotle in which you disagree with his viewpoint.

16 Imagine what would happen if instead of being an attractive force, gravity was a repulsive force that pushed objects away.

   Construct three diagrams showing what could happen to things around you if this was the case.

MODULE 7.3 Practical investigations

SPARKlab alternative available for this activity.

1 • Look out below!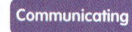

Purpose
To investigate if heavier objects fall faster than lighter ones.

Timing 15 minutes

Materials
- metre ruler
- Blu Tack
- foam or rubber
- a number of unbreakable objects of different mass
- sheet of butcher's paper
- 50 g mass
- electronic balance

SAFETY Be careful not to drop objects where they could fall on someone.

Note: If possible, use a motion sensor or light gates to complete this experiment more accurately.

Procedure
1. Copy the table below into your workbook.
2. Measure the mass of each object and record the masses in your results table.
3. Predict what will happen when each object falls. Record your predictions in the table.
4. Mark a height of 2 metres on a wall with a piece of Blu Tack. Place some foam or rubber at its base. This is your 'drop zone' to test how fast each object falls.
5. Drop the 50 g mass and another item from the height marked on the wall as shown in Figure 7.3.13.
6. Record whether the object landed at about the same time, slower or faster than the 50 g mass. Repeat the test if you are unsure.
7. Repeat, using the 50 g mass and every object to be tested, and record your results.
8. Drop the 50 g mass and the sheet of A4 paper (held horizontally) and record your result.
9. Crumple the sheet of paper into a loose ball and repeat the test.
10. Finally, scrunch the loose ball into the tightest ball you can and do the test again.

Results
Record all your masses, predictions and measurements in your table. Give your table a title.

Review
1. How accurate were your predictions?
2. Did most objects fall at the same rate as the 50 g mass, or did the objects fall faster or slower?
3. a Which object fell the fastest?
   b Propose a reason why this was the slowest.
4. a Name the objects that fell faster than the 50 g mass.
   b Why do you think this happened?
5. Propose a reason why the 50 g mass was used in every experiment.
6. a Summarise how the shape of the sheet of paper changed how it fell.
   b Explain why.
7. Draw a conclusion for this activity.

Speed of falling objects

Falling object	Mass (g)	My predictions Will fall the same/faster/slower than the 50 g mass	Landed about the same time as 50 g mass	before the 50 g mass	after the 50 g mass

FIGURE 7.3.13

308 PEARSON SCIENCE 7 2ND EDITION

MODULE 7.3 Practical investigations

• STUDENT DESIGN •

2 • Robocopter investigation

A robocopter is a paper construction that spins as it falls when it is dropped from a height.

Purpose
To make a robocopter and then determine how one variable affects the time that it takes the robocopter to fall.

Timing 45 minutes

Materials
- sheets of cardboard
- ruler
- pencil
- scissors
- stopwatch
- paperclip

SAFETY — A Risk Assessment is required for this investigation.

Procedure

1. A template for a robocopter is shown in Figure 7.3.14. The completed model is shown in Figure 7.3.15. To build your robocopter, draw a copy of the template onto an A4 piece of cardboard (cut long ways).
2. Cut along solid lines and fold along dotted lines as shown by the arrows.
3. Place a paperclip at the base to complete the robocopter.
4. Drop this robocopter from the same height three times, timing how long it takes to fall in each case.
5. Now investigate what affects the drop time of the robocopter. First, decide which variable you will change. You could:
   - change the length of its blades
   - add more paperclips to its base
   - make different-sized robocopters
   - make robocopters from different thicknesses of paper or cardboard.
6. Write your procedure in your workbook.
7. Assess any risks that your procedure might involve and what you might do to minimise those risks. Show your teacher your procedure and your assessment of its risks. If they approve, then collect all the required materials and start work.

Use the STEM and SDI template in your eBook to help you plan and carry out your investigation.

Results
Record your results in a table and show these in a graph.

Review
1. Which forces act on the robocopter when it is falling?
2. a Construct a conclusion for your investigation.
   b Assess the method you used in your investigation.

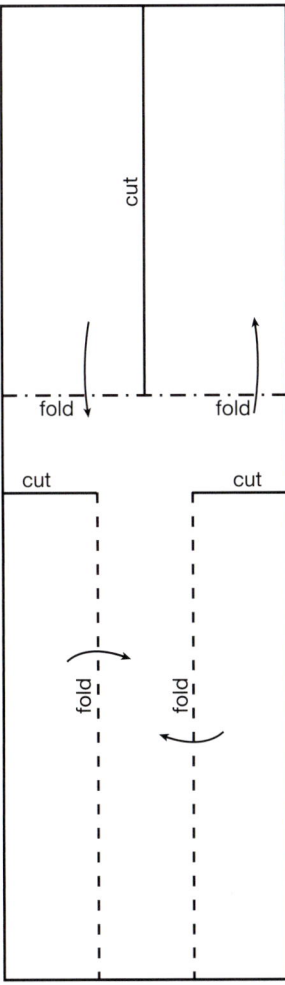

FIGURE 7.3.14

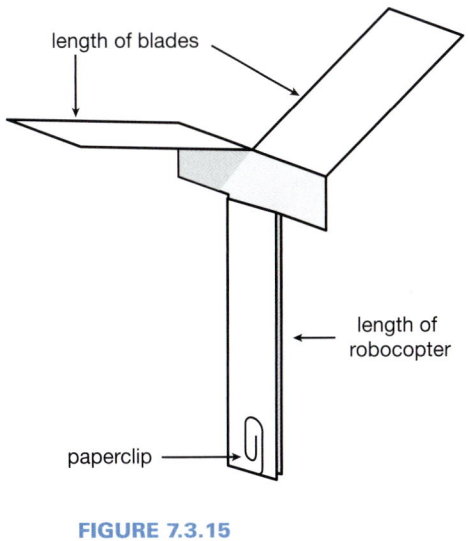

FIGURE 7.3.15

CHAPTER 7 • FORCES **309**

MODULE 7.3 Practical investigations

• STUDENT DESIGN •

3 • Marble run

Purpose
To build a structure that will apply different forces to a marble.

Timing 60 minutes

Materials
Students could select materials such as:
- elastic bands
- wooden ramps
- springs
- balloons
- cardboard boxes
- cardboard tube
- funnels
- icy-pole sticks
- marble

SAFETY
A Risk Assessment is required for this investigation.

Procedure
1. Design a structure that will cause a marble dropped onto or into it to speed up, slow down, change direction, and finally come to a stop.
2. In your workbook, draw a diagram of the structure you plan to build.
3. Before you start any practical work, assess your structure and how you will build it. Assess any risks that your procedure might involve and what you might do to minimise those risks. Show your teacher your plan and your assessment of its risks. If they approve, then collect all the required materials and start work.

Use the STEM and SDI template in your eBook to help you plan and carry out your investigation.

Results
Record your observations about the journey of the marble.

Review
1. Assess how effective your design was in making the marble speed up, slow down, change direction and finally stop.
2. Propose any improvements you could make to your design.

310 PEARSON SCIENCE 7 2ND EDITION

MODULE 7.4 Magnetic and electric fields

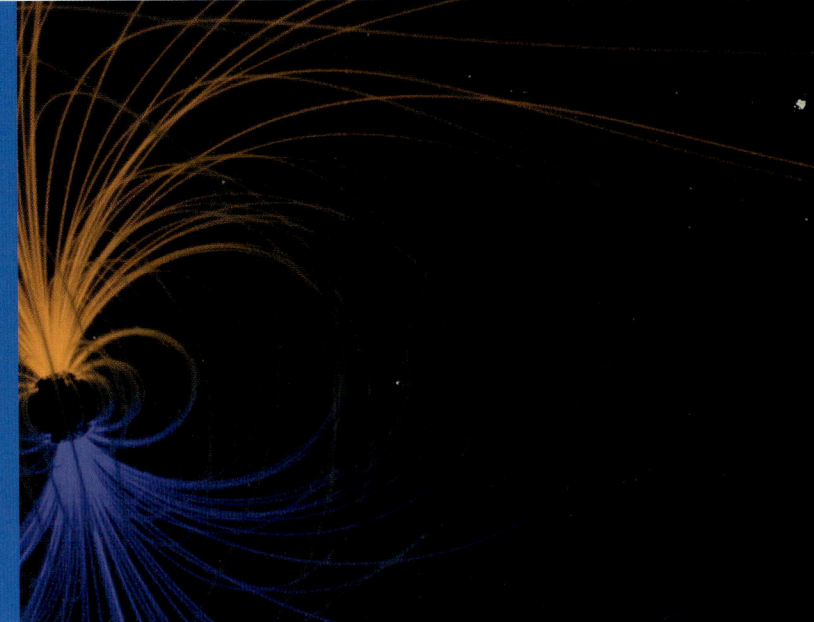

This image shows the shape of the magnetic field around Earth. Where the lines are closest together, Earth's magnetic field is strongest. This happens near the north and south poles. Earth's magnetic field protects us all by deflecting harmful charged particles from the Sun or channelling them down towards the poles. Magnetic and electrostatic forces are non-contact forces around us.

Magnetic fields

A magnet attracts materials containing the metals iron, cobalt or nickel. Steel contains iron, and so steel is also attracted to a magnet. Materials not made from iron, cobalt or nickel are not magnetic. The horseshoe magnet shown in Figure 7.4.1 attracts the steel filings from a distance away.

FIGURE 7.4.1
This horseshoe magnet attracts only the steel filings from a pile of steel and copper filings. The copper is left behind.

science 4 fun

Seeing magnetic field lines

Can you see a magnetic field?

Collect this…
- collection of magnets
- thin books
- stiff, transparent plastic
- white paper
- iron filings

Do this…
1. Place a bar magnet on a sheet of paper.
2. Put the plastic sheet over this and flatten its edges with some books.
3. Sprinkle about a teaspoon of iron filings onto the plastic sheet.
4. Lightly tap the sheet to spread the iron filings. What pattern can you see?
5. Gather up all the iron filings and then test a different magnet.

Record this…
1. Describe each pattern you saw.
2. Explain why you think these formed.

CHAPTER 7 • FORCES 311

This happens because the steel filings were positioned within its magnetic field. A **magnetic field** is the space around a magnet where a magnetic force is experienced. The steel filings were pulled by a magnetic force in the direction of the magnetic field.

The ends of a magnet are called **poles**. The poles are where a magnet's field is the strongest. If a magnet floats in water, then one end spins to face the Earth's north pole. This end is the north pole of the magnet. The opposite pole of the magnet is the south pole. If a magnet is cut in half, each half still has a north and a south pole.

A magnetic field is normally invisible to us. Its shape and strength can be determined either by passing a compass around a magnet, or by examining a sprinkling of iron filings around a magnet. Figure 7.4.2 shows that magnetic field lines point from the north to the south pole.

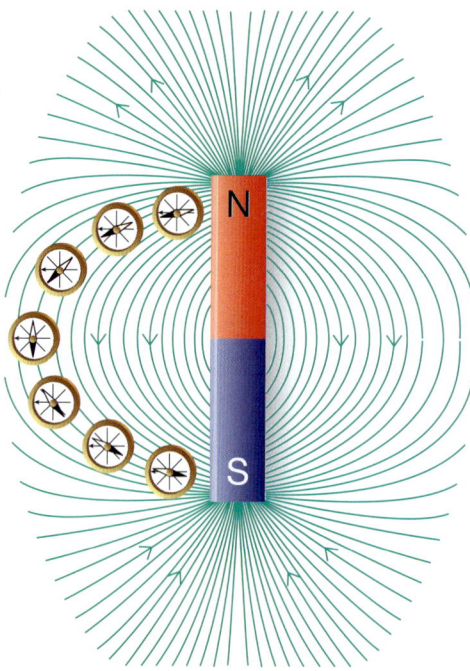

FIGURE 7.4.2 Magnetic field lines do not cross, and always run from the north to the south pole of a magnet.

Magnetic field lines:
- show the direction that a compass would point
- always run from the north pole to the south pole
- do not cross
- represent a strong magnetic field when they are bunched closely together
- represent a weak magnetic field when they are spaced further apart.

SciFile

In-built navigation
Many animals, such as honeybees, dolphins, tuna, whales and pigeons, contain tiny crystals of a magnetic material in their brains or stomachs. These act as tiny internal compasses, preventing the animal from getting lost and helping them find their homes.

Attraction and repulsion of poles

Magnetic poles may be attracted to each other, or repelled by a magnetic force. Poles that are the same are called like poles. Like poles repel each other, pushing them apart. Poles that are different are called unlike poles. Unlike poles attract each other, pulling them together. These situations are shown in Figure 7.4.3.

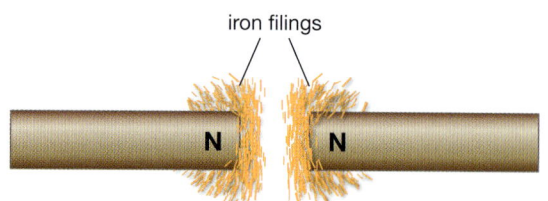

North and north poles repel, pushing each other away.

South and south poles also repel.

South and north poles attract, pulling together.

FIGURE 7.4.3 The movement of iron filings reveals the attraction or repulsion of magnetic poles. Unlike magnetic poles attract and like magnetic poles repel.

SciFile

Floating on air

The repulsion of magnetic poles can make things float. This is called magnetic levitation. Maglev trains float about 10 cm above their tracks. They can reach speeds of 500 km/h because they operate with very little friction.

Magnetic domains

The metals iron, nickel and cobalt are attracted to magnets. Scientists believe that inside each of these metals are tiny magnetic particles called **domains**. Each of these acts like a mini-magnet, and has a north and a south pole. In a piece of magnetised iron, the domains all point in the same direction. This makes the metal act like a magnet. The domains in a piece of unmagnetised iron point in random directions, as shown in Figure 7.4.4.

Prac 1 p. 319

Temporary and permanent magnets

If you stroke an iron nail many times in the same direction with a bar magnet, then the nail begins to act like a magnet itself. This happens because you have pulled all of its domains into line. After a while, the effect wears off and the domains point in random directions once again. In this case, the nail is called a **temporary magnet** because it only acts like a magnet for a short period of time. **Permanent magnets** can be made by hitting or heating the metal to make the domains stay in this arrangement.

Magnets made from soft iron lose their magnetism more easily than magnets made from cast iron. If a magnet is heated or dropped, its domains may be knocked out of alignment, destroying its magnetism. Data stored on the magnetic strip on a credit card can be lost when placed near a strong magnetic field.

Electricity flowing through a wire creates a magnetic field around it. If the wire is wound into a coil, it produces a much stronger magnetic field. Inserting a piece of iron inside the coil increases its strength even further. Such a device is called an **electromagnet** and is shown in Figure 7.4.5. It acts like a bar magnet. An electromagnet is a temporary magnet, because when the electricity in the wire is switched off, the magnetic field is also switched off.

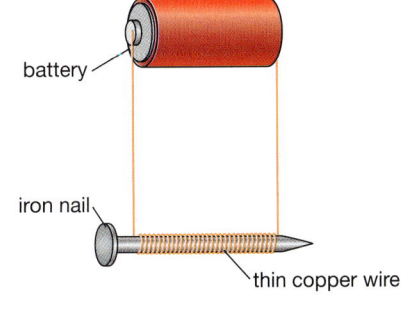

FIGURE 7.4.5 An electric current in the wire creates a magnetic field. This field can be turned on and off with the current.

Prac 2 p. 320   Prac 4 p. 322

FIGURE 7.4.4 Domains are like mini-magnets. When they line up, they form a magnet with a north and a south pole. When they point in random directions, the metal has no magnetic properties.

SciFile

An unexpected discovery

In 1820, the Danish scientist Hans Oersted (1777–1851) told his students that he did not believe in any link between magnetism and electricity. He placed a compass near a wire through which an electric current was flowing. To his surprise, he saw the compass needle move! Oersted realised that electricity in a wire creates a magnetic field around it. He described the year of his great discovery as the happiest year of his life!

CHAPTER 7 • FORCES   **313**

Uses of magnets

Magnets and electromagnets are used in many everyday devices and are used in most modern technologies. They are in every household appliance that has an electric motor. They are used to store information in computers and tablets, and on EFTPOS and credit cards. Figure 7.4.6 shows some examples of how magnets are used.

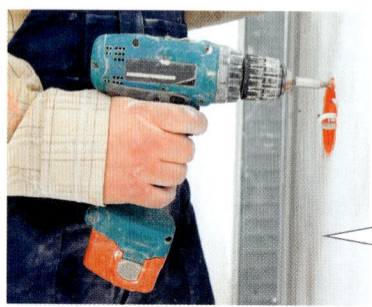

Drills, hairdryers, food processors and remote controlled toy cars have electric motors containing an electromagnet.

Credit cards store information on a magnetic strip.

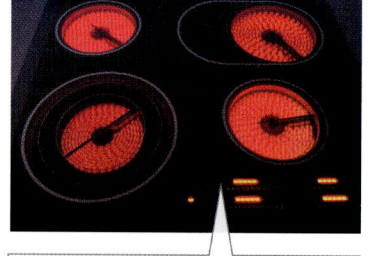

Induction cooktops use electricity to focus a magnetic field above the points on the cooktop where the food is heated. Pots and pans used on the cooktop must be made from iron or steel.

All speakers produce sound due to the vibration of a central cone which contains an electromagnet.

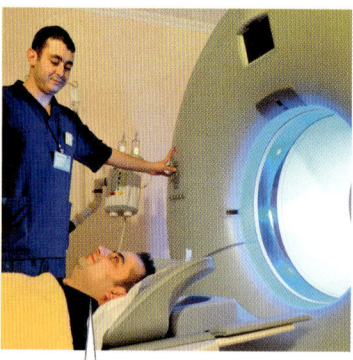

An MRI (magnetic resonance imaging) machine is used to look inside the human body. The patient lies inside a donut-shaped electromagnet. Diseased tissue behaves differently from normal tissue in a magnetic field.

FIGURE 7.4.6 Magnets have many uses.

Earth's magnetic field

Earth itself has a magnetic field. It behaves as though it has a huge bar magnet in its centre like that shown in Figure 7.4.7. Scientists believe Earth's magnetic field is generated by molten rock moving inside Earth's core.

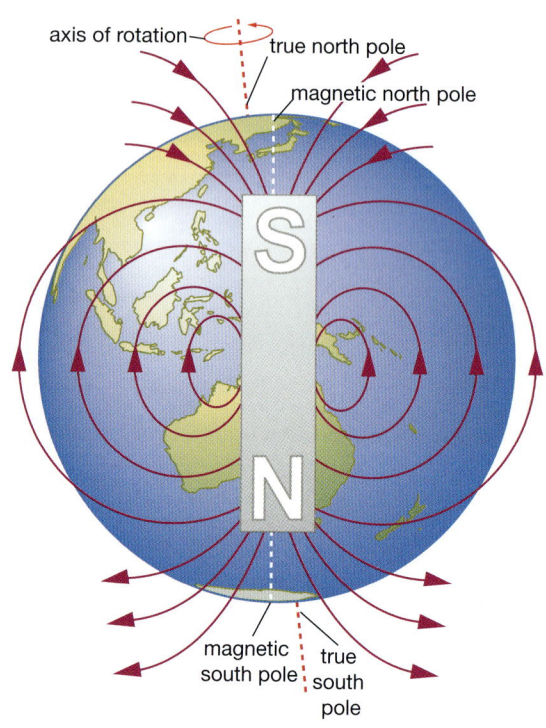

FIGURE 7.4.7 Earth's magnetic field behaves as though there was a giant bar magnet inserted inside the Earth. The magnetic poles of north and south are flipped upside down compared to Earth's north and south poles.

Electric fields

The force of gravity acts on objects inside the Earth's gravitational field. A magnetic force acts on objects within a magnetic field. An **electrostatic force** acts on objects within an **electric field**. An electric field exists between objects that have different electrical charge. An electric field is the reason that electric current flows in an electric circuit. To understand an electric field you need to know about atoms.

What is an atom?

All substances are made up of tiny particles called **atoms**. Atoms themselves are made up of even smaller particles called protons, neutrons and electrons. Neutrons are found deep within an atom in a region called the nucleus. They have no charge. Protons are also found in the nucleus and have a positive charge (+).

Electrons move in the space around the nucleus as shown in Figure 7.4.8. They have a negative charge (–). Usually an object has equal numbers of protons and electrons. It has no overall charge and is said to be neutral.

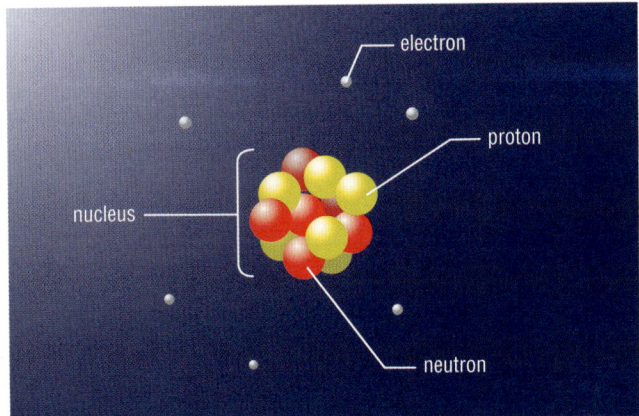

FIGURE 7.4.8 An atom consists of three types of smaller (subatomic) particles, called protons, neutrons and electrons.

Charging up

If one material is rubbed against another, electrons may move from one substance onto the other. If this happens, the number of protons and electrons in each is no longer balanced. Some materials, such as plastic, rubber and wood, will build up charge when rubbed with another substance. Such materials are called electrical **insulators**. Electrons cannot flow freely through them. The reason electrical wires are covered with plastic is because plastic is an effective electrical insulator. Metallic objects do not build up charge, because electrons can flow through them. These materials, such as a copper electrical wire, are called electrical **conductors**.

Electrons move from a silk cloth onto a balloon when the two are rubbed together (Figure 7.4.9). The silk cloth has lost electrons and is now **positively charged**—it has more protons than electrons. The balloon has gained electrons and is **negatively charged**—it has more electrons than protons. When an object becomes charged, it is said to have **static electricity**.

A force field called an electric field exists around any object that is charged. Any charged object positioned within this field will experience a force, called an **electrostatic force**.

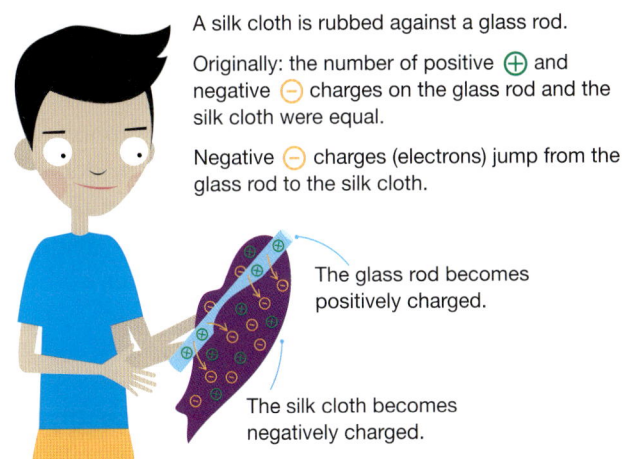

FIGURE 7.4.9 Electrons are rubbed from the glass rod and jump onto the silk cloth. As a result, the glass rod becomes positively charged and the silk cloth is negatively charged.

Figure 7.4.10 shows what happens when these charged objects are placed next to each other. If placed inside an electric field, two objects with different types of charge will attract each other, while those with the same type of charge will repel. Note that a charged object may also attract a neutral object.

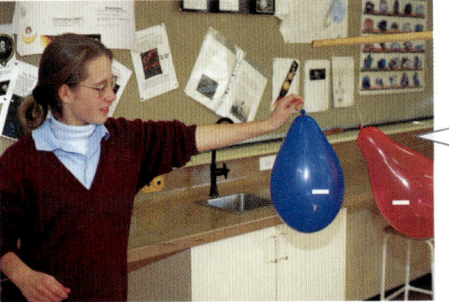

FIGURE 7.4.10 Objects with like charge are repelled, and objects with unlike charge are attracted.

A machine called a Van de Graaff generator separates positive and negative charge by friction between a moving rubber belt and a plastic pulley. Negative charges are released to flow through to the ground, while positive charges are transferred onto the dome of the generator. The girl touching the dome of the generator in Figure 7.4.11 becomes positively charged. Her hair stands up because each strand of hair is repelling the hair around it!

Static discharge

Static electricity describes a build-up of charge. If you walk across carpet on a dry day and touch a metal door handle, you could get a shock. Friction between your feet and the carpet rub electrons from the carpet onto you, making you and the carpet both charged. Normally, this charge gradually leaks back out of your shoes to the ground, or into the air, and you become neutral once more. If there is a big build-up of charge, or if you wear rubber-soled shoes that stop the charge from escaping, extra electrons can jump from you to the metal door handle as a spark. You feel this as a small electric shock. If you were to touch another person while charged, electrons would jump onto this person and you would both feel a static shock.

Prac 3 p. 321

AB 7.8

FIGURE 7.4.11 Each strand of this girl's hair is positively charged and is repelling all of the hair around it.

SciFile

Super sparks

Lightning is a giant spark caused by a build-up of charge in a cloud during a thunderstorm, dust storm, bush fire or a volcanic eruption. A flash of lightning can travel at 140 000 km/s. There is enough energy in a single lightning strike to keep a light bulb glowing for a year!

MODULE 7.4 Review questions

Remembering

1. Define the terms:
   a. magnetic field
   b. insulator
   c. electrostatic force
   d. electromagnet.

2. What term best describes each of the following?
   a. the north and south ends of a magnet
   b. a magnet that only acts for a short while
   c. a material that allows electrons to flow through them.

3. Which of the following words correctly complete the following sentences?
   a. A magnetic force is a contact/non-contact force.
   b. As you get closer to a magnet, the size of the magnetic force increases/decreases.
   c. A north pole of one magnet is attracted to the north/south pole of another magnet.
   d. A magnet is strongest/weakest at its poles.

4. List five places you could find a magnet in your home.

5. Atoms consist of two types of charged particles. What is the name of:
   a. a positively charged particle?
   b. a negatively charged particle?

6. A plastic ruler loses electrons when it is rubbed with woollen fabric. After rubbing, will the ruler be positively or negatively charged?

7. In the science4fun activity on page 311, iron filings are sprinkled around a bar magnet. Draw a diagram to show the magnetic field you would expect.

Understanding

8. Explain why a steel ball bearing is attracted to a magnet.

Applying

9. Will the magnets in Figure 7.4.12 attract or repel?

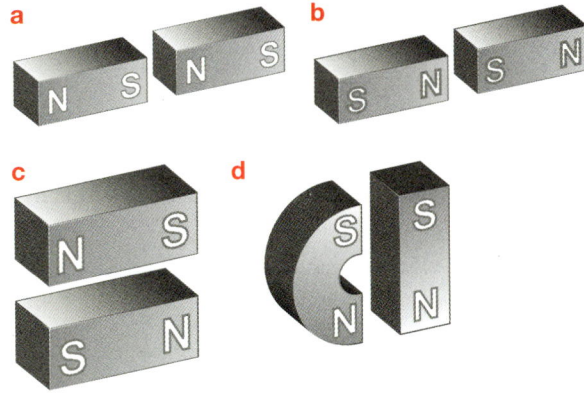

FIGURE 7.4.12

10. a. Identify the direction a compass would point if it is placed at X in Figure 7.4.13.
    b. i. In which position, X, Y or Z, would an iron nail be attracted to the magnet with the most force?
       ii. In which of these positions is the magnetic field strongest?
       iii. How do you know this from the diagram?

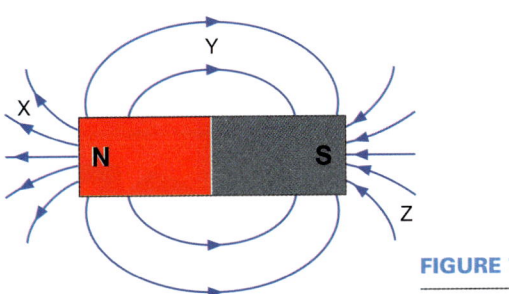

FIGURE 7.4.13

11. In Figure 7.4.14, identify the:
    a. positively charged object
    b. negatively charged object
    c. neutral object.

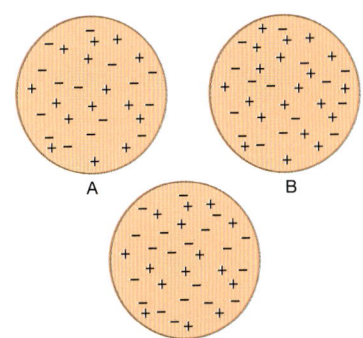

FIGURE 7.4.14

CHAPTER 7 • FORCES 317

MODULE 7.4 Review questions

12 In each of the following situations, identify which two surfaces are rubbing together to produce static electricity.
   a Hundreds-and-thousands stick to the walls of the plastic bottle in which they are stored.
   b After driving to a shop, you get a shock as you close the car door.
   c Your clothes crackle as you lift them out of the clothes dryer.

Analysing

13 The bar magnet and the horseshoe magnet shown in Figure 7.4.15 are attracted to each other.
   a Analyse Figure 7.4.15 to identify whether each of the combinations A and B will attract or repel.
   b State whether you needed more information to decide if combination B attracted or repelled.

Combination A

Combination B

FIGURE 7.4.15

14 Classify each of the following materials as an electrical conductor or an electrical insulator.
   a aluminium foil
   b polystyrene cup
   c plastic ruler
   d glass rod
   e copper pipe
   f rubber hose.

Evaluating

15 Drivers are asked to turn off mobile phones while putting petrol in a car. Propose a reason why.

16 Ralph and Julia are walking along the red carpet to an Academy Awards ceremony. Upon touching a gold banister, Julia receives a nasty static shock.
   a Analyse why Julia got a shock.
   b Propose ways in which she could prevent this from happening again.

Creating

17 Lying on a bench in front of you is nail A, which is not magnetised, and nail B, which has been treated to become a temporary magnet.
   a Construct a diagram to show the possible domains inside nails A and B.
   b Construct another diagram to show how you would expect the domains of nails A and B to look tomorrow.

MODULE 7.4 Practical investigations

1 • Magnetic shielding *Planning & Conducting* *Evaluating*

Purpose
To test which materials a magnetic field can pass through and which materials block a magnetic field.

Timing
15 minutes

Materials
- 50 g mass
- paperclips
- cotton thread
- Blu Tack, Plasticine or sticky-tape
- bar magnet
- retort stand, bosshead and clamp
- sheets of different materials such as cardboard, plastic, aluminium foil, iron, steel, tin, wood, glass, copper

Procedure
1. Set up the equipment as shown in Figure 7.4.16.
2. Find the maximum distance that can be left between the paperclip and the magnet before the paperclip falls.
3. Insert each different material between the paper clip and the magnet and record what happens in your results table.

Results
In your workbook, construct a table like that shown below to record your observations. Include a title for your table.

Material	Paperclip stayed/dropped

Review
1. In terms of the strength of a magnetic field, explain why the paperclip fell when the distance between it and the bar magnet increased.
2. Which materials allowed a magnetic field to pass through them?
3. Which materials acted as a magnetic shield?
4. Magnetic fields can damage sensitive electronic equipment. Propose a use for materials that act as magnetic shields.

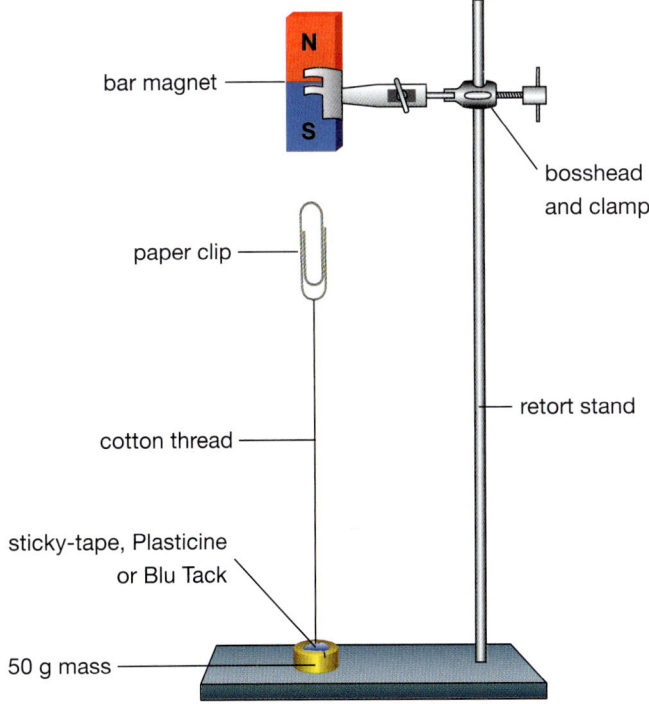

FIGURE 7.4.16

CHAPTER 7 • FORCES **319**

MODULE 7.4 Practical investigations

2 • Making an electromagnet

Processing & Analysing **Evaluating**

Purpose
To make an electromagnet and test how its strength can be increased.

Timing 30 minutes

Materials
- 6 V lantern battery or a power pack
- large nail (at least 7 cm long)
- compass
- paperclips
- switch
- 2 insulated wires (one long) with alligator clips
- retort stand
- bosshead and clamp
- piece of string about 30 cm long

SAFETY Take care when connecting your circuits.

Procedure
1. Copy the table from the Results section into your workbook.
2. Test to see if the nail on its own will pick up any paperclips.
3. Suspend a paper clip from a retort stand so that it hangs just above the benchtop.
4. Connect the shorter wire from the battery or power pack to the switch.
5. Carefully wind the long wire 10 times around the nail as neatly as you can. Make sure that you only wind the wire in one direction along the nail.
6. Connect one end to the switch and the other to the power supply as shown in Figure 7.4.17.
7. Set the power pack to 6 volts DC.
8. Press the switch down and record the minium distance the paperclip was positioned before it deflected towards the electromagnet.
9. Repeat steps 4–7 increasing the number of coils as shown in the table.
10. Test which end of the nail is the north pole and which is the south pole using a compass.
11. Reverse the connections to the power supply and repeat step 10.

Results
Record your results in a table like this. Include a title for your table.

Number of turns on wire	Minimum distance before deflection (cm)
0	
10	
20	
30	
40	
50	

Review
1. State the effect of the number of turns of the wire on the number of paperclips picked up.
2. Describe what happened to the poles of the electromagnet when the connections were reversed.

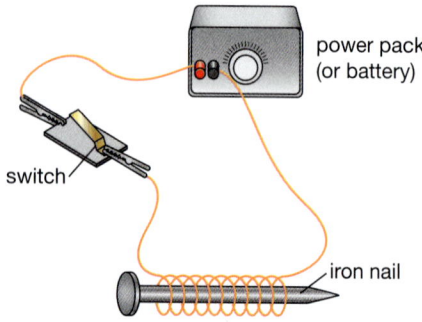

FIGURE 7.4.17 Setting up your circuit with the electromagnet

MODULE 7.4 Practical investigations

3 • Investigating static electricity

Planning & Conducting · **Evaluating**

Purpose
To explore static electricity.

Timing 15 minutes

Materials
- plastic comb
- sheet of paper
- woollen material
- balloons
- string
- retort stand and clamp

Procedure
1. Rub the plastic comb vigorously on the woollen material. Bring it close to some tiny pieces of paper. Write down what happens.
2. Turn a water tap on and carefully turn it down to get the finest stream that you can of steadily flowing water. Rub the comb with the woollen material and hold it close to the stream of water. Draw a diagram to show what you observe.
3. Blow up a balloon and rub it with the woollen material. See if you can make the balloon 'stick' to the wall.
4. Blow up a second balloon. Attach a piece of string to each of the balloons and then tie these to a retort stand. Rub both balloons with the woollen material. Draw a diagram to show what happened.

Results
Record your observations for each step in the procedure.

Review
1. Explain why you could pick up the pieces of paper with the comb.
2. Describe what happened to the stream of water when the charged comb was brought near to it.
3. Why did the water behave in this way?
4. Propose an explanation for your observations in the two balloon activities.

CHAPTER 7 • FORCES 321

MODULE 7.4 Practical investigations

• STUDENT DESIGN •

4 • Magnetising a nail

Purpose
To magnetise a nail and test a related variable.

Timing 30 minutes

Materials
- nail
- bar magnet
- paperclips

Procedure
1. Design an experiment that will magnetise a nail by stroking it repeatedly (in the same direction) with a bar magnet.
2. Decide on a variable to investigate. You could investigate:
    a. how the number of strokes given to the nail by the magnet affects the number of paperclips picked up, or
    b. if the time the nail remains magnetic varies for the number of strokes made.
3. Write your procedure in your workbook.
4. Before you start any practical work, assess your procedure. Assess any risks that your procedure might involve and what you might do to minimise those risks. Show your teacher your procedure and your assessment of its risks. If they approve, then collect all the required materials and start work.

Use the STEM and SDI template in your eBook to help you plan and carry out your investigation.

Results
Record your observations.

Review
1. Outline what is happening inside the nail:
    a. when it is being stroked by the permanent magnet
    b. when it loses its magnetism.
2. Construct a conclusion for your investigation.
3. Assess the method you used in your investigation.

Extension: Build a magnetic sculpture
Build an interesting sculpture by using at least one magnet and objects containing iron such as paperclips, nails or washers. The sculpture can be supported underneath or from above by one or more magnets. Once you have created your sculpture, take photographs of it from different angles. Annotate your photographs to label and explain the forces that hold the sculpture together. Before commencing your design, ensure that you have conducted a risk assessment.

MODULE 7.5 Simple machines

Whenever you use scissors or use a handle to open a door, you are using a simple machine. Simple machines include levers, ramps, wedges, screws, pulleys, wheels and gears. Simple machines make a job easier by changing the size, direction or speed of a force.

Machines and force

A simple machine is a device that makes a job easier to do. For example, the job of lifting the sound equipment in Figure 7.5.1 into the van is a difficult one—the equipment is heavy so a large force is needed to lift it. The job is much easier if a ramp is used—the force required is reduced and so the task becomes easier.

FIGURE 7.5.1 Loading and unloading heavy sound equipment would be almost impossible without the use of a ramp.

science 4 fun

Turning on a tap

Can you turn on a tap without its handle?

Collect this...

a tap that has a handle that can be unscrewed

Do this...

1. Place a plug in the sink to avoid losing any parts down the drain.
2. Carefully unscrew a tap.
3. Place the screw, handle and cap on the basin.
4. The tap should now just be a spindle, or an axle.
5. Try to turn on the tap using just your hands.
6. Offer a challenge to your friends and family. Can it be done?

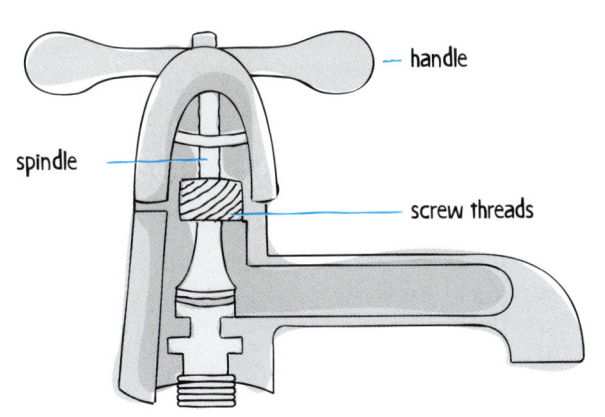

Record this...

1. Describe what happened.
2. Explain why you think this happened.

CHAPTER 7 • FORCES 323

The force you need to apply to get a job done is called the **effort**. In this case, a ramp reduces the effort needed to lift the sound equipment into the van. The **load** is the force actually required to do the job. For the sound equipment, the load is its weight.

Simple machines work in three different ways. They can:
- change the size of a force
- make things speed up
- change the direction of a force.

Force multipliers

Lifting a car to change a tyre would require a huge effort. For most of us, this task would be impossible despite it being a small distance. However, a jack makes the task easier. You apply a small force to the handle of the jack, but wind it over a very long distance. This is shown in Figure 7.5.2. In the same way, a crowbar can be used to shift a rock that would otherwise be too heavy to move. Machines used in this way magnify the force you apply to do a job. These machines are known as **force multipliers**.

FIGURE 7.5.3 A crowbar acts as a lever. The lever increases the force that you can supply making it easier to move the rock.

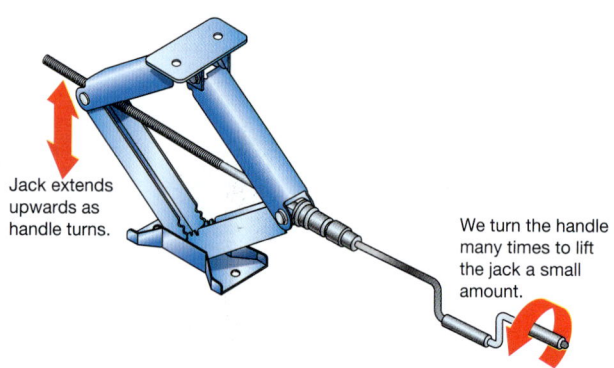

FIGURE 7.5.2 To lift a car you use a small force to turn the handle of a jack through a very large distance.

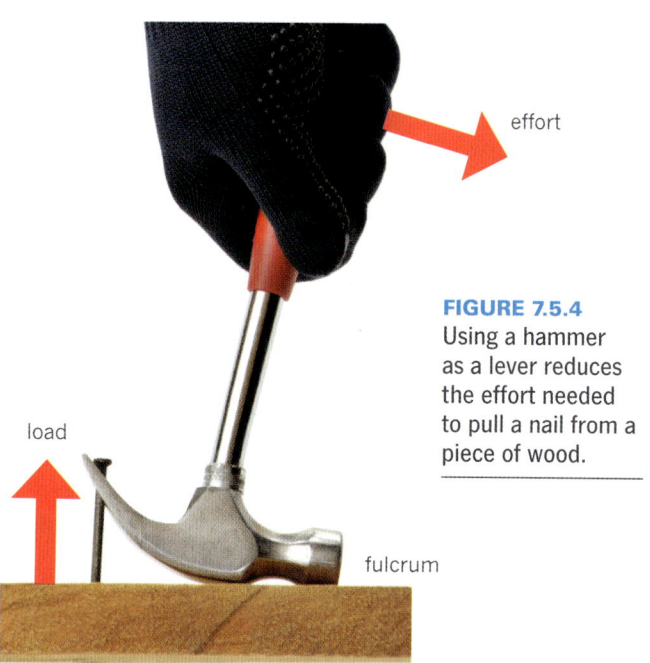

FIGURE 7.5.4 Using a hammer as a lever reduces the effort needed to pull a nail from a piece of wood.

Levers

A **lever** is a simple machine that is made of a long, rigid object, such as a stick or metal rod. It also needs a pivot or **fulcrum** about which it rotates. Most levers are force multipliers. The crowbar in Figure 7.5.3 is an example.

Figure 7.5.4 shows how the claw of a hammer can be used as a lever to pull a nail (the load) out of a piece of wood. If you used just your fingers, then the effort required would be so high that the task is nearly impossible. Using a teaspoon to remove the lid of a coffee tin multiplies force in the same way (Figure 7.5.5).

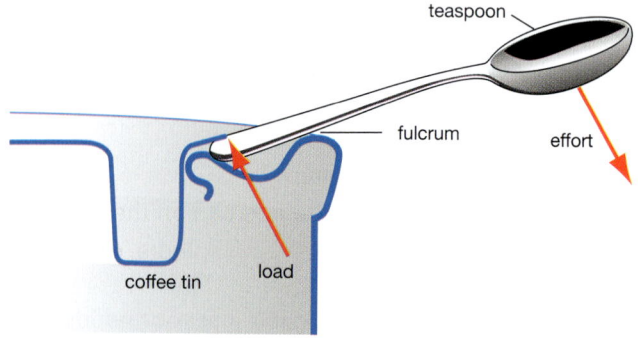

FIGURE 7.5.5 The teaspoon is a lever that multiplies the force, making it easier to remove the lid from the tin.

When you use a lever as a crowbar, or use a teaspoon to lift a lid from a tin, you are using a **first-class lever**. First-class levers have the fulcrum positioned between the effort and load forces. The trolley shown in Figure 7.5.6 is a first-class lever because the fulcrum (the axle that has the wheels attached) lies between the load that is being carried and the effort force the woman applies to the trolley. When you use a first-class lever, the lever moves through a larger distance than the load. In doing so, the force applied is increased. Other first-class levers are pliers, tin snips, hedgecutters and scissors.

If the load is positioned between the fulcrum and the effort, then the lever is called a **second-class lever**. This also acts as a force multiplier. A wheelbarrow is an example of such a lever. By lifting the handles a greater distance than the load, the force applied is increased. This is shown in Figure 7.5.7. Other second-class levers include bottle openers, paper guillotines and nutcrackers.

Prac 1 p. 331

AB 7.9

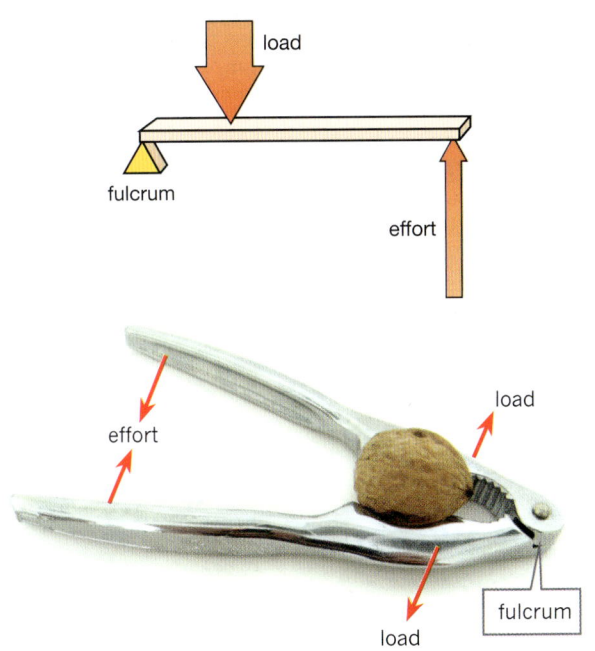

FIGURE 7.5.7 A second-class lever has its fulcrum positioned at one end of the system and the effort at the other. These levers also act as force multipliers.

Wheels

The centre of a **wheel** is called its **axle** and the outside of a wheel is its **rim**. This is shown in Figure 7.5.8 on page 326. A wheel on an axle is a special type of lever—each spoke of the wheel is a lever, the axle is the fulcrum and the wheel rim is the outer end of the lever. Figure 7.5.9 on page 326 shows how a wheel can act as a force-multiplier. When you apply a force to turn on a tap, the handle acts as a wheel. It increases the force you apply at its centre, allowing the axle to turn.

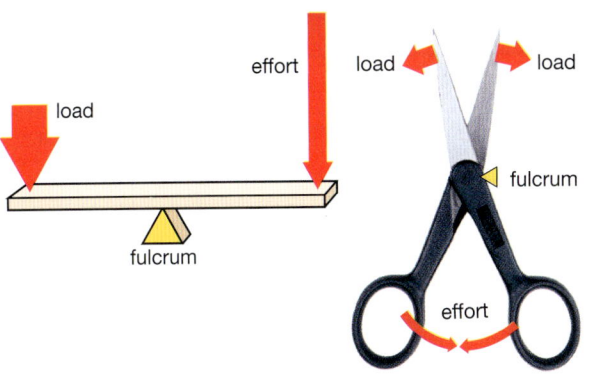

FIGURE 7.5.6 A first-class lever has its fulcrum positioned between the effort and the load. These levers act as force multipliers.

STEM p. 335

CHAPTER 7 • FORCES **325**

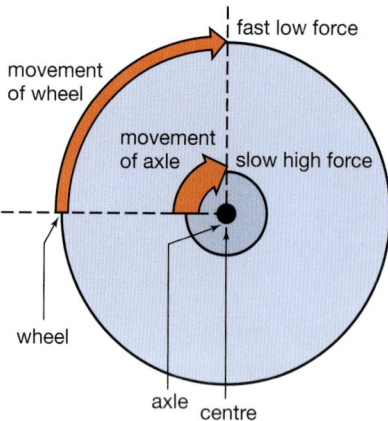

FIGURE 7.5.8 The rim of the wheel rotates with greater speed than the axle in its centre. As the wheel turns, the force at its centre is larger than the force at its rim.

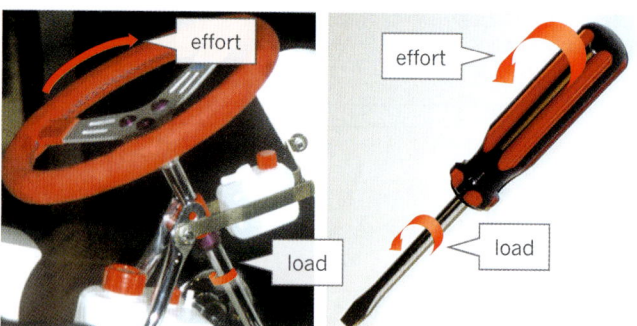

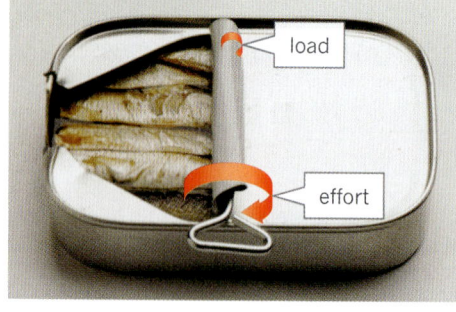

FIGURE 7.5.9 In each of these situations, a wheel is used to multiply force

Gears

Prac 2 p. 332

Gears are wheels that have teeth around their rim. Gears can mesh directly together, or be joined by a chain, such as on a bicycle or in the overhead cam shaft in some car engines. A set of gears that are connected is called a **gear train**. When one gear turns, the gear it interlocks with also turns, but in the opposite direction. The gear that supplies the force is called the **driving gear**. The gear that is connected to this gear is called the **driven gear**.

If the driving gear is smaller than the driven gear, then the combination acts as a force multiplier. The larger cog will rotate more slowly, but the force it delivers is much larger. This gear combination is called gearing down and is useful when you need a large force (Figure 7.5.10). For example, it would help a car get up a hill or help in winching it out when it is bogged.

FIGURE 7.5.10 Gearing down makes the driven gear rotate more slowly than the driving gear, but with greater force.

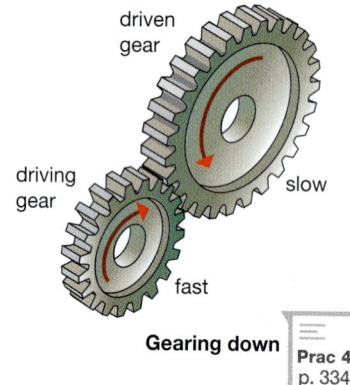

Gearing down

Prac 4 p. 334

Inclined planes

While levers, wheels and gears can multiply a force to make it larger, **ramps** or **inclined planes** are force multipliers that *reduce* the effort force needed to do a job. Ramps make it easier to shift heavy sound equipment into vans. They also make it easier to climb a mountain. This is why roads wind up mountains. Ramps reduce the effort force required, by making you travel further. The longer the ramp, the less steep it will be. It will be easier to climb but you need to go further.

Screws

Prac 3 p. 333

A screw has a double inclined plane winding around it. This spiral is called the thread. A screw is easy to screw into wood but you need to turn it many times with your screwdriver. This can be seen in Figure 7.5.11.

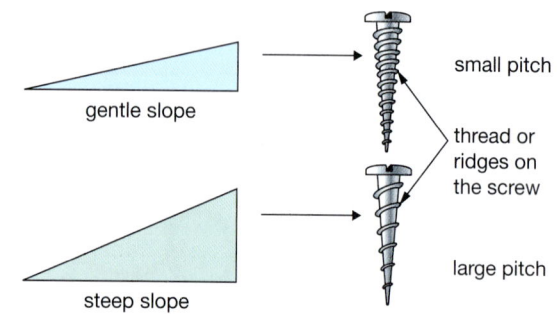

FIGURE 7.5.11 The pitch of a screw is the spacing between its thread. The screw with the small pitch has a longer spiral inclined plane and requires less force to be screwed into wood.

Speed multipliers

A machine can also make something move faster than otherwise possible. A machine such as the egg beater shown in Figure 7.5.12 is called a **speed multiplier**.

Tennis racquets, cricket bats and golf clubs are levers that are used as speed multipliers so that they hit balls at high speed. They are examples of **third-class levers**, with the effort positioned between the fulcrum and the load. This is shown in Figure 7.5.13.

FIGURE 7.5.12 The beaters spin much faster than the handle turns in this speed-multplier.

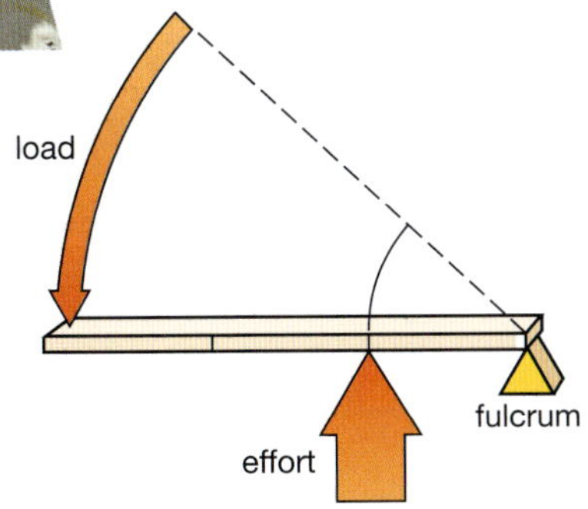

FIGURE 7.5.13 Cricket bats are third-class levers. They are speed multipliers.

AB 7.8

When using a broom, you apply a large effort force to the handle. The handle moves though a much shorter distance than the end of the broom, which moves much faster, but with less force. The broom acts as a third-class lever. It has traded an increase in force for an increase in speed.

Gears can also act as speed multipliers. If the driving gear is larger than the driven gear then the combination acts as a speed multiplier. This happens because one turn of the large cog makes the smaller cog spin a number of times. This gear combination is called gearing up. It is useful when using an eggbeater, where you require the beaters to spin faster than the handle turns. This is shown in Figure 7.5.14.

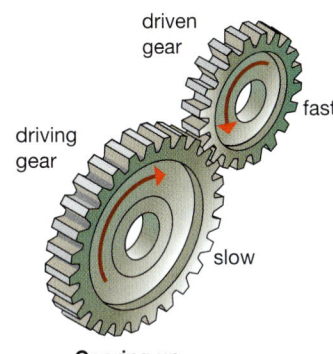

FIGURE 7.5.14 Gearing up makes the driven gear spin faster but with less force.

Changing the direction

A machine can also change the direction in which a force acts.

Wedges

Imagine trying to bite into an apple without your front teeth. Your front teeth, called *incisors*, cut like a knife. These are simple machines called **wedges**. A wedge is a double inclined plane that moves through another object. Wedges are used to split objects because they change the direction of a force by 90° and increase its size. When an axe is pushed downwards, the wedge of the axe head pushes the wood apart, as shown in Figure 7.5.15. Pins, needles, nails and doorstops are all examples of wedges.

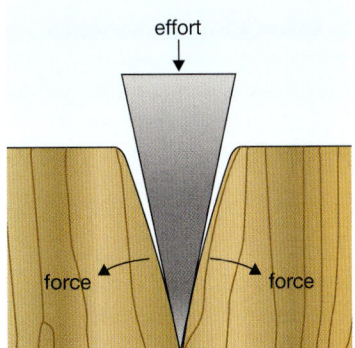

FIGURE 7.5.15 A wedge changes the direction of a force, splitting an object.

CHAPTER 7 • FORCES 327

Pulleys

Sometimes it is necessary to change the direction of a force. To lift a set of Venetian or Roman blinds, it is much easier to apply a downwards force on a cable than to try to lift it upwards from a height. A simple way of doing this is to use a **pulley**. A pulley is a wheel with a groove around it into which a rope or chain can move. Pulleys can also be used as force multipliers if more than a single pulley is used. The single pulley shown in Figure 7.5.16 changes the direction, but not the size of the effort force required to lift a load. Using two pulleys halves the size of the effort force required. In this case, the force is applied over a greater distance.

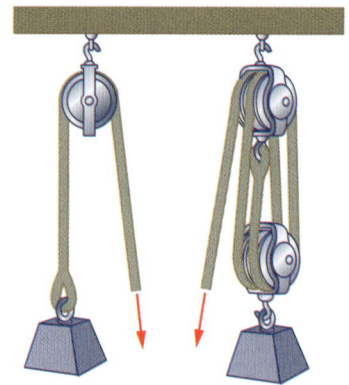

FIGURE 7.5.16 The arrangement shown on the right provides four times the force of the single pulley on the left.

Working with Science

WIND TURBINE TECHNICIAN

With the growth of renewable energy, there is an increasing need for people skilled in the installation, maintenance and repair of renewable energy technology, such as wind turbines. Many jobs in renewable energy industries are still relatively new and so opportunities are expected to grow rapidly over the next ten years.

Wind turbine technicians are responsible for the installation, maintenance and repair of wind turbines. An understanding of how wind turbines work and the forces that act on them is an important part of this job. The blades of the turbines have a curved shape, like aeroplane wings, to capture as much wind energy as possible. The blades rotate because of forces caused by wind flowing over them. These forces cause the gears inside the wind turbine to spin, powering the electricity generator.

To become a wind turbine technician, you will need to complete a Certificate 4 in large-scale wind generation. You can also gain the necessary skills by completing an apprenticeship as an electrician or mechanic, followed by on-the-job training to learn the specialist skills needed for working with wind turbines. Wind turbine technicians often work outdoors, sometimes at great heights (Figure 7.5.17)! Technicians may also work in manufacturing facilities, ensuring that the equipment involved in the manufacturing of turbines is running smoothly and that the parts of the turbines are assembled correctly (Figure 7.5.18). As a wind turbine technician, you get to work in an exciting new field while playing an important part in making our society more sustainable.

Review

1. Why do you think opportunities in the renewable energy sector are expected to increase?
2. What skills do you think are important for a wind turbine technician to have?

FIGURE 7.5.17 A wind turbine technician servicing a turbine. Often this job involves working at great heights.

FIGURE 7.5.18 A wind turbine technician working inside a factory making turbines

MODULE 7.5 Review questions

Remembering

1. Define the terms:
   a. load
   b. fulcrum
   c. axle
   d. gears
   e. pulley.

2. What term best describes each of the following?
   a. the force you need to apply to do a job
   b. inclined plane
   c. the outside of a wheel
   d. the gear that supplies a force
   e. a series of connected gears.

3. What are three ways a machine can make a task easier?

4. Which of these statements are true and which are false?
   a. A lever is a simple machine that can increase the effort supplied to get a job done.
   b. If using a crowbar to lift a tree stump, then the tree stump is called the effort.
   c. A crowbar used as a lever rotates about a point called the fulcrum.
   d. When using the claw of a hammer to pull a nail out of a piece of wood, the hammer acts as a force multiplier.

5. Recall which class of lever multiplies speed.

6. State which simple machine could be called a:
   a. double inclined plane
   b. spiral inclined plane.

7. List two examples each of a wheel being used as a:
   a. force multiplier
   b. speed multiplier.

Understanding

8. Most levers used in ball sports are third-class levers. Explain why.

9. A tennis player serving a ball will toss it into the air and reach upwards to hit the ball. How does this increase the speed of their serve?

Applying

10. Identify whether each of the following machines makes a task easier by increasing the size of a force, speeding something up, or changing the direction of a force.
    a. axe
    b. crowbar
    c. hand drill.

11. Ping uses a chisel to lift the lid from a paint tin. Identify what acts as the:
    a. load
    b. effort
    c. fulcrum.

12. Identify the following as first-, second- or third-class levers.
    a. load positioned between the fulcrum and the effort
    b. effort positioned between the fulcrum and the load
    c. fulcrum positioned between the effort and the load.

13. Copy the table below into your workbook. Identify how the simple tasks shown are usually completed, the types of simple machines used to perform these tasks and how these tasks could be performed without these simple machines and write your responses in the table.

Simple machines

Task	How we do this task	Type of simple machine involved	How we could do this without this machine
opening a tin			
opening a door			
cutting paper			
turning on a tap			
opening a pencil case			
beating eggs			

MODULE 7.5 Review questions

Analysing

14 Classify the following as an inclined plane, wedge or screw:
 a corkscrew
 b axe
 c electric fan
 d car park ramp
 e chisel
 f escalator.

15 Classify the objects shown in Figure 7.5.19 as first-, second- or third-class levers.
 a for the scales
 b bottle opener
 c tweezers
 d for the hammer.

FIGURE 7.5.19

16 a Copy each diagram in Figure 7.5.20. Analyse how each object operates and label the position of the fulcrum (F), load (L) and effort (E) on each diagram.
 b Which class of lever is shown in each diagram.
 c State whether each is a force multiplier or a speed multiplier.
   i for the shovel
   ii fishing rod
   iii pliers.

  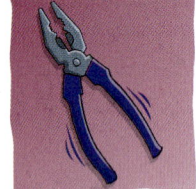

FIGURE 7.5.20

17 Copy the three gear trains from Figure 7.5.21. Analyse the direction of rotation and speed of each gear and show these on your diagram.

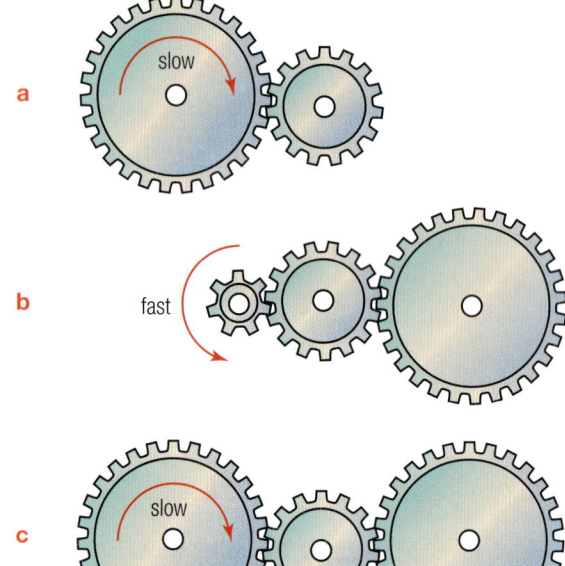

FIGURE 7.5.21

Evaluating

18 Propose a reason why a tap without its handle is nearly impossible to turn on or off.

19 The person shown in Figure 7.5.22 needs to get to the top of this dam wall. There are two options: climb straight up or use the stairs on the right.
 a Identify which will be the easiest way to the top.
 b Justify your choice.

FIGURE 7.5.22

330 PEARSON SCIENCE 7 2ND EDITION

MODULE 7.5 Practical investigations

1 • Modelling a see-saw

Purpose
To investigate how the effort force required to balance a load on a see-saw is affected as it is moved closer to the fulcrum.

Timing
60 minutes

Materials
- metre ruler
- stiff cardboard square
- 2 plastic cups
- slotted masses
- masking tape
- scissors

Procedure

1. Copy the results table below into your workbook. Alternatively, construct a spreadsheet with similar columns.
2. Use the scissors and ruler to score two lines so that the square is divided into thirds. Bend the cardboard to make a triangular prism to use as a fulcrum, as shown in Figure 7.5.23.
3. Position the ruler so that the fulcrum is halfway along its length.
4. Tape one of the plastic cups at one end of the ruler, so that its centre sits at the 10 cm mark, and a second cup at the 90 cm mark.
5. Put 100 g of masses in the first cup and measure how much mass needs to be added to the second cup to balance this.
6. Repeat this process with the centre of the second cup positioned above the 85, 80, 75, 70, 65 and 60 cm marks along the ruler.

Results
Record all measurements in your results table or spreadsheet.

Review

1. Was more or less mass required to balance the load as the effort force moved closer to the fulcrum of the see-saw?
2. Have you have experienced this yourself on a see-saw?
3. Calculate the missing values in your table or spreadsheet by carrying out the following calculations:
   - column 3 = column 1 × column 2
   - column 6 = column 4 × column 5
4. State whether the values calculated above are similar. Explain your result.

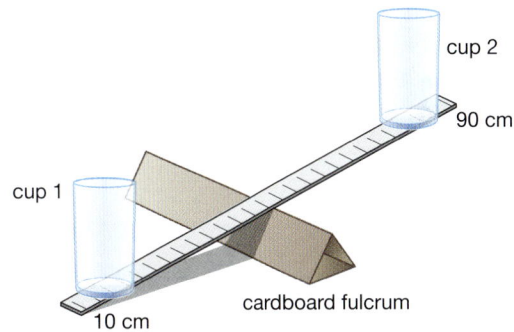

FIGURE 7.5.23

Balancing a see-saw

1	2	3	4	5	6
Mass in cup 1 (g)	D_1 (distance of cup 1 from fulcrum) (cm)	Mass in cup 1 × D_1	Mass in cup 2 (g)	D_2 (distance of cup 2 from fulcrum) (cm)	Mass in cup 2 × D_2
100	40			40	
100	40			35	
100	40			30	
100	40			25	
100	40			20	
100	40			15	
100	40			10	

MODULE 7.5 Practical investigations

2 • Using a wheel and an axle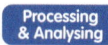

Purpose
To build a simple machine consisting of a wheel and an axle.

Timing
30 minutes

Materials
- 250 mL beaker or tin can
- 2 paperclips
- length of stiff wire
- sticky-tape
- 100 g mass
- string

Procedure
1. Set up the equipment as shown in Figure 7.5.24a. Tape the two paperclips to hold the wire axle in position.
2. Try to lift the 100 g mass by twisting the wire around using your thumb and index finger.
3. Remove the paperclips and remove the wire. Bend the end without the masses to form a handle, as shown in Figure 7.5.24b.
4. Reassemble the equipment and try to lift the masses by turning the handle.

Review
1. How difficult was it to lift the masses using the straight piece of wire.
2. Why did bending the wire make the task easier?
3. This handle is acting as a lever. Explain why turning the handle provides the force advantage needed to lift the mass.
4. Identify three places you have seen systems similar to this being used to provide a force advantage.

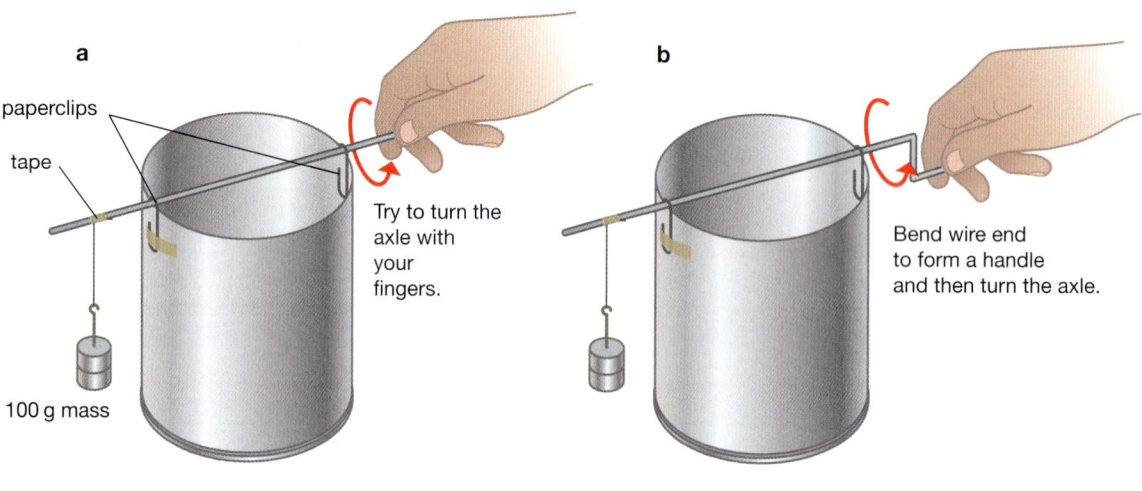

FIGURE 7.5.24

MODULE 7.5 Practical investigations

3 • Using ramps

Purpose
To measure the force required to lift a cart vertically and to lift it using ramps of differing slope.

Timing
30 minutes

Materials
- trolley
- spring balance (or force sensor)
- a number of books or a couple of blocks or bricks to elevate ramp
- wooden ramp
- spring balance
- protractor

Procedure
1. Copy the results table into your workbook.
2. Position a plank of wood on a pile of books (or a brick and some books) to make a ramp that is about 10 cm high, as shown in Figure 7.5.25.
3. Attach the trolley to a spring balance (or force sensor). Carefully lift it vertically until its rear is level with the height of your ramp. Record this weight as the load force.
4. Measure the angle of elevation of the ramp and its distance from the base to the pile of books. Record these values in the table.
5. Slowly drag the trolley up the ramp to the pile of books. Record the effort force required.
6. Repeat steps 4 and 5 for four different angles of the ramp. Measure the new ramp length and effort force each time.

Results
Record all measurements in your results table.

Effort to lift mass up a ramp

Angle of ramp (°)	Distance along ramp (cm)	Effort to pull trolley up ramp (N)

Review
1. Which ramp required the greatest effort force—the ramp with the large or small angle?
2. Explain why this occurred, considering how the distance of the ramp varied with the changing angle.
3. List three situations in which using a ramp at a shopping centre is useful.

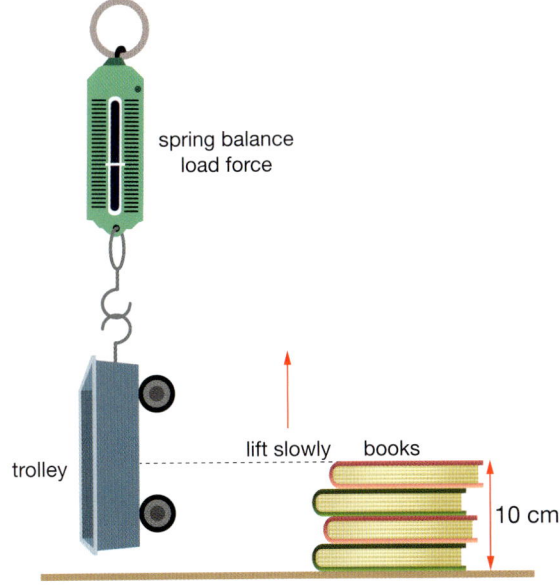

FIGURE 7.5.25

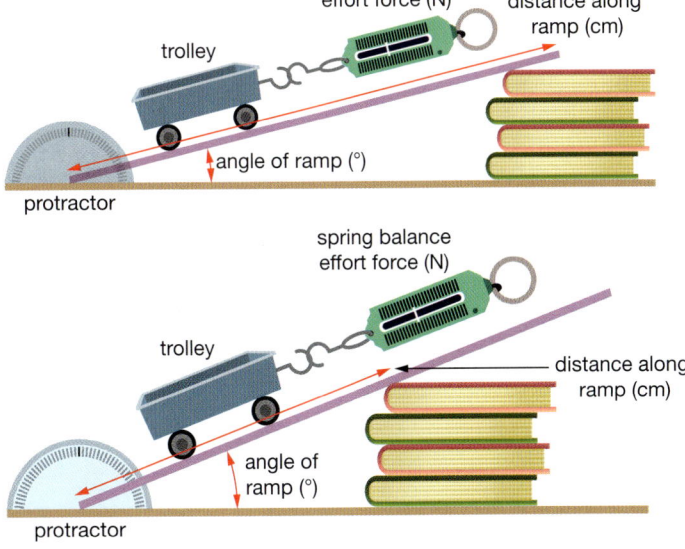

CHAPTER 7 • FORCES 333

MODULE 7.5 Practical investigations

4 • Investigating bicycles

Purpose
To examine the gearing combinations of a bicycle.

Timing
45 minutes

Materials
- geared bicycle
- broom handle
- piece of chalk

Procedure
1. Copy the results table below into your workbook. Alternatively, construct a spreadsheet with similar columns.
2. Lift the rear of the bicycle off the ground and support it against two stools or benches, as shown in Figure 7.5.26. You may need to ask a friend to hold the front of the bike to keep it stable.
3. Select the first gear, so that the chain wheel is on the smallest sprocket and the rear sprocket is on the largest.
4. Make a mark with chalk on the rear tyre. Slowly turn the pedals one revolution and count how many revolutions the rear wheel makes in this time.
5. Record this data in the first row of your table.
6. Count the number of teeth on the front and rear sprockets and enter this data.
7. Repeat steps 3–6 for another four gear combinations.

2. Fill in column 5 by completing the following calculation:
   - column 5 = column 3/column 4

Review
1. a Identify which gear combination is best suited to riding:
   i uphill
   ii along a flat, easy road.
   b Justify your choice.

FIGURE 7.5.26

Results
1. Record all your findings in your results table.

Gear ratios

1 Combination number	2 Number of turns of rear wheel for one turn of pedals	3 Number of teeth on chain wheel sprocket (N_1)	4 Number of teeth on rear wheel sprocket (N_2)	5 Gear ratio $\frac{N_1}{N_2}$
1				
2				
3				
4				
5				

MODULE 7.5 Practical investigations

How does a yo-yo work?

Background
For her birthday, Rachel was given a yo-yo. It took a bit of practice for Rachel to flick her wrist so that the yo-yo string unwound and then brought the yo-yo back up into her hand. Rachel brought the yo-yo to school and asked her science teacher how yo-yos work.

Instead of explaining to the students, Rachel's teacher brought ten yo-yos in the next day and asked the students to try to explain how a yo-yo works.

Problem
Your task is to use your knowledge and understanding of forces to explain to another year 7 student how a yo-yo works.

Engineering design process
In your investigation:
- filming the yo-yo may enable you to slow down the images to work out how the yo-yo works
- manipulating the yo-yo by hand as if it were operating in slow-motion may help to work out how it works
- if possible, dismantle the yo-yo to examine the axle and method of string attachment.

Present your findings in a written report, an oral presentation or by producing a video.

Lifting that crate

Background
Stan's warehouse for imported car parts is near a river. With a possible flood coming he needs to raise his heavy crates of car parts up to the higher shelves. Unfortunately, his forklift truck has broken down and will not be fixed before the floodwater arrives. Stan has some rope, metal poles, plastic pipes, wheel rims, tape and the wood from old crates. The warehouse has strong metal framing from which his rope can be attached (Figure 7.5.27).

FIGURE 7.5.27

Problem
Your task is to design a system Stan could use to lift his heavy crates off the floor. If time allows, you might even build a model of your solution.

Materials
Modelling materials such as:
- string for rope
- LEGO rods for pipes and wheel rims
- ice-cream sticks for wood
- any other materials supplied by your teacher

Engineering design process

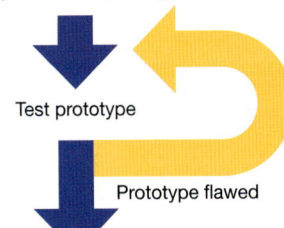

FIGURE 7.5.28 Engineering involves the application of science to design, construction and maintenance of structures, machines and devices.

Hints
- How high would the crates need to be to avoid floodwater?
- Can they be lifted and supported in progressive amounts or is one lift better?
- Can the curved surface of pipes be used for another purpose?
- How were heavy object lifted in factories and worksites before electricity and hydraulics were invented?

CHAPTER 7 • FORCES 335

CHAPTER 7 Chapter review

Remembering

1. Which of the following statements are true and which are false?
   a. Gravity is a contact force.
   b. Weight is measured in kilograms.
   c. The north pole of a magnet will attract the north pole of another magnet.
   d. The magnetic field of a magnet is strongest at its poles.
   e. A proton has a negative charge.
   f. An electric field exists around a charged particle.
2. List four examples of a pushing force.
3. Name a surface that has little friction.
4. Is an electromagnet a temporary or a permanent magnet?

Understanding

5. Explain how a non-contact force can act on something without touching it.
6. Dropping a magnet could destroy its magnetism. Why?
7. If a comb pulled through your hair becomes negatively charged, predict the charge of your hair.

Applying

8. The diagrams shown in Figure 7.6.1 show forces acting on objects A, B, C and D.
   a. Identify whether the forces are balanced or unbalanced in each case.
   b. In the case of any unbalanced forces, predict the direction in which the object will move.

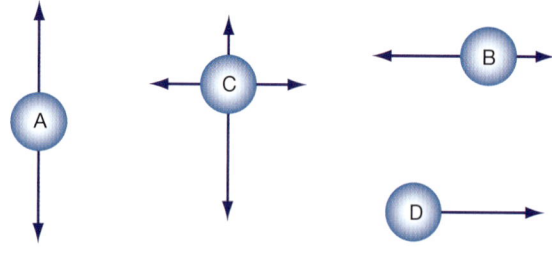

FIGURE 7.6.1

9. One gear is rotating anticlockwise. It is connected to a second gear. Predict the direction that the second gear will turn.

Analysing

10. Compare:
    a. mass and weight
    b. friction and gravity
    c. the force between like poles of a magnet and the force between unlike poles
    d. a force-multiplier and a speed-multiplier.
11. a. State the class of lever acting in each situation in Figure 7.6.2. Letters represent the following: e = effort, f = fulcrum, l = load.
    b. Classify which act as force multipliers and which act as speed multipliers.

FIGURE 7.6.2

12. Analyse the combination of gears shown in Figure 7.6.3.
    a. If gear 1 rotates in a clockwise direction, state which direction gears 2, 3 and 4 will rotate.
    b. If axle 2 is rotated, identify whether gear 1 or gear 3 will turn faster.

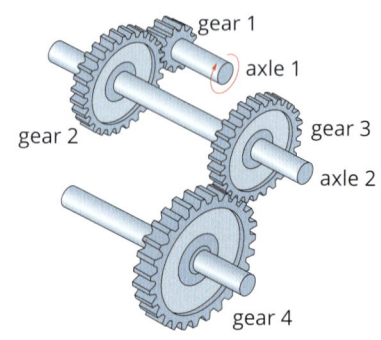

FIGURE 7.6.3

CHAPTER 7 Chapter review

13 Analyse the force diagram in Figure 7.6.4.
 a State in which direction the boat is moving.
 b Predict what will happen to the speed of the boat when many fish have been caught in the net.
 c If the boat is travelling at a constant speed, compare the size of the thrust and drag forces acting on the boat.

FIGURE 7.6.4

Evaluating

14 Mariah flicks a coin across the stone benchtop in her kitchen. Later that day, she tries to flick the same coin across sand at the beach.
 a Predict which coin would travel the greater distance.
 b Justify your prediction.

15 A length of wire is used to make coils A, B and C shown in Figure 7.6.5. An iron nail is inserted into coil C.
 a Propose which of the three coils would produce the strongest electromagnet when connected to a power supply.
 b Justify your choice.

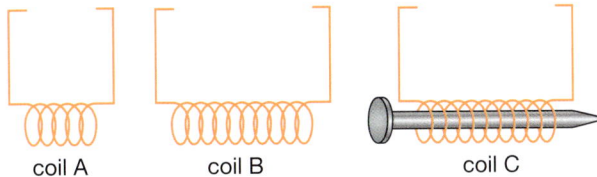

FIGURE 7.6.5

16 Use Figure 7.6.6 to answer the following.
 a How many pulleys are being used by the system?
 b It is so much easier it will be to lift an object using such an arrangement. Propose reasons why.

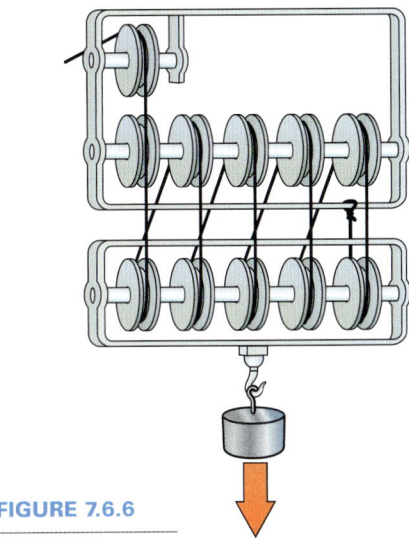

FIGURE 7.6.6

17 a Assess whether you can or cannot answer the questions on page 279 at the start of this chapter.
 b Use this assessment to evaluate how well you understand the material presented in this chapter.

Creating

18 Construct a diagram to show an arrangement of gears in a gear train to act as a force multiplier.

19 Use the following ten key terms to construct a visual summary of the information presented in this chapter.
 gravity
 weight
 mass
 force
 force field
 friction
 motion
 magnetic field
 electric field
 simple machine

CHAPTER 7 Inquiry skills

Research

1 *Questioning & Predicting* *Communicating*

Some animals move through water as they swim, some animals move through air as they fly and some animals move over land as they run.

a Find images of at least three animals of each type listed above. Describe the outer covering of each of these animals. Propose how these layers and the shape of the animal assists it in reducing friction as it moves.

b Search to find and download footage of three animals in motion. Describe the shape of the animal in motion. Do any of these animals have a streamlined shape while moving?

c Draw a diagram of a new type of animal that either swims or flies. Explain which features it has that assist in reducing friction as it moves.

Present your research in the forms indicated in each part above.

2 *Evaluating* *Communicating*

You may have heard of the term 'zero gravity' to explain what happens to astronauts on a mission in space. Research what this term means.

a Define the term 'zero gravity'.

b Describe situations in which zero gravity would exist.

c Search for footage of astronauts in a zero gravity environment. Explain how astronauts train to prepare their bodies to tolerate zero gravity conditions.

d Various experiments have been conducted in zero gravity environments. Describe two such experiments.

e Design two experiments that you would like to see performed in zero gravity. Explain why you chose these experiments.

Present your research in digital form with links to relevant videos.

3 *Questioning & Predicting* *Communicating*

Earth's magnetic field has long been used as a navigation guide by people and various species of wildlife.

Research to find:

a an image showing the structure of Earth's magnetic field

b what scientists believe causes Earth's magnetic field

c what protection is provided by Earth's magnetic field

d the meaning of the term 'geomagnetic reversal'

e evidence of past geomagnetic reversal

f predictions about how Earth's magnetic field may change in the future.

Present your findings in digital form.

4 *Questioning & Predicting* *Processing & Analysing*

Write down a list of your favourite toys that you have ever played with.

a Do any of these toys move, or have moving parts? List the toys that you've mentioned that do have move moving parts.

b Design your own toy with moving parts.

c Draw a series of diagrams showing how your will construct your toy, what it is made from, how much it will cost to build.

d With permission, construct your toy.

e Create a brand name, packaging and even a marketing plan for your toy.

f Do you need to modify your design so that the parts move more smoothly or so that the toy works better? Make a note of any changes you make.

g Show your toy to your classmates and explain to them which forces act to make your toy move and also which simple machines are incorporated in your toy.

Your class could vote on a 'People's Choice' award winner for the best toy in your class.

CHAPTER 7
Inquiry skills

Thinking scientifically

1 Siobhan finds two horseshoe magnets in her school laboratory that do not have their poles marked correctly (Figure 7.6.7). One has poles labelled A and B, while the other has poles labelled X and Y. She tests each using a third horseshoe magnet and finds the following combinations attract.

FIGURE 7.6.7

Knowing that opposite poles attract, select which of the following pairs of poles will attract:

A   X and B;   Y and A
B   X and A;   X and B
C   Y and A;   Y and B
D   X and A;   Y and B

2 Look at the three blocks of wood resting on different surfaces, as shown in Figure 7.6.8. If you were to pull each by its hook, propose which block would:
   a   move with the least friction
   b   move with the most friction:
      A   Block A
      B   Block B
      C   Block C

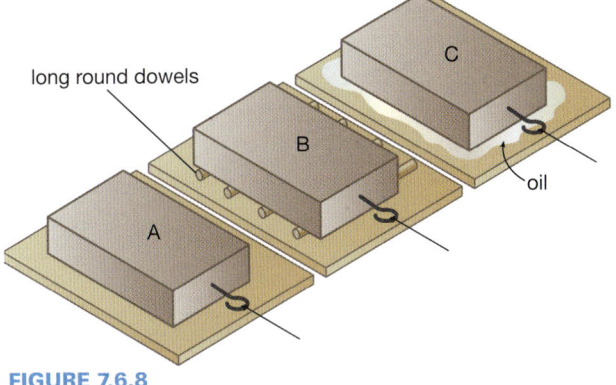

FIGURE 7.6.8

3 The total force acting on an object can be found by comparing the overall horizontal and the overall vertical forces. A box is acted upon by three forces as shown in Figure 7.6.9.

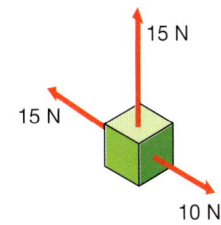

FIGURE 7.6.9

   a   In which direction will the box move as a result of these forces?
      A   upwards and to the left
      B   upwards and to the right
      C   downwards and to the left
      D   downwards and to the right
   b   Draw the block with three arrows as shown in Figure 7.6.9 in your workbook.
       Draw two more force arrows on the block, which together add an additional combined force of 10 N upwards on the block.
   c   Redraw the original block with the three forces. Draw four additional forces that have no overall effect on the motion of the block.
   d   Repeat part c but draw six new force arrows.
   e   Draw a new block with no forces acting on it. Add five force arrows to the block such that the net force acting is 20 N to the right.

4 From the mid-1990s to the present, the installation of car airbags has become more widespread in motor vehicles. Figure 7.6.10 on page 340 shows the uptake of different types of airbags and the uptake of ESC, or electronic stability control. In the time frame that these safety features have become more common in cars, the number of deaths on the road has halved. Figure 7.6.11 on page 340 shows the estimated reduction in fatalities linked to driver, passenger and side airbags and to ESC.
Figure 7.6.12 on page 340 shows the estimated reduction in fatalities due to these and other factors.
   a   Can it be assumed that the introduction of airbags and ESC alone has resulted in the reduction of deaths on Australian roads in the past 20 years?
   b   In which year were passenger airbags standard in 40% of cars?
   c   In 2007, driver airbags were standard in about half of all cars sold. How many years later were passenger airbags standard in half of cars sold?

CHAPTER 7 • FORCES   339

CHAPTER 7 Inquiry skills

FIGURE 7.6.10

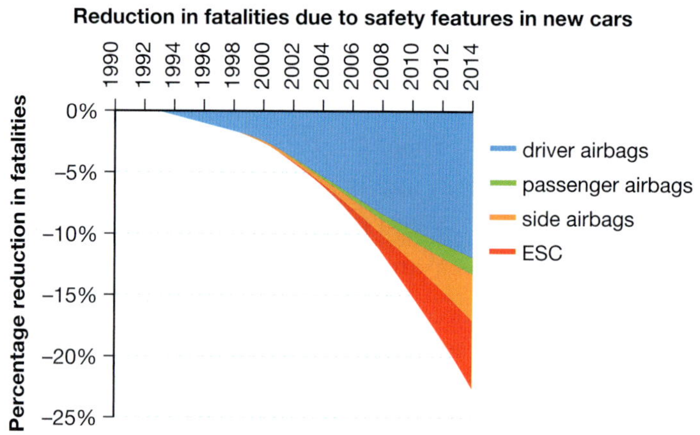

d List the four car safety features studied in Figure 7.6.11.
e Describe what each of these four car safety features are. Research if you are not sure.
f State which one is believed to have had the largest effect in reducing fatalities.
g Propose three reasons why this may be the case.
h List the five factors that have contributed to reducing the road toll, as shown in Figure 7.6.12.
i State how each of these factors makes driving on the roads safer.
j The graph in Figure 7.6.12 shows data from 1990 to 2014.
On this graph, 'vkt' is vehicle kilometres travelled.
  i The wearing of seatbelts was made compulsory in Australian states and territories by 1973. Predict whether the number of deaths on the roads per 1000 vehicles would have been higher, lower or about the same as the level as 1990 in the 1960s.
  ii Justify your answer above.
  iii Research to find whether you were correct.

FIGURE 7.6.11

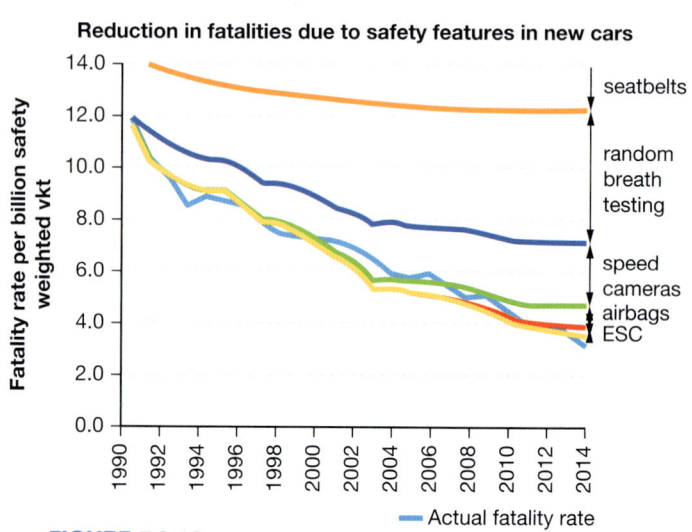

FIGURE 7.6.12

CHAPTER 7 Glossary

acceleration: increase in speed (verb: accelerate)

air resistance: or drag: friction that acts on an object moving through the air

atoms: tiny particles that make up all matter

atom

axle: shaft on which a wheel rotates

centre of mass: a point where you can imagine all of an object's mass is concentrated

conductor: substance through which electrons can flow, such as metal

contact force: force that acts between two objects that touch or are in contact, for example friction

deceleration: decrease in speed (verb: decelerate)

domains: small regions inside a magnet that each behave as a mini-magnet, with a north and a south pole

driven gear: the gear that receives force from a driving gear

driving gear: the gear that supplies force to another gear

effort: force applied to a lever to overcome the load

electric field: region around a charged object in which another object will experience a force

electrostatic force: force experienced inside an electric field (also called electric force)

first-class lever: lever with effort and loads located at each end, and fulcrum in the centre

first-class lever

force: a push, pull or a twist that can change an object's motion

force field: region of space in which an object will experience a non-contact force

force multiplier: machine that increases the force applied for a task, such as a first-class lever

force

friction: force that acts against an object's motion

fulcrum: point about which a lever pivots

gears: a wheel with teeth used to turn another gear wheel

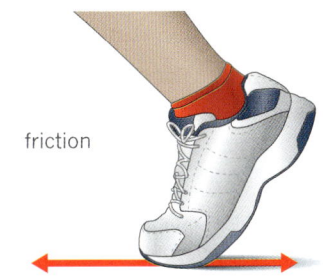
friction

gear train: a system of interconnected gears

gravitational field: region of space in which an object will experience a force due to gravity

gravity: force of attraction between any two objects, for example between the Earth and a person

inclined plane (ramp): a simple machine that reduces the effort needed to lift a load by increasing the distance through which it acts

inertia: the tendency of an object to resist change in its motion

insulator: substance through which electrons do not flow, such as plastic

inclined plane

CHAPTER 7 • FORCES 341

CHAPTER 7 Glossary

lever: simple machine consisting of a rigid rod that pivots about a point

load: a force, often a weight, on a lever or material

magnetic field: region around a magnet in which a magnetic force is experienced

mass: the amount of matter in a substance (measured in kilograms)

negatively charged: having more negative charges (electrons) than positive charges (protons)

newton (N): unit used to measure force

non-contact force: force that acts on an object from a distance

permanent magnet: a material that remains magnetic for a long time

poles: ends of a magnet, may be a north or a south pole

positively charged: having more positive charges (protons) than negative charges (electrons)

pulley: a wheel with a groove over which a rope or cable can slide, used to change the direction of a force

ramp: an inclined plane used to help lift an object

rim: outer edge of a wheel

second-class lever: lever with the fulcrum located at one end, the effort at the other and the load in the centre

simple machine: a device that makes work easier by changing the size or direction of a force. Examples are ramps and levers.

speed multiplier: a machine that requires a small movement of an effort to produce a large movement of a load, such as a third-class lever

static electricity: a build-up of electric charge

temporary magnet: a material that keeps its magnetism for a short time

terminal velocity: the point at which a falling object ceases to accelerate, but falls at constant speed, because its weight is balanced by air resistance

third-class lever: lever with the fulcrum located at one end, with the load at the other and effort in the centre

traction: grip

wedge: a double inclined plane that moves through another object, changing the direction of force

weight: the force of gravity pulling on an object; measured in newtons (N)

wheel: a type of lever with an axle acting as its fulcrum

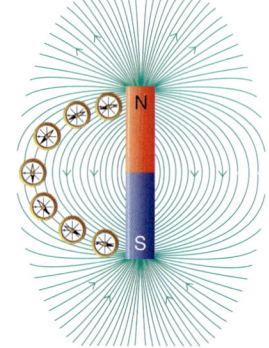
magnetic field

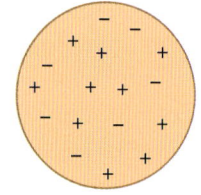
negatively charged

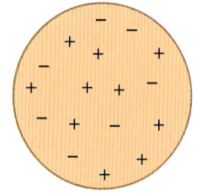
positively charged

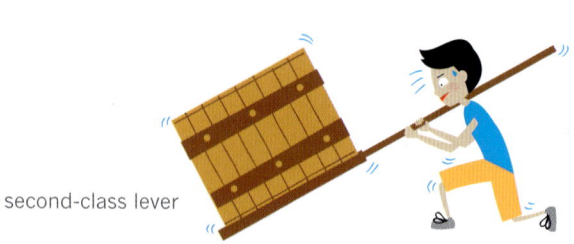
second-class lever

terminal velocity

third-class lever

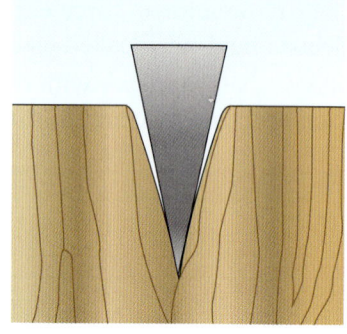
wedge

AB 7.11

342 PEARSON SCIENCE 7 2ND EDITION

CHAPTER 8

Earth in space

Have you ever wondered...

- how we know that the Earth moves around the Sun and not the Sun around Earth?
- why Earth or the Moon don't just spin off into space?
- why we see changing amounts of the Moon in the night sky?
- what causes day and night?
- why we have seasons?

After completing this chapter you should be able to:

- explain why different cultures had different stories for what they saw in space
- describe how telescopes and space probes provided new evidence about space
- research developments in the understanding of astronomy
- describe how different models of the solar system developed
- outline how gravity keeps planets in orbit around the Sun
- compare the orbit times of Earth and the Moon
- compare times for the rotation of Earth, the Sun and the Moon
- model how solar eclipses, lunar eclipses and phases of the Moon depend on how Earth, the Sun and the Moon are arranged in space
- explain why different regions on Earth experience different seasons.

This is an extract from the Australian Curriculum
Victorian Curriculum F–10 © VCAA (2016); reproduced by permission

MODULE 8.1 The night sky

Look into a clear night sky and you will see stars, cloudy blurs of light made up of even more stars, and most probably part of the Moon. A few of those starry points of light aren't stars at all but are planets. A couple of 'stars' might even shoot across the sky. They aren't stars either, but meteors. The night sky is Earth's view of the rest of the universe, its stars, constellations, planets, dwarf planets, moons, meteoroids, asteroids and comets.

science 4 fun

Liquid craters

Meteorite strikes have marked the Moon with many craters. Many have peaks in their centre. What forms them?

Collect this...
- water
- drinking glass
- drinking straw

Do this...
1. Put a small amount of water in the glass.
2. Place one end of the straw in the water and then block the other end with your finger.
3. Keep your finger on the straw while you remove it. It should be holding some of the water.
4. Release the pressure of your finger so that a couple of drops fall back into the glass.
5. Carefully observe what happens to the surface of the water as the drop falls in, particularly at its centre.

Some meteorites have so much energy that they melt the Moon's rock, causing it to slosh around and to form a small peak in the centre of the crater. Droplets form a similar peak when they hit liquid water.

Record this...
1. Describe what happened.
2. Explain why you think this happened.

Observing the night sky

Without a telescope, most people can see about 2000 stars in the night sky. The exact number depends on the weather and on light conditions. If you are in the city and it is a cloudy night, you will not see as many stars as you would on a clear night in the country, away from light pollution. Also, a bright full Moon will reduce the number of stars you can see.

Not all those bright points of light are the same: some have different colours, some are much brighter than others and some move at different speeds. If you use a telescope, then some of these differences become even more apparent. These visible differences arise because not every point of light in the night sky is a real star. While most points of light are stars, a handful are planets, and a few might be meteoroids or comets.

The objects seen in the night sky are known as **celestial** objects. A scientist who studies celestial objects is known as an **astronomer**.

The Moon

When it is visible, the Moon is the biggest and brightest object in the night sky. The Moon doesn't make its own light but acts like a giant mirror in the sky, reflecting sunlight down to Earth. This is the light you see. Sometimes you will see the Moon's full face (known as a full Moon) with its craters and 'seas'. At other times, you will only see half of it (a quarter Moon) or a slice of it (a crescent Moon). These different views of the Moon are known as its **phases**. These are shown in Figure 8.1.1.

The Sun lights up half of the Moon but on Earth we don't always see that half: what phase you see depends on how the Moon, the Sun and Earth are arranged in space.

Prac 1 p. 350 | AB 8.2

SciFile

Close but you can't see it!

Proxima Centauri is not far from Alpha Centauri, a double star system that forms one of the pointers leading to the Southern Cross. Proxima Centauri is so close to Alpha Centauri that it is sometimes considered to be part of the same star system. You can see Alpha Centauri in Figure 8.1.2. However, Proxima Centauri itself is so faint that it cannot be seen with the naked eye.

FIGURE 8.1.2 After the Sun, Proxima Centauri is the closest star to Earth. Proxima Centauri is near Alpha Centauri but it is too faint to see in this image.

FIGURE 8.1.1 Several images of the Moon and its phases recorded over 30 days are combined in this composite. The cycle repeats itself every 30 days (roughly one month).

Stars

Stars are massive burning balls of hydrogen gas. Hydrogen comes from nuclear explosions. A type of nuclear reaction called a fusion reaction converts hydrogen into helium. Nuclear reactions release enormous amounts of energy as heat, light and radiation.

The nearest star to Earth is the Sun, being 'only' 150 million kilometres from us, which is still very far away. At this distance, the light and heat from those nuclear explosions takes just over 8 minutes to reach us.

The other stars you see in the night sky are much, much, much further away. After the Sun, the next closest star is Proxima Centauri. It is approximately 40 million million kilometres away and it takes 4.2 years for its light to reach us on Earth. The other stars you see are even further away—the light from some of them takes millions of years to reach us!

The Milky Way

A band of light runs across the night sky from one horizon to the other. In ancient times, people thought that this looked like a road made of milk. That's why it was named the **Milky Way**. You can see it in Figure 8.1.3. Scientists now know that this white band is the light from more than 200 billion stars. Most of these stars are too far away to be seen distinctly or individually from Earth, but their combined glow is one of the most spectacular features of the night sky.

SciFile

Starry, starry day

The stars are always there in the sky whether it's night or day. However, you can't see them in daylight because they can't compete with the intense brightness of the Sun.

Planets

Planets are very different from stars. They are balls of rock or gas that orbit (move around) the Sun. There are no nuclear explosions on the planets and so planets do not make their own light. Instead, they reflect light falling on them from the Sun. This allows us to see them in the night sky. They're seen as points of light that look very much like real stars.

Figure 8.1.4 shows the planets that travel around the Sun. Together, they form the **solar system**. Although the planets of the solar system are far from Earth, they are much, much closer to us than the stars.

Mercury, Venus, Earth and Mars are the closest planets to the Sun. These are known as the **terrestrial** (meaning Earth-like) planets. All these planets are rocky with a hard surface. Mercury, Venus and Mars are relatively close to Earth and are often seen in the night sky as a bright or coloured points of light.

FIGURE 8.1.3 A long time-exposure image of the Milky Way. The light pollution caused by buildings and street lighting makes it difficult to see in the city.

FIGURE 8.1.4 The eight planets of the solar system can be classified as either terrestrial or gas giants. Pluto is a dwarf planet.
(The planets in this image are drawn to scale but the distances between them are not.)

346 PEARSON SCIENCE 7 2ND EDITION

Mercury and Venus are usually visible before dawn or just after. They are often called morning or evening stars, even though scientists know that they are not really stars. At these times, Venus is the brightest 'star' in the sky. Mars appears as a red-coloured 'star'.

The outer planets–Jupiter, Saturn, Uranus and Neptune–are huge balls of gas with small and rocky cores. For this reason, they are commonly known as the **gas giants**. While Jupiter and Saturn can be seen as 'stars' with the naked eye, Neptune and Uranus can only be seen from Earth using a telescope.

Prac 2 p. 351

Other things you might see

The Moon, stars and planets are not the only things you might see in the night sky. Other things are up there that look like stars too.

Artificial satellites

Artificial satellites orbit (travel around) Earth, looking like stars travelling slowly across the night sky. They have been placed in orbit as space stations and for purposes such as communication, for observing the weather on Earth's surface, and for navigation. The International Space Station (ISS) makes its own light, but this is too dull to be seen from Earth. You see satellites because they reflect sunlight back to Earth. You can see the ISS and another satellite in Figure 8.1.5.

FIGURE 8.1.5 A time-exposure image of the International Space Station (ISS) and another satellite moving across the sky. The solar panels of the ISS reflect sunlight making it almost as bright as Sirius, the brightest star in the night sky.

Shooting stars

You may have seen something that looks like a star shooting across the night sky. Most burn out before they hit the horizon. These 'shooting stars' are space rocks burning up in our atmosphere as they plunge towards Earth.

A small rock in space is called a **meteoroid**. Meteoroids can range in size from a grain of sand to a rock 10 metres across.

Occasionally, the path of a meteoroid will bring it close enough to Earth for it to be pulled in by Earth's gravity. As the rock falls through Earth's atmosphere, it reaches speeds of more than 15 kilometres per second! As it falls, the meteoroid quickly compresses the air in front of it, causing the air to heat up. This in turn heats up the rock, much like when your bicycle pump gets hot when you quickly pump up a tyre. The enormous heat generated turns the meteoroid into a blazing fireball known as a **meteor** or 'shooting star' (Figure 8.1.6). Most meteors are so small that they burn up completely in the atmosphere. This is why most shooting stars fizzle out before they reach the ground.

However, if a meteor is large then part of it might reach the ground before it has completely burnt up. The part that reaches the ground is called a **meteorite**. Most meteorites are small, but on very rare occasions Earth is struck by a large meteorite. Occasionally, these large meteorites are **asteroids** that have strayed from the **asteroid belt**. This belt is a band of rocky objects that orbit the Sun between Mars and Jupiter. The destruction the meteorite causes depends on its size. Smaller meteorites form craters while larger ones can have devastating effects. For example, there is strong evidence that a major meteorite impact caused the extinction of the dinosaurs 65 million years ago.

FIGURE 8.1.6 A meteor burning up as it travels through the atmosphere.

CHAPTER 8 • EARTH IN SPACE

SciFile

Russian strikes

In 2013, a meteor exploded at a height of 30 kilometres above the city of Chelyabinsk in Russia, shattering windows and injuring at least 1200 people. Astronomers estimate that the meteor had a mass of around 10 tonnes, was about 3 metres in diameter and travelled at a speed of 50 000 km/h! In 1908, an even bigger meteor exploded above the largely uninhabited region of Tunguska, Russia, devastating more than 2070 square kilometres of forest.

SciFile

Meteors from comets

Astronomers usually don't know when a small meteoroid might hit Earth's atmosphere. This makes the appearance of most 'shooting stars' very unpredictable. However, some meteors are caused by Earth passing through debris left behind by comets. These are much more predictable events. Sometimes they form meteor 'showers' like the one in Figure 8.1.7.

FIGURE 8.1.7 A time-exposure image of a meteor shower. The image was taken by using a longer-than-usual exposure time. Meteor showers happen when Earth passes through the debris left by a comet.

Comets

Comets are part of the solar system because they also travel around the Sun. Comets don't appear often but when they do they are among the most spectacular sights in the sky (Figure 8.1.8). **Comets** are 'dirty snowballs' made of ice mixed with carbon dioxide and other substances. They have a head (known as a coma) and a long shining tail. One of the most famous comets is Halley's Comet. It reappears in the night sky approximately every 76 years. Its most recent appearance was in 1986.

FIGURE 8.1.8 The spectacular Comet McNaught crossed the skies of both the northern and southern hemispheres in 2007.

MODULE 8.1 Review questions

Remembering

1. Define the terms:
   a. fusion reaction
   b. phases of the Moon.
2. What term best describes each of the following?
   a. the nearest star to Earth
   b. a rock that falls through Earth's atmosphere but does not reach the ground.
3. Name the bright band of light that can be seen in the night sky.
4. a. How many stars are visible without a telescope?
   b. List factors that affect the number of stars able to be seen.
5. List the:
   a. terrestrial planets
   b. gas giants.

Understanding

6. Explain why moonlight can be considered to be sunlight.
7. Why are planets sometimes mistaken for stars?
8. Calculate the year in which Halley's Comet is likely to be next seen from Earth.

Applying

9. A drop of water is dripped into a glass of water.
   a. Predict the pattern that would result.
   b. Use your prediction to explain why craters formed when meteors struck the Moon.
10. The table below shows the average distances of the planets of the solar system from the Sun. Assume that all the planets are lined up in order from Mercury to Neptune.

    Use this information to:
    a. name the closest planet to Earth
    b. list the planets from closest to Earth to most distant from Earth.

Analysing

11. Contrast:
    a. a planet with a star
    b. a star with the Milky Way
    c. a meteor with a meteorite
    d. a meteoroid with a comet.

Evaluating

12. You see many bright points of light in the night sky.
    a. List the different types of things they could be.
    b. How likely is it to see each type? Rank them in order from most likely to least likely.
13. A meteor and a comet look similar in many ways. What would be a way of telling them apart?
14. Propose reasons why there are very few photos or videos of individual 'shooting stars' but lots of meteor showers.
15. Figure 8.1.9 shows Meteor Crater in Arizona, USA. Its name is scientifically incorrect.
    a. Why?
    b. Propose a better name for it.

FIGURE 8.1.9

16. It would be easy for astronauts to move about on the surface of Mars, but it would be impossible for them to do so on Jupiter. Propose reasons why.

Creating

17. Joe wants to demonstrate why planets 'shine' in the night sky using a torch, a mirrored disco ball and a basketball. Construct a diagram showing how he could do it.

Average distances of the planets of the solar system from the Sun

Planet	Earth	Jupiter	Mars	Mercury	Neptune	Saturn	Uranus	Venus
distance from Sun (millions of km)	150	778	228	58	4498	1427	2870	108

CHAPTER 8 • EARTH IN SPACE   349

MODULE 8.1 Practical investigations

1 • Simulating impact crafters

Purpose
To model the surface of the Moon by forming impact craters and simulating erosion. Examples of impact craters can be seen in Figure 8.1.10.

Timing 45 minutes

Materials
- 4 cups of damp sand or flour
- small plastic box or tray (such as a lunch box or take-away food container)
- several marbles or ball bearings (of various sizes if possible)
- tweezers
- piece of tissue paper or cloth
- large sheet of plastic (to clean up mess)
- digital camera or mobile phone with camera function

Procedure
1. Lay out the tray on the large sheet of plastic or set up outside.
2. Fill the tray with flour or sand to a depth of 2–3 cm. Keep at least one cup aside for later.
3. Drop a marble or ball bearing into the flour or sand to make an impact crater.
4. Using tweezers, carefully remove the marble or ball bearing. Avoid changing the shape of the crater.
5. Repeat steps 3 and 4 with marbles of different sizes from different heights until a pattern of overlapping craters has been formed.
6. Sketch or photograph the crater pattern.
7. Simulate volcanic activity by sprinkling the remaining flour or sand over a section of the crater pattern. Sketch or photograph this section.
8. Simulate erosion by lightly dragging the tissue or cloth over a section of the tray.
9. Sketch or photograph the crater pattern.
10. Simulate earthquakes by lightly tapping the side of the tray.
11. Drop several more marbles or ball bearings.
12. Sketch or photograph the crater pattern.

Results
If you took photos, print them out and label important features that you see in them.

Review
1. Can you tell from the crater patterns you made which craters were formed earlier and which were formed later? If so, explain how.
2. What effect do you think the following events would have on the shape and pattern of impact craters on the Moon if they happened after the craters were formed?
    a. volcanic activity
    b. earthquakes.
3. How would your answers to question 2a be different if the events occurred before the craters were formed?
4. Use this information to explain how astronomers can use observations like those in question 2 to write a history of the Moon's landscape.
5. Use information gained from this activity to predict what astronomers could learn from the pattern of impact craters on a moon or a planet.

FIGURE 8.1.10 Impact craters on the Moon's surface

MODULE 8.1 Practical investigations

2 • Toilet paper solar system

Purpose
To construct a scale model of the solar system that shows the distance between the planets.

Timing 30 minutes

Materials
- 300-sheet roll of toilet paper
- pen or pencil (not a felt-tipped pen)
- small stick or length of dowel

Procedure
This investigation should be done outside in an open space at least 30 m long.

1. Insert the piece of dowel through the centre of the toilet roll and hold it at either end so the toilet roll can unroll smoothly. Unroll a little of the toilet roll. At the very start of the first sheet, draw and label the Sun as shown in Figure 8.1.11.
2. Unroll the toilet roll a little further. At the end of the fourth sheet, draw a small planet. Label it Mercury.
3. The table below shows where you need to draw and label Mercury and Neptune. The scale being used here is 1 sheet = 15 million kilometres or 1 : 15 000 000. Using this scale, calculate the number of sheets you need to mark the distance from the Sun of each of the remaining planets. Neptune should be drawn at the edge of the final sheet on the roll.

Scale of distances of solar system

Planet	Distance (millions of km)	Toilet sheets
Mercury	58	4
Venus	108	
Earth	150	
Mars	228	
Jupiter	778	
Saturn	1427	
Uranus	2871	
Neptune	4498	300

Review
1. List:
   a the four terrestrial planets
   b the four gas giants.
2. Which planets are closest to each other? Are they the terrestrial planets or the gas giants?
3. The asteroid belt is about 450 million kilometres from the Sun. Identify and mark on your toilet paper solar system where the asteroid belt would be found.
4. Compare this model solar system with Figure 8.1.4 on page 346. Discuss why pictures like this are not drawn to scale.

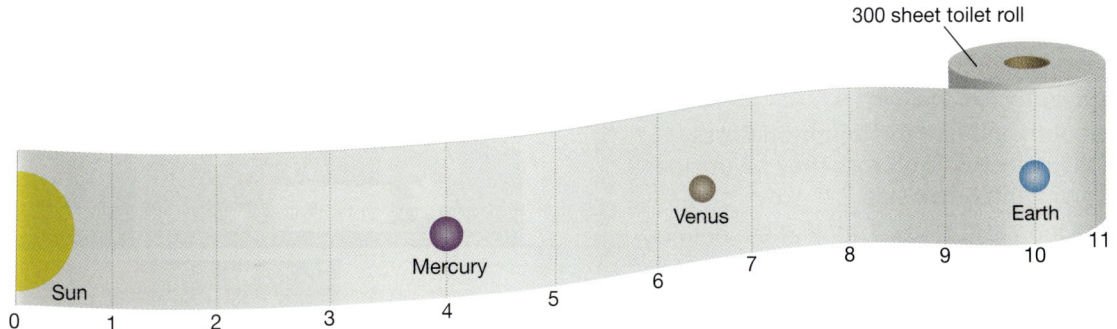

FIGURE 8.1.11

CHAPTER 8 • EARTH IN SPACE 351

MODULE 8.2 Discovering the solar system

We now take it for granted that Earth and its seven planetary neighbours orbit the Sun. However, this is a relatively new idea. Our understanding of the solar system and Earth's place in the wider universe has changed through time. Changes have happened because of the ideas, discoveries and new inventions of scientists from different countries and diverse cultures.

science 4 fun

Skywatch

Collect this...

sky map (from Pearson Science 7 Activity Book Worksheet 8.2, or similar)

binoculars (if available)

Do this...

1. Wait until the Sun has been down for at least half an hour.
2. Find a spot outside where you can see the sky and where there are as few street and house lights as possible.
3. Face south and find the Southern Cross and the pointers. The Cross may be upside down or lying on its side.
4. If the Moon is in the sky, look at the details of its surface (use binoculars if available).
5. Use the sky map to identify as many constellations as you can.

Record this...

1. Describe what you saw.
2. Explain how some stars might actually be planets or something else.

Constellations

Throughout history, different groups of people in different parts of the world have looked at the same stars and grouped them together in different ways. The pictures and patterns they have recognised have varied from one culture to another. These patterns are known as **constellations**. The Southern Cross is a constellation that can only be seen all year round in the southern hemisphere. For this reason, its five stars appear in the flags of a number of countries located south of the equator (Figure 8.2.1).

FIGURE 8.2.1 The flags of Australia, Papua New Guinea and Samoa

352 PEARSON SCIENCE 7 2ND EDITION

Structure of the solar system

Explaining the motion of the Earth, Moon, planets and stars has been a puzzle that has taken many centuries to solve. Every day, the Sun, Moon and stars rise in the east and set in the west. By itself, this evidence suggested that the Sun, Moon and stars all travel around Earth. However, the planets move differently from the stars. Since ancient times, **astronomers** have seen that the five visible planets (Mercury, Venus, Mars, Jupiter and Saturn) take months or years to travel across the night sky from east to west. Their motion holds the key to our understanding of the structure of the solar system and Earth's place in it.

The geocentric model

To many ancient astronomers, the motion of the Sun, Moon, stars and planets suggested that the Earth was at the centre of the universe with everything orbiting around it in circular paths. This model is shown in Figure 8.2.2 and is called the **geocentric model**. This model puts the Earth (*geo-*) at the centre (*-centric*) of the universe. The Greek philosopher Aristotle (384–322 BCE) clearly described the geocentric model in the third century BCE. Since this model matched everyday experience, his ideas were generally accepted. However, not all astronomers agreed.

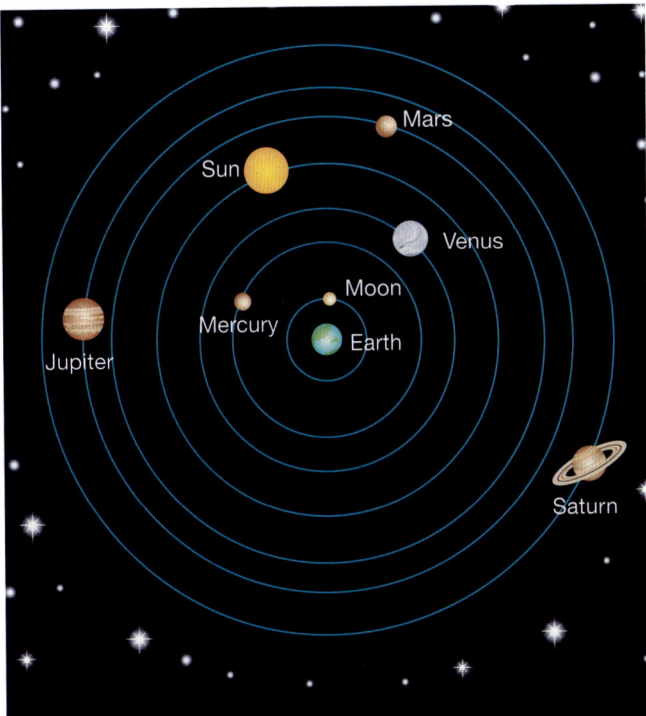

FIGURE 8.2.2 The geocentric model places Earth at the centre of the universe. The Moon, Sun, other planets and stars all revolve in orbits around it.

The heliocentric model

In about the second century BCE, the Greek philosopher Aristarchus (310–230 BCE) suggested that the Sun and not the Earth was the centre of the universe. This model is known as the **heliocentric model** (*helio-* = Sun) and is shown in Figure 8.2.3.

However, predictions made with the heliocentric model did not match astronomical observations of the time. This is why very few astronomers supported Aristarchus or his model.

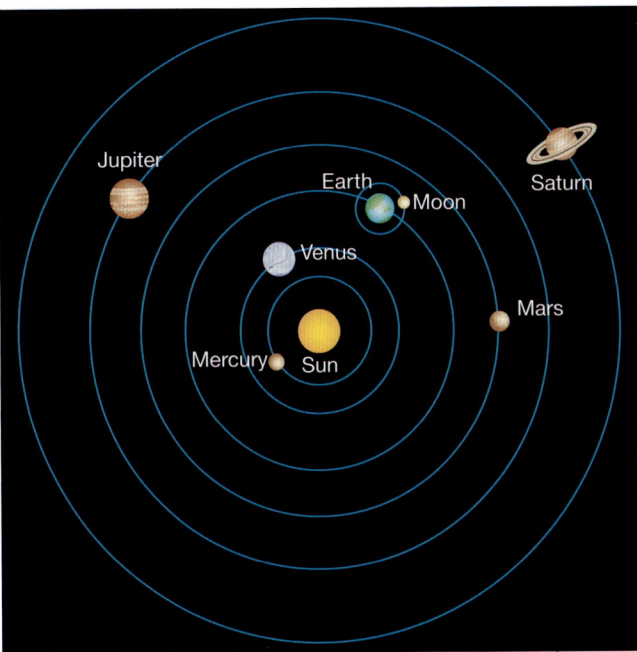

FIGURE 8.2.3 The heliocentric model of the solar system places the Sun at its centre. The Earth and other planets revolve around it.

Retrograde motion

Although the geocentric model made sense to the ancient astronomers, they observed that the planets sometimes seemed to turn around and move backwards! The section of the planet's path at which it reverses its direction (Figure 8.2.4) is known as **retrograde motion**.

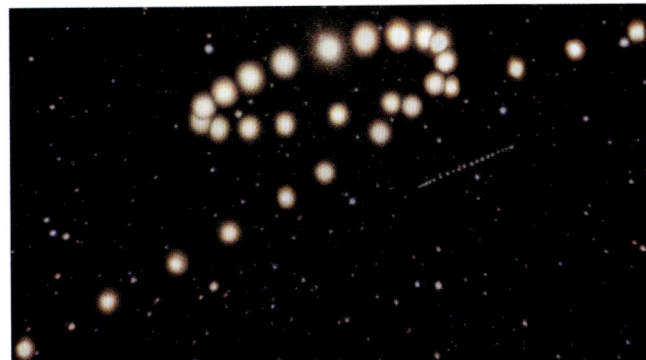

FIGURE 8.2.4 When viewed over a couple of months, the motion of Mars seems to loop back on itself: it shows retrograde motion.

CHAPTER 8 • EARTH IN SPACE   **353**

In the second century CE the Greek philosopher Claudius Ptolemy (100–170 CE) refined the geocentric model so that it could explain retrograde motion. In Ptolemy's model, each planet rotated on its own separate circle called an 'epicycle'. The centre of the epicycle orbited the Earth (Figure 8.2.5).

Ptolemy's refinements did not agree perfectly with observations but it was close enough. Most scientists in Europe accepted his version of the geocentric model. Support for the geocentric model was so strong that in 1543 a book by Polish mathematician Nicholas Copernicus (1473–1543) supporting the heliocentric model was banned in many countries.

Copernicus used the heliocentric model to explain retrograde motion. He assumed that all the planets orbited the Sun at different speeds. This would change their relative positions when viewed from Earth, sometimes making them appear to move backwards.

The telescope challenges ideas

Before Italian scientist and mathematician Galileo Galilei (1564–1642) built his telescope in 1609, astronomers viewed the night sky with nothing more than their own eyes. Galileo used his telescope to discover:

- craters on the Moon (Figure 8.2.6)
- the rings of Saturn
- the four largest moons of Jupiter. This showed that not everything in the universe orbited Earth.
- that the planet Venus went through phases just like the Moon. This observation could only be properly explained if Venus was orbiting the Sun and not Earth.

Galileo's observations led him to challenge the geocentric model and instead support the heliocentric model of Copernicus. Galileo lived in Italy at a time when religious authorities were very powerful. For centuries, some passages of the Bible had been interpreted as meaning that Earth is at the centre of the universe. Galileo's ideas and outspoken manner brought him into conflict with the authorities and he was imprisoned and banned from publishing his ideas and from writing to other scientists.

Galileo relied on his scientific technique and observations and not on the accepted way of thinking of his time. For this he is recognised as the 'father of modern science'.

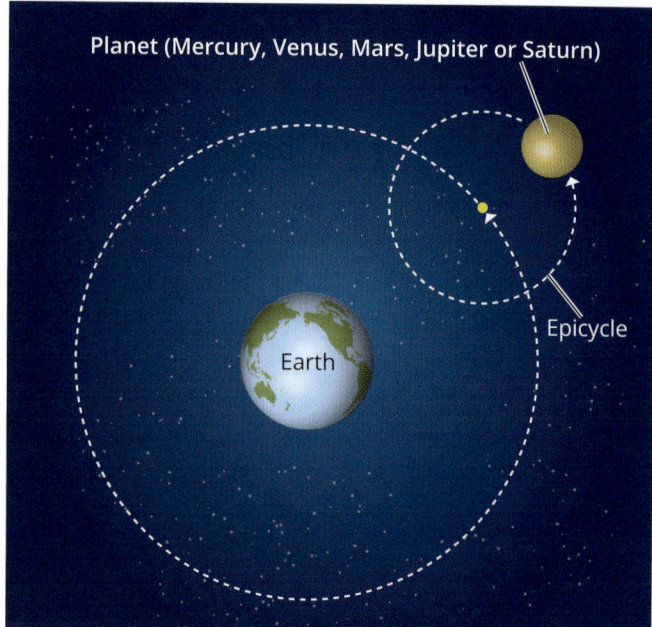

FIGURE 8.2.5 In Ptolemy's revised model of the universe, each planet travelled in a circle called an epicycle centred on a point that orbited the Earth.

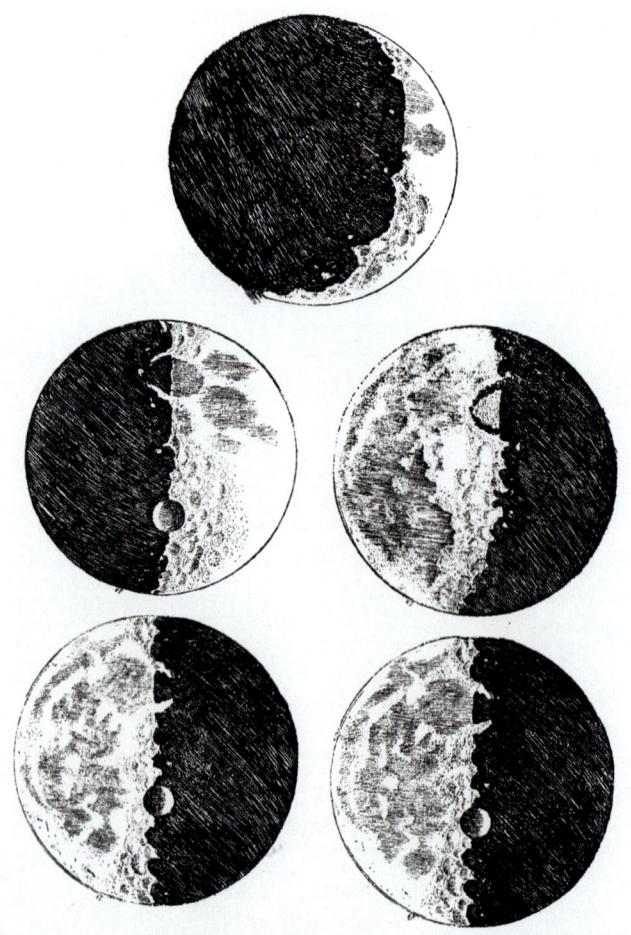

FIGURE 8.2.6 Although Galileo did not invent the telescope, he was the first person to use it for astronomy. These are some of his drawings of the Moon in different phases and its craters that were visible.

In 1596, the German mathematician Johannes Kepler (1571–1630) produced a heliocentric model that closely matched existing astronomical data. His model assumed that planetary orbits were elliptical (oval-shaped) rather than circular. This was a revolutionary idea—at that time, circles were believed to have special, almost mystical, properties. Like Copernicus and Galileo before him, Kepler was fiercely attacked by religious authorities. However, these authorities did not have as much influence in Germany as in countries like Italy, where religious figures such as the Pope were very powerful.

Figure 8.2.7 shows the great English scientist and mathematician Isaac Newton (1642–1727). In 1687, Newton proposed a law that described the force of gravity. It was known as the universal law of gravitation and it explained how the heliocentric model would work. With such convincing evidence, support for the opposing geocentric model quickly disappeared.

FIGURE 8.2.7 Isaac Newton (1642–1727) developed laws that explained forces, gravity and the motion of the planets. He is considered to be one of the greatest scientists of all time.

Discovering the outer planets

The planets Uranus and Neptune cannot be seen with the naked eye and so a telescope was required to discover them. The German-born British astronomer William Hershel (1738–1822) used a telescope in 1781 to discover the planet Uranus, and German astronomer Johann Galle (1812–1910) used one to observe Neptune in 1846.

SciFile

What's causing that?

The existence of Neptune was predicted before it was actually seen! In 1845, the French astronomer Urbain Le Verrier and Englishman John Couch Adams both used their telescopes to track the orbit of Uranus. They noticed that it was a little 'warped'. This could only happen if another planet (Neptune) was further out, pulling Uranus a little towards it.

Discovering the dwarf planets

Pluto was discovered in 1930 by American astronomer Clyde Tombaugh (1906–1997). It was quickly classified as the ninth planet of the solar system. In 1992, it was then found that Pluto was part of the Kuiper Belt, a band of relatively small objects orbiting the Sun at the outer edge of the solar system. Over the next 10 years, other Pluto-sized objects were discovered. Some of these are shown in Figure 8.2.8.

FIGURE 8.2.8 The Kuiper Belt contains a number of dwarf planets and similar-sized objects.

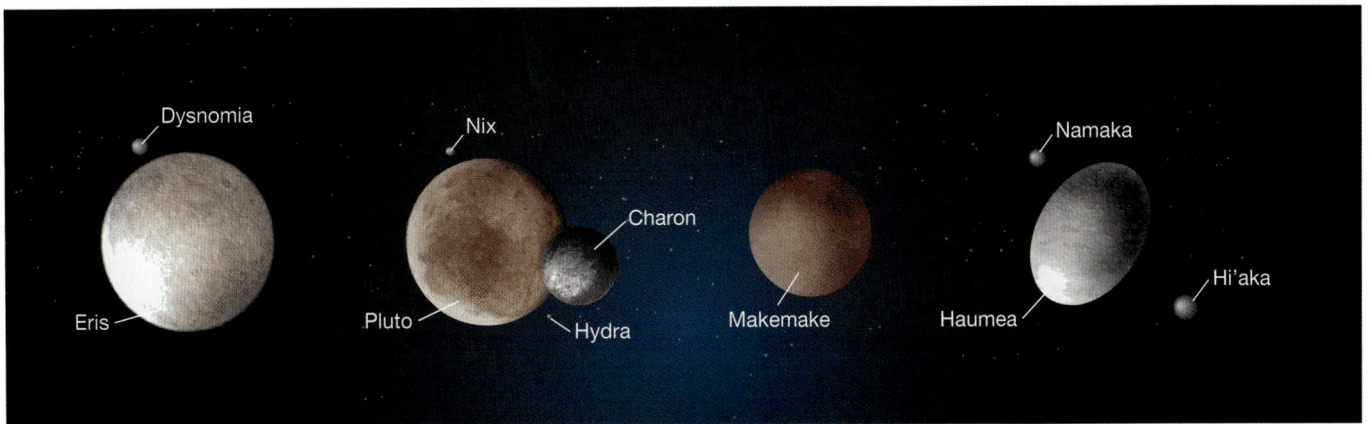

CHAPTER 8 • EARTH IN SPACE   **355**

For astronomers, this raised a difficult question—if Pluto is a planet, then should these objects be classified as planets too? If so then the solar system would have at least 12 planets!

In 2006, the International Astronomical Union solved this problem by defining a planet as a celestial body that:

- is in orbit around the Sun
- is nearly spherical (round)
- has enough gravity to clear the neighbourhood around its orbit of dust, rock and other objects.

Pluto orbits the Sun and is roughly spherical but it is part of the Kuiper Belt. This means that it has failed to clear its orbit. For this reason, Pluto is no longer considered to be a planet but is now classified as a **dwarf planet**. Haumea, Eris and Makemake are also classified as dwarf planets, as is the asteroid Ceres located in the asteroid belt between Mars and Jupiter.

Prac 3 p. 362

Exploring the solar system

The development of rockets in the mid-twentieth century allowed us to leave Earth and explore the solar system directly. The Apollo missions that landed on the Moon between 1969 and 1972 had human crews. Apollo XI was the first to land. You can see one of its astronauts (Buzz Aldrin) on the Moon's surface in Figure 8.2.9.

Since these missions, humans themselves have not travelled outside Earth's immediate orbit. All other space probes to the Moon and beyond have been without human crew, although many have carried robots.

Some space probes have landed or crashed onto the planets or their moons. Others have flown by, taking photos and measurements as they did so. These missions continue to this day—one of the most recent being the *New Horizons* probe. It landed its rover on Mars in 2012. In 2015, it went into orbit around Pluto sending back the most detailed photos ever taken of this dwarf planet.

Most of the missions of the twentieth century were sent by the USA or the USSR (now Russia). However, twenty-first century space exploration has become truly international, with countries such as India and China investing in their own space programs. The programs of countries such as France, Germany and Italy are coordinated through the European Space Agency.

Space exploration has allowed astronomers to make many important discoveries about the solar system that would have been impossible using telescopes alone. These include the following discoveries:

- Moon rocks have a similar composition to those found on Earth. This suggests that the Moon was once part of Earth.
- Water once flowed on the surface of Mars, depositing minerals such as gypsum.
- Jupiter has more than 60 moons ranging in size from Ganymede, with a diameter of about two-fifths that of Earth, to unnamed chunks of rock barely a kilometre across.
- One of Jupiter's moons (Io) is still volcanically active, sending plumes of material shooting hundreds of kilometres above its surface.
- The rings of Saturn appear solid when viewed from Earth but are made of countless pieces of rock ranging in size from dust to chunks metres across.
- The planet Uranus has a magnetic field that is, strangely, tilted at 60° to the angle of the planet's rotation.

Prac 1 p. 360   Prac 2 p. 361

FIGURE 8.2.9 Buzz Aldrin from Apollo XI on the surface of the Moon

SciFile

Still a planet to some

In 2009, the government of Clyde Tombaugh's home state of Illinois, USA, 'overruled' the International Astronomical Union. Within the state of Illinois at least, Pluto is still considered a planet and March 13 (the anniversary of its discovery) is celebrated as Pluto Day.

SCIENCE AS A HUMAN ENDEAVOUR
Nature and development of science

Interpreting constellations

Different cultures look at the sky in very different ways. To some, the stars might form a hunter, a saucepan or a canoe, while other celestial objects might be seen as an emu in the sky (Figure 8.2.10).

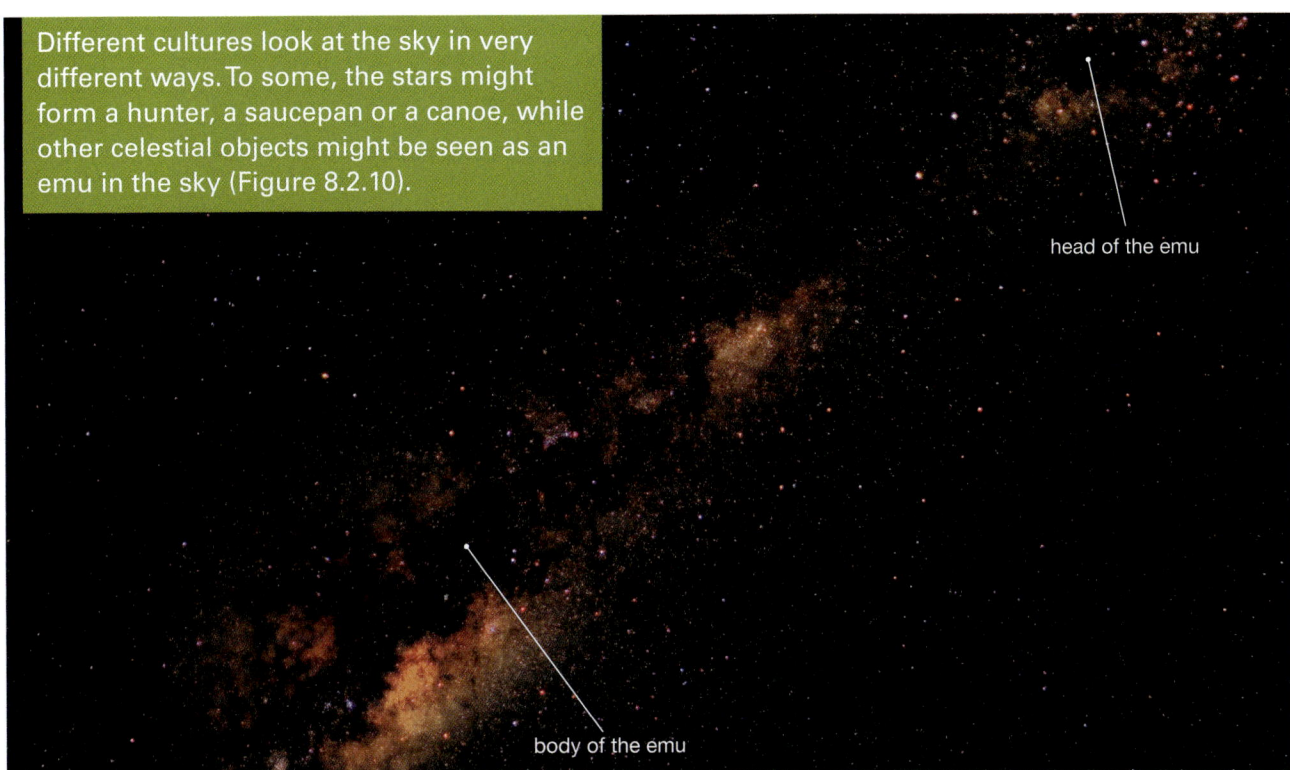

FIGURE 8.2.10 The Aboriginal Emu-in-the-sky constellation is seen by looking at the dark clouds of dust between the stars rather than the stars themselves.

The zodiac

The ancient Greeks looked up at the patterns in the night sky and recognised familiar objects such as a scorpion, a bull and a lion. They gave special importance to the twelve constellations called the zodiac because they are the only constellations that the Sun appears to move through. These are the 'star signs' of astrology and are still known today by their Greek names such as Scorpio, Taurus and Leo. Figure 8.2.11 shows the signs of the zodiac with the dates traditionally associated with them.

20 January–18 February	Aquarius
19 February–20 March	Pisces
21 March–19 April	Aries
20 April–20 May	Taurus
21 May–20 June	Gemini
21 June–22 July	Cancer
23 July–22 August	Leo
23 August–22 September	Virgo
23 September–22 October	Libra
23 October–21 November	Scorpio
22 November–21 December	Sagittarius
22 December–19 January	Capricorn

FIGURE 8.2.11 The zodiac is made up of 12 constellations.

Different cultures, different constellations

When looking for patterns in the stars, people are naturally reminded of objects they are familiar with from everyday life. It is not surprising that people from different cultures with different lifestyles would identify different constellations.

CHAPTER 8 • EARTH IN SPACE   357

SCIENCE AS A HUMAN ENDEAVOUR

For example, consider the group of stars in Figure 8.2.12. The ancient Greeks called this group of stars Orion after a famous hunter from mythology. He is shown in Figure 8.2.13. The bright stars at the corners represent the hunter's hands and feet, the group of stars across the middle is his belt with a scabbard (a sheath or cover for the sword) sticking out of it. However, from the southern hemisphere this image appears upside down! For this reason, many Australians don't see a hunter but instead see a saucepan. As Figure 8.2.14 shows, Orion's sword is the handle of the Saucepan. The Yolngu people of the Northern Territory know this group of stars as Djulpan or the canoe, shown in Figure 8.2.15. Here, the sword/saucepan handle represents a fishing line trailing behind the canoe in the water.

FIGURE 8.2.13 Orion, the hunter

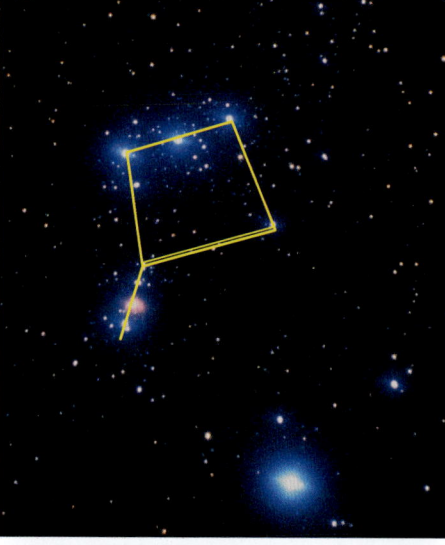

FIGURE 8.2.14 The Saucepan

FIGURE 8.2.12 Orion is easy to identify in the southern sky.

REVIEW

1. List four constellations of the zodiac.
2. Explain why the ancient Greeks and the Yolngu people saw different shapes in the same set of stars.
3. The Yolngu people identified the three bright stars in the centre of the constellation Djulpan as three fishermen sitting in a canoe. Identify what these three stars represent in the:
   a. ancient Greek constellation Orion
   b. the modern Australian Saucepan.
4. The Emu-in-the-sky constellation is considered unusual compared with many other constellations. Explain why.

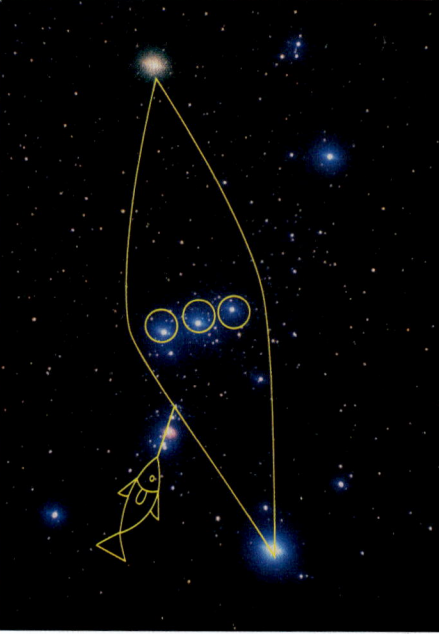

FIGURE 8.2.15 Djulpan, the canoe

MODULE 8.2 Review questions

Remembering

1. Define the terms:
   a. heliocentric
   b. constellation.

2. What term best describes each of the following?
   a. apparent reversal of the direction of motion of a planet across the night sky
   b. spherical object in orbit around the Sun with enough gravity to clear its orbit.

3. Name three scientists who contributed to the development of the heliocentric model of the universe.

4. Name a star or constellation that can only be seen all year round in the southern hemisphere.

Understanding

5. Why is Pluto no longer considered a planet?
6. Explain why Aristotle's model of the universe is described as geocentric.
7. What caused Galileo to challenge to the geocentric model and support the heliocentric model of Copernicus?
8. Explain why the heliocentric model was not originally accepted when it was first proposed by Aristarchus in the second century BCE.
9. Describe retrograde motion.
10. Explain why Ptolemy modified the geocentric model.

Applying

11. Identify an observation made by Galileo that suggests that not everything orbits Earth.
12. Earth's Moon is approximately the same size as Pluto. Use the definition of the International Astronomical Union to explain why the Moon is not classified as a dwarf planet.

Analysing

13. The asteroid belt is a collection of rocks of various sizes that orbit the Sun between Mars and Jupiter. The largest of these asteroids is known as Ceres. It is spherical with a radius of about 500 km (about half that of Pluto). Use the International Astronomical Union's definitions to classify Ceres as a planet or a dwarf planet.

14. The main illustration on page 352 shows the ancient Greek god Atlas carrying the universe on his back. Compare this to Figure 8.2.16, which shows how scientists in the sixteenth century thought the universe was constructed.

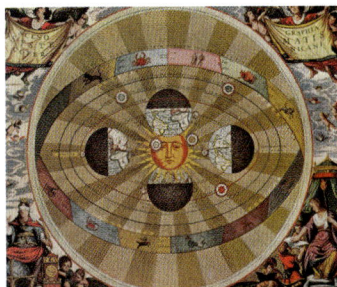

FIGURE 8.2.16

   a. Which of these pictures portray the following?
      i. geocentric model
      ii. heliocentric model.
   b. Justify your answer by referring to specific features of each illustration.

Evaluating

15. The term 'Copernican revolution' is sometimes used to describe any big shift in understanding. Propose a reason why.
16. Newton claimed that his achievements in explaining the solar system were due to the fact that he 'stood on the shoulders of giants'.
   a. Name some of these giants.
   b. Propose reasons why he made this claim.

Creating

17. a. Construct a diagram for a new constellation that would fit the star pattern shown in Figure 8.2.17. (You don't need to use every star.)
    b. Name your new constellation after what you think it looks like.

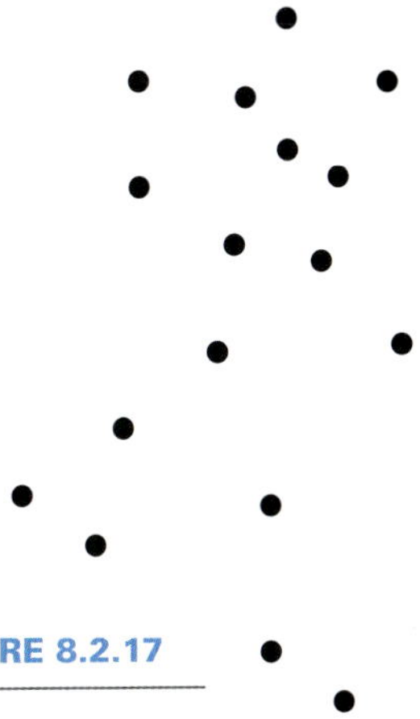

FIGURE 8.2.17

18. Construct a poster or presentation to explain to a group of younger students why Pluto is no longer considered to be a planet.

MODULE 8.2 Practical investigations

1 • Constructing a telescope

Purpose
To construct a simple telescope.

Timing
45 minutes

Materials
- 2 biconvex lenses (which curve outwards on both sides) of different focal lengths (the greater the difference in focal lengths, the greater the magnification of the telescope)
- 2 retort stands with clamps (or similar) to hold lenses
- marker pen

SAFETY Do not point your telescope at the Sun.

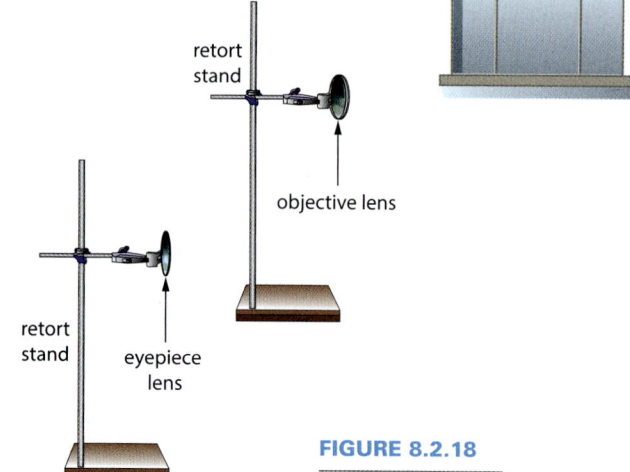

FIGURE 8.2.18

Procedure
1. Use the SkillBuilder below to determine the focal length of each of the biconcave lenses. Record each focal length in your workbook.
2. The fatter, more curved lens should have the shorter focal length. Make it the eyepiece of your telescope. The flatter, thinner lens should have the longer focal length so make it the objective lens.
3. Clamp or tape each lens into a retort stand. Adjust the stands so that both lenses are at the same convenient height to look through.
4. Arrange the stands in line with each other so that the objective lens faces a distant object. For example, you could look through the window. Look through the eyepiece lens to see the image in the objective lens.
5. Add the focal lengths of the two lenses together. Place the retort stands so that the distance between them is equal to this distance.
6. Look through the eyepiece lens. Sketch the image you observe.
7. Reverse the telescope (i.e. look through the objective lens). Sketch the image you observe.

SkillBuilder

Determining focal length

To determine the focal length of a biconcave lens, follow these steps:
- Hold your lens so that lots of light can enter it (perhaps stand in sunlight).
- Hold a blank sheet of paper behind your lens.
- Move your lens slowly back and forth (alternatively, move the sheet of paper back and forth) until the light passing through the lens has focused to a single bright point. Figure 8.2.19 shows what is happening.
- Measure the distance between the lens and the sheet of paper. This is the focal length of your lens.

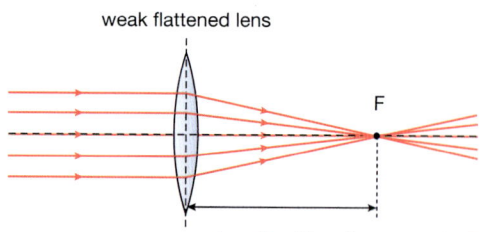

FIGURE 8.2.19 Parallel rays of light are brought together at a point called the focus (F) on the other side of a convex lens. The greater the curve of the lens, the stronger the lens is and the shorter its focal length, or distance between the lens and the focus.

360 PEARSON SCIENCE 7 2ND EDITION

MODULE 8.2 Practical investigations

Results

1. Record the focal lengths of each lens then add them together.

   Fatter, more curved lens = _____
   +
   Flatter, thinner lens = _____
   Sum of focal lengths = _____

Review

1. Describe the image sketched in step 6. The magnification of the telescope is how much it has increased the size of the image (such as doubled, tripled). Estimate the magnification of your telescope.
2. Contrast the images sketched in steps 6 and 7.
3. Figure 8.2.18 shows the equipment used in this prac in three dimensions (3D). Construct a scientific diagram that shows it in two dimensions (2D).

---

2 • Improving the telescope

Purpose
To improve the simple telescope constructed in prac 1.

SAFETY
A Risk Assessment is required for this investigation.

Timing 120 minutes

Procedure

1. Design a telescope that will be better than the one constructed in prac 1.
2. Sketch your planned telescope in your workbook. Before you start building it, assess its design and construction. List any risks it might involve and what you might do to minimise those risks.
3. Show your teacher your design and your assessment of its risks. If they approve, collect all the required materials and start work.

Hints
In your design:
- consider using curved mirrors instead of lenses for the objective
- try changing the focal lengths of the objective and eyepiece to alter the magnification of the telescope
- design apparatus that will allow the telescope to be kept still and focused on an object in the sky. An example is shown in Figure 8.2.20.

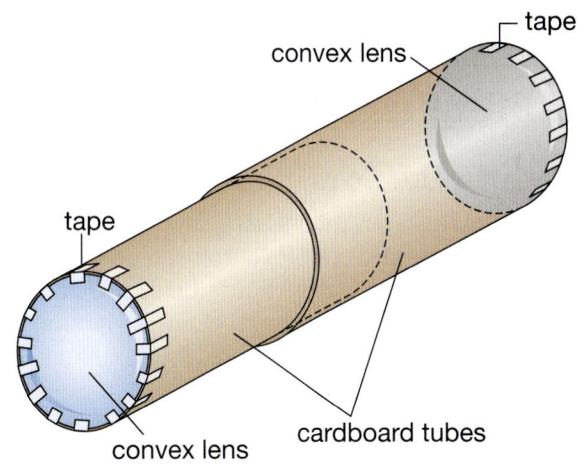

FIGURE 8.2.20

Review

1. Compare the image observed using your telescope with the ones observed using the simple telescope constructed in prac 1.
2. Estimate the magnification of your telescope.
3. Evaluate the success of this investigation. Was your telescope an improvement?

CHAPTER 8 • EARTH IN SPACE 361

MODULE 8.2 Practical investigations

3 • Visiting dwarf planets *Planning & Conducting*

Purpose
To use simulation software to observe a number of dwarf planets.

Timing 30 minutes

Materials
- computer or tablet computer
- a planetarium program or app such as GoSkyWatch Planetarium, SkyGlobe, Celestia or WorldWide Telescope

Procedure
1. Set the program to show the sky as it will appear at 8 p.m. tonight from your home town.
2. Search for Ceres.
3. Zoom in until the image of the dwarf planet fills the screen. Sketch it.
4. Zoom out to identify and sketch any moons orbiting the dwarf planet.
5. Repeat steps 2–4 for other dwarf planets, such as Pluto, Eris, Makemake and Haumea.

Review
1. List the three characteristics of a planet.
2. Dwarf planets are not classified as planets because they do not have one of the characteristics of a planet. Describe the feature that most dwarf planets lack.

SkillBuilder

Finding the South Pole

In ancient times, navigators used the Southern Cross to locate the South Pole. You can do this too. First you need to locate the South Celestial Pole. This is the point in the southern night sky around which all the stars seem to rotate. You can find it using two different methods:

Method 1: Draw a line through the main axis (i.e. the vertical line) of the Southern Cross. Extend this line from the bottom of the cross for a distance equal to four times the height of the cross.

Method 2: Extend the main axis. Construct another line out from the middle of the pointers as shown in Figure 8.2.21. The South Celestial Pole is where the two lines meet.

Once the South Celestial Pole is located, drop a line to the horizon; where it hits is the South Pole.

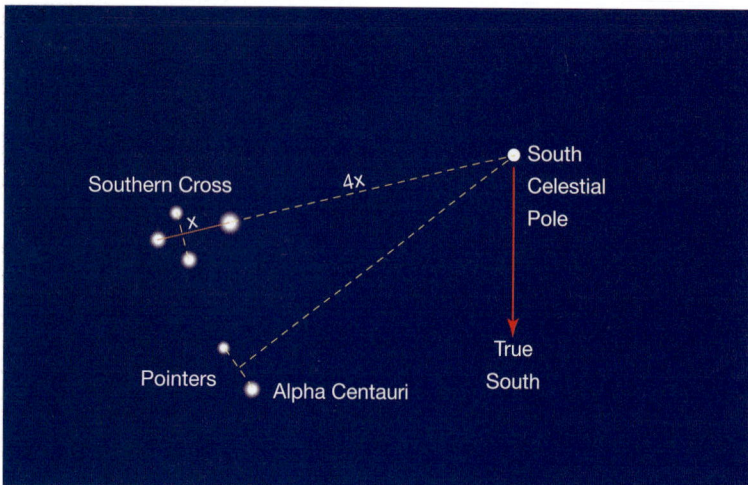

FIGURE 8.2.21 How to use the Southern Cross to find the South Pole

MODULE 8.3 Gravity and orbits

Gravity is the pulling force that causes rain to fall and rivers to flow to the sea. Gravity also causes the planets of the solar system to orbit the Sun, the Moon to orbit Earth and spectacular rings to orbit Saturn.

Gravity

While some forces make contact with the objects that they push or pull around, other forces act without touching. These non-contact forces act instead through force fields. As Figure 8.3.1 shows, magnets have magnetic force fields around them that attract objects containing iron. They also push or pull around other nearby magnets.

Gravitational fields

Around every mass is a **gravitational force field** that attracts other masses. This attractive force is gravity, and it attempts to pull masses together. Matter is the stuff that everything is made up of, and matter has mass. You have mass, as does the person who is sitting next to you, the chair you are sitting on, and the pen you are writing with. They all have their own gravitational fields, and all of them are attracting each other. This force of gravity and its attraction is most obvious when you fall off your chair! The force of gravity between you and the Earth has pulled you both together!

FIGURE 8.3.1 Iron filings align (line up) with the field lines around a magnet. The strong field lines between these magnets will pull them together.

CHAPTER 8 • EARTH IN SPACE 363

The effect of mass

Gravity is a force caused by mass. The bigger the mass, the stronger its gravitational field and the more it attracts other masses nearby. However, gravity is a very weak force, and a lot of mass is required before any attraction is noticeable: people, pens, chairs, and even cars, buildings and ships, are not massive enough to have much effect on other masses. This is why you don't get pulled towards the person sitting next to you or to a large skyscraper that you are walking past. Gravity is only noticeable when one of the objects is really massive, such as a planet, moon or star. These objects have strong gravitational fields around them that attract anything else that is nearby, including you. Earth has a gravitational field that attracts other masses towards its centre. This is shown in Figure 8.3.2.

The effect of distance

The gravitational fields around planets, moons and stars weakens rapidly as you move away from them. This makes Earth's gravitational field a little weaker on the top of its highest mountain (Mt Everest), than at sea level. However, the difference is too small for you to notice and can only be detected by extremely sensitive instruments. By the time you get to the Moon, Earth's pull is weak, much weaker than at Earth's surface.

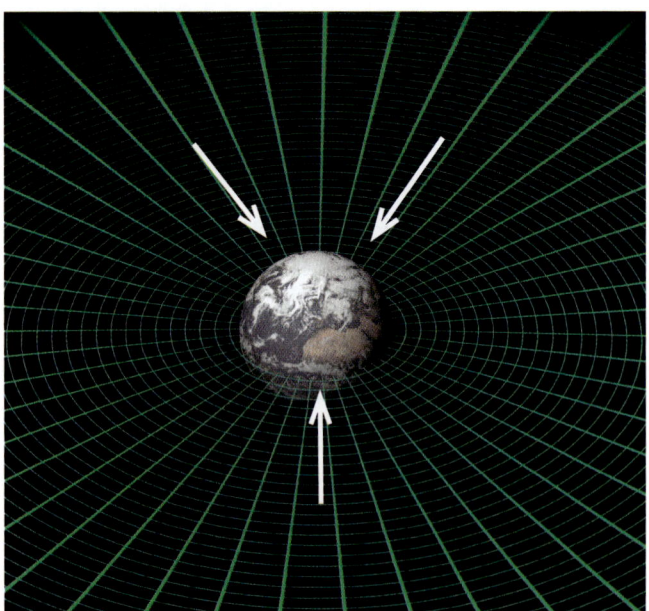

FIGURE 8.3.2 Gravitational field lines fan out from Earth (green) and the white arrows show the direction a mass will move when in the gravitational field of Earth.

 Prac 1 p. 370   STEM p. 372

STEM 4 fun

Gravity-powered machine

PROBLEM
Can you create a machine that is powered by gravity?

SUPPLIES
- paper cups
- string
- drinking straws
- icy-pole sticks
- glue
- paper
- tape
- paper rolls
- toothpicks (large and small)
- anything else you may need

PLAN AND DESIGN Work out what information you need to solve the problem. Design a solution and draw a diagram. Make a list of materials you will need to make your machine. Write down a plan including the steps you will take.

CREATE Follow your plan. Draw your solution to the problem. Create your solution using materials you have gathered.

IMPROVE How do you know it solves the problem? Keep a record of what works and what doesn't. What could work better? Modify your design to make it better. Test it out.

REFLECTION
1. What area of STEM did you work in today?
2. In what career do these activities connect?
3. How did you use mathematics in this task?

Orbits

The gravitational fields around planets, moons and stars are often strong enough to trap other masses so that the masses travel continuously around them in a path known as an **orbit**. For example, Earth and the other planets of the solar system are trapped by the gravitational field of the Sun and so they orbit it. Likewise, the Moon keeps orbiting Earth. This is shown in Figure 8.3.3. At least 63 moons orbit Jupiter, and millions of rock fragments, ice and dust particles form rings that orbit Saturn.

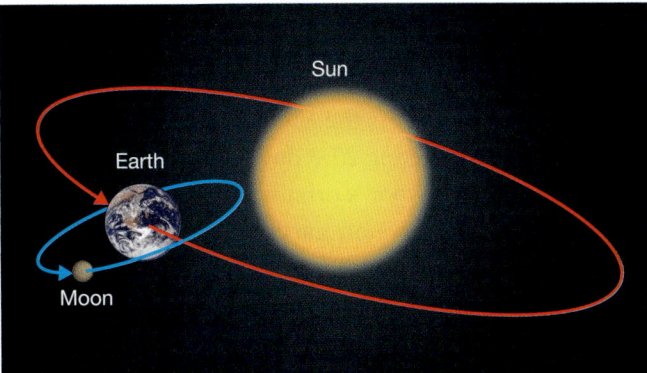

FIGURE 8.3.3 Earth is trapped by the Sun's gravitational field so it orbits the Sun. Likewise, the Moon is trapped by Earth's gravitational field so it orbits Earth.

Objects that are in orbits like this are known as **satellites**. The planets of the solar system are natural satellites of the Sun, and the Moon is a natural satellite of Earth. Earth also has many artificial satellites, which have been placed in orbit by us humans. Some are used to transmit information such as internet and telephone conversations, while others scan the Earth for everything from erosion and bushfires to espionage (spying). The largest artificial satellite in orbit around Earth is the International Space Station (ISS), shown in Figure 8.3.4.

FIGURE 8.3.4 The International Space Station (ISS) is a huge artificial satellite orbiting Earth. It has a crew of six on board at most times.

Prac 2
p. 371

SciFile

Dog in orbit

In 1957, a dog named Laika was sent into orbit by the USSR aboard *Sputnik 2*. The Russians wanted to test whether living things could survive a launch into space and the lack of gravity there (Figure 8.3.5). Laika died from overheating a few hours into the mission, but her body completed another 2750 orbits. *Sputnik 2* and Laika's remains disintegrated on re-entry into Earth's atmosphere five months after launch.

FIGURE 8.3.5 A stamp remembering Laika, the first dog to go into orbit

Explaining orbits

Imagine you are on a really, really tall mountain. You have a handful of tennis balls and drop one. Of course, the ball will fall and land by your feet because gravity pulls it downwards. When you throw the ball horizontally, it still falls but it takes a curved path to the ground, landing at a distance away from you. Now imagine that you could throw the ball so fast that it kept on falling, never hitting the Earth. If you could do this then the ball would be in orbit. The ball would then keep 'falling' around Earth forever, needing no extra push or power to keep it orbiting (Figure 8.3.6 on page 366).

An orbit like this can only happen outside Earth's atmosphere because there is no air resistance and therefore nothing to slow the satellite down.

CHAPTER 8 • EARTH IN SPACE **365**

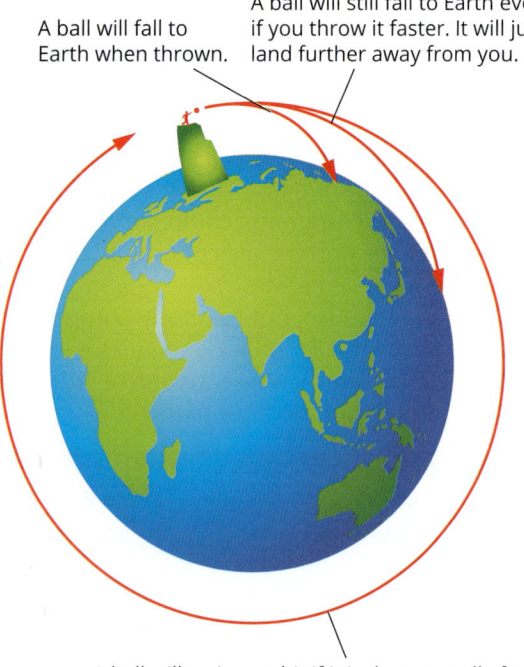

FIGURE 8.3.6 Throw a ball slowly and it will land back on Earth. However, if you throw it really fast, then it will continue to fall and keep missing the planet. The ball will then be in orbit around Earth.

Orbits in the solar system

Orbits are elliptical in shape. **Ellipses** are oval-shaped closed loops. Some are long, thin ovals while others are almost perfect circles. For example, the orbits of Venus, Earth and Neptune around the Sun are nearly circular. Mars, Jupiter, Saturn and Uranus have more elliptical (stretched) orbits. Mercury and the dwarf planet Pluto have even more elliptical orbits. Comets from deep space are sometimes trapped by the gravitational field of the Sun and sweep around it in long thin orbits. Comets often orbit in a plane very different from that of the planets. A typical orbit of a comet is shown in Figure 8.3.7.

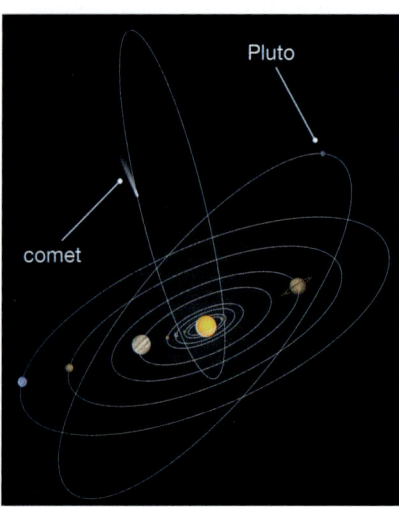

FIGURE 8.3.7 The dwarf planet Pluto and most comets orbit in different planes from the rest of the solar system.

The Moon's orbit

The Moon takes 27.3 **days** to orbit Earth. This is known as a **sidereal month**. As the Moon orbits, it also rotates (spins) on its axis, taking 27.3 days to complete one rotation. Since the Moon's orbit time and rotation time are exactly the same, we on Earth only ever see the same face of the Moon (Figure 8.3.8). We never see its rear.

FIGURE 8.3.8 It doesn't matter where you are on Earth, this is the only face of the Moon that you will ever see.

Phases of the Moon

On Earth we see the same face of the Moon but we don't always see it fully lit. Sometimes only half of its face is lit. At other times we see nothing at all. The different shapes that we see are known as phases of the Moon (Figure 8.4.9 on page 378). Phases happen because the Moon's orbit constantly changes the arrangement of the Moon, Earth and the Sun in space. Half of the Moon always faces the Sun but on Earth, we don't always see the part being lit.

SciFile

Unstable orbits

If a satellite is travelling too slowly then it will slowly spiral in towards Earth. This is what most artificial satellites eventually do. Likewise, if a satellite is travelling too fast then it will slowly spiral outwards. The Moon is travelling at 1 km/s, a little too fast for its orbit. This allows it to stray 3.8 cm away from Earth each year!

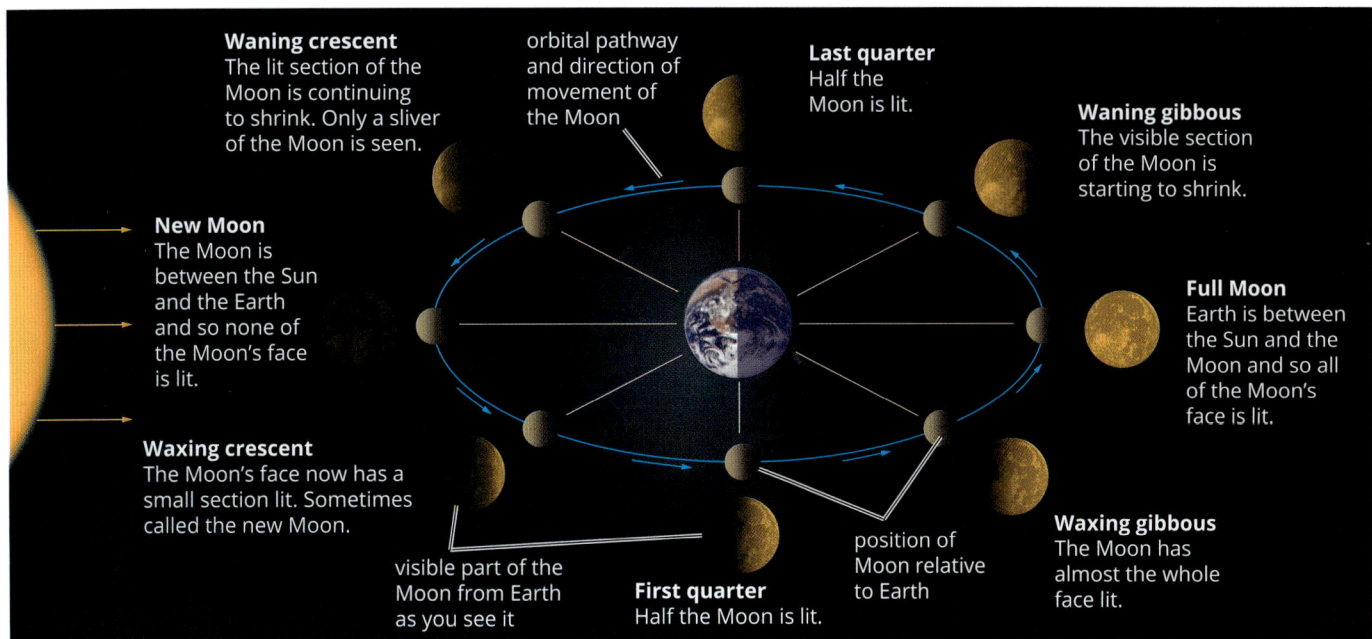

FIGURE 8.3.9 The phases of the Moon depend on where it is in its orbit around Earth. The larger moon image shows how it looks from Earth. The small moon images show where it is in the orbit.

What we see of the Moon's face depends on the where the Moon is in its orbit and how much of its face is receiving light. You can see how this happens in Figure 8.3.9.

Eclipses

Sometimes the orbits of the Moon around Earth and Earth around the Sun cause all three bodies to align so that the Moon blocks sunlight from reaching Earth, or Earth blocks sunlight from reaching the Moon. When this happens, an eclipse occurs. **Eclipses** are caused by a celestial body completely or partially blocking sunlight from reaching another celestial body. Eclipses can be solar or lunar.

Solar eclipses

A **solar eclipse** occurs whenever light from the Sun is blocked by the Moon, casting a shadow onto Earth. The Moon is too small to block light from the Sun over the entire Earth, and so its shadow falls on only part of Earth's surface (Figure 8.3.10 on page 368). Some regions experience a complete eclipse because they are under the full shadow known as the **umbra**. Other regions are under a less dense shadow known as a **penumbra** and so they will experience a partial eclipse. Meanwhile, the rest of Earth experiences daylight as normal.

science 4 fun

Drawing ellipses

Can you draw an accurate ellipse?

Collect this…
- 2 pins
- sheet of cardboard or thick pad of paper (such as your workbook)
- length of string or cotton
- pencil or felt-tip pen

Do this…
1. Stick the pins well apart into the cardboard or pad of paper.
2. Tie the string or cotton into a loop so that it fits loosely over the two pins.
3. Use the pencil or felt-tip pen to stretch the loop out.
4. Keeping the loop tight, 'orbit' the pins with the pencil or pen, drawing as you go.

Record this…
1. Describe what happened.
2. Explain how this relates to the shape of orbits.

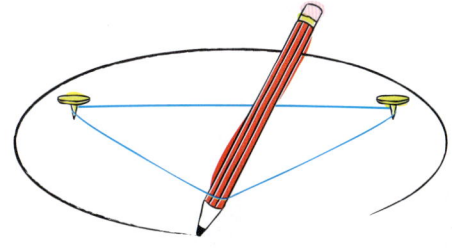

CHAPTER 8 • EARTH IN SPACE   **367**

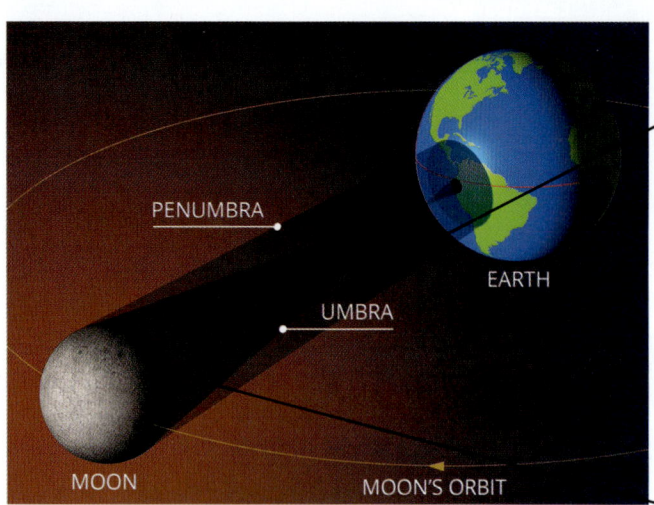

FIGURE 8.3.10 The Moon's shadow only covers a small part of the Earth's surface. Only these shadow regions will experience a solar eclipse.

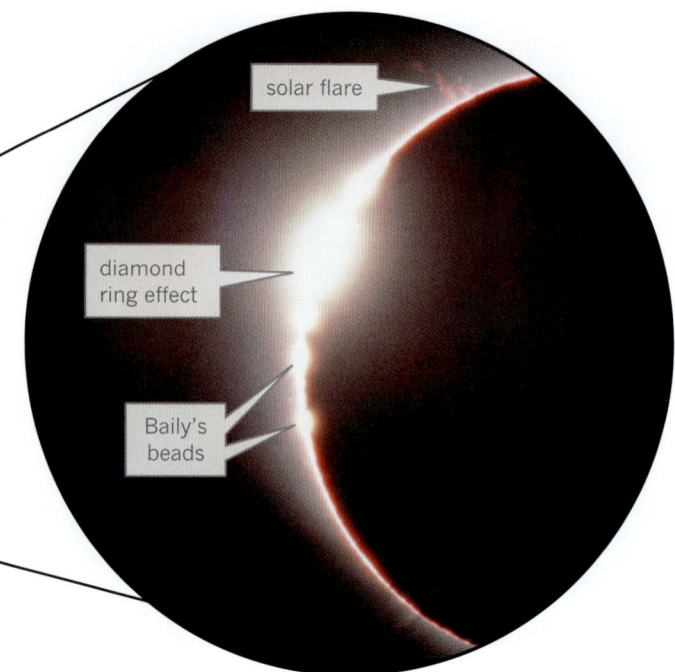

FIGURE 8.3.11 This photo shows the moment just before a solar eclipse, as seen from Earth. It shows a solar flare, the diamond ring effect (the last burst of sunlight) and Baily's beads (sunlight shining down lunar valleys).

Astronomers use solar eclipses to view the corona or very outer layer of the Sun, and the solar flares that burst from it. You can clearly see a solar flare in Figure 8.3.11.

Lunar eclipses

During a **lunar eclipse**, the Earth blocks light from reaching the Moon. As the Moon passes along its orbit, it first passes through Earth's penumbra, causing a partial lunar eclipse. It then moves through the umbra, forming a total lunar eclipse, before moving back into Earth's penumbra and then back into the sunlight. Figure 8.3.12 shows how this happens. In Figure 8.3.13 you can see what the Moon looks like when the Earth's shadow passes across it during a lunar eclipse.

SciFile

Eclipse myths and legends

The ancient Chinese and Vikings both thought that a lunar eclipse happened because the Moon was eaten: the Chinese thought a dragon did it, while the Vikings thought that a wolf ate it. Some American Indian tribes instead thought a bear was wandering through the sky, fighting the Moon whenever it blocked the path.

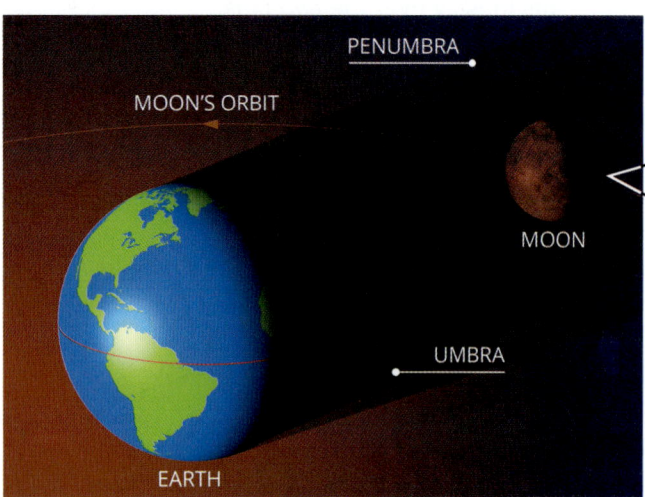

FIGURE 8.3.12 A lunar eclipse passes through different stages depending on what part of the Earth's shadow it is passing through.

FIGURE 8.3.13 Five images of the Moon during a total lunar eclipse. The Moon does not disappear completely while it is in the umbra because it is lit by a little sunlight bent by Earth's atmosphere.

MODULE 8.3 Review questions

Remembering

1. Define the terms:
   a. orbit
   b. gravitational force field
   c. ellipse.

2. What term best describes each of the following?
   a. an object in orbit around another object
   b. when light from the Sun is blocked by another object like the Moon or Earth
   c. different views of the Moon as seen from Earth.

3. List two examples of forces that act through a field.

4. Name one thing that is currently pulling you with a strong gravitational force.

5. Name one:
   a. natural satellite of the Sun
   b. natural satellite of Earth
   c. artificial satellite of Earth.

Understanding

6. One way of constructing an ellipse is shown in the science4fun activity on page 367. Predict what would happen to the shape of the ellipse if the drawing pins were placed closer together.

7. How can you show the following?
   a. the magnetic field around a magnet
   b. that a gravitational field exists where you are right now.

8. Explain why you aren't pulled towards a wall despite there being a gravitational attraction between you and it.

9. Explain why a satellite does not need to be powered to keep it in orbit.

10. Draw a diagram to explain why we see phases of the Moon.

Applying

11. Use the internet to find a photo of Saturn and its rings taken by the unmanned *Cassini* spacecraft in 2006.
    a. What are the rings of Saturn made of?
    b. Use the idea of falling to explain why the rings don't fly off into space
    c. What would happen to the rings if they slowed down for some reason?

12. Use the idea of umbra and penumbra to explain why only parts of Earth experience a solar eclipse.

Analysing

13. Contrast:
    a. a natural satellite with an artificial satellite
    b. the orbits of Pluto and comets with the orbits of the planets.

Evaluating

14. *Gravity always pulls you down.* Assess whether this statement is true, false, or a bit of both.

15. Rank the following places from the one that would have the strongest gravity to the place with the weakest gravity.
    A. on the top of Mt Kosciusko (NSW), the tallest mountain in Australia (2228 m above sea level)
    B. at the top of Q1 tower (Queensland), the tallest building in Australia (323 m above sea level)
    C. on Bells Beach (Victoria) (sea level)
    D. on the banks of Lake Eyre (South Australia) (15 m below sea level).

16. When half of the Moon is visible, its phase is not called a half moon but a quarter moon. Propose a reason why.

Creating

17. The Moon orbits the Earth in 27.3 days but solar and lunar eclipses don't occur every 27.3 days. Instead, we usually see the Moon in one of its phases.
    a. A full Moon occurs whenever we see all of its face lit by the Sun. Construct a diagram showing how the Sun, Moon and Earth might be arranged so that a full Moon occurs without causing a lunar eclipse.
    b. A new Moon happens when the far-side of the Moon is lit and we on Earth look at its unlit side. Construct another diagram that shows how this might happen without causing a solar eclipse.

MODULE 8.3 Practical investigations

1 • Go jump!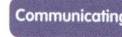

Each planet in the solar system has a different mass and this means that each planet pulls you down with a different gravity. Different gravities mean that you should be able to jump different heights on different planets—you will jump higher on planets with weak gravity and lower on planets with strong gravity. This assumes that the surface is solid!

This activity should be performed in groups of four.

Purpose
To calculate how high you could jump on another planet.

SAFETY
Make sure someone holds the hands of the person jumping.

Hypothesis
Where in the solar system do you think you will be able to jump the highest and where will you find it difficult—will it be Earth, the Moon, Mercury, Venus, Mars, Jupiter, Saturn, Uranus or Neptune? Before you go any further with this investigation, write a hypothesis in your workbook.

Timing 45 minutes

Materials
- metre ruler or tape measure
- calculator

Procedure
1. Choose a safe and clear space, perhaps outside.
2. One of your laboratory partners needs to hold the metre ruler vertically, with the 'zero end' touching the ground.
3. Another needs to be crouched down, with their eyes level with the ruler.
4. Stand next to the ruler and jump as high as you can.
5. Your lab partner needs to measure the height your feet got to in the jump.
6. Repeat two more times and record your jump heights.
7. Swap roles so that everyone in your group has a jump.

Results
1. Copy the results table shown below into your workbook. A sample calculation has been completed for you. Alternatively, construct a computer spreadsheet that looks something like the table.
2. Calculate your average jump height by:
   - adding: jump 1 + jump 2 + jump 3
   - dividing: by 3.
3. Calculate the height you could jump on the Moon and other planets by:
   - dividing: your average jump ÷ gravity.

   Record your predicted heights in your results table.

   Alternatively, use your spreadsheet to complete the calculations for you.

Review
1. Identify the celestial body/bodies on which you could jump:
   a. the highest
   b. the lowest
   c. about the same as on Earth.
2. Find the world records for various athletics, such as high jump and pole vault, then calculate what they would be on the other planets.
3. Astronauts on the Moon were able to jump higher than on Earth but not as high as you calculated above. Propose reasons why.

Jump heights

Name of jumper	Fred	Freda	Jim	Jane
jump 1 (cm)	58			
jump 2 (cm)	62			
jump 3 (cm)	49			
jumps 1 + 2 + 3 (cm)	58 + 62 + 49 = 169			
average jump (cm)	168 ÷ 3 = 56			

Gravity compared to Earth's		Predicted jump heights (cm)			
Earth	1	56/1 = 56			
Moon	0.17	56/0.17 = 329			
Mercury	0.38	56/0.38 = 147			
Venus	0.91	56/0.91 = 62			
Mars	0.38	56/0.38 = 147			
Jupiter	2.36	56/2.36 = 24			
Saturn	0.92	56/0.92 = 61			
Uranus	0.89	56/0.89 = 63			
Neptune	1.1	56/1.1 = 51			

MODULE 8.3 Practical investigations

2 • Orbits

Purpose
To use a model of an orbit and to determine the effect of changing gravity.

Hypothesis
Which satellite do you think will orbit faster—a satellite around a planet with high gravity or a satellite around a planet with low gravity? Before you go any further with this investigation, write a hypothesis in your workbook.

Timing 45 minutes

Materials
- plastic casing of ballpoint pen or short length of plastic or metal tubing
- string or strong cotton thread
- rubber bung with hole
- washers
- large open area

SAFETY
The rubber bung will be travelling fast in wide circles so make sure you wear safety glasses at all times and that you have plenty of room.

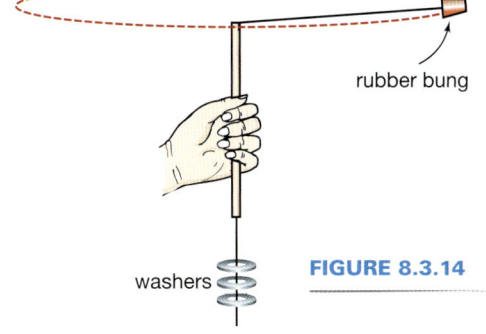
FIGURE 8.3.14

Procedure
1. Tie the string or cotton thread securely to the rubber bung by passing it through the hole a number of times and then knotting it tightly.
2. Pass the string or thread through the tubing and tie a couple of washers on the other end, as shown in Figure 8.3.14.
3. Find a large open area and swing the rubber bung horizontally around your head.
4. Swing it at a speed that keeps the washers at a constant level below the tubing.
5. Add more washers and repeat.
6. Carefully observe what happens to the speed and radius of the 'orbit' as more washers are added.

Review
1. Identify which part of this model represents:
   a. a satellite in orbit
   b. the force of gravity
   c. the planet around which the satellite orbits.
2. What happened to the speed and radius of the orbit when the gravitational pull of the planet was increased?
3. a. Construct a conclusion for your investigation.
   b. Assess whether your hypothesis was supported or not.

3 • Modelling • STUDENT DESIGN •

Purpose
To construct a model that shows how the orbit and rotation of the Moon affects what we see from Earth.

Timing 60 plus minutes

Materials
To be selected by students

Procedure
1. Choose one of the following and design a model that will show why:
   - on Earth we only ever see the one face of the Moon
   - we see phases of the Moon
   - solar or lunar eclipses occur.
2. Before you start any practical work, assess your model. List any risks.

Hints
Your model could be:
- a digital animation
- a physical model (for example made of balls and a light source)
- a role play (for example with people moving about to represent Earth, Moon and Sun).
- Use the STEM and SDI template in your eBook to help you plan and carry out your investigation.

Review
1. Assess how well your model demonstrated your chosen phenomena. For example, what did it show well and what were its limitations?
2. Compare your model with those of other groups. How could your model be improved?

CHAPTER 8 • EARTH IN SPACE 371

MODULE 8.3 Practical investigations

Build a mobile from recycled materials

 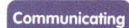

Background
Sophie has always loved mobiles. Her parents remember when she was a toddler how much she enjoyed watching the mobiles hanging from her bedroom ceiling, moving in interesting ways. At primary school Sophie made a model solar system in the form of a mobile. At secondary school she has been learning about forces including gravity.

Problem
Your task is to design and build a mobile of multiple recycled items. Once you have constructed your mobile you should take a photo of it and explain why it must be hung through the centre of gravity. Create a poster or slideshow presentation outlining the method you used to create your mobile.

Use a flow chart and labelled diagrams to show the stages of design and construction. Use your knowledge of forces to explain how the mobile remains balanced like the one in Figure 8.3.15.

Materials
You have access to:
- wire
- nylon thread
- cotton thread
- coat hangers
- hard and soft plastic
- wood scraps
- tennis balls
- marbles
- fishing sinkers
- string
- fishing line
- scissors
- sticky-tape
- modelling clay
- corks
- safety pins
- paperclips
- drinking straws
- paper
- cardboard
- pliers
- wire cutters

Engineering design process
- Identify the problem that needs solving.
- Brainstorm solutions to identify the different designs using the materials you have on hand.

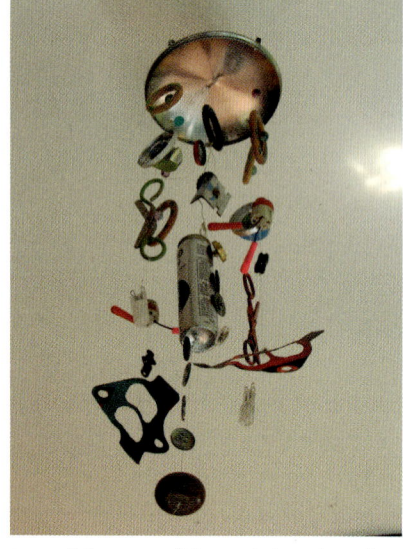

FIGURE 8.3.15 A large mobile sculpture hanging from the ceiling

- Before you commence your investigation you must conduct a risk assessment and write down safety measures that you will follow to keep yourself and other students safe. See the Activity Book Science toolkit to assist you with developing a risk assessment.
- Summarise your investigation in a scientific poster or slideshow presentation using flow charts and labelled diagrams.

Engineering design process

Identify problem
↓
Brainstorm solutions
↓
Design and build prototype
↓
Test prototype → Evaluate and redesign
↓
Prototype flawed
↓
Communicate successful solution

FIGURE 8.3.16 Engineering involves the application of science to design, construct and maintain structures, machines and devices.

372 PEARSON SCIENCE 7 2ND EDITION

MODULE 8.4 Earth

Earth's atmosphere and distance from the Sun give it the perfect conditions for life, allowing it to sustain millions of different species on its surface and under its seas. Earth rotates on its own axis, making the Sun appear to rise daily in the east and set in the west. Earth tilts on its axis and also orbits the Sun, giving the planet its different seasons.

science 4 fun

Simulating seasons

What happens when sunlight falls on Earth at an angle?

Collect this…
- torch
- sheet of paper (preferably graph paper or with a grid)
- 30 cm ruler

Do this…
1. Place the sheet of paper on the floor or on a desk or table.
2. Hold the torch 30 cm from the paper and shine its light directly onto the paper.
3. Trace around the 'pool' of light.
4. Repeat, but this time direct the torch so that its light falls on the paper at an angle.
5. Once again, trace around the 'pool' of light.

Record this…
1. Describe what happened.
2. Explain why you think this happened.

The Earth in space

Every day the Sun appears to rise in the east and set in the west, as do the Moon and stars. The Sun doesn't really move this way. Neither do the Moon or the stars. Instead, the Earth itself is spinning from west to east, making it appear that the Sun, Moon and stars move the other way (Figure 8.4.1).

FIGURE 8.4.1 Every five minutes another photograph was taken to produce this image of the Sun setting in the west.

CHAPTER 8 • EARTH IN SPACE **373**

Day and night

An imaginary line called the **axis** runs through the Earth from the North Pole to the South Pole. Earth rotates (spins) about this line, from west to east. The time taken for any planet to rotate about its axis is referred to as its **day**. Earth takes 24 hours to complete one rotation, and so one day on Earth is 24 hours. During this day, the Sun rises once in the east and sets once in the west.

As Figure 8.4.2 shows at any time half of the Earth is bathed in sunlight. This half experiences day. The other half is in the dark and so experiences night. As the Earth rotates, some regions move into the light and others move out of it.

This causes the Sun to rise and set at different times in different regions. Those further to the east experience sunrise and sunset before than those in the west. For example, the sun rises in Melbourne about 30 minutes before it does in Adelaide. Likewise, the sun sets in Brisbane about 2 hours before it sets in Perth. To ensure that sunrise and sunset occur at roughly the same time across the country, Australia has three basic time zones (Figure 8.4.3).

The year

Like all the other planets in the solar system, Earth orbits the Sun. It travels at an average speed of 108 000 km/h and takes $365\frac{1}{4}$ days to complete one orbit. A complete orbit is called a **revolution** and is shown in Figure 8.4.4. The time taken by a planet to revolve around the Sun is known as its **year**. For Earth, a year is $365\frac{1}{4}$ days. The quarter day makes setting up a calendar very difficult and so a calendar year is normally taken as 365 days. However, every four years the calendar needs to 'catch up', so an extra day is added to make a leap year of 366 days. This extra day is 29 February.

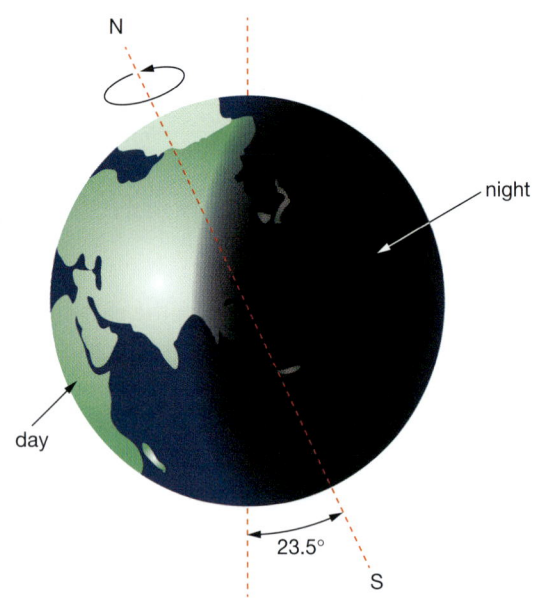

FIGURE 8.4.2 A day is the time it takes for Earth to spin around on its axis once completely.

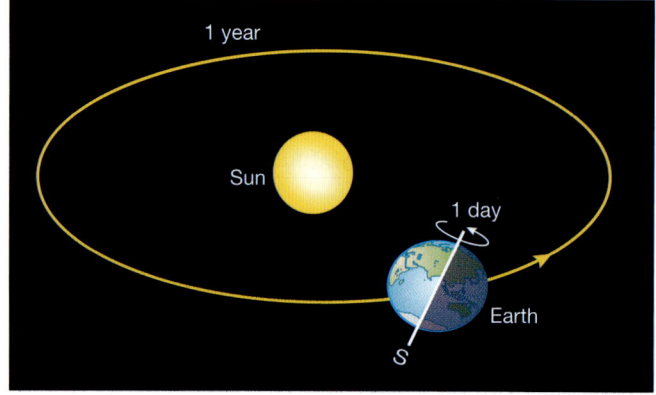

FIGURE 8.4.4 A year is the time it takes for Earth to completely revolve or orbit around the Sun. A day is the time it takes to rotate completely on its own axis.

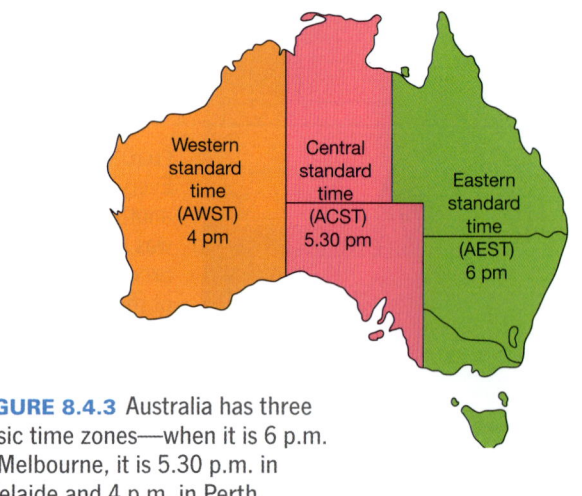

FIGURE 8.4.3 Australia has three basic time zones—when it is 6 p.m. in Melbourne, it is 5.30 p.m. in Adelaide and 4 p.m. in Perth.

SciFile

Feeling dizzy?

Earth spins once per day but we don't all travel at the same speed. The equator is furthest from the axis so anyone living there is travelling the fastest (1670 km/h). The further from the equator you go, the slower your speed. For example, Cairns speeds along at approximately 1600 km/h, Sydney at 1380 km/h and Hobart at 1240 km/h. The axis passes through the North and South Poles, so anyone there simply turns around on the spot!

SkillBuilder

Leap years

Every fourth year is not always a leap year. Use the following key to predict whether a year is a leap year or not.

Can the year be divided by 400 exactly?	If yes, then go to 2.
If not, can the year be divided by 100 exactly?	If yes, then go to 1.
If not, can the year be divided by 4 exactly?	If yes, then go to 2.
1	It's a normal year.
2	It's a leap year.

Worked example

Problem
Was 2016 a leap year?

Solution
Thinking: Can the year be divided by 400 exactly?

Working: 2016 ÷ 400 = 5.04
No

Thinking: Can the year be divided by 100 exactly?

Working: 2016 ÷ 100 = 20.16
No

Thinking: Can the year be divided by 4 exactly?

Working: 2016 ÷ 4 = 504
Yes

504 is a whole number and so 2016 is a leap year.

Try yourself
Calculate whether the following years were/will be leap years.

a 2015
b 2020
c 2100

Seasons

If the plane in which Earth revolves around the Sun is thought to be horizontal, then Earth's axis is not vertical. Instead it tilts at an angle of 23.5°. This tilt gives us our **seasons**, summer, autumn, winter and spring. As Figure 8.4.5 shows, some parts of Earth point towards the Sun. This exposes them more, so that the sunlight falling on them is more concentrated. These parts experience summer. Other parts of Earth point away from the Sun. In these regions the sunlight is spread over a larger area. This results in lower temperatures and winter.

Earth exposes different parts of its surface to the Sun as it moves along its orbit. Australia experiences summer from December through to March because this is when the southern hemisphere is pointed towards the Sun. Meanwhile, the northern hemisphere is pointing away from the Sun and is experiencing winter. The situation reverses six months later.

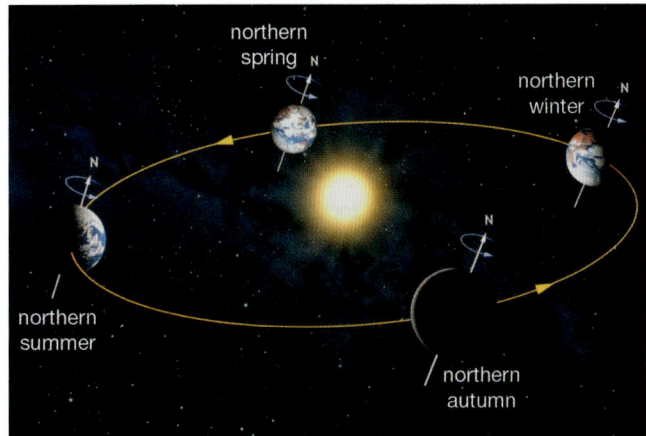

FIGURE 8.4.5 Earth's tilted axis causes sunlight to be more concentrated on some parts of Earth than others at different times of the year. This causes the seasons.

In summer, Earth's tilt causes the Sun to be more vertical in the sky at noon than in winter. This causes:

- more hours of sunlight in summer than in winter
- the position on the horizon where the Sun rises and sets to change slightly each day
- short shadows in summer and long shadows at exactly the same time of day in winter.

In summer, sunlight falls nearly vertically. Heat is concentrated but can easily be blocked by eaves and verandas. Winter is colder because sunlight is more angled, spreading its heat over a larger area. You can see how this happens in Figure 8.4.6.

Prac 3 p. 382

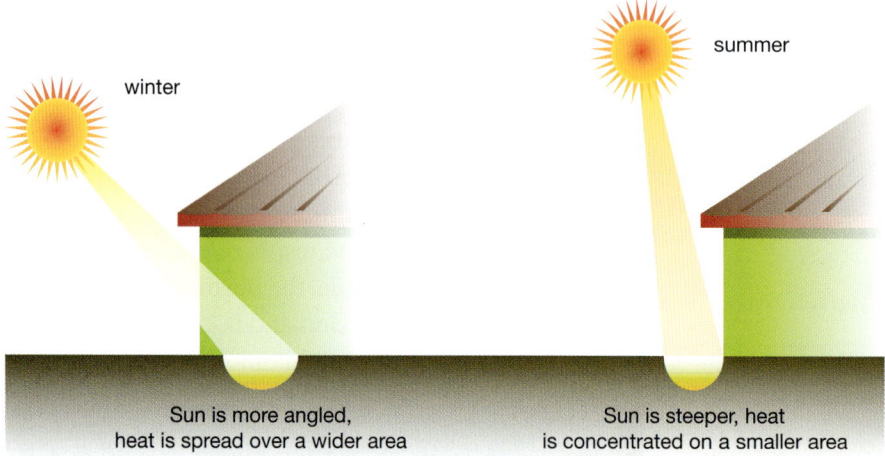

FIGURE 8.4.6 Architects and builders design eaves and verandas to block sunlight in summer and admit it in winter.

Working with Science

AVIATION SAFETY
Airspace controller

Observing the skies is a big part of an airspace controller's job. Airspace controllers (also known as air traffic controllers) are in charge of controlling the flow of aircrafts to ensure the airspace is safe and orderly. They do this by communicating with pilots via radio and using computer and radar technology to monitor the airspace (Figure 8.4.7). Airspace controllers are responsible for assisting pilots in emergency situations and directing aircrafts during take-off and landing. Airspace control centres work closely with the Bureau of Meteorology to stay alert to weather conditions and direct air traffic during storms.

Airspace controllers must be able to make quick, accurate decisions, have excellent computer, maths and communication skills, a good understanding of weather patterns and good spatial awareness. To become an airspace controller, you need to complete a Diploma of Aviation (Air Traffic Control). Training is also provided by Airservices Australia and the Royal Australian Air Force (RAAF).

FIGURE 8.4.7 An airspace controller monitors aircraft activity using computer and radar technology and radio communication.

Review

1. Why do you think an airspace controller's job is important?
2. Why would it be important for an airspace controller to have a good understanding of weather patterns?

SCIENCE AS A HUMAN ENDEAVOUR
Nature and development of science

Rotation in the solar system

Earth rotates on its axis once per day and the Moon takes 27.3 days to rotate on its axis. Other bodies in the solar system rotate on their axes too.

FIGURE 8.4.8 Being gaseous, different layers of Jupiter can rotate at different rates. This photo of Jupiter (and its largest moon Ganymede) was taken by the unmanned spacecraft *Cassini* in 2000.

Without other evidence, it might seem logical to think that the Earth doesn't move and that the Sun revolves around it from east to west. Early civilisations thought just that. Some even thought that a brand new Sun was 'born' each morning, only to 'die' that evening.

We now know that what we see is caused by Earth rotating on its axis from west to east, making the Sun appear to move in the opposite direction. If we could look down onto Earth's North Pole from space, then it would appear that Earth was spinning anticlockwise around it.

The other planets in the solar system spin on their axes too. All but Venus and Uranus spin like Earth, from west to east, in an anticlockwise direction when seen from their 'north' poles. Venus spins in the opposite direction. Uranus is even stranger—it is tilted over onto its side and rotates in a different plane to everything else in the solar system!

SCIENCE AS A HUMAN ENDEAVOUR

Mercury, Venus, Earth and Mars are terrestrial or rocky planets. Having a solid surface means that everything on the surface rotates at exactly the same rate. For example, everywhere on Earth takes one day to rotate and everywhere has a day that is 24 hours long. Likewise, everything on the Moon takes 27.3 days to complete one spin.

The outer planets of Jupiter, Saturn, Uranus and Neptune are not solid but are gas giants. Being gaseous, different regions in these planets are able to rotate at different rates. This gives many of the gas giants a layered appearance (Figure 8.4.8). Table 8.4.1 shows that time taken for the equator and higher latitudes of each gas giant to rotate once. The shorter the time, the faster that part is rotating.

TABLE 8.4.1 Times for rotation of the Sun and planets. The minus sign for Venus and Uranus indicate that they rotate in a different direction.

Celestial body	Equator	Higher latitudes
Sun	24.5 d	35.0 d
Mercury	58.6 d	58.6 d
Venus	−243.0 d	−243.0 d
Earth	1.0 d (24 h)	1.0 d (24 h)
Mars	24.6 h	24.6 h
Jupiter	9.8 h	9.9 h
Saturn	10.2 h	10.6 h
Uranus	−17.2 h	
Neptune	16.1 h	

In 1610, the English astronomer Thomas Harriot (1560–1621) used the recently invented telescope to sketch sunspots on the Sun's surface. A year later, German astronomer Johannes Fabricius (1587–1616) observed that sunspots move across its surface, suggesting that the Sun rotates too. You can see this in Figure 8.4.9. In 1625, another German, Christopher Scheiner (1573–1650), used sunspots to measure the rate of rotation of the Sun at its equator. He noted that the rest of the Sun seemed to rotate more slowly.

In the early twentieth century, the Sun's rotation rates were measured accurately. These studies proved that the northern and southern hemispheres of the Sun spin differently. The Sun rotates in the same direction as most of the other bodies in the solar system—from west to east or anticlockwise as seen from its 'north' pole.

REVIEW

1. Compare the rotation rates of Earth, the Moon and the Sun.
2. Why does Jupiter have different rotation rates while Mars has only one?
3. Compare the rotations of Venus and Uranus with everything else in the solar system.
4. What evidence was used to prove that the Sun rotated?

AB 8.7

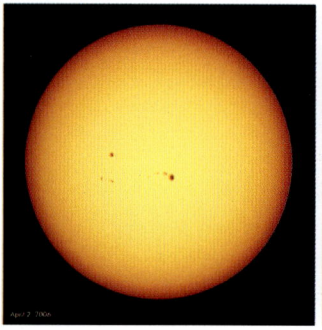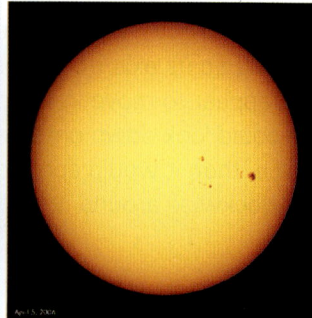

FIGURE 8.4.9 These photographs show the Sun over four days in 2006. Sunspots can be seen moving left to right, suggesting that the Sun is rotating on its axis.

MODULE 8.4 Review questions

Remembering

1. Define the terms:
   a. 1 day
   b. 1 year
   c. 1 revolution.
2. Which direction does the Earth spin in—east to west or west to east?
3. How many days are there in the following?
   a. 'normal' calendar year
   b. year as defined by Earth's orbit
   c. leap year.

Understanding

4. Explain why Adelaide is half an hour behind Melbourne while Perth is two hours behind Melbourne.
5. a. Why do some people only have a birthday every four years?
   b. What date is their birthday?
6. Predict which would produce the largest 'pool' of light in the science4fun activity on page 373.

Applying

7. Calculate whether the following years were/will be leap years or not.
   a. 1896
   b. 1900
   c. 2225
   d. 2400
8. In Figure 8.4.10, identify the part(s) of Earth (A, B, C or D) experiencing:
   a. summer
   b. winter
   c. a day in which the Sun is always in the sky
   d. a day in which the Sun never appears.

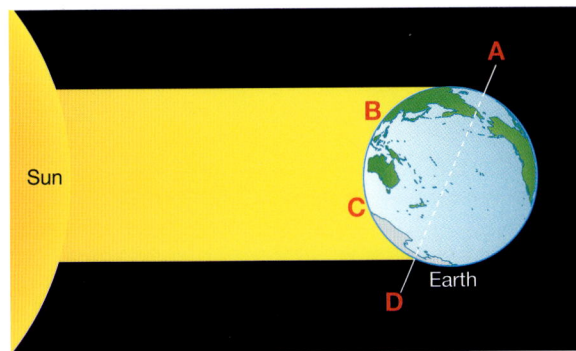

FIGURE 8.4.10

Use the following key for questions 9 and 10.

A	21 March	C	21 September
B	21 June	D	21 December

9. The summer solstice is the date when we receive the most daylight. The winter solstice is when we have our longest night. Australia is in the southern hemisphere. Use Figure 8.4.5 on page 375 to predict which of the dates above mark our:
   a. summer solstice
   b. winter solstice.
10. The equinox marks the dates each year that everywhere on Earth spends equal times in daylight and in the dark of night.
    a. How many equinoxes occur each year?
    b. Use Figure 8.4.5 on page 375 to predict the dates for each equinox.

Analysing

11. We can only celebrate the New Year at 12 a.m. (midnight) because our calendar years are rounded off at either 365 or 366 days. If we used $365\frac{1}{4}$ days for our calendar year, then New Year's celebrations would have to be celebrated at different times each year.
    a. Calculate how many hours there are in one quarter of a day.
    b. The New Year began at 12 a.m. this year. If the calendar year was $365\frac{1}{4}$ days long, calculate the time it would occur:
       i. next year
       ii. the year after that.
    c. Calculate how many years would pass before the New Year returned to 12 a.m.
    d. Use this example to explain why the length of a calendar year is rounded to 365 or 366 days.
12. China has no time zones, despite being a country as large as Australia. Compare what a day would be like in its east and in its west.
13. Propose what would happen to the seasons if Earth's tilt suddenly changed to:
    a. 0° (no tilt at all)
    b. 45° (more than now)
    c. 10° (less than now).
14. Neptune's axis tilts at 29° and takes 165 Earth years to orbit around the Sun.
    a. Compare Neptune's tilt with that of Earth.
    b. Explain why Neptune's tilt gives it four seasons.
    c. How long is a year and a season on Neptune?

CHAPTER 8 • EARTH IN SPACE 379

MODULE 8.4 Practical investigations

1 • Day and night

Purpose
To model day and night on Earth.

Timing 45 minutes

Materials
- balloon
- string or cotton
- felt-tip pen
- access to a globe
- access to a bright light (such as a projector, spotlight, data projector or similar)

Procedure
1. Blow up your balloon and tie it off so that no gas can escape. This is your Earth, and its tied-off end represents the North Pole.
2. Tie a length of string or cotton to the North Pole.
3. Use the felt-tip pen to draw on the balloon the position of the equator, South Pole and International Date Line.
4. Use the globe to check the shape and position of the major continents and copy them onto the balloon. Make sure you include Australia.
5. On Australia, write a large E on the east coast and a large W on the west coast.
6. Hang the balloon by the string in front of the bright light and slowly turn it from the 'west' (W) to 'east' (E) as shown in Figure 8.4.11.

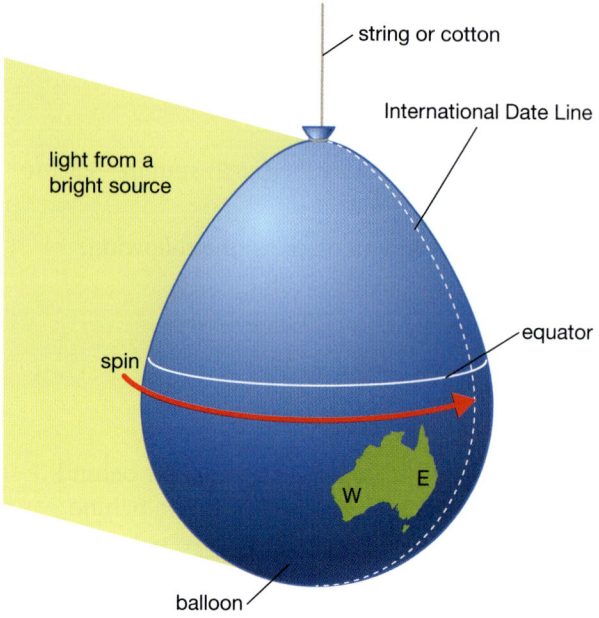

FIGURE 8.4.11

Review
1. The Sun rises in the east and sets in the west, but you rotated your 'Earth' in the opposite direction. Why?
2. State which coast of Australia:
   a. first came into 'daylight'
   b. was the last to move into 'night'.
3. Perth is in a different time zone from Melbourne, Sydney and Brisbane, being two hours 'behind' them. Use your model to explain why different time zones are needed in Australia.
4. Assess how accurate this model is in showing Earth, its spin and its day.

MODULE 8.4 Practical investigations

2 • Make a sundial

Purpose
To construct a sundial.

Timing
30 minutes plus one sunny day

Materials
- sturdy sheet of cardboard or scrap timber
- sheet of A4 scrap paper
- sticky-tape
- felt-tip pen
- watch or clock
- compass (optional)

SAFETY A Risk Assessment is required for this investigation.

Procedure
1. Roll up the A4 sheet of paper lengthwise to form a cylinder.
2. Secure it to the sheet of cardboard with strips of sticky-tape so that it stands upright (Figure 8.4.12).

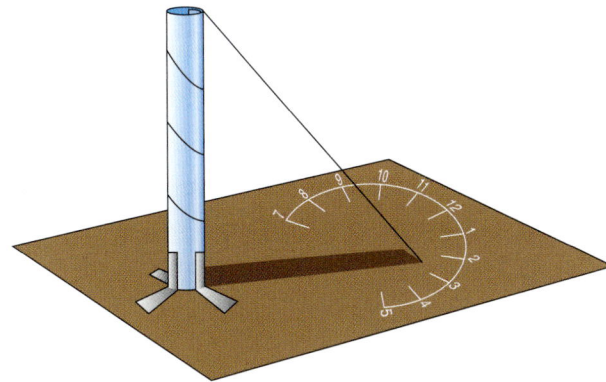

FIGURE 8.4.12

3. Place your sundial in a spot where it gets sunlight most of the day.
4. Every hour, use the felt-tip pen to mark where the shadow falls on the cardboard or timber sheet. Write the time next to its mark.
5. To make your sundial more accurate:
   a. Use a compass to find exactly where north is.
   b. Use an atlas or search the internet for the latitude of where you live. For example, Melbourne is 38°S. Use a protractor to measure out this angle and tilt the base so that it slopes away from north at this angle (Figure 8.4.13).

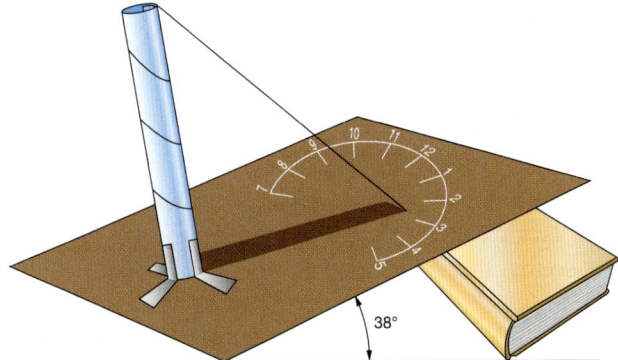

FIGURE 8.4.13

Review
1. a. Will 9 a.m. be on the west side or east side of your sundial?
   b. Justify you choice.
2. Tilting the sundial made it more accurate. Propose a reason why.

CHAPTER 8 • EARTH IN SPACE **381**

MODULE 8.4 Practical investigations

SPARKlab alternative available for this activity

3 • Angles and temperature

Purpose
To test whether the angle of sunlight affects the surface temperature on Earth.

Hypothesis
Which do you think will heat up a thermometer faster—a lamp shining directly over it or a lamp shining at an angle? Before you go any further with this investigation, write a hypothesis in your workbook.

Timing 45 minutes

Materials
- lamp (such as a microscope lamp)
- 2 thermometers
- 2 blocks of wood
- black plastic
- sticky-tape

SAFETY The lamp will get very hot so avoid touching it.

Procedure
1. Cut out two small identically sized sheets of black plastic and tape them onto wooden blocks so that they make pockets.
2. Secure a thermometer in each pocket, ensuring that it is touching the plastic sheet. Tape the thermometer to the board to secure it.
3. Place the two blocks the same distance from the lamp. Figure 8.4.14 shows the set-up.
   - Block A: Lay one block flat on the desk so that the light from the lamp falls on it at an angle.
   - Block B: Use some books to chock up the other block so that it is at an angle to the desk and the light falls directly on it.
4. Turn on the lamp.

Results
1. Record the temperature of each thermometer every minute for at least five minutes.
2. Place your results in a table like the one shown below. Give your table a title.

Time (min)	Block A	Block B
1		
2		
3		
4		
5		

Review
1. Identify which block (A or B) showed the greatest increase in temperature.
2. Identify which block (A or B) modelled the surface of the Earth in:
   a. summer
   b. winter.
3. Use your results to propose a reason why:
   a. the tropics are found near the equator
   b. icebergs are only found near the poles.
4. a. Construct a conclusion for your investigation.
   b. Assess whether your hypothesis was supported or not.

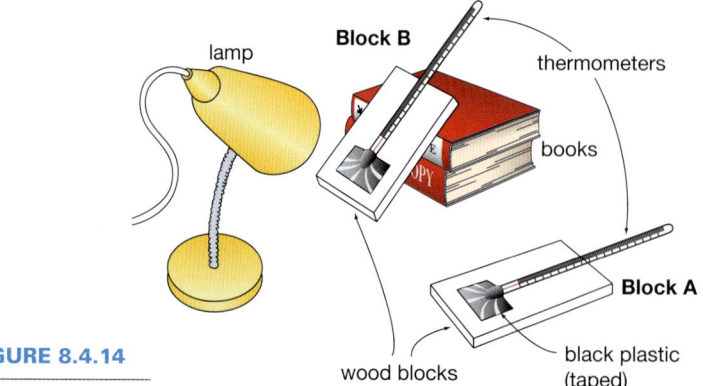
FIGURE 8.4.14

CHAPTER 8 Chapter review

Remembering

1. Define the terms:
   a. ellipse
   b. Earth's axis
   c. satellite
   d. umbra.

2. What term best describes each of the following?
   a. a mass completing a revolution around Earth
   b. a complete rotation of Earth on its axis
   c. different shapes of the Moon
   d. when the Moon blocks the Sun.

3. Name two important people who supported:
   a. the geocentric model
   b. the heliocentric model.

4. What evidence caused the geocentric model to be dropped in favour of the heliocentric model?

5. Draw a diagram that shows what retrograde motion is.

6. Draw a diagram showing the arrangement of the Sun, Earth and the Moon during a lunar eclipse.

Understanding

7. Describe what a 'shooting star' really is.

8. Explain why comets and meteor showers are often observed together.

9. One set of planets is also known as the rocky planets. Which planets are most likely to belong to this set?

10. Outline four important observations that space missions to the planets have brought.

11. Why does Earth experience four seasons each year?

12. Describe how the day and year are related to Earth's movement.

13. Predict what the world would be like if there were no time zones and everywhere was all at exactly the same time.

Applying

14. You are about to fly between Perth and Sydney. Identify where in your flight gravity will be:
    a. the least
    b. the greatest.

15. Sanjay is a Year 7 student. He roughly sketched the diagram of the solar system shown in Figure 8.4.15, but forgot to add labels and didn't draw every orbit. Identify which of the orbits he drew most likely represents that of:
    a. Earth (an inner planet)
    b. the Moon
    c. Neptune (an outer planet)
    d. Pluto
    e. Halley's comet.

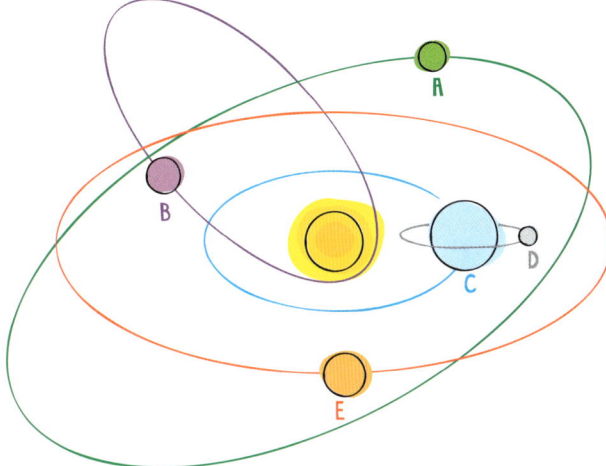

FIGURE 8.4.15

16. Everything around you has its own gravitational field.
    a. Identify what mass affects you the most.
    b. Explain why other things like the wall or the person sitting next to you don't influence you much.

17. Imagine that you shoot a gun horizontally off a tall mountain, the bullet going so quickly that it goes into orbit around Earth. It could be extremely dangerous if you stay on top of the mountain. Propose a reason why.

Analysing

18. Compare:
    a. a star and a planet
    b. a comet and a meteor
    c. revolution and rotation of a planet
    d. a solar and lunar eclipse.

19. Classify the model presented in Figure 8.4.15 as either geocentric or heliocentric. Justify your answer.

20. Calculate whether you were born in a leap year or not.

CHAPTER 8 Chapter review

Evaluating

21 Neptune and Uranus were the last planets to be discovered. Propose a reason why.

22 The International Space Station (ISS) shown in Figure 8.4.16 orbits Earth 340 km above its surface. On board, astronauts float around in 'weightless' conditions. Two Year 7 students are arguing about what this means. Joe says this proves there is no gravity at the height of the ISS. Sarah disagrees, saying that there must be gravity at that height.
   a Use the evidence given above to deduce whether there is any gravity at the height of the ISS.
   b Justify your response.
   c Some scientists prefer to use the term 'microgravity' to describe these conditions rather than weightlessness. Assess whether microgravity is a better term.

FIGURE 8.4.16

23 a Assess whether you can or cannot answer the questions on page 343 at the start of this chapter.
   b Use this assessment to evaluate how well you understand the material presented in this chapter.

Creating

24 A mnemonic is a way of remembering the order of something. Construct your own mnemonic to help you remember the order of the planets of the solar system. See the Worked Example on page 266 for more information.

25 Use the following ten key terms to construct a visual summary of the information presented in this chapter:

stars	constellation
gravity	orbit
ellipse	Sun
Earth	Moon
umbra	comet

AB 8.9

CHAPTER 8 Inquiry skills

Research

1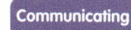

A number of spacecraft have flown by or successfully landed on asteroids or meteors. Some have even attempted to sample dust and gases from these objects. Choose one of these spacecraft (e.g. *Vega 1, Vega 2, Near Shoemaker, Galileo, Hayabusa, Deep Impact, Rosetta* and *Dawn*) and find:
- which space agency ran the mission
- when the mission was launched
- which comet or asteroid it visited
- what data it returned and what scientists learned from it
- what eventually happened to the mission
- where the spacecraft is now.

Present your research as a poster or digital poster designed to explain the value and importance of this type of scientific expedition.

2 Processing & Analysing | Communicating

In January 2016, scientists announced the discovery of a new planet with an orbit well beyond that of Pluto. Explore this discovery to find out:
- the radius of the new planet's orbit
- the evidence that was used to discover it
- names that have been proposed for the new planet.

Which name do you think would be best? You can choose one of the names suggested by others or propose one of your own.

Present your findings as part of a letter or email to the International Astronomical Union (IAU) in support of your preferred name for the planet.

3 Planning & Conducting | Communicating

Research the 1908 or 2013 meteor explosions above Russia. Find:
- a map showing where it happened
- photos or video of the meteor or of the devastation.

Present your research as two email attachments that can be sent to your teacher.

4 Processing & Analysing | Communicating

Investigate the formation of the Moon. Find:
- how it was formed by a collision between Earth and a smaller planet
- evidence for this collision
- the name of the smaller planet
- diagrams or animations showing how it might have happened.

Present your findings in digital form.

5 Planning & Conducting | Communicating

Al Battani was a tenth century astronomer who accurately measured the length of the year. Research Al Battani to find:
- his full name, years and place of birth and death
- where he lived and worked
- the length of the year as determined by him
- his other scientific and mathematical achievements
- the name of the Moon crater named after him
- how he has been honoured in science fiction.

Present the information you find as a series of dot points.

6 Planning & Conducting | Communicating

Research times zones and seasons by finding:
- what the UTC and International Date Line are and why they are needed
- a map showing the main time zones that exist around the world
- the location of the International Date Line
- how long a day and year are on the other planets of the solar system
- the axis tilt of other planets in the solar system
- whether other planets in the solar system experience seasons.

Present your research as a Word document that includes relevant maps and tables.

CHAPTER 8 • EARTH IN SPACE **385**

CHAPTER 8 Inquiry skills

Thinking scientifically

The Bayer system is used to name stars within a constellation. It uses the Greek alphabet to name them, with alpha (α) being the brightest star. Beta (β) is used for the next brightest, gamma (γ) for the next and so on.

The two pointers of the Southern Cross are α-Centauri and β-Centauri. In another constellation are Alpha-Cygni and Beta-Cygni.

The first six letters of the Greek alphabet are α (alpha), β (beta), γ (gamma), δ (delta), ε (epsilon) and ζ (zeta).

1 Use this information to:
   a state which of the following stars would be brightest:
      A α-Centauri
      B β-Centauri
      C Alpha-Cygni
      D Beta-Cygni
      E α-Centauri AND Alpha Cygni
      F β-Centauri AND Beta Cygni
      G α-Centauri is brighter than β-Centauri and Alpha-Cygni is brighter than Beta-Cygni but there is not enough information to tell whether α-Centauri is brighter than Alpha-Cygni or whether β-Centauri is brighter than Beta-Cygni.
   b explain why you cannot compare the brightness of α-Centauri and Beta-Cygni.

2 Stars are named in order of decreasing brightness using letters of the Greek alphabet. Use this information to identify which of the following lists its stars in the correct order from brightest to least bright.
   A α-Crucis, δ-Crucis, Gamma-Crucis, Zeta-Crucis
   B β-Geminorum, Beta-Crucis, β-Cygnis, Beta-Orionis
   C δ-Geminorum, δ-Centauri, δ-Cygni, δ-Crucis
   D β-Geminorum, Gamma-Geminorum, Delta-Geminorum, ε-Geminorum.

3 Density determines whether an object sinks or floats. Basalt rock has a density of around 3.0 g/cm while the density of pure water is 1.0 g/cm. These densities suggest that a lump of basalt will sink when placed in water. The average density of a human is 1.01 g/cm. We are slightly denser than water and so will sink very slowly into it. The table below shows the density of the eight planets of the solar system.

TABLE 8.5.1 Density of planets

Planet	Density (g/cm^3)
Mercury	5.427
Venus	5.204
Earth	5.515
Mars	3.934
Jupiter	1.326
Saturn	0.687
Uranus	1.27
Neptune	1.638

Use the following key to answer parts a to d below:

A   Mercury, Venus, Earth, Mars
B   Mercury, Venus, Earth
C   Jupiter, Saturn, Uranus, Neptune
D   Saturn

a Identify the planet(s) that are most likely to be rocky.
b Identify the planet(s) you would most likely sink into.
c Identify the planet(s) on which a lump of basalt would sink.
d Identify which of the planet(s) would float on water.

CHAPTER 8 Glossary

artificial satellites: satellites placed into orbit by humans

asteroid belt: a group of rocks that orbit the Sun in a band between Mars and Jupiter

asteroid: an irregular rocky object in orbit around the Sun between the orbits of Mars and Jupiter

astronomer: a scientist who studies the stars, planets and other celestial objects

axis: the line connecting the North Pole with the South Pole. Earth rotates around this axis.

celestial: relating to the sky or to space

comet: a ball of ice, dust and rock that orbits the Sun in a highly elliptical orbit

comet

constellation: a group of stars which form a recognisable pattern in the night sky

day: the time a planet takes to rotate once completely on its own axis

dwarf planet: a small celestial body that is in orbit around the Sun and is nearly round in shape but with insufficient gravity to sweep its orbit clear of other bodies (which is a criterion of being called a planet)

eclipse: the total or partial obscuring of one celestial body by another

ellipse: oval shape

gas giants: the large planets of the outer solar system: Jupiter, Saturn, Uranus, Neptune

geocentric model: model of the universe with Earth at its centre

gravitational force field: invisible field that causes masses to be attracted to each other

heliocentric model: model of the universe with the Sun at its centre

lunar eclipse: when the Earth blocks sunlight from reaching the Moon

meteor: a meteoroid that enters Earth's atmosphere, usually creating a bright streak across the sky as it burns up; a shooting star

meteor

meteorite: a meteor big enough for part of it to hit the ground

meteoroid: a small particle or body of rock that orbits the Sun near Earth's orbit

Milky Way: the galaxy in which our solar system is located

orbit: path a planet takes around a star, or a moon or artificial satellite takes around a planet

penumbra: less dense shadow of an eclipse

phases: different shapes of the Moon as seen from Earth

planet: roughly spherical ball of rock or gas that orbit (move around) the Sun. They do not generate their own light.

retrograde motion: apparent loop-like motion of the planets as seen from Earth

retrograde motion

revolution: one complete orbit around the Sun

satellite: object in orbit around another larger object

seasons: on Earth, summer, autumn, winter, spring; caused by the tilt of a planet's axis

sidereal month: the time the Moon takes to complete one orbit of Earth (27.3 days)

solar eclipse: when the Moon blocks sunlight from reaching Earth

solar system: the Sun and all the planets, satellites, asteroids, comets and other bodies revolving around it

terrestrial: Earth-like, rocky. The terrestrial planets are Mercury, Venus, Earth and Mars

umbra: full, dark shadow of an eclipse

year: the time a planet takes to revolve once around the Sun

AB 8.8

Index

A

acids 8, 44
adaptations, organisms 185–6
    advantages for animals 186
    advantages for plants 186
agriculture
    Australia 212–13, 229, 263
    palm oil 211, 215
    see also food
air resistance 294, 303–4
analogy model 53
animal kingdom 237–49
animal phyla 238
animals
    adaption advantages 186
    and fire 202–3
    as consumers 196
    as organisms 184
    biological control 204–7
    characteristics of kingdom 256
    classification 228–68
    classification problems 245–6
    controlling 204–7
    crocodile 185, 230–1, 243
    dingo fence 204
    eagles 194
    fish 242
    possums 34, 214
    quoll 185–6, 196
    rabbit proof fence 205
    rabbits 195, 207
    Tasmanian devil 196
    threatened species 189
    vertebrates 241
    see also Australia; classification, using; life/living things
Antarctica, science research 9
aqueous solution 141, 167
aquifer 115
asteroids 347
astronomy
    Aristarchus 353
    Aristotle 353
    Copernicus 354
    described 3
    Galileo Galilei 354
    Kepler 355
    Ptolemy 354
atmosphere 89
atoms 56
    structure 314–5
Australia
    agriculture 212–13, 229, 263
    biological control 204–7
    cane toads 207, 231
    cattle 213
    classification 228–30, 266
    dingo fence 204
    energy reserves 102
    fire 202–3
    Great Artesian Basin 115, 129
    habitats, organisms 184–6
    indigenous classification 267–8
    indigenous water use 128–9
    indigenous weather classification 271–2
    introduced species 204–5, 207, 229
    logging 211
    mining 212
    rabbit plagues 207
    rabbit proof fence 205
    regrowing forest 189
    renewable energy 103
    salt-tolerant wheat 212–13
    uranium reserves 102
    water management 123–9
axes, graphs 24

B

bacteria 46
    as organisms 184
    monera kingdom 255
balances (equipment) 6
bar graphs 23–5, 33
beakers 6, 8, 21
biodegradable 46
biodegradability 46–7
    plastics 47
biogas 103
biological adaption/conservation 9
biological control 204–7
biology 3–4
biomass 103–4, 110
biosphere 187
boiling point 42, 63
bonds, particle 54–5, 62
Brownian motion 57

Bunsen burner 8, 12, 13
    lighting 7
    parts 6–7
buoyancy 80
bushfire *see* fire/bushfire

C

carbon capture and storage 95
carbon dioxide 89, 94–5, 100, 102, 107
cells, organisms 255–6
centrifuging blood 153
changing state 61–9
    see also states of matter
chemical properties 44
chemical reactions 46
chemicals, equipment 6
chemistry described 3
chemists 34
chromatography 159–60
classification, using 227–78
    agnatha 242
    amphibians 243
    animal phyla 238
    annelids 240
    arthropods 241
    aves 243
    chondrichthyes 242
    chordates 241
    classes 265–7
    cnidarians 239
    constructing dichotomous key 233
    crocodiles 230–1
    described 228–9
    echinoderms 239
    families 265–7
    groups change 229
    illustrated example 232
    introducing keys 231–3
    keys 231–3
    mammals 244
    molluscs 240
    nematodes 240
    orders 265–7
    osteichthyes 242
    platyhelminths 240
    poriferans 238
    reptiles 243
    taxonomy 231

why classify? 230
    see also kingdoms
classification systems 262–72
    common names 263–5
    history of classification 262–3
    indigenous 267–8
    indigenous compared to biological 268
    levels 265–7
    standardising names 264
climate change 2–4, 9, 18, 34, 107
cloning 2
clouds 113
coal 87, 94–5 100, 101–2
coal seam gas 95
column graphs 23–5
comets 348
communicating in science 23–30
compression characteristics 43–4, 54
conclusion, scientific report 26
condensation 64
    in distillation 162
    water cycle 114
conductivity 43
conical flasks 6, 8
contact force 292–3
continuous measurements 24–5
controlled variables, described 32
cooling, and changing state 61–4
cross-section 8
crystals 161
curve of best fit 25

D

data, displaying *see* displaying data
density 42, 70–80
    and mass and volume 71, 72
    and particle packing 70–71
    floating and sinking 73
    formula 72
dependent variables
    described 32
diagrams 15, 26
diesel fuel 102
diffusion 56
disciplines, science 4
discrete groupings 23–5
displaying data 23–6, 33
    graphing changes of state 64

distance, units 16
domains, magnetic 313
drawing equipment 8
drought 201

E

Earth
    atmosphere 89
    axis 374
    biosphere 187
    magnetic field 311, 314
    seasons 375–6
    water cycle 112–22
    see also Earth resources
Earth in space 343–82
    Moon 345
    planets 346–7
    Sun 373–6
    stars 345–8
    the night sky 344–51
    see also solar system
Earth resources 85–138
    energy 100–111
    global energy solutions 107–8
    natural 86
    renewable and non-renewable 86–99
    water cycle 112–22
    water management 123–32
    see also resources
earthworms, classification 240
eclipse
    lunar 368
    solar 367–8
ecology/ecologists 3, 34
ecosystems 187
    and fire 202–3
    controlling animals 204–7
    energy flows 195, 197
    habitats and organisms 194–200
    impacts on 201–9
    natural 201
    pond 197
    sustainable 201–2
ecotoxicology 45
electric fields *see* magnetic and electric fields
electricity, as energy source 94–5, 102–8
    see also magnetic and electric fields

El Niño 122
energy
    changing state 61–4
    food chains 195, 197
    fossil fuels 87, 101–2
    friction 295
    geothermal 106
    hydroelectricity 103
    in solids 54
    light 195
    nuclear 102
    ocean 105
    particle model 53
    science-based employment 106
    solar 104
    use per person, globally 101
    wind 105, 111
    see also Australia; energy resources
energy flow, food chains/webs 195, 197
energy problems, global 107–8
energy resources 100–111
    energy demand 101
    fossil 101–2
    non-renewable 87, 101–2, 107
    nuclear 102
    renewable 100–111
    see also resources
environment
    factors shaping
    organism adaption 187
    protecting 171
    see also pollution; toxic chemicals
equipment, scientific *see* scientific equipment
erosion 92
ethanol 104
evaporation
    air temperature/movement 116–17
    changing state 61–3
    separating soluble substances 161
    slow and fast 164
    water cycle 114
evidence *see* scientific evidence
experiments 15
    and fieldwork 15
    communicating results 23–30
extinct 201, 210

F

fair test 32
farming *see* agriculture
fields *see* magnetic and electric fields
fieldwork 15
filtering 151–2, 168
fire/bushfire 4
    fuel-reduction burning 202–3
    modern use 202–3
    traditional use 202
flatworms, classification 240
foam 42
focal length, determining 360–1
food
    biodegradable 46
    renewable resource 88
    urban farming 214
    see also Australia
food chains and food webs 194–200
    apex predator 197
    decomposers 196
    energy flow 195, 197
    food chains 195–7
    food webs 197
    predators and prey 194–5, 207
    primary consumers 196
    producers/decomposers/consumers 195–7
    scavengers 196
    secondary consumers 197
    tertiary consumers 197
food web *see* food chains and food webs
force multipliers 234–6
forces 279–342
    and change in motion 281
    and simple machines 323–8
    balanced 282
    between particles 54
    changing direction 327–8
    comparing mass and weight 302–3
    contact 292
    defined 280–5
    drawing 282
    electrostatic 314–5
    friction 292–300
    gears 326–7
    gravity 301–10
    lever 324–5
    magnetic and electric fields 311–22
    measuring 281
    non-contact 302, 363
    pulleys 328
    push/pull 280
    reducing impacts of 283
    sports science 305
    terminal velocity 304
    unbalanced 282
    wedges 327
    wheel 325–6
    see also friction; gravity
forests 87–8, 189, 211
fossil fuels 87, 101–2
    fracking 95
freezing point 42, 61, 64
    change of state 63–4
friction 292–300
    as contact force 292
    factors affecting 293
    reducing 294
    swimsuits 295
    unwanted 294
    useful 293
fulcrum 324–5, 327
fungi 46, 188, 196
    kingdom 254

G

gases 42–4
    atmosphere 89
    characteristics/properties 44, 55
    coal seam 95
    cooling 64
    density 71
    diffusion 56
    explaining 55
    fracking 95
    LPG 102
    natural 87, 95
    organism survival 185
    suspensions 143
gears 326–7
geology 3–4
geothermal energy 106
glassware 6, 8, 22
graph types 23–6
    plotting 33
    software 23
    summary of features 25
gravity 301–10
    and distance 364
    and orbits 363–72
    as non-contact force 302
    falling 303–4
    force caused by mass 364
    gravitational fields 302, 363–5
    mass and weight 302–3
greenhouse gases 102
groundwater 115

H

habitat 184
    requirements 185
    Sumatran animals, endangered 211
habitats and interactions 183–226
    adaptations 185–6
    animal control 204–7
    biological control 204–7
    crocodiles 185
    environmental conditions 187
    living places 184–9
    living together 187
    see also organisms
health
    bacteria 255
    centrifuging blood 153
    in ecosystems 194
    water treatment 168
heat
    and changing state 61–4
    and density 71
    biomass 103–4
    in distillation 162
    removing 63
    renewable energy source 103–6
    see also temperature
heating equipment 6–7
height, units 16
hotplates 6–8
humidity 116–17
hydroelectricity 103
hypothesis
    developing 32
    scientific report 26

I

ice, and water 73, 113
icebergs 73
identifying variables 32

independent variables
　　described 32
indirect evidence 56–7
industry, effects of 210–20
　　agriculture 212–13
　　logging 211
　　mining 212
inertia 283
information designers 26
insoluble substances, separating 149–54
　　centrifuging 153
　　decantation 150
　　filtration 151
　　gravity separation 150
　　magnetic separation 150
　　sieving 151
investigating *see* planning investigations; 'Practical Investigations' book examples
irrigation 124–5
　　drip 125
　　flood 125
　　spray 124

J

jellyfish 239

K

keys, classification 231–3
　　dichotomous key 231, 233
　　strong keys 233
kingdom/s
　　animal 237–49, 256
　　characteristics of all five 256
　　comparison of characteristics 256
　　described 238
　　fungi 254, 256
　　monera 255–6
　　organisms classified into 265–7
　　plant 250–3, 256
　　protist 254–6

L

laboratory 2–8
　　descriptions of 5
law, and science 18, 160
length, units 16
levers 324–5
Liebig condenser 162

life/living things
　　as renewable resource 88
　　dependent on natural resources 86
　　needs of 185
　　see also animals; kingdoms; plants
line graphs 24–5
line of best fit 25
liquids 42
　　characteristics/properties 43, 54
　　densities 71
　　diffusion 56
　　explaining 54
living places 184–93
logging *see* forests

M

machines, simple *see* simple machines
magnetic and electric fields 311–22
　　charging up 315–16
　　electric fields 314
　　magnetic domains 313
　　pole attraction/repulsion 312
　　static discharge 316
　　see also magnets
magnetic field lines 312
magnets 311–4, 363
　　temporary/permanent 313
　　uses 314
mass
　　and density 70, 72
　　and gravity 302–3
　　and volume and density 71–2
　　gravitational force field 363–5
　　is not weight 72, 302–3
　　measuring 6
　　units 16
materials *see* scientific equipment
matter
　　and density 70
　　and mass 72, 364
　　states of 43–4
measurements 15–17, 22, 26
　　and observations 15
　　taking accurate 17
　　units 16
melting, change of state 61
melting point 62
meniscus, reading 17

meteorites 344, 347
method of a scientific report 26
metric system 16
microscope 56
Milky Way 346
minerals 91–2
mixtures 139–82
　　and solutions 140–42
　　purifying water 166–73
　　separating insoluble substances 149–54
　　separating soluble substances 159–65
　　suspensions 143
　　types 140–48
　　water 167
　　see also insoluble substances, separating; soluble substances, separating; solutions (of substances)
models in science 52–3
Moon 345
　　in space 373
　　lunar eclipse 368
　　orbit 366
　　phases 366–7
　　solar eclipse 367–8
motion
　　and forces 282
　　Brownian 57
　　see also forces
multicellular 256
multipliers 324–7
　　force 324–6
　　gears 326–7
　　inclined planes 326
　　levers 324–5
　　pulleys 328
　　speed 327

N

natural resources 86
　　see also Earth resources
Newton 280
nitrogen 89
non-biodegradable 46
non-renewable energy sources 101–2, 107
non-renewable resources
　　rocks/minerals 91–2
　　soil 92

INDEX **391**

nuclear fission 102
nuclear fuels 102
nuclear fusion 345
nuclear waste 102

O

observations
    and measurements 15–17
    in classification 232–3
    discrete groupings 23–4
    displaying 23–5
    qualitative/quantitative 15, 232
    reports 26
oceanography 9
oceans
    energy from 105
    pollution 154
    water cycle 112–14
optical illusion and measurement 15–16
orbits 363–72
    and time 374
    explaining 365
    in solar system 366
    Moon 366–7
    satellites 365
    unstable 366
    see also gravity
organisms 184
    adaptations of 185–6
    animal kingdom 238
    cells 255–6
    classifying Australian 266
    kingdom characteristics compared 256
    need for food 194–5
    scientific naming 264–5
    sustainable ecosystems 201
    symbiosis 187
    symmetry 239
    see also kingdoms
oxygen 89, 167
ozone layer 18

P

parasites 240, 242
particle model 53
particles 53–5
    and density 71
    and heat 61
    atoms 314–5
    bonds 54–5, 62
    cooling 63–4
    electrons 314–5
    neutrons 314–5
    protons 314–5
    see also bonds; energy; heat; temperature
petrol 101–2
pH 44
photosynthesis 89, 195
physical properties 42–4, 70–80
physics 3–4
pie graph (sector graph) 24
planets 346–7
    see also Earth in space; solar system
planning investigations 31–6
    conclusion 33
    developing hypothesis 32
    developing procedure 32–3
    displaying results 33
    equipment 33
    identifying variables 32
    teamwork 31
plants
    adaption advantages 186
    and herbivores 196
    as organisms 184
    as producers 196
    biological control 206
    classifying, employment 244
    conifers 253
    cyads/ginkgos 252
    ferns 251–2
    fire 186, 202–3
    flowering 253
    how to take cuttings 217
    irrigation 124–5
    kingdom 250–3
    mosses/liverworts 251
    native vegetation 189, 212
    prickly pear 206
    renewable resource 87–8
    seed-producing 252–3
    stomata 116
    water cycle 114, 116–17, 127
Plimsoll lines 80
poles, magnetic 312
pollination 253
pollution 45–7, 94–5, 102, 107, 154
practical investigations 14–22
precipitation 113–14
pressure 55
procedure of a scientific report 26
properties of substances *see* substances, properties
psychology described 3
purpose of a scientific report 26

Q

qualitative observations 15
    in classification 232
quantitative observations 15
    in classification 232

R

rain gardens 127
rate of reaction 44
recycling 47, 93, 150, 171–3
renewable energy sources 103–6
renewable resources
    air 89
    forests 87–8, 189
    living things as 88
    sunlight 90
    water 90
reports 23–30
    graph types 23–5
    structure 26
    tables 23
resources
    conserving 93
    debating use 94–5
    human-made 87
    natural 86
    see also Earth resources; non-renewable resources; renewable resources
results of a scientific report 26
risk *see* safety and science
rocks 91–2, 115, 128
roundworms, classification 240

S

safety and science 6, 8, 14
    assessing risks 33
    aviation 376
    ecotoxicology 45
    science and the law 18
    sources of advice 8
safety, car 284–5
safety flame, Bunsen burner 7

satellites
    artificial 347
    natural 365
saturated 114, 142
scanning tunnelling microscope (STM) 56
science
    and classification 230
    and sport 305
    as important 2–3
    branches 3–4
    models 52–3
    safety rules 8
science and the laboratory 2–8
science employment and careers see 'Working with Science' examples
science sub-branches (disciplines) 4
scientific equipment 5–8, 26, 33
scientific evidence 18
    indirect, and particles 56, 57
    uses of 18
scientific naming of organisms 264
    comparison with indigenous naming 268
scientific reports see reports
scientific work 1–40
    see also 'working scientifically' examples; 'Working with Science' examples
scientists
    and observations 18
    Antarctica 9
    as investigators 2, 31–9
    climate, Sarah Harris 4
    what they study 2–4
Seabin solution (pollution) 154
seas see oceans
sector graph (pie graph) 24
separating substances see insoluble substances, separating; soluble substances, separating
sewage
    classifications 169–70
    drinking recycled 172–3
    septic tanks 170
    treatment plant 169, 176
shooting stars 347
simple machines 323–35
    and force 323–6
    effort 324–5
    gears 326

    levers 324
    wheels 325
SI units 16
'SkillBuilder' examples
    bilateral symmetry 239
    calculating density 72
    determining focal length 360–1
    graphing changes of state 64
    how to filter 152
    identifying boiling 63
    leap years 375
    lighting Bunsen burner 7
    radial symmetry 239
    reading a meniscus 17
    symmetry in organisms 239
software use 23
soil 92, 114, 189
solar cells 104
solar energy 104
solar panels 94, 104
solar system 346–7, 352–72
    constellations 352
    dwarf planets 355–6
    exploring 356
    geocentric model 353
    gravity and orbits 363–72
    heliocentric model 353
    retrograde motion 353–4
    rotation in 377–8
    structure 353
    see also Earth in space; gravity
solids 42
    calculating volume 74
    characteristics/properties 43, 54
    densities 71
    explaining 54
solids, liquids and gases 43–4, 52–60
solubility 43, 140
soluble substances, separating 159–65
    chromatography 159–60
    crystallisation 161
    distillation 162
    evaporation 161
solutions (of substances) 140–42
    common types 141
    concentrated/dilute/saturated 142
    folding a filter paper 152
    solutes/solvents 141, 167
    see also mixtures

South Pole, finding 362
space see Earth in space
space science 9
species
    diversity 210
    endangered 210
    extinction 201–2, 204
    in sustainable ecosystems 201
    introduced 204–7, 229
    naming 264
    rare 210
sponges, classification 238
spores 251
sports science 305
spreadsheets 23, 26, 31
starfish, classification 239
stars 344–8
    interpreting constellations 357–8
    see also Earth in space
states of matter 43
    changing state 61–9
    characteristic properties 52–5
    water 116
steam 64
storing water
    dams and reservoirs 124, 169
    tanks 123
sublimation 62
substance reactions 44
substance/s
    insoluble/soluble 140, 149–65
    pure 140, 167
    versus mixture 140
    see also insoluble substances, separating; soluble substances, separating
substances, properties 41–84
    biodegradability 46
    changing state 61–9
    density 70–80
    impurities 161–2
    non-biodegradable 46
    physical and chemical 42–51
    solids, liquids and gases 43–4, 52–60
    see also insoluble substances, separating; soluble substances, separating
Sun/sunlight
    and Earth 373–6
    and Moon phases 367
    and time 374

biomass 103–4
day and night 374
food chains 195–7
photosynthesis 195
renewable resource 90
seasons 375–6
solar eclipse 367–8
solar energy 86–7, 104
'water cycle' 114
see also Earth in space; orbits; solar system
sustainability
    ecosystems 201–2
symbiosis/interdependence
    commensalism 188
    mutualism 188
    parasitism 188

T

tables, reports 21, 23–4, 26, 33
taxonomy 231, 237–8, 255
teamwork 31, 34
technology
    alternative 93–5
    car safety 284–5
    fire monitoring 203
    new 2
telescope 354
    constructing 360
temperature
    and biodegradability 47
    and changing state 61–4, 162
    and energy 54
    bacteria tolerance 255
    units 16
    versus time, graphing 30, 64
    water cycle 116
    see also heat
test-tube 8
thought model 53
tidal energy 105
time
    day/night 374
    units 16
    year 374
    zones 374
topography 117
toxic chemicals 45, 47, 95, 154, 212
transpiration 114–17
trees *see* forests

U

unicellular 256
units of measurement 16, 280
universe, the 344–8, 354
    interpreting constellations 357–8
    see also Earth in space
urbanisation 214
using classification *see* classification, using

V

variables 32
    see controlled variables; dependent variables; independent variables
vegetation *see* plants
velocity, terminal 304
vibration
    change of state 62–4
    particles 54–5, 62
volcanoes 91
volume
    and mass and density 71–2
    of oddly shaped objects 74
    measuring 6

W

wastewater treatment 169–73
    blackwater 169–70
    greywater 169–71
    recycling 172–3
    uses of recycled 173
    see also sewage
water
    and ice 73
    changing state 61–4
    desalination 122, 169
    displaced 74
    drinking 167, 168
    fresh water 113
    groundwater 115
    hydroelectricity 103
    need for 167
    percolation 114
    purifying 166–73
    recycle sewage, drinking 172–3
    renewable resource 90
    reverse osmosis 169, 173
    springs 129
    storing 123–4
    stormwater 126–7
    tidal energy 105
    treatment 168
    see also condensation; evaporation
water contamination, fracking 95
water cycle 112–22
    factors affecting 115
    groundwater 115
    humidity 116
    landscape 117
    vegetation 117
water management 123–32
    changing vegetation 127
    indigenous 128–9
    irrigation 124–5
    moving water around 125–6
    spray irrigation 124
water purification 107
water turbine 108
water vapour 43, 64, 89, 114–16, 162
weight 70, 281
    is not mass 72, 302–3
wheels 325–6
wind energy 105, 111
windmills 105
wind turbines 105
wind turbine technician (science-based employment) 328
Wollemi pine 253, 267
working scientifically 1–40
'working scientifically' examples
    communicating 23–30
    enquiry process flowchart 37
    planning an investigation 31–6
    practical investigations 14–22
    science and the laboratory 2–8
    scientists in Antarctica 9
    wind turbine technician 328
'Working with Science' examples
    airspace controller 376
    ecotoxicologist 45
    electrical and renewable energy engineer 106
    green chemist 143
    information designer 26
    plant classification 244
    urban farming 214

Z

zoology 4, 34